MANUSCRIPTS OF THE MARQUESS OF BATH
Volume V
TALBOT, DUDLEY AND DEVEREUX PAPERS

Historical Manuscripts Commission
58

CALENDAR OF THE MANUSCRIPTS OF
THE MOST HONOURABLE
THE MARQUESS OF BATH
PRESERVED AT
LONGLEAT, WILTSHIRE

Volume V
Talbot, Dudley and Devereux Papers
1533-1659

Edited by G. Dyfnallt Owen, Ph.D.

LONDON
HER MAJESTY'S STATIONERY OFFICE

I S B N 0 11 440092 X*

PREFACE

This volume completes the series of calendars devoted to the manuscripts of the Marquess of Bath.

The thanks of the Commission are due to both the late and the present Marquesses for the unfailing generosity with which they have made their papers available for the purpose of these publications. The Commission's gratitude is also expressed to successive agents, secretaries and librarians at Longleat who have facilitated access to the papers.

CONTENTS

	Page
Preface	v
Introduction	1
The Provenance of the Papers at Longleat calendared by the Commission	1
The Talbot, Dudley and Devereux Papers	3
Summary of MS Volumes calendared	18
Talbot Papers 1569-1608	20
Dudley Papers 1558-1608	136
Devereux Papers 1533-1659	228
Index	293

INTRODUCTION

The Provenance of the Papers at Longleat calendared by the Commission

It is now over one hundred years since Alfred Horwood visited Longleat on behalf of the Royal Commission on Historical Manuscripts. His account of the manuscript riches that he found there appeared in 1872, in the Appendix to the Commission's *Third Report* (pp. 180-202).

In 1904 appeared the first detailed *Calendar of the Manuscripts of the Marquis of Bath preserved at Longleat, Wiltshire* (HMC 58 : *Bath I*), which dealt with the contents of what Horwood described as the 'Duchess of Portland's Box'. These were papers brought into the Thynne family by Lady Elizabeth Bentinck, daughter of the 2nd Duke of Portland and grand-daughter of Edward Harley, 2nd Earl of Oxford. Lady Elizabeth married Thomas, 3rd Viscount Weymouth (later 1st Marquess of Bath) in 1759. The 1904 volume describes papers relating to the sieges of Brampton and Hopton Castles during the Civil War (1643-46); Harley papers covering the period 1660-1738, but concerning principally the politics of Queen Anne's reign; and correspondence of the 2nd Duchess of Portland, including letters from the poet Edward Young, 1740-65, and Mrs Elizabeth Montagu, 1749-85.

The second volume, published in 1907, calendared letters and papers of the period 1515 to 1772, beginning with papers purchased by Robert Harley, 1st Earl of Oxford, and ending with further items relating to the Duchess of Portland.[1] This was followed in 1908 by a third volume, devoted to the papers of Matthew Prior preserved by his patron Lord Oxford.

The fourth volume, which did not appear until 1968, dealt with the *Seymour Papers 1532-1686*, another collection that reached Longleat through a marriage alliance. In 1672 Thomas Thynne (1640-1714, created Viscount Weymouth in 1682) married Lady Frances Finch, daughter of the 3rd Earl of Winchilsea, and granddaughter of the 2nd Duke of Somerset and his wife Frances. The last-named died in 1674, having appointed her grand-son-in-law Thynne an executor of her will.

The Dudley and Devereux manuscripts, calendared in this fifth and final volume of Bath MSS, also owe their presence at Longleat to Frances, Duchess of Somerset. Though a Seymour by marriage, she was by birth a Devereux, and the co-heir of her brother Robert Devereux, 3rd Earl of Essex, who died in 1646. Their grandmother was Lettice Knollys, the wife firstly of Walter Devereux, 1st Earl of Essex, and secondly of Robert Dudley, Earl of Leicester. Lettice, Countess of Leicester, died at Drayton Bassett, near Tamworth, in 1634, and the papers relating to both her first and her second husband passed first to her grandson and then to his sister, the Duchess. When the Duchess in her turn came to draw up her will, she left her personal estate at Drayton entirely to her 'grandson Thomas Thynne', and also expressed the wish that he should purchase the manor of Drayton from her executors, which he did.[2] The Dudley and Devereux papers were presumably moved to Longleat in 1682, when Thynne succeeded his cousin in the family inheritance.

The presence at Longleat of two volumes of original MSS relating to the Talbot Earls of Shrewsbury is less easily explained, although here too there was a family connection. Frances, Duchess of Somerset, had been the second wife of the second Duke. His first wife, by whom he had no issue, was Lady

---

[1] See Horwood's description under 'Letters Etc. in the Library'.
[2] *Bath IV, Seymour Papers*, pp. 234-35; PCC Wills 1677, PROB 11/355/133.

Arabella Stuart, a relative (through the Cavendish family) of the Talbots. She was in fact the niece by marriage of Gilbert, 7th Earl of Shrewsbury; and the Talbot MSS at Longleat include letters from her to her uncle.

The Talbot family papers descended to Henry Howard, 6th Duke of Norfolk, who in about 1677 deposited fifteen volumes of them in the College of Arms.[1] Other material was, however, retained by the antiquary Nathaniel Johnston (1627-1705), who had spent several years going through the Duke's archives at Sheffield Manor for his work on the Talbot Earls of Shrewsbury. Edward Bernard's *Catalogi Librorum Manuscriptorum Angliae* (1697) lists Johnston's collection of MSS, among them 'Two volumes of Original Letters writ to and from George, Gilbert and Edward Earls of Shrewsbury, and the noble Ancestors of the Families of Cavendish of Devonshire, and Newcastle, the Lady Arabella Stuart, and other eminent persons in the Courts of Q. Elizabeth, and K. James I' (Tom. 2, part 1, pp. 99-100).

If these are the volumes in question, they may have been acquired by Lord Weymouth, because of their family interest, at some time after Johnston's death in 1705. A number of other Shrewsbury MSS, previously in Johnston's custody, were acquired by Lambeth Palace Library between 1705 and 1715.[2] Still other Talbot MSS, intermingled with Johnston's own papers, descended to his son, and afterwards passed by purchase to the Frank family, of Campsall, near Doncaster.[3]

Johnston made copies from both the volumes of Talbot MSS now at Longleat for his MS 'Lives of the Shrewsburys', of which there is a fair copy in the Longleat library. (The 'Lives' in Johnston's own hand, with original Talbot MSS found in them, are now in Sheffield Central Library).

In the 1870s the Rev. J.E. Jackson printed various sixteenth century Longleat papers in the *Wiltshire Archaeological and Natural History Magazine*.[4] Twenty-six letters of Lady Arabella Stuart, dating from August 1603 to November 1608, were included by Emily Tennyson Bradley in her *Life of the Lady Arabella Stuart,........containing a collection of her Letters, with notes and documents from original sources...*(2 vols., 1889). Those letters have consequently not been reproduced in detail in the present volume. Since the late nineteenth century surprisingly few of the materials calendared or summarised here have appeared in printed form.

In 1910 the late Geoffrey Baskerville was invited to prepare a calendar of the bound volumes of Seymour, Talbot, Dudley and Devereux papers at Longleat. They were deposited for this purpose in the Public Record Office by the 5th Marquess of Bath, and by 1914 Mr Baskerville had made considerable progress. He had transcribed or summarised the Talbot, Dudley and Devereux volumes, and had drafted a calendar of the first eleven volumes

[1] See G.R. Batho, *A Calendar of the Shrewsbury and Talbot Papers, Volume II, Talbot Papers in the College of Arms*, 1971: HMC Joint Publications Series No. 7, with the Derbyshire Archaeological Society (Record Series No. 4). For four volumes of autograph letters, 1513-1723, remaining at Arundel Castle see F.W. Steer, *Arundel Castle Archives*, Vol.I, 1968, pp.199-207, reprinting interim handlist No.11, 1965.

[2] Catherine Jamison, *A Calendar of the Shrewsbury and Talbot Papers, Volume I, Shrewsbury MSS in the Lambeth Palace Library*, 1966: HMC Joint Publications Series No. 6, with the Derbyshire Archaeological Society (Record Series No. 1), pp. vii-viii.

[3] HMC *Sixth Report*, 1877, App., pp. 448 ff.; Janet D. Martin, 'The Antiquarian Collections of Nathaniel Johnston' (Oxford B. Litt. thesis, 1956); *Sheffield City Libraries Cat. Arundel Castle MSS*, 1965, pp. 181-222.

[4] 'Longleat Papers', Vol. XIV (1874), pp. 192-216 and 237-253, and Vol. XVIII (1879), pp. 9-48; 'Amye Robsart', Vol. XVII (1878), pp. 47-93.

of Seymour papers.

At this point the work was interrupted by the First World War, and the papers were returned to Longleat. It was not until 1938 that the project was revived and the papers brought again to London. After the lapse of a quarter of a century Mr Baskerville was reluctant to resume work on the calendar, and it passed to Dr Marjorie Blatcher (Mrs S.T. Bindoff). She found that the Seymour papers would by themselves fill a printed volume, so the Talbot, Dudley and Devereux papers went back once more to Longleat. The Dudley and Devereux volumes were returned by way of Cambridge where they were microfilmed as a wartime precaution for the Library of Congress (Reel Nos. Bath 66-70).

After the publication of the Seymour calendar in 1968, the task of preparing a calendar of the Talbot, Dudley and Devereux volumes from the Baskerville transcripts devolved upon the present editor.

The Talbot, Dudley and Devereux Papers

I

In 1568 George Talbot, 6th Earl of Shrewsbury, married Elizabeth Hardwick, better known as Bess of Hardwick, a Derbyshire widow of considerable fortune whom three husbands had already failed to survive. In the following year he was entrusted with the custody of Mary, Queen of Scots, and enjoined not to allow his courtesy and esteem for her royal person to obscure the fact that she was a political prisoner. In less than twelve months one of the greatest and wealthiest noblemen of England had, unwittingly no doubt, made himself vulnerable to the ambitions and intrigues of two of the most fascinating women in the realm.

The first years of his marriage, and custody of the Scottish Queen were pleasant and uneventful, and the Earl's loyalty to the Crown and attachment to his wife most exemplary. As marks of Queen Elizabeth's favour he was appointed Privy Councillor in 1571 and created Earl Marshal of England in 1573 in the place of Thomas Howard, 4th Duke of Norfolk, arraigned and executed for treason the previous year. His peace of mind was disturbed, however, and with good reason, when in 1574 the Countess of Shrewsbury, with an arrogant disregard of political consequences, chose to arrange a marriage between Charles Stuart, the Earl of Darnley's brother, and Elizabeth Cavendish, one of her daughters by her late second husband Sir William Cavendish, of Chatsworth, Derbyshire.

If the Countess had conveniently forgotten that the bridegroom was brother-in-law to Mary, Queen of Scots, now comfortably lodged in the Earl of Shrewsbury's home at Sheffield, it was a fact that would loom large in Queen Elizabeth's assessment of what she regarded as a piece of effrontery and a matrimonial conspiracy for the advancement of the Cavendish family. The Countess was clapped into the Tower of London, where she was joined by the Countess of Lennox, mother of Charles Stuart, who had connived at the rather precipitate marriage. Elizabeth's suspicions even alighted on the Queen of Scots as having encouraged the union, although Mary had never concealed her distaste for the whole Darnley family. The Earl of Shrewsbury thought it advisable to clear himself of complicity by throwing all the blame on his wife. [1] Elizabeth found it politic to accept his protestation of innocence,

[1] G.R. Batho, *op. cit.*; p.96.

3

and eventually the Countess was released.

From this time onwards a coldness crept into the relations between the Earl and his wife, and increasing estrangement finally led to an open breach and the retirement of the Countess to Chatsworth. The Earl became convinced her first concern was the prosecution of the fortunes of her own children, and his obsession on this point had the effect of dictating his attitude towards his sons and daughters. The fact that the former did not share his quarrel with the Countess enraged him, and the slightest demonstration of friendship for his wife was denounced as an intolerable infraction of filial duty (p.26).

The mutual bickering and recriminations between husband and wife soon became the talk of town and Court. The Earl did not seem to care whether the domestic dispute reached the proportions of a national emergency. His good friend at the Court and Queen Elizabeth's favourite, Robert Dudley, Earl of Leicester, found it difficult to reason with him on the matter. What was even more symptomatic of Shrewsbury's apparent irrationality in the whole business was his tactless way of badgering the Queen with complaints about his wife's behaviour (p.40). And this at a time when complex state problems such as the dangerous situation in the Netherlands, the subversive activities of Catholic conspirators at home and troubles in Ireland were occupying her mind and playing on her nerves.

The bitter wrangling between the two parties was further inflamed by rumours that the Earl was enjoying a degree of intimacy with the Queen of Scots which could not be justified, excused or explained by fourteen years of constant attendance on an ageing but still attractive woman. Mary had no doubt as to the identity of the person who was disseminating them. In a letter to Mauvissière, the French Ambassador, in October 1584, she complained of the 'malicieux déportemens et mensonges en mon endroict'[1] of the Countess of Shrewsbury and of her sons Charles and William Cavendish, and demanded that they should be brought before the Privy Council to answer for their scandalous gossip. It is evident that the Queen of Scots had put up with these defamatory innuendoes for some time, since she wrote her letter of protest after her removal from the Earl's care - in itself the culmination of a series of pinpricks that had annoyed Shrewsbury and caused him to feel somewhat humiliated.

It is unlikely that Elizabeth took the rumours seriously. But, while not questioning the devotion of the Earl to the Crown, and to herself in particular, she had not been reluctant to criticise occasionally the manner in which he exercised his authority as guardian of the Queen of Scots. In 1582 she had written to him to express her annoyance that, whereas she had given her consent that Mary should be allowed to visit the spa of Buxton in Derbyshire only once that year, Shrewsbury had authorised a second visit unknown to the authorities, and that furthermore he was permitting the Scottish Queen to hunt and fish at her pleasure (p.40). Neither could the Earl have failed to notice the veiled censure in a further message from Elizabeth that he should cancel an assembly of the freeholders of the Peak Forest, convened by him, because of their Catholic sympathies. She informed him that she was apprehensive of 'what inconvenience maie followe of this assembly of so manie people by reason of the neerenes of the place to Buxtons where your chardge (the Queen of Scots) presently remayneth' (p.50).

For the moment Elizabeth confined herself to merely registering her

[1] A. Labanoff, *Lettres Instructions et Mémoires de Marie Stuart*, Vol. VI (1844), p.37.

displeasure, as the Scottish Queen had recently submitted certain proposals for a better understanding between her and her 'sister' of England. A year later, when hopes of an improvement in their relations had evaporated, the Earl distinctly felt a wind of change blowing coldly upon him from the direction of Whitehall. During a temporary absence from Sheffield, his place as keeper was taken by Sir Ralph Sadler, and despite Shrewsbury's hint that any removal of Mary from Sheffield would entail considerable trouble and expense, he was ordered to arrange the conveyance of her person, her staff and her baggage to Wingfield Manor, within a few miles of Matlock in Derbyshire. What caused him more chagrin, perhaps, was the fact that his appointment of a certain Mr Bentall to be Gentleman Porter to the Queen of Scots was peremptorily disallowed by Elizabeth, who distrusted the man and instructed the Earl to find a more reliable person (p.52). Finally, Shrewsbury was relieved of his onerous, and by this time irksome, duties as Mary's keeper in the autumn of 1584. He did not see Mary again until October 1586, when he was one of the Commissioners at her trial in Fotheringhay Castle. Four months later he presided at her execution there.

Not that he was allowed to forget his long association with the Queen of Scots or some of its more immediate consequences. When provisions grew scarce at Wingfield Manor late in 1584, it was Shrewsbury who was asked by the Government to find enough victuals to keep Mary and her household from near starvation (p.53). Such a request for assistance would meet with a wholehearted response from a nobleman like Shrewsbury when his chivalrous sentiments were stirred. But the New Year brought a message from Whitehall which aroused totally different feelings in him.

Elizabeth had been informed that plate, hangings and other household goods had been sent from Scotland for the service and personal comfort of the Queen of Scots while she was in the Earl's custody, and wished to know what had become of them and some other materials supplied by her own Wardrobe. In a highly irascible mood, the Earl snapped back that no plate or draperies of any kind had been received from Scotland; and that, as for the Crown stuff, he had already returned 'xix peces of hangings which were verey sore spoyled' but not half as damaged, he protested, as his own household furnishings which the Queen of Scots and her servants had ruined during their long residence at Sheffield. He added, for good measure, that it was high time that Elizabeth and the Privy Council thought of rewarding him suitably for his meritorious services as keeper (p.53). What he got in hard cash was £50 for supplying Mary with twelve days' diet (p.54). But that, perhaps, did not matter, for by this time Shrewsbury was engrossed in his feud with his wife and the Cavendish children, and was hoping to win Elizabeth over to his side.

Released from the distractions of the Queen of Scots' presence, Shrewsbury had all the time at his disposal to harass his wife, and the protracted quarrel came to a head with his stopping of her allowance and the revocation of a deed of gift to her sons, Charles and William, of all the lands he held in her right. In return, William ransacked the mansion at Chatsworth of its principal furnishings, and went so far as to deny his stepfather a night's lodging there (pp.52,54). The Earl retaliated by invading the estate with his servants, breaking the windows of the house, and creating havoc in the gardens and parks.

This public exhibition of aristocratic bad temper may have been one factor in bringing about what the Earl most earnestly desired - the intervention of the Queen herself. However, it took a form which gave him an unpleasant shock. The case was referred to Lord Chancellor Bromley and the two Chief Justices, but upon a personal appeal by the Countess of Shrewsbury, Elizabeth decided to exercise her own notions of justice in the matter. To his consternation Shrewsbury was told that the Queen regarded the Countess as the more injured of the two parties and that she dismissed his reasons for separation as flimsy and unconvincing. He was also ordered to restore his wife's property to her, retaining only £500 worth for himself. Elizabeth tried to sweeten the pill by declaring that the whole purpose of her arbitration was to effect a reconciliation between husband and wife (p.55). Moreover, she went out of her way to treat Shrewsbury's son, Lord Talbot, with special kindness, which the Earl appreciated to the extent of agreeing to her request that he should contribute £1000 towards the discharge of Lord Talbot's debts (p. 60).

But on the possibility of a reconciliation he was obdurate. He told the Queen that he would have none of it (p.61), and did not conceal his antagonism in a letter to the Countess full of bitter reproach and harsh criticism. He also dealt such a rebuff to the Earl of Leicester, who had attempted more than once to patch up the quarrel, that Dudley hurriedly dropped the matter (p.63). The Earl's resistance to pressure from Court and friends was not entirely to his disadvantage, for it provoked the Countess into behaving in a manner which cost her, and gained him, some sympathy. Even Elizabeth, irritated by her importunities and complaints, gave her a downright snub on one occasion (p.64). Nevertheless, the current continued to run against Shrewsbury.[1] His law suits against the Cavendish family were definitively brought to a halt by the Queen's order in 1586, and he was brusquely reminded from time to time of his obligation to implement the terms of Elizabeth's arbitration award. He even found it possible, at the Queen's express wish, to pay a visit to the Countess which passed off more harmoniously than he may have anticipated. But if he ever contemplated some form of reconciliation with her, he had never taken any positive step towards it when he died in November 1590.

II

Concurrently with the dissensions that broke up the marriage between the Earl and Countess of Shrewsbury, there went a similar campaign of mutual vilification and hostility between two families of a lower social standing in the landed hierarchy of Derbyshire. Squabbles among the squires would be the appropriate title of one chapter at least in the history of local government in any part of seventeenth century England. Derbyshire was certainly integrated into the general pattern of pugnacious and ambitious country gentlemen competing for prominence and power in local affairs, and using violence and intrigue to gain their ends. To enlist the active sympathy and connivance of an influential member of the nobility was one method that commended itself. It added lustre to what was too often a dubious cause, and provided a cover under which a more forceful way could be devised of dealing with an opponent. Sir Thomas Stanhope of Shelford may have thought so when he decided to engage the Earl of Shrewsbury in his quarrel with Sir John Zouche of Codnor Castle.

The Earl did not need much persuasion for he and Zouche had already fallen foul of one another as far back as 1571, when the latter had disrespect-

[1] Francis Bickley, *The Cavendish Family* (1911), pp. 19-30.

6

fully ignored a request from Shrewsbury that he, as High Sheriff of Derbyshire, should convene a meeting of Justices of the Peace. More recently he had further provoked the Earl by intriguing against him at a critical moment when the Countess of Shrewsbury was jeopardising her husband's position at the Court by marrying her daughter to Charles Stuart.[1]

An opportunity to pay off old scores came in 1577. There were complaints circulating throughout the shire that Zouche had failed to account for the money and armour given to him to equip some of the inhabitants at the time of the rebellion in the North in 1569. One of his principal accusers was Sir John Stanhope who acquainted Shrewsbury with the alleged embezzlement of public funds which the Earl, in his turn, immediately communicated to the Privy Council. The Earl of Bedford was reported to have espoused Zouche's cause, which only made Shrewsbury the more determined to support Stanhope, but not to the extent of identifying himself completely with his faction. It was a wise precaution, for Stanhope was indiscreet enough to make some offensive remarks about Zouche's wife and other members of his family. Stanhope was summoned before the Privy Council and forced to withdraw them unreservedly. To hammer home their disapproval of his behaviour, the Lords of the Council issued strict orders that controversies between him and Zouche were to cease there and then.[2] A year later the Council enforced this prohibition by removing a case which Stanhope had brought against Zouche from Derbyshire to the Queen's Bench in London. It was a warning that he was to leave Zouche alone, and Stanhope construed it as an indication that Shrewsbury, although a Privy Councillor, was either unable or indisposed to lend his influence on his behalf.

Whether this was true or not, the next few years saw a reversal of the situation which showed how fickle and unstable country gentlemen could be in their friendships and enmities, and how the pursuit of personal advantages dictated the one and the other. Having ostensibly laid Stanhope low, Sir John Zouche may have reflected that he had nothing to gain by maintaining bad relations with Shrewsbury, and took the first step towards a reconciliation. He shrewdly exploited the differences between the Earl and the Cavendish family by allying himself with the political faction in the shire which supported Henry Talbot, the Earl's son, and Henry Cavendish (the eldest and only one of the Countess of Shrewsbury's sons who adhered to the Earl in the family dispute) in the election of knights of the shire in 1584. The principal opposing candidate was Sir Charles Cavendish, the Countess's third son, between whom and Shrewsbury feelings were particularly hostile.[3] Zouche's advances were not rejected, and two years later he was on sufficiently amicable terms with the Earl to be able to ask him a favour.[4] On the other hand, Shrewsbury lived long enough to witness a serious breach in the old friendship with the Stanhope family, for shortly before his death there was a quarrel between Sir Thomas Stanhope and Gilbert, Lord Talbot, who succeeded his father as 7th Earl of Shrewsbury in November 1590.

Whatever were the causes of the initial dispute, it broke out afresh in 1592. A complaint reached the Privy Council that Stanhope had erected a weir in the River Trent near Shelford, which was prejudicial to the livelihood of the

[1] G.R. Batho, *op. cit.*, p.101.

[2] *Acts of the Privy Council of England, Vol. X: 1577-1578* (1895), pp.165-66.

[3] The returns for this election are not available, but the fact that both men were elected to the Parliament of 1586 suggests that they may have been successful in 1584 as well.

[4] G.R. Batho, *op. cit.*, p.135.

local fishermen and other poor persons. Stanhope protested that the charge had been engineered by Shrewsbury's supporters with his connivance, and that many people whose names were associated with the complaint had not been consulted beforehand nor their approbation requested and obtained (p.103). Shrewsbury counter-attacked by submitting to the Council an attested certificate that Stanhope had impugned his honour by insulting him and his servants (p.104). Once again the Queen was told of altercations in which an Earl of Shrewsbury was involved, and was patently annoyed by the affair. And once again an Earl of Shrewsbury discovered to his mortification that former royal favours did not necessarily predispose the Queen to accept his version of events. Elizabeth insisted that the case should be determined by a Commission of Sewers. What was more ominous, she was inclined to give credence to Stanhope's accusations that the Earl and his friends were guilty of dubious practices. This galvanized Shrewsbury into writing letters to his friends at the Court in which he showered Stanhope with invective, but their replies must have put him out of countenance. They unanimously advised him to drop his differences with Stanhope and seek a reconciliation, adding that Elizabeth herself had expressed such a wish. But like his father, the Earl did not take kindly to the idea of reconciliation when he felt himself misjudged and discriminated against, and the royal wish was ignored.

1593 was a year of Parliamentary elections, but this time the alignment of opposing factions was different from that of 1584. The Earl, in defiance of his father, had retained the closest relations with the Countess of Shrewsbury and her sons throughout the long years of wrangling and vituperation, and he now decided to throw his full weight behind Sir Charles Cavendish who aspired to be chosen knight of the shire for the county of Nottingham. It was an ambition which Sir Thomas Stanhope was anxious to frustrate if he could. The two parties met face to face in Nottingham on election day, but Sir Thomas, the older and wiser - and possibly the inferior in point of numbers - of the two leaders, withdrew to the Shire Hall, leaving Sir Charles and another to be elected unopposed (p.117).

A head-on collision had been averted at Nottingham, much to the relief of the Privy Council, but there were less public methods of settling accounts. Two events made it inevitable that sooner or later one side would challenge the other to a duel. The first was an incident at Newark, when during a hunt meeting some of Stanhope's men, so it was alleged, 'set up vile pictures of the Talbot'.[1] The other was an abusive letter sent by the Earl of Shrewsbury's wife to Sir Thomas Stanhope, in which she compared him unfavourably with a toad and wished him every conceivable tribulation in this world and perpetual hell fire in the next (p.119). But it was not Sir Thomas who issued a challenge. That came from Sir Charles Cavendish, eager to defend the honour of the Earl, his stepbrother and patron, and it was directed to John Stanhope, Sir Thomas's son and heir. What followed almost amounted to a well-staged farce.

After a series of messages between the two, a rendezvous was arranged at Lambeth Bridge, the weapon agreed upon and seconds nominated. The parties met at seven o'clock in the morning, but a preliminary frisking of young Stanhope revealed that he was wearing a doublet thick enough to resist a rapier thrust, and he was ordered not to fight in it. Sir Charles considerately offered to fight in his shirt, but Stanhope refused to remove his doublet on the

[1] *Acts of the Privy Council of England, Vol XXIV : 1592-1593* (1901), p. 78.

grounds that he was suffering from a cold. Suspecting that his opponent was just being difficult, Sir Charles then proposed that Stanhope should borrow his waistcoat to keep himself warm, and get on with the duel. Even this charitable offer was rejected, and eventually Stanhope returned to London by boat leaving a frustrated Sir Charles on the banks of the Thames (p.120).

This was not the end of the matter. A few weeks later John Stanhope and a number of servants were ambushed in Fleet Street by a party of Shrewsbury's and Sir Charles's followers. In the ensuing brawl one of Stanhope's men was badly injured, and the affray was reported to the Privy Council. Stanhope produced enough evidence to incriminate his assailants as the instigators of the attack upon him, and they were committed to the Marshalsea prison.

This act of violence convinced the Queen and her Council that Shrewsbury was more at fault than Sir Thomas Stanhope in the controversy between them. And it was Sir Thomas that emerged victorious. An order from the Council in 1593 warned his opponents to leave him in peace and to keep their hands off the weirs erected by him on the Trent near Shelford.[1]

III

By the end of 1559 it was evident that Lord Robert Dudley was the unchallenged favourite of Queen Elizabeth, and that her barely concealed infatuation for him had invested Dudley with a position of special eminence and influence at the Court and in state affairs. He was constantly in Elizabeth's company at Whitehall, entertained her to suppers in St James's Park, and accompanied her to Greenwich, Gillingham, Cobham and elsewhere in the neighbourhood of the capital, besides performing his regular duties as Master of the Horse to the Queen (p.136). At the same time, foreign ambassadors and visitors of princely rank from the continent were finding it advisable to cultivate the goodwill if not the friendship of the favourite, and he was a frequent guest at their dinners, and took part with varying luck in the games of chance that followed (p.138). Meanwhile, he was expected to attend City functions, to act as official host on state occasions, to take part in jousts, and participate in the almost daily sessions of the Privy Council. To be fit enough to cope with these multifarious activities, Dudley made a point of regularly playing tennis.

This was the kind of life that appealed immensely to him, and being sure of the Queen's affection, he plunged into it with all the confidence and ebullience of a young man - he was 27 years of age at the time. Occasionally he was able to think of his wife, Lady Amy Dudley, who preferred to live in the country, and pay her a visit, which both seem to have genuinely enjoyed. There was only one problem that distracted him periodically, but he was far from being the sole nobleman in England irritated and frustrated by lack of funds. Despite the liberal gifts of land bestowed on him by the Queen, Dudley found it impossible to meet the expenses of his household in the country and the bills which he incurred in London. By 1561 he had had to borrow money to the tune of £14,000 from various merchants and lenders. But by that time other and more momentous matters were forcing themselves upon his attention.

Dudley's ascendancy at the beginning of the reign was initially an assurance to Philip II, King of Spain, that for the moment he had nothing to fear from the accession of Elizabeth to the throne of her sister, and his late wife, Queen

[1] *Acts of the Privy Council of England, 1592-1593*, p.441.

Mary. Indeed he might have been pardoned for thinking that he could hope to win Dudley's collaboration, since the favourite had taken part in the great Spanish victory over the French at St. Quentin three years previously and had lost a brother in the battle. Philip may have reckoned too that the French capture of Calais would rekindle the old antagonism of the English towards France, and make them oblivious to his policy of consolidating his hold on the immense territorial heritage left to him by his father, before proceeding to extend his political influence, as well as the spiritual jurisdiction of the Catholic Church, wherever he could. He failed to see that, in the long run, these objectives were bound to excite the suspicions of the English, already apprehensive of their security and religious liberties. The expulsion of the French expeditionary force from Scotland in 1561, with the help of English troops, should have warned him that Elizabeth would not tolerate the intervention of a continental power in affairs this side of the Channel. Similarly her meddling on behalf of the Huguenots in 1562, during the first stages of the civil war in France, not only showed where her religious sympathies lay. It also demonstrated that she was not averse to undertaking a little intervention of her own in continental affairs if circumstances warranted such a step.

But diplomatic and military operations were, for the moment, of peripheral interest compared with the intense speculation concerning the marriage prospects - and intentions - of the English Queen. At home there were persistent rumours that she was secretly affianced to Dudley. Some circles approved of it, although the mysterious death of Lady Amy Dudley was too opportune an event not to be related by hostile quarters to an alleged scheme of the favourite's to remove one obstacle to his marriage with the Queen. In any case, attitudes in England were generally dictated by the benefits or disadvantages that would accrue from such a union to rival politicians and colliding Court factions.

Abroad, the Queen's marriage meant something more than that, not least in the Netherlands. Here there was much discontent with Spanish rule, and the slowly increasing Protestant element was alarmed by the possibility of a union between Elizabeth and the King of Spain or one of his Austrian cousins. This would no doubt preserve the cloth trade which linked England and the Low Countries commercially, but, on the other hand, it was likely to lead to the spread of the Spanish Inquisition throughout the Netherlands and the ultimate suppression of heresy, since English neutrality would be guaranteed by the marriage. France, with her own internal troubles, had little time to consider the matter. But even the Guise family, for all their sympathy with Spain, may have had second thoughts about a dynastic union between England and the Spanish-Imperialist axis. For one thing, it would militate against their own policy of prosecuting the claims of their niece, Mary, Queen of Scots, to the English throne with a view to bringing the country within the orbit of Catholic but primarily French influence.

At the beginning of 1563, both Houses of Parliament sent addresses to Elizabeth urging her to marry, an indication that public opinion was perturbed and wished the Queen to take some positive action (p.166). This may have convinced Elizabeth that it would be more proper and expedient to exploit her position as an unmarried queen in the national interest than to indulge herself in emotional scenes with Dudley, especially as the latter had alienated some of her closest advisers and was apparently unpopular with nobility and ordinary citizens alike (p.168). She proceeded to define the new relationship between her and Dudley in her own shrewd and independent way. By proposing that he should become the husband of Mary, Queen of Scots, as she did in 1563, Elizabeth hinted that there could never be any question of marriage between her and Dudley. And by creating him Earl of Leicester in the following year she made it clear that she rated his person and qualities much higher than her subjects did.

As to her own matrimonial intentions, the Queen prevaricated over them so cleverly that almost a decade passed before serious negotiations were begun to attach her to a definitive marriage alliance. During these years Leicester remained in high favour. Further grants of land, together with licences to export woollen cloth, enabled him to overcome financial difficulties resulting from his extravagant habits, and the radius of his influence gradually extended over most matters of national importance and impressed itself on all classes. The Mayor and Aldermen of Bristol were probably not alone in their assumption that the Earl was powerful enough to pressurize the Parliament of 1571 into repealing a private statute passed by its predecessor, and which was not to the liking of the corporation of that city (p.173). Even places as remote as Denbighshire in North Wales did not escape Leicester's attention. There the formidable Sir John Salusbury of Lleweni, who feared no man and harried his opponents, found it wiser to acknowledge the Earl's control over local government in Denbigh and to desist from provoking his officers and friends in the countryside (p.189).

Leicester had never displayed any particular anti-Spanish bias at the Court and in the Privy Council, but by 1570 his opinions had changed and his assessment of the internal problems and foreign dangers of England had inclined him towards an understanding with France. There, at least, the Queen had potential allies in the Huguenots, and even the King of France, Charles IX, and his mother Catherine de Medici, in their fear of Guise machinations, were not averse to better relations with England. One advantage to Elizabeth of such a rapprochement would be to head France off from stepping in where England feared to tread too heavily at the moment, that is in the Netherlands, which had revolted against Spain. The Queen did not wish to commit herself irrevocably to their cause, but merely to supply the insurgents with enough money and men to maintain their struggle. French intervention would have the adverse effect of upsetting her policy of a flexible and adjustable support.

The Queen therefore made a convincing show of welcoming the proposals initiated by Catherine de Medici that she should marry her son, the Duke of Anjou, and negotiations were opened in Paris and London. Whatever his personal feelings in the matter - and they may conceivably have been coloured by the fact that he too was contemplating marriage[1] - Dudley supported them with apparent enthusiasm. At least he was regarded in France as being one of the most prominent and active persons in furthering the marriage (p. 177), and the French King went out of his way to express his gratitude to Leicester (p.178). There was some talk of sending the Earl to Paris to expedite the talks and resolve certain differences (p. 186), but the visit did not materialize.

That both the French and English Governments realized the political necessity of a more tolerant attitude towards one another was amply demonstrated by their mutual desire to continue with the marriage negotiations

---

[1] For his alleged marriage to the widow of John, 2nd Lord Sheffield, in 1573, see G.E.C., *The Complete Peerage.*, Vol. VII (1929), p.550 and n.

despite two events which could have postponed or possibly terminated them. When the Duke of Anjou decided that Elizabeth was not serious and withdrew his suit, his place was immediately taken by his brother d'Alençon, later Duke of Anjou but more familiarly known as 'Monsieur', again at the suggestion of Catherine de Medici. Neither were the talks broken off, despite the indignation felt in England, at the news of the massacre of St. Bartholomew. They were prolonged for another eight years, punctuated and enlivened by the dramatic appearances of Monsieur at Whitehall. On one occasion at least, his representative in London was wined and dined by Leicester and other notables, a reception marred by a tactless post-prandial observation by the Earl of Bedford (p.24). Nothing emerged from the talks, but they helped to create a friendlier atmosphere between the two kingdoms and an absence of armed conflict between the two Crowns for the next fifty years.

One factor which cannot be overlooked in an analysis of Leicester's actions and ideas during this period was his ardent championship of Protestantism. From dallying with Spanish ambassadors and the pro-Spanish faction at the Court, he suddenly developed an interest in theological controversies and a tolerance of reformist and nonconformist views of people like Cartwright, which may not be entirely unconnected with his appointment as High Steward of Cambridge University. The fact remains that both on political and religious grounds he took up a somewhat severe attitude towards the practice and promulgation of the Catholic faith, even to the point of suspecting papist affiliations and doctrinal aberrations amongst his own chaplains where they did not exist (p.175). He certainly displayed partiality towards that section of the clergy who disliked church ceremonies and too much ritual, by his support of Perceval Wyburn, a Puritan divine, who had left his college at Cambridge to become preacher and reader at Northampton. There he publicly advocated reform within the Church of England, and earned the censure of the Bishop of Peterborough. When Leicester requested that Wyburn should be afforded every help and protection in his post, the Bishop refused point-blank to assist him or countenance his preaching (p. 185). On the other hand, the Earl was careful not to allow his religious enthusiasm to outrun his political discretion and, above all, to rouse the Queen's irritability where Puritanism was concerned. He was circumspect enough, for instance, to approve the choice of Dr John Still, Master of St. John's College, Cambridge, and an uncompromising supporter of the established church, to uphold the Protestant cause in the disputations between Protestants and Catholics at Schmalkald in 1578 (p.199). Like a good Protestant he kept a copy of Foxe's *Book of Martyrs* in his library at Wanstead (p.208). And he would have felt pleased that his services to religion had not gone unnoticed and unappreciated, if ever he got round to reading the tract on 'Godlie fame' dedicated to him by Thomas Lupton, a miscellaneous writer, and in which his Christian qualities were eulogized (p. 218).

While the Queen was enjoying the adulation and gallantries of her 'petite grenouille' as she playfully called her suitor, the Duke of Anjou, Leicester had plunged into matrimony again. On 21 September 1578 he secretly married Lettice, widow of Walter Devereux, 1st Earl of Essex, with whom he had been on very intimate terms even during the lifetime of her husband (p.205). Some time elapsed before the Queen heard of the marriage, when she proceeded to treat the Earl as if he had committed a personal affront to the Crown. But her mood of resentment passed, to the extent at least of advertising to the world that she did not question his political fidelity to her. At her request he accompanied Anjou to Antwerp in 1582 (p.206). Later she allowed herself to be swayed by his importunity into appointing him to the command of the English expedition to the Low Countries in 1585.

The Queen's choice met with the approval of the Dutch, but more important to Leicester, it appeared to confirm that his influence over Elizabeth was as strong as ever. One way of impressing this fact on the Netherlands was to arrive there with all the pomp and display that a numerous and imposing retinue could create (p.208). It also partly explained his assumption that the Queen would or could not seriously oppose his acceptance of the Dutch offer to make him Governor of the United Provinces. There was no doubt about the genuineness of Elizabeth's indignation when she heard the news, but the Earl had rightly calculated that she would consider it inadvisable to interfere with the arrangements and thereby hinder the objects of the expedition. By August 1586, he was high in her favour once again (p.68), although his insufferable arrogance lost him his popularity with the Dutch while his ineptitude as a military commander lost the Dutch a number of important strongholds and towns. Neither was he much concerned about the plight of his English soldiers. His recall to England was followed by the mutiny of the garrison at Ostend out of sheer desperation because of official negligence and indifference (p.215).

Leicester had very few more years to live, and it is conceivable that they were not particularly happy ones. Elizabeth continued to make much fuss of him, and he basked in the sunshine of her popularity, especially during the exhilarating days before and after the destruction of the Spanish Armada. But he could not have failed to observe that her eyes did not fix themselves unwaveringly upon him as in the old days. Elizabeth had seen, and been impressed by, the good looks and youthful vitality of Leicester's stepson Robert Devereux, 2nd Earl of Essex, then 22 years of age. Whether Leicester chose to regard this as merely an indication of the Queen's benevolent interest in a member of his family for the sake of old friendship; or whether he foresaw in it the inevitable decline of his influence over her is conjectural. But it would have been interesting to know how he construed the letter which Essex wrote to him on 28 August 1588 (p.216). In the event it does not matter, for the Earl died a few days later at his house in Cornbury, Oxfordshire, on his way to Kenilworth where he had spent some of his happiest and most carefree hours with Elizabeth in the past.

IV

That there was a portrait of Walter Devereux, 1st Earl of Essex, hanging in Leicester House (p.222) recalled the days when he was on friendly terms with the Earl of Leicester before the latter began to take a more than neighbourly interest in his wife, Lettice Devereux. There was no question of rivalry between the two men for the Queen's favour or a place of influence at the Court. Essex's concern was with the consolidation of his position as a land magnate in West Wales and Staffordshire, but, above all, it was Ireland and the opportunities of playing a decisive role in the affairs of that kingdom, that engaged his attention throughout his short life.

His chance came in 1573, when the situation in the turbulent province of Ulster was threatening to lead to complete lawlessness and the domination of the O'Neill sept, which would have spelt the end of any control over that part of Ireland by the English Lord Deputy and his Council in Dublin. Essex submitted certain proposals to the Queen with a view to his undertaking, as a private adventurer, the pacification and colonization of Ulster. After careful consideration Elizabeth agreed to a joint enterprise, the Earl and herself to share the expenses estimated at £63,000 (p.242). Strict injunctions were issued to Essex as to how he was to organise the expedition, to deal with the native Irish and their leaders, and to establish a system of defence and administration in Ulster after its reduction (pp. 241,242). To encourage him in the initial stages of the military preparations, the Queen lent him £10,000 out of her own pocket.

The Earl lost no time in trying to infuse others with his own enthusiasm and readiness to gamble on the success of an expedition adequately equipped to bring to heel the 'wolves and foxes' of Ulster, as the Queen's instructions disparagingly described the Irish. There were always volunteers to be found for this kind of enterprise which promised booty and rewards, but Essex clearly planned to draw on his own resources to provide men and money. The freeholders and tenants of his wide estates were the first to receive appeals for support which would testify to their loyalty and sense of duty both to him and the Crown.

The response was mixed and varied from one part of the country to another. In West Wales, where Devereux influence was unchallenged, there was, surprisingly perhaps, little disposition to follow the Earl in his venture. Some Pembrokeshire tenants, mostly gentlemen, were prepared to go (p.236), but there was talk of compulsion to raise volunteers in Carmarthenshire (p.237). The position was slightly better in Herefordshire, where gentlemen's sons were more eager for adventure and enticed by the prospects of making their fortunes in Ireland, and footmen could be recruited on some of the Earl's manors (p.237). Elsewhere it was relatively easier to obtain contributions in money than to enrol volunteers, although at Keyston, Huntingdonshire, the Earl's tenants resolutely opposed his demand for £100 and offered £40 instead (p.237). His tenants at Sapperton, Gloucestershire, were also glad to be relieved from further badgering by collecting £30 as a gift (p.240).

The expeditionary force, which Essex had raised mainly through his own exertions, soon succumbed to the usual unstable conditions of politics and warfare which bedevilled the policy of the English Government in Ireland. The Lord Deputy, Fitzwilliams, refused to cooperate with the Earl, the actual invasion of Ulster petered out into desultory skirmishing owing to lack of provisions and the prevalence of disease, Essex's plan of sowing dissension between the Irish and the Scots in the province failed, and not even the devastation of the O'Neill lands and a despicable act of treachery on the Earl's part served to turn the thoughts of the Irish towards submission. At home the Privy Council was critical, the Earl of Leicester, for personal reasons, aligned himself with the opposition, and the Queen vacillated between supporting the expedition and calling it off. In 1575 Essex sent a strong protest to the Privy Council in which he vindicated his actions in Ulster and warned the Government that a dissolution of his army would be tantamount to a surrender of the province into the hands of the Irish (p.245). The Queen showed her appreciation of his services by appointing him Earl Marshal of Ireland, but two months later she informed him that the Ulster scheme was at an end.

Essex returned to England and made his way to the Court where he persuaded the Queen to allow him to assert his right to all the lands in Ulster which she had granted him the previous year. He sold many of his estates to raise the necessary funds for this second venture, a costly affair since he personally had to defray the expenses of those who accompanied him (p. 246). He arrived in Dublin in July, but had only time to pay a short visit to Ulster before being taken seriously ill (p.247). He had hopes of recovering sufficiently well to be able to travel to the family home at Lamphey, but died on 22 September 1576. From Dublin his embalmed body was carried all the way by boat and litter - and on his servants' backs where roads were impassable - to Carmarthen, where it lay in the castle for 50 days before being buried in the Church of St. Peter's (p.248).

V

Robert Devereux, 2nd Earl of Essex, was nine years old when his father died, leaving him a reduced patrimony and heavy debts in England and Wales, and various estates exposed to Irish raids in Ulster. He became the ward of Lord Burghley, the Earl of Sussex, the Earl of Huntingdon and others who sent him to Cambridge University at the age of 10, but withdrew him from that seat of learning four years later partly because his expenses continually exceeded his allowance - a bias towards prodigality which the Earl was to show over and over again during his life. He was placed under the care of the Earl of Huntingdon, President of the Council of the North, whose household was conducted along more austere lines than Essex had known at Cambridge. Later, he was permitted to go to the ancestral mansion at Lamphey, and there he behaved like a generous young nobleman, extending liberal hospitality to the squires of the neighbourhood and reviving the old association between his family and the shires of West Wales (p.251).

It was the Earl of Leicester, his stepfather, who then took him under his wing, and Essex found much to admire and emulate in the older man, not least his extravagance. His success at the Court , which went to his head, encouraged him to scorn economy as much as he did his rival, Sir Walter Ralegh, and he soon found himself encumbered with debts. They were not all his, however, for the Queen, although captivated by his physical attractions, insisted that he should be held responsible for the repayment of more than half of the £10,000 which she had lent his father for the Ulster expedition (p.252). Gradually the Earl edged himself into the position of acknowledged favourite and was thus able to enjoy priority in the matter of the Queen's bounty. Land and money came his way, as well as the much coveted farm of sweet wines (p.256). But even these grants and others could not prevent him from amassing £30,000 of debts (p.257), although he could have claimed that some of them had been incurred during his military services in Portugal and Spain, where he had shown much personal courage.

In the intervals between participating in naval and military operations of which the most spectacular was the capture of Cadiz in 1596 (p.264), Essex had his hands full with the same kind of duties and commitments shouldered by the Earl of Leicester when he was the Queen's favourite. Apart from attending on Elizabeth and being present at Privy Council meetings, he had foreign envoys and visitors of distinction to entertain, an expensive business sometimes (p.254) - formal and informal dinners to arrange; a mass of personal matters constantly called for his attention. Like his stepfather, the Earl showed an intelligent interest in politics and religion, and took some pains to become conversant with the trend of events abroad in which he was ably assisted and instructed by his friend and secretary, Anthony Bacon, brother of Francis Bacon, and a man hardly rivalled in his knowledge of foreign affairs.

Essex strongly advocated the continuation of the war against Spain after the defeat of the Armada, and was a firm supporter of the alliance with France. Whoever could help in furthering these objects was *persona grata* with him; for instance, Don Antonio, the pretender to the throne of Portugal, and Antonio Perez, former secretary to the King of Spain. Both were political refugees in England, but were useful for their intimate knowledge of Spanish affairs, their hatred of Philip II, and, in the case of Don Antonio, as a rallying point for anti-Spanish and nationalist sentiments in Portugal. Essex took a special interest in Perez, paying him a salary and watching over his health (p. 260), and finally sending him to Paris as an English agent.

The failure of a second expedition in 1597 to seize the Azores and capture the West Indies treasure fleet, and Essex's incompetence as commander of the expedition, did much to diminish his reputation as a military leader, and encouraged his rivals and enemies at home. This may have made him more amenable to the suggestions of Francis Bacon that he should pay greater attention to events in Ireland, especially in Ulster, where his estates had been half ruined by the incursions of the rebellious Irish and were now being further threatened by the increasing power of O'Neill, Earl of Tyrone (p.262). When the English Government decided in 1598 to send a punitive force to reduce Tyrone to submission, the Queen, after some hesitation, appointed the Earl to be its commander as well as Governor General of Ireland. His troops were superior in number to those whom his father had led to Ireland in 1573, but the obstacles to military success were as insuperable as ever. Thwarted by the Irish Council in Dublin, he wasted time and lives in the south instead of attacking Tyrone, and when eventually he advanced into Ulster his position was too weak to do more than negotiate with the rebel. Having already flouted the Queen's instructions in certain matters, Essex aggravated his offence by signing an unauthorised truce with Tyrone, and abandoning his command to hurry home and burst dramatically into the Queen's bedroom at Nonsuch.

The Queen's affection for the Earl may have stretched to pardoning this impertinence but she could hardly condone the flagrant dereliction of duty committed by him in leaving his army, particularly as she had forbidden him to do so. He was not allowed to return to Ireland but kept in strict seclusion, with the possible danger and indignity of being brought to trial in the Star Chamber. His counsellor, Anthony Bacon, attempted to console him by detecting a silver lining to the clouds which were darkening the prospects of the Earl's rehabilitation (p.267). But it was not visible to Essex, who in the extremity of despair spoke of finding greater consolation in religion (p.268). For once, Essex was nearer to the mark than Bacon. In a specially constituted court at York House, he was formally indicted for contempt and disobedience, and his vigorous speech in his own defence failed to save him from being stripped of all his offices of state (p. 276). However, no charge of disloyalty was pressed against him, and within a few weeks he was set at liberty.

He enjoyed his freedom from constraint for about six months, during which time he prepared his reckless plan to regain his old position at the Court by force, and failed miserably to achieve it. (p.277). It was an act of irresponsibility which forced Queen and Government to realize that the Earl could not only be imprudent as he had been in Ireland, but positively dangerous to the state. And by the same token he forfeited the sympathy of the common people who had acclaimed him as the paragon of loyalty and the champion of the Protestant cause against Spain. His execution in February 1601 therefore aroused little emotion, except perhaps in Elizabeth who, it is said, was prepared to pardon him if Essex had appealed for clemency. The fact remains, however, that she did not choose to restore his son and heir, Robert, in blood and honour even after a decent interval of time.

SUMMARY OF MS VOLUMES
CALENDARED

The manuscripts selected for the present edition were bound into volumes at the British Museum, in the late nineteenth century. A brief summary of the contents of each volume calendared is given below. In the case of the Talbot MSS, the two bound volumes represent the whole of the original Talbot papers at Longleat, with the exception of a few documents relating to Derbyshire. As regards the Dudley and Devereux papers, however, the bound volumes are supplemented by a mass of deeds, estate records and other papers not reproduced in this edition. These loose papers, amounting to some eleven thousand items, were sorted shortly after the First World War by Mr I.H. Jeayes, who arranged them by county and placed them in eight blue boxes.

Talbot

I Correspondence of George Talbot, 6th Earl of Shrewsbury 1574-87. 297 ff. *(Calendared)*

II Correspondence of George, 6th Earl, and Gilbert, 7th Earl of Shrewsbury 1569-1608 (mainly 1588 onwards). 311 ff. *(Calendared)*

Dudley

I Correspondence of Robert Dudley, Earl of Leicester 1559-72. 248 ff. *(Calendared)*

II The same *c*1570-88. 327 ff. *(Calendared)*

III Miscellaneous papers relating to the Earl of Leicester 1559-1601, including accounts 1559-61, a deposition concerning his marriage to Lady Essex in 1578, and various petitions and financial papers. 209 ff. *(Calendared)*

IV The Earl of Leicester decd. Papers 1588-1608, with a few earlier letters and accounts (1560-87). 215 ff. *(Calendared)*

V Inventory of Leicester House 1580. 16 ff. *(Extracts)*

VI Inventory of Leicester House 1583 (revised to 1589). 45 ff. *(Extracts)*

VII Inventory of Leicester House 1584 (revised to 1588). 56 ff. *(Extracts)*

VIII Inventory of household effects at Wanstead 1585. 33 ff. *(Summarised)*

IX Copy of VIII above.

Xa Two inventories of plate at Leicester House n.d. and 1586. 10 ff.

  b An inventory of the contents of a chest at Leicester House 1586, and an inventory of Kenilworth, Leicester House and Wanstead taken after the Earl of Leicester's death (1588). 41 ff. *(Extracts).*

XI General inventory, Kenilworth, Leicester House, Grafton Court and Wanstead, taken after the Earl's death (1588) 1585-88. 126 ff. *(Summarised)*

XII Wardrobe account 1571-74. 33 ff. *(Noted)*

XIII Wardrobe inventory 1588. 25 ff. *(Summarised)*

XIV Household and personal accounts Dec 1558-Dec 1559. 41 ff. *(Extracts)*

XV The same Dec 1559-April 1561. 42 ff. *(Extracts)*

XVI Survey and rental June-Oct 1563. 139 ff. *(Summarised)*

XVII Rental June 1566 (lands received by exchange with the Queen in 1564). 189 ff. *(Summarised)*

XVIII Estate surveys 1579-81. 52 ff. *(Noted)*

XIX Survey of Drayton Bassett estate 1584. 25 ff. *(Noted)*

XX Schedule of title deeds *post* 1586 (additions dated 3 July 1590). 65 ff. *(Noted)*

Devereux

I Correspondence of the 1st, 2nd and 3rd Devereux Earls of Essex 1572-1641 (mainly 1572-75, 1590-98 and 1609-41). 378 ff. *(Calendared)*

II Papers relating mainly to the public life of the 1st and 2nd Earls of Essex 1571-1608. 330 ff. *(Calendared)*

III Accounts, estate surveys and legal papers 1536-1638. 288 ff. *(Calendared)*

IV Legal and estate papers 1627-59. 331 ff. *(Calendared)*

V The 1st Earl of Essex decd. Papers and accounts 1576-86. 80 ff. *(Calendared)*

VI 'The Booke of the Impost of Wynes' (account of duties farmed) 1593-94. 62 ff. *(Extracts)*

VII Copies of papers relating to the 2nd Earl 1599-1601, with a copy of 'Leicester's Commonwealth'. 149 ff. *(Extracts)*

VIII Report (1619) on sales of Crown lands (1561-71) and Thomas Gardiner's accounts. 62ff. *(Summarised)*

IX Notes concerning the Bourchier, Ferrers and Devereux families and their estates *c*1620-30. 64 ff. *(Noted)*

X Steward's account book, household of Henry Bourchier, 2nd Earl of Essex 1533-34. 48 ff. *(Extracts)*

TALBOT PAPERS
1569-1608

THE EARL OF LEICESTER TO THE EARL OF SHREWSBURY

1568-69, March 3. 'I have long forborne to wryte unto your Lordship, and the cause hath bin that I have bin so troubled with the colde as I have not with myne owne hande bin hable to wryte to any of my frendes, and have therefore stayed this bearer Mr Candishe the longer here, by whom though I had no great matter of newes to wryte other then such as himself can declare unto your Lordship, yet coulde I not let him passe without thies fewe lynes whereby to imparte unto your Lordship my most harty commendations and withall to put you in mynde of the advise I gave your Lordship at your last being here, which I doo not heare but you doo well observe, and the longer your Lordship dooth so, the more wilbe your owne safety and the better service you shall doo her Majestie and your countrey.

And nowe to returne to Mr Candishe. I doo not thinke your Lordship hath a more faithfull nor assured frende than he is unto you, and for myne owne parte the more (I assure your Lordship) I am acquainted with him the better I lyke him, prayeing your Lordship therefore to contynewe your good favor towardes him, and to give him credit for the reporte of our occurrences here, wherof my leysure serveth not to wryte at large.' At the Court.

Signed ½p. (Original Letters II/87)

THE EARL OF SHREWSBURY TO THE EARL OF LEICESTER

1574, June 26. 'My very good Lord. Wheras one Chester, in tymes past my pardener throughe great misdemeanure and approved falshoode in conveyinge this Queens (of Scots) letters too and fro, was banishte my howse and the whole cuntrey besydes. Wherupon wandring masterles up and downe in places knowne utterly refused, at lengthe gott into my Lord Bedfordes service, who, at the only report of so lewde a fellowe, wrytes to my wyfe in his behalfe for sertaine wages detayned, wherin he dothe not onely helpe himselfe, having every penny justly paid him, but my Lord Bedforde seemes much too credulous in that respecte. Wherfore upon this discourtesie I thoughte good to give you to understand that if it comes to your Lordships hearing you may the better knowe what to say therin. For he that will not spare to wryte of Chesters word will peradventure spare as little to speak when occasion servethe. But I thinke if the Queens Majestie understode my Lord Bedfordes entertayning eny suche, she would not lyke well therof, and I am very sorie to heare the same. Neverthelesse except at eny tyme.....impart it unto you.....I request ther be......spooke.' Sheffield.

Copy Torn Endorsed in the Earl of Shrewsbury's hand: 'The coppy of my letter to my L. of Leycester toucheth the....my L. Bedforde wrytt to my wyf.' (Original Letters I/1)

THOMAS GREVES TO THE EARL OF SHREWSBURY

(1574) August 3. So far as I can learn none of the ladies and gentlemen who are now at Buxton leave before Monday week, except Sir Thomas Cecil who goes next week, and then 'Mr Secretary shall be placed in his chamber.' Yesterday there came from Chatsworth 5 hogsheads of beer and ale, of which two were delivered to Mr Cecil, two to 'My Lady Mildmay' and one to Lady Norris. I perceived that my Lady 'Susons' grudged much that she was without it. I gave her some rabbits to make her equal with the other ladies. I have given Mr Secretary some sheep and six bottles of wine from you, for which he was very thankful.

You ordered me upon the delivery of letters sent from Mr Mildmay to my Lady his wife, to find means that she would write to him again and your Honour would see them. Directly upon the receipt of these letters she sent one of her folk with letters to Mr Mildmay telling him of the care you had had of her at Buxton, leaving her your own furnished lodging, for her man made me privy to part of her letters. She told me today to write to you and ask you to send some tips of a stag's horn, for Mr Doctor Beech, who is come with Lord Essex, told her they would be very good for her. Lady Norris asks for two or three casks of your bread. I gave her six jugs of wine and two bottles of ale to her and Lady Mildmay who were glad of it 'for here ys no wyne worthe drinkinge.' Buxton.

P.S. 'The strangers which be at Buxton at this present:
My Lady of Essex
My Lady Norris
My Lady Mildmay
My Lady Susans Bowssor
My Lady Wyllobe
My Lady Gresham
My Lady Margaret, the Earl of Bedfords daughter.
Mrs Morreson, my Lady of Bedfords daughter with divers other gentlewomen
Sir Thomas Smyth
Sir Thomas and Lady Syssils
Sir Thomas Stanhope
Mr Doctor Astley
Mr Doctor Bayle
Mr Leverett
Mr Allington
Mr Digby and his wife which came with my Lady of Essex, all lodged within the house and all their meat dressed within the house except Mr. Secretary which hath his meat dressed at Heathcoks House.'

Holograph Addressed: 'To my Lord at Sheffeld manor give this.'*Endorsed:* Company at Buxton, 1574. 3pp. (Original Letters I/139)

(?WILLIAM) CAVENDISH TO THE COUNTESS OF SHREWSBURY

(1576 or before) November 19. He requests her to procure from her husband the loan till Lady Day of his house at 'Cowlhar (bor)' (Coldharbour) for Lady Mary Sidney, 'of the condition of whose ability to requite both your courtesies therin, as I know you both fully resolved, so of the ready thankfulness of her mind in all such honourable offices of virtue I assure myself you possess no less assurance: besides the which you shall, as it were, whet and refresh the memory of both my noble Lords, her brothers, with continuance of my Lords and your lasting friendship to their house.' From the Court.

Holograph Addressed: To the Countess of Shrewsbury at Sheffield Castle. 1 p. (Original Letters II/285)

On the same page is a holograph note from Lady Mary Sidney to the

Countess of Shrewsbury expressing a hope that the above-mentioned favour may be granted at the request of her cousin Cavendish. Overleaf there is a holograph note from the Countess of Shrewsbury to her husband. 'My none, I se my Lady Sedney ys desyrus to have your howse thys winter. Yf yett plese you that she have yett apone condecyone that yf you com to London your selfe then you may have yet apone ii days warnynge to be made redy for you, yett were not amisee. I am of opinyon you shall not come there afore Ester. God grant you may be ther then yn good sorte. I wyll sett my workes yn as good order as I can, and come to you of Saterday come senett, and soner yf you se causse. If you lend your howse I pray you synnyfy your plesure to Bylbrowe by thys barare, your fotteman, who brought me thys letter. Farewell my deare none.'

SIR CHARLES CAVENDISH TO THE EARL OF SHREWSBURY

(? Before 1577) I beseech you to appease my Lady's mislike to me through this crooked misfortune, which was but ill-luck, and I will set it down as it chanced. I having no disposition to stir abroad, left my chamber and Mr Hungatt accompanied me, his men and mine went to dinner, he and I practising the sword and target a good space and then left. The man that now is hurt came to us seeing those and having a special fancy to be playing. He spake against the target, commending the buckler for the better defence and offence, and took up a foil and a target. I told him that with my single rapier I would be too hard for him, and playing it him upon the ribs under his target, the second time I offering to thrust his thigh and he for his casts, as he thought, put down his target; in which time I turned the point over which 'lyght' him in the eye. So that he fell, which amazed me greatly, for if ever in my life I played more cooler or with better discretion, both the man's master and myself be greatly deceived. But, God be thanked, he is well amended and in no danger of any 'lyme'. Once again I humbly beseech your earnest means to my mother, for I protest I desire not to live to have the least frown of her, much less to be in her disgrace; and except it be done by your Lordship, whose wisdom I know can temper this conceit of hers, I shall rest in doubt not to be restored to her favour, which I hold dear above all things.

Holograph Addressed: To the Earl of Shrewsbury, Earl Marshal. *Seal* 1p. (Original Letters II/283)

The misunderstanding between the Earl and Countess of Shrewsbury began in 1577. See Francis Bickley, *The Cavendish Family*, p.21.

THE PRIVY COUNCIL TO THE EARL OF SHREWSBURY

1577, June 17. We thank you for preserving peace in the late quarrel at Derby between Sir John Zouche and Sir Thomas Stanhope. We have ordered the former to give us an account of his doings, and shall take such further order in regard to him as will preserve her Majesty's peace and your honour. We understand that the Justices of the Assizes have been dealing with the matter, and have ordered them on their next coming down to the country to take some order therein. Greenwich.

Signed: Lords Burghley, Lincoln, Sussex and Bedford, Sir F. Knollys and Sir F. Walsingham *Endorsed:* '17 Junii, 1577. The Lords of the Counsayle to George, Erle of Shrewsbury touching the quarrell betwixt Sir Thomas Stanhope and Sir John Zouche.' 1 p. (Original Letters I/2)

1577-78, January 12. I ask you to bestir yourself at Court to help me in my cause against Sir John Slouche (Zouche), who has the ear of the Earl of Bedford and works very earnestly. 'Therefore your Lordship must now awaken your spirit.' The Privy Council's letter (of January 2) directed to four Justices of the Peace of Derbyshire (to enquire into Sir John Zouche's doings at the last musters) is useless to me. Sir T. Cockin is wholly Zouche's, Sir Humphrey Bradborn is a simple and soft person and will be over-ruled unless he is looked to. Mr Rodes goes to London, and Mr Francis Curson is the only man you can trust; and he is very flexible and perhaps his hand was dipped in the same pie (i.e. the embezzlement of funds at the musters) You must send for them, and without threatening or entreating them, give them to understand that you reported Zouche's proceedings to the Council on the complaint of the country. But deal privately and do not let the interview get to Zouche's ears. You might also get some wise friend to tell them plainly what their duty is to perform in your behalf. In any case it is quite necessary you should be at the trial, for it is in many respects truly spoken, *Faciem hominis, faciem leonis.* The Vice-Chamberlain tells me that the Earl of Bedford is come to London on purpose to support Zouche. Your servant Germayne Ireton was mixed up in the affair. You might send him to Yorkshire on her Majesty's affairs, so as to prevent his being called as a witness. Please make enquiry as to how much, if any, money was returned by Zouche.

PS. 'Yf your Lordship for want of helthe be nott in ease to goo uppe when you thinke good, my thinkes then it were very convenient that my Lady tooke the travell. And your Lordship knoweth that women with women can worke best, specially such one as my Lady whose wisdome and discrete cours can sufficiently deale with the best of them, by this with her Majesty or the Counsell or the other ladies about her Highnes. And so may she prepare the way for all thinges and return so instructed and leave such a plott for you behind her and worke your frendes for you in suche good order, as att your one comyng thear shalbe no difficulty att all, but that every thinge may goo as you would desier. And this was my Lord of Leicester's advise and speche to me in somer.' Shelford.

Signed   The postscript holograph   Endorsed in Gilbert Talbot's hand: '12 Ja. 1577.   Sir Thomas Stanhope to my L, my Father.   Very pollitique.' 4pp. (Original Letters I/4)

'THE SAYING OF SIR THOMAS STANHOPE'

1577-78, February 16. 'I have not intended to doe nor have written or sayd anything wherebie my Lady Souche shoulde or ought to be taken to be an unhonest woman, neither can I of my knowledge charge her to be an unhonest woman, nor meane to doe aniething to that ende.

I knowe not that William Souche ever ment to destroie the children of Sir John Souche, neither did ever meane to charge him therewith, neither can I say that Sacheverell dyd report any such thing of William Souche.'

Notes in margin in another hand: 'Sir Thomas Stanhope's letters were produced before the Lords of the Counsail which was directly contrary to boothe these things. This is registered in the Counsell Booke.'

Draft? 1p. (Original Letters I/6)
   (See *Acts of the Privy Council*, 1577-78, p.166)

THE EARL OF LEICESTER TO THE EARL OF SHREWSBURY

(1579) September 10.   I have received your letters and have written lately to you such news as the time afforded as well of Monsieur's being here and his departure again, as also of Irish news.   For the first I can say no more for that we are not acquainted with any further disposition of her Majesty, and hereof your Lordship shall trust me and believe I speak truly and unfeignedly to you. Yet hath it been hard to myself here that many things are done and as much past whereof I should be a witness: but believe me, my Lord, I know no more but that he is departed even as he can hitherto, for anything past here.

For the other matter of Ireland, though the chief rebel be dead, yet it goeth not well there, for I think there be few other than rebels at this day.   Her Majesty hath sent some forces and means to send more, and, good my Lord, take heed of bruits and tales.   You will not believe what tales and lies are spread abroad; it is for no good.   I hear of them from all parts of the realm, and as well to touch her Majesty as those about her.   We have had some brabbles here of late; this bearer shall tell you of them.   Havering.

Holograph   Wafer seal   1¼pp.   (Original Letters II/272)

THOMAS BAWDEWYN TO THE EARL OF SHREWSBURY

1580, May 8.   One Owen Jones, attending on the Lord Treasurer, has obtained from her Majesty the wardship of one Sherbrooke, and he denies that you have any claim.

The Earls of Northumberland, Kent, Worcester, Rutland, Southampton and the Lords Paget and Buckhurst, accompanied by the Comptroller and a great number of other gentlemen, passed through Cheapside the 7th of this instant from their lodgings to the *Castle* in Fleet Street, where they dined together.

There is a commission out from the Council to examine and punish the Papists of Lancashire, Cheshire and Yorkshire for such abuses as they have committed in hearing of masses and other misdemeanours since the speeches of Monsieur his coming.

The agent for Monsieur dined with Lord Leicester yesterday, where after some speeches of the ancient wars between England and France, Lord Bedford called to remembrance your noble progenitor and urged him very often with the French proverb used to terrify their children: 'The Talbot doth come, the Talbot doth come'.

The said Frenchman looks for his dispatch today or tomorrow.   All that look for Monsieur's coming declare what a good prince he is, and commend him for giving advertisement what foes this land has in the Pope and King Philip.   They say further that he has been offered with the daughter of Spain the lands which were given to the Emperor for the ransom of the captive French King, besides the Low Countries and the sum of 300 crowns for the payment of his debts.   The Pope will give to the value of 2000 crowns *per annum*, the Kingdom of Avignon in the land of Savoy.   Yet his zeal is so great with the Queen that he will forsake all to be her Majesty's husband, and he intends to send over ambassadors with perfect conclusions if her Highness will so like.   In respect of that hindrance which otherwise he should incur, others say there is no such matter, but that all things are already ended by consent of them, and that he shall marry the Duchess of Lorraine.

By reason of the plague which is in the Spanish army and camp, it is scattered but not dissolved.   Whether the same shall arrive, it is for anything we do there so doubtful as it was in the beginning.

Burnell, whose bands (bonds?) I have , has been once again before her Majesty; she has made Mr Dale his solicitor with the Lords.

PS. Mr Doctor Masters doth desire you to take regard hereafter you do not meddle with mechiachow the root, by taking whereof many have incurred great extremities, namely the wife of Sir Thomas Cecil as he doth affirm.

You have no need to send into Shropshire until my coming, for we are proceeding here for a third jury also.

I do trust that Mr Walsingham's daughter shall do well. London.

Holograph 3pp. (Original Letters II/94)

(THE COUNCIL OF THE NORTH) TO RICHARD NORTON

1580, May 13.   We have received your letter enclosed in one from the Lord President, and observe that you think yourself unable, by reason of ill-health, to take up the appointment.   In that case, you must appoint your brother William and your son Edmund, duly furnishing them with armour, tents, corslets, bows etc. 'The use hath bene to have xxx harquebusses in the hundreth, xxx pikes and the rest bowes and bills. Your pikemen shuld have corslettes, your harquebusses nede smal armor, but a moryan, sleves of maile yf they may be hadde, and swordes and ther peces, and for suche harnes as your men shuld have besides corslettes, we think cotes of plate wilbe the best allowed.' The matter requires great speed: do not therefore fail in any wise.

PS. We send you herewith a new commission and have added no names therein to the intent the men may be set forth with the most speed that may be; and for carriage, we have not known any man charged therewith but the captains for the bands.   York.

Copy 2pp. (Original Letters I/9)

THE EARL OF LEICESTER TO THE EARL OF SHREWSBURY

1580, June 19.   I recommend the bearer Somerset the herald to your notice, who desires to thank you for your consent in procuring for him his present position.   From the Court.

Holograph Addressed: 'To the right honourable my very good L. and cousin the Erle of Shrewsbury'. *Endorsed:* 'Erle of Leycester, 1580, 19 June' 1p.   (Original Letters I/13)

THE EARL OF LEICESTER TO THE EARL OF SHREWSBURY

(1580) June 26.   'My good Lord, with my most hartye thankes for your honorable and frendly intertaynment at Buxstons. I am to pray your Lordship not to think any thing in me for not wryting soner unto you, specyally touchinge the matter at Chatsworth, which your Lordship told me of: but touching these matters, first your Lordship shall understand that at my coming thether I found my Lady in very great grefe and laing all blame from her self, chardged dyvers with evyll offyces done betwene you, she altogether seking her justyfication, and desired nothing more than that she might be charged with some particularyties. I did as much as I could avoyde to deal your waye, the rather for that I was to departe so sone, onlye I am than to vyssett hir as her Majestie had comaunded me, and to lett her knowe how sorry she was that any such brech shuld be betwene your Lordship and hir. She answered styll the fault was not hirs, she protested all innocencye toward your Lordship, craving nothing but to be charged with some partyculer matter, but she never yet could be. Whereuppon I was so bold to tell hir of some thinges which I hard of, which she shuld overshute hirselfe in, as well in un-

25

mete speeches toward you, as otherwyse: amonge other thinges I sayd yt was reported she shuld threaten your Lordship, as though she knewe thinges by you that she could harme you yf she lysted, which I did marvell that so wyse a woman wold use to her husband. To this she answered very calmely, saing: "I think ther ys no creature able to say yt of me, nether had I ever the thought to deale that way with him, and yet," sayth she, "both my self and my children ar made now to be chefe instruments of yll servyce toward the Queenes Majestie in all matters cast uppon them, which I hope wyll not be provyd. As for my Lord, my husband, God forbid I shuld use any such speeches against him." And so semed therin to me to be farr from any such intentyon, but she told me of dyvers hard dealings that had bin used toward hir, as one was, that she had byn as yt were slyted before your servauntes, and openly made an exclamation of hir to hir owne face coming from chappell, which she greved at and yet doth. Than I told hir further that I hard she had sent your Lordship a message uppon a very smale cause, by which she shewyd herself not to owe you any further obedyence or dewtye, that hir love was gone, etc. To this she semed much trowbled and told me yt was not so, but thus much ys trewe, "that your Lordship sending the lytle Lady Arabella to me, being a thing I desired much the contrary and that she might stay still with my daughter Talbott, and in his message did use his comandment for hir abode with me. I answered indede that my Lord delt hardly with me, and dyd use me strangely in many thinges, not as thoughe I were his wife, but in such sort as were inough to alyanatt the hart and dewty of any wyfe, and," sayth she, "I think I wylled my sonne Talbott to wryte such wordes of grefe, finding his so exstreme and unaturall dealing with me, and," quoth she, "my sonne ys here, though a prisoner only coming to take his leave of me, and his wyfe, taking hir jorney further to London." And theruppon coming into hir gallery brought me to him in a chamber wher he and his wyfe was, and told me howe he came that night late thether and wold away agen that present night and overtake me or I cam to the Court, as he dyd in dede, and he was very loth that he was knowne to be ther, and therfore I stayed not with him so long as the wryting of these lynes. Thus have I told your Lordship upon myne honor and truth the somme of our doings at Chatsworth, having that my Lady ernestly desired me to be an humble meanes to her Majestie not to think amysse of hir before she shuld finde somme just matter proved against her. And yf her Majestie wold be a gracious instrument to quallyfie your Lordships great dyspleasure, as she had sent her word by her sonnes and others that she wold. And this much more I think good to lett your Lordship understand that, being at Leycestre ther came to me from hir Majestie by post, thinking to find me at Buxstons, dyrectyon from hir self to comand me to have delt very ernestly in hir name with your Lordship, as also with my Lady, which your Lordship doth well remember. I had some notyce of ii or iii dayes or I departed Buxstons, and as I have reported to your Lordship as nere as I can what was the chefest matter that passed betwene my Lady and me, so must I say in troth I found her most desirous and most wylling to have your good favor above any worldly thing.

Now, my Lord, somwhat touching your owne causes which your Lordship comytted unto me. I have not fayled fully to declare them unto her Majestie as well som thinges that greved you as others that moved you to desier her Majestie's presence, and that you were in good hope that her Majestie wold have grauntyd you your many and longe petitions that way or now, for ther was no earthly thing you desired more than to see and speake with her Majestie. I did also lett her know how many causes of grefe you had uppon brutes and tales that came fliing down to the great touch of your honor and credytt. I doe finde her Majestie very willing that your Lordship shall have your desier to come upp to her. And for other reports or tales she doth pray your Lordship not to trowble your self with them for ye shall well perceave that she wyll do nothyng but that shall be to your honor and good. And that your faythfull and loyall dealing ys not unthankfully bestowyd, as at your coming ye shuld better perceave, and to my seming she doth meane ye shuld come very shortly, which yf wyshing could shew, I have wysht yt at this present, for her Majestie is even now in consultation of those matters that your Lordship and I conferred on. And I did imparte unto her how your Lordship and I did joyne in opinion concerning those matters. Of this your Lordship shall hear more very shortly from me. I will not forgett to vyssett you often.

Touching myslyke of my Lord Talbott for his going to Chatsworth, truly my Lord, all thinges dewly considered, your Lordship doth deale hardly to be so offended for that matter, his wife being ther and with child, and to come secretly bycause he wolde avoyde the note your Lordship dyd charge him with, which was to give open countenance in coming thether, which he refrayned as well to satysfye your Lordship as only to se his wyfe and departing from hir so sone. And truly, my Lord, he ys fully bent in all obedyence and dewty to seke you and obey you, and doth draw himself and his wyfe thence for that only purpose. And your Lordship I knowe wyll not refuse wyllingly the fonte of the blessinges of God, which is the comfort of your owne flesh and blood, your child and him that must succede you in your honor and place yf he lyve, specyally that ys forward and so lykely to prove well as he ys in the opinion of all men: which I speak to your Lordship without flatterye, he ys as well thought of of all sorts of good men as any noble man in England ys. Her Majestie hath also conceved a very good opinion of him. He ys only now shadowed and darkened by the want of your Lordships father lyke coun-tenance and favor, which yf hit may please to shew and to use him as all your frendes thinkes him worthye of, your Lordship shall have the greatest good and comfort therof. I can but lament the noble man's hard case to se how he is perplexed with such dyffycultyes, as he ys almost no way able to helpe, and only I find him disposed to applye him self from all other comforts and conten-tations. Good, my Lord, think yet somtymes what I was bold to say to you at Buxstons touching this matter. I am suer ther was never any that spake with a more syncere minde towarde you and your howse, wherof ye know I have no smale interest to seke the well doing therof, neither shall ye ever finde any kinsman or frend that hath byn more carefull both for ye and them than I have byn. And so wyll I take my leave and comend your Lordship to the grace of God.' Richmond.

PS. 'I cam hither to ye Court uppon Tewsday last. Her Majestie, God be thanked, never better for her health.'

Holograph Addressed: 'To ye right honorable my very good L and cousin the Erll of Shrewsbury, L. Marshall of England and one of the lords of her Majestie's Privy Councell' *Endorsed:* 'E. of Leicester, about the Countess. 1580.' 5pp. (Original Letters I/16)

FRANCIS, LORD TALBOT, TO THE EARL OF SHREWSBURY

1580, June 30. Since my last letter, the Prince de Condé and the French Ambassador have seen her Majesty, Lord Leicester, the Vice-Chamberlain and Secretary Walsingham. The Lord Treasurer has been much in London but is now at Court, and the Lord Chamberlain has gone to his house at Newhall. I hear he is very sick. Lord Grey goes to Ireland as Deputy, Lord and Lady Warwick to the Wells in Warwickshire. Lord Leicester goes to Kenilworth within the next three or four days for a short stay. 'The Quenes Majestie hathe ben sycke of a could, but now well receovered, thankes be to God.' Forgive this short letter, but I have been very sick these 3 or 4 days with such an extreme pain in my head that I am not able to hold open my eyes. Say ows (? Say House).

Holograph Addressed: 'To my lord my Father.' 1p. (Original Letters 1/19)

LORD BURGHLEY TO THE EARL OF SHREWSBURY

1580, August 10. 'The Quenes Majesty hath commaunded me to gyve your Lordship on hir behalf in chardg that your Lordship do look very circumspectly to your great chardg, which although she thynketh of common order you will doo, yet hir Majesty wold have you to understand that at this present she fyndeth it more necessary for you to do than at any tyme these 7 yeres. The particularityes which move hir Majestie, I assure your Lordship I am not made acquaynted withall. But it semeth by her Majestie's speeches that she has intelligence gyven hir sondry wayes that it is ernestly intended both within the realme and without that very shortly the Quene ther shuld ether by slight or force escape from you.

And now therefore, my good Lord, you shall do well to have regard to such as you suffer to come neare to the sayde Quene, or how hir company shall wander abrode, or have frequent conversation with such in that contry as may be suspected. This new suspicion of hir Majesty is very suddenly risen, for not manny wekes past hir Majesty began to conceave better of the Quene, by reason of hir last courteous letters, than she had before done, and therefore some short tyme will make proof whither the new causes of suspicion are grownded uppon matter of weight. But howsoever it be, your Lordship shall do well to be very circumspect and to be curious herin, and so I take my leave of your Lordship.'

The occurrents of this time are these:

In France La Fère must soon surrender to the King unless it is relieved by a foreign army. Anjou wants peace, but cannot get it unless the King of Navarre will surrender his towns. This he will not do because hitherto, when towns have been surrendered, the Governors have slain all the Protestants in them. The Commissioners for the marriage are appointed, but the Queen delays admission of their coming till the Civil War is ended.

In Ireland Lord Baltinglass, a young man and sworn servant of the Pope, is broken out. Lord Kildare is gone against him, and Lord Grey wants 500 men to assist him. Lord Desmond is driven into the mountains of Munster; his only hope now is from Spain.

The Queen's navy is increased with new ships. The King of Spain is entered into Portugal; Don Antonio cannot long hold out. D'Aubigny rules all in Scotland. The Low Countries are minded to give themselves to Monsieur d'Anjou. Oatlands.

Holograph 3pp. (Original Letters I/21)

(SIR) FRANCIS WORTLEY TO THE EARL OF SHREWSBURY

1580, August 11. In answer to your letter of the 10th instant, Hallamshire has as yet no particular charge set upon it, but is referred to your consideration to be assessed as parcel of the Wapentake. We levy as many men in every Wapentake according to the proposition I sent you taxed upon them. The Lord President will be at Wakefield for three days on Saturday. Halifax.

Holograph Addressed: 'To the Earl at Buxton.' 1 p. (Original Letters I/23)

(SIR) FRANCIS WORTLEY TO THE EARL OF SHREWSBURY

1580, September 5. The Archbishop and the Lord President today went hence towards Southwell to sit on ecclesiastical causes, the President to Mr Lees at Hatfield 'to his bed', and the Archbishop (as is said) to Mr Gargravis. The President will be back on Saturday, Lord Ewry is supplying his place. Mr Thomas Barneby of Burnby brought young Bosevyle to York to prove Godfrey Bosvile's will. Mr. Thomas Barneby is constituted guardian. Lord Darcy, Mr Wentworth, Mr Lea and Mr Holmes have rated your lands in the Wapentakes of Strafford and Tickhill, for the furnishing of soldiers, very near to the third part of the Wapentakes. This I consider unreasonable, and when I get home I will do my best to get order taken therein. York.

Holograph Addressed: 'To the Earl at Sheffield.' 1 p. (Original Letters I/25)

THOMAS BAWDEWYN TO THE EARL OF SHREWSBURY

1580, September 11. 'I have ben at the Court with Bawkin his horses and have declared your request to Mr Walsingham, whoe did sende twoe of his cheffest survauntes to take the vewe and to yeld him an estimate of the saide horses wyche withe theire furniture are valued under the price which was set downe for the hobbye, as this bringer can informe yowe.

The saide Master Walsingham hathe mooved her Majestie yet once againe for the money dewe unto yowe for the diat of yowre charge and many speeches did pas, but in conclusion Mr Walsingham did delyver that he was not a frende unto the quiet of the state whoe did put her Majestie in minde to abate the allowance. For, saide he, iff it be goonne or be taken awaye, howe can my Lorde mainteine his people aboute him, and yf she be not sene unto she wyll presentlye escape. I beseche youre Majestie, let not the pinchinge and sparinge of a thousande pounde by yere worke suche extremeties in this cause as they have doonne in others to late to be called backe: as it lyeth presentlye to be perceaved in Ireland and other places, and assure yourselfe this unquietnes in Scotland dothe tend to soome purpose. And yet if no suche thinges were or had happened, I wolde not keepe so dangerous a guest for to gaine *de claro* so muche money as my Lorde hathe allowed him. For yf in time it sholde happen that she sholde escape, let her be never so vigilantlye seene unto, yet youre Majestie wolde thinke a suspicion styll in me and call me to triall of that wiche I did never offend in, and therefore let these causes move yowe. Wherein she hathe taken a pause and so Mr Secretary standeth in good expectation to have it the next bill, which was my Lord Treasurer his opinion, as heretofore I have written unto yow.

Master Wilson dothe entende a jorney to Duram before Michaelmas. It is good yowe byd him welcome to Rufford, and that yow doe see all thinges well ordered at Sheffield. I can not tell what her Majestie's pleasure maye be, but I am promised, iff his viage dothe holde, I shall have fowre dayes warninge by his men. The saide Mr Secretary hath also dealed with her Majestie for yowre diat money. He saieth she made him a very straunge aunswere, but yf Mr

Walsingham can not obtaine he wyll see what he can doe.'

I enclose the articles of agreement between the Low Countries and Monsieur. La Fère in France still holds out: the King has moved his camp to the upper side of the town.

'Soome say that the English house in Rome is dissolved by the pope for that theye promised him that rebellion sholde be in this lande, whyche is not fallen out. Howsoever it be, manye of the same Italionated merchauntes have latelye arived here and are apprehended.' London.

Holograph Addressed: 'To my Lorde. The Corte dothe come to Richmond on Monday, part of the stuffe was sent to Winsor, but there cam a countermaunde. The parliament dothe not holde untyll October.' 2pp. (Original Letters I/27)

THOMAS WILSON TO THE EARL OF SHREWSBURY

1580, September 17. I received your letter of the 6th of September only today, owing, it seems, to the negligence of the post at Stamford or elsewhere. I will send it tonight to your servant and the packet according to direction. 'I am glad there are so few papistes about yow. Conformitie in religion cawseth quietnes in conscience universallie, and would God that charitie did more abownd. Yesterdaie Monsieur de Buy, elder brother to Monsieur de Plessy, came to the Court from Monsieur to take a resolute answer for this great matter of the mariage. I am not hable to saye any thyng touching the sequele, but as God wyl, al shal be.'

As for news from abroad. The Prince of Orange is much blamed by the multitude for the loss of Bouchain. A reward of 25,000 crowns is offered by King Philip for the capture or killing of the Prince.

In Ireland several captains have been killed in an attack on the baron of Baltinglass, 'I praye God our own men, I meane of the meaner sorte, had not more desire to spoyle than intention to beare armes justly upon their paye, for repressyng of the rebels. Greadie desire to get hindreth thexecuting of justice as it should bee.' At the Court in Richmond.

Holograph Addressed: 'To the Earl. In Darbyshyre at his manor of Shefyld.' *Endorsed* 'Mr Wilson. 1580, 17 Sept.' 2pp. (Original Letters I/29)

LORD MOUNTEAGLE TO THE EARL OF SHREWSBURY

1580, October 6. A request for £150, part of the sum due to him from the Earl. Harwood.

Holograph 1p. (Original Letters I/31)

THOMAS WILSON TO THE EARL OF SHREWSBURY

1580, October 20. 'I have receaved the great packet, which I wyl cawse presentlie to bee sent according to the direction, the same conteynyng nothyng but the parties affayres. The parliament is proroged to the 24 of November, which is 20 daies longer, that the Commissioners in France, who are looked for here, maye have the longer tyme and to bee here at the bigynnyng, Mr Staffre being sent thether for that purpose. It is reported that the French Kyng should be dangerously sicke of a bloodie flux, and that he hath sent the Queene Mother to Dolynville, where he lyeth, being a place of pleasure. Monsieur is at Jarnacke with the King of Navarre to make a peace for hym uppon surrender of such townes as those of the religion are held. In the mene season St Jhon D'Angeli is besieged where it is thought the Prince of

Condye is, and also Strozzi, who was thought should have gone to the defense of Portingale when no such thing was ment, doth now keepe Rochel frome vytayles, and so to furnyshe them yf they wil not yeeld. King Phillipe enjoyeth Portingale as quietlie as he doth Spayne. Out of Irland there is nothing yet knowen synse the arrival of the straungers there and my Lord Deputie goyng agaynst with gaie face. When any newes be come, your Lordship shal understand the same with the first' At the Court in Richmond.

Holograph Addressed: 'To the Earl at Sheffield' 'Delivered at the Court 20th of November (October?) at 9 of the clocke in the forenoon. Recd Walton at Cros at six at afternoon, 20 Oct. Recd Ware XX Octobris at eyght in ye nyght. Recd. Huntingdon the 21 of October at 8 in the mornying.' 1p. (Original Letters I/35)

The Earl of Leicester to the Earl of Shrewsbury

(1580) Saturday, December 3. 'I have received your letter which I dyd imparte to hir Majestie, and she lyked well your Lordship's removing of Martyn, but somwhat offended with me that I had omytted one parte of hir pleasure, which was that your Lordship shuld send him upp hether with message or commandement. Assuredly, my Lord, I did not so understand at her Majestie's handes and so I told her, for yf I had I wold aswell have signyfied theone as theother to your Lordship. Then it semed her Majestie was dowbtfull whether she have yt dyrectyd to me or to Mr Secretary Walsingham, who I suppose hath remembered yt. Quoth she: "Yf not ye shall wryte agayn to my Lord", sayth she, "that he cause Martyn to come upp, and yf he send him ether to you or to Secretary Walsingham." Whereby your Lordship may now perceave her playsure ys that you send Martyn hether, which I am sewer your Lordship wyll do accordingly, albeyt I assure your Lordship I know no further matter than I wrote in my last, whatsoever ys further knowne to her Majestie.

Now, my Lord, though I dowbt not but the newes be come to your eares or now, I cannott lett pas to signyfie the good successe God hath geven to Lord Grey in Irland agaynst the late dayngers arived there. About the 5th or 6th of the last month he cam thether with a 1000 souldyers, horse and footemen. He found ther her Majestie's shipps which had both ordynaunce and other provyssions for a siege, being sent of purpose to mete him ther, and he imedyately planted his battery and within ii dayes he forced them simply to yeld without condycyons. They were newe 600 Italians and Spanyardes, as well appointed men as any could be and as gallant souldyers in all aparaunce, very well furnysshed and vyttalled for a long tyme, and inough to have kept out 6 tymes as many as my Lord had with him; but so amazed were they as the fort and princypall men to the number of xii being taken to mercye, the rest were cutt in peces to the number of 600 and odd. I trust hit wylbe a warning how theyr fellowes attempt the lyke. My Lord Grey lost only one man, which was Mr John Cheke, a querry under my rule, a tall valiant gentleman he was. And thus much I thought good to signyfie unto you coming but Thursday night late last to her Majestie.'

Holograph Addressed: 'To the right honorable my very good Lord and cousin the Erle of Shrewsbury.' *Endorsed in the Earl of Shrewsbury's hand:* 'Answered the 12 of Dec. 1580.' *and in another hand:* 'L. °Leicester 1581 (sic) Irish newes.' 3 pp. (Original Letters I/37)

Gilbert Talbot to the Earl of Shrewsbury

1580-81, January 29. 'Yesternyght Mr Secretarye Walsyngham sente for me into his chamber and toulde me that your Lordship myghte thynke discurtesye in him that he hadd not wrytten unto you of so longe, yet that the falte was not in him but in her Majestie who for thes xvi dayes hathe ever putt him of, and wolde never gyve him any resolute answere touchynge those thynges which he moved for your Lordship, espetially for the wonted allowance of monye for the dyett of your charge. Wherin her Majestie hathe often requyred that before he and Mr Secretary Wyllson sholde in one lettere lett your Lordship understand that her Majestie wyll not contynew any suche for- mer allowance but to requyre you to be satisfyed with the one halfe thereof, to which mynde she can not be removed from. Nevertheless for that Mr Secretarye thynkethe it not fytte that your Lordship sholde satisfye your selfe therwith, he hathe forborne to wryte after that manner. Yet did her Majestie dyrectly so commande him to doe. The which he wylled me to lett your Lordship to understande, and withall that his opinion is that your Lordship sholde no more sue for the allowance. He layed dyvers examples before me, to shew her Majestie's unwillingnes to departe with any monnye but upon nessesitie inforced, as in this matter of Scotland, wherin he saythe hir Majestie shalbe forced to spende above xx thousande poundes before thinges be brought to that passe for the safetye of her Majestie and her realme that they were in before when 11 thousande poundes wolde have kept it as it was, which daly was shewed her Majestie yet colde she not be brought to disburse it, with dyvers other such lyke examples. Wherfore he advysethe that your Lordship wolde presently sue for sum landes in fee farme, so much as you thynke con- venyent, which sute he saythe her Majestie can no wayes suppose to be great- ter than it is, as commonly she dothe other sutes, and so it can be no hyndrance of other sute of importance hereafter for recompence of your service. This he wysshethe sholde be moved in consyderation only of your present charges for the kepynge of your charge; he wysshethe therfore that your Lordship, if you so lyke it, wolde wryte to him to this effecte. That seeynge you perseave her Majestie's great and urgent occasions are suche as she is constrayned to disburse daly infynyte sums of money, that you will press her no further for the contynuance of your wonted allowance, and yet not beynge able any way to defray and beare so great expences which you are forced to be at in the fyn- dynge of her and suche chargeable provisions for her saftye as you are at, you are moste humbly to beseche her Majestie to have consyderation of and not leave you the only unhappy man that ever did her faythfull and trew service, all others being most grasciously and lyberally rewarded, and altho you can chalenge by desertes lyttel or nothinge, yet in all trew faythfull service towardes her and perfyte discharge of all the trust that ever her Majestie reposed in you, you dare and doe compare with any man that lyveth, and you nothinge doubte but that her Heyghnes will have good remembrance of this your xi yeares service, of the great adventure therby of your selfe and all that you have, of your bondage by abode all this whyle, in effecte, in one place, depryved of the comforte of your frendes company and sosietye wherewith every man taketh felicity, with a number of such lyke great inconvenyences, all which you will leave to her Majestie to consyder and in tyme to recompence, so that as well your chyldrens' chyldren may reverence her Majestie by her lyberality to you now for your trew service, as yourselfe hathe presente cause to honor her for her most good and grascious opinion of you, in all other thynges never havynge yet bene burtheness unto her, nether sutor for any other recompence: and now seeyng you are no wayes able to beare the charges of that Lady's kepynge and provision for her saftie, you are to requyre him that he will move her Majestie to bestowe on you (so much as you shall thynke good to name) in fee farme, wherin ther can be no hynderance to the revenew of the Crowne, or any delay to her treasure, and for the recompence of your service you truste herafter her Majestie will consyder. This is the effecte of all that I can remember this noble gentellman requyred me to acquaynte your Lordship with of his opinion, and also that your Lordship wolde wryte your letters severally to my Lord of Lecester, to my Lord Treasurer and to Mr Vic-chamberlaine and to Mr Wyllson, lettynge them know that uppon sum consyderations you have determyned not to presse her Majestie any further for the wonted allowance, and therfore have desyred Mr Secretarye Walsingham to move her Majestie to graunte you so much in fee farme, for that he was accustomed to obtayne your allowance: requyryng eche of them partycularly to be furtherars therin, etc. When he had ended this, uppon further talke and conference, he sayde that he wolde assure me uppon his faythe and credyte that her Majestie had a moste parfyte sounde opinion both of your Lordship's and my Lady's love and fydelitye towardes her, nevertheless she was perswaded that the S(cots) Q(ueen) dothe beare a great sway with your Lordship and my Lady and all your house, and that the longe contynuance of acquayntance with her hathe bredd in you bothe a great good lykynge of her: the which, althoughe her Majestie dothe not very well lyke, yet doth she thynke and assure her selfe that withall you bothe doe carry that faythefull harte and love to her Heyghnes which becometh you. And this did Mr Secretarye tell me, as he sayde, as one who he lovethe and trusteth, and was contented that I sholde, as of my selfe, make your Lordship privye thereunto, so as he myghte not here therof againe. Yet, if it pleasethe your Lordship in sum letter to him, knowynge well the messenger, to gyve him harty thankes for his moste frendly advyse and playne delyuge with me, wherunto I have made you pryvye, I thynke he wyll take it very well.

Immediately after this, I imparted to my Lord of Lecester his advyse to your Lordship touchinge your movynge her Majestie for sum landes in fee farme, the which he lyked very well and agreed with his opinion in every thynge. Then I asked him how muche landes he thought was convenyent for your Lordship to demande, and he sayde, seeynge that it was but in consyderation of your presente charges about the kepynge of your charge and not in recompence of your servyce, he wysshed you wolde request but two hundred poundes in fee farme.

I omytt all my answers and replycations to Mr Secretarye, for that it wolde make too longe a letter, but I trust your Lordship knowethe that according to my pore wytts, I omytted nothynge that I thoughte convenyent. In thes matters I desyre to knowe your Lordship's answere so sone as it pleasethe you. By poste it may not be sente, therfore if your Lordship wolde sende upp any ydell boddy with your letters, I thynke the charges were not evyll bestowed. I omytt all other matters for my next letters, and so now doe sease, most humbly besechynge your Lordship's and my Lady's daly blessynge with my wanted prayers for your Lordship's long contynuance in all honor, moste parfyte healthe and longe lyffe.' At my lodgings in Westminster, at the sign of the *Half Moon* in a grocer's house.

PS. 'I here that Baldwyne is comme, but I have not yet seene him, nether sent he to me yet.'

Holograph Seal (a talbot) *Addressed:* 'To my Lord.' *Endorsed:* 'Lord Gilbert to my Lord concerning the Q. of Scots allowance. 29 Jan. 1580.' 3pp. (Original Letters I/39)

(THE EARL OF SHREWSBURY) TO SIR FRANCIS WALSINGHAM
1581, April 11. 'Good Mr Secretarie. This Ladys talour Jukes, yet with

much adoo, is despached, and she lothe to lett him departe, desyryng to retayne styll all that come to her, she caused him to make sondry thinges for her which hathe bene his staye. I made him to be truly loked unto, yett can I nott answer but that they moghte use sum practis with him. I know them so well and there cunnynge delynges as I can not be of other opynion....tourne to there owne hurt......So desyring to here from you of her Majesties good and gracious consideration towardes me, I wyll for thys tyme seas troubling you but with this lords gret paquett.' Sheffield.

Draft Amended and illegible in parts Endorsed: 'The coppy of my letter to Mr Walsyngham conserning Jukes the talore, the 10 of April 1581.' 1p. (Original Letters I/42)

THE EARL OF RUTLAND TO THE EARL OF SHREWSBURY

1581, May 9.   He is writing on behalf of the bearer, John Nevell, who is in debt to Shrewsbury.   He is endeavouring to arrange matters with Nevell's father, and is in London for that purpose.   London.

Signed   1 p.   (Original Letters I/42)

LADY GRACE CAVENDISH TO THOMAS BAWDEWYN

(Before May 19, 1581)   I thank you most heartily for writing to Mr Cavendish and me of the state of this troublesome world, and now I am to entreat you to do me a pleasure, which is this.   Mr Cavendish is very willing to have me go to London with him now, if it would please my Lord to give me leave. But because he himself waits upon my Lord, he will not take me with him without it be my Lord's pleasure, but he is very willing and desirous to have me go, and thinks it very fit for him that I should. Now I am to desire you to move my Lord that he will grant his consent that I may go, or that his Lordship will not be offended if I come after, for Mr Cavendish will be well pleased with it. I desire to go for some causes I will tell you when I see you, and one cause for that I would willingly take some physic. I have had of late such extreme pain and giddiness in my head as I would willingly take some remedy for it now at the beginning least hereafter it will be more painful to me. My request is so reasonable as I trust by your good means I shall obtain it, which if I may do I shall think myself greatly beholding to you. Therefore, good Mr Baldwyn, do your best to obtain it. Mr Cavendish's charges will be all one with me or without me. Thus, hoping for a good answer from you, I bid you heartily farewell.   Tutbury.*   *Undated*

Holograph   1 p.   (Original Letters II/291)

LADY GRACE CAVENDISH TO (THE EARL OF SHREWSBURY)

(1581) May 19.   'In most humble wyse my duty remembrede. It may pleas your Lordshipe to understande that I have receved the forty pounds it pleasede your Lordship to bestow of me for the whych I most humbly thanke your Lordship. It cam in very good tym for that my fesicke hath byn sum thynge chargable to Mr Candysh, but I hope to receve great good by it. I have since my cominge forth of the dyut byne twys at the Court, wher her Majestie spoke very graciously to me askinge me for your Lordship, and tould me she harde lattly from you and that you wer very well, she thankede God. Thus haveinge not any thynge els worthy the writing to your Lordship at thys tyme, but humbly desiringe your Lordships dayly blessinge for Mr Cavendyssh

---

*   *See* following item.

and me, do most humbly take my leve with my prayers for your Lordships helth and long lyfe. Your Lordships most humble and obedyent daughter.' Shrewsbury House. *Undated*

Holograph *Addressed:* 'To my Lord.' *Endorsed:* 'Lady Grace Cavendish, 19 May 1600*(sic).*' 1p. (Original Letters II/76)
See *H.M.C. A Calendar of the Talbot Papers in the College of Arms*, ed. G.R. Batho, p.115, G76.

THE EARL OF NORTHUMBERLAND TO THE EARL OF SHREWSBURY

1581, May 19. He requests permission to see the marriage covenants between his uncle, Lord Percy, and Shrewsbury's aunt. From my house in Saint Martin's.

Holograph 1 p. (Original Letters I/44)

SIR FRANCIS WALSINGHAM TO THE EARL OF SHREWSBURY

1581, May 28. He is writing on behalf of John Wigley, of the hundred of Wirksworth, co. Lancaster, whose goods have been seized by the Earl's officers. Whitehall.

Signed 1 p. (Original Letters I/46)

SIR CHRISTOPHER HATTON TO THE EARL OF SHREWSBURY

1581, June 17. He is writing on behalf of one Tasser, to whom the Queen has granted lands in certain manors of the counties of York and Derby of which Shrewsbury is Lord Steward. From the Court at Whitehall.

Signed 1 p. (Original Letters I/48)

LORD BURGHLEY TO THE EARL OF SHREWSBURY

1581, August 6. He thanks him for his last letter 'by which I perceave your contynuance of your good opinion of my good will towards you'. He thanks him also for the two fodders of lead which proved very useful.

'Now, my Lord, at this present we have here no gret matters to wryte of. I thynk your Lordship hath hard how Campion the Jesuit was taken in Barkshyre at one Yate's house and 3 other massyng priestes with hym. He is in the Tower and stiffly denieth to answer any question of moment, havyng ben corrected before my Lord Chancellor, my Lord of Lecester and Mr Vice-Chamberlain at my Lord Chancellor's house.

Ther was this weke a masyng priest named Everard Duckett that, being apprehended, was charged with traytorous wordes and thereof convynced, mainteining the Pope's action to be lawfull in publishyng against hir Majesty an excommunication and a sentence that she was not a lefull quene nor her subjects bound to obey her, for which falt he was condemned and suffred as a traytor.

If any of these late apprehended priestes shall do the lyke, the law is lyke to correct them; for these actions are not matters of rellygion but mearley of estate tendyng dyrectley to the deprivation of hir Majesty from hir Crown, wherin God send hir a long possession. Hir Majesty was purposed to have removed to Rychmond, but the plage is in a house at Mortlack, and so I thynk she will tarry x or xii dayes and then to Otelandes and so to Wyndsor, without makyng any speciall progress.

Your Lordship may here of Don Antonio entitlyng hymself K(ing) of Portugall, who now lodgeth at Baynard's Castell, as I thynk by meanes of my Lord of Lecester. I never as yet saw hym, but some of my Lordes of the Counsell that hath spoken with hym report hym to be very wise and modest, slow but grave of speech, and he meaneth to try his fortune, to be a Kyng or nobody. He hath very rych jewells, having in France taken upp gret somes of monny wherwith he hyreth shippes and men both in France and England, to repayre to the Isles of Azorres, wherof the gretest and strongest named Terceras holdeth for hym, as he sayth; but the Spanish Ambassador sayth no.

As yet, since the Secretary departed into France, we have not hard from hym, supposyng that as he was directed to speke first with Monsieur d'Anjeu, so he being far from Parris, that is at St Quyntyn's neare to Cambray, so he is stayed from spedy dispatch hyther.

I pray your Lordship, commend me to my Lady, your wiff.' Greenwich.

Holograph *Endorsed in Shrewsbury's hand:* 'My L. Tresurer's letter of the 6 of August 1581.' 3pp. (Original Letters I/50)

Lord Chancellor Bromley and Lord Treasurer Burghley to the Earl of Shrewsbury

1581, December 1. They inform him that the subsidy which he is to pay amounts to £133:6:8, at the rate of 2/8 in the pound for his lands, according to the grant made by Parliament to the Queen on January 16 (1581), and that Thomas Fortescue and William Phillips of London have been appointed collectors. They request immediate payment.

Signed 1p. (Original Letters I/52)
See *H.M.C. A Calendar of the Talbot Papers in the College of Arms,* ed. G.R. Batho, p.117, G.101.

The Earl of Leicester to the Earl of Shrewsbury

(?1582) May 23. 'My very good Lord. I have read your letter whearby I understand of your good health and present recovery of which I am most hartily gladd, and shall pray God for the long contynewance therof.

But for matter of my cousin Gilbert, I perceave hit doth not a lytle trowble your Lordship styll. But synce your Lordship doth find that hit hath ben the mallyce of others and no desart nether in him nor your Lordship, you shuld well satysfye yourself, spetyally for that hir Majesty ys well resolved that they wer the partes and devyces of lewde personnes as may appere by the order taken, the principall albeyt ther be not so much severytye used as your Lordship doth look for, seeing the manner of thes doings toward you. Yet seing yt can no way be found that yt hath any further roote but even spronge out of this our lene braunch that was your Chaplen, and whether to pick thank and gett reward for nede or to work dyspleasure for mallyce and cannott yet gett albeyt both ys to be supported to be the end of his interest. But for that the face of his pretence caryeth another shewe, your Lordship must in some parte quallyfie the uttermost of your expectation for all that he deserveth. The rather because her Majesty doth both deall and conceave gratyously toward yourself, notwithstanding all ungracious devices uttered, which I must confes to some princes might have bridd more surprize than hath any way entred into her Majestie, which your Lordship must take as a pece of satysfactyon, and I dowbt not but shall be more fully performyd, otherwyse also to your Lordship's greater contentation. And I am well assured her Majestie ys so well satysfied touching my cousin Gilbert as I do wyshe your Lordship rather to let him come agayne to the Court then to remain styll thear. For yt was not his being here that bredd the dyspleasure, but your ill happ to have such a varlett in your sewyer as ther, here or any whear, wold have donne this he did, as you may perceave by the manner of yt. Thus waiting present lesure wyll byd your Lordship farewell.'

PS. 'The good fellow Cor. hath made today ernest menes to speak with me agen, and I mene this day or tomorrow to hear what he wyll say.'

Holograph Endorsed: 'Earl of Leicester, 23 May about 1582.' 1p. (Original Letters I/56)

MARTIN BIRKHEAD TO THE EARL OF SHREWSBURY

1582, June 21. Our sitting at York for this time comes to an end, and I sup-pose the next sitting will begin immediately after the next assizes. 'I receyved a letter from my Lord President to Mr Wortley and myself to agre Mr George Saville and the parson of Thornell if we canne. We hope that my Lord President wilbe here at the next sitting.

A preacher hath written to me that one William Wharton, an old man (whome I thinke your Lordship knoweth), being requested by a great nomber of gent. to sitt at the table with theyme (for that he could kepe theyme good talke), he answered and said: I shall then tell you lyes as the preachers do in the pulpitt. I have showed the Counsell hearof that he may be punished according to his desertes (if it be proved against him).' York.

Holograph 1 p. (Original Letters I/58)

(AUDLEY DANNETT) TO (THE EARL OF SHREWSBURY)

1582, July 23. Since my last of the 16th instant, His Highness and the Prince of Orange arrived at Bruges on the 17th and were well received by the Burgomasters and the town, and by those 'of the Francg as they call them', who take it well that Bruges is visited before Ghent. Monsieur writes to promise those of Ghent to come there shortly, but it is doubtful if he will do so, finding them 'ung petit trop haut a la main.' Yet they may receive him well notwithstanding his mass 'which in that place is very odious.' Today the Assembly of the provinces meets him to decide on the payment of the army and its place of employment. On Saturday, the 21st, the Prince was himself in the Townhouse trying to get money provided for the army, 'But that argument was nothing pleasaunt and the P. that knoweth these people must be gayned by perswasion and not by force, knoweth not, as I have heard say, howe to behave himself to wynne them.'

The camp on the other side are ready daily to mutiny for want of pay, and this notwithstanding the heavy taxes which are levied, 'but the most parte seeke their owne particular and neglect the common busines which in tyme is thought will be their overthrowe.' It is said that his Highness has hitherto sustained his own charges. 'And nowe when he hath assembled great forces to their succor, and that men should be encouraged by a pay to do some service, thease people drawe backe as though all the burden should lie on his Highnes shoulder. The Duke himself beareth all with patience, but his people have much ado to forbeare to speak at the lest.' Things will go badly unless the Assembly does its duty. Reinforcements from France arrive daily; it is given out that the Duke will shortly take a general muster of the camp on the con-dition that money is provided in the mean time, otherwise some great disorder will ensue.

The enemy is said to have passed into Flanders, and to intend to attack us before we are ready. 'And truly here in thease tymes of service the deliberations are very slowe especially in any thing that asketh money.'

It is said that the King of Spain will crave aid of the Princes of the Empire at the Diet against his Highness for intruding on his possession.

On Friday six spies were arrested in the town, the chief being one 'Salceedoe, a Lorrainist borne but a Spaniard by his father, who was killed at the massacre of St Bartholomew for a Huguenott (being as it is said a Papist) for a certein peice of grounde in Lorraine which the Cardinall could by no meanes gett of the said Spaniard. The sonne being left very rich by the death of his father, in short tyme spent all and was of late hanged in effigie at Roan for a coyner of false money, and is reported for a man geven to all kinde of naughtines, and therupon absented himself out of France; till of late he came to this towne recommended by the Duke of Lorraine to his Highnes' service. In the small tyme of his being here, he practised the conveying away of the yonge Counte of Egmonde to the enemy, who as it should seeme did encline therto. He is now commaunded prisoner to his owne lodging in this town. This Salceedo hath had the torture, and as it is said hath confessed some other bad enterprise which I can not learne as yet.' There are said to be here 2000 French footmen, 1500 Reiters and 700 French lances. 2000 Swiss, certain pietons and great store of horsemen under Prince Daulphin are expected. The enemy is said to be much stronger, both in number and goodness of their horsemen. Bruges.

Copy Endorsed: '23 July, 1582. Copie of Mr Dannets letter.' 4 pp. (Original Letters I/60)

Cotton Gargrave to the Earl of Shrewsbury

1582, July 27. I received today the commission for the subsidy in the West Riding and send it on to you to know your pleasure as to the places and times you will appoint for the taxation thereof. It is to be finished before August 25. Nostell.

Holograph Addressed: 'To the Earl at Sheffield.' 1 p. (Original Letters I/62)

The Earl of Leicester to the Earl of Shrewsbury

1582, August 1. He is writing on behalf of the bearer, one Harvy, his servant, in his suit with Roger Beckwith. At the Court.

Signed, with holograph postscript 1p. (Original Letters I/64)

The Earl of Sussex to the Earl of Shrewsbury

1582, August 8. 'My good Lord, I receavyd at my comyng home your Lordships letters, with a letter to your Lordship and another to my self enclosed, for the which I do most hartely thank your Lordship, and do returne to you herewith your owne letter with the wrytyng enclosed. And do very hartely pray you that if eny letters come at eny tyme to me from Mr Secretary, your Lordship will open them, for that I do desyer you should have knowledge of eny thinge cominge to me from him duryng my abode here, and if it be your pleasure to looke on them before they come to me, it wyll save the labor in judging of them to your Lordship after I have receaved them; for my meanyng indede is your Lordship should see them if they conteyne eny matter worth the syght. Your Lordship doth wysely to asserte the forthecomyng of your charge and not to provyde for the nexte, nowe that your self shall see lyklyhood to performe. And so, my good Lord, beyng thoroughly weryed with my travell this daye, I take my leave.' Buxton.

Holograph Seal 1 p. (Original Letters I/66)

(Sir) Thomas Markham to the Earl of Shrewsbury

1582, September 11. He offers his condolences on the death of Francis, Lord Talbot, and regrets that he (Markham) had not been on better terms with him. Woodhouse.

Holograph 1 p. (Original Letters I/68)

Sir Francis Walsingham to the Earl of Shrewsbury

1582, September 26. 'My verie good Lord. Ffor that I knowe your Lordship cannot but be desyrous to understand howe thinges do passe in Scotland and what successe this late action doth take, as a matter wheron your libertye dothe also depend, being nowe stayed there to have a carefull eye unto your Ladys proceedings, I have therfore thought good to send your Lordship a coppye of the last advertisments we have received from thence. By the which you may perceave that thinges stand not yet in so good termes as weare to be wished, which I fear me wilbe the cause of your longer stay from hence then yourself and as many of your frendes her - as would be glad to see you - do desier, among which none doth more earnestlye wishe for that tym then myself, being yet altogether unknown to your Lordship by sight. I send your Lordship also a coppye of Sir George Caryes letter to her Majesty conteyning the Kings answer to hir message, by the which you may judge of what rare towardlynes that yonge prince is and howe dangerous an enemye therfore he would prove unto England yf he should happen to runne any other coorse. And so I commend your Lordship to God.' Windsor.

Signed 1p. (Original Letters I/70)

Jas. Blythman to the Earl of Shrewsbury

1582, October 14. 'I have manye tymes thought upon your honor's words spoken unto me the fyrst of September laste upon your brydge at your castell in Sheffeld, that you were werye of me and that I was werye of your Lordship.

I have syns bothe day and nyght stodyed howe I myght take the cours I myght no more werye your good Lordship, and as I thynke yf my chyldren may have your Lordships favor and helpe, the matter is already brought to pas.' He asks for help in the matter of his suit against Lacy.

Holograph 1p. (Original Letters I/71)

The Earl of Pembroke to the Earl of Shrewsbury

1582, November 2. He offers condolences on the death of his brother-in-law, Francis, Lord Talbot, and requests that his sister's jointure be paid over to him, and if possible increased, according to the terms of his father's will. Salisbury.

Signed 1p. (Original Letters I/73)

Henry Talbot to the Earl of Shrewsbury

(1582) 17th. 'Your Lordship shall understande that I have accordinge unto your direction made Mr Vicechamberlaine aquainted with the copie of the letter directed unto her Majestie; the which when he had perused, he founde that it was too sharpe in two pointes, the one is almost in the beginninge where your Lordship writeth that your wives speeches that are both infamous and wiked shoulde be better hearde then yours. This sentance will, as he sayeth, drive her Majestie into collor, for she hath alwas saide that there was one case lefte open for your Lordship, and therfore she woulde take it in verie bad parte that you shoulde flatly condemn her of partialitie towards your wife. And therfore your honorable frende doth say, that seeinge your Lordship is to deale in a matter of souche importance and with soe souttle and perilous an adversarie (as your wife), he woulde wishe you not to write any thinge that may move her to anger, but to write fully your minde with all humilitie. The seconde pointe the which he doth dislike is in the ende of the letter, where you desier to receave a favor from her Majestie by the discharge of your enemies; this he sayeth to be verie harde, for if her Majestie doo say she hath received a letter from your Lordship and so doo geve it to your wife, she that hath soe perilous a heade (as he saith your wife hath) will answere and saie: Now your Majestie may plainely see that my Lord doth seeke nothinge else but the distrouction of mee and mine, for he sayeth only the disgrace of his enemies will satisfie him. Those twoe thinges this honorable mane doeth thinke fit to be altered, and therefore I have by his advise sente bake her Majesties letter, the which will doe verie moutche good if in those twoe pointes it be qualefied. And thus in haste I ende, cravinge pardon.' Richmond.

Holograph Addressed: 'To my Lord.' *Endorsed:* 'Henry Talbot. (?) Dec. 1582. About the Countess.' *(This may be a later endorsement of the 17th century)* 1 p. (Original Letters I/75)

Lord Burghley to the Earl of Shrewsbury

(1582) 'My Lord: the Quenes Majesty hath willid me to advertise yow that she understandeth by letters out of France that the Quene of Scottes frendes maketh vaunt that your Lordship hath of late gyven hir liberty to hunt and to fish at hir will, and that she is more lusty now than she was these seven yeres, and that she hath hir minde in all thinges. Wherunto, though I answered for your Lordship that I thought these wer some derived news of the splene ether against the Quene of Scottes or ageynst your Lordship to furder hir removing from yow, yet hir Majesty did assure me uppon hir honor that she had the sight of letters wrytten out of France, but by whom they are wrytten I know not, but she charged me to write ernestly to your Lordship.

She also sayth that she heareth that the Quene of Scottes was twise this sommer at Buxtons, and yet hir Majesty gave license but for on tyme.

From Scotland I understand that both the Kyng and sondry lordes of his Counsell begyn to mislyke of the Erle of Lennox for his relligion, and so meane to stopp his procedyngs*. The Kyng of Scottes also hath sent word to the borders that strayt peace shall be kept uppon the frontyers.

Don Antonio, entitled Kyng of Portugale, hyreth sondry shippes here to send succors to his islandes, but untill we may know that the French Kyng will manifestly ayde hym, his preparations here shall stay.'

Holograph 1 p. (Original Letters II/274)

The Earl of Shrewsbury to Lord Burghley

1582-83, January 22. Concerning a bond of £500 forfeited by Roger Beck-

* Lennox left Scotland for France towards the end of 1582.

with of Selby on whose encumbered lands the Earl has a reversion. He asks Burghley also to deal with 'our lead matters' because it redounds generally to the benefit of the poor in Derbyshire. Sheffield.

Signed, with a holograph postscript asking that his long drawn-out suit to the Queen may be settled. 1p. (Original Letters I/77)

HENRY TALBOT TO THE EARL OF SHREWSBURY

1582-83, March 5. 'The iiiith of this present I was by her Majestie commanded to requier your Lordship not to passe againste Berisforde with your *scand (alum) magnat (um),* but her Majestie saide that seeinge these matters were committed unto her to ende, she woulde not therfore have the lawe to determine theme, but she required your Lordship to let theme passe untill your coumming ouppe, at which tyme, if your Lordship coulde prove that Ber(esford) had spoken any thinge to the prejudice of your honor, her Majestie saide he shoulde be a spectacle to all other vilaines; and fourther her H(ighness) saide that louke what she had spoken unto your Lordship, she woulde not breake one jotte therof, nether woulde shee eather for the prayer or requeste of any geve eare to any newe motion, but accordinge as she had promised your Lordship at your departure, soe she doeth and will continewe. Moreover, her H. bad me signefie unto your Lordship that she was your phisition, and therfore she desired to see her patient whome she wished as well unto as to any man in all her realme, and that your Lordship, she saide, shoulde finde at your nexte comminge. Lastely her Majestie comendeth her unto your Lordship and desireth you to thinke that she both doeth and will have as great a care of your honor and welldoinge as you yourselfe can have, and therfore desireth your Lordship soe to acounte.

Fourther your wife desired her Majestie that she mighte have mor witnesses examined towchinge the valewe of your Lordships five houndereth poundes, and the lot and cope, but her Majestie doth passe her over unto the Lord Treasurer and Mr Secretarye whom, she saide, were to determine these causes, wherefor your wife went presently unto the Secretarye (whoe at that tyme was presente) and required him as aforesaide, but he answered that he woulde talke with the Lord Treasurer, and toulde him what your wife required. Whereuppon I was caled for, and they both willed me to let your Lordship understande, howe that your wife had besoughte her Majestie that certen witnesses might be examined whome she kepte in towne for that pourpase, and seeinge those matters were by her Majestie referred unto theme to be examined, eather by ii Masters of the Cancherie, one for your Lordship and an other for the Ca (ve) ndishes, or else by somme poublique examiner; and they saide that your Lordship after examination had, mighte (choose) whether you woulde make them any restitution or noe, and herein they requier to knowe your answere with speede. Colharbor.

Holograph Addressed: 'To the Righte honorable my good lorde and father, ther (le of Shrewsbu) rie, Earle Marshall. Good Mr Baylie, I pray you convay this letter to my lo. with speede.' *Endorsed:* 'Henry Talbot to the Earl, 1582.' 1 p. (Original Letters I/79)

THE EARL OF LEICESTER TO THE EARL OF SHREWSBURY

1582-83, March 21. 'My good Lord, I trust we shall se you here shortly, for so I perceave by her Majestie that she looketh to have you here at St Geo (rges) feast next, whereof I am most gladd for dyvers respectes. I dyd lately wryte to your Lordship that I had procured my Lord Talbott to come upp, and I look for him here shortly except your Lordship stey him, which I wold not wishe because yt importyth him greatly to com as I have again written unto him. God send your Lordship health to performe your jorney to se hir Majestie.' From the Court.

Holograph 1 p. (Original Letters I/81)

LORD OGLE TO THE EARL OF SHREWSBURY

1583, April 20. 'Wolde God I ware at that libertie as I might accomplisshe our desires (as undeserved of my partie) that your second sonne might marye my oldest daughter, whoose mariage hath beene in suspence almost these twoo years, not yet determyned. Than shoulde your Lordschipp well perceave your inwarde good will of request should be thankfully accepte. But within xx daies I looke for ane fynall ende of my lorde of Northumberlands preten-sed mynde towchinge suche articles as es ministred to hym in that behalfe, and than shall your honoure have furder knowledge (the drefte therof shall be no longer). And in the meane tyme what your honor thynketh meate (the first with your honoure provided withall) for me and my callynge to doo for my younger dowghter and her mariage, I am to accept in good parte and by your honors advise, ffor thei er the ympes I have most comforte in and joye. And the greatest care to bestowe them well (seinge God of his goodnes haith deter-myned to me no otherwise) for the honor of the house thei er extracted of, as yet standynge to this day whole and sounde. And to be matched with the like, what pleasure might I have to frequent theire companie that so had maried theme: a thinge that was not a dalye joye but a furderer of a longe and adop-ted life.' Bothole.

Signed 1 p. (Original Letters I/83)

SIR FRANCIS WALSINGHAM TO THE EARL OF SHREWSBURY

1583, May 7. 'My verie good Lord. Your Lordship maie fynde yt strainge that youe have not yet heard from me since my brother Beales returne: the cause wherof hath proceded for that I could not till yesternight get her Majesties resolution towching yowr repeire hether: who fyndinge nowe by offers made by the Queene of Scottes to be of good importaunce and suche as requier to be well considered of and in no waye to be neglected, dothe thinke meete to dispatche one of her Councell together with my brother Beale to deale further with the said Queene about the same, wherein for that her Majestie dothe also mean to use your Lordships service, she dothe therfore praye you to dispose yourself to staie yet some tyme there, which I suppose will not be longe for that her Majestie dothe purpose the dispatching of the said Commissioners within sixe or seaven dayes. And in the meane while her Majesties pleasure is you should let the Queene understand howe she hathe taken order for the repeire of certen Commissioners unto her to treate further with her about the said offers, who shall come furnished with suche commission and directions in that behalf as she shall have no just cause to mislike therof.

Coronell Steward and Mr Colville had audience yesterdaie, who did assure her Majestie of the K (ing) their masters synceare good will and affection towardes her and the amity of this Crowne, and that he meant whollye to depend uppon her good and frendlye advice and counsell in his greatest and most importaunt causes. Some requestes thei did also propound unto her Majestie, wherewith I have not yet ben made acquainted, but as thinges proceede further so will I not faile but to imparte the same unto your

Lordship.' London.

Holograph   Endorsed in Shrewsbury's hand: 'Mr Walsinghams letter of the 7 of May. 1583.'   1p.   (Original Letters I/85)

(SIR) HENRY COBHAM TO THE EARL OF SHREWSBURY

1583, June 18.   I perceive it is your pleasure that your sons Edward and Henry should return to you.   I am sorry to be deprived of their company, but hope you will be satisfied with their growth and disposition.   They have lately been in some other parts of France, at Orleans, in Poitou and in Brittany as far as Nantes.   Paris.

Holograph   Seal   Addressed: 'To the Earl at Sheffield.'   1 p.   (Original Letters I/89)

SIR FRANCIS WALSINGHAM TO THE EARL OF SHREWSBURY

1583, July 20.   'My verie good Lord.   Whereas I did of late wryte unto your Lordship that I thought the begunne treaty with the Scotishe Quene would be a staie by reason of some alteration happened in Scotland wherein yt was lykely she had ben a doer, her Majestie being since advertised that all thinges ther remayne quiet and in good termes, doth meane nowe that the said treaty shall go forward as by her own letter youe shall further perceave within a daie or two, whereof I have thought good to geve your Lordship knowledge aforehand to thend youe may theruppon stay the sending of the letter I did advise you to wryte unto her Majestie to be licensed to make your repeire hether.

Howe thinges passe in foreign partes your Lordship shall perceave by the enclosed occurauntes.'   Greenwich.

Signed   Endorsed in Shrewsbury's hand: 'Mr Secretaries letter of the 20 July, 1583.'   1 p.   (Original Letters I/91)

SIR THOMAS STANHOPE TO THE EARL OF SHREWSBURY

1583, July 23.   You are to understand that Zouche, Harper, Ralph Sacheverell and the rest are doing all they can to prevent you at the choosing of the Coroner.   They have sent into the Peak to stop your friends coming and into Scarsdale to get Sir Godfrey (Foljambe) on their side.   They pretend that you have a friendship for Zouche, notwithstanding all his malice against you. Pray bring all that are bound to you by living, love or office to this election, and above all be at Derby for it yourself.   I hope to bring you as many 'voicis' as Sir John Zouche does.

Signed   Seal   Endorsed in Shrewsbury's hand: 'Mr Stanhope's letter.' 1p. (Original Letters I/95)

SIR THOMAS STANHOPE TO THE EARL OF SHREWSBURY

1583, July 27.   You have done well to make enquiries as to who are on your side in the matter of the Coroner.   Have you asked my cousin Gresley?   You doubt whether the election of a coroner is in the hands of commoners or only freeholders.   I take it it is the same as with the choosing of a knight of the shire, which is by the freeholders only; because the statute says the electors must have some proper interest in the shire, which the commoners can only have through their landlord who can remove them at any time, and who would, in any case, produce disorder.   If you cannot be at Derby yourself, at least pretend you are coming so as to deceive the other side. I myself (lame though I am) will be there with my son and servants at 8 on Thursday morning to attend you or Lord Talbot as the case may be.   Shelford.

PS. Pray let me have a buck; all mine I shall bestow on my friends on Thursday.

Signed   Seal   1 p.   (Original Letters I/97)

SIR GODFREY FOLJAMBE TO THE EARL OF SHREWSBURY

1583, July 28.   Consenting to the appointment of Mr Stephenson as Coroner.   Walton.

Signed   1 p.   (Original Letters I/99)

THOMAS BAWDEWYN TO THE EARL OF SHREWSBURY

1583, August 1.   We arrived at Bothal Castle last Monday and were well entertained by Lord and Lady Ogle. The house is a castle 'battled, and not unlike to Nether Haddon where Mr John Manners doth dwell', but for situation and building much better, the park, woods etc as good. If it were situated in Derbyshire and not in Northumberland, it would be worth £1000 a year besides the coal-pits.

The gentlewoman is to our liking, well brought up, not tall but of very good complexion, and well connected.   Lord Ogle would settle on his daughter Jane (if she were to marry Mr Edward Talbot) his baronies of Ogle, Bothal and Hepple and all his lands in England.   In return he demands for her an allowance of £400 a year during your life and the house at Selby. Lady Ogle opposes the passing of her inheritance . You must write to her. · Lord Ogle says he cannot afford to give them further allowance than their meat and drink, as he is in debt to the Earl of Northumberland. We recommend you to accept his terms which seem very reasonable. Please let us know your answer at once. Annewick.

PS. 'The newes of Scotland for any thing I can lerne do stand at one staye hard against our frendes there and well for them that are secured to the French.'

Holograph Endorsed: 'Baldwyns letter to the Erle concernyng the mariage of Mr Edward Talbot with the Lo: Ogles daughter. To be kept.' *3pp.* (Original Letters I/101)

T. FOULLER TO THE EARL OF SHREWSBURY

1583, August 10.   I have received letters from the Court dated the 6th from his Lordship (? Gilbert, Lord Talbot) blaming me because he has had no answer from you.

Secretary Walsingham goes to Scotland for certain, Lord Hunsdon to Berwick. Sir Walter Mildmay is not likely to come to you yet. Mr Stafford goes to France in Sir Henry Cobham's place. We must see what can be done to bring the Scots King to (us) of himself and his lords also. 'My Lord the Erll of Leycester is growne lately in great favor with the Quenes Majestie, suche as this ten yeres he was not in the lyke to the utward showe, and yet not vi weekes since he was in great disgrace abowt his maryage, for he opened the same more playnly then ever before.' Woodhouse.

Holograph   1 p. (Original Letters I/103)

SIR JOHN DANVERS TO GILBERT, LORD TALBOT

1583, August 12.   Concerning the wardship of young Mr (Talbot of Grafton) to Mr Scudamore.   Astle.

Signed   Endorsed: '12 Aug. 1583. Sir John Danvers concerning young Mr Talbot of Grafton, warde to Mr Scudamore.'   *Addressed:* 'To the Lord Talbot.'   2pp.   (Original Letters I/105)

GILBERT, LORD TALBOT TO THE EARL OF SHREWSBURY

1583, August 26.   I thank you for permitting me to sell lands in Somersetshire and Gloucestershire in order to pay off my debts, and I ask pardon for my offences.   'In my laste letter to your Lordship I prayed my brother Harry Talbot to sende to your Lordship I wrote that her Majestie, uppon my reporte to her (according to your Lordships direction) sayde she wolde wryte shortely therof.   And 3 dayes synce Mr Secretarye delyvered me this inclosed, which he tolde me was to that effecte and told her he had order to have wrytten it a good whyle before, but omytted it thorow his other continuall busynes ffrom a weeke after your Lordship wente tyll within this 4 dayes I have bene at the Courte.   Her Majestie was greatly trobled with the rendering upp of Andwerpe, at my cumminge from thence, and my Lord Tresurer, who then was at Tibolles sumwhat ill of the goute, was sente for, and so my Lord of Lester to returne to the Courte, and it is thoughte that her Majestie shalbe forced of very necessitye to sende sum great person with great forces presently for the defence of Hollande and Zealande, or else they will (oute of hande) follow Andwerpe and be lykewyse rendered upp to the Prynce of Parma.   Sum doe assuredly thynke that my Lord of Lester shalbe sent shortly.   Sir John Smyth sholde have bene sente to the Prynce of Parma, but beynge reddy to have received his dispatche is stayed uppon this newe conference purposed when the Lordes that are sente for are mett.   There is no other newes that I here of worthe wrytynge to your Lordship.   Her Majestie is now at Wymbolton, Sir Thomas Scycilles house, 3 or 4 myles from Nonsuche, but this nyght or tomorrow returnes againe to Nonsuche, where it is thought she will tarry till Mychailmas.'   Mile End.

Holograph   Addressed:'To my lord my Father.'   2pp.   (Original Letters I/107)

ELIZABETH, COUNTESS OF SHREWSBURY TO (GEORGE, EARL OF SHREWSBURY)

(? 1583 or before) August 26.   My Lord, the innocency of my own heart is such and my desire so infinite to procure your good conceit as I will leave no ways unsought to attain your favour, which long you have restrained from me, and in all duties of a wife I beseech you not to ruin with a settled condemnation of me; for my heart cannot accuse itself against you, neither is there anything alleged against me that deserves separation.* My Lord, how I have rendered your happiness every way were superfluous to write, for I take God to witness my life should ever have been adventured for you, and my heart, notwithstanding what I have suffered, thirsts after your prosperity and desires nothing so much as to have your love. Alas! my Lord, what benefits it you to seek my trouble and desolation or wherein does it serve you to let me live thus absent from you? If you will say because now I love you not, I know, my

---

* The Countess of Shrewsbury separated from the Earl and retired from Sheffield to Chatsworth in 1583. See Bickley, *The Cavendish Family*. p.23.

Lord, that hatred must grow of something, and how I have deserved your indignation is invisible to me. If you will say I or mine have touched you in duty of allegiance, first I protest there is no such thing; and what can you have more than that her Majesty justified you and us, the Lords at the Council, I and my sons clear you; or how can it in reason be thought I should forget myself so greatly being your wife, and my daughter wife to your eldest son? My Lord I beseech you give me liberty to come unto you. I doubt not but in every particular to satisfy you as my innocency will manifestly appear, and then I trust you will quiet my heart, receiving me into your favour, for you only may do it. So I end, beseeching the Almighty God to prosper you and bless me with his grace and your favour. Your humble wife most faithful. From my lodging in Chancery Lane.

Holograph Addressed: 'To my Lord my husband, the Earl of Shrewsbury.' 1p. (Original Letters II/267)

ROBERT BEALE TO THE EARL OF SHREWSBURY

1583, August 27. 'Yesternight I receved this packett from the French Ambassador, which her Majesties pleasure ys that I shold send unto your Lordship. Mr Seton and Courcelles are arrived in London and yesterday had ther Lordships passeport to go into Fraunce. Sir Walter Mildmay is (gone) to London and appointed to attend here when her Majesty shalbe returned about x dayes hence, for so much time she mindeth to spend at Gilford, Dorking and Sunninghill in hunting. And by that time we trust to here sumwhat of Mr Secretaryes negotiation out of Scotland. I wold to God that that of your Lordships and Sir Walter Mildemayes had taken better successe, for then in my simple opinion many inconveniences might have bin prevented or redressed, which I think will ensewe and be veary dangerous, yea remedilesse. The Lord preserve her Majesty and direct her to take that course that may be for the advancement of his glory, her own safty and the benefitt of this realme.'

Although I be no great dealer in the matters of this world, yet shall I be glad to do you any service.

I have prepared a box of aloes for you, which I will send when it is possible. Oatlands.

Holograph 2pp. (Original Letters I/109)

THE PRIVY COUNCIL TO THE EARL OF SHREWSBURY

1583, August 28. In accordance with the Queen's commission, they appoint him Commissioner for the maintaining and keeping of horses in the county of Derby, and order him to begin his duties at once. Oatlands.

Copy Names of Lords Burghley, Lincoln, Léicester, Hunsdon, Warwick and Sir C. Hatton. *Endorsed*: 'A copie of the Counsailes letter of the 28 of August for musters etc.' 1p. (Original Letters I/111)

SIR FRANCIS WALSINGHAM TO THE EARL OF SHREWSBURY

1583, October 2. 'I most humblie thanke your Lordship for the honorable care of me by sending Mr Baldwin to visit me. I fynd my greefe of the faule to be somewhat greater this daie then yt was yesterday: notwithstanding I am put in good hope by my phisityon that the payne will leave me by the helpe of a plaster that he hath applyed to my side, so as I hope to be hable to wayte uppon your Lordship tomorrow at Worshoppe, wher I wilbe bould to continew all daye, being nowe forced to alter my coorse of the expedition that I thought to have made in my returne to the Courte, which I have excused to her Majesty by a dispatche that I sent away this day.' Hatfield.

Signed 1p. (Original Letters I/113)

QUEEN ELIZABETH TO GEORGE, EARL OF SHREWSBURY

1583, October 19. 'By the Queene. Right trusty and right welbelovid cousin and counsailor, we greete you well. Where we have of late bene given to understand from our principall Secretary of the good and honorable intertaynment which he hath of late receavid at your handes at Woorsop. Forasmuch as we doo assure our selfe that the same was principally don for our sake, who have good cause to be very carefull of his well-dooing, being so good and faithfull a servant and counsailor unto us, as we know him to be: we could not forbeare but to give you our right hartie thankes, and by our own letter signifie unto you in how acceptable parte we take the same your good usage. Assuring you that bothe therof and of sondry other your like good desertes towardes us we shall not be unmyndfull as occasion therof shal be ministred.' 'At our mannor of St James.'

Signed 1p. (Original Letters I/115)

THE EARL OF LEICESTER TO THE EARL OF SHREWSBURY

1583, October 22. 'My good Lord, I have received your letter by which I understand styll the good affectyon remayning in your Lordship toward me, and of which I have always made that assured accompt that both long aquaintance and nere kindred persuaded me to, and the rather for that my nowne conscyence knoweth I have most faythfully deserved yt even from the beginning by all the frendlyest meanes I could shew yt by: and doe think myself not least beholding unto you in geving such notyce of by practysers to hinder the course of that which you for no respect wyll allowe, no more, God wylling, shall I, to the least hindrance of that good wyll I have alway born you.For your Lordship and I both shall have reason not to take them our frendes that wolde seeke to severe suche frendes as we are and ought to be, not only for the comfort of our selves, but even for the better servyce of our prince and sofferayn: nether can I se what ground the conningest of them can justly take to seke breache betwene us; for God be thanked ther ys no cause or cullor of cause I can imagyn wherein they may gyve matter so lyttle as suspytion betwene us; for as we be kinsmen and old frendes, so have we no sutes or quarrelles one to other, nether cause of envye nor yet dysdaine. So that I hope God wyll not suffer either of us to be so blind as to lett any at least, that will not doe good, yet to doe any harme betwene us; for my parte I dare right well, assuring myself and your Lordship, and the rather for that I have passed the brunts of many practyses and practysors and therby the more aquainted and the better armyd for them. I pray your Lordship be so to. And touching that parte concerning the unkindnes of my lady your wyves dealing, truly my Lord I am sorry with all my hart for yt, for I know yt myt be a great grefe unto you that any cause of devision or myslyke should groe that way: and the more wheir so great love and good wyll was and heretofore hath byn between you: only I may lament yt, for yt ys not for me or any to enter into those causes betwene you, but wyll pray to God to send you that comfort that justly you ought to have.

My Lord Talbott hath byn here and her Majesty hath used him very gratyously and surely since his coming. I perceave he hath quallyfied some matters well, and I must say truly of him, he doth carry him self as wysely and dyscretely as any man in England can do, both to your Lordships great honor and his owen, and I am gladd of yt with all my hart to se him doe so well. God grant him his grace always; your Lordship, no doubt, shall have great comfort of him. He doth expect shortly Drury, and by him your Lordship shall at more length have of the late causes fallen out here synce your departure of my Lord Pagett and Cha: Arundell. Hit is known and so confessed by my Lord of Northumb (erland) that he was the dealer for this conveyance over, and that he lykwise rec (eived) Ch. Pagett into his howse not longe synce, coming out of Fraunce uppon a practyse, as ys by some others confessed. The matters seme much to touch my Lord, and her Majesty doth take yt verye ill, and yf they fall out trew against him that he and others ar charged with, she hath just cause to be offended. Thus my good Lord I have held you to long, but I trust you wyll also bear with my syldome wryting, having byn of late very busye, yet not unmyndfull of your Lordship, always most reddy to do you all the pleasure I can, being of late in som hope that we shuld have your Lordship here in these partes, for so her Majesty told me sondry tymes. The Lord God have you always in his saveguard.'   At the Court.

Holograph 3pp. (Original Letters I/119)

SIR HENRY COBHAM TO THE EARL OF SHREWSBURY

1583, December 4.   He has returned from France, and is sending 'theis too small toyes....as a payre of sweete gloves and a stomacher of the birde vulture.' London.

Holograph 1p. (Original Letters I/117)

FRANKPLEDGE

1583. Memorandum of a view of frankpledge held at Ashford until Michaelmas 1583, when Mr William Cavendish held a court in his right and Sir Charles his brother, and that until that day all profits and rents were paid to the Countess their mother.

1p. (Original Letters I/121)

SIR FRANCIS WALSINGHAM TO THE EARL OF SHREWSBURY

1583-84 March 11. 'My verie good Lord. Her Majesty hath by Mr Sommer willed me to signifye unto your Lordship that where she understandeth there have ben some reportes made unto youe that she should enter into some sinister conceapt of your faithfull and loyall disposition to her house, she prayeth you to be perswaded that she caryeth that honorable opinion of you that your longe and dutyfull service doth well deserve, and as she hath above her signing written loving and affectionate so rather to accepte the same as an assured testimony of her gratyous and princely disposition towardes you, then to give credit or be discomforted with the false suggestions of those that would be glad to breede some distrust and jealousy betwen so loving a soverayn and so faythfull and well deserving a servaunt.' London.

Signed 1p. (Original Letters I/124)

JOHN SAUNDERS AND WILLIAM BROKE TO ANDREW DOTTIN, THE ELDER

1584, April 12.   They report some lewd speeches made by Watkin Davy against the Earl of Shrewsbury. Davy alleges that he had lain two years in the Tower for the Earl's cause and was often examined by counsell about the consenting of the conveying away of the Queen of Scots; and that if he had not at that time stood the Earl in good stead, the latter would have found himself in difficulties. It would be well that the Earl should be made acquainted with this. Lewe.

1p. (Original Letters I/128)

Lord Burghley to the Earl of Shrewsbury

1584, April 19. 'My very good Lord: being acqueynted with the comming of this bearer, hir Majesties servant Mr Will. Wade, I cold not but by hym send my most harty commendations and salute your good Lordship with these few lynes. His occasion of comming is to accompany one sent from the French Kyng at the sollicitation of the Duke Joyeuse to speak with that Quene, to make some easy bargan for a right due to hir as Dowager of France, uppon a purchas of a signory by the Duke which is holden of some higher signory, parcell of hir dower. As I here the due to hir is about 30,000 crownes, but it is ment to obteyne of hir a diminution therof, which I thynk not so resonable to demand of hir as it is resonable for the Duke, being such a favorit of the French Kyngs, to yeld all that is hir dew; but the Quene is so wise as I thynk she will provyde for hir self as they do for themselves.

My Lord, of late I did tell your sonn, Mr Talbott, that he should se your Lordship here shortly, and so I then thought, for your license to come was both agreed and, I think, signed. But alteration followed, as manny tymes in a sommer morning we thynk assuredly for a fayre daye, but a change followeth. The beror hereof was the son of one Mr Armigell Wade that was a clerk of Counsell in Kyng Edwards tyme; the yong man is very discret and of good practise.' Westminster: 'with a better hand than a foote.'

Holograph Endorsed: 'The L. Treasurers letter the 19 of Aprill 1584. sent by Mr Wade coming down with one for the Duke of Joyeuse to the S(cottes) Q(uene).' 1p. (Original Letters I/130)

The Earl of Shrewsbury to Sir Francis Walsingham

1584, June 23. 'Good Mr Secretarie: having received your letters of the xvith of this instant, I doo perceive therebie that her Majestie is contented to referre the tyme of this ladies going to Buxtons to me when I shall thinke mete, whither I meane to make more spede with her, for that my stuffe and other thinges which I sent thither for my Lord of Leicesters coming is yet stayed there for the same purpose. And for the departure of the Frenche man hir servaunt, I thinke yt most convenient yt were before hir going to Buxtons, which is like to be about Twesdaie or Wensday come sevenight, if I here not to the contrarie from you in the meane tyme. And for her abode there I thynk yt will be about a fortenight or thereabout, for I am of opinion that she will make the more haste thence when I shall put her in hope of her Majesties gratious dealing with her, and that the treatie is like to go forwardes; if yt be not long of herself and some indirecte delaing discovered in the meane while, whereof I will wish her to have great care, and have told her that her best course were to submit her self unto her Majestie, and that the King her sonne should use no violent meanes against thes distressed noblemen.

I thanke you for your comfortable newes and good hope you put me in of my repaire to her Majesties presence, which is the thing I most desier.' Sheffield.

Copy. The last paragraph is apparently meant to be erased. *Endorsed:* 'The copy of my letter of the 23 of June 1584 to Mr Secretary Walsingham about the Scottishe Quenes going to Buxtons.' 1p. (Original Letters I/132)

SIR FRANCIS WALSINGHAM TO THE EARL OF SHREWSBURY

1584, July 10. 'My verie good Lord: Her Majesty understanding by the reports of certen gentlemen latelie come from thos partes that your Lordship hath appointed a great assemble of the freehoulders of the Forest of the Peake to be heald the fourtenth of this moneth at (*erased*) within two or three myles of Buxtons, and (*torn*) the inhabitantes thereabouts are for the most parte backward and ill affected in relligion; doubting therefore what inconvenience maie followe of this assembly of so manie people by reason of the neerenes of the place to Buxtons where your chardge presently remayneth, her Heighnes hath willed me to signify unto your Lordship that her pleasure is yf any suche assemblye be by you warned as is alleadged, you should in any case unwarne the same in respect of your chardge.' Richmond.

Signed 1p. (Original Letters I/133)

W. PATTEN TO THE EARL OF SHREWSBURY

1584, July 25. He has received from Mr Baldwin a packet of 52 letters written to and from the Earl's father concerning his proceedings as Lord President of the North. 'From my house in Aldersgate Street.'

Holograph 1p. (Original Letters I/135)

THE EARL OF LEICESTER TO THE EARL OF SHREWSBURY

(1584) August 2. 'My good Lord: I do thank you for the care you take for the loss of my yonge sonne which was indede, my good Lord, great to me for that I have no more and more unlyke to have, my growing now old, but the wyll of God must be obeyd in all thinges whatsoever, for he doth all for the best.

Touchinge the keeping of your justice court, I have hard more of yt after the wryting of my letter to your Lordship from Richmond than at the wryting therof I dyd, for than the brutes were somwhat straunge. And truly, my Lord, I have greatly myslyked and must utterly that manner of dealing. I dyd never imagyn that any such cause wold have byn geven, but I feare thes be yll instruments such as wylbe cause to harm more their frends than themselves; for yf but themselves yt were the least matter, and I doe beleave your Lordship doth ges rightly at them. Your Lordship doth honorably to respect him that hath mached with your owen daughter, and he ys to be cheryshed that doth show himself to carry his dewty toward you in that sort, and for dyvers good benyfytts also done by your Lordship to him. So, my good Lord, I besech you have lyke care of your owne sonne, for, my Lord, I know that ther lyveth not a more carefull nor a more loving child, and of late hath taken that course which I am persuaded wyll lyke you, and to please you hath fully framed him self therto. Your Lordship must a lytle examyn him by your self, and the more bear with him when he doth apply himself in the end to you. For, my Lord, who bare more affection in this world to his wyfe then you dyd a longe while, and at whose hands wold your Lordship have easily beleavyd any hard conceat of her, na whome wold ye have lovyd that shuld have gone about yt; and truly my Lord, yt was a virtuus mynd tyll you had found very manyfold just causes to the contrarye: and so well I think styll of your Lordships good mynde as without just cause you wold not alter it. Now, my Lord, yf your sonne hath settled the lyke lote unto his wyfe, wold your Lordship, except he doe know some just cause, alyanatt him self from her. God forbyd, for yt ys heavye in the sight of God for any person to seke separation betwene man and wyfe. God hath joyned them and therfore without good cause no man can separatt them. And for your sonne, yf he obey your Lordship in all other dewtyes, I trust you wyll be his good Lord and father, as you have byn, and as I am sure hever fourth he wyll deserve to be. For my part I have these many yeres byn your very faythfull and trewe frend and as carefull every way for the well-doing of your self and your house as any frend or kinsman lyving could be; and I trust your Lordship hath always so thought or ells you have donne me the more wronge, for examyn all partes and circumstances of my doinges towardes you since my first aquaintance, and I hope you wyll find no man in this realme hath had a pore frend more carefull than myself hath byn. How other later frendshippes may now a days make them I know not, but yt suffyceth me to know what I am and have byn to your Lordship.

For your dealing of William Candysh in carrying awaye the stuffe from Chatsworth, in my opinion was a very fond and foolysh parte. Such children oftymes doth ther parents more harm than good, and redynes to entercept benefyttes from others more doth make them to forgett both reason and dewtye. But your Lordship ys wyse and can tell best how to order and reforme those causes. They be within the lymytts of your authorytye, and so wyll pray to God to dyrect you always with his holy spyrytt, and commend your Lordship to the same in som haste. Your Lordships assured cousyn.

PS. I have byn absent from the Court ever synce my son dyed and wylbe Thursday next or I com thether.'

Holograph 3 pp. (Original Letters I/137)

SIR FRANCIS WALSINGHAM TO THE EARL OF SHREWSBURY

1584, August 11. 'My verie good Lord: yesterday as I offered unto her Majesty the instructions of Sir Rafe Sadler who is to departe hence about the latter end of this weeke or the beginning of the next, Her Majesty willed me in her name to signify unto your Lordship that forasmuch your chardge hath now lyen long at Sheffield Castell, she thinketh meete your Lordship should remove her to Wynckfeld before you set forward, there to remayne all the tyme of your absence. Which I thinke is done cheefly in respect of the gentlemans health that shall supply your place, who being now very ould and his body accustomed to a good ayre where his owne howse standeth, may be annoyed by the closeness of the howse at Sheffield.' Oatlands.

Signed ½ p. (Original Letters I/141)

Underneath in the Earl of Shrewsbury's hand is a draft of his reply:

'Good Mr Secretary: I thank you most hartily for the advertisement you have gyven me of Sir Rafe Sadler his cetting (?) forwards hither. Wherupon I doo presently wryte unto her Majestie a most ernest letter to thend I may spedily repair unto her presence, as well in respect of the season of the yere much importuning my helth as for the exceeding desyr I have to imparte unto her self many things for her Majestys service, and touching my own estat, praying you most hartily to further the same with all good offices you may, for in no other thing can you gyve me more assured proffe of your frendshippe than in this. As to the remove of my charge to Wyngfield, syth it hathe bene

51

onely propounded, as you wryt, but for Sir Rafe Sadlers helthe in respecte of the good eyre there, and the closeness of Sheffield Castell wher you thought that I was, I have thought good now with all speed to advertise you that I remove me at my house in Sheffield Park wher (yf yt shall be so lyked) I think he shall find as good and open ayre as at any house I have, and therfor until your answer again therunto I have staide the remove wherin you will nott beleve what a penefaull toyling there must be in the transporting of this the whole household.......baggage.

Notwithstanding I do take order in the mean tyme that all provisions and preparations there as tyme will give leve be redy for the purpose wyche can nott be soner than I may reseve your answer. And thus wishing you as to myself, I cease.'

THE EARL OF SHREWSBURY TO THE EARL OF LEICESTER

1584, August 20.   I thank you for your letter of the 14th of August. William Cavendish denies in part the charges against him, but I shall bring substantial proof of my allegations.

As to the grant under my hand and seal for the quiet enjoying of lands, etc, which Mr Cavendish produces, consideration must be had of the time of its making, the considerations for which it was made, and the possession of the thing granted.

In any case he had no right to come to Chatsworth by night and convey away the principal stuff, and that on two occasions. It was only my lenience after the first occasion that encouraged him to repeat the offence. Now my wife pretends she is wholly dependent on her son and his allowance. To conclude, 'I am towardes my sonne and my wief' as in my former letters to you, and so will continue. Sheffield.

Copy Endorsed: 'A copy of my Lords letter to my Lord of Lecester.'   2 pp.   (Original Letters I/143)

SIR FRANCIS WALSINGHAM TO THE EARL OF SHREWSBURY

1584, September 4.   'My verie good Lord: uppon the receipt and viewe this daye of the orders sett downe by you and Sir Ralphe Sadler for the better custodie of your chardge to be committed to him in your absence, findyng Mr Bentall appointed gentleman Porter and to have the chiefe chardge of the gates, I call to remembrance a verie speciall poynt which I forgott to require Mr Somers to signifie to Sir Ralphe Sadler to thend he should impart the same to your Lordship: and that was, howe her Majestie had (uppon what information or by whome I know not) a verie hard opinion of the sayd Bentall, and therefore that shee dislikyng him you should beware not to put him in anie place of trust about your chardge. Wherfore before your Lordships departure from your howse hitherwards, you shall doo well in anie wyse to appoynt some other person of trust, of whom no dislyke may be conceaved by her Majestie, to that place of gentleman Porter. I have not yet aquainted her Majestie with your letter receaved this daye. And thus I humbly commend your Lordship to God.'   Oatlands.

Signed   1 p.   (Original Leters I/145)

SIR FRANCIS WALSINGHAM TO THE EARL OF SHREWSBURY

1584, December 17.   'My verie good Lord. Ther is a despatche come this daie from Sir Rafe Sadler by the which her Majesty is advertised that the Queene cannot yet be brought to yeld to be removed untill the returne of Nau unto her, who cannot be readie to depart hence untill Mondaie next at the soonest, and that they are therfore lykely to be utterly unprovided of vittals. Thoughe her Majestys officer there be employed to make provisions, the barenes of the country is such unles by your Lordships meanes the want therof may be supplyed; and therfore her Majesty hath willed me in her name to pray your Lordship that you will send further order to your officers to make newe provisions though yt be at hir owne chardge, that may serve during the tyme that the said Queene shall yet continue at Wingfield.' At the Court.

Signed Endorsed in the Earl of Shrewsbury's hand: 'Mr Secretarys letter of 17 December 1584.' 1 p. (Original Letters I/147)

SIR FRANCIS WALSINGHAM TO THE EARL OF SHREWSBURY

1584, December 19. On behalf of his servant, Tomson, and his claims in a suit. From the Court.

Signed 1 p. (Original Letters I/149)

SIR FRANCIS WALSINGHAM TO THE EARL OF SHREWSBURY

1584, December 21. The Lord Chancellor will not be ready to hear your suit against your wife till Wednesday next. From the Court.

Signed ¼ p. (Original Letters I/151)

LORD CHANCELLOR BROMLEY

1584-85, January 16. Order of Lord Chancellor Bromley, appointing the 8th of February next for the examination of witnesses touching the case of George, Earl of Shrewsbury, *versus* Sir Charles Cavendish and William Cavendish.

Copy Large paper 1 p. (Original Letters I/154)

THE EARL OF SHREWSBURY TO LORD BURGHLEY

1584-85, January 30. 'My very good Lord. I have resayved a letter from your Lordship wherin I understande that her Majestie ys informed of certeyne plate, hangings and other moveables sent by the Erle of Murrey out of Scotland unto the Scottishe Quene when she was in my custodie, and that her Majestie wold know what ys become therof: the which I think very strange for to my knowledge since her commynge she never receaved any stuf or other thinges from him. Moreover your Lordship doth desire in your letter to have a note of the stufe that came out of her Majesties Warderobe to Tutberie for the use of the Scottishe Quene, part whereof, as ys informed unto your Lordship, shuld be delivered unto my wief. Truly, my Lord, that ys an unjuste report, for at her departure from Winckfeld I did delyver unto Mr Chancellor xix peces of hanginges which were verey sore spoyled; besides they have maid suche wast of my hanginges and dyvers other thinges that onles her Majestie stand my good and gracious Ladie, I am not able to support so great losses that I have many wayes sustayned by that chardge, the which now are apparant unto her Majestie and to you my Lords of the Councell. And seyng that her Majestie doth most bountyfully reward them that have donne her service, I therfor, havinge served her in the highest degre, do hope liekwise to tast of her Majesties most gracious bounty, the which, if I can not, I must not impute the faulte unto her Majestie but unto my owne evill happe, for the world may therby thinke my desertes hath merited nothinge; which will turne to my great grief and discredit, wherof I hope her Majestie will most graciously consider. And thus trusting to your Lordships favor herein, I bid you most hartely farewell.' Chelsea.

Signed, with holograph postscript: 'I have sente your Lordship a note of the stuffe which my servant hathe delyvered and what hath bene wasted within this xvi yeres.' *Endorsed:* '30 Jan. 1584. E. of Shrewsburys answere to your letter.' *Addressed:* 'To the right honorable my very good Lord, the Lord Burghley, L. Treasurer of England.' 1 p. (Original Letters I/156)

(THE EARL OF SHREWSBURY) TO QUEEN ELIZABETH

(After February 8, 1584-85)* I must inform your Majesty that the suit between me and the Cavendishes has been heard before the Lord Chancellor and the two Chief Justices. Their only evidence was that of my wife's servants and a secret instrument written by her own hand without witness: I had many warrants duly registered or copied. I cannot attend upon your Majesty 'being now so greeved with the colicke and stone', but would make two requests:

(1) to enjoy the benefit of my title. When I made the deed to the Cavendishes, I did it not for their benefit but for that of my wife, under the belief that she would do the duty of a wife. Yet she has animated her sons 'not onlie with force to keepe me from a nights lodginge in one of the houses, but also with slaunderous speaches and sinister practises to dishonor me.'

(2) to have leave to go into the country, both on the grounds of health and for the satisfying of divers whose services I have used for the keeping of the Queen of Scots. I beseech your Majesty to give me some remembrance of your good liking for my long service. Chelsea.

Copy Endorsed 'Copies of letters written by the Erle of Shrewsberie to her Majestie 1585.' 3pp. (Original Letters I/207)

JOHN TALBOT TO THE EARL OF SHREWSBURY

1584-85, February 10. Concerning his appointment as executor to the Earl's lately deceased sister, Lady Wharton. Mitcham.

Signed 1p. (Original Letters I/160)

ORDER

(Before February 15, 1584-85) Order signed by Lord Burghley and Sir Walter Mildmay to Robert Petre to pay the Earl of Shrewsbury the sum of £51:8:4 for the 'diet' of the Queen of Scots for one week and five days (at the rate of £30 a week) from December 1-16, 1584.

Copy Annexed is the acquittance of Christopher Copley on behalf of the Earl and dated 15 February, 1584-85. *Endorsed:* 'The copy of my lord of Shrewsburies last order for the Scottes Quenes diete.' ½p. (Original Letters I/162)

GILBERT, LORD TALBOT, TO THE EARL OF SHREWSBURY

1585, Easter Tuesday (April 13). I thank you for the tun of wine you have sent to Welbeck. My belongings shall be moved from Rufford to make room for you. The parson of Ekring threatens not to renew the lease of his parsonage 'but it is thought a courteouse letter and a token of a rundelet of Malmesea will doe muche with him...I must crave pardone for I am but fayntye and quyckly werye: I am in fear of my fytte agen this nyghte.' Mile End.

---

* See *supra* p.53.

Holograph 1p. (Original Letters I/164)

LORD CHANCELLOR BROMLEY TO THE EARL OF SHREWSBURY

1585, April 29. 'My Lord. I have reseved letters from my Lord of Leycester touchinge the causes betwene your Lordship and my Lady, your wyeff, wherupon I wold gladly taulke with your Lordship. Wherfore yf it wod please your Lordship to come to me tomorow in the mornyng abowte seven of the clocke to my howse, or else to sytt with us att the Starr Chamber tomorow and thare dyne with us, I shall make you aquaynted therwith.'

Holograph *Endorsed in the Earl of Shrewsbury's hand:* 'Mr Lorde brought me this letter.' ½p. (Original Letters I/166)

THE EARL OF LEICESTER TO THE EARL OF SHREWSBURY

1585, April 30. 'I have showed your letter to hir Majestie which she did thorowly peruse. Her highnes for the first parte touching your fidellytye she nether dowbtyd of yt at any tyme, nor hath shewyd at any tyme but to be fully perswaded therof, and so hath made knowen from her self to your Lordship. Touching the order betwene my Lady and you that she hath sett dowen and your Lordship doth seme to think hard, her Majestie sayth that in such cases, being sufferayn and hed over her subjects, she ys uppon complaintes to gyve justyce with equyty to all persons; and in this cause of my Lady your wyves, she findes ii great matters for hir both in honor and equyty to consider of: the one ys the putting away and seperating of yourself from your wyfe, whome you have long and many yeres very lovingly and honorably interteyned tyll within these fewe yeres that the breach betwene her and the Q. of Scottes felle owte, by whose practyse though not dyrectly (with) your self, yet using some instruments *(torn)*...you, her Majestie doth think great dysp (ite) ys grown toward her, and yet your Lordship not meaning to doe yt for that Q's sake, but other matters (layed) before you to withdrawe your love from my Lady ys for them a good cullor. And the rather her Majestie ys bould to think thus for that for she never yet hard or could find suffycyent matter layd against hir *(torn)*....so hard and extreame a breach to be made betwene a man and his wyfe, and albeyt ther be ordynary places and courses for tryalls of such matters betwene party and partye, yet her Majesty hath that regard to you both, being in the best rank of her subjects, your wyfe by your place being cauled therto and making her piteous and lamentable complaint to her Majestie to take the order of this cause into her own gracious hands, whereby she dyd meane to have brought the chiefe and principall point she had most care of to a better pass than yet yt ys, which was to have had a godly and crystyen reconcylement betwene you as man and wyfe.

The seconde matter ys, for such dedes and grauntes as your Lordship hath conveyed to my Lady at sondry tymes under your hand and seall, was sought to be made frustratt, which her highnes did commytt to the grave consideration of my Lord Chancelor and others her lernyd juges, which cause she sayth resteth in this sort, as they all think the meaning of your Lordship was that my Lady should enjoye all those gyftes, but for want of one only cerymony in exstremytye of lawe your Lordship might take some advantage with extremyte of lawe, her Majestie dyd think reason to quallyfie with taking notwithstanding so much of my Ladys lyving from her as shuld make upp to your Lordship £500 yerely.

These be the ii reportes moveth her Majestie to sett down the order as she hath done. As for the lands nomynated by my Lady and was sent to your

55

Lordship to consider of, her Majestie doth not meane to bynd your Lordship precysely to accept of those parcels, but that you should have such as may be thought convenyent and resonable to perform the full valew sett down by her Majestie. And to this effect I am comanded to wryte to my Lord Chancelor to deale with your Lordship and my Lady lykewise, that your Lordship myslyking her offer may have to your satisfaction otherwise; for truly, my Lord, you must not think that her Majestie doth this for specyall favor more to my Lady than to you, but I have shewyd you the very cause she doth think my Lady hath receved some hard dealing, and doth not fynd suffycyent matter to chardge hir touching your self that she should be so turned away. And for my parte I besech God, except your Lordship have of your own knowledge indede very just and knowen cause, that he wyll move your hart to doe that which with a good conscyence shalbe most acceptable in his sight. For surely, my Lord, those transitory, worldly thinges will have an end, and the judgement to come must both fear and look for. That judge will spare no person, and blessed be they that shall most sincerely seke to walk in his commandments. Good my Lord, think of this and bear with those playn speches which I have often used unto you. The Lord doth know no man lyving hath delt with truer good wyll and frendshipp then I have alway done: yea, I curse them that I may know that wold ye evyll. Seke your chefe *(torn)* in heaven, and trew honor here in earth, which your Lordship cannot but have in ernest sekyng the first. And so to that God I comytt you who can graunt you both.' The Co(urt).

Holograph 3pp. (Original Letters I/168)

SIR FRANCIS WALSINGHAM TO THE EARL OF SHREWSBURY

1585, May 16. On behalf of Richard Arnold, a Gloucestershire tenant of the Earl's. Barne lands.

Signed ½ p. (Original Letters I/170)

GILBERT, LORD TALBOT, TO THE EARL OF SHREWSBURY

1585, August 8. 'At my nexte cominge hither to the Courte after your Lordships departure, which was in the beginninge of this weeke paste, I did declare unto her Majestie how exceedinge muche your Lordship made me know I was bounden unto her, and delyvered partycularly everye parte therof that your Lordship had sayde unto me. And so confessinge the infinite comforte that it was to me, gave her Hyghnes most humble and dutyfull thankes, all which she toke in very good parte, as myghte be; and protested that your Lordship had perfytely remembered in the moste thinges even her very wordes, and made repetition agen therof her self, bothe of her owne speches and your Lordships answeres. And after sayde, that she had apoynted your Lordship to sende her worde (so sone as you were returned home) how you had passed your jornea, which she loked every day to here of. And wolde then lett your Lordship understand how very well she toke your Lordships reporte of her goodnes to me and your kepinge promis with her therin. It pleased her to tell me in what sorte your Lordship had carryed yourself in sondry matters of counsell, and espetially in thos of the Low Countreys, and what earneste perwations your Lordship used to her, to forsee the great dangers to her in the realme if she did not presently ayd and succore them bountifully: and recyted many of your wordes to her therin, commending your Lordship excedingly for it, and protested she thought and knew she had not a more faythfull counsellor then your Lordship amongst them all.

I heare by my brother Harry that my Lorde of Lester wryteth unto your Lordship by this bearer, and I suppose he will wryte the truthe of suche matters now in hande, as I and others here of by chance, one at another, many tymes untrew. Therfore I thynk I sholde troble your Lordship in vayne to wryte any thynge of them at this tyme.' Nonsuch.

Holograph Seal 2pp. (Original Letters I/172)

THE EARL OF LEICESTER TO THE EARL OF SHREWSBURY

(1585) August 17. 'My very good Lord. I am very sorry that I could not aswell come to se you as thus to wryte to you: but in very troth I was fully determyned to have stollen uppon your Lordship, and even this day I have receavyd letters from my Lord Tresorer and Mr Secretary that her Majestie doth now agayne meane to use my service in the Low Countreys. But all this had not held me from seing you, but that yt was my hap a Wensday last to have my horse fall uppon me in such sort as I assure your Lordship I am not able to ryde, no not to goe but ledd, which wyll not only hold me from your Lordship but also to make that spede to the Court which otherwyse I wold doe. Though Antwerp be lost, as your Lordship hath hard, yet yf her Majestie take the matter to hart and deale accordingly, ther ys lyffe inough. Howe this matter shall procede, you shall hear from me very shortly.

In the meane tyme, my good Lord, I wold have byn glad yf so happy occasion might have servyd that I might only have putt you in mynd my non self of the great desyre I have alway had to se my Lady and you together, which I pray God may be, and as farr as my pore credytt doth stand with your Lordships, I must nedes wyshe the good success of so godly and good a cause; not dowbting but your good Lordship doth frame yourself to lyve ever in the sight of God, preserving the pleasing of him before all flesh and blood or worldly respectes.

The principall newes I hear now of ys that the matters of Fraunce goo yet well and the Duke of Guyse in no good case; the greatest part of the realme and gentlemen doe now stand for the King of Navarre.' 'From Kenilworth: very lame yet and removing this day away.'

PS. Thanks for favour to Thomas Trentham. 'Sir Charles Cavendyshe was with me before my coming forth. I do se that gentleman most desyrous of your favour and good opinion, and above all thinges to se your Lordship and my Lady his mother together ageyn. He regardeth nothing so much as that.'

Holograph Endorsed: 'E. of Lecester about the Countess, Aug. 17 1586 *(sic)*'. 2pp. (Original Letters I/244)

GILBERT, LORD TALBOT, TO THE EARL OF SHREWSBURY

1585, September 17. I thank you for your offer to buy Sutton of me for £2,300 towards the payment of my debts, but I cannot get my Lady's consent or that of my wife. She protests she would only have £200 *per annum* clear, and that even if this sale were to take place only half my debts would be paid. 'And wher your Lordship wryteth that yf she denye me this good and helpe in my distresse, the care and difference betwyxte a naturall father and stepmoother will then appere (which I stuck not in the ende playnely to tell her)', she said that you would see to it that I got the worst of the bargain. 'And further she alledged that hitherunto she fyndeth smale hope of your Lordships reconcilement to her, but daly cause to doubt that your Lordship will styll seke her ruine and destruction.' She says if you had possession of Sutton you would encourage her tenants in those parts against her as you have done in

Derbyshire. 'And in conclusion absolutely refused to graunte me any of her estate to that ende.'

Her discontent with me is great. 'Neverthelesse she saide for that she will prove that trew which she hath harde your Lordships selfe heretofore say to me, which was yf she loved me (as well as if she were my owne naturall mother), she will bestow as muche on me presently towardes payment of my debtes (tho' she cause one of her sonnes to sell sum of theyr purchased landes) as your Lordship will doe, whatsoever it be; albeit she saythe. as your Lordship doth beste know, you are more able to gyve a pounde then she a penny.'

My days of payment are now at hand and I put myself at your mercy, resolved to change my manner of living, and never more to trouble you with such entreaties. I thank you for the £100 received for me for this Michaelmas quarter. At the Court at Nonsuch.

Holograph 3 pp. (Original Letters I/174)

THE EARL OF SHREWSBURY TO GILBERT, LORD TALBOT

1585, September 24. 'Sonne Gilbert Talbot.' I have received your letter of the 17th instant. I had understood from your former messenger Ratcliff that the sale of Sutton would all but pay your debts and that they amounted to £3000. 'But nowe you sing another song, as though my wief should better knowe of your debtes then your self dooth by your wyves instruction, for now you saye that Sutton will paie but half your debtes, as they geve out and you wryte.' As for my wife's refusal, 'belyke....she assures her self she shall overlyve me, which I knowe both mother and daughter hoope of, and yet they maie be both deceived, for the lyves of all are in the handes of God.' They were quite willing to sell the estate to others, but not to me. 'And now I must tell you trulie I never ment to bye yt, but to trye the cankerednes my wife and yours beares me, which is manifest, and forsooth to bleare your eyes withall she makes the worlde believe she will be contented her sonne Charles Cavendish shall sell all his landes in Darbishire to relieve you and her wantes, and he hath very kyndely offered them to me to sell, whome I am assured after my death you mynde to recompence his kyndnes double both to my wife and him, but I will provide and meete therwith as I may.' As to her saying she has only £200 a year, I know that she and her two younger sons have nearly £4000 a year, so that her excuse was but a simple shift, 'but if you be not too much blynded you maie discover them.' You have tried to deceive me over this sale. 'For myne owne parte I never durst deale in lyke tearmes with my father, nor make any meanes by motion or otherwise for the sale of anie landes in his lief-tyme, though my allowance was small and not past half so much as yours, and my charges great bothe at home and in sondry forrein services, the least bur-then whereof you never yet soo muche as felte. And truly but for her Majesties sake I woulde never have bene brought to condiscend to geve my consent to my child to sell my land soo longe as I live.' But you must get some nobleman or councillor to be bound to me 'for with grief I thinke yt and must tell you plainlie, I have found your regard of your woord and promise soo litle to me (what yt is to others I know not) as I cannot trust you that you shall presentlie come into the countrye and lyve there as is most fitt for you and not trouble me further hereafter. I will over and besides that you can gett of the best chapman for that land' give you £1000 in reasonable time in payment of your debts. In the last year you have had in money and lead and by my toleration nearly £2000, besides your maintenance and allowance £800 money. 'Theis are no small matters and howe you should soo spend all this and bring yourself soo farre into debte I cannot but mervail, and with grief thinke of yt. Well, in hope of better hereafter, for her Majesties sake I will doo thus much nowe, which you knowe is a gret deale more then your behavior and desertes have geven me cause. As to yourself I referre yt, yet will doo good against ill and praie God to blesse you and woorke that in you which nowe I fynd not.' Sheffield.

Signed Addressed: 'To my loving sonne Gilbert Talbott.' 2¼pp. (Original Letters I/176)

Annexed f.175 is a copy of the above letter endorsed: 'Copie of a letter to the L. Talbott of the 24th of September 1585 in answere of his of the 17th of the same.'

SIR FRANCIS WALSINGHAM TO THE EARL OF SHREWSBURY

1585, September 26. Concerning the musters in the Earl's lieutenancy which, owing to the unseasonableness of the harvest, are to be omitted this year. The Deputy-Lieutenants and Muster-Masters are merely to view the men enrolled and report on them and their arms. From the Court at Nonsuch.

Signed, with a holograph postscript: 'Your Lordship by the inclosed occurrentes lately sent owt of Ffraunce may perceiyve howe malytyowsley the great potentates are bent agaynst this poor yle. I hope God wyll confownde their devysses and defend her Majestie.' 1p. (Original Letters I/180)

On back is a draft of the Earl's instructions to the Deputy-Lieutenants etc to carry out the orders conveyed in the Secretary of State's letter.

MUSTERS

(?1585) October 1. Draft order from (the Muster-Master of Derbyshire) for a view of horses, armour, etc, at Derby on Monday, October 1.
1p. (Original Letters I/206)

THE EARL OF DERBY TO THE EARL OF SHREWSBURY

1585, October 2. He is sending a list of persons guilty of trespassing in the royal forest of Macclesfield, and asks that they may be dealt with. New Park.
Signed ½p. (Original Letters I/182)

GILBERT, LORD TALBOT, TO THE EARL OF SHREWSBURY

1585, October 12. 'I sholde presume to troble your Lordship over muche to answere every parte of your Lordships letter. Therfore omyttinge the reste, will beceche leave for thos thinges which moste nerely touche me, as where your Lordship wrytethe that Sir Charles Cavendishe offerethe to sell all his landes in Darbyshire to releve me and his moothers wantes with, which your Lordship supposethe I have a meaninge another day to recompence. I proteste before God that there is no suche thynge intended for any manner of releefe to me (albeit my Lady did once offer, as I thynke I wrote to your Lordship, that she wolde gyve me towardes payment of my debtes as muche as your Lordship wolde, tho' she caused her sonnes to sell sum of theyr landes for it). Nevertheless my meaning was never that he or any other sholde so farr be harmed for me, what other shyfte soever I made, but whensoever your Lordship shall know that I make any bargane or pass any promis to any man for recompence ageinste suche future tyme, then will I acknowledge to have deserved your Lordships uttermoste disfavore for ever.'

I am doing my best to get the highest price possible for Sutton. As to the bond to a nobleman, 'I truste your Lordship thynkethe me nether so simple or lewde as that I wolde for any gayne notefy myselfe to any suche person, to have so lyttell credytt with your Lordship as to thynke I will not be more obedient to you by the bondes of God and nature then for all other bondes that the worlde can bynde me in.' I hope to come to the country when I have settled with my creditors.

'Two dayes agoe her Majestie tolde me that your Lordship had sente her worde that for her sake you wold bestow a thousande poundes of me towardes payment of my debtes, saying that my brother Harry hadd tolde her so from your Lordship. And she was assured (she sayde) your Lordship did it to please her with, and so she toke it and had bydden my brother Harrye to gyve your Lordship thankes for it from her, and straytly commanded me to doe the lyke, which if it please your Lordship to make knowne unto her I shall be very glad. I semed to be otherwise ignorant thereof and confyrmed all I colde that I was suer your Lordship did it only for her Majesties sake. She also sayde she was suer your Lordship did it the rather to inhable me to serve her here, which I denied not but also confyrmed it. She shewed me a fayre jewell your Lordship had lately sente her, and sayde she toke the thousand poundes that I should have as well geven to her as the jewell, with many wordes of her thankefullnes to your Lordship she ended.' I beseech you to let me have the money soon, or at least a piece of paper which I may show to my creditors, to get them to prolong my credit till it comes.

'Yf it were not in respecte of my debttes, and that before my L. of Lesters goynge over I can not possible take order for them, I wolde have bene an humble sutor to your Lordship for your leave to have gon with him, but my contience will not suffer me to goe any whether till I have freed myselfe out of this miserye of debtte, that then I may take an other course to lyve within my compasse.' At the Court (at Oatlands *erased*).

Holograph 3 pp. (Original Letters I/184)
Annexed f. 186 *is a copy of the last part of the letter with the following post-script* (*not in the original*): 'Your Lordship dateth this letter ffrom the Court at Otelandes, where your Lordship putt out Ottlandes in your letter, and so yt is from the Court. I dare nott putt in Richmond because my hand may be descerned from your Lordships, and also my thinkes yt very wel as yt is now all of your own hand.' *Large paper* 1p. *Endorsed*: 'October 1585. The seconde coppy of my letter to my Lord.'

SIR FRANCIS WALSINGHAM TO THE EARL OF SHREWSBURY

1585, October 12. Lady Shrewsbury's chief complaint against you is that you maintain other men's suits against her in Derbyshire and Shropshire. I hope to hear from you that she is deceived by false report in the matter. Richmond.

Signed ½p. (Original Letters I/190)

THE EARL OF SHREWSBURY TO QUEEN ELIZABETH

1585, October 23. I grieve to hear that the matter between me and my wife, which was so long debated before the Lord Chancellor and the two Chief Justices, is again called into question, 'in the which she nor her sonnes wanted anie meanes to further her purpose, and inforced ye profe of one deade by a sorte of purjured and suborned personns, her owne servantes, therby intending (if God had not revealed their practise) most coningly to have taken from me all her landes and goodes which she was seased or possessed of. Yet after report made to your Majestie by the Lord Chancellour and the Judges of the secrecie of the cause, it pleased your highnes to declare your roiall pleasure and commandment betwixt us, that I should have of my wiefes landes vc^{li} by yeare and she to have the rest of all her landes and lyvinges, wherwith (though it seemed hard) I have settled and contented myself and hath suffered her and her children to injoye all the residewe of her landes and lyvinges which is better then mmm^{li} by yeare. Howbeit still she crieth out to your Majestie and consell that I have broken your highness's order, and daylie troubleth you, mindinge therby most wikedly towardes me to imprint in your princlie minde some deepe concept of disloiall and undutifull disposition towardes your Majestie, which pratize of hers being divulged throwe your Majesties Realme as rumores hertofore spred of me hath bene by her and her ministeres to my great dishonor, she hopeth they will tak such rotte and successe as make you my heavie lady and by her cuning devises work my over-throwe, as she and others desires if they maie be harde and beleaved. The good opinion that your Majestie hath of me in performinge your highnes order and my dutie towardes your Majestie I will never deceave nor forget, nothing doubting that my wiefes sclandarous speaches (though they be never so maine) can spoile me of your Majesties gracious and favourable good lykinge. The declaration of your Majesties pleasure did never touche nor release accions commensed against her children nor servants nor pament of anie money receaved by me, for I accompt them mine owne and by your Majesties lawes I ought to have them. Howbeit since your order I have left the receit therof to her and her children and doth not medle noe more with anie of them; yet I have paid them since my coming into the countrie all I received above vc^{li} by yeare assigned me by your Majestie according to my word to the Lord Chancellour and the Lord of Leiceter. The grief that my wife hath conceived can not be removed nor the acusations therof taken awaie, for her unsatiable desire is suche which I am acquented with, that her owne and a great parte of mine would never satisfie her greadie appetite. Therfor the troubles that aforetime I have indured at her handes are admonitions sufficient to advise a man of reason or els I wish not to be pitied of your Majestie nor desires my lief. Thes thinges I doubt not but your Majestie will consider and favoure my quietnes in my ould age, that I maie the better and longer serve you like a noble man under whos obedience I will sett upp my rest. As the lyving God knoweth unto whos mightie protection I commend your Majestie, beseking the almightie God bless and save you from all your enemies.' Sheffield.

Copy 1½pp. (Original Letters I/192)

THE EARL OF SHREWSBURY TO THE COUNTESS OF SHREWSBURY

1585, October 23. 'The offences and faltes that you have committed against me, which noe good wief would doe, wher admonitions sufficient to all men in their mariage, and though you desire to be chardged particulerlie to thend you maie know your faltes, I nede not to expresse them, they be so manifest to the world; and yf I would hidd them, your behaviour and conditions hath laid them open. There can not be anie wief more forgetfull of her dutie and lese carfull to please her husband then you have bene, nor anie more bounden nor have received greater benefittes by her husband then you. The particulers I will not expresse but doe leave them to the time till that God will send his grace to make you confesse them. In that I loved you and did manie good thinges for you and was loth that the world should see your behaviour, it maie be judged that I wolde still so have continued if you had not sought all meanes both at home and abroade to offend me. Ther nede not manie wordes. I have sene throwlie into your devises and desires. Your unsatiable gredie appetite did bewraye you. Your owne living at my handes could not content you, nor yet a great part of mine which for my quietnes I could have bene contented to have geven you, but this was short of the mark you shott at and yet doe. Your faire wordes are (? nought) but forme. They have the showe and tast they have had, though they appeare butifull yet they are mixed with a hidden poison. But assure yourself I will avoide so near as I can my owne harme. I am and wilbe pleased with her Majesties order (though it semed harde), for you best knowe that your living was never ment to your children during my lief. But seing it fals out so, you must be likewise contented with that for your mantenance and pament of your debtes that her Majestie hath assigned, which is a great portion and none of your callinge hath the like. You chardge me with an untruthe that I doe enter into your livinge, meaninge your childrens, as it semeth. I content myself with her Majesties order and intendeth to hold the £500 lande by yeare during our lives. You wer ever in miserie, but yet sufficientlie furnished to buy landes for your children. Marie! You now wanted the helpe and so shall desyre you hadd to paie for it. I enforce not your children to sell land, but yf your wilfulnes and their pride be such as cannot be manteyned without sale of your landes, I do not rejoyse in it, nor assuredlie I am not sorie for it.

I mervell to see your earnestnes, as you pretend by your letters, to be with me. You can not forget ther was books drawn by our counsell, and about the agrement I did mete your children before the L. Chancellour, the L. of Leiceter, and all your griefs were then recited, as well the release of my sutes commensed against your children and servants for my goodes and sclanderous rumors spred by them of me in divers parts of this realme, for whom no good wif would aire open her mouth. As for our cohabitation with having all your living at my disposition during the same and divers other thinges as by the tales appereth, to which I answered then as I will answer you, that yf ever I think good to tak you agane (for you went awaie voluntarilie not turned awaie by me as you saie, and when I sent for you, you said I should send twise for you or you would come), I will have both together without any exceptid, either of signification on your part or of mine. But herof you made me noe recitall in your letters that you are contented that I shall have the disposition of your lyving, but assure yourself the one without the other I will never have. The malicious mindes that your children doe beare to me I cannot awaie with all; it can not be but you must favoure your children, therfore howe dangerous it wher for me to be compassed about with you and theim when after me you shall leape into my seate, the most ignorant maie judge. And here I ende protesting before the Almightie God that I doe not this for anie malice to you or anie partie, but that in my ould age I desire my securitie and quietnes and would not have it troubled during my lief.' Sheffield.

Copy *Endorsed*: 'The copie of my letter to my wief the 23 of October 1585.' 2pp. (Original Letters I/194)

THE EARL OF SHREWSBURY TO SIR FRANCIS WALSINGHAM

1585, October 23. My wife and her children pester the Queen and Council with their imaginary griefs, but seldom get to 'particularities which I am able to answere agreable with my place and honor, the like whereof hath not ben offered to a man of my cotte by a woman of so base a parentage and her children.' They should not be heard or believed. I must answer because I am charged with breaking her Majesty's order. I deny this: (1) in respect of the lands in dispute; (2) of the money which they say I received; (3) of my wife's charge that I maintain other men's suits against her. She gives no names 'but she showes herself no changeling and still continues the same she hath begone.' Sheffield.

Copy   Endorsed: 'The copie of my letter to Mr Secretarie Walsingham the 23rd of October, 1585.' 2pp.   (Original Letters I/196)

LORD OGLE TO THE EARL OF SHREWSBURY

1585, October 24.   I thank you for the £100 loan and desire to borrow £100 more. I hope you will not be offended that your son and his wife stayed with me so long, but it was my wish on account of the extreme weather.   Bothal.

Signed   Endorsed: 'My Lord Ogels letter.'   1 p.   (Original Letters I/198)

GILBERT, LORD TALBOT, TO THE EARL OF SHREWSBURY

1585, October 24.   My uncle, Mr Roger Manners, has told me of the good effects of his suit to you on my behalf.   My only delight will be to be commanded and employed by you.   I hope to come to the country when I have settled with the creditors and disposed of the Somersetshire estate profitably. 'And then having your Lordships good concente to joyne in the assurance of your estate, I doubte not but to obtaine bothe my Ladyes and my wyves also, altho they both well know and with grefe consider (as I also have no less cause) that if God sholde take me away, bothe my wyfe and my three pore lyttell daughters shall therby be beggared.'   I thank you on my knees for the thousand pounds.   Richmond.

Holograph   1½ pp.   (Original Letters I/200)

THE EARL OF LEICESTER TO THE EARL OF SHREWSBURY

1585, November 15.   'My good Lord.   I have receved your letter which I have longe lookyd for, in respect of a letter I wrote a month or 6 weekes synce to your Lordship uppon your veary frendly and curteous offer to pleasure me now toward my voyage in any sort you could.   Wheruppon being desierous to have had forty or fiftye such good archers as I know were easily to be founde among your tenants and servants, I was bold with your Lordship therin; but for that I dyd not hear in long tyme from you and my jorney hastened by hir Majestie, I have provided me now sufficiently of such archers I requyred, and soe doe pray your Lordship, specyally for that in this your letter also ther is no mencyon made of them, to bear with my former request, which in truth I dyd chiefly presume uppon by your courteous offer unto me.

As touching your Lordships request to me for no further dealing in moving reconcyllyation betwene my Lady and you, I doe very willingly yeld therto. Albeyt that I dyd was honest and Christyanly and not unfytt for any frend your Lordship hath in good sort to have delt as farr as I have done; confessing in (truth) yt ys not matter for man to mo (ve) in without your own good lyking, which yf I were to tarry as I am to goe out of the realme, I wold not any more intrude myself therin, much less being absent as I shalbe. Nether had I dealt so far as I have done wyshing the good end I dyd betwene you but for the honor and love I have long born to your Lordship and your howse, whereof I have made a good proofe as any frend or kinsman whosoever he be in England. And so commending your Lordship to the protectyon of the Almighty, I will take my leave of you meaning, God wylling, to take my jorney within these 7 days.'   At the Court.

Holograph   2 pp.   (Original Letters I/202)

1585, November 30. 'I have resayved your Lordships answere of my letters on the 19 and 23 of November, and letters written to her Majestie and to the Erle of Lecestre which Mr Talbot hath delivered. The Quenes letter was delivered by Mr Talbot the 27th of this instant to her owne handes as she walked abroad on the grene at Richmounde, but therof as yet we understande nothinge of her likinge or dislikinge, but we hoope to resayve answere this day or tomorow. We were constrayned to folow the Erle of Lecestre from the Court to London for his letters. Suche preparation and busynes ys about the Erles despatche for his voyadge into the Low Countries as to few or no private causes any answere ys geven. He hath returned your Lordship answere by his letters, but how your Lordships offer ys accepted of him I can writ no certyntye; but Mr Talbot told me that the Erle said he conceyved great comfort of your Lordships kinde letter then yf your Lordship had geven him thre thowsande poundes. I was with him at the delivery of your letter, but I could not come to his presence but this day. He says he will speke with Mr Talbot and me. The Countess contynueth the same in her complayntes that she hath bene, and lately in a matter hath trobled her Majestie about pulling down of a wall (as she informed) procured by your Lordship. The Quene of her self remembering how she had herd by petityon of the countriemen of commons inclosed, said to the Countes: 'Madam, so longe as you had the Erle of Shrewesburies good contenance and favor, they durst not medle with it, but they seying you in disgrace with your husband, they have pulled it down of themselves,' and thus excused your Lordship. She will be spied out in the ende, I hope to her shame. Clearke hath labored earnestly to get the injunctyon dissolved, but at my laynge at the Court I have spoken with the L. Treasorer (who as yet is very weake).' I cannot hear of any further information as to our opponents' proceedings in the suit.   Coleherbent.

Holograph   Seal   1p.   (Original Letters I/204)

(THE EARL OF SHREWSBURY) TO (QUEEN ELIZABETH)

(1585)   I am right sorry that your Highness is so continually troubled with my wife's complaints touching me, whose desire to have is so importunate that although her living be more than any of her calling, she does not rest to devise by all skill how to draw your Highness to great liking of her insinuations. I thank you for hearing my part, and am contented with the £500 of land assigned me, so long as my wife is contented with the residue for her maintenance. To save further trouble I want my part to myself. I have done many good things for my wife and her children, and they have requited me evil. I hear now she is lodged in your Majesty's Court of purpose daily to trouble you with these unnecessary toys, and to withdraw you from your weightier affairs. And although I have reposed such a certain and assured confidence in your Majesty's goodness and justice that she shall little prevail; yet the show and opinion of her, being so continually in your presence, and of those which are about you, is construed to be to my discredit and prejudice. And therefore, under your Majesty's favour and correction (I speak as a husband), it were more seemly for her to contain herself at home than in such sort to trouble your Majesty, and discountenance him of whom she received and has all the honour and most of the wealth she enjoys.

Copy   Endorsed: 'A copy of a letter written to the Queen by the Earl of Shrewsbury.'   2½ pp.   (Original Letters II/259)

SIR CHRISTOPHER HATTON TO THE EARL OF SHREWSBURY

1585-86, January 1. 'My very good Lord. Her Majestie, understanding by my Lord Talbott your sone, with what fatherly kyndnes you have lately extended your goodnes towardes hym in the performance of your promyse for the thousand poundes which you have geven hym toward the payment of his debtes; and in honorably acknoledginge a fyne of some part of the landes in the West Country where in your Lordship had interest, and wyll favorably profitt (as her Majestie hopeth) whatsoever is in that behalf as yet unfinished, it hath pleased her Highnes to conceave and interprete that your Lordship hath vouchsafed these fatherly kynde partes of your love and affections towardes hym the rather for her sake and for the honorable concept which she houldeth of his vertue and merit. In which respect she hath expresly commaunded me to yelde unto your Lordship, in her name, her manifold most pryncely thankes, and withall to assure you that the more you shall cherishe and favor such a sone, the more your Lordship shall advance her honor and your owne reputation, beeing to her Majestie and the State a very sufficient servant, and to your self a comfortable staff in your ould yeares, not unworthy, in respect of the hope and towardlynes in hym to succeede his most honorable and great auncestours. And herin her Majestie desyreth your Lordship to remember what woordes she spake of hym and the opinion which she delyvered of hym to yourself at her (*sic* your) last being with her, which, her Highnes willed me to tell you, is synce increased through the experience and increase of his merit and service. I assure you, my good Lord, your honorable dealinge with hym hath greatly contented her Majestie, who in her gratious favor is glad to see you comfort and incourage hym in his honorable disposition and course of service with your fatherly love and kyndnes.' From the Court at Greenwich.

Signed Endorsed: 'Sir Chrestopher Hattons letter to my Lo. my father by her Majesties express commandment most favourably on my behalf.' 1 p. (Original Letters I/209)

SIR CHRISTOPHER HATTON TO THE EARL OF SHREWSBURY

1585-86, January 6. 'My very good Lord. Uppon intelligence geven me by your sone Mr Talbot of his repayre to doo his dewtie unto you, I have thought it an office, whereunto I confesse I am bounde, to visite your Lordship with these fewe lynes, and in the same to commend to your honorable good opinion all the service that so poore a frende here may doo you with all faythfull and trewe devotion.

Synce my Lord of Leycesters arrivall in the Lowe Countries we have receaved no advertisement from those partes of any moment; and from France no occurrentes but ordinary, ymportinge nothing in effect but a wavering in constant disposition in the Kinge, some tymes to harken to peace, and sone after, uppon sudden occasions, inclyned agayne to war; making his preparations accordingly both of Swissers and Almayns, whereof he expecteth dyvers companies to come to hym shortly, and so doth the King of Navarre, who indevoureth dayly to increase his power and to gather forces to answere hym; and so doth Duke Memorancie whose fortune in some late attemptes agaynst the Kings forces hath ben prosperous and of good successe. Her Majestie, as Mr Talbott can tell your Lordship, is well disposed in her health, and so he left her, which I beseche God may long contynue, to her gratious contentation and the comfort of all that faythfully love and serve her.' From the Court at Greenwich.

Signed 1½ pp. (Original Letters I/211)

JOHN MANNERS AND SIR FRANCIS WILLOUGHBY TO LORD BURGHLEY AND SIR FRANCIS WALSINGHAM

1585-86, January 12. In accordance with your instructions and a commission from the Chancery, we here examined today certain witnesses with regard to the dispute between the Earl of Shrewsbury and the Cavendishes. The Earl sent word that he would not assent to our proceeding with the second article, the Cavendishes insist on our dealing with the articles as they stand. We therefore ask your wishes. Ashford.

Copy Endorsed 'The copie of John Manners and Sir Francis Willoughby their letter to the L. Tresorer and Sir Francis Walsingham, principall secretarie to her Majestie.' 1 p. (Original Letters I/215)

THE EARL OF DERBY TO THE EARL OF SHREWSBURY

1585-86, January 18. In favour of Richard Davies, a servant to his son, Lord Strange. Lathom.

Signed ½ p. (Original Letters I/213)

LORD STRANGE TO THE EARL OF SHREWSBURY

1585-86, January 21. On behalf of Richard Davies, one of the Earl's tenants. Lathom.

Signed 1 p. (Original Letters I/216)

THE PRIVY COUNCIL TO — — — — — —

1585-86, January 31. Giving instructions that in the case of one [*name erased*] dying, who is now very sick, his moveables should be protected from ill disposed persons. At the Court.

Seal 1 p. *The signatures torn off and the address erased. It appears to be a copy and to refer to the Earl of Shrewsbury's illness.* (Original Letters I/122)

CHRISTOPHER COPLEY TO THE EARL OF SHREWSBURY

1585-86, February 2. Mr Talbot arrived here yesterday and was heartily entertained by my brother Rayner. It was your pleasure that I should tell you what I could about Mr Talbot's liking or disliking of the gentlewoman, and also my own opinion what I thought of her. 'I do thinke it my part to describe the maide as she ys. Her yeares are verey tendre, not of thage of xv years till midsomer next, of a very good stature, somethinge hier then my Ladie Grace, and therwithall smale, beautyfull ynough, wise for her yeares and modestly governed, educated under my sister, an ancyent vertuous gentlewoman, one of the daughters and heires of Sir John Constable, deceased.... She is not unfytt for a very good matche.' Pray let me brother Rayner know your decision 'sith he hath broken very good offers for the preferment of his daughter.' Kymelton.

Holograph 1 p. (Original Letters I/218)

THE EARL OF SHREWSBURY TO GILBERT, LORD TALBOT

1585-86, February 17. 'Gilberte Talbot. I have accordinge to your requeste sent my letter herin to Mr Vice Chamberlin, wherein I have requested him to geve her Majestie humble thankes for her gracious remembrance of me, and for her Majesties goodnes towardes you, which I praye God your service maye deserve att her Majesties handes; and so having performed your requeste and sent you his letter that you may deliver hit yourself, doe bide you farewell, prayinge to God to bless you'. Sheffield Castle.

Signed ½ p.   (Original Letters I/220)

QUEEN ELIZABETH TO THE EARL OF SHREWSBURY

1585-86, March 5. 'Right trustie and right welbelovid cousin and counsellor, we greete you well. We could not uppon this present occasion of writing but let you understand howe glad we weare to heare (having ben, as we weare informid, reducid to so weake an estate through your late sicknes) of your good recoverye, assuring you that no frend or kinsman you have, of thos that pretend most to love you, was more glad therof then our self.

We have long desired, for your owne good and quiet, that all matters of difference between the Countesse your wife, her sonnes and you, might be brought to some good composition; for which purpose we have appointed the L. Thresorer and the Secretary to do their best endevor for the accomplishing of the same, so as we would be loth that anie thing should faule out, by presenting of matters in coorse of lawe, that might any way interrupt our good intent and meaning in that behalf. And therefore whereas the last yere, when we toke the mediation of the cause in controversy betwin you into our handes, we did order that there should be a staie made of all proceedings in lawe against the said Countesses servants and sonnes, being now geven t'understand that you have an action to be tryed at the next Assises in our countyes of Derby and York against William Cavendish, the saide Countesses sonne, and one Basseford her servant, against whom (as we are informid) the witnesses that are producid be such as have other actions and sutes in triall with him and are besides men of no good name or credit, we cannot but pray you again, as a thing we looke you will performe, that you do staie your proceeding against them, for that we would be glad that all causes of controversie betwin you should receave some end rather by way of mediation then by sute of law, assuring you that we wishe yt cheefely for your good, without any intent or meaning that by this staie your credit should be any way towchid, wherof we are no lesse carefull then of our owne, as you shall well understand at the tyme of your repeire hether, which we are put in hope by your sonne Henry Taulbott wilbe about Easter; and to thend the same may not be impeachid therewith through the indisposition of your body, we cannot but both advise and pray you to have an especyall care that thoroughe could or disorder of dyet you cast not yourself into a relapse.'   Greenwich.

Signed under privy signet   1 p.   (Original Letters I/222)

INSTRUCTIONS FROM THE EARL OF SHREWSBURY TO HENRY TALBOT, TO BE SHOWN TO THE LORD TREASURER AND SECRETARY WALSINGHAM

(1585-86, March 18)   The Countess's petition for more witnesses to be opposed on the ground that the evidence was taken by the last Commission; of the four articles, three have been examined. As to the second about the lead ore (which they call lath and cope) the Earl has accounted to Sir Charles Cavendish about the rents. The matter was not part of the Queen's order, and the Earl cannot agree to any further examination. 'Also I wold have you to move the Lords that I be not further pressed with anie further demaundes, for I am resolved not to yeld to more then I have alredie done.'

Endorsed: '15 March, 1585. Instructions for Mr Henry Talbott.' 1p. (Original Letters I/224)

SIR FRANCIS WALSINGHAM TO THE EARL OF SHREWSBURY

1586, April 7. 'My very good Lord. I would not omit th'occasion that is now offered to acquaint your Lordship with the present state of thinges aswell at home as abroade. At home her Majestie some few dayes before Easter, her Majestie was dryven to kepe her chamber, being troubled with a mild defluxion of the rheum, but is nowe, thanks be to God, in perfect good health, wherof I do the rather geve your Lordship knowledge because I knowe you will take comfort by it.

At this last assises in Devonshire, we heare there hath happened the lyke accident thorough the infection of the ayre comming from the prisonners that fell out in lyke case four yeares past at Oxford; by meanes whereof fyve or six of the principall justices in the country, among which Sir John Chichester and Sir Arthur Basset be named and sayd to be dead, besides Mr Baron Flowerdew, one of the Justices of Assise, and dyvers other persons of good welth and reconning in the sayd county.

For forren matters we heare that in Scotland the King professeth to be altogether at her Majestys devotion and wholly bent to do any thing that may be for her contentment and the stablishing of mutuall good frendship and unity betwin the two Crownes.

In Fraunce they seeme to have put on a full resolution to prosecute the King of Navarre and thos of the relligion with all extremity, who notwithstanding are in good hope to be speedily releeved out of Germany where the princes protestant beginne nowe to be more carefull of the maintenance of the common cause then hertofor they have ben, forseeing that yf the King of Navarre miscary ther staffe is then next the doore.

Of Sir Francis Drakes successe and proceedings in the Indias, we have good newes by advertisements out of Spayne; as that he hath taken dyvers townes of great importance and much treasure, and armed a great number of the stoutest Indians against the King; but herof tyme only is to confirme the truth.

For the matters of the Lowe Countryes the displeasure that her Majesty had of late mantained against my Lord of Leycester for his acceptance of the governement is now well qualified, and her Majestie hath now restored him to her wonted good opinion and favor which she hathe for his comforte signifyed unto him by her owne letters and seeketh now to grace and countenance him as much as she can, having written lykwyes to the States to cary that respect and affection still towardes him that the place wherin he representeth her owne person and his dutyfull love and devotion towardes her do require, so as I hope thinges will henceforth go better there then hitherto they have done. Of late there have fallen out two mutinyes among our souldiers for want of pay, which inconvenyence is meant hereafter to be avoyded for the tymely sending over of such supplyes of treasure as are requisit for the satisfying of them.' Greenwich.

Signed 2pp. (Original Letters I/226)

THE EARL OF LEICESTER TO THE EARL OF SHREWSBURY

(? 1586) Good Friday. I rejoice to hear from my friend Mr Herbert of your good amendment in health. The best service you can do your friends is 'to be quyett and merry and not to be overpressed with any grefe or conceattes, rather cast uppon your frendes any burden that they may bear for you.' I thank you for your honourable dealing touching your royalty and manor of Cambton. At the Court.

Holograph 3 pp. (Original Letters II/23)

THE EARL OF LEICESTER TO THE EARL OF SHREWSBURY

(1586) May 1. 'My very good Lord. Since I wrote to you and my Lord Chancelor by her Majesties comandment and lykwyse to my Lady, your wyffe, I receved this day my Ladys answer touching the requests your Lordship made for the lands in the west, or for the Peak Forest etc. My Lady being, as she sayth, most desyrous of a quyett end, specyally with hope to recover your Lordships good favour, though desperatt as the world doth thinke yt, she ys well content your Lordship uppon certyn condytions, which are not in my conceat but reasonable, that your Lordship shall have ether the western landes or the Peak Forrest alone; and bycause your Lordship shall perceave she meaneth that you should have the full of that her Majestie hath asigned yf your Lordship shall not lyke to take ether of them with the condytions she wyll offer. Your Lordship shall at your choyse ether take her your farmer or some other wey sufficyent to answere your yerely £650 clerely, or els to take which of those shall please you in lew of £500 yerely rent. So that yf your Lordship shall not lyke of the landes with these condityons your Lordship shall yet have £500 a yere gayned. Thus much I thought good to advertyse your Lordship of, as I have done my Lord Chancelor lykwyse.' At the Court.

Holograph Endorsed (not in contemporary hand): 'E. of Leicester, 1586, May 1, concerning the Countess.' 1 p. (Original Letters I/228)

THE EARL OF SHREWSBURY *VERSUS* THE COUNTESS OF SHREWSBURY

1586, May 8. 'Certain thinges pronounced by her Majestie in the presence of we whose names ar underwritten, by her Majesties commandement ar ordered to be performed by the Erle of Shrewsbury in the causes of controversie betwixt him and the Countess his wife.' At Greenwich the 8th day of May, 1586.

The writers Burghley, Walsingham and Bromley, recommend:

(1) That the Earl content himself with the £500 of land assigned him by the Queen's former order.

(2) That the Earl pay to the Cavendishes the £2000 claimed by them in respect of profits of the lands at variance.

(3) 'Where it was before ordered that all sutes commenced by the sayd Erle against the said Countesses sonnes and servants or any of them should cease; contrary wherunto the said Erle proceded in his sute then dependyng against one Henry Beresford, the said Countesses servant, the said Erle obteyned verdict against him at the last assises in the Countie of York; wherein nevertheles her Majestie was sithens content, at the said Erles request, that judgement should pass upon that verdict, for that the Erle alledged that his honour was interested in the cause; her Majesties pleasure is that the said Erle shall content himself with the judgement only without taking advantage for dammage therby receved being but a matter of profit, without further troubling or molesting the said Beresford or his sureties any wayes by reason of the said action or judgement.' Nor is he to enter into any action against the Countess etc. for matters past.

(4) The Earl not to displace any of the Countess's tenants.

Endorsed: 'Her Majesties order betwene the Erle and Countess of Shrewsbury.' 1 p. (Original Letters I/230) F.232 *is another copy of the above. 2 pp.*

QUEEN ELIZABETH TO THE EARL OF SHREWSBURY

1586, May 12. 'Beinge caried with an earneste desire sithens the first dislike fallen out betwene you and the Countesse your wife, to see all matters as well of unkindnes betwene you as of variance otherwise betwene you yourselfe and her younger sonnes, by our mediation brought to some good end and accorde, both in respecte of the place we holde, whiche requireth at our handes that we should not suffer in our realme two personnes of your degree and qualitie to live in suche a kinde of divided sort, as also for the speciall care we have of your selfe, knowinge that theis variances have greatlie disquieted you whose yeares require repose, speciallie of the minde; we have of late thought hitherto noe such effectes have folowed of our mediation in that behalfe as we loke for (although we hope better therafter), speciallie touchinge the matter of unkindnes; calling unto us both the Lorde Chauncellor, for that he had direction before, together with our cousin of Leicester, to deal betwene you and the said Countisse and her sonnes touchinge the perfectinge and putting of our former order in due execution, and the Lord Tresurer and our Secretarie whom we appointed this laste winter to procede in the same cause, with your sonne Henrie Talbott and your servant Copley, for that the former order by us entended was not then brought to a quiet end, and upon due consideration had, as well of the matter ytself restinge in our memorie, as of their reportes and opinions to us declared for the full perfectinge and accomplishing of our former order, thought good in the presence of the said Lord Chancelor and Tresurer and Secretarie to pronounce our order betwene you touchinge the pointes in variance, whiche our pleasure is to be observed as is specified and conteyned in a schedule herinclosed, subscribed by the said Lord Chancelor, Lord Treasurer and our Secretarie.' Greenwich.

Copy Endorsed: 'A copy of her Majesties letter the 12th day of May, 1586.' 1p. (Original Letters I/7)

THE EARL OF SHREWSBURY TO LORD BURGHLEY

(1586, May 23) In answer to the Queen's letter of May 12, 1586. Sheffield Manor.

Copy Endorsed: 'A copie a letter to be sent to the L. Trusurer from the Earle of Shrewsburie about the Countess.' 2 pp. (Original Letters I/11) (See *H.M.C. Salisbury MSS*, Vol. III. pp. 142-3)

SIR CHRISTOPHER HATTON TO THE EARL OF SHREWSBURY

1586, June 30. 'According to your Lordships request I delivered unto her most excellent Majestie the writing brought unto me by your servant Mr Beeston. Her Highnes hathe been pleased to peruse the same, and thereuppon thinkethe it very fitt that the parties which have subscribed unto it sholde be stayed and further talked withall. By meanes whereof there is lyke to falle owte the more satisfaction both unto her Highnes and to your Lordship.' From the Court at Greenwich.

Signed ½ p (Original Letters I/234)

GILBERT, LORD TALBOT, TO LORD BURGHLEY

1586, July 24. 'Right honorable and my espetiall good Lord. Knowynge how very greatly I am bounde to your Lordship for your late favores above any other, I purposed to have attended on your Lordship my selfe this day to have acknowledged the same, with humble petition for continuance thereof, but that I am ernestly intreted by letters from my Lady Russell to mete the Erle of Ormonde and his Lady at her house at Donington Castell nere Newberry tomorrow at night, meaninge to goe thitherwardes this afternoone.

How your Lordship founde my Lord my father or left him disposed to-wardes me on Fryday last I knowe not, but I greatly doubte that his Lordship, suspectinge that this late nobell and godly act of her Majestie on my mother-in-lawes behalfe (which before went so muche agenst his harte) hath bene fur-thered by sum of my good frendes at my sute, the rather or in respecte of me is more offended with me then before. So as if I sholde now attende on him I sholde be in gretter perell of the tempest of his wordes then before (the feare and terror wherof hath bene the only cause of this forbearance), which also by my comminge to his Lordship nowe might be conceved to have proceded oute of my mother-in-lawes disjoynte with my Lord, which beynge now united agen I theruppon presently make repayre. Nevertheles if your Lordship have founde no alteration in my Lord towardes me, but that he will be pleased (as once he did) to promis your Lordship on his honor to forbeare to chastyse me with any extreme rygour of wordes; and yf your Lordship doe not thinke thes reasons before alledged be suffitient to withhoulde me from him yet for a whyle longer, I will be reddy with all humility to him and faythfull affection to your Lordship to follow your direction therin, which I protest I rather desyre to be guyded by then any mans whosoever. And how farr herin your Lordship will vouchsafe to directe me to use my Unkell Roger Manners, I will be a sutor to him to performe.' At Doctor Gilberts house not far from Powles.

PS. 'I have directed this bearer to come this night to me to Colbruck.'

Holograph   Addressed: 'To Burghley at Tybells.' 1 p. (Original Letters I/236)

THOMAS BAYLY TO THE EARL OF SHREWSBURY

1586, July 27. 'May it please your honor. I have thought it apperteyninge to my dutie, wherin I stand most bound unto your Lordship, to geve you to un-derstand of the prosperouse aryvall of Sir Francis Drake at Portsmouth with his fleete, his expedition beinge in most honorable wyse accomplished, and he with the same fleete and companies as readie and, thanked be God, as able for any furder service as when he went out. Wherein he hath showed such a president of good conduct and government as may not only redound to the honor and encoragement of our nation but to the astonishment of thenemye, who never had the like pece of service performed synce first the Indies were found, though some one jorney thither have cost him tenn tymes so much. Neyther hath he nor anie other prince had so greate thinges done by so fewe handes, the particularities wherof synce now I cannot set downe as their worthines requireth I have thought better to saie nothinge therin then a little, only this by your Lordships favore and no more. Outward bound we loked on the coost of Spaine and Canaries, burned and sacked the cytie of St Jago with the townes of Domingo and Praia of Capo Verde, the brave cytie of St Domingo in Hispaniola and the stronge cytie of Cartagena in Peru. Whom-ward we tooke and razed the fortresse of St Johns with the towne of St

Augustine in Florida, and so passinge along that coast and falling upon Wingandecoa we brought awaie such forlorne contreymen of ours as at Sir Richard Grenefields departure thens were ther left behind to smale purpose. And yf wind and wether would have permitted us, we had not failed to have taken all such Spaniards as fyshed this year at Newfoundland, which place we could not sease throw contrary windes. So as we directed hither where we ar all, thanked be God, in saftie, but three of our shippes, viz, the *Sea Dragon,* the *Talbote* and the *White Lyon,* who by violence of wether were forced to sea from the roode at Wingandecoa, leaving there on land behind them attendinge upon our general there captaines and gentlemen with many other of their companies, whereof myself am one, in some want and distresse had not the generall, by whose commandement and for whose gard we were there, releved the same with such honorable curtesie as myself could not have wished for. The shippes we loke for them here every houre, and there is no doute of there saftie yf God be pleased, who in greate mercy hath loked upon us all in this action, upon the conclusion whereof yf the expectation of some adventurers therin (who perhaps more respect there private pence then publique welth or honor) be not satisfied to the full, lett them blame the causers or causes of so longe and manifold lettes and delaies used in the dispatching therof whereby thenemye hadd so long a tyme to fortifie to prevent or to provyde for the saftie of theire treasure and things of most price, so as we by all likely hood could loke for no better then blowes or bare walles. Notwithstandinge, it pleased God to favor and furder us that we found some unrype burdes upon the nestes which we toke not without some good scrachinge and spoiled the same as before, insomuch that yf (accordinge to the Spaniardes owne computation) we have endamaged them upon the coste of Spaine to the value of 300,000 ducats, and have by that proportion spoiled them in the Indies to the value of 300 millions at the least in castles, tounes, shippes, gallies, souldiers, slaves, treasure, marchandise, vittels, munition and 300 peces, 200 of them beinge brasse, and as good ordinance for canon, cuveringe, basilisto etc as any in England. Some other good thinges will also be found in this our fleete, I hope sufficient to yeld a reasonable good content to every honest mynde, as shortly, God willinge, I shall more at large enforme your Honor, hopinge in the meane tyme your Lordships accustomed goodnes will accept in good worth these fewe and rude lynes.' 'Written in hast upon the sea by the Ile of Wight abord the admirall the *Bonaventure,* the best conditioned shipp of the world.'

PS. 'I besech your Honor, let Massy or some other write to my father that all is well with me, I thank God.'

Holograph 2 pp. (Original Letters I/238)

Sir Francis Walsingham to the Earl of Shrewsbury

1586, July 28. 'My very good Lord. I have receavid your Lordships letter conteyning the manner of the order, as you conceave yt, that her Majesty hath lately taken betwin the Countesse your wyfe and you, wherein your Lordship desyreth t'understand whether you have taken her Majestys meaning a right or no. For aunswer wherof yt may please you to consider that thorder being set downe by her Majestys self, she might easely conceave offence against me yf I should without her knowledge or privity take uppon me to interpret her wordes or meaninge in the matter, espetyally because I may mistake or forget some of the pointes of yt: as indeede I do not well remember that some of the thinges set downe by your Lordship weare at all mentioned or spoken of by her Majesty. Nevertheles, yf your Lordship do thinke good that

I move her Majesty in yt, I will not fayle to do yt, meaning nevertheles to forbeare the same untill I heare further from your Lordship, Besides, for that my Lord Thresorer was also present when her Majesty set downe the sayd order, yt were fitt his Lordship should also be made acquainted with your request, who meaning to be now at the Court within a day or two, I will not fayle, yf your Lordship shall lyke of yt, to deale with him in that behalf.' Barn Elms.

Signed   Endorsed in the Earl of Shrewsbury's hand: 'Mr Secretarys letter of the 28 of July concerning my speches with her Majestie inne my L. Tresorers and Mr Secretarys presence.' 1 p. (Original Letters I/240)

LORD DARCY TO THE EARL OF SHREWSBURY

1586, August 9. He requests indulgence for the bearer, Francis Scrimgar, a young man who, misled by evil company, has been hunting in the Earl's grounds at Kimberworth. 'Praying to God to deliver you from your enemies and send your Lordship to Sheffield.' Aston.

Signed   Endorsed in the Earl of Shrewsbury's hand: 'Francis Scrimgrours confession to me therle of Shrewsbury, the 9 of August 1586.' *and in another hand:* 'My Lo. Darcys letter of the 9th of August, 1586, touchinge my hunters.' ½ p. (Original Letters I/242)

SIR CHARLES CAVENDISH TO MARY, LADY TALBOT

(1586) September 27. I can give you no great news since there is none stirring. His Excellency uses me very well, asked often times for my Lady and their agreeing, but has heard they have fallen out again, which I understand not in any case. But it is believed here. My Lord North asked very kindly how you did with yourself, and says he is a little in my Lord Talbot's debt which he will shortly come out of.

I thank God I am very well, and see no more necessity here than London affords, for all things are exceeding plentiful. If you will have any understanding of the last broil here,* my Lord's letter will tell you as much as I know in effect. So being in some haste by reason of the bearer's haste I wish you the greatest good that ever any creature possessed. I pray you remember my most humble duty to my Lord of Ormond. And so I take my leave. From the camp before Zutfen. *Undated.*

Holograph   Addressed: to the Lady Mary Talbot. ½ p. (Original Letters II/281)

FOTHERINGHAY

1586, October 13. 'The Lordes and others of the Counsell that came to Ffotheringaie this 13 of October 1586.

Lords and others of the Counsell:

L. Chancellor. Sir Thomas Bromeley.
L. Treasurer. L. Burghleie.
Erle Marshall. Erle of Shrewsbury.
Erle of Derbie.
Erle of Warwick.
Mr Comptroller. Sir James Croft.
Mr Vice Chamberlaine. Sir Christopher Hatton.

* Possibly a reference to the battle in which Sir Philip Sidney was mortally wounded on September 22, 1586.

Mr Secretary Walsingham.
Mr Chancellor of the Duchy. Sir Raffe Sadler.
Mr Chancellor of the Exchequer. Sir Walter Mildmay.

Erles and barons:

Erle of Oxford. L. great Chamberlaine.
Erle of Kent.
Erle of Worcester.
Erle of Rutlande.
Erle of Cumberland.
Erle of Pembrook.
Erle of Lincolne.
Viscounte Mountague.
L. Bergeinie.
L. Zowche.
L. Morlie.
L. Stafford.
L. Graie.
L. Lumleie.
L. Sturton.
L. Sandes.
L. Wentworth.
L. Mordant.
L. St John.
L. Compton.
L. Cheinie.

L. Chief Justice of the Kings Bench.
L. Chief Justice of the Common Please.
L. Chief Baron.
Justice Gowdie.
Justice Peream.'

Endorsed: as above. 1 p. (Original Letters I/33)

LORD CHANCELLOR BROMLEY TO THE EARL OF SHREWSBURY

1586, October 22. 'My verie good Lord. This day I came hyther to the Courte and repayringe to her Majestie to doo my dewtye after our longe and tedious jorney, her Highnes made me acquaynted with your letter of request to be excused in respecte of your infirmitie of your attendaunce at London upon Tuesday next for fynishinge of the commyssion concerninge the Quene of Scottes, where her Highnes sheweth her selfe desyrous to have had your presence. And therfore (my Lorde) yf possibilie you can, I woulde advyse yow not to be absent, and herin her Majestie willed me to wryte unto you. And soe prayinge God to send you good health, I leave further to trouble your Lordship.' Windsor.

Holograph Endorsed: 'Answered 23 of October 1586.' ½p. (Original Letters I/246)

LORD BURGHLEY TO THE EARL OF SHREWSBURY

1586, October 22. 'My honorable good Lord. I was even strycken with greff of mynd when your servant Mr Beson brought your letter, signefyeng your stay at Stilton by occasion of your payne, and afterward hir Majesty tellyng me how it greved hir that your Lordship shuld be absent on Tewsday, I sayd that your Lordship had wrytten to me and that I shuld declare your opinion for that cause which we hard at Fodrynghay to be agreable with myn. Nevertheless I se hir Majesty very sorry that your Lordship shuld be absent at that daye lest ther might be of the malicious some sinister interpretation, but I answered that seing your absence was to be known to procede of Gods visitation with sycknes, and I had good authorite to answer for your Lordship as I wold for myself, I hoped there shuld be no harm to your cause. Wherfor to conclude, if God shall permitt your Lordship to be hable to be on Tewsday in the fornoone, I wold be most glad, but if that cannot be I pray your Lordship to wryte to me, that wher uppon conference with me we both thought the Scottish Quene had not cleared hir self by hir answers for the matters wherewith she was charged, for compassing and imagining the Quenes Majestys deth, that your Lordship wold if you war present delyver your sentence so to be, and therfor in your absence coming by infirmitie, you both require and authorise me to delyver your opinion to be ageynst the sayd Quene of Scottes. And this my opinion, I nevertheless (give) to your good Lordship to do that you shall think mete, which if you shall by wrytyng signify, I wish your Lordship wold send it to me by post.' Windsor.

Holograph *Endorsed:* 'Answered the 23 of October 1586.' 1 p. (Original Letters I/248)

LORD BURGHLEY TO THE EARL OF SHREWSBURY

1586, October 26. 'My very good Lord. I did on Tewsday at night receave your Lordships letters, on to hir Majesty, on to my self privatly, the thyrd joynt to my Lord Chancellor and me. The Quenes letter I did this day delyver to hir Majesty, who accepted your Lordships letter very thankfully, and yesterday in the Star Chamber when all the Commissionars amongst which no one ther wanted only your Lordship and my Lord of Warwyk both uppon on cause, war assembled and had pronounced ther sentences all in one manner, to chardge the Q. of Scottes with privete of the conspiracy and with the compassyng and imaginyng also of dyvers thynges tendyng to the hurt and distruction of her Majestys person, my Lord Chancellor and I did declare by readyng of your Lordships letter your sentence conform to the generall sentence of all the rest Commissioners; and then it was ordered that ageynst Monday next the process with this sentence shuld be put in wrytyng in form of a record, to the which it is ment that we all shuld put to our names and seales.

Tomorrow the Parlement shall be proroged untill Satyrday, at which tyme hir Majesty will come from Lambeth to Westminster and so retorn to Lambeth and tarry untill Monday fornoone, and then havyng allowed of the Speaker, she meaneth to retorn to Rychmond, and I wish to hear of your Lordships amendment to be hable to come towardes London by that tyme. Praying your Lordship to advertise me what hope I may gyve of your coming.' Westminster.

Holograph *Endorsed in the Earl of Shrewsbury's hand:* 'The L. Treasurers letter of the 26 of October, 1596. Answered from Stilton.'* 1 p. (Original Letters I/250)

* Presumably the letter printed in Lodge, *Illustrations of British History* II p333.

LORD BURGHLEY TO THE EARL OF SHREWSBURY

1586, October 27. 'My very good Lord. Sence my letters wrytten yesternight and sent by post this present daye, I understand by the judges that were in commission with us that although your Lordships letters sent to my Lord

Chancellor and me, wherby your Lordship hath declared your sentence concerning the Scottish Quene, is in matter sufficient and agreeth with all our sentences delyvered oppenly on Tewsday last at the Star Chamber, yet because our commission conteaneth a form of chargyng of hir accordyng to the Statute and that we are to follow in wordes the same forme and that our sentence is to be entred of record in one form of wordes; therfore they have considred of the form of your Lordships letters, the trew copy wherof I do now send your Lordship with an enterlyneation of some thynges to be altered in form, and I have also sent to your Lordship in a paper apart such wordes as ar to be inserted into a new letter in place of those that ar underlyned. And so I remitt to your Lordships consideration to cause your letter to be wrytten to my Lord Chancellor and me, as your former was and of the same date, with the chayngyng only of so much as I have underlyned, and in place therof to wryte the other sentences conteyned in the other paper herincluded. And I pray your good Lordship to retorn this your answer by post.' Westminster.

PS. 'This fornoone the Lords of Parliament appeared and did adjorn the parliament untill Satyrday, and on Monday the Speaker is to be presented.'

Holograph Endorsed: 'Answered the 29th of October, 1586.' *Address, headed*: 'For the Q. Majesties affaires at Stylton or Huntingdon.' *Signature only in Burghley's hand:* '27 Oct, 1586 at London at 7 at night.' *Note:* 'Recd at Waltham 28 day at 8 in the nyght. Huntyngdon the 29 day at past 9 in the forenone.' 1 p. (Original Letters I/252)

SIR FRANCIS WALSINGHAM TO THE EARL OF SHREWSBURY

1586, November 3. 'My verie good Lord. The inclosed I receaved in a pacquett from Sir Edward Stafford, and for that I doe not knowe how greatly it importeth your Lordship to have it with speede, I thought good to send the same unto you by post.

Our Parliament hath yett brought nothing fourthe worthie of your Lordships knowledge. I will not faile as thinges shall fall out to acquaint your Lordship with our procedinges. Ther is an Ambassador dispatched out of Scotland unto her Majestie for twoe pourposes. The one to use some offices of mediation from the King for his mother. The other that the sentence against his mother maie be so quallified as maie in no sorte prejudge his pretended tytle. There is one also looked for from France to move her Majestie to staie proceading against the said Quene. All good men do hope that her Majestie will not be carried by their persuasions from the doing of that which shalbe for her owne preservation and her good, and for that of all (her) servantes. And so I most humblie take my leave.' Barn Elms.

PS. 'Yesterdaye I receyved newes to my infynyte greafe of the deathe of Sir P. Sydney. Her Majestie hathe lost a rare servant and her realme a worthye membre.'

Signed, the postscript holograph Endorsed: 'Answered the 5th of November, 1586'. 1 p. (Original Letters I/254)

SIR FRANCIS WALSINGHAM TO THE EARL OF SHREWSBURY

1586, November 10. 'My verie good Lord. I most humblie thanke you for your late honorable and comfortable letter written unto me. And according unto my promise your Lordship shall understand touching our proceeding here in parliament, that reporte being made unto them of the foule matters wherewith the Scottishe Queene is charged; which being considered by both the upper and lower house, they are both agreed to joyne together in petition unto her Majesty that execution maie be donne according to justice for the cryme, without the performance wherof they apparantlie see that nether her Majesties safetie nor the quiett of this realme can well be maintened.

Mr Keith, the Scottish Ambassador, who useth the office of mediation for the said Queene is this daie appointed his audience. The other whom we expect for the like pourpose out of France named Monsieur Bellievre is not yet arrived here, but is on his journey hetherwardes, and come to Calles. We doe not heare that they come furnished with other matter in substance then complementes for facions sake, which we hope shall not divert nor lett our pourpose of thorough prosecution of this cause.' London.

PS. 'The Erle of Leycester is dayly looked for, yet her Majestye dothe not lyke of his retorne untyll some person of qualytye may be sent over to supplye his place. The Lord Graye hathe ben named therunto, but he pleadethe dysabylyte.'

Signed, the postscript holograph Endorsed: 'Answered 13 November, 1586'. 1 p. (Original Letters I/256)

LORD BURGHLEY TO THE EARL OF SHREWSBURY

1586, November 12. 'My very good Lord. I long much to heare of your ease from payne and of your good amendment. Hether is come one Mr Kyth from the King of Scottes to require hir Majesty to forbeare any furder procedyng ageynst the Quene of Scottes untill the King his master may be informed further of hir cryme, and to send some of his Counsell hyther. Secondly he requireth that nothyng be doone to the prejudice of any title of the King.

This latter is granted. The former can hardly be granted without her Majestys perrill and discontentation of all the parliament, wher the sentence ageynst hir is allredy confirmed, and petition redy this daye to be exhibited at Rychmond by 21 lordes temporall, 6 lordes spyrituall and xl of the Comens house for to require her Majesty that execution may follow.

One Bellievre is coming from the French Kyng also to intreat for hir, but it is lykly the Quenes Majesty will rather trust hir own nobilite and Comens in ther counsells for hir surety, than any forrayn princes that have no naturall interest in hir Majesties lyff. And tomorrow Sir Dru Drury is sent to Fodrynghay to asist Sir Am (ias) Paulett being sick both of an ageu and his gout from the which ennemy I am hitherto fre, but I dare not assure myself from his mallyce any long tyme.' Westminster.

Holograph No endorsement as to answer, but it was answered on the 17th. (See *H.M.C. Salisbury MSS* Vol.III, p.195) 1 p. (Original Letters I/258)

LORD BURGHLEY TO THE EARL OF SHREWSBURY

1586, November 14. 'My very good Lord. Sence my last wrytyng on Satyrday in the morning ther was with hir Majesty at Rychmond xxvi lords temporall, the 2 Archbishopps and 4 other bishopps from the higher howse, and xl of the Comens howse, authorised by both the houses to exhibit a petition to hir Majesty conteaning an affirmation of the sentence of the Scottish Quene to be just and lawfull, and an ernest petition to publish the same and also to procede to execution. The Lord Chancellor for the Lords and the Speaker for the Comens in two severall orations expressed the same largly. And her Majesty made a prinsly, wyse and grave answer not only to the admiration of all that hard it, but to the drawyng out of teares out of manny eies. The conclusion was that she wold be advised of her procedyng and commend hir self to be directed by Gods spyritt.

This day hir Majesty hath determyned to send to the Scottish Quene the Lord of Buckhurst, havyng with hym Mr Beale, the Secretary of the Counsell in the North, one, as your Lordship knoweth, well acqueynted with hir causes. They shall declare to hir how the sentence is passed, confirmed in Parliament and now required to be fully executed, so as the Quene of Scottes is to resort to God to expect what it shall please hym to inspire into our Quenes hart concerning this cause.

Sir Dru Drury as I thynk is gon this day to assist Sir Amias Paulett uppon advertisement of his infyrmyte, from which I perceave by his letters this evening that he is now fre, and so I hartely wish your Lordship to be, and so I hope shortly to heare of you, consideryng the great though dangerous evacuation by your so manny vomitts wherof your Lordship did lately advertise me. I stay to send your Lordships signett untill I may have a speciall man of trust to carry it.' Richmond.

Holograph 1 p. (Original Letters I/260)

LORD BURGHLEY TO THE EARL OF SHREWSBURY

1586, November 30. 'My very good Lord. It is long sence I wrot to your Lordship or hard from you, but on my part truly the impediment is lack of lesure, being of late tyme and yet still more toyled with the care of hir Majestys affayres than I was these manny yeres.

Here are Ambassadors from France and Scotland to press hir Majesty to stay furder procedyng ageynst the Scottes Quene. From France a very grave counsellor named Bellyevre, one of gret estimation for his wysdom and vertue, and so commended by all men. He hath had once audience and used much speeche to move hir Majeste, but he was answered that if the French Kyng understood hir Majestys perill, if he loved hir as he pretendeth, he wold not press hir Majesty to hazard hir liff. The Scottes Ambassador, one Mr Kyth, being but a yong man useth gret ernestnes but with small reson.

My Lord of Buckhurst was sent to the Scottish Quene to declare to hir that the sentence was gyven ageynst hir, and that the parlement required the publication and execution therof, and offred hir to have some dyvyne to instruct hir. She refused instruction and desired to have license to make her will, which was granted. Whyther she look to dy or no, I know not.

The sentence was subscribed yesterday by all the Commissioners that were here at parlement, and I have answered for your Lordship that you (will) not fayle but to sign it at any tyme, and so I left a space for your name.

The Session shall be proroged on Fryday next, as I thynk, but I must ryde tomorrow to Rychmond and theruppon hir Majesty will conclude. I thynk it will be proroged untill mid February or March.

I thynk on Frydaye our sentence shall be published by parlement, which will trooble our ambassadors. And so, my good Lord, for lack of leser, but not of good will, I end.

I have commanded on of my servants to wayte on your Lordship to offer your Lordship any venison at my commandment.' Westminster.

Holograph Endorsed: 'Answered the 4th of December, 1586.' 2 pp. (Original Letters I/262)

LORD BURGHLEY TO THE EARL OF SHREWSBURY

1586, December 1. 'My very good Lord. Though ther hath bene a good long trewce betwixt your Lordships commen ennemy and myne, yet of late he hath broken out with me not into a full warr, but with a skyrmyshyn brawl, as your sonn Mr Henry Talbott can report: and now I heare your Lordship is entred into a severance of hostillite and ar only uppon your gard, but I wish your Lordship as perfect a peace as I desyre for myself. Thus much, my good Lord, to mint some myrth with payne. If your Lordship shall lyke to prove in your litter to fynd a dryer soyle, my house of Burghley shall be at your commandment, wher out of the ston pittes noe humor cometh to norrish the gout.

After I fell syck about 7 or 8 dayes, I shewed to hir Majesty your last letter for the wise care you shewed for hir savety, by shewyng ii lynes of your Lordships own hand added to the body of the letter wrytten by your secretary. Hir Majesty was so much contented therwith as she wold nedes read it twyse hir self to dyvers of her Counsell with great allowance of your Lordships judgement. I do send your Lordship the late proclamation for publishing of the sentence wherewith her Majesty was very well satisfyed. What will follow, a few dayes will declare. Hir Majesty is greatly pressed by the French and Scottish to stay furder action. God must direct hir therin, which I must desyre to be for hir honor and hir savety.

And thus, my good Lord, I pray you pardon my hasty scriblyng.' Richmond.

Holograph   Endorsed in the Earl of Shrewsbury's hand: 'The L. Tresurers letter.'   1 p.   (Original Letters I/266)

SIR FRANCIS WALSINGHAM TO THE EARL OF SHREWSBURY

1586, December 2.   He thanks the Earl for his letter and that of his deputy-lieutenant, Mr John Manners. He advises him to use his judgment in the matter of deferring the musters to the spring.

'For the state of our proceding here, your Lordship shall understand that certeine principall persons being chosen as Committies out of both houses were sent to be humble suitors unto her Majestie that she would be pleased to geve order for the execution of the Scottishe Queene; to whom she made answeare that she was loath to proceade in so severe a course against the said Queene as the taking awaie of her lief, and therefore praied them to thincke on some other waie that might wourcke both hers and their suertie. The parliament after long deliberating uppon this answeare retourned their comitties unto her Majestie to lett her understand that they, having duelie considered thereof, sawe no waie of safetie but by thexecution of the said Queene, and therefore praied her Majestie that the same might be performed. Hereuppon her Majestie is contented, thoughe she yealded no answeare unto this latter reply of theirs, to geve order for the publishing of the proclamation, and it is hoped that she wilbe moved at their earnest instance to proceade throughlie in the cause. The parliament is appointed this daie to end, and is adjourned untill the moneth of Januarie next.' London.

Signed   Endorsed in the Earl of Shrewsbury's hand: 'Mr Walsinghams letter concerning the musters.'   1¼ pp.   (Original Letters I/264)

THE PRIVY COUNCIL TO THE EARL OF SHREWSBURY

1586-87, February 3.   Informing the Earl that the bearer, Robert Beale, has with him the commission (for executing the Queen of Scots), which is to be shown first to the Earl of Kent.   Greenwich.

Signed: ten signatures. *Endorsed in the hand of the Earl of Shrewsbury's secretary:* 'Broughte by Mr Beale with the comysion the 7th of February, 1586 at Orton Longvile; with him came Sir Drewe Drurye and the 7th day went to Fothringham, and the 8 of Februarie 86 executed the Scotts Quene accordinge to the said comysion.

Mr Andrews, the Sheriff of Northamp-sheere, I sent to bring her downe to execution, and so I charged him with her both lyving and with her dead corpes.'   1 p.   (Original Letters I/268)

(Printed in *Wiltshire Archaeological Magazine*, Vol. XIV (1874) p.242. See also *H.M.C. Salisbury MSS*, Vol. III, pp.216-218))

THE PRIVY COUNCIL TO THE EARL OF SHREWSBURY

1587, April 3.   Touching the release from prison of Nicholas Clarke against whom the evidence is insufficient.   Greenwich.

Signed: six signatures.   1 p.   (Original Letters I/270)
(See *Acts of the Privy Council*, 1587-8, pp. 16, 18, and 140).

SIR FRANCIS WALSINGHAM TO THE EARL OF SHREWSBURY

1587, May 23.   The Privy Council desires you to send Lancelot Blackurne, the seminary priest, to London for trial 'as he will doe hurte and infecte the countrie by being there.   He is to be lodged in the Marshalsea prison.

'I declared unto her Majestie your Lordship being at Wingefield to vissitt your wief, which had been before reported to her, whereof she shewed to have a verie good liking for your Lordships carefullnes to satisfie her request therein.   And withal that it might please God so to dispose of your harte that the former good love betweene you might be renued.'   From the Court at Nonsuch.

Signed   Endorsed: 'Mr Secretary for the sending up of Blackborne, 23 Maii 1587.'   (Original Letters I/272)
(This letter is an answer to one of the Earl of Shrewsbury's dated May 16. See Cal.S.P.Dom., 1581-90, p.411.)

THE PRIVY COUNCIL TO THE EARL OF SHREWSBURY

1587, May 25.   Concerning the complaint of John Molineux of Carlton-in-Lindrick against Sir Jervis Clifton.   Nonsuch.

Signed: six signatures.   *Endorsed:* 'The Councells letter for the matter betwixt Sir Ger. Clifton and Mr Mollineux.'   *Inclosed f.276 is a copy of Molineux's petition to the Privy Council.*   ½ p.   (Original Letters I/274)
(See *Acts of the Privy Council*, 1587-8, p.88.)

LORD BURGHLEY TO THE EARL OF SHREWSBURY

1587, June 19.   'My very good Lord.   I might be ashamed to have forborn from wrytyng to your Lordship if my lamenesse of both my handes had not bene the stay.   And therfor, good my Lord, I pray you make more accompt of my hart than of my handes, for whylst I shall lyve I can mak you good assurance of my hart, in sycknes or in helth; but of my handes or my fete I can not make any firm promise.

Of hir Majestys health, of her intention to come to Thebalds the 27th hereof and to abyde ther, as she sayth, a fortnight or three wekes; of my Lord of Lecesters redynes to pass to the Low Countres, I dowt not but your Lordships sonn, Mr H. Talbott, can advise your Lordship.

There is also ernest motions made to us from the Duke of Parma for a treaty of peace, which suerly, my Lord, was most necessary for this Crown and realm, and so I pray God we may have his blessyng to receave it being offred to us very frankly.

I am dayly pressed by my Ladys 2 sonns the Cavendishes to heare such matters as remayn undecyded betwixt your Lordship and them. Wherof I cold be content to be eased, being so otherwise toyled as I have scant lesur to breath.'   Greenwich.

Holograph Endorsed: 'The L. Tresurer, 19 Junii, 1587.'   *Addressed, but not in Lord Burghley's hand, to the Earl of Shrewsbury after having been first addressed by mistake to Lord Buckhurst.*   1 p.   (Original Letters I/277)

THE EARL OF LEICESTER TO THE EARL OF SHREWSBURY

(1587) June 21.   'My most assured good Lord.   My great hope I had at my last wryting unto you to have sene you this somer ys now clean altered thorough her Majesties comaundement to make my hasty repayre to the other syde of the sea; and the soner by occasion of the sige of Sluce which ys a place of very great importance.   And as I am most wylling and reddy to obey all her Majesties commandments, spetyally for her servyce, so am I sorry that my spedy departure ys such as I cannot take leave of my dere good Lord and frend, protesting to your Lordship in the word of a faythfull man, you have not a truer nor a faster frend in all England than I am to you.   And I pray God to send me alway good tydinges of your well doing, and yf it shall please God to suffer me to lyve to retorn home ageyn, your Lordship shall finde me to the end the same I have professed toward you, wyshing yt were in me to substytute in my place such a one as may carye the same affection to you that I doe. Nevertheless I have spoken with my Lord Chancelour who is my assured good frend, and I doe find him well disposed to shew your Lordship all the frendshipp any waye he can wherin your Lordshipp shall have any cause to use him.   I have had spech often of late with her Majestie touching your Lordship, and fynd her very gratyously and constantly resolvyd toward you.

The Erll of Rutlands matter for the forrest doth stey uppon your Lordships last sending, but yf you may think yt good, in my opinion your Lordship shall doe well to make the noble man, being your kinsman, so nere to be beholding to you, spetyally for that he taketh he had your consent before.

I have presumed much uppon your Lordship at this present, having taken your barge to make me a lytle galley to skowre the shallow ryvers, but I wyll bespeake your Lordship another to be made for you, but you se how bold I am with you who is beholding inough many ways alredy to your Lordship.   Thus my good and dere Lord, having none other meanes to take my leave, I doe here kyss your handes.'   From the Court.

PS.   'Tomorrow morning I take my going hence.'

Holograph Endorsed: 'L. Lecester.   21 June 1587.' $2\frac{1}{2}$ pp.   (Original Letters I/279)

LORD BURGHLEY TO THE EARL OF SHREWSBURY

1587, June 23.   I desire to continue my good will towards you now just as I frequently did 'by reason of your only chardg.'

'I am here in Court occupyed with publyck matters, and yet some tyme privat matters of them whom I love and lyk are not neglected by me. Amongst other noble men in Court I do often behold your Lordships sonn the Lord Talbott, who doth manny tymes come to my company.   I consider whose sonn he is and how plentifully God hath endewed hym with manny mo vertews and ornaments for a noble man to succede in your state whan God shall be pleased to call you to hym than any (I will saye to avoyde comparison, than almost any) noble man of his byrth hath in England.   And truly I am greved to se hym lyve so privatly as he doth, and I do thynk that he lyveth owt of lyff and comfort by reason he hath not sufficient mayntenance to uphold the degre answerable to your state and honor. And remembryng with my self how the wyntar afore this, whan your Lordship and I cam togither in a coch from Wyndsor, I did intreat your Lordship to have compassion of his estate, being depely then indetted and as I saw by hym full of discomfort by his unhabilite to discharg it, specially seing it did grow uppon him even as a disease will do if it be not cured in tyme; and at that tyme I had, after some arguments of contradiction, a very fatherly and comfortable answer gyvyng me good hope of your releyvyng of hym out of his dett than, so as hereafter he wuld lyve without fallyng into any the lyke, and so I did afterward comfort hym and in a sort assure hym of your releff. And truly untill now of late I did thynk that your Lordship had shewed your fatherly liberallite uppon hym, but lately I have had cause to doute thereof, and theruppon I did ernestly inquire of hym in what estate he stood in for discharg of his former dettes, merely remembryng to hym that I dowted his last sommars intertaining of hir Majesty very honorably wold torn hym backwardes ageyn, though I dowted not but your Lordship had accordyng to the hope your Lordship gave me delyvered hym of his old dette. But to this my speche I cold receave no answer to satisfye me, presuming by the silence he used, with some ernest token of sadnes, that he was not by your help delyvered of his old dettes, so as I accompt his case very hard; and as I did afor resemble it to a growyng disease, that in suffrance of his estate to be as it was eaten with the burden of interest, your Lordship shall by delaying of your help, mak both his burden increase and your help also less hable to releve hym if you do not add your cure in convenient tyme. My good Lord, accept this my longe letter in good part. I do not so much respect hym as I do your own honor. Thynk it is your honor, that your sonn lyve in honnor and reputation. I myself have a sonn or ii. I assure your Lordship, I accompt that which they expend in honnest sort to be my comfort, and as it war myne own expence. We fathers must tak comfort of our chyldren, to se and provyde for them to lyve agreable to our comfortes. But my good Lord, accept my wrytynge meant as well for the honor of an Erle of Shrewsbury as for a Lord Talbott. And so with my paper I end, praying your Lordship that I may have some comfortable answer.'

Holograph 3 pp. (Original Letters I/281)

THE FUNERAL OF MARY, QUEEN OF SCOTS

1587, August 1. 'The order for the buriall of the Scottishe Quene, the first of August, 1587, at Peterborough:

Two yomen Conductors with black staves in theire handes.
Pore women ii and ii to the number of 44.
The Standerde borne by Sir Andrewe Marvell.
Gentlemen in cloakes ii and ii to the number of 42.
Then the ii Sewers.
Then the ii chapleynes.
Then the Deane of Peterboroughe.
Then the bushoppes of Peterboroughe and Lincolne together.
Then the greate banner borne by the lord Compten.
Then the helme by an herald.
Then the Sworde by an other.
Then the Large (*sic* Targe) by an other.
Then the Coate of Armes by an other.
Then Clarencieux kinge of Armes and with him a gentleman usher.
Then the bodie borne by xii yomen in blacke coates.

The lord Dudley
The lord Mordant
The lord Willoughbie
The lord Sheffeld
} these 4 barons to be assistants to the bodie.

Sir George Hastinges
Sir Thomas Cicill
Sir Edwarde Mountague
Sir Edwarde Dyer
} these 4 knights to beare the Canapie.

William FitzWilliams
Edwarde Griffyn
Thomas Brudenell
— — — — Saunders
George Lynne
Edwarde Elmes
Roberte Wingfeld
Edwarde Watson
} these 8 esquieres to beare the banner rolles.

Garter principall kinge at Armes and with him a gentleman usher.
Then the Countesse of Bedforde ladie cheif mourner and the ladie Graie her trayne bearer.
The Earle of Rutland
The Earle of Lincolne
} these ii Earles assistantes to the cheif mourner.
The Countesse of Rutland the 2 mourner.
The Countesse of Lincolne the 3.
The ladie Barkeley the 4.
The ladie Dudley 5.
The ladie St John de Bassinge 6.
The ladie St John of Bletsoe 7.
The ladie Hastinges 8.
The ladie Cicill 9.
The ladie Mountague 10.
The ladie Cromwell 11.
The ladie Dyer 12.
The ladie Nowell 13.
After these cheif mourners ii yomen with blacke staves in theire handes.
Then all the wailinge women ii and two to the number of 34.
Then the yomen in blacke coates to the number of 166.

Note that the hearse with the paynters worke and fees will come to cccc^{li} and the dyet ccc^{li} so that all the whole some of this buriall will come to the some of mcccc^{li} at the least.

Cheif mourner xii yardes
ii earles x yarde a pece
ii countesses x a pece
} at xxx^s the yarde.

ii Bushoppes
v Barrons
v Baronesses
} viii yardes a pece at xxvi^s the yard

vi Knightes
vi ladies
The Deane
The Master of the Wardrobe
Garter
Clarencieux
iiii Scottesmen
} vi yardes the pece at xx^s the yard.

83

iiii Scottes women ⎫
ii gentlemen ushers ⎬ vi yardes the pece at xx^s the yard.

ii Chapleynes vi yardes a pece
ix Esquires ⎫ v yardes
v heraldes ⎬ a pece
ii Sewers 4 yardes a pece
xxiiii waylinge women 4 yardes a pece   at xxvi^s the yard.
iiii Scottes women 4 yardes a pece
xiiii Scottes men theire clokes iii yardes & dem. a pece

xiiii gentlemen servantes to the lordes and
ladies to eche of theyme for theire cloakes   at vi^s 4^d the yard.
iii yardes and dem.

166 yomen to eche of theyme one yard and a   at x^s the yard.
half for their cotes

44 por women to eche of theyme for theire   vi^s viii^d the yard."
gownes iii yardes at

2 pp. (Original Letters I/283)

The Privy Council to the Earl of Shrewsbury

1587, October 9. Order to the Earl as Lord Lieutenant of Derbyshire and Staffordshire to take a view of the trained men of those shires, and to send an immediate return to the Queen of the numbers available for the defence of the realm. Richmond.

Signed: 8 signatures. *Endorsed*: 'Recd by John Worsley the 16 of October, 1587.' 1½ pp. (Original Letters I/285)
(See *Acts of the Privy Council*, 1587-8, pp. 252-4)

Henry Cavendish to (The Earl of Shrewsbury)

1587, October 10. Pleading his poverty and asking the Earl as a last resource to be allowed to lease his estate of 'Meadowplecke'. Tutbury.

Signed Addressed: To my Lorde.' 1p. (Original Letters 1/287)

H. Goodere to Lady Talbot

1587, October 10. To explain that he is put to the extra charge of 5 marks a week by the maintenance of 'my Ladye Arbella,' at Newgate Street. She and her ladies are well. Newgate Street.

Signed Addressed to: 'The Ladie Talbott at the Courte.' 1p. (Original Letters I/289)

Queen Elizabeth to the Earl of Shrewsbury

1587, November 3. In order that the frontiers of Scotland may be defended against any possible incursions and invasions, we have ordered the force to be in readiness and have appointed the Earl of Huntingdon as Lieutenant-General of the North with orders to make ready an army. If the forces of Scotland are so increased by men and money out of foreign countries, you are authorised to levy forces out of other counties than those of the North, including Derbyshire and Staffordshire, of which you are Lord Lieutenant. You are to put in readiness 300 footmen from the former and 400 from the latter county, under gentlemen of experience; two parts to be armed with the arquebus and long-bow, the rest with pikes and bills, and send them to the Earl at his request. Beyond this a force of demi-lances is required. You are to furnish 34 with horse and lance, to be charged upon both shires in due proportion. Ely House.

Signed, privy seal 2 pp. (Original Letters I/291)

LORD BURGHLEY TO THE EARL OF SHREWSBURY

1587, November 26. 'My very good Lord. I have receaved your Lordships letter of the 17th of this month, by which it appeareth your Lordship hath both noted and taxed the scilence that hath bene betwixt us both, by lack of wrytyng on to the other. My Lord, I can not deny but ther hath bene silence for wrytyng, but no oblivion of my frendshipp and dutifull good will to your Lordship. Trew it is I have of late bene so oppressed with busynes, now by Mr Secretarys absence, and by the heapes of affayres that this busy tyme bredeth and therwith joyning my late extreme anguishes in my whole body, as I assure your Lordship on my fayth I have not once delt with frend or servant in any particular cause of my own these ii monthes; nether have I wrytten any privat letter to eny frend that I have farr or neare this long tyme; and for these 14 dayes I have not without payne subscribed any letter and yet have I endyted all matters of weight that hath passed from hir Majesty or the counsell and even now the whole burden is forced uppon me, that I assure your Lordship I am weary to lyve. But all this percase will not satisfye your Lordships gelosy coming of abundance of frendshipp, the which on my part I fynd not deminished, and yet I will mak no doubt of yours, besechyng your Lordship to accept these my hasty scribled lynes for a knollydg of my constancy.' From my cooch in my house neare the Savoy.

PS. 'I nede not certefy your Lordship of my infyrmyte, for I am ashamed that all London knoweth it to be notorious by our manny argumentes, and Westminster Hall can wytnes the lyke, where I have bene forced to be absent most part of this long while.'

Holograph 1 p. (Original Letters I/293)

QUEEN ELIZABETH TO THE EARL OF SHREWSBURY

1587, December 5. The Earl of Huntingdon has been appointed our Lieutenant in the North parts. You are to supply him with such soldiers from among your tenants in Shropshire and Staffordshire as he may require, and to put your son Lord Talbot in command of them. Ely House.

Signed: 'Under our signet.' ½ p. (Original Letters I/295)

(THE EARL OF SHREWSBURY) TO (QUEEN ELIZABETH)

(? 1587) 'It may please your most excellent Majestie to understand that beynge visited with my old enemye the goute at the commynge downe of my sonne Henri Talbot, and therewithall greatly payned in so muche that I feared no recoverye wold have bene before warm wether, yet your Majesties most gracious and comfortable wordes and message sent me by my sonne hath renewed and quickened my vitall spirits wherby the rest of my parts of my bodie are strenthened, that since the acceptation therof I fele myself amended and delivered for this yeare (as I hope) from all his violent assalts. For the which I rendre unto your most excellent Majestie my most humble and harty thanks. No application of medicine or mynistration of phisike wold have wrought that cure in so short tyme as your Majesties most gracious speches hath mynistered reliefe and helpe unto me, that I fynd my bodie will shortly be able and stronge to do your Majestie any service that your Highnes shall commande, unto whos protection and government I submit myself.

Beseching the Holy Trinytie to endew your Majestie with the most riches of his glorie and contynew in you a longe prosperous and most happie reygne over us.'

Copy *Endorsed*: 'Copies of letter to the Quene, the Vice-Chamberlayne and Mr Secretarie' 1 p.   (Original Letters I/297)

THE PRIVY COUNCIL TO THE EARL OF SHREWSBURY

1587-88, January 14.   Acceding to his request that Richard Simpson, a seminary priest, may be committed to gaol to be tried at the next assizes.   From the Court at Greenwich.

Signed: by Hatton, Burghley, Leicester, Croft, Heneage and Walsingham.   ½p.   (Original Letters II/3)

SIR FRANCIS WALSINGHAM TO THE EARL OF SHREWSBURY

1587-88, February 27.   'My verie good Lord.   Being desired by my Lord Steward to convey unto your Lordship this inclosed letter and his, I thought good withall to lett your Lordship understand that on Sondaie last, as we conjecture, the Commissioners embarked at Dover, soe as we doe shortlie looke to heare from them of ther proceadinges in this charge. We are advertised that the preparations of Spaine are in that forwardnes as they wilbe readie to sett fourth by thend of Marche.   Her Majestie doth therefore contynue her force on the seas, having ordered Sir Fra. Drake to repaire with his fleete to the coast of Spaine to withstand that nothing be attempted either against Ireland or Scotland, and in case they have a meaning to come into the narrowe seas, that ther my Lord Admyrall shall enconter them with his strength.   Your Lordship shall also receave herewith such occurentes as were last sent out of France. And so I humblie take my leave.'   London.

Signed   ½p.   (Original Letters II/5)

THE EARL OF LEICESTER TO THE EARL OF SHREWSBURY

1587-88, March 3.   I cannot but send a message of good wishes by your son Edward, who is shortly going down to you.   At the Court.

Holograph   ½p.   (Original Letters II/7)

LORD BURGHLEY TO THE EARL OF SHREWSBURY

1587-88, March 3.   'My very good Lord.   Perceavyng by hir Majesty that she wold wryte to your Lordship hir self, in a kynd sort both to understand of your helth and to assure your Lordship of your contynuance of hir favors, I cold not forbeare, without condemning myself, but to wryte a few wordes to your Lordship specially, to acknowledg my self redy at your commandment with my office of frendshipp or duty, and so I pray your good Lordship to accept me.

For news, though I thynk your children lyvyng about this Court do usually advertise yow, yet I will also acqueynt your Lordship with some forrayn news as we have them reported.

Collonnell Skenk, serving the States, kepeth Bonna still, beyond Collen, uppon the Rhyne, and therby kepeth the passage of the ryver at his commandment, to the great annoyance of all the King of Spaynes party.   But now the Duke of Parma sendeth the young Count Charles Mansfeld with 38 ensignes to recover the town if he can, which will prove a long and chargeable work, but therby the Duke of Parma shall be weakened to do any great enterprise.

About the x of January, Maximillian, the Emperors brother, who had sought to be chosen Kyng of Polonia and so was by a faction of Polonia chosen, was taken in a battell prisoner by the Chancellor of Polonia, who took part with the Prynce of Sweden, whom the greater part of Poleland had chosen ther Kyng, being the son of the daughter of Sigismond, King of Poleland.

We heare that 2 cantons of the Swises, that have bene allweise papists, ar become Protestants.

We heare from Ganua that the Marquis Sta Croce is dead, who was apoynted the Generall of the Kyng of Spaynes gret army, which will work some stey in the hast that the Kyng of Spayne makith to sett owt his army which he pretended shuld be by the 25th of March. Within thes x dayes Roland York the traytor dyed miserably, beyng rotten with the pocks, and his body thrown into the stretes, a just reward of God.

Our Commissioners stayed at Dover from the 2 of February unto the 26th, and that day they passed to Ostend.

Mr Controllor, goyng in a small passynger alone, was constrayned by wynd to land at Dunkyrk, where he was fested, lodged and defrayed of all charges by the Governor, and so was he also at Newport, in both which towns the people made great exclamation to have peace with England, and determined to have generall processions, wher contrarywise the Hollanders can nether heare willyngly of peace nor yet have power to make warr.

Ther is a good order taken for redress and satisfaction upon the borders of all injuryes, and hope that peace will be ther kept, so as we do call home 400 of our soldiers that went out of Yorkshire.

Thus your Lordship seeth that I have as my leser may serve me scribled to your Lordship such odd news as at this present I know.' Greenwich.

PS. 'Sir William FitzWilliam hath this daye taken his leave to depart towardes Ireland to serve as Lord Deputie ther.'

Holograph   2 pp.   (Original Letters II/9)

LORD BURGHLEY TO THE EARL OF SHREWSBURY

1587-88, March 6.   As to the debts of your son, Lord Talbot, I beseech you to help him. 'Your Lordship is the father and my Lord Talbott is your sonne and heyre, your Lordship endowed by God's goodnes and your owne wisdome with much larger possessions then your Lordships father or anie your ancestors of longe time; your sonne in all partes endowed with giftes meete to succeade such a father, hath lesse to live on than can maintaine his estate meete for your honnor, and in this age, wherin all thinges are increased to darthe, unpossible to live out of debt, as in former times your Lordship and other lordes, heires apparantes, might have done with half that which nowe is commonlie allowed.' You say that your body is so feeble that you are distributing 'some portions to your frendes and other poore children, looking for more thankes of them than of your owne children.' I am sorry for your weakness, 'and yet I can measure the same by my self, even at this time beinge with this long cold winter weake and as you are, but I dowbte not but a nosegaie of cowsleppes or damaske roses of your owne gatheringe shall recover all your strength lost this winter, as I am in good hope to recover the like for myself.' I am sure that your good deeds to the poor will purchase you a happy place in heaven for ever, but think of your children too, and relieve your son of the debt which is as a 'cancre growing.'

You charge him with being in league with his 'fast frend', your wife, but I know that he always laboured for her reconciliation with you. I find that he is willing to observe faithfully any conditions you may make.   Greenwich.

Signed   3 pp.   (Original Letters II/11)

LORD CHANCELLOR HATTON AND LORD TREASURER BURGHLEY TO THE EARL OF SHREWSBURY

1587-88, March 15.   Giving notice that the Earl of Shrewsbury is liable for the first payment of £133:6:8, at the rate of 2^s8^d in the pound, as his share of the subsidy granted by the present parliament, and requesting him to have it paid to the Collector, Peter Houghton, at his office in Fenchurch Street.   London.

Signed   1 p.   (Original Letters II/13)
  (See *H.M.C. A Calendar of the Talbot Papers at the College of Arms*, ed G.R. Batho, p.140, G.378)

LORD BURGHLEY TO THE EARL OF SHREWSBURY

1587-88, March 17.   I have received your letter of the 13th of March concerning the office of the forest of Sherwood, about which there is a dispute between you and Lord Rutland. I cannot just now approach her Majesty for I am now absent from Court, 'uppon knolledge of God's pleasure to call to his mercy out of this world, and from my comfort, the surest, the oldest, yea the first frend that ever I had. I cold not endure the affayres of the Court nor of cite, nor of my own famyly, but by provision of hir Majesty I have bene here at my house, or rather in my chamber at Theobalds, and so mynd to contynue for a season if hir Majesty shold so favorably permitt me, and though I can not my self travell to the funerall at Burghley, yet I am a little both with comfort and discomfort occupied to perform the duty of such a sonn as old Tobias had whom he commanded to laye his mother by his father, and so hath my mother required me, who hath two yeres made her will and than did actually dispose all that she had, savyng her litle apparell necessary for her liff, so as now a good tyme before her deth she had no care to dispose anythyng, and therfor varryng from the form of all other wills, she hath sayd, 'I have gyven' and not 'I do gyve', which example, God sendyng me grace, I mynd to follow as my degre will suffer me. Good my Lord, you se the infirmite of nature thus to overshoote my self in wrytyng herof as I do.'

As to Sherwood Forest, Scryour, the late Lord Rutland's man, was with me this morning. He denied that Lord Rutland only held the office on your suffrance, and said that at Lord Leicester's request the Queen had granted the office and keeping of Nottingham Castle to Sir Thomas Manners to the use of the young Lord Rutland; and I am sure that Lord Leicester would not impeach you in any right that you have.

You acknowledge the receipt of a letter under my hand but not written by myself. 'What shall I answer to your cold reply to my so ernest request for your son.' *It was only through lack of leisure that I did not write myself, and I grieve that my earnestness should offend you.   From my lodging at Theobalds.

Holograph   3 pp.   (Original Letters II/15)

SIR FRANCIS WALSINGHAM TO THE EARL OF SHREWSBURY

1587-88, March 23.   On behalf of Thomas Chaloner, a servant of Lord Derby's, who is applying for the post of herald in Ireland.   The Court.

* See *supra*, p.87.

Signed ½p. (Original Letters II/17)

SIR FRANCIS WALSINGHAM TO THE EARL OF SHREWSBURY

1587-88, March 26. We hear reports of your sickness. I am sending my servant to enquire. From the Court at Greenwich.

Signed ½p. (Original Letters II/19)

THE PRIVY COUNCIL TO THE EARL OF SHREWSBURY

1588, April 2. 'Wheras the Quenes Majestie is daylye geven to understande of the continuance of the great preparations of the Kinge of Spayne, which are thought to be intended towardes these partes, her Highnes, beinge desirous to understande the generall estate of the forces of the whole realme, hath caused such certificates to be viewed as have ben sent hither from suche as have ben heretofore appoynted Lieutenantes in sondrie countyes of this realme. Forasmuch as uppon the viewe of suche certificates as have ben sent from your Lordship of your doinges, it is thought that the same are not in suche order as her Majestie is desirous to have observed generallie by your Lordship and other the Lieutenantes. We have thought good to send unto you herein inclosed a note of suche defaultes as are conteyned in your former certificates, and which we are desirous to have amended, and lykewise a paterne and forme of a certificate, in what sorte and order the same shoulde be now made, and appoynted to be observed by others, which we praie you to retorne unto us accordinglie with all the speede that maye be. And we are further to lett you understande that her Majesties pleasure is that you geve present order unto the Captens of bothe horsemen and footemen to see their bandes complete, as also for the trayninge of their severall bandes, especially the Shott: havinge regarde that the same maye be don with as greate ease to the countreye as maye be, by causing the said Captens, especiallie of the footemen, to trayne their shott bothe in convenient numbers and at apt times, according to the former direction geven in that behalf.' Greenwich.

PS. 'You shall cause the men appointed to be sent into Ireland to be in a readines that uppon anie occasion they maie be speedelye sente thether.'

Signed: by Lord Chancellor Hatton, Lords Burghley, Leicester, Howard, Sir Thomas Heneage, Sir Francis Walsingham and J. Wolley. 1p. (Original Letters II/21)

SIR FRANCIS WALSINGHAM TO THE EARL OF SHREWSBURY

1588, April 10. Recommending Thomas Lane, late servant to Sir Philip Sidney, for the office of pursuivant, if the (senior) pursuivant should be appointed to the office of Somerset Herald void by the death of Robert Glover. At the Court.

Signed Enclosed in II/27 1p. (Original Letters II/25)

THE EARL OF LEICESTER TO THE EARL OF SHREWSBURY

1588, April 11. As your deputy (in the office of Earl Marshal) I recommend William Seager, portcullis pursuivant, for the post of Somerset Herald, it being the custom for the 'eldest' pursuivant to receive such an appointment. I enclose a letter from Sir Francis Walsingham on behalf of a man of his. Wansted.

PS. 'This man of Mr Secretarys (is) a very able man and hath long geven himself to this kynd of knowledge.'

Signed, with holograph postscript ½p. (Original Letters II/27)

QUEEN ELIZABETH TO THE EARL OF SHREWSBURY

1588, April 17. Permitting his absence from the approaching feast of St George by reason of his sickness.

Signed ½p. (Original Letters II/29)

GILBERT, LORD TALBOT, TO THE EARL OF SHREWSBURY

1588, May 7. 'Beynge yesternighte (which was the nexte Munday after I parted with your Lordship) come hither to London safely with my carryage (I thanke God), and this nexte morninge returninge down certayne nagges which I brought with me, I colde not omytt this duty of wrytynge to your Lordship, albeit I have not yet sene any one of my frendes synce my cuminge: whereby I am but meanely furnished of any matter of worthe to informe your Lordship; but suche as one of my folkes tolde me I will make boulde to wryte to your Lordship.

Her Majestie meaneth this day to goe to Wansted to see my Lorde of Lester, who hathe bene ther syck this fortnighte.

The Kynge of Denmarke dyed about a fortnighte or 3 weekes synce, wherwith her Majestie is greatly greved, for that he was a moste constante, well affected prynce towards her as she had in Chrystendome. And that nation beynge so furnished with tale shipps and strengethe by sea as yt may compare with any other, may therefore anoy us moste yf it be not governed by our frendes. The yonge Kynge, sun to him who now is dedd, is about 14 yeres of age.

Within these fewe dayes ther is growne at Courte and here in London sum better expectation of sum good conclusion of peace then was before. Our commissioners and thers mete often, and very shortly it is thought they will growe to resolution. In the meane tyme, my Lorde Admirall remaynethe at the Courte, havinge her Majesties Navy in redines. Sir Francis Drake is also there, havynge his flete reddy also in the Weste, but bothe of them are to goe to sea or altogether to stay, as this treaty of peace falethe oute.

Sir John Norris, Sir William Reade, Mr Frobyshyr and others suche who depende on actions of warrs are here also expectynge the succes therof. Captayne Skynke (who my Lord of Lester knyghted in the Low Countreys) came to this towne on Fryday laste. Here is also an Italian Marques, who as my man tells me was lately taken prisoner by sum who served under Sir William Reade, and that he is now brought over hither by Sir William Reade who kepes him as his prisoner.

Your Lordships letters to my Lord Tresurer and Mr Secretary I will deliver this nyghte or tomorrow. The other to my Lord of Lester will be sumwhat the longer undelivered for that her Majestie is now this day to be with him, and tyll she be returned from Wansted I thynke the tyme unfytt.' Coleman Street near Moorgate.

PS. 'Synce the wrytynge of this above the King of Scottes hath very lately bene a jorney or progresse all alonge his borders from agenste Barwyke all towarde westewarde, as is thought only to take order for the performance of peace and all good order there, as he promised before my Lord Chamberlanes coming from Barwyck. This newes came hither but two dayes synce.

These latin verses inclosed my man showed me yesternighte. Dyvers suche coppyes were founde in the Exchange; fyrste the four upper verses were founde, and two days afterwarde this one verse in answere was ther lett fale in

90

many coppyes also.'

Holograph 2pp. (Original Letters II/31)

THE EARL OF LEICESTER TO THE EARL OF SHREWSBURY

1588, May 30. Some here are working for title of dignities, as Mr Ffynes for the Lord Say and Mr Nevyle for the Lord Bergavenny. Requests authority to deal with them in the Earl of Shrewsbury's absence. At the Court.

Signed ½p. (Original Letters II/33)

ROBERT BEALE TO THE EARL OF SHREWSBURY

1588, June 4. I grieve to hear that you are offended with my letter to you concerning Mr Holland the preacher. I protest my loyalty, for I am no curious busybody or censurer of any man's actions. The good will that I bear to good ministers may have stirred me to write over earnestly. From the Court.

Signed 1 p. (Original Letters II/35)

THE PRIVY COUNCIL TO THE EARL OF SHREWSBURY

1588, June 15. We are advertised that the King of Spain's navy is abroad. See to it that the captains and soldiers of the trained bands (in Derbyshire and Staffordshire) are not absent, but that they may be ready at an hour's notice, upon pain of being committed to prison for forty days. Take a private view of them; have the beacons watched; the authors of all false rumours and tales sought for and punished. A Provost Marshal is to be appointed to punish vagabonds. Greenwich.

Signed: nine signatures. 1 p. (Original Letters II/37)
(See *Acts of the Privy Council*, 1588, p. 126)

QUEEN ELIZABETH TO THE EARL OF SHREWSBURY

1588, June 18. As Lord Lieutenant of Derbyshire and Staffordshire, he is to assemble the gentlemen of the two counties and to get them to furnish, on this extraordinary occasion, a larger number of men than is due from them for the defence of 'countrey, liberty, wife, children, lands, life and (that which is especially to be regarded) for the profession of the true and syncere religion of Christ.' Greenwich.

Signed 1 p. (Original Letters II/39)
The same letter addressed to the Earl of Pembroke, as Lord Lieutenant of Wiltshire, is printed in *Wiltshire Archaeological Magazine*, Vol.XIV, p. 243.

THE EARL OF KENT AND OTHER COMMISSIONERS FOR THE EXECUTION OF MARY, QUEEN OF SCOTS, TO THE EARL OF SHREWSBURY

1588, June 26. 'Beinge crediblie enformed that all the reste of the proceedings against the late Scottish Queene were enrolled and recorded, save only the commission directed unto your Lordship and me, the Earle of Kent, for her execution: forasmuch as it importethe your Lordship and us all, your and our posterites, that were any doers in the cause to have it enrolled, to be able to shewe sufficient warrant at all times for our dischardge. Uppon conference amongst our selves we have thought good that a petition should be framed to her Majestie for that purpose, wherto we have sett our hands at this present, for that after the terme I, Sir Amyas Paulett, minde to repaire into Somersetshire and the rest of us shall not have such an opportunyte of meetinge againe. And so sende it unto your Lordship here enclosed, trusting that your Lordship will joyne with us therin. Nevertheless, our meaninge is not to require this of your Lordship contrary to your good likeinge. But if your Lordship shall not thinke good to subsigne it, we praie your Lordship to retorne the said petition unto us, who minde to procede therin without your Lordships good likeinge firste had; nor would have don this unles the aforesaid cause of our dispersing abroode from London had now moved us therunto.' London.

Signed: Earl of Kent, Sir. A. Powlet, Thomas Andrewe, W. Davison, Robert Beal. ½p. (Original Letters II/41)

GILBERT, LORD TALBOT, TO THE EARL OF SHREWSBURY

1588, July 13. I send this by the son of Mr Brian Lascelles. Things here remain much as they did. 'It is certeyne that ill wether and the great visitation of sycknes and deth that happened in the Spanyshe Navy did lately sever and separate theyr shyppes. But where they are now or whether they are joyned and mett together agen or not, I thynke (at this present) is not here knowne.' All our preparations against invasion still hold. I heard lately that you are likely to be made Lieutenant-General of the Army for the guard of her Majesty's person, and that you would be summoned to London for the purpose. But the matter can only have been privately mentioned to her Majesty and not formally moved for by the Privy Council. I was dining yesterday with the Lord Chancellor, and he protested he knew nothing of the matter. He said your name was mentioned among others, but that after Lord Hunsdon was resolved on, he never heard you named in that behalf. If I may speak my poor opinion I think you should not come up unless there is an invasion (which I hope will not be attempted in this realm this year). I told you that three great councillors had promised to move her Majesty for the reversion of your offices for me. But the Lord Treasurer is fallen sick of the gout at his house in the Strand, and will not come to Court till my departure. I think it is useless for me to wait. The matter of Welbeck goes better. I hope to leave on Tuesday next, making very easy days' journeys. Coleman Street.

PS. All the chief recusants here are this day sent towards Ely, where they are to be kept in the Bishop's house as close prisoners until it be known what will become of these Spanish forces. My cousin John Talbot is one of them. Sir Thomas Cornwallis and Lord Vaux are alone left in London, I think in respect only of their bad health.

Holograph 2 pp. (Original Letters II/43)

THE PRIVY COUNCIL TO THE EARL OF SHREWSBURY

1588, July 17. We have received your letters of the 15th of this month certifying the apprehension of two seminary priests and of other recusants, and we observe your zeal for the advancement of true religion by the rooting out of such seditious and traitorous persons. Her Majesty sends you grateful thanks, considering the notable mischiefs wrought by such lewd and wicked persons and the hurt and danger thereof in these doubtful times. We have written to the Justices of Assize of the county of York to proceed with the said priests at the next assizes according to the law, for their conviction, condemnation and execution. Please send them at once under a safe guard to the sheriff of the county, the place of execution to be as you shall direct. The rest are to remain as they are until we send further order, except the daughter of Sir Thomas Fitzherbert who is to be given in charge of some person in the county well affected in religion, according to your discretion. Meet persons are to be appointed to keep the house of Sir Thomas Fitzherbert and to take the harvest and other profits. All his goods are to be assessed and an account thereof rendered to us. Richmond.

Signed: Lord Chancellor Hatton, Lord Leicester, Sir Thomas Heneage and Sir Francis Walsingham. 1 p. (Original Letters II/44)

THE CONTENTS OF LORD COBHAM'S LETTER TO (SIR FRANCIS WALSINGHAM)

1588, August 1. 'That they arrived at Calles the 1 of August and did expect and desire safe passage as soon as might be. And if her Majestie would bestowe a fewe lynes of Gordon for his well using them, it would be well taken.

That the Capten of Bullein would be friended and curteouslie used, or else he might prove a bad neighbor.

That the Capten of the Galleasses (that was sett upon Calles sandes) was the sonn of the Viceroy of Valentya and was called Don Hugo de Moncada, and that his shipp was one of the best of all the galleasses.

That Sir William Stanley was imbarqued upon Tewesdaie, and divers other companies of Spaniards and Italians, but for that the Spring is past, it is thought they are discharged againe or shall be untill the next Spring.

That the Duke is there, and I was informed that there landed a nobleman of Spaine to hasten there coming forth, but fynding them nothing reddie, told Monsieur La Motte that if he weare in Spaine he should (lose) his hedd and the D(uke). These wordes were openlie spoken. The rest I referr till we meete.

The Flushingers have taken a galleas, called *St Phillipo*, as it is reported here.'

Copy Endorsed: 'The copie of my Lord Cobhams letter to Mr Secretary, 1 August 1588.' 1 p. (Original Letters II/467)

THE PRIVY COUNCIL TO THE EARL OF SHREWSBURY

1588, August 13. Her Majesty has received news that the Spanish fleet, having taken its course northward, is come to a place in Scotland called Moray Firth, and has landed some men there. Because it is as yet not known whether they intend to land them to win over the disaffected elements in that realm, or mean only to stay to take in fresh water and to supply themselves with whatever other necessaries that country can afford, the Earl is directed to furnish for service in the north parts 300 foot from the county of Derby, 400 from the county of Stafford and 34 lances, who are to be instantly sent at the Earl of Huntingdon's demand. From the Court at St James.

Signed: Lord Chancellor Hatton, Lords Burghley, Derby, Howard, Sir T. Heneage, Sir A. Powlet and J. Wolley. 1 p. (Original Letters II/47)

(See *Acts of the Privy Council*, Vol.XVI, 1588, p.231)

THE EARL OF HUNTINGDON TO GILBERT, LORD TALBOT

(1588) September 2. I send this by Mr Edward Stanhope though I have little to advertise, 'all matters, to my knowledge, standynge nowe at a staye, yet so, in my opinion, as I doo wyshe that we may not over soone thynke all the storme to bee clearly blowne from us. Tho yt weare trew in deede, which I perceave manye doo thynke, the Spanyshe fleete to be returnyd home, but I take yt to bee rathyr a conjecture then that any can of certeyntie affirme yt. Before my cumynge from Newcastle I dyd take order that the best knowledge which coulde bee gottyn of them in Scotland by sendynge of a man to the Northe shulde be obteyned, which I truste wyll bee don and sent with speede, yf in my expectation I bee not deceavyd.' York.

Holograph *Addressed*: 'To the ryghte honorable my verrye good lord and coosyn, the Lord Talbot.' 1 p. (Original Letters I/49)

Queen Elizabeth to the Earl of Shrewsbury

(1588, after September 6) 'My very good old man. Your letters written upon the good succes that it plesid God lately to send us against those that sought utterly to destroye us, were very welcom, and as thankfully acceptid on our parte as ye can expect of your souverain who no less acknowledgeth your good and faithfull harte than ye have plainly sett fourth the same in your said letters by your most dutifull offer of all that ys yours evin to your lyves. Which we trust God will reserve to assist and preserve us against any the lyke or other attempts that may be heerafter intendid, he having of his mercy delyverid som of our ennemyes upon that part of the coste of Irland where (not many yeeres since) they had as good payment as now they have had. For which Gods goodnes we pray you with us to be continually thankfull. As for other matter conteynid in your said letters, although we doo therin accepte and acknowledge your carefull mynde and good will, yet we rather desire to forbeare the remembrance therof as a thing wherof we can admitt no comfort otherwise than by submitting our will to Gods inevitable appointment, who, notwithstanding his goodnes by the former prosperous nues, hath nevertheless been pleasid to keepe us in exercise by the loss of such a parsonage so deere unto us: which though it be a most sharp stroke unto us in particular, yet we accompte it the greater in respect of the publick. And so we end with great thanks unto your self for your care to have mett with any thing that might have happenid in those parts where you are. Assuring you that we contynue the same you left us towards you and all yours, as this messenger can more at large tell you (for sending of whom unto us we thank you), adding furder this remembrance unto you, that we have good regard to your helth upon the approche of the cold season. Our thanks also to my lord of Derby we referr to be given to him by you in our name.'

At top of letter: 'Your verey loving souveraine Elizabeth R.'

Signed *Addressed*: ' To our right trusty and right well beloved cousin and counsaylor the Earle of Shrewsbery.' 1 p. (Original Letters II/57)

(See letter printed in Lodge, *Illustrations of British History*, II. p.377 and dated September 6,1588)

The Privy Council to the Earl of Shrewsbury

1588, September 22. Mr John Fitzherbert, his son and the old massing priest are to be removed from the Earl's house and conveyed to gaol. St James.

Signed: Archbishop of Canterbury, Lord Chancellor, Lords Howard and Hunsdon, Sir T. Heneage and J. Wolley. ½ p. (Original Letters II/51)

(See *Acts of the Privy Council*, Vol.XVI, 1588, p.286)

LORD BURGHLEY TO THE EARL OF SHREWSBURY

1588, November 4.   As your deputy (Marshal) I have filled up the post of Lancaster Herald by the appointment of Nicholas Padie and that of Rougecrosse is given to one Raven.   For that of Norrey the name of Edward Knight, the oldest herald, is mentioned, and for his place that of James Thomas, now Bluemantle.   From the Court.

PS. 'I am glad that the parlement is proroged to February, for that I hope that your Lordship havynge past the two wynter months of December and January shall have license from our common enemy to be here with her Majesty and your good frendes.   On the ninth hereof hir Majesty will oppenly go to Powls or Westminster to gyve publyck thankes to God for his miraculous goodnes in overthrowing of our mortall ennemyes and the sworn ennemyes of Christ; the same notion is met to be celebrated through the whole realm the same day, if knowledg may come in tyme, for it was concluded but yesterday in counsell.

All our frendes in Scotland, in Denmark, in the Low Countres, in all the Contreys of Germany that are Protestantes, have performed this in great solemnite, and our ennemyes in Spayn and Itally made solemnities uppon the false first bruits that was forged in France by Mendosa.

The Spanyards that wracked in the north of Ireland with two shippes and one galleas coming on land ar greatly wasted; ther two shippes being broken, they repared the galleas and filled her with as many of the choysest as she cold hold and went to the seas, and within six houres she was broken uppon a rock in sight of the land and all the men perished savyng five.   Fifty of the others that went not away submitted themselves to two of the Quenes captayns and are brought to Drogheda.   Ther ar amongst them many sons, brothern and cossyns to the greatest of Spayn.   Ther do yet remayn about 1000 dispersed in the north of Ireland; against them the Lord Depute is gon with a good force.

We have stayed the men that wer redy to have gon out of Wales and other parts.'

Signed, with the postscript in Burghley's hand 1 p. (Original Letters II/53)

GILBERT, LORD TALBOT, TO LORD BURGHLEY

1588, December 29.   He requests him to further his suit for the reversion of his father's offices and for the farm of Welbeck.   Rughford.

Holograph 1 p. (Original Letters II/55)

QUEEN ELIZABETH TO THE EARL OF SHREWSBURY

(? 1588 *or* 1589) 'My very good old man. I doubte not but you doo now evin long to heare from us, considering we have not this good while written anything unto you. The cause therof hath bene the only stay for a convenient messenger that might be most acceptable unto you; such a one as this little yong postillion we think will prove, whome as we have chosen to be the messenger for bringing this letter unto you, so wold we have you to receave the same as a most sure and faithfull messenger to express the contynuance of your gracious souverains good opinion and favour, as largely as your self can wish, toward you: whom you shall be also assured to finde will allways reserve one eare open for you against any blast that may be procured to be soundid in the other against you, if any such occasion should be offred. Your good usage toward the widow your daughter-in-lawe (wherin you shew your self like to your self), that is, an honorable noble gentleman, we pray you contynue, and receave our very harty thanks for the same. And because we assure our self that in your prayers you are not unmindfull of us, so doo we also pray God to keepe unto us in helth such a faithfull noble subject, as we have allways found of you, and to deliver you from your auncient ennemy the gowte.'

At top of letter: 'Your verey lovinge soveraine, Elizabeth R.'

Signed Endorsed: 'Q. Elizabeths gracious letter, 1588'. ½p. (Original Letters II/59)

GILBERT, LORD TALBOT, TO THE EARL OF SHREWSBURY

(1588) Regarding the 'showing of the books of the subsidy' to the Earl of Shrewsbury. Sir Thomas Stanhope has carried up his book to certify. Rufford.

Holograph 1 p. (Original Letters II/61)

THE PRIVY COUNCIL TO THE EARL OF SHREWSBURY

1588-89, January 6. 'Whereas of late certain articles have been exhibited unto us in the behalf of Sir Walter Asheton, knight, against Anthony Kynnerslie, gentleman, your Lordships servant: wherin the said Kynnerslie, beside other matters alleged against him, is charged with not receiving the Communion and that some of his children are not baptized, wherof as yet he hath not cleared himself in such ample sort as were convenient, in respect of the grievousness of the matters laid against him. Forasmuch as your Lordship hath been already made acquainted with the said causes, having heretofore entered into the hearing and examination therof, we have thought good to desire your Lordship, sending for the said Sir Walter Asheton, knight, to attend you and likewise the said Kynnerslie, to proceed to the full hearing and examination of the matters on either side to be alleged and hereupon to make some final good end of all matters in controversy between them, as your Lordship in justice and equity shall think fit. And whereas we are likewise given to understand that the said Kynnerslie hath an action in the case against Sir Walter Asheton, we do not think fit that matter shall be prosecuted any further. Wherefore we pray your Lordship to take order with the said Kynnerslie accordingly. And if any of the parties shall not be conformable to your Lordships order and direction in any of the controversies between them, then we pray your Lordship to advertise us, in whom the fault is and with your Lordships opinion therein, that we may take such further order as shall appertain.' Richmond.

Signed: Lord Chancellor Hatton, Lords Howard and Hunsdon, Sir T. Heneage, Sir F. Walsingham and J. Wolley. 1 p. (Original Letters II/63)

LORD BURGHLEY TO THE EARL OF SHREWSBURY

1588-89, January 18. 'My very good Lord. I am sure your Lordship hath hard of my long affliction by the gowt, both in my hands and fete, wherof I am not yet fully recovered, and therfore I hope your Lordship hath thought me excusable for not wrytyng to your Lordship of long tyme, for in truth this my right hand which I now aventure to use to your Lordship hath bene unhable this month to wryte any lynes without payne, and now I wryt not with ease, yet I am mynded to have it to serve you as your hart and body also shall.'

I thank you for your New Year's gift. 'And now, my Lord, fyndyng by my own experience whan I am but at London absent from the Court, how common reports are scattered of the actions at the Court, I thynk also such un-certen reports are brought or wrytten into the contrey, wherof I know your Lordship wold know the truth also. Therfore I will scrible to you as it war in a heepe the occurrentes here of the Court.'

It is true that the Duke of Guise and the Cardinal of Guise are slain by the King's command for conspiring the King's deprivation and so to have attained the Crown. It is found that the Duke of Guise had a pension of 150,000 crowns from the King of Spain, and had received many great sums these three years past for himself and his confederates.

The King sought to kill the Duke's brother, the Duke of Maine, but he is escaped from Lyons, and so has the Duke of Aumale from Paris. The Marquis of Elboeuf, the Cardinal of Bourbon, the Bishop of Lyons, four presidents of Paris and other places are taken. Paris is in an uproar, yet they have sent 12 persons to the King to regain favour, but the King delays to answer them and, I think, will punish some of the heads for expelling him from Paris, and will bring them low. Orleans rebelled, but the King had the citadel kept for him and thereby, as I hear, the city is mastered. The King has put a great number to the sword, and so I think he will use Lyons. 'The first judgment of God is lyke to fall uppon these 3 towns, for they war the great authors of the massacres a few years past.'

The Queen Mother is certainly dead of a long sickness. The King's wife is said to be also dead. The Cardinal Bourbon is so old and sick, he cannot long endure. The King, notwithstanding this proceeding against the Guisards, proceeds as sharply as his business will permit against the King of Navarre who, notwithstanding, has won divers towns in the late troubles.

As to domestic news, the Parliament shall certainly hold: the purpose to borrow some money of the realm must needs also hold. For though it is likely that the Parliament will yield some subsidy, yet it cannot be answered conveniently before this time twelvemonth.

Her Majesty, finding a great want of noblemen for Parliament, is minded to create some earls and some barons.

Your son, Lord Talbot, and Lord Strange shall also be called to Parliament. Sir H. Grey, Sir Robert Sydney, Mr Richard Fynes, shall be also called as barons. Sir John Perott is either to be called to Parliament or to be controller. Sir Edward Cleare is also named as a baron.

'Hir Majesty had some speche with me, to call me to some other degre, but I have shewed hir Majesty just cause to leave me as I am, havyng cause to diminish my lyvlihood by provydyng for my younger son; and besyde that, I am meter to be lett down into my grave than to be sett up any higher; and for these and many other reasons I hope I have satisfyed hir Majesty, although your Lordship may percase here some other report.'

When I had wearied my hand I received your letter concerning the Wardship of one Wastness, but 3 days ago Lady Hunsdon sued her Majesty for it. Pray let me know what your right to it is.

'And so, my good Lord, fyndyng my hand utterly weary', I and all your friends will be glad to see you in health. Richmond.

Holograph 4 pp. (Original Letters II/66)

THE QUEEN'S LOAN

1588-89, January 28. Writ of privy seal for a loan of £50 addressed to Margaret French, dated Richmond, January 28, Elizabeth 31 (1588-89).

(Original Letters II/93)

The Privy Council to the Earl of Shrewsbury

1588-89, January 31.   Regarding the raising of the loan in Nottinghamshire and Derbyshire.   Whitehall.

Seven signatures 1 p.   (Original Letters II/69)
  (See *Acts of the Privy Council*, Vol.XVII, pp. 59 and 60.)

The Privy Council to the Earl of Shrewsbury

1588-89, January 31.   We enclose letters from the Queen under the privy seal directed to divers persons whom we think of ability to lend her Majesty such sums as are specified.   Your deputy-lieutenants are to cause the justices to send for such, and first by way of friendly persuasion to get them to lend the money within a month.   If they refuse the justices are to take bond of them to appear before the deputy-lieutenants who are likewise to use gentle persuasion.   If they still persist in their refusal, they are to let them understand that enquiry will be made by commission and a jury of the true value of their lands and goods, a return of which is to be made to the Privy Council and Exchequer to remain there of record, by which in time to come her Majesty may justly cause them to be rated both for subsidies and all other ordinary charges, musters and otherwise levies of men for service of the realm, and not by such low and favourable rates as now are accustomed; and to that end we require that the names of such recusants be certified unto us that such order may be taken with them for their wilfulness in such times of service as these are.   You are to certify to us of any who have come to London or removed into some other county, and those absent from their homes are to leave directions to their wives and servants to send them word when they are to appear before the justices.   Sir George Chaworth is named collector for Nottinghamshire, John Manners for Derbyshire and Richard Bagot for Staffordshire. Whitehall.

Signed: Lord Chancellor Hatton, Lords Burghley, Hunsdon, Howard, Buckhurst, Sir James Croft, Sir Francis Walsingham, Sir T. Heneage and Mr Wolley. 2 pp.   (Original Letters II/71)
  Enclosed is a form for the appointment of collectors to be issued by the Lord Lieutenant.

Order from the Privy Council

1588-89, February 8.   Orders conceived and set down by the Lords of the Council by her Majesty's direction to be put into execution for the restraint of killing or eating of flesh, as well by the Lord Mayor within the City of London and other officers of the several liberties, as by the Lords Lieutenant of the several counties.

Large paper 1 p.   *Enclosed in* II/79   (Original Letters II/77)

The Privy Council to the Earl of Shrewsbury

1588-89, February 9.   Ordering him to exercise his diligence in causing the Queen's orders (enclosed) to be obeyed as to the restraint of eating meat in Lent.   Whitehall.

Ten signatures ½p. (Original Letters II/79)

William Herbert to the Earl of Shrewsbury

1588-89, February 22.   I thank you for the honourable token which I received of Mr Herne.

Our present news here. Yesterday Lord Henry Howard was committed to the keeping of the Master of the Rolls, Lord William Howard to the keeping of Mr Edward Cordell, and the Countess of Arundel confined to her own house. Today the Lord Chancellor and the Lord Treasurer dine with Mr Secretary Walsingham at Tower Hill and from there go to the Tower in the afternoon, so that some think an arraignment will follow shortly.

Sir John Norris and Sir Francis Drake with the rest of the captains of that journey have taken their leave of her Majesty on Thursday. Notwithstanding, they were sent for again and some stay made, but I think they shall go forward out of hand. There will be some hundred sail of shipping of all sorts, and some twelve or thirteen thousand men. So God prosper them.

Scanty news comes from France, because the great towns of Picardy and Normandy hold for the League. Only Boulogne and Calais hold for the King in that part and Dieppe in Normandy. The lower town of Boulogne is taken by the Leaguers lately, and the high town is like to follow. It is feared the King has a great commission in Rome to treat with the Pope for the end of it all. It is thought and feared they will agree. The King never sent here since the action. The Duke of Parma lieth with some forces upon the borders of France ready to take part with the League. Here is no particular news but the death of the Earl of Worcester and Sir William Wynter, and bill for a double subsidy to be paid in two years agreed upon, and so till the next safe messenger. I must write somewhat at large if I like him. London.

PS. The young Earl of Northumberland, your Honour's neighbour, is a fine gentleman and a wise, and of good courage and begins to be a good courtier, and is like to live. Your Lordship may conjecture the rest.

Holograph 1 p. (Original Letters II/81)

LORD DARCY TO THE EARL OF SHREWSBURY

1588-89, February 25. I regret to hear that a man of mine, a lewd fellow named Kendall, has been trespassing on your liberties. I have ordered him to be discharged from my service. Westminster.

Signed ½ p. (Original Letters II/83)

ROBERT LEE TO THE EARL OF SHREWSBURY

1588-89, February 26. Complaining of the negligence of the late and present sheriffs of Yorkshire in not effecting the arrest of one Mr Eastoft. Hatfield.

Signed 1 p. (Original Letters II/85)

GILBERT, LORD TALBOT, TO THE EARL OF SHREWSBURY

1588-89, March 3. 'I can advertize your Lordship of no espetiall matter at this tyme, more then I thynke your Lordship is informed alredy by sum of the nether house touchinge two bylls, the one agenste purveors, the other agenste certayne abuses in thexchecker: wherin her Majestie toke offence, which hathe bredd sum stirr bothe by her Majesties espetiall dislyke of certayne yonge gentlemen who have bene muche busyer bothe in thes bylls and others then they needed. And also by them in the nether house who thynke that we in our house deale sumwhat hardly with them to refuse the reding of suche bylls whatsoever as they have passed and doe send unto us. This day we are to receve answere from the nether house to her Majesties message. What shall then cum therof I will by my next advertise your Lordship.

I here that order is geven for the inditement of the Earle of Arundell, which if it be so, then it is very lyke his areignment will not be longe after, which I here is entended to be at the ende of this parliament. Within thes two or three days we loke for the byll of subsydyes to be broughte into our house, after the which I hope we shall quickly make an ende. There is a byll in the nether house againste the non-residentes of the clergy and agenste pluralities, wherin dyvers pure fellowes are very whott and ernest. Amongeste whome Mr Beale hathe made a very sharpe speche, which is nothynge well lyked by the Busshoppes. Dyvers artycles are preferred unto the nether house for reformation of the booke of common prayer and suche lyke matters, but the Speker dare not rede them, for that her Majestie espetially forbad that any suche matters sholde be delte in the fyrste day when she was at the parliament house.

I am forced to ende, for that this bearer Mr Nevell of Grove, your Lordships servant is in haste, and my tyme is to gyve attendance at the parliament house.' At Mr Caswells house near Clements Inn.

Holograph Seal 1½pp. (Original Letters II/89)

GILBERT, LORD TALBOT, TO THE EARL OF SHREWSBURY

(1588-89, March 10) I have been trying either for love or money to get for you particulars of my uncle Roger Manners's book. I cannot find the information you want about the tithe corn within the parish of Sheffield belonging to Worksop Abbey.

Mr Hatton sends you thanks for the lead.

'The Parliament is daly loked to ende, so that I can wryte your Lordship no other certayntye therof.' At the Court.

Holograph 1p. (Original Letters II/91)

E. STANHOPE TO GILBERT, LORD TALBOT

1590, May 22. Concerning the commission of Mr Floyd for the transporting of saltpetre, and concerning the difficulties of raising the provision of money for her Majesty's household in the shire (of Nottingham). 'Experience partly teaches me already to see that they who do so unwillingly pay (it), being the highest to be respected and have been in effect at every sessions perswaded to it these 4 or 5 years, will more hardly be drawn to yield to so great a sum for the transporting of salt petre and necessaries therunto appertaining, casting upon themselves that the president therof may lay divers other public burdens of more importance upon them.' Grays Inn.

Signed Addressed: 'To Lord Talbot, as Deputy Lieutenant of Nottinghamshire'. *Endorsed:* 'Mr Edward Stanhope to my Lord concerning Floyd, the saltpeter man.' 1p. (Original Letters II/96)

JOHN STANHOPE TO GILBERT, EARL OF SHREWSBURY

1590, November 22. 'My very good Lord. The maner of gret prynces is fyrst they saye (in lyke accydents) to condole and then to congratulate, and because yt is fytt that poor men should immytate theyr betters, I thynke yt not amysse to bewayle with your Lordship the losse of your honorable father, whose wysdome and loyaltye hath both mayntayned and encresed the honor of his ancestors, and after a longe well spent lyfe hath lefte, I hope, a quyett and honorable estate to such as succeedyng hym by course of nature I dowbt not but wyll excede hym in the glory of his house and all other perfectyons.

The Quene yesterdaye as sone as she sawe me after dynner tolde me whatt a losse she had had of so grete a parson as both for his lykyng and fydelytye to her self and her Estate had (now?) lost his felowe behynde hym and that she thanked hym (much) for, was that he left one so suffycyent to supply his place as she could the better bear with the mysse of hym. Very late at nyght she used the lyke wordes agayne to Mr Vice-Chamberlayn and myself, Mrs Kydmore beyng only by, and in very truth Mr Vice-Chamberlayn replyed gretly in your Lordships commendatyon. Now, my good Lord, to tell you that a grete number of your poor frendes and others ar gladd of any advancement of your honor were nedeless, for such hath heretofore ben your caryadge as hath longe synce enabled you to more then you shall now receave; and herin pardon, I pray you, the love I beare you yf yt be carefull you shuld proceade both to contynue and encrese the honor hertofore gyven you for, as I protest, I know your dispositytyon fraught both with honor and a besemyng curstosye, so as owt of your self nothyng can be loked for butt good, and that yt ys both strengthened and assysted with the stoote feloshipp of an honorable wyse ladye, yett such is and shalbe the gretnes and such wyll and must be the concurse of men of all sortes unto you, as your eares which must nedes be open, shall hear mens severall humors laying open one anothers imperfectyons, to wourke yf yt maye be the goodnes of your owne mynde to a wary and jelus concete of such as perhapps not havyng lyke opportunytye at all tymes, nor so harde an humor at any tyme, or otherwyse so devoted to love and serve you to theyr uttermost.

Your Lordships experience and judgmente hath noted, I kno, that in others of lyke qualytye, which wyll not now be impertynente for yourself to remember, and that your caulinge must be accompanyed with the love of manye, both of sundry degres and of severall condytyons yourself best knoes, whose inwarde frendshipp thoughe yt be fytt to be retyred to such choyce persons as both tyme and troth had confyrmed in your love, yet must ther be above a passadge for men of wourth and vertue to ayme unto the favor of your good countenaunce, wher in the constancye of your garmente they may settle the hope of theyr well doynge. My Lord, yf the Lord Talbott had had any enemyes, which I protest I kno not, or yf some of testie temper had showed more stomacke, or yf conceytes of anye unkyndnes hath made sho of straungnes, lett the Erle of Shruesberye forgett and forgyve them, and for such lett his gretnes and goodnes be knowne as yt neyther feares the malyce of an enemy, nor wyll refuse the good wyll of a frend. My Lord, yf I be bolder then I shuld or busyer then I nede, impute yt to the lybertye I have hertofore usurped and to the love I ever meane to beare you, of whose well doynge every way I shuld be the prouder for many respectes, and the rather for that I shuld be the apter to beleve myself an other tyme.

Sir, the Erle of Essex, I thynke, shall have the justyceship of an Eyr, my Lorde Chamberlaine doth stande to be Chamberlaine of the Chequer, and Mrs Care stands for her husbande. Of Erle Marshall I neyther heare of sutor nor lyklyhood. The Quene, I thynke, will dysmyse the Vi(count) Turynne with all love and kyndnes and is thought her contrybutyon wylbe rated at £30,000 and 5000 men. If they hast not the more the King of Spayne will mar theyr market. Marye and most of your Lordships frends be in healthe. Emongest the rest Mrs Mackwyllyames desyres humbly to be remembred to your Lordship and my honorable lady, to whom yf yt plese you to present my humble service I wylbe as redy to performe yt as to offer yt.'

Holograph   Torn in places   Endorsed: '22 November, 1590 John Stanhope

101

to my Lord of congratulation.' 2 pp. (Original Letters II/98)

T. KITSON TO THE EARL OF SHREWSBURY

1590, November 22. I came to Barnet on Thursday at five o'clock at night and made full account to be at London by seven, but if my life had lain of it I could not get a horse till three o'clock in the morning, so that it was five o'clock on Friday before I came. I went presently to Burghley House and got Mr Maynard to deliver your letter so soon as ever my Lord's chamber door was opened, which, when he had read it he presently sent for Mrs Cecil and by her did presently advertise her Majesty. He sent for me into his chamber and asked me how long my Lord did lie in any extremity before his death, and when he died, with divers such like questions, and when he dismissed me he said he would write to your Honour at large. Mr Markham told me this day that he would write to your Honour by this bearer what he hath done.

I pray God your Honour may like the apparel, which this bearer brings and especially the doublet and hose, because it was not of such stuff as your Honour would have had, for here is none of the kind to be got that was thought fit for your Honour. For the other suit we let it rest till we know your Honour's further pleasure, for your Honour told me that the other cloak should be of unshorn velvet and we all take it that your Honour meant uncut velvet; wherefore we humbly desire to know your Honour's pleasure by your next letters. I lie by Mr Foster's wardrobe in Philip Tasker's house at the sign of the Talbot. London.

PS. I gave your Honour's message to Mr Herne who protests he is at your Honour's devotion, but I do not believe him. He makes himself to be a poor man and says that he has little in his keeping, but the world thinks otherwise.

Holograph Endorsed: '22 November, 1590. Mr Thomas Kytson, my Lords servant to my Lord. Concerning my Lords pleasure to be known touching a suit of apparel of velvet for his Lordship, whether to be of unshorn velvet or of uncut velvet.' 1 p. (Original Letters II/100)

THE EARL OF SHREWSBURY TO LORD BURGHLEY

(? 1592) May 30. My Lord of Essex is willing to join with me in compounding all quarrels between my brother-in-law, Mr H. Cavendish, and Mr William Agar. I make bold to ask you, when they appear before you tomorrow, to persuade them to refer 'all the matter of quarrell and pyke betwyxt them' to Lord Essex and me, 'so as if it myght be, they may be bounde by your Lordship and the rest of the R(ight) Ho(norable) Borde to performe what order we shall sett downe betwyxt them for the observyng of the peace.' Bishopsgate Street, London.

Holograph Endorsed: '1592.' 1 p. (Original Letters II/102)

SIR THOMAS HENEAGE TO THE EARL OF SHREWSBURY

1592, August 24. My Lord, I can prove my love to you no better than by letting you know what I hear that concerns you and what is fit for you to take heed of.

This other day I found the Council Board was possessed with a complaint against Sir Thomas Stanhope for erecting a weir called Shelford, which by the certificate of a number of hands, whereof some be of calling and my kin, should appear to be very prejudicial to many poor men and a destruction of fish. This complaint now I find answered by Sir Thomas Stanhope to the great 'toche' of such as have complained, for he affirms that the weir was made with your father's and your consent, and that this complaint has been exhibited without the knowledge or consent of many of those whose names are subscribed by the practice and procurement of one Tailor without cause or reason, which some guessed to be of your Lordship's setting on. And his letter being credited, this was thought to be a very hard kind of dealing with a gentleman. Whereupon letters are sent to Lord Willoughby and others to examine this matter; and Tailor is sent for up to be examined; of all which I did think it my part to give your Lordship notice; to whom withal I give this charge upon the love I bear your Lordship, that you take no particular knowledge hereof by me. And so I commend me humbly to your Lordship and likewise to my Lady, whom I love and honour more than any lady in the north of England, be as jealous as it pleaseth you of it. At the Court at Mr Dolmans at Newbery.

PS. My Lord of Essex has a warrant signed for the fee farm of £300 per annum out of the (royal) parks.

Holograph Endorsed: '24 of August, 1592. From Mr Vice-Chamberlaine touching Sir Thomas Stanhopes weare.' 1 p. (Original Letters II/104)

THE EARL OF SHREWSBURY TO THE PRIVY COUNCIL

1592, August 28. 'My very good Lordes. For that I have allwayes heretofore found in all my occasions great favour at your Lordships handes, I do therefore make boulde to troble your Lordships with the information of a greate abuse offered unto me by certayne prowde, false and unmeete wordes lately uttered of me by Sir Thomas Stanhope, and sutch as I would not beare, but seeke to redresse my selfe as I were able by somme other waye then complaynte, had I not bene depelye charged by hir most roiall Majesty at my last attendance on hir Highnes, when I tooke my humble leave (upon occation of speache of that person) that yf he or any of his adherentes should forgett themselves in any sorte towardes me, that then I should speedily lett hir Majesty understand yt, that she might right me (for so yt pleased hir most gratiously to protest), before I should endevour any other redresse of my selfe, which hir Highnes sayde might perhapps breede somme unquietnes here in this countrey. Now this commandement beinge thus layde upon me, I dare not disobey, but humbly yeildinge my selfe to the performance therof (how contrary soever yt be eyther to my nature or desyre, being now thus greatly provoked), I shall beseche your Lordships to make hir Highnes privy to the effecte of this note enclosed, wherby your Lordships may perceyve what his wordes of me were, and then in your wisdomes and honorable dispositions to judge how farre I am divers wayes therby touched. My good Lords, my longe sufferinge his former insolent courses towardes me causeth him thus now to presume, and I am credibly enfourmed (by somme who are oft in his company) that he is of opinion that any indignity or wronge that shalbe offered unto me here in the country wilbe rather acceptable at the Court then otherwise. And so in deede yt shold seeme he conceyveth by his manner of proceedinge with me, but I hope well that therein he shall fynde himselfe farre deceyved, or els I would accompt my selfe a most infortunate man. For I do assuredly trust that in this my obeyinge hir Majestys commandment she will performe hir most gratious wordes in that behalfe, and not suffer my pore honor and reputation (which above my lyfe I desyer may be preserved to do hir service and honor) to be thus wounded. And I shoulde esteme myselfe a most unworthy man of all hir Highnes former gracious favours and unmeete to be imployed in any of hir services hereafter, yf I should endure and putt upp sutch disgraces. Thus beinge much greived and ashamed, the necessity of the case inforceth me to troble your Lordships in a matter of this nature, I doe take my leave and commytt your Lordships to the protection of the Lorde Allmighty.' At Worksoppe my house.

Holograph Copy Endorsed: '28 August 1592. A coppy of my letter written to the L. Tresurer, Ld Admirall and the Ld Chamberlen upon sutch speaches uttered of me by Sir Thomas Stanhope at Fletchers house.' 1p. (Original Letters II/106).

ENCLOSED

The copy of the certificate in question in the Earl of Shrewsbury's hand.

The 17th day of August 1592, Robert Kydman and John Knott being at Mr Fletchers house in Stoke Bardolph, Sir Thomas Stanhope came thither about eight of the clock in the morning, having with him three of his servants, viz, Thomas Gylbert, Robert Grey and Thomas Swyndell, each of them having a forest bill or Welsh hook of four yards length or thereabouts. Sir Thomas Stanhope asked if Mr Fletcher were at home, who presently coming forth unto him, Sir Thomas said: 'I understand that two of my Lord of Shrewsbury's men are come hither, who would speak with me.' Fletcher answered: 'There be two of my Lord's gentlemen in my house, but I know not any occasion that they have to speak with you, but if it please you I will let them understand what you say.' And thereupon calling them forth, Sir Thomas Stanhope said to Kydman: 'Would you speak with me?' Kydman answered that he desired not to speak with him, neither had he anything to say to him. Then presently after, amongst other speeches, Sir Thomas said: 'My Lord preferreth lies,' and afterwards repeated it again. Kydman answered: 'My Lord preferreth nothing but truths,' and then Sir Thomas proceeding in speeches said 'My Lord is no Lieutenant' and after that he said: 'If my Lord come hither, sure I will meet him, but he will not come him self.' Then Kydman said: 'My Lord, I think, will take other courses.' Sir Thomas said: 'I care not what course he can take.' And then he asked Kydman if he meant to come upon his ground. Kydman said he would hold that way that was lawful for him. Sir Thomas replied: 'If you do otherwise, I will keep you off, if I come.' Then Kydman left him.

Subscribed are the signatures of: Francis Fletcher, Robert Kydman, John Knott, Thomas Nycholson, Samwell Willcock, William Pearson, *with a note signed by:* The Earl of Shrewsbury, Sir Charles Cavendish and Francis Needham *certifying the above to be a verbatim report.*

A further report signed by: Fletcher, Nycholson, Willcock and Pearson.

Fletcher remaining still by Sir Thomas Stanhope, Sir Thomas Stanhope said: 'This is my Lord's malice against me.' Whereunto Fletcher answered: 'My Lord doth not malice you nor any man; neither will he do anything but what he may lawfully.' By God,' said Sir Thomas, 'if he do, I will unlaw it if I can.' Then Fletcher said: 'The matter is to be heard before the Privy Council, and what their Honours determine, my Lord will willingly obey.' 'I cannot tell,' said Sir Thomas, 'what he will willingly do.' Fletcher then said: 'My Lord is a subject.' Sir Thomas answered: 'That is his grief, he is sorry for that.' And after many other speeches, he departed, the wife of the said Fletcher and his servant being much affrighted at the manner of his coming thither.

Endorsed: '17 August, 1592. The copy of the certificate of Sir Thomas Stanhopes speeches touching the Earl of Shrewsbury sent up to the Ld Treasurer,

Ld Admiral and Ld Chamberlain within a letter to them of the 28 of August, 1592.' 2 pp. (Original Letters II/107)

(Original Letters IV/110 is another copy to the same effect in another hand, with the autographs or marks of the witnesses and the additional signature of Christopher Blundeston. 1½pp.)

LORD BURGHLEY TO THE EARL OF SHREWSBURY

1592, September 11. Your letters to the Lord Admiral, Vice-Chamberlain and myself about Sir Thomas Stanhope's misusing of you have come into my hands. The Lord Admiral is still absent, but the Vice-Chamberlain and I have perused them with the evidence you send. I laid them before her Majesty, who thought you justified if the evidence were true. But she observed that some of the witnesses were your men. Sir Thomas Stanhope is to be sent for if he is able to travel. His friends report that you have called him names, such as knave. I must be bold to tell you that there have been disorderly proceedings among certain towns and people; that names were subscribed at the request of others, knowing nothing of the matter, and my Lord Sheffield testifies by his letter that many of these have told him so; and so does one Tailor of Gainsborough, who subscribed to the bill, confess that he was hired for money to go from town to town to get the subscriptions. It would be well for you to have answer to this. Sudeley Castle.

Signed 1 p. (Original Letters II/112)

SIR THOMAS HENEAGE TO THE EARL OF SHREWSBURY

1592, September 11. My good Lord. Most good will useth least ceremonies. And as I have a property more plain perhaps than pleasing, so use I not to those I most love to show another face of things that concern them than in very truth I find them.

Your Lordship's letters, brought me by Mr Talbot, I had no good occasion before this day to acquaint her Majesty with. Who, when she had heard me begin to read them, misliking (methought) the matter, grew weary of the circumstances, but when I showed her the difference of the abilities of your Lordship and Sir Thomas Stanhope to serve her Majesty, the justice of your desire, the assurances you made of her Highness's promise and the patience you used upon the hope of her goodness, howsoever it seemed to me, she could have the quality of his usage qualified. She told me very confidently that if it were true he had so forgotten himself, he should answer it, and your Lordship should be well satisfied, whose honour (considering your love to her) it was fit for her to regard. Whereupon I told her Majesty that I was sure her grace in doing your Lordship that justice, would infinitely bind you and not a little guard you. More than this of these matters I cannot yet show your Lordship. And though I was not ignorant how before this Sir Thomas Stanhope was sent for, yet I thought fit, by telling her Majesty of your letter, to sound her disposition, which I have opened to your Lordship truly as I found it, and now only advise you to carry no other conceits, nor show in letter or message to this place than that you are fully persuaded that her Majesty, out of her princely nature and justice, will do you right and regard your honour, which I will ever further to the utmost of my ability. Wherewith humbly commend me to your Lordship and my Lady, whom I love and to whom I owe service. At the Court at Sudeley.

Holograph Endorsed: '11 Sept. 1592. From Mr ViceChamberlain touching Sir Thomas Stanhopes misusage of me.' 1 p. (Original Letters II/114)

1592, September 20. I thank you for your letter of the 11th, whereby I perceive that my letter to your Lordships has been shown to her Majesty, and that she well allows of my manner of proceeding. Touching the witnesses your Lordship shall understand what they are to me, for you wrote that her Majesty enquired somewhat of you thereof. Francis Fletcher is a gentleman and owner of the house whither Sir Thomas Stanhope came in that bravery when he used those unmeet speeches of me; he was eldest son of old Mr Fletcher of Gray's Inn, whom, I suppose, your Lordship knew. This gentleman is my servant as a retainer. Robert Kydman is one of my domestic servants. John Knott is none of my servants, nor ever did in any sort belong to me, neither did I ever see or hear of him before I saw his name to the testimony; he has spent good time in service in the wars, as may appear by a note here-inclosed under his hand. The other three belong to Fletcher and I know nothing of them. Thus two only are my servants, not three as your Lordship suggests. There can be no manner of just exception to the credit of these of witnesses. Like testimony were sufficient in law in the highest degree of trial of the greatest subject within this realm. I thank her Majesty for sending for Sir Thomas Stanhope to answer his misusage of me, and I hope I may receive satisfaction from your Lordships. Where your Lordship writes that some of Mr Stanhope's friends make report that I have in divers places given reproachful speeches of him, as calling him 'knave' and such like, I beseech you to get better proofs, for your Lordship shall find that I am very wary what I say of my gentleman, though I confess I think as contemptibly of that man's conditions as I do of any man's of his calling that lives. It is given out by his dependents that so long as he lives I shall never be Lord Lieutenant of Nottinghamshire, that the way to increase his credit is to oppose himself to me, as he does. As to the Lieutenancy, though I well know there is nothing that in the vulgar opinion (through all this country) makes men to conceive as they do that my credit with her Majesty is very mean, yet so long as she shall not hold me worthy of it I will not desire it. Only with all humble earnestness I can crave that I may not be forced to swallow up such indignities in my country as never any of my ancestors did, and which would make me contemptible to the world, and I look to her Majesty to regard my poor honour, which I dedicate wholly to her service. And your good Lordship, whom from my youth hitherto I have always found to have been a lover and favourer of my house (besides your particular affection and infinite favours to myself) and who has promised under your own hand to be as a father to me in advice and affection, I earnestly beseech you to be my friend and favourer in this as in all other my honest, reasonable and just causes.

As to the first complaint against the weir, how disorderly however it was procured, I was not privy to the setting it on foot, as the testimony of the parties themselves, which I sent to your Lordship by Sir Thomas Wylkes, shows. As to the disorder, I am able to prove that Sir Thomas Stanhope's certificate was either indirectly or unlawfully procured, as I showed in my letter of the 9th of August. Some of the farmers of fishing, fishermen and boatmen of those parts, repaired to me with suit to move your Lordships therein to such effect as I did: all which I will prove. Of late I know you have received another complaint from a multitude of people dwelling above the weir. Nevertheless, I think they will be as well satisfied to have the matter examined by a Commission of Sewers (which is the ordinary course for reforming such disorders and annoyances) as by any other means. Worksop.

Holograph Endorsed: '20 Sept. 1592. Erl of Shrewsbury to my Lord.' 3½ pp. (Original Letters II/116)
(This is the original letter of which a copy appears as folio 423 on p.172 of *Calendar of Talbot Papers in the College of Arms,* ed G.R.Batho.)

THE EARL OF SHREWSBURY TO [SIR JOHN PUCKERING, LORD KEEPER]

1592, September 23.   I lately received your Lordship's letter in answer to one which I wrote to you concerning a weir of Sir Thomas Stanhope's, and now I am advertised from the Court that upon the exhibiting of a new complaint to the Lords of the Privy Council subscribed by a multitude of people against that said weir, their Lordships had written a letter to your Lordship for the granting a Commission of Sewers for the due determination of the matter. And for as much as the choice of the Commissioners is very greatly to be respected and that I am assured there lives not a more politic person in the handling of his own private causes than Sir Thomas Stanhope, who will leave no means unattempted that he may hope will serve his turn (albeit I assure myself no politic device can withdraw your Lordship from ministering equal and indifferent justice to all men), I make bold hereby in the name of thousands of my country people most earnestly to beseech your Lordship's especial care of the Commissioners, that none may be who are either akin or allied to him, or of kindred to any so near to him as Mr John Hollice, his son-in-law, is.   Those dwelling near the river Trent in the shires of Lincoln, Nottingham, Derby and Stafford would be meetest.

The matter is of great moment, and I dare boldly affirm concerns as many or more of her Majesty's tenants and subjects than ever any weir did that was erected since her Majesty's reign.   I commend this to your grave consideration.   For my own part, although it is that gentleman's pleasure to give out that I further this matter against him only for malice, I know in my own conscience the untruth thereof, and that it is the general good that I seek.   I make small account of any such reports.   Worksop.

PS. I am credibly informed that Sir Thomas Stanhope has given out that if it should cost him many thousand pounds, but he would keep up his weirs.
Holograph 1 p. (Original Letters II/118)

LORD HOWARD OF EFFINGHAM TO THE EARL OF SHREWSBURY

(1592) September 27.   I have received your letter of the 19th of September and perceive by it of a former letter from you to the Lord Treasurer, Lord Chamberlain and myself, which by reason of my absence I was not acquainted with.   But now by this letter of yours I perceive the undutiful and unadvised dealing of Sir Thomas Stanhope towards you.   I did not rest after the receipt of your letter to know of my Lord Treasurer what course had been held for the satisfying of your Lordship.   He tells me that Sir Thomas is sent for, a course best for your honour, which I will always maintain during my life.   I regret that sickness has prevented me from visiting you and my Lady.   Oxford.
Holograph Endorsed: '27.7.92. From the Lord Admirall touching Sir Thomas Stanhope.' 1 p. (Original Letters II/119)

THE EARL OF SHREWSBURY TO LORD BURGHLEY

1592, October 5.   I received lately a letter from Ratcliffe wherein he writes that at his attending your Lordship at Woodstock at her Majesty's (visit) there, your Lordship commanded him to let me understand that her Majesty was greatly displeased with me for two causes informed against me. The (first) was that where 800 men certified against Sir Thomas Stanhope's weir, it is since confessed by divers of these men that they set their hands to that certificate at the instance of some of my servants, not knowing nor having any cause so to do but to pleasure me. The other was that on a Saturday night some of my servants came **to the town of Derby, and in my name (as Steward** of the town) warned all the burgesses that they should assemble the next morning, being Sunday, in a church before divine service, and that they did there meet, being called by a bell, and were solicited from man to man to sign the roll that was last sent up and to add the Common Seal.

Since my servants advertised me of this, I have received a letter from you from Oxford written the 27th of September, in the first part of which you tell me that Sir Thomas Stanhope is sent for if his health will allow, or otherwise so as he may be able to clear himself: in the second part you inform me in writing what you told Ratcliffe in words of the undue gathering together of them of the town of Derby in an unmeet place and time, my servants' soliciting from man to man, the long roll sent up by Mr Needham to be subscribed. I am informed that Sir Thomas Stanhope has complained of these things both to the Privy Council and to his private friends at Court. I have, therefore, asked the Council to send me the charges that I may send up my answers, and that after due trial of the truth thereof the fault may be punished on whichever side it is.

In the mean time it is a great grief to me that her Majesty gave credit to the first information before hearing my answer; especially remembering who is my adversary, a man perfectly known by all men who rightly know him to be as full of all sleights and subtleties and to use them as much in all things that may serve his own turn as any whosoever; and knowing what an instrument he has in his brother, Mr Michael Stanhope, so near to her Majesty as that he may fill her ears with such reports as the other shall devise. I cannot but greatly doubt that he who has not stuck to inform so manifest an untruth as that of the assembling and meeting of them of the town of Derby in a church, will not leave there. And the rather I have to suspect so, for that it was told me within these 24 hours that Sir Thomas Stanhope, speaking of those matters of unkindness lately happened between Mr Thomas Markham and me, said he could if he list teach Mr Markham an easy way to become quit with me. The other, with whom he was speaking, asking him by what means: 'Marry', quoth Sir Thomas Stanhope, 'lett him tell the Queen that the Earl of Shrewsbury is a Papist, and then see who can get it out of her head.' And this, in good faith, my Lord, was lately very credibly told me and I will seek to get further proof thereof. I am the more apt to believe it because Mr Markham has often told me the speeches Sir Thomas Stanhope used to him at the time he was furthest out with my honourable cousin, Edward, the Earl of Rutland, viz., Sir Thomas Stanhope advised Mr Markham to inform her Majesty of a matter concerning that expressing a thing of great moment (which, if it had **been true, in likelihood would have utterly discredited him with her Majesty).** Mr Markham answered he knew it not nor was able to prove it, for if he could he would inform her Majesty thereof. The other replied in these words: 'That is all one; there is colour and likelihood enough therof; put it once into her head and it will never be removed.' And although Mr Markham and I be not in those terms of familiarity that we have been, and that, as I hear, Sir Thomas Stanhope and he met this other day at Hardwick my mother-in-law's house, where they two were reconciled, yet I doubt not but Mr Markham will confess so much in substance as I here affirm. I have often heard him say, if he be asked thereof by such a one as he (*torn*) will answer, and if it be true it is not only a manifest proof of his malicious and dangerous disposition, but also it shows he carries not that reverend opinion of her royal Majesty that becomes him, to conceive that an information, being once put into her head, will be believed athough there be no direct proof thereof. Whereas the world knows that there was never prince (both by nature and judgement) more apt to afford all men their due trial without which she condemns none, either in her own princely opinion or otherwise, whereof few or none have had better proof than myself, having heretofore been as deeply wronged by most false reports to her Highness as any other; with the remembrance whereof I am exceedingly comforted, assuredly hoping that her Majesty will be the same gracious lady and Sovereign towards me (if any like lewd reports happen to be brought unto her hereafter) as she has been heretofore.

I thought it best to advise you thus of the evil disposition of my adversary, who sought to make the Privy Council believe that these errors were committed (as appears from letters of Lord Sheffield otherwise) by my means, whereas it is evident from the testimony of Somerscales and Sawre of Gainsborough, which I sent up, that I never heard or knew of that matter as of any intent that any man had to complain who dwelt above the weir, until long after it was subscribed, and then by chance was shown me in London. As for the Derby meeting, if I cannot disprove it very directly and apparently, then let me close my credit with your Lordship. And whether I follow this matter against him more of stomach than for any needful cause, it will best appear when the Commission of Sewers shall sit, if the commission is impartial. For his lewd speeches of me which he is sent for to answer if he is able to travel (as no doubt but he is, for these seven years past, I can assure your Lordship, he has not travelled so much in the like time as he has done in these two or three months past, and often 30 miles in a day: and yesterday he was at the Sessions in Newark, which is eight or nine miles from his house and home again the same night), I will not doubt but that her Highness in her princely nature and gracious disposition will right me and regard my poor credit. Worksop.

Copy Endorsed: '5 of October, 1592. A copy to my Lord Treasurer touching Sir Thomas Stanhope's complaint of me.' 2½pp. (Original Letters II/21)

See *H.M.C. A Calendar of the Talbot Papers in the College of Arms*, ed. G.R.Batho, p.171, H.405.

THE EARL OF SHREWSBURY TO (SIR THOMAS HENEAGE)

1592, October 6. I am advertised of the charges brought against me and my servants with regard to the Derby assembly. I am sure her Majesty will not condemn me unheard. I have asked the Privy Council to let me and my servants answer the charges. Until then I beseech you to move her Highness to suspend her conceit thereon for her judgement. The Earl repeats the story of the conversations between Sir Thomas Stanhope and Mr Markham, the influence of Michael Stanhope at Court, and Sir Thomas Stanhope's fitness for travel. Worksop.

Copy Endorsed: '6 of October 1592. A copy to Mr Vice-Chamberlain touching Sir Thomas Stanhope's complaint of me.' 2 pp. (Original Letters II/123)

LORD HOWARD, LORD BUCKHURST AND SIR THOMAS HENEAGE TO THE EARL OF SHREWSBURY

1592, November 3. We are sorry to understand the extreme differences lately grown between you and Sir Thomas Stanhope, the continuance of which can only bring troubles, malice and mischief, and will end by taking away all hopes of reconcilement between you. Surely you must think of this, as one of the great personages of this commonwealth, and Sir Thomas, a gentleman of such credit and strengthened with that special favour from her Majesty which his near friends possess at Court. You will spend your whole time withstanding your adversaries in this cause, and be deprived of the great and honourable hopes of serving her Majesty, which your birth and desires would in short time have brought upon you.

We are thus moved to interpose ourselves for the compounding of this cause and pray you that all matters of difference may cease and stand in suspense until by the persons of you both here in Court we may be thoroughly informed of the same. At the Court.

Signed: Lords Howard and Buckhurst and Sir Thomas Heneage. *Endorsed:* '3 November 1592. A letter from the Ld Admiral, Ld Buckhurst and Mr Vicechamberlain to my Lord to motion of compremyse betwixt my Lord and Sir Thomas Stanhope.' 1½ pp. (Original Letters II/125)

LORD BUCKHURST TO THE EARL OF SHREWSBURY

1592, November 3. 'My very good Lord. Although by a joint letter from my Lord Admirall, Mr Vicechamberlain and meself, I have moved your Lordship to some frendly end of this bitter varians betwixt your Lordship and Sir Thomas Stannop, yet, bearing to your Lordship so unfained love as I doe and knowing how important the same is and may be to your Lordship, I have thought good, even by these few also, very ernestly to wish your Lordship to yeld to have good course therin; for we that live here in court and see how matters are handled and do pass, shall surely much better judge of these thinges than you that ar so far from the sight and dealinges of this place, assuring your Lordship (if I can judge anything at all) that the continuall presens of thes two brethren in court, with the nere place that they have with her Majestie, and that which is above all the rest, the especial favour which her Highnes doth beare unto them, will alwaies prevaile with so greate advantage against you, as it will not be possible, neither for you nor your frendes to cary this caus in that course of good succes which peradventure you expect and hope for. Besides, to deale plainly with your Lordship, I see by profe that whether it be by reason of your absens or of the greate favour which they receave from her Majestie, upon which as you know most mens eies in court are fixed, they are so mightely frended and favored in Councell, as it wilbe hard, except your caus be marvelous plain and just, to win any cours of advantage against them there, so as assure your Lordship (things standing as they doe) if you have any open or secret enemies as either in respect of envie or malice I know not who is free, and specially sitting in this comonwelth upon so hie a place of honor, welth and dignity as you doe. Undoubtedly your Lordship can never do them so grete a pleasure, nor your self so much harme, as to norishe and continue the quarels of these contentions betwixt you; wherby, assure yourself, they shall never want meanes and matter enough prively here in Court to wound you, being one of the grete daungers and infelicities of this place, that even the meanest may do us more hurt then peradventure the gretest can do us good. And your Lordship must also remember that in the policie of this comon rivale we ar not over redy to adde increse of power and countenans to such quiete personages as you ar; and whan in the country you dwell in you will nedes enter into a war with your inferiors there, we think it both justis, equity and wisdome to take care that the weaker part be not put downe by the mightier.

Thus, my Lord, you se how plainly and boldly in my true love I write unto you, being most desirous that this troblesome caus (which without some good course I feare may become the hindrans of your best fortune) might be brought to the hering and compounding of us your true frendes who, dout you not, will have that regard which shall fit, without prejudice to the honor and reputation of either and certenly to unfained love to bothe. And upon this fundacion I hope we shall build a happie work, both of frendship, quiet and profit to your selfes and of no small contentacion and comfort to all your frendes besydes. And if in fine we may knit a fast knot of unfained frendship betwixt you, as it shall no dout prove best to him and his, so shall it not be the lest honor, strength and benefit that may come unto yourself, to possess the assured love of so many gentlemen of worth, welth and wisdome, as by him self, his frends and kinsfolke shall so be had unto you. And thus, my Lord, wishing all honor, hapines and contentacions unto you, I end.' From the Court.

Holograph Endorsed: '3 November, 1592. A private letter from my Lord Buckhurst to my Lord, moving a compromyse betwixt my Lord and Sir Tho. Stanhope.' 2½ pp. (Original Letters II/127)

LORD HOWARD OF EFFINGHAM TO THE EARL OF SHREWSBURY

(1592) November 5. Very great means were used to me and to your good friend Mr Vice-Chamberlain to join with my Lord Buckhurst in a letter to you and in another to Sir Thomas Stanhope, which we have done. The reason we did it was this — the means made by his best friends and also by some others of no small account who protested that none loved you more than they or grieved more of the unkindness that has been.

I protest before the Lord as I would have of my soul to God and my honour in this world that I shall have a deep care of your estate and honour: but when I see that you are ever ready to be called to that place that many of your ancestors possessed, I should be loth that any cause should stay it, and albeit that her Majesty, as I know, has that due respect of you as one of your place and calling, yet you know that in all times and in all princes' reigns they who have had their kin and friends near unto the prince have always found favour of the prince for them. I see that to any who well or much they are favoured by her Majesty, yet it is not hard for another that 'frendethe' not them, though they be much meaner, yet they are able to hinder any good fortune unto them.

Now in these two letters to you and Sir Thomas we have had due respect to you and have written plainly to him; and nothing we have done can give you cause of mislike. If you will write to me in private as well as an answer to our joint letter, I will do for you what is in my power. What would our adversaries have put in her Majesty's ears if we, your poor friends here, had refused the means we took? That we were rather nourishers of the unkindness than qualifiers. Assure yourself that there is no one in the world that I love and honour more than your Lordship. At the Court.

Holograph Endorsed: '5 November, 1592. A private letter from my Lord Admiral to my Lord for a compromise with Sir T. Stanhope.' 2 pp. (Original Letters II/129)

1592, November 10.   With regard to the Derby affair, I wrote to the Privy Council that I might be directly charged with it.   I have had no answer from their Lordships, but am now informed that Mr Michael Stanhope has shown them a letter from one Walton of Derby, the Archdeacon, to Sir Thomas Stanhope touching the matter.   Mr Michael Stanhope says he has returned this letter to his brother, and although he was commanded to send for it again, I verily think it will not be brought, nor that the matter therein can be justified.   I am told it is false and untrue, and if duly examined will discover the malicious practices of Sir Thomas Stanhope and the lewdness of Walton, whom I am well able to prove to be no other than a very hypocrite and bad man, being beneficed by Sir Thomas and a very ready and fit instrument for him.   I am greatly grieved to see my adversary have this scope and be suffered to charge me with what he list to invent: yea and so, as some times it comes to her Majesty's ears, yet I am not allowed to answer it.   I am not conscious of having overshot myself in all my disputes with the gentleman.   I beseech you to listen to my answer from this bearer, who has full instructions.   I refer my wrongs to your consideration.   In view of my quarrels with Sir Thomas, I beg that an impartial sheriff may be appointed this year for Nottinghamshire. The bearer will tell you who are those whom I except.   Sheffield Lodge.

Holograph   Endorsed: '10 Nov. 1592. Earl of Shrewsbury to my Lord by Mr P. Every.' 2 pp. (Original Letters II/131)

THE EARL OF SHREWSBURY TO LORDS HOWARD AND BUCKHURST AND TO SIR THOMAS HENEAGE

1592, November 12.   I received yesterday by the bearer William Hanlett your joint letter of November 3, and should have been greatly perplexed at it had it not been for your long continued favours and kindness towards me. Thus I am persuaded that these letters have been wrought from your Lordships by the importunity of some who are either altogether partial to the adverse party, or ignorant in the causes, rather than that they proceed of your voluntary desires, as thinking this agreement betwixt me and my adversary thus to be made were either agreeable to equity, in respect of the causes in question, or did other than impugn my credit in respect of the extreme wrongs which I have hitherto sustained.   I am quite sensible of the mischiefs which this contention may bring to me, of the place Sir Thomas Stanhope's friends hold at Court, and of the great ease, quiet and safety which the compounding and ordering of it would mean to me.   But I cannot see how to commit to any compromise such reproachful, malicious and dangerous speeches and courses as he has uttered and practised against me.   So that unless some public course is taken for repair of my honour and credit, I think my reputation can never be repaired.   As to the weir, he tried to make her Majesty and their Lordships think I oppose him out of malice.   I assure you, my wish is only to relieve a multitude of poor creatures which the weir undoes. Why then should I fear the ill-will either in Court or country (of which you put me in mind) either of himself or his friends and followers?   I only desire due trial and course of law usual in such matters; when neither favour at Court nor practice in country will avail them.   As to the speeches, I cannot bring such foul disgraces to myself: I prefer an open foil to a smothered dishonour.   I pray you therefore not to think me wilfully transported in these matters.   I should hate myself ever after if I did not follow an open and plain course.   I implore you to further the due and orderly course of law that the world may still hold you patrons of justice.   Sheffield Lodge.

PS. My delay in answering is due to the fact that I only got your letter of the 3rd on the 11th. Beside, the messenger told me he left his horse lame at Stamford, and was returning by Sir Thomas Stanhope's, so for more speedy conveyance I sent the answer by my own servant.

Copy Endorsed: 'The copy of my answer to the Ld. Admiral, Ld. Buckhurst and Mr Vicechamberlain touching a compromise with Sir T. Stanhope.' 2½ pp.   (Original Letters II/133)

(THE EARL OF SHREWSBURY) TO (LORD BUCKHURST)

1592, November 13.   I have received your private letter to me besides the joint letter, which I have answered, giving my reasons for not compromising with Sir Thomas Stanhope. I have thoroughly thought out all the reasons and advantages which you mention. I know by experience how matters are handled at Court and the credit the gentleman's brothers have with her Majesty. But I repeat my only desire is, first, that I may be charged with the offences informed against me by Sir Thomas and his adherents, as the Archdeacon of Derby (a very bad fellow); and, secondly, that the Commissioners of Sewers will enquire about the weir, that being the ordinary course for trial and redress of all such disorders and abuses within this realm. As to the speeches, I only ask for ordinary law and justice. You say that in a war of this sort, it is thought agreeable to justice that the weaker party be not put down. I do not deny this, but my case is that my inferior grievously misuses me. Can I have no remedy?   Sheffield.

Copy Endorsed: '13 November, 1592. The copy of my private letter and answer to the Lord of Buckhurst touching a compromise with Sir Thomas Stanhope.' 2 pp.   (Original Letters II/135)

(THE EARL OF SHREWSBURY) TO LORD HOWARD OF EFFINGHAM

1592, November 13.   I acknowledge your private letter and the joint letter. As to my answer to the latter, I hope Lord Buckhurst may not mislike it. I am in no manner of doubt of your Lordship and Mr Vice-Chamberlain. I cannot have Sir Thomas Stanhope's misusing of me smothered or shuffled up. (The Earl here recapitulates his wishes as to the weir and other matters as in his letter to Lord Buckhurst.) Sheffield.

Copy Endorsed: '13 November, 1592. The copy of my private letter to the Lord Admiral.' 2 pp.   (Original Letters II/137)

(THE EARL OF SHREWSBURY) TO (SIR THOMAS HENEAGE)

1592, November 13.   I received your private letter with the joint letter. I fully concur with your grave and most friendly opinion, but my course is so clear that I need fear no cunning practices on my adversary's part. If I am not extremely blinded in my own cause, my desires are most reasonable. I only wish for justice in respect of the weir and the speeches. My kinsman, Mr John Talbot, told me (as it seems you told him) about the letters to which your hand was required, but refused; a part most well becoming yourself, in your wisdom. It seems strange that those others, who were not at the other former direction, should join in a letter to countermand the same, merely on a motion of an agreement between me and my adversary. I have written to ask for their reasons. I lately wrote to you, by Mr Evers, to ask you to move her Majesty for an 'indifferent' sheriff for Nottinghamshire.   Sheffield.

PS. My wife sends her friendly commendation with hearty wish of better health to my Lady Heneage than the last time you wrote of her to me.

Copy Endorsed: '13 Nov. 1592. The copy of my private letter to Mr Vicechamberlain.' 1½ pp. (Original Letters II/139)

LORD BUCKHURST TO THE EARL OF SHREWSBURY

1592, November 22. 'Right sorofull I am, my very good Lord, that my second desier to have conjoined with other in the compounding of those differences betwixt your Lordship and Sir Tho: Stannop have taken no better succes: yet might I yeld to those wise and waighty reasons which your Lordship both in your general and particular letters hath remembred to withhold you from the same, being assured that your Lordship doth better know your own case than me self, and therefore in your wisdome can best advise your self. I must confes I do much honor and love your Lordship, and for divers respects am so tied to the house of Sir Thomas Stannop as I can not but love and wishe wel unto the same. But in this case, being not able to do good to both I am resolved to do hurt to neither, though it were in my power: and to abandon all medling on either side except it be to do good offices to either. And thus, my good Lord, remaining nevertheles as much your Lordships as in all true love and affection I can unfainedly trew, I end.' From the Court.

Holograph Endorsed: '22 November, 1592. Ld Buckhursts letter leving to deale betwyxt me and Sir Thomas Stanhop.' 1 p. (Original Letters II/141)

SIR THOMAS HENEAGE TO THE EARL OF SHREWSBURY

1592, November 27. 'My honorable good Lord. Having been over much occupied in busynes commanded me, I have had lytle leasure to answere your Lordships sondry letters, which wold well have contented me. And now by the absence of my Lord Chamberlayne, not freed from many thinges that cumbre me, I must crave your Lordships pardon, thoe I wryte not so largely as otherwyse I might to your Lordships better satysfactyon; and the rather because as I have doone, so I meane to do, in delyvering myne opynion and knowledge of thinges that concerne you, to Mr Evers to whome your Lordship by your letter have requyred me to gyve credyt.

Toching thinges that be past. As I joyned with my Lorde Admirall and my Lord of Buckehurst in myne opinyon, that yt was best for your Lordship to end your differences with Sir Thomas Stanhope by the mediatyon of your frendes that love you and regard your honor; so, tho I cannot be of other opinion by lookyng unto the nature of this place and how this matter hath been caried and still ys wrought; yet knowing how much (you that be great) tender your honor, and beleeving that every wise man understandeth and judgeth best of his own case, I forbeare to perswade you from that which best pleaseth you, and will remaine *usque ad aras* a fast and trewe frend to your Lordship in what course soever you like best to hold, ether in this or anything that shall concerne your Lordship; which mind made me to refuse to sette my hand to a letter which my Lord Admyrall and my Lord of Buckhurst wold have wrytten to my Lord Keeper to have staed the Commyssyon of Sewers. And upon hearing my poore reasons for refusal therof, they both thought yt very inconvenient to wryte. So having now nether leasure nor likying to wryte to your Lordship that I wold be glad to telle you, I rest ready with all good will to serve you and my Lady no lesse than your Lordship, commendyng me humbly to you both.' At the Court.

Signed 1p. (Original Letters II/143)

114

1592, November 29. I have asked the bearer, my brother-in-law Sir Charles Cavendish, to tell you how deeply my credit is touched by the lewd speeches of my adversaries. Sir Thomas vaunts that he has answered my charges. The matter of the weir interests multitudes of people and not me (save in a fishing or two), but my adversary has so intermixed the great cause with our private quarrel as to make them to appear one. Under which colour the Commission (of Sewers) is stayed, and the people in these parts begin now to conceive and utter that the weakness of my credit in Court is the cause of the continuance of their exceeding hurt in the country, for never before was the lawful course for redress in such cases stopped. I enclose therefore a few lines which I ask you to deliver to her Majesty, in the name of the long friendship your Lordship has shown me. Long before my father died you were the chief means to withdraw the suspicions which were conceived of me by the Highest, and were afterwards the honourable mediator to reduce me to my father's good favour when I wanted it. I cannot forget your kindness in the matter of my debts; or your grave and friendly advice at my coming to Court both these last times. You have been my best friend in my causes since, as that of Sir George Savyle, my brother-in-law. All my friends at Court together have not done a tenth part of what you have done for me; all which I say not to flatter or curry favour with you.

And now, being thus far waded into these particularities, I cannot forbear (though more plainly than wisely) to let your Lordship know that I am much grieved to hear (as I do by many) that one of your Lordship's (who I never wronged to my knowledge in my life) should in these present matters (wherein my credit is so deeply touched) join with my adversaries to displeasure me, but as he doth (if it be true which I both generally and particularly hear) work against me without any desert on my part against him, I beseech you to bear with my folly in opining thus much to you, as I crave the continuance of your former favours and wonted love towards me. Sheffield Lodge.

Holograph Endorsed in Burghley's hand: '29 November, 1592. Erle of Shrewsbury.' 3 pp. (Original Letters II/145)

(Folio 499 on p.175 of *Calendar of Talbot Papers in the College of Arms* is a copy of this letter.)

LORD HOWARD OF EFFINGHAM TO THE EARL OF SHREWSBURY

(1592) December 6. I waited to answer your Lordship's letter till I could have opportunity to speak with her Majesty, which I did. I assure you that she has a gracious and princely respect to you, showing great love and affection. Yet must it not be known that I have dealt so privately in this case, but as a public man in my place, and so leave it to your wisdom.

Since your last letters Sir Thomas Stanhope has written to the Board that a servant of yours has been at Derby, Nottingham, Gainsborough and other places, asking them to appoint him to solicit their cause here before the Commission of Sewers. The Board wishes you to suffer them bring their own cause, as also the unkindness between you and Sir Thomas Stanhope, to follow it themselves and not by your servants. You have sent a most wise and discreet gentleman, Mr Evers, to deal in your cause. I took a copy of some of his writings about Sir Thomas Stanhope's speeches, which I will use if I can to recover your favour (with the Queen).

Of our news here, the Duke of Parma is dead in this manner. Being at Arras he went to Avylay, three miles thence, hunting, though he had long been sick and weak. After hunting he came to dinner in the village and ate reasonably well. Presently after dinner, even as he rose, he fell down dead, without even speaking a word. The river of Antwerp is shut up; this is confirmed in three several ways and is no doubt true. There came two months past to Brussels from the King of Spain the Count of Foyntes, the best soldier the King has of a Spaniard; he should have gone with the army into France because the Duke was so weak. This Count has been this long (while) at Brussels, and yet did never send nor write unto the Duke, which is thought very strange.

The death of this Duke is like, in my opinion, to breed some alteration in those parts, and I believe will be a cause of a long stay of the army to go into France, which will serve the French King's purpose well, for at this time he was not well provided to encounter a great army.

There are also letters come from Barton from Constantinople that upon the solicitation of the French King the Turk makes this year a great army to trouble the King of Spain. He has not only banished him that came from the King of Spain, joined with one that came from the League out of his dominions, but hearing that they were gone to Ragusa, sent to them charging them not to suffer them to tarry there; so as no Basha dare speak unto the Turk in their behalf. This will trouble the King of Spain much and make him end his ambitious wars in Christendom and seek to keep his own.

By letters out of Spain we find that all people generally are in miserable want, and the King himself driven to ask of his people, the which was never asked of a King, which was of every 'henykey' (a bushel and a half) of wheat or other corn that came to the mill to be ground, a Spanish royal, which would have mounted to five or six millions. This he would have had during the wars, but it was flatly denied him. As I have news you shall ever be acquainted with it if it be worth the writing.

Holograph Endorsed: '7 December, 1592. From the Lord Admiral.' 3 pp. (Original Letters II/147)

LORD BURGHLEY TO THE EARL OF SHREWSBURY

1592-93, January 27. 'My vearie good Lord. It maie seeme straunge unto you if yowe have trewelie herd of my dangerous late sicknes, in which I have not been hable of a good time to write or to endite longe letters from myself, being not yet recovered, that I shoulde entermeddell to write to your Lordship at this present nothing pertinently to me but in respect of affection and good will unto yowe. But yet by the common report both in Court and Citie, it is said that your Lordship meaneth to be at Nottingham on Mondaie next with sum great extraordinarie companies to urge the countie to make choise of Sir Charles Cavendishe your brother-in-law, though noe possessioner within the countie, and of Mr Pierpoint, a gentleman not well reported for religion, to be knights of the shire for this parlement: whereas if the countie might have theire free libertie, theire are sondrie others fitt for the place against whome noe exception might be had. But nowe, seeinge the time is so short, and to move yowe to alter your determination, I think not reasonable, I onlie wishe that your Lordship would have vearie good regard that if anie contention should thence arise betwixt the gentlemen and freeholders of the countie, your Lordship would use your honorable wisedome and accustomed temperance to staie all quarrells that maie be dangerous to the breache of peace: or slanderous to anie partiall proceeding in the election hereof. And for this purpose also I am sumwhat the rather moved for that I heare of quarrelous brabbles betweene Mr Holles and Jarvis Markham, the one being sonne-in-lawe to Sir Thomas Stanhope, and the other a dependant upon your Lordship, which would be ended either by composition or both parties bound to the peace untill a convenient time of examination of the cawse. And thus praieing your Lordship to interpret my meaning according to the good will and love I beare you, I take my leave.' From my house in Westminster.

PS. 'Your Lordship answers at your commandment, but not to wrastel at this tyme. I will thank your Lordship for your gret New Yeres gift.'

Signed, with holograph postscript Addressed: To the Earl as Lord Lieutenant of Derbyshire. *Endorsed*: '27 January, 1592. My Lord Tresurer to my Lord touching a report of my coming to Nottingham with extraordinary companyes.' 1 p. (Original Letters II/151)

THE EARL OF SHREWSBURY TO LORD BURGHLEY

1592-93, January 30. Yesterday as I was on horseback coming out of Nottingham from the election of the knights for the shire, the post-boy of Newark brought me your letter of the 27th, whereby I find your care and good affection to me to be continued. I will deliver you all my proceedings in that matter, to stop false rumours. On Sunday night last, the day before the County Court, I came to Nottingham attended by my own servants, under 80; but the High Sheriff and most of the Justices of the Peace, hearing of my coming, did indeed meet and accompany me to the town. By the way I was told by many of my friends that Sir Thomas Stanhope had gathered thither all his servants and very many of his tenants, who were to be in readiness with extraordinary weapons, whereupon was supposed that some great breach of the peace would be offered. Wherefore I was no sooner alighted but I required the Sheriff and all the Justices that they would all have especial care for the preservation thereof. And in like manner I sent two to the Mayor requiring him to do the like, by having a good guard of his townsmen well furnished to suppress any disorder that might be offered. The next morning was delivered to the Sheriff a letter from three or four of the Privy Council taking knowledge of a quarrel between Mr John Hollis and Mr Jarvis Markham, charging him and all those Justices of the Peace there present to see her Majesty's peace duly observed. Howbeit we had all taken such order in that behalf the night before as we could add nothing thereto upon view of that commandment. The freeholders were very many, which moved the Sheriff, upon good advice given by two or three very sufficient councillors at the law there present, as Mr Cardinall, a Justice of the Peace there and one of her Majesty's Council at York with two others, to adjourn the County Court from the Shire Hall within the town to her Majesty's castle, for that the said hall would not have contained the fifth man who had a voice in that election. So in the Castle Court the election was made (at the time limited by the Statute) of Sir Charles Cavendish and Mr Philip Strelley, with one voice of all, without contradiction of any one man. At the same time, as I heard, Sir Thomas Stanhope and Mr Thomas Markham, with none but their sons and servants (unless they procured the two coroners to stay with them) sat in the Shire Hall, but we after our election and dinner done departed the same night in as quiet and peaceable manner as could be imagined. Now, my Lord, for Sir Charles Cavendish, who as you write is thought to be no possessioner in that county, he has two lordships there called Kirkby and Hardwick well worth £400 a year, besides some freehold lands of his own purchase, and then at Kirkby he is both assessed for the subsidy and has kept servants and family a long time. For Mr Strelley, son and heir to Sir Anthony Strelley, I think no just exception can be taken against him. As for my brother-in-law, Mr Peirpoint, though I am sure there is no cause why he should be suspected for religion now, howsoever heretofore, yet neither he nor I had ever meaning that he should stand for one in this election. Whereby you may well perceive how ready my adversaries are to spread out any falsehoods or untruths whatsoever if they think the same may any way serve their turns. You refer to some 'quarrelous brabbles' between Mr John Hollis and Mr Jarvis Markham, wishing it to be ended either by composition or the parties bound to the peace until some convenient time for the examination of the cause. The one is impossible, so exceeding fierce has the matter already proceeded to: but the other is very necessary to prevent the great mischief that is otherwise likely to ensue. For myself, I having only the common authority of a justice of the peace there and one of them being my professed foe, I am of all others most unmeet to deal therein. Howbeit, if your Lordship, continuing the great care you have always for the preservation of the peace, shall think good to lay upon them either your own commandment or any other joined with you, I think it very necessary and the rather in respect of a great meeting upon a match of hunting appointed to be at Newark on Monday next the 5th of February, where it is given out that both those gentlemen will be, and great parts is supposed will be taken on both sides. And therefore it will much better effect your Lordship's intention therein if such commandment came unto them by that time. The report of your great sickness has been exceeding rife in these parts, and much more than I hope it was, but I have been always able to satisfy all such as have spoken with me thereof, for I have received from my servant in London weekly advertisement of your state of body, he being charged to enquire every second or third day at your house.   Worksop.

Copy Endorsed: '30 January, 1592. A copy of the answer to the Lord Treasurers letter touching the knights of the parliament and the quarrel between Jarvis Markham and John Hollis.' 2 pp.   (Original Letters II/153)

NOTES OF CORRESPONDENCE BETWEEN SIR CHARLES CAVENDISH AND JOHN STANHOPE
1592-93, February 7 to March 16.

7 February, 1592-93. Sir Charles Cavendish challenges in writing John Stanhope upon the villainy at Newark to supply his father's inability to maintain by sword the detestable act.

8 February. Sir Charles reiterates his former challenge, and hastens his acceptance upon Stanhope's excuse by word of infirmity in his leg, and upon his promise to answer the challenge, his leg once being recovered.

8 February. John Stanhope's refusal of the challenge as not knowing what to maintain, and promising that he and another gentleman would accept any challenge sent from any that had quarrel with his father, whom Sir Charles would second.

10 February. The lie given by Sir Charles to John Stanhope upon words in his letter justifying his father's life, in which letter he had refused Sir Charles's challenge.

14 February. The prohibition of the Lords that Sir Charles should prosecute his quarrel with John Stanhope no further by himself, his servants or his friends.

14 February.   John Stanhope's acceptance of the former challenge, with promise to send further about the same at his best opportunity and after the parliament.

26 February.   Sir Charles's promise to make a reasonable answer when John Stanhope should proceed in his acceptance of the challenge, withal remembering him that his letter of acceptance bears the same date as the Lords' letter and yet was delivered 9 days after, which causes suspicion that he would abuse their Lordships with an ante date.

16 March.   John Stanhope's acknowledgment that he never refused Sir Charles's challenge, but had always accepted it by word to Sir Charles's man that carried the first challenge and by all letters since, and that he was now come up to London for that only purpose.

Note, in another hand: 'All these above were in writing sent from one to the other.'   1 p.   (Original Letters II/158)

THE COUNTESS OF SHREWSBURY

1592-93, February 10.   'The message sent by the Countesse of Shrewsbury, wife of the now Earle of Shrewsbury, unto Sir Thomas Stanhope, knight, by Humphrey Chedell, the 10th of February, 1592, and by him delivered to the said Sir Thomas Stanhop.'

Tell Sir Thomas Stanhope from me that he is a reprobate and his son John a rascal, and that the child that is yet to be got shall rue it.

The message sent from the said Countess to the said Sir Thomas Stanhope to his house by one Williamson and George Holt, two of her servants and delivered by Williamson.

My Lady hath commanded me to say thus much to you, that though you be more wretched, vile or miserable than any creature living, and for your wickedness become more ugly in shape than the vilest toad in the world and one to whom none of reputation would vouchsafe to send any message; yet she hath thought good to send thus much unto you that she can be contented you should live and doth no way wish your death, but to this end: that all the plagues and miseries that may befall any, may light upon such a caitiff as you are, and she doubteth not but the same will light upon you and that you shall live to have all your friends forsake you, and without your great repentance (which she looketh not for because your life hath been so bad) you will be damned perpetually in hell fire.

With many other opprobrious and hateful words, which we could not remember because he would deliver it but once (as he said he was commanded), but said that if he had failed in anything it was in speaking it more mildly and not in terms of such disdain as he was commanded.

Attested by: Edward Stanhope, John Stanhope, George Lacock, Thomas Gilbert, Henry Dodding, Richard Cowoppe, John Hollywell, Lawrence Southorpe and Roger Holme.

A note (by the Earl of Shrewsbury's secretary) to the effect that this copy was sent by Sir Thomas Stanhope to the Earl with a letter of heinous complaint, but the truth of these messages is otherwise in divers points, yet the most thereof of true in substance.

Endorsed: 'A note of two messages sent by the young Countess of Shrewsbury to Sir Thomas Stanhope, knight, 1592.'   1 p.   (Original Letters II/149)

(*Part of this message printed from another copy in* Lodge's *Illustrations of British History,* Vol.I, pp.xviii and xix.)

MR HENRY NOWELL'S REPORT OF THE PROCEEDINGS OF SIR
CHARLES CAVENDISH AND MR JOHN STANHOPE

(1592-93, March).   About three or four of the clock 16 March came Mr
John Townesend to Sir Charles Cavendish in the Earl of Shrewsbury's house
with this message, viz: 'My cousin John Stanhope has sent me to you to tell
you that he accepts your challenge, and that if you be willing to perform them
he appoints the time to be tomorrow morning at seven o'clock, the place of
meeting to be Lambeth Bridge, with single rapiers only, and after search
made there, to ride from thence to what place you both should best like; that
other weapons should be brought by Mr John Stanhope as he shall think good,
which he will take what you do leave; and that either of you should be accompanied only with a gentleman to search you indifferently, or with a servant to accompany you forward and to hold your horses.' Sir Charles wished
that they might fight in their waistcoats without doublets, which was agreed
upon by Mr Townesend's consent, but Sir Charles refused to have his weapons
brought into the field by his adversary: but if Mr John Stanhope would appoint the weapons and their length, Sir Charles would come appointed accordingly, and instead of servants if Mr Stanhope would bring a gentleman he
would bring his cousin Jarvis Markham. Mr Townesend answered that he had
commission (if Mr Jarvis Markham were named) to name his cousin Hollis on
the other party, whom he would undertake to bring. Upon this point Mr
Henry Leake was sent with Mr Townesend to bring back answers, there
arising some difference about Sir Charles's speech between Mr Townesend
and Mr Henry Leake. At their coming to Mr John Stanhope, Mr Townesend
returned again to Sir Charles to be resolved of his meaning, wherein he
satisfied him, desiring that the time might be altered to five o'clock in the afternoon. But if Mr Stanhope would not consent thereto, Sir Charles would
perform the first time. It then chanced that Mr Henry Nowell was with Sir
Charles at this last coming of Mr Townesend, whom Sir Charles desired to go
with Mr Townesend to conclude finally, which he did.

Upon Friday at Mr Nowell's first coming to Sir Charles, Mr Townesend
came to Sir Charles and said that he had authority from Mr Stanhope to
nominate a gentleman to accompany them to the field, if Sir Charles named
any one. Sir Charles named Mr Jarvis Markham. Mr Townesend named Mr
Hollis. Mr Nowell went with Mr Townesend to Mr John Stanhope to certify
him of the gentleman before named to accompany them to the field, who
nevertheless that he had authorized Mr Townesend to nominate Mr Hollis
(which Mr Townesend ayed) denied to have Mr Hollis with him for causes to
him known.

It was further committed to Mr Nowell by Sir Charles that he should offer
(if required) their single adventures to the field, which Mr Stanhope rather
accepted than to take Mr Hollis with him; which determination Mr Nowell
repeated to Mr Stanhope and Mr Townesend, the full agreement whereof Mr
Nowell was to return to Sir Charles.

Mr Stanhope, having appointed Saturday morning at seven o'clock, to
come to the place of search, it was desired by Sir Charles it might be five
o'clock in the afternoon; whereto Mr Stanhope answered that though a
challenger should be always ready, yet he agreed to the motion. After the
full circumstance of bringing them to the sword was agreed upon, which way,

namely to fight at the single rapier, length of weapon, search at Lambeth by Mr Townesend and Mr Nowell, then to ride alone or to go by water, the resolution whereof was referred to their coming to Lambeth. This was that passed on Friday.

Upon Saturday morning Mr Townesend came to Mr Nowell and told him that Mr Stanhope was afraid that they had mistaken him in that point of going into the field alone, wherein he was deceived as Mr Townesend did then and can witness with Mr Nowell. Mr Nowell wished Mr Townesend to go to Mr Stanhope and to remember him that it was otherwise agreed of; whereunto he answered that if he named not his man yet he intended it, which being related to Sir Charles Cavendish, nevertheless the two precedent offers being revoked, Sir Charles accepted it.

Mr. Townesend wrote to Mr Nowell that Mr Stanhope would not have their men to fight but to be beholders, except Sir Charles would; whereunto Sir Charles granted upon this condition, that they should stand afar off, otherwise his man should fight.

At five of the clock Sir Charles came to Lambeth Bridge with his servant, whom Mr Nowell desired to hover upon the water until the coming of Mr Stanhope and the rest: who being come, Mr Townesend and Mr Nowell went to demand of Mr Stanhope whether he would go by water or land, who would not resolve till there had been search of either: whereupon Mr Nowell desired that Mr Stanhope would go into a house which he did, where, searching Mr Stanhope's doublet he found it of great thickness and so hard quilted as Mr Nowell could hardly thrust a knife through it. Whereupon Mr Nowell told him the doublet was strange 'and though you are not armed, yet the doublet is not to be fought in', and thereupon desired Mr Townesend to feel it, who affirmed the same. Mr Nowell and Mr Townesend having certified this to Sir Charles, Sir Charles offered to fight in his shirt, but Mr Stanhope refused it, saying he had taken cold; which speech Mr Nowell delivered to Sir Charles who answered Mr Nowell and Mr Townesend that he was come to fight and would offer condition according: whereupon he sent word to them that he would lend Mr Stanhope his waistcoat to keep him warm and fight himself in his shirt, which being by them certified Mr Stanhope refused. This being told Sir Charles, he referred himself to Mr Nowell and Mr Townesend, that notwithstanding, if they thought it fit, he would nevertheless fight. Whereupon Mr Townesend and Mr Nowell replied they thought it unfit and very unequal, after which Sir Charles staying till Mr Stanhope's boat was past, returned to London.

Endorsed: 'The report of Mr Henry Nowell of the proceedings of Sir Charles Cavendish and Mr John Stanhope.' $1\frac{1}{2}$ pp. (Original Letters II/159)

JOHN STANHOPE TO THE PRIVY COUNCIL

1593, April 6. Asks for permission to return to the country on business connected with his estate. Sends some notes on the recent affray in Fleet Street, the desperate state of his servant, and asks that the assailants may be apprehended. Warns their Lordships of the manifold intentions and murderous threats of his adversaries.

Signed Endorsed: '6 Apr. 1593. John Stanhopes letter to the Privy Council.' $\frac{1}{2}$ p. (Original Letters II/155)

(1593, April 9)   May it please your Lordships to peruse these notes about the affray made upon Mr Stanhope and his men in Fleet Street on Wednesday, the 27th of March, by the Earl of Shrewsbury's followers, and also the particulars about the shameful wounding of his man who at this present, having 4 or 5 mortal wounds, lies in great danger of his death.

(1)   It will be proved that on the Wednesday morning aforesaid, one Henry Leake, gentleman, with a troop of the Earl of Shrewsbury's and Sir Charles Cavendish's men went up and down Cheapside seeking and enquiring for Mr Stanhope, and understanding he was gone from thence, they forthwith went up Fleet Street to 'forlay' his way.

(2)   It will be proved that sixteen of this company having swords, daggers and gauntlets, and seven or eight of them bucklers, entered the tavern in Fleet Street called the *Three Tuns,* and called for a room to drink in, but would have none but one next the street, where Henry Leake principally appointed in every corner of the window one to watch, and when Mr Stanhope came they cried: 'Yonder comes Stanhope, to it, to it', and so rushed all down the stairs with swords prepared upon him.

(3)   Then it will be proved that Henry Leake, whom Mr Stanhope's testimony describes as a tall black man in a long black cloak and after fetched away by the guard, was the most forward and that he said, seeing Mr Stanhope come: 'Yonder he comes, I will make him dance Trenchmore.'

(4)   Item, it will be proved that Godfrey Markham was one of the 'forlayers' of this match, and that he passed twice or thrice by Mr John Stanhope as he was coming down, and that when the fray was he could not come out because his nose bled.

(5)   Item, concerning the affray and filthy murder offered to his servant, James Jaques, this will be proved, that Mr Stanhope's weapons and his men's being undrawn, the whole company pressed upon them, being but five, and that his said servant, being villainously struck down by a prentice and assaulted before and behind, one Swinerton, Mr Henry Cavendish's man, struck at him, being down so eagerly that he broke his sword upon him, and one other of Mr Henry Cavendish's men, who it is said attends him in his chamber, did stab the said Jaques as he proffered to rise up again.

(6)   Item, the said Jaques himself says that he heard the aforesaid Swinerton say: 'Kill him, kill him', and that six or seven struck and thrust most furiously at him amongst whom Bastard Leake was most forward. The said Jaques is a man of seventy-four years of age, and at this present in more expectation of death than of life.

(7)   Item, to prove that this was wilful and fore-intended murder, if it please God this hurt man die, it will be avowed that some of the assailants said they had rather make sure work of the old man than of any two of the other men.

(8)   Item, it will be proved that one in a greenish wash-coloured doublet and hose struck at Jaques three times very eagerly when he was down, which man is known though not his name.

(9)   Item, it will be proved that one Gill, a fishmonger dwelling at Broken Wharf came to the *Three Tuns* and there drank a pint of sack with one Bery, the good man's brother of the house, enquiring of him whether the old man was dead or no, saying that one of them who did wound him was his near friend, and forthwith he sent the said Bery to the barber in Chancery Lane who had first dressed him, to enquire what news.

The names of the witnesses will be sent at your Lordships' request, and Mr Stanhope will inform you of his adversaries' threats and how his life is in danger.

In primis, it will be proved that Henry Leake aforesaid, walking in Paul's on Tuesday afternoon the 27th of March, told many gentlemen whom he met there that there he looked for Mr Stanhope, and that he should never be quiet till he had imbrued his dagger, with many other braving, vainglorious and threatening speeches, which are let pass because he himself is not a man to be feared but in regard of a greater person.

Item, it will be proved by a dweller in Fleet Street that two men standing by the shop (whom he thinks to belong to the Earl of Shrewsbury) had these speeches one with the other: 'that this matter would never be ended without the death of Sir Thomas Stanhope or his son.'

Item, it will be proved by a householder and his wife in Fleet Street that Godfrey Markham and five or six of Sir Charles Cavendish's men were at his house on Wednesday aforesaid (after the affray made upon Mr Stanhope), who said that the quarrel would never be ended till Sir Thomas Stanhope or his son were slain.

Item, it will be proved that the same men said moreover that if they had met with Mr Stanhope beneath the Conduit, that the Earl of Shrewsbury's part would have had more friends, which shows how well they had laboured the streets; and further they said they would not attempt him more in the streets, but they would take him in the field or elsewhere.

Item, the said Markham said to a gentleman of good worth that Mr Stanhope had abused the Earl of Shrewsbury, and therefore he would be revenged on him. This childish threat Mr Stanhope reckons not of, but he sets it down to your Lordships with reference to the party Markham follows.

Item, the said Markham bravingly said to one of the guard that if he had killed John Stanhope he would not care if he were hanged the day after.

Item, it will be proved that one of Sir Charles Cavendish's men answered a friend of his, who had speech with him about the beastly wounding of James Jaques, that now the matter was but in beginning. The other replied: 'Nay, but the Council will set better order', to which Sir Charles Cavendish's man answered, 'that neither the Council could do it, nor all England.'

Item, it will be proved that a gentleman (who said he loved the Earl of Shrewsbury well) meeting James Jaques and another man of Horsley, to whom the gentleman was well known, told them that the Earl would pull down Sir Thomas Stanhope's house and his sons' over their heads and murder them and all their followers, and not leave one of the Stanhopes alive, and that when he came back again he would raise all the power he had and make an insurrection, but he would do it. 'If he do so,' said Jaques, 'he were best beware his head, for the Queen is above my Lord.' 'Tush', said the gentleman, 'he cares much for that; he will do it, let them all say what they will.'

Mr Stanhope has other good proofs how the Earl's men dog some of his father's men in the streets, and that every day they lie in wait for him, insomuch as wanting sufficient company to affront their numbers, he is restrained within his lodging, neither can he come forth without great hazard of his life, to present these his humble complaints to your Lordships.

Thus his life is in danger, and every day in respect of his country habitation and the universal greatness of the Earl of Shrewsbury, he shall be liable to the snares of his forepromised destruction. He prays your Lordships to take knowledge of these murderous threats.

The names of such of the principal actors in the fray made upon Mr

Stanhope in Fleet Street as are yet at liberty:

Henry Leake, gentleman; Godfrey Markham, the Earl of Shrewsbury's man; Thomas Swinerton, Mr Henry Cavendish's man; one whose name is supposed to be Colborne, waiting upon Mr Henry Cavendish in his chamber; one that was committed to Newgate and bailed whose name I know not; one other that was bailed by one Alyson in Fleet Street.

Endorsed: '9 Aprilis, 1593. John Stanhopes articles exhibited to the Privy Council.' 3 pp, *with note* 'Exam: per W. Waad.' (Original Letters II/156)

PHILIP STRELLEY TO THE EARL OF SHREWSBURY

1593, May 23. I must acquaint you with some speeches lately uttered to me by one Edmund Richardson, a shoemaker of Nottingham. He says that one John Fulwood, a man of Sir Thomas Stanhope's, came to his house on Saturday, February 10th, and walking in his garden talked of the accidents which had happened at Newark that week. Richardson said to Fulwood: 'John, I pray God that thou be not guilty of this crime in defacing of my Lord Shrewsburys arms', who answered: 'Ned, by my troth I am not, but I suspect some, for that the same night that my master and we came from Newark, early the next morning Robert Pygin (servant to John Stanhope) being my bed-fellow, rising before me in the morning came again unto me into my chamber and said that this night there had been some work somewhere, for that Francis Jakes gelding and John Rooes gelding have been ridden this night by some that they reek again and I pray God that thy horse hath not also been ridden'. Fulwood further said that Lawcock was a subtle and crafty fellow. Richardson will justify these speeches to you if you think them of any moment towards finding out that most detestable villainy committed against your honour. He thinks further that if Fulwood were well examined and assured that Sir Thomas Stanhope should not harm him hereafter, and that he might have your favour, he could and would utter the whole practice, for he is either acquainted with it or else could name the author of the same. Newstead.

Signed Endorsed: One Fullwood's knowledge of two horses that were brought in 'sweetyng' the night the villainy was done at Newark. *Addressed:* To the Earl at his house in Broad Street. 1p. (Original Letters II/161)

THE EARL OF SHREWSBURY TO LORD BURGHLEY

1594, May 7. 'My especiall good Lorde. This morninge in my way homewardes I called at your Lordships house, wher I founde the two swete ladyes, with the other fowre your grandchyldren, in good health, whose innocent prayers for your Lordship will (I hope) kepe you longe to live, to continew your moste honorable and naturall care towardes them. A finer chylde have I not sene then Sir Robert Cecills sonne. I was boulde to wyshe your Lordship amongest them. I beynge boulde also to make a survey of your Lordships house founde few thynges wherwith I was not before acquaynted, savinge the new conduite in the inner courte which is not yet fully finished. Ther is a smale pece of payntynge in one parte therof, the which Sir Charles Cavendish and I doe suppose weare far better to be lefte unpaynted, the stone of it selfe beynge pur whyte marble, which nedes no arte of counterfaytynge. Of this we were boulde to deliver our opinion to Mr Fades, your Lordships servant, and stayinge here at Chesthunt for an hower or two, doe crave pardon in wrytynge therof to your Lordship. As also to inform your Lordship that I understand it is determined by my Lord Keeper for certayne that the complaynte exhibited by Sir Thomas Stanhope agaynste sondry of my servantes and frendes touchynge a supposed riott at the weares at Shelford shall be hard in the Star Chamber on Fryday next, wherupon some of them have made earnest sute to me to become a sutor to your Lordship to be pleased to admytt them your presence ther, if so you may, for they are throughly perswaded your Lordship espetially (althoughe they have no cause to doubte of any of the reste in case of justice) will loke depely into the matter, and accordinge to law and equity will pronounce your sentence therin. Thus your Lordship sees how bouldly I presume upon your Lordship unto whom I rest very affectionate in all trew sincerity. And do pray to the Allmighty longe to preserve you in most perfyte health, to lyve to see more yeres than any of your kyndred.' At your Lordships house at Chesthunte.

Holograph Endorsed: '7 May, 1594. Erle of Shrewsburye to my Lord.' 1 p. (Original Letters II/163)

SIR CHARLES CAVENDISH TO THE EARL OF SHREWSBURY

1594, September 15. I hope to meet you on September 23 at Gilling Castle, on a visit to the lands you have paid for, where I think you will be forced to lie two nights because Mr Francis Metham's house is marvellously little. The nephew Thomas Metham is no less ready in business than the uncle, and I shall give notice to the gentleman. 'I trust he shall one day doe both your Lordship and yours service or else wiekcome dandy will come upon him. My fiddelynge cosen I have some tyme misliked; he is well gone since he cannot be as becometh him.' Lord and Lady Ogle thank my sister for the red deer. My wife sends her humble duty. Bothall Castle.

PS. 'The hawke your Lordship bestowde of me Philipe hath dispatched; she is gone into Southsex accordynge unto the prase. I take it he flew her foule, but Mr Wetherington and others heare say noe, otherwyse Philipe had gon into Suffolk.'

Holograph 1 p. (Original Letters II/165)

JOHN BOVY TO THE EARL OF SHREWSBURY

1596, July 30. It is reported among Sir Thomas Stanhope's friends, in some secret, that he is not like long to live, and at these Assizes his son, Mr John Stanhope, was 'inthronised' in our shire also a Justice of the Peace, and I have heard it secretly given out that this is done to the intent he may enjoy the office of Custos Rotulorum after his father's death, wherefore it shall be fit that your Honour have some care thereof. The office is absolutely in the gift of the Lord Keeper of the Great Seal, albeit sometimes her Majesty may bestow it. After the death of Sir Francis Leek, Sir John Zouche made very earnest and special means unto her Majesty by the Earl of Bedford, deceased, for the office of the Custos Rotulorum in Derbyshire, and had a grant thereof by her Majesty, but Sir Thomas Bromley, then Lord Chancellor, told her Majesty that he had made a former grant of the office belonging to him to bestow of right, and he hoped her Majesty would not impeach his grant. Whereunto her Majesty yielded, and so Mr Manners had the office and still enjoyed the same. If it please my Lord Keeper to bestow the office upon your Honour or at your Honour's denomination, this may be a precedent to his Lordship if any question arise about it. I pray God send your Honour good success in all your honourable affairs, and especially in this your intended voyage, that it may be happily achieved and graciously accepted. Nottingham.

Holograph 1 p.   (Original Letters II/167)

Sir Matthew Arundel to the Earl of Shrewsbury

(1597) May 23.   '*Nimis familiaritas parit contemptum*: that I kno right well, if eny way I be more sawcy then well becometh me, I kno your honorable construction will not altogether lay it to the custom of my cuntry, that as Thomas Marcham was wont to say, 'Westerne men were too forward', but will somewhat regard your owne mayntenance of my former boldnes and partly under the correction of so favorable a judge, I may as truly say as playnly meane, I kno no man that ether will please my poor humor but the Erle of Shrewsbury nor who I wold be so bold withall as with him selff, my consciens warranting my presumtion by the feeling of myne owne hart. Now, Sir, after this long proloug, this is my short tale. I have no one worldly delight that feedes my melancoly moste but the breeding of a horse, and ther was no one horse in England I so wel lyked as your Lordships black Turk (myne own being ded I had of my Lord Treasorer) howbeit his lyttlenes did nothing please me. I was bold to lett you kno by my servant my want of a stallion, the tyme of the yeere being far spent. I think it both a far jorney and very casual to send two mares so far for a covering. So unsure and uncertayn your bowntifull offer of my choice or my mans for covering my mares is no less dutifully and thankfully taken (of me poor sole) thus most honorable offered from your self with the *caveat* you gave of your jenetts broken wynd, of whose triall what a broken-wynded horse wil do I leave to this years proff and wish (as to my self) that your mares may as aptly conceave of him as some of myne have done with my Turk, being broken wynded, albeit I verily think and kno he will deceave many. If this yere he get you colts I know you wilbe pleased; if he get you none, not worth the feeding. I kno he is a fyne horse and right jennett, otherwise you wold never have brought him over. If after this covering tyme be past you will lett me feede him this wynter, that do beleve my feeding of a broken wynded horse, I will hope and therewith greatly delight my selff that the next yeere I shall have some colts of his begetting, and your Lordship have many many yeeres after, and I the meane tyme but your horse keeper, to whome only I could afford a stowping or els to no earthly wight, her Majesty only excepted. *Dixi*. I pray God send you long life, increase of honor, and to your good wife and my speciall good lady I humbly beseech you I may be most humbly commendyd.   Your Honors poore welwiller (though *tremontano*).'   Wardour.

Holograph   Endorsed: '23 Maii, 1597. Sir Matthew Arundells letter for my bay jennett.' 2 pp.   (Original Letters II/169)

The Information of Mr Agard against Mr H Cavendish

(1597, October 22)   A note to say that Mr Agard has informed in the Exchequer against Henry Cavendish and his servants upon the statute of retainers and liveries, and had a verdict and judgment there: that a writ of error was sued in the Exchequer Chamber on the ground that the Exchequer is not mentioned by the statute as a court in which such offenders shall be punished: and that there is no record in that Court of any judgment given there at any time in the like case, though sundry informations have been exhibited.

There follows a note, dated October 24, 1597, in the Earl of Shrewsbury's hand, with reference to the above, beginning: 'My very good Lord (Burghley)', to say that this note was sent him by the counsellors of his brother-in-law Henry Cavendish, and that Agard had procured their verdict before Cavendish ever heard of the suit, and to ask Burghley's favour under these circumstances.

Endorsed: '22 October, 1597. The Erle of Shrewsbury. Touching the information of Mr Agard against Mr H. Cavendish upon the Statute of Retainers.' 1 p. (Original Letters II/171)

Sir Charles Cavendish to (the Earl of Shrewsbury)

1599, June 5. 'In most humble wyse, etc. Havinge nothinge but rusticall stuff, I can only returne humble thankes for your Lordships many letters. My Lord Lumley sawe a fatt bucke wich cam from Sheffylde, admired the greatnes and fatnes as it was well worthy. I offered to half-bake it and to send it after him, which his Lordship accepted, and this bearere or whom your Lordship shall please maye deliver it, and he sayde heare your Lordship and my sister shulde be at the eatynge; this berer had bin soner dispached but the venison was warme, not in case to cary. They did discharge their parts very well, the younger will not serve out of London, I thinke he meneth your Lordships house, soe that I must continew my request to Mr Kydman to healpe me to a good coke, for I have gotten one out of an alehouse from Mansfylde that can dress meat and drinke well. Mr Gervas Mark(ham) and Mr Pipe cam to me of Sonday last about three in the afternoun, stayed supper and retorned to Walinge Welles to beade. My cosen Markham entered into many discourses about Sir Thomas, and toulde me your Lordship had spoken with a man of his, and had sent him worde by the same man that Sir John Hollice had licence to travell, but that it was only to goe freely to the endynge of the difference between them. We handeled many poynts of that matter, but if he understoode me noe better then I did him (as I suppose he did not) ther is noe mistakinge for I conceved nothinge, havinge nothinge delivered but confusednes. I think he meaneth to send by message ore to writt unto him very shortly for he spake determinately both wayes. He spake of Calice, Deap, of Scotlande agaynst my Lord Scropes government, and of that part of Scotlande that lyeth agaynst Sir Rob: Caryes government to be the places that he will tender him, but not resolvedly. I shulde be glad to be no further acquainted with his course and his wayes; if he com I cannot refuse to heare him, but he shall take his owne wayes. Your Lordship last writt after the holydayes makes me both sory and glade of your Lordships doubfulnes to come downe, sory in respect I shall not of long attend you, and glad because I imagin ther is som comfortable lyght cominge towardes you, though it be not yet well decernable.' Welbeck.

Holograph 1½ pp. (Original Letters II/173)

The Privy Council to Sir Charles Cavendish

1599, July 5. The Queen has been informed of the late accident between you and Mr John Stanhope. This is to warn you at your peril against further disorder on the part of yourself, friends or servants. The same direction has been given to your adversary. The High Sheriff has been directed to take bond of you for the keeping of her Majesty's peace. From the Court at Greenwich.

Signed: seven signatures. *Copy Endorsed:* '5 Julii, 1599, Copy of the Lords of the Counsails letter to Sir Charles Cavendish.' (Original Letters II/174)

Sir Charles Cavendish to (The Earl of Shrewsbury)

1599-1600, February 3. 'Since my letter to your Lordship touchinge the levy of mony towards the fore horse this shier is to make and that therin I thought I was freed, now by this inclosed your Lordship may see howe thos two justices have handeled the matter for Mr Shreeve disclaimeth from the burthen, and if the gentlemen think much to be ratede by thos used by your Lordship in Darbyshier, being in all respects as they are, with what more right may the better sort of this shier resin that the meanest shall governe the best, who dispose thinges accordynge to ther privat humors and not with that indiferency as becometh them. I wysh ther weare a good Leaftenant heare as other shiers have, and then I hope we should have as good delinge as our neygbore shiers have.' Welbeck.

Holograph 1 p. (Original Letters II/175)

E. Wingfield to — — — — —

(*? temp* Elizabeth) November 8. Yesterday Mrs Blagrew was buried who truly, God be praised, made a very good end, and at my coming from the church I heard my Lady Arbella was come for her sweet cousin, and when I came to the coach she was to my Lady Arbella, who looked very strangely, which made me much to marvel; and at my coming down the steps I met Mrs Humfreson who sware to me she knew not of my Lady Arbella's being here, and she prayed me to write to you not to be offended with her coming, which she swears was by chance. God reward your Ladyship for the charity you show to my niece Busshe.

Holograph Endorsed: 'To my Lady. E. Wingfield concerning Lady Arbella.' 1 p. (Original Letters II/294)

Lady Arabella Stuart

1603, August 14 to 1608, November 8. A collection of letters, twenty-six in number, from Lady Arabella Stuart to the Earl and Countess of Shrewsbury and others.

(Original Letters II/188-257)

(Printed in E.T. Bradley *Arabella Stuart*, Vol.I, p.232, and Vol.II, pp. 176-222)

The Earl of Pembroke to the Earl of Shrewsbury

(1604) October 3. All the news here is that a great ambassador is coming from the King of Poland, and his chief want is to demand my Lady Arbella in marriage for his master. So may our princess of the blood grow a great Queen, and then we shall be safe from the danger of mis-superscribing letters. Hampton Court.

PS. You must pardon my short writing, for I am half drunk tonight.

Holograph Seal Endorsed: '3 October, 1604. E. of Pembroke.' 1 p. (Original Letters II/224)

Edmund Lassells to the Earl of Shrewsbury

(1605, April 12) The young Princess,* as it is yet determined, shall be christened at Greenwich this day fortnight, which I think is the 26th of April. The Duke of Hulster we hear shall be godfather, and two of our own great

---

* Princess Mary *b* 1605 *d* 1607.

ladies, but which we know not yet. St George's Feast is held at Whitehall because it shall not pester the house at Greenwich before the christening.

Holograph   Seal   Imperfect   Endorsed: '11 Marcii 1605. Mr Lassells.' ½ p.   (Original Letters II/184)

THE CAVENDISH FAMILY

1605-6, February 3 to 1606, June 30.   Letters to the Earl of Shrewsbury from members of the Cavendish family, chiefly on money matters.

(Original Letters II/234, 238 and 240)

SIR CHARLES CAVENDISH TO THE EARL OF SHREWSBURY

1606, May 24.   'Gilbert Dickenson cam hyther of Monday last, the next day he and I arrived at Sheffylde about a 11 supposinge to have founde your bayly ther, by whom I thought first to have bin instructed and after to have determined what course to houlde. He went the day befor to Darby, soe I had nobody to joyne with me, Mr Wingfylde beinge at Nott., Rich. Heete kepinge his chamber but of the mendynge hand as they saye. (*Marginal note:* died yeasterday being the 30 of this moneth). I presently went (befor I allighted) to the house by the bake syde and enteringe the house I found Jhon Bouth at the dore upon the street syde, both dores havinge a garde upon them. I desiered Jhon Bouth to come in, and soe excludynge the unnessesary I declared unto them the cause of my comminge and your Lordships favor to them, together with your Lordships resonable desiers without prejudice or disturbance to any of them, and alsoe my sisters desier of good agrement amoungest them, and the oulde mans request unto hir to settle peace amoungest them if any disagrement shulde happen, with many thinges more over longe to writt. The thre brothers semed to lyke exceedingly therof, prayed for your Lordship, my sister and all yours, with some tears and frivelous tales of the oulde man, the(y) began to play the courtier with me in ther grose but significant flattery. I desiered that we myght fall to the busines, soe I, Jhon Bouth and the thre brothers went into a chamber next the hall wher was many arkes and cofers, but on great chest was only full of bookes of accountes and conveances of all sortes, Fra. Dickenson took up parceles and began to read. I toulde them that course was never to mak an ende, and therfor wished that all writynges and bookes whatsoever shulde be saufly layde up, and that hear-after when your Lordship cam into the country the(y) myght advisedly be perused and distributed to whom the(y) belonged, savinge ther fathers will ore any other writynges that the present use therof was necessary. Fra. D. an-swered thos thinges his father delivered with his owne handes befor his death. Heringe that, I knewe (which I more then suspected befor) all was gon. Then sayd I, we need the less to looke of this, which was nothinge but art in him, as though he had not seen them befor. Soe they weare content I shulde lock upe the chest, the rest had nothinge but trash in them, soe I left a man ther and went up into a chamber wher was many papers filed and hunge in the roof, and only one bigg trunke full of writynges wich I stired not but locked it up agayn. After this we went into the chamber wher the oulde man dyed, full of arkes, cofers, trunkes, boxes, barrels and capaple thinges of divers formes. I found the bookes, papers and conveances to ryse so infinitly for fewe chestes was without, and seinge a great stronge prese standinge ther I moved that all the bookes and writynges myght be put together in that press, soe one lock woulde serve for all. The(y) weare content, notwithstandynge we filled it full and one resonable bigg cofer besydes. I sent for Kellam to make a staple and a claspe to hange the lock one, which he presently performed, soe I locked them both upe and seled them with my seale and have the keays heare with me. Ther was good store of course sheetes newe, and many oulde toyes, ther was good store of candles, otmeale, ould swety apparell and such lyke, but noe penny of mony but vi pondes in an arke with thre lockes, on at ether end, and one in the myddest and a falce bottome. This six poundes belongeth to an other who trusted the oulde man to keape it, and in an other smale box we found a litle silver rynge worth som iii^{d} accompanied with a towpeny peece. Ther was in an other ark some silver spounes, som thre oulde boules. I found noe conveance belonginge to any of them savinge on of half an aker to Gilb. and some acquittances which Fra. Dickenson was busy to lay apart. I toulde him that the(y) also concerned your Lordship because many thinges may be caled to memory, the parties name and the some beinge sett downe, and desiered that if the(y) had any others that they woulde bringe them in at your Lordships comminge into the country, which the(y) promised they woulde. When I had ended this search, I toulde them I founde Mr Bayly had advisedly sett a wacth upon the house, but because I understoode it brede variety of speach in the country I woulde acquant them with my intent and desiered to knowe ther opinions therof. The gard I woulde take away, yet it was necessary and resonable also that your Lordship shuld have thes writynges keapt to your satisfaction, which I sawe not howe it coulde be done except I placed one ther to that purpass, who shulde be such a one as them selves shulde lyk, and that they myght have one for them to keape the other company, and nothinge to be don without the privity of both. They lyked very well therof; soe I have placed ther your servant Rogers, biddynge him to repayre to Mr Bayly upon any alteration, whos house is at the next dore. But I doubt it will prove like the wacthinge of Lambeth after Cardenal Poles death, as wyse men as Rogers beinge sett ther, who upon the search found nothinge but ould shues and buskins. Thus somwhat after 3 I went to a good dinner at the Castle, only Jhon Bouth keapt me company; towardes the latter endynge cam Gilbert D. After he had dinen he began to discours (non beinge present but we thre) howe that his mother leaft unknowinge to his father 300^{l}, that his father had often toulde him that he alwayes had 300^{l} in angels in that falce bottomed ark, howe his father had mad unto him a bonde to be payd within one moneth after his death of 200^{l} and that his fathers will was he shulde have an equal part with the rest, but they say now my father mad noe will, but only by worde, his brothers beinge the only witnesses, that they say ther was not above 120^{l} in gould wherof they had delivered to his wyfe 50^{l} and as much money as to make that 50^{l} - 120^{l}, which thay perswaded hir was more then was dewe unto him, and she belevinge them moved him to be content therewith. After all this he desiered my opinion what was best to be don, for he had leaft him only 8 poundes of the rack, half an aker and 3^{l} in a lease. William D. had 14 pondes land and Fra. 30^{li}, but methought he was mor cherfull then when we cam to the towne. I toulde him I thought that he could take noe hurt by some delay, for tym woulde discover more then he knew then, that he was heare at the Common lawe and had your Lordships favor, therfor it were good to be well advised befor any conclusion. He sayd they had provided a supper for him and gave him good wordes and soe he took his leave for that nyght. In the tyme of our search I somwhat observed Gilbert, and methought he was somwhat out, for somtymes he woulde say to his brethern, My masters, I know not what, and stope ther; and at an other tyme, My masters, I know not how yow have dealt with me. William D. answered, You are well dealt withall. That eveninge Greves toulde me that one Wilson

130

toulde him that ther was 3 horse loden with culbasketes covered carlesly with strawe sent to Rotheram to F.D. house, som sayd 3 som 4 som 6 lodes. I supposinge it had bin a secritt byd Greve say nothinge therof but to bringe that Wilson to me. The next morninge Mr Bayly cam erly to me and toulde me all the country knew it, and that 3 lodes went to Rotheram and thre lodes to Winkebanke where Fra. and William dwelt. Presently after can (*sic*) in Gilbert excedynge cherfull, and sayd they had alredy consented to pay him his bond of 200¹ and to give him 200¹ more, that he caused William yeasternyght to send for his fathers dett book and all the(y) will acknowledge in gould ore silver is 380¹ and 500¹ in good dettes. Nay, sayde I, Gilbert yow will finde more for elce 400¹ will prove a great share out of 880¹ , but methought it grewe myghtely in on nyght. I pray God they may behave themselves as they ought to your Lordship; all I see is that this huge quantity of writynge may doe yow some service. William and Fra. divers tymes sayd in the search that ther father sayd divers tymes in his sicknes that he would give all he had to have hade som fewe wordes with my sister. I urged them what the(y) thought it was, whether he gave noe wordes that they myght gess what it myght be. They sayd noe, and as often as they spake it I still urged them but the conclusion is nothinge. For your husbandry, I harde of litle, but Mr Hordes worke hath done great hurt as they say, producinge quantety of russhes in the orcharde I was, and the younge trees prosper excedyngly and the oulde beare great quantity of frute. The newe orchardes in the lytle park is replenished with 700 trees, beinge only invironed with a hedge, but if it be not paled ore waled befor winter, it wilbe in danger to be spoyled for ther is much harme done alredy. The trees yow sent from London prosper, all excedyngly fare better than at Worsupe. But nowe Philipes plasheth your abricotes agaynst the was (?wall), he findeth great inconvenience by mice to brede in the loose wall by his boughes that are nipt and eaten ther. It were good if the other weare layde with clay. For your hunters we doubt the pardon will healpe them as som say heare, but I thinke not because it is don within the limitation.' Welbeck.

Holograph 4 pp. (Original Letters II/236)

Sir Charles Cavendish to the Earl of Shrewsbury

1606-7, January 30. Regarding a controversy between the Earl of Shrewsbury and Sir Robert Swift about Hatfield Chase. Its bad state at present, 'the deere are in a manner decayed, the fizants gonn, the meere spoyled.'

Holograph 1 p. (Original Letters II/242)

The Earl of Shrewsbury to Henry Cavendish

1607-8, January 4. I will give you advice on legal difficulties in connection with leases and entail arising out of the anticipated death of Elizabeth, Dowager Countess of Shrewsbury. When I was at Hardwick she ate very little and not able to walk the length of the chamber betwixt two, but grew so ill at ease as you might plainly discern it. On New Year's Eve when my wife sent her mother's gift, the messenger told us she looked pretty well and spoke heartily, but yesterday my Lady wrote that she was worse than we left her, and Mrs Digby sent a secret message that her Ladyship was so ill as she could not be from her day nor night. I heard that direction is given to some at Wirteley to be in readiness to drive away all the sheep and cattle at Ewden instantly upon her Ladyship's death. These are the reasons which move me to advise you, considering how like it is that when she is thought to be in danger your good brother will then think it time to work with you to that effect, and God forgive me if I judge amiss. I verily think that till of late he hath been in some hope to have seen your end before hers, by reason of your sickliness and discontent of mind. To conclude, I advise you not to accept any offer which may bind you to him. You have not been forgotten to my Lady neither for yourself nor for Chatsworth, but we have forborne to tell you, knowing that one of your brother's chief means to keep us all so divided one from another has been speeches and letters which have heretofore passed among ourselves. I entreat you to keep what I have written to yourself, and let this messenger be witness, after you have well perused it, of your burning it. Sheffield.

PS. You should write to him kindly, but not engage yourself. They persuade my Lady that upon her death you intend to enter the house and seize all. If you take upon you to think her in danger, she will hear of it, and think that you have spies to advertize you thereof; therefore, in any case seem not to think so to any creature.

Holograph Addressed: To my very good brother, Mr Henry Cavendish, at Tutbury. *Endorsed:* 4 Jan. 1607. A letter from my Lord to Mr Henry Cavendish. 2 pp. (Original Letters II/246)

HENRY CAVENDISH TO (THE EARL OF SHREWSBURY)

1607-8, January 8. I received your letter of the 4th of January on the 7th. Your Lordship may set the fortune, for one hour before your Lordship's footman arrived at Tutbury, the gentleman that has dealt between my Lord Cavendish, my brother and me, and has taken a world of pains in it, came likewise to my house. He was in haste and I was fain to call him to my bedside, where he made many persuasions. I had knowledge that your footman was come with a letter. I asked him to stay until I could be ready when we could discourse further in the great chamber. In the interim I read your letter. My brother's offers were £5000 in money, £500 a year for four years. I know my entail as well as any lawyer can beat it into my head, and I know the foundation to be weak and easily overthrown. My brother's offers would allow my debts to be paid, and given me his friendship and no expectation of suits or law brabbles betwixt us; then an increase of £500 for four years, which would have served me well till God had sent more, my ambition being no greater than I thank Jesus it is. But out of affection to you I have set all this aside and refused the offers. But in consequence my wife and I need your help. We have always been tractable to you, and made four several journeys to London to our great charge.

We heard of your being at Hardwick lately and of your meaning to return thither shortly. We hope that you and my mother will bear us in remembrance. I return your letter hereinclosed. Tutbury.

Holograph 2 pp. (Original Letter II/248)

STATEMENT CONCERNING THE DEATH OF ELIZABETH, COUNTESS OF SHREWSBURY

(After February 13, 1607-8) That the late Countess* reported, and that not long before her death, she also showed hereself to be much offended with some, for that the well was poisoned and yet broth was made with that water.

That Mrs Digby has reported that the Countess, at the time of the making of the supposed nuncupative codicil and not long before her death, did by

* Elizabeth, Countess Dowager of Shrewsbury died on February 12, 1607-8.

word will and bequeath to her son Sir Charles Cavendish either the sum of £4000 or 4000 marks of money.

That about that time she showed herself willing to give £100 to (*blank in MS*) and that it was then told her either by Lord Cavendish or some other person then present that she might not nor could she give it. That Mrs Digby states the Countess made no will, but only gave something by word; that she did by word will £2000 to William Cavendish, son of Lord Cavendish, and £2000 to his daughter Frances. That in the March before her death she said in the presence of Lord and Lady Katherine Cavendish she would give Sir Charles Cavendish £4000 or £5000.

That the said Lord Cavendish was so fearful and so unwilling that the new Countess should have any private conference with the late Countess, that he desired Mrs Digby to use some means to get the new Countess from her Ladyship: and once that his Lordship showed himself so to be was in her last sickness, his Lordship and Sir Charles Cavendish standing then in her Ladyship's chamber by the fire; and that Mrs Digby's answer to his Lordship then was that supper was coming up and that therefore the said new Countess would not have any time for anything.

That the said late Countess told Lord Cavendish and others that suits were drawn on and kept on foot to continue dislike, etc. *Undated*

2 pp. (Original Letters II/295)

See also *H.M.C. A Calendar of the Shrewsbury Papers in Lambeth Palace Library*, ed. Catherine Jamison, p.196, 710/61.

MARIE DE SETON TO MARY, COUNTESS OF SHREWSBURY

1607-8, February 22. 'Madame: Votre honneur m'excusera s'il luy plait de ce que je ne vous escrive de ma main, estant incomodité d'un caterre qui m'est tombe (sur) le bras droit. Et aussi si je ne m'acquite de ce debvoir en Englois, pour avoir oublié le peu que j'en avois apris le vingt trois ans que je suis sortie du pais, mais non (*torn*) que je vous ay augmente pas l'honneur de votre favorable lettre. Je ne doute, Madame, que le Roy et la Reine et les princes leurs enfants ne vous faict souvent souvenir de la joie qu'eust eue la Royne leur mere de ceste veue. Helas! Madame, elle n'eust este entière, les voyant d'autre religion que la sienne. Car c'estoit, soit dire, avec larmes qui se pouvoient juger de sang procedant du coeur qu'elle n'avoit qu'un enfant, que chacun pouvoit (*torn*) luy estre chere. Mais qu'elle aymeroit mieux choisir (estre) prive de tel bon heur que d'estre si infortunee que d'avoir porté en son ventre le fleaux de l'Eglise. (*Torn*) Eux qui estoient pres de la feue Majeste s'enhardioent de luy reponder ce que St Ambroise dit a Sainte Monicque, mère de Saint Augustin, qu'un fils si douloureusement pleure ne pourroit perir. Je suplie la bonté divine, comme c'est mon debvoir, qu'ainsi soit. Quant à vous, Madame, à l'exemple de ceste bien heureuse Marie de l'Evangile vous avez choisie la meilleure part. De quoy j'ay un extreme joie, esperant que se grain ne sera infructueux, mais s'estandra par toute votre heureuse posterité. J'avois envoiee par un gen(tilhomme) Englois qui partit d'icy quant le Roy fut receu en (son) Royaulme d'Angleterre quelques toknes adressant à vous Madame, et à Madame Arbella, et depuis escrit à la dite dame par home expres la supliant de presanter au Roy la lettre où je requerois sa Majesté avoir compassion de la ruine que j'ay entre aultres encourue des guerres (continuelles?) qui ont este en ce Royaulme, et suivie d'un proces qui m'aflige encore, mais n'ayant receu nulles responses je ne m'atendois pas à l'honneur qu'il luy plait (*torn*) en votre lettre. Dequoy je luy baise humblement les mains ne m'osant ingerer plus a davantage. Quant a Monseigneur votre mari j'ay toujours estimé de son bon et honorable naturel. Par l'experience de la memoire qu'il faict de moy, pauvre recluse en un monastere, je luy en demeure toute ma vie tres humble servante. Et à mesdames, ses filles, qui m'excuseront, s'il leur plait, de ce que l'incomodite du maladie en quoy je suis, pour le presant me faict manquer à recognoistre en particulier l'obligation que je leur ay de l'honneur qu'elles me font par votre lettre. Pour vous, Madame, je m'estimerois bien heureuse si ma bonne fortune eut este telle de vous faire quelque agreable service. Comme j'en avois tousjours desiré depuis notre premiere cognoissance, vous remerciant tres humblement de votre courtoise offre que j' амploirois volontiers à porter quelques bonnes parolles envers le Roy pour moy consernant le suict pour lequel j'avois suplié Madame Arbela de presanter une lettre à sa Majesté, comme pouvez avoir veue cy devant. Mais en cas se vous fut trouble ou empesche je ne voudrois pour rien du monde vous donner ceste paine. Et sur ceste verité je vous baise tres humblement les mains, vous demeurant à jamais, Madame, votre tres humble et afectionee à vous servir.'

Signed Addressed: 'A Madame la Contesse de Choresbery.' *Endorsed*: Mrs Seton. February, 1607. 2 pp. (Original Letters II/250)

Henry Cavendish to the Earl of Shrewsbury

1608, April 4. We came to London on April 3. My Lady Arbella, the elder Countess of Arundell, my Lord and Lady of Arundell, the little sweet Lord Matravers, my Lord and Lady of Pembroke we heard were all well. Lady Pembroke came today to welcome her aunt and me, poor soul, to London. London (Shrewsbury House) Broad Street.

Holograph 1 p. (Original Letters II/252)

Henry Cavendish to (the Earl of Shrewsbury)

(1608, April) 'On Sunday last I wyshed I could have sent your good Lordship a dovve with a lettar under her wynge to have advertysed your Lordship of shuch newes as cam very strange to me abowte the howre of ix in the morninge. At what tyme my Lord Cavendish sent to me by hys man Smythe to excuse hym that he had not made me pryvy of hys soones maryage to the Lorde of Kyllose hys daughtter * (now after vi yeares I have learnte hys name to be Lord of Kynlosse), the reason was he had great enymyes, and yf yt had byn made publyke he myght have byn crossed, and the cheyfe cause he so machched (*sic*) hym was to strengthen hym selfe agaynst hys adversaryes. I wyshed all myght prove to all theyr comfortes. My Lady Arbella was thear at dynner, and my Lady Cavendish the Barones, and so wear they at supper and both daunced in rejoycynge and honour of the weddynge. The bryde ys meetly hansom as they say, of a redd hayre and about xii yeares of age. Helas poor Wylkyn, he desyred and deserved a wooeman alredy groene, and may evell staye xii weekes for a wyfe, much lesse xii monethes. They wear bedded togeather to hys great punyshment some ii howres. The next mornynge I wayghted of my Lady Arbella at Whyte Haule and in taulke with her Ladyship I towlde her honour I thaught yt was she that made the mache, which her Ladyship denyed but not very earnestly, affyrmynge she knew nothynge of yt tyll that mornynge the maryage was, and that she was invyted

---

* The marriage between Christian Bruce and William Cavendish took place on April 10, 1608.

to the weddynge dynner. I tould her Ladyship much my bettars would thynke so as I did, and x thowsand besydes. That nyght, when as I was sett at my booke very earnestly (*marginal note*: after ix of the clocke), one of myne cam to me and tould me thear was a man of my Lord Cavendish desyred to speak with me. I badd brynge him up, who after some ceremony and excuse that he was but a servant, served me with a supina into the Chauncery at my Lord Cavendish hys suyte, and I am to appeare within xiiii dayes after (*marginal note*: the 14 day of April is the right day), yt seemed very strange to me. At the fyrst I thaught yt was somethynge abowte my Lady owr mothers wyll, but certaynely by skylfull men I am assured yt cannot be so; but that yt ys for somethynge towchynge my intayle. I shall greatly lacke your honourable Lordship or my honourable Lady my systar, or Sir Charles, hear in towne. My Lorde, my brother, ys too wyly polytyke and too skylfully experymented for me, and that I dowbt most, ys *tropo ponderoso* for me, but I have no remedy but to abyde hys worst. When I had made thys full poynte I was cauled to supper, and so lefte wrytynge to your good Lordship tyll this mornynge, in which interim I have learned for certayne truthe that my unkynd injuryous brother hath exhybyted a byll in to the Chauncery agaynst me, almost as full of lyes as of lynes, pretendynge that I gooe abowt to cutt of my intayle, to dyshynherytt my ryght heyres, and dyvers other thynges, and desyres to be releeved in that Cowrte that I may not have the cowrse of the common law to shue forthe a fyne and recovery, alledgynge many faulse reasons, as faulse as God ys trew. I am counceled not to appeare as yet, nor to take owt a coppy of hys byll, by some whom your Lordship dooth trust. It ys verely thaught he hath assured my lande upon the Crowne, Thys day Mr Kynge, Mr Hersy and Mr Deane dooe intertaynge cowncellors for me. I am so unfytt and so unapt for these law matters as thys onely matter dryves me into shuch agony, dyscontentment and perturbation of mynde as wyll lessen my tyme. God revenge my wronge of them that be causers of yt.

I receyved your honours lettar dated the xth of Apryll, sent by Mr Fox, for the which I most humbly thanke your good Lordship. I have not as yet talked with Mr Hamon, your Lordships man, towchynge the money your Lordship so honorably lendes me, which I have now more neede of then ever. And I hope in Jhesus my cruell brother shall not have hys wyll of me altogeather to hys lykynge.' *Undated*

Endorsed: 'Mr Henr. Cavendysh, sans date, y^t his brother Wm marrys with the Lord of Kinloses d^r.' 1½pp. (Original Letters II/287)

DUDLEY PAPERS
1558-1608

1558, December 20 to 1559, December 20. Book of Accompt of moneys received and paid by William Chaunsye *or* Chancy to the use of Lord Robert Dudley from 20 December, 1 Elizabeth to 20 December, 2 Elizabeth.

The receipts (f.1) amount to £2540:5:6.

The payments which are not dated include:

(1) 'Forin expenses and charges with rewardes,' including *inter alia:*

'For cariage of your stuff from Somersett House to Hithall, 16^d'

In reward for the Queen's New Year's gift, a gilt cup, 38^s.

Many rewards to Lord Derby's servants for bringing hawks.

To the watermen who rowed the Queen to Chelsea, 12^s 8^d.

'To Mr Hampden for your part of the supper made unto the Quene in the parke at St James, £7:18:2', besides other expenses connected with setting up tents there.

To my Lord of Pembroke's servant for bringing a hat, 3^s 2^d.

To the yeomen of the barge for rowing the Queen's Highness at one time, and your Lordship another time, 25^s 6^d.

'To the vitteling wyfe by Christs Church for Edmund Burd and Frances coming from Saint Quentans, 58^s.'

For your servants' dinner when your Lordship dined with my Lord of Pembroke, 12^s.

For their supper when you supped with Sir William Pickering, 10^s.

To Lamens, one of your Lordship's players, 40^s.

For our dinner at London, your Lordship dining with the 'Master of the Rowells', 10^s.

For carriage of bedding and hangings to 'Mr Skottes of Camerwell', 10^s.

To my Lord of Norfolk's man bringing your Lordship a hound, 5^s.

To the Clerk of the Signet for your Lordship's warrant for the mantle and the hood with 20^d for the writing, 8^s 4^d.

Paid for writings made between Foster and Detersall for £300:20^s.

To Gemynie the Frenchman for an instrument of astronomy, £10.

For our dinners, your Lordship going to Tower Wharf to receive the Ambassadors, 24^s 8^d.

Ditto your Lordship's dining with the French Ambassador, 22^s.

For our boat hire, your Lordship going to fetch the French to Court, 3^s 4^d.

For balls for your Lordship in the play at Westminster, 18^d.

Under the heading 'Windsor at thinstallation' are, among other items:

'For your L. Offering there, 2^s.

'To the heralds there for the fee for the instalment, £37:5:4.'

To the servants at the house where your Lordship lay at Windsor, 19^s.

For hackneys to Windsor, £8:8:4.

To your Lordship's players for their charge at 'Thestelworthe' that night they played before your Lordship at Kew, 4ˢ.

To the surgeon for letting your Lordship's blood, 10ˢ.

Boat hire when your Lordship went to the *Old Swan* to dine with the French Ambassador, 5ˢ 8ᵈ.

To 'Partridge' for service done at divers times, given unto him for reward when your Lordship won the wager of my Lord of Pembroke coming from Kew, £8:8:10.

To Mr Willowby your Lordship's chaplain, 40ˢ.

To servants for hanging your lodgings at Greenwich, 15ˢ 2ᵈ.

For my boat hire to London, being sent thither about the despatch of my Lady, 8ˢ.

To the watermen that carried your Lordship to London with my Lord Chamberlain and back again to Greenwich, when your Lordship hunted in St James's Park, 12ˢ.

To Dunkin for his boat hire, being sent to Whitehall with your taffeta nightgown, 4ˢ.

Boat hire to London when your Lordship supped with Mr Gresham, 5ˢ 8ᵈ.

For your men's lodgings, the Queen's Highness lying at Greenwich by the space of four weeks, 7ˢ 8ᵈ.

There follow further expenses at Dartford, Rochester, 'the Queens Majesty being at Gillingham'. Reward to the boys of the Kitchen at Cobham, 'the Queen lying there'.

Carriage of your Lordship's tents from London to Otford, 77ˢ 8ᵈ.

Servants' dinners 'when the Queens Majesty dined with Sir Percival Hart', 4ˢ 4ᵈ.

Lodging etc. of your footmen at Horsely, the Queen being there, 2ˢ 6ᵈ.

For 'rabond pointes' for your caparison against the running at Horsely, 12ᵈ.

For our dinners at Greenwich, your Lordship being there 'to sey your Armor', 5ˢ 4ᵈ.

For horsemeat etc. at Nonsuch, your Lordship being there, 22ᵈ.

For a hen which the spaniel killed, 7ᵈ.

The sum of foreign charges to the end of October is £935:4:6. Further charges under this heading for November and December amount to £21:16:5, one of the items being 'a looking glass sent to my Lady by Mr Forster'.

(2) Charges of apparel and goldsmith's work, which include:
'a salt given to Mr Knevetts child at the christening, 58ˢ 6ᵈ.
Ditto, to my Lady Cheaks chuld, 100ˢ.'

Sum total up to end of October is £524:16:5, and for November and December £45:3.

(3) Diet.
6 boxes of codymokes given to my Lady Clinton.

Paid for our dinners, your Lordship dining with Mr Forster christening his child, 22ˢ.

Boxes of 'comfetts' and other sweetmeats for my Lord of Derby, 4ˢ.

For 'banketing stuff' prepared at the Queen's Highness being at your Lordship's tent within the park, £6:14.

For spices bought by the cook when your Lordship rode to my Lady's, 22ˢ. (The places mentioned on this journey are Waltham, Ware, where the night was spent, and Buntingford).

Charges of your supper at Eltham, 117^s 10^d.

Sum total up to end of October is £83:13:10, and for November and December £12:14:8.

(4)   Necessary provision, such as furniture, utensils etc, £63:14:5.

(5)   Charges for livery, £91:8:8.

(6)   'Pleying Monnye', including *inter alia:*

Paid to Sir Raffe Bagnell for money which your Lordship owed him, £4.

Delivered to you at Mr Harrington's house which you lost at play, 60^s.

Delivered to you at play, being in your gallery with my Lord Admiral and others, £12:13:4.

To Mr Hide, when you played at cards at his own house, 40^s.

Paid to your Lordship's hands the 8th of April, playing in your chamber with my Lord of Norfolk, the Earl of Sussex and others 20 crowns; on the day that your Lordship went to Eltham another 20 crowns, £12:13:4.

To my Lord of Hertford for money which your Lordship lost, £40.

Delivered to your Lordship in Mr Comptroller's chamber to play at the tables, 10^s.

Delivered at Cobham 'being at dyse' with my Lord of Sussex and others, £6:3:4.

Money borrowed of Mr Thomas Warcoppe at the 'Duke of Swethelands', £4:6:8.

Sum total is £109:7:10.

(7)   Payments, not before mentioned, one item being:

To the French gardener at Kew, 20^s.

(8)   'Prestes', £13:18:10.

The grand total amounts to £2589:2:7$\frac{1}{2}$, leaving a balance due to Mr Chancy of £48:16:7$\frac{1}{2}$, with the signatures at the end of John Dudley, R. Horden and William Kynyatt, auditors.   A few other unimportant memoranda are added on ff.38-41.   The volume includes several entries relating to 'my lady' viz Amy Robsart, Lord Robert Dudley's first wife.   These have been printed in the *Wiltshire Archaeological Magazine*, Vol.XVII, 1877, p.84.

Small Folio   Vellum covers   ff.41   (Dudley Papers XIV)

GEORGE GILPIN TO LORD ROBERT DUDLEY

1558-9, March 6.   'Att my fyrste commyng hyther which is abowte fowre dayes paste and ever sence tyll the Kynges returne frome Monse which wasse yesternyghtt, theare hathe bene a full talke that the peace was certeyne. This daye ytt is communed to be moore dowbtfull for that by reason the Frenche Kynge wyll nott surrendre Callesse owr commysshoners wyll not agree to the peace, and theye saye thatt the Kynge withowte us wyll in no wyse make any peace; with all thoughe I doo beleve, yett doo I see sutche owteworde synes, and I heare sutche talke as forse me to beleeve thatt yf thay dydde not thynke the leavynge of Callesse in the Frenchmens hands too ympoorte this contrye as muche as England, thay woolde sure conclude a peace whatt some ever we dydde; but I perceyve some of the wysyst of them too be of oppynyon thatt yf a peace be made and Callesse lefte in the Frenchmens handes, ytt wyll never be kepte 2 yeares too an ende, for thatt the Frenche Kinghe havynghe sutche an entrye into Flanders and sutche an advantayge of the seaes wyll be redy upon every lightt occasion for too fall owte agayne.

The magestreets and rulers heare seme to murmure mutche att the alteration which thay thynke wyll be of relegion in owr contrye, the commune sorte for the moost parte as ytt semythe doo rayhther dyssyre ytt then otherwyse. Yett yff a peace be concludytt, ytt is lyke thatt great persecution wyll follow heare, for the spretuall doo yernystely traveyll for ytt, and of late have forbydden many books amongst which nombre Erasmus wurkes are includytt.

Thay have heare very delygent and spedy advertysements owte of Englande of all the prosedynghes theare, and are very inquysytyve too understand whatt is sayd and thoughtt in England concernynghe the maryenghe of the Quenes Majestie. The Poope is now mutche comendytt heare for thatt he hathe of late banysshed the Cardinall Carraffa and a nother of his nephewes owte of Rowme, and hathe dysmyssed them of thayre dygnyties.' Brussels.

Holograph 3 pp. (Dudley Papers I/11)

SIR JAMES CROFT TO LORD ROBERT DUDLEY

1559, April 10. Commending the case of the bearer, 'a gentlewoman widow' whom 'my lorde your father (whose soule God pardon) favoured well.' She will declare her own cause, 'and then I doubte not but her estate which the goodnes of your owne nature, which I have knowen all wayes to be favorable to women, dothe assuer me that she shall fynd favor at your handes.' Berwick.

Signed Wafer seal Addressed: 'To the right honorable and my very good lorde the Lord Robarte Duddeley, Master of the Quenes Majesties horsse at the Court.' *Endorsed*: 'April 1599. Sir James Croft.' 1 p. (Dudley Papers I/13)

LADY HASTINGS TO LORD ROBERT DUDLEY

(1559) May 5. 'Good brother. I here that God hath yncresed you with honor syns my departure. I praye lett me desyre you to be thanfull (*sic*) onto hym. I pray you esteem my lord as I am sure he geveth you cause thoughe peradventure he usyth not soche flateryng behavyour as many wyll do unto prosperyte. Brother, I wold you wold help to mak hym better able to wayte which I assure you he dessyreth but necessyte wyll dryve hym a waye unles you do kepe hym.' Sonnyng Hyll.

Holograph Wafer seal Endorsed: May 1559. 'My Lady Hastings' 1 p. (Dudley Papers I/14)

LORD HASTINGS TO LORD ROBERT DUDLEY

(May 6, 1559) Asking him to move the Queen to let him enjoy his offices in the West where he had served her sister. Lady Hastings wrote yesterday to the same effect.

Holograph Endorsed: 'May, 1559, Lord Hastings' 2 pp. (Dudley Papers I/16)

THE EARL OF PEMBROKE TO SIR ROBERT DUDLEY

1559, May 18. 'I cannot but vearey thankefully receave your Lordships frendly sending. So am I sorry to understand by this berer that your Lordship hath not yet altogether escaped your ffytt. I have bene at the Court according to my promisse saving that I hard the Ffrentche would not be ther so sone as they were looked for. Besydes that I was glad I might passe a fewe mo dayes in this hollsome ayere (wher I would your Lordship had some occasion that I might se you) for the better recovery of my helthe, having bene somewhat ackrased sithens my coming hither .... I take my leave untill Satterday next.' Hendon.

Signed, in capital letters PENBROKE. *Wafer seal* 1 p.   (Dudley Papers I/18)

THE LORD TREASURER TO LADY TALBOYS

1559, June 24.   Warning her to pay £40 due for the last subsidy before August 22.

Signed   1 p.   (Dudley Papers III/133)

LORD JOHN GREY TO LORD ROBERT DUDLEY

1559, July 2.   On the Queen's blood-letting, etc.   Haufnaker.

Holograph   Wafer seal   1 p.   (Dudley Papers I/20)
(Printed in *Wiltshire Archaeological Magazine*, Vol.XVIII (1879) p.23)

SIR JAMES CROFT TO LORD ROBERT DUDLEY

1559, July 7.   'At first the Councell moved me to the abatement of the Quenes chardges having consyderacion to the good guardyng of this towne, and then I abated one hondereth and fyftie horsemen.   And syns they have at two sondrye tymes cessyd fotebands without my knowledge ... and now they go about to put away all armor.   I must speke somewhat colerykly, as well may yt be sayde to kepe a towne of warr without wall or rampert as men of warr to be without armor.   Something I have written to declare my opynion, but yt comythe alwayes to late, for they make me not privy till they have fyrst determyned.   Your Lordship hathe very well advized me in soche weightye matters to advertise the Quenes Majestie, whiche thing her Highnes lycensed me to doo at my departyng from the Courte.   But nowe the Councell hath determyned, yt ys to late to wryte for you know the peryll therof, and this secrasye I must put into your handes.   Assuredly the doers of these matters are eyther careles or els they understand not the state of thinges here.   I shall be glade according to my dutye to advertyse my opynion to the Quenes Majestie for the servys here, for at wynter when I trust to be at the Courte plainly to declare what I thinke, but without her Highnes supportacion a poore man can not medyll with so waighty matters.   But if my opynion were askyd in tyme the Councell might be perswaded to order these matters without offence, but who so movythe to revoke anything that they have don puttythe the worlde on hys hede.   Yf yt be your pleasure to have the copyes of soche letters as I have wrytten for this towne, I will send them to you; of these things that I have written, collect that which you thinke mete and bestowe yt where yt may doo good.   And this thing in especiall, I beseche your Lordshippe to be meanes there be no more demynishement or alteration here without good deliberacion.   I refer your Lordshippe to other letters which I have written to Mr Treasorer bering date hereof, wherein I desier your favor and furtheraunce.   Mr Treasorers letters cometh after theis because I send them by a servaunte of myne who travelethe the ordinary jorneis.   Mr Richard Lee hathe written to the Queenes Majestie to have some noble man to see the workes here, whiche both he and I doo wishe might hapen unto your handes, knowing that you wolde reporte the trothe for that which you shall see, and though your travell may be something painefull, I doubt not but your self shall confesse that you shall have no cause to repent your coming hether.'
Berwick.

140

Signed Wafer seal Endorsed: 'Julii 1559. Sir James Croft.' 3pp. (Dudley Papers I/21)

SIR RICHARD LEE TO LORD ROBERT DUDLEY

1559, July 9. I have written to the Queen to ask that some nobleman (I hope your Lordship) may inspect the fortifications here and report direct to her Majesty. 'And without some witnes of my doings, I thinke not myne owne report sufficient in so weightie a matter.' Berwick.

Signed Wafer seal Addressed: 'To the right honorable the Lorde Robert Dudley, Master of the Quenes Majesties horse, and one of the most noble order of the Garter, Knyght, give these at the Court.' *Endorsed*: 'Julii, 1559. Sir Richard Lee.' 1 p. (Dudley Papers I/23)

LADY DARCY TO LORD ROBERT DUDLEY

1559, July 11. Thanking Dudley for taking her son Robert into his service. Wevenho.

Holograph 1 p. (Dudley Papers I/25)

SIR NICHOLAS BAGENAL TO LORD ROBERT DUDLEY

1559, July 12. I urged my services to the Queen when, as the Lady Elizabeth she removed towards Hatfield, to King Edward as Marshal of Ireland where I raised 400 men on my own lands to serve the King without charge, 'all which lands saving the town of Carlingford afore I had it lay in effect waste and maintained thieves and rebels.' And when King Edward was dead Sir George Stanley procured my said office of Marshal, whereby I so lost my credit and countenance as my neighbours being wild and savage people spoiled my said lands and tenants.

Sir Ambrose Cave also claims £20 a year which I was obliged to give to buy off his original claim to the Marshalship. I ask that the Queen will send a commission to inquire into my doings in Ireland which were by sinister means reported to the Council. I have sent over purposely into Ireland to get a horse or two for her Majesty's saddle. Llanver beside Carnarvon.

Signed 3 pp. (Dudley Papers I/27)

WILLIAM EURE TO LORD ROBERT DUDLEY

(1559) July 14. 'The Busshop of Dearolme beyng now set forward to London, and hearyng sey that he will not swear, wherby I suppose shortly his temperallyties shalbe in the Quenes hyghnes hand', I ask you to procure for me the Stewardship of Wardell (parcel of the said temporalities) from the Queen. Wytton.

Holograph Wafer seal Endorsed: 'July, 1559. Mr Eure.' 1 p. (Dudley Papers I/29)

GEORGE GILPIN TO LORD ROBERT DUDLEY

1559, July 15. 'The greate joy and triumphe thatt wasse in hande and prepayryng shortely to have bene in this Courte ys now mutche weakened by reason of these sorafull newis of the deathe of the Frenche Kynge, whiche as semythe the Kynge of Spayne dothe take very heavely, and ytt is thowghtt wyll sett of his voyage into Spayne for this somer. I thynke his deathe hathe mutche alltered theyre dyssengnaes as well in this contrye as in France; the priests and other religious persones are very sory for his deathe, dowtynge they have loste one of theyre cheffe pyllours.   Too heare the dyscourses and repoorts of these men heare which they make of our contrye, ytt wyll greve any trew Englysshman; they doo nott lacke very delygent advertysements frome thence, which by many is redely reported too the wurste exposytion.   I pray Godde gyve all men grace too be faythefull and trewe, for the contrayry is hoped of as ytt semythe by thayre commune talke.   The deathe of the French Kynghe doth make them somthynghe allter thayre style and I treste wyll doo moore.   The Spanyards arre mutche moore besye in thayre spytefull tallks then ayther this contrymen or any other nation.   The Kynghes Majestie is reteared frome the towne of Ghent too an abbaye abowte a leaghe thence and hathe prolonged the gevynghe of the flese for xv dayes.'   Antwerp.

Holograph   *Addressed:* 'To the right honourable and my singular good lorde, the Lord Robert Dudley, Master of the Horse to the Quenes Majestie, this be delivered in London.'   *Endorsed:* 'George Gilpin.   July 1559.'   1p. (Dudley Papers I/31)

The Earl of Derby to Lord Robert Dudley

1559, July 15.   Is looking out for a 'lyome' and suitable greyhounds which he will send 'when the Quenes highnes shalbe in progresse.'   He also informs him that 'a spar-hawke I have reydy for your Lordship so good I trust as any is withyn this shier, which shalbe sent so sone as she is furth of the mewe.'   Knowsley.

Signed   1 p.   (Dudley Papers I/33)

Sir Ambrose Cave, as joint Lieutenant for Warwickshire and Commissioner for administering the Oath of Supremacy, to Lord Robert Dudley

1559, July 16.   'It maye please you to be advertised of the state of this country whiche apperid unto me.   Beynge at the Assyses at Warwick, after the procedings of sondry comissions, I perceyvid the contreis good inclinacon to quietnes like true and obedyent subjects in all respects.   And wheras for thexecution of the chardge committed unto us, resolved of certeine gentelmen to be officers unto us, as Mr Fysher for one who by reason of his attendaunce can not well take it upon him, in whose stede Sir Richard Varney, a gentilman mete to serve in that behalf wolde willingly endevor himself for Warwicksheir yf yt please you to appointe or require him by your letters to take the chardge upon him.   I dyd also imparte thother to Mr Neythermylle, who is willinge to do dylygent service therin, beynge apt to exeart it.   So I suspended bothe thone and thother untill I here further from you in that behalf.   The great takynge light at the late Bishopps and from Oxforde preists in the countrey, contynew in their accustomed obstinacie behavinge themselves verie ill and disobediently.   Wherfor if the visitors do not shortly com amongest them I feare least it will breed a dangerous divicon, wherof God defend us.   The Deanes of Worcet[r] and Lichefeld are hidd or fledd and so parson Comterforde, as I am informed.

About ten daies hense I shall understande what the subsidie will amount unto; we shall have moche to do to make it reache to the laste, for the welthiest and substancialest men be deade and departed and their goods dyvided into dyvers porcons so as they shall answere for subsidie verie little or nothinge.   For our endevor in that behalf we have appointed to sytt together in every hundrethe as at Stratford upon Avon on Mundaie and Teusdaie, at

Warwick Wednesdaie and Thursdaie, at Stonley Fridaie and Saturdaie next, and Mondaie and Tuesdaie next ensueyng at Collehull; for the subsidie of Coventree is no commission sent. I have written for it to Mr Secretary.' Duddeston.

Signed Addressed: 'To the right honorable and my very goode lorde, the Lorde Robert Duddley, Knyght of the noble order of the Garter and M^r of the Quenes Majesties horse, geve theise with sped.' *Endorsed* 'July 1559.' Amb. Cave.' 1 p. (Dudley Papers I/36)

DONATO RULLO TO LORD ROBERT DUDLEY

1559, July 16.   I write to complain that two officials of yours have seized two of my horses for the Queen's stable. I thought to ask for redress through the medium of the Earl of Bedford and Mr Secretary Cecil. *Ma havendo inteso in questa hora che V.S. è venuta qui a Londra per non essere molestato dalli predetti ministri,* I appeal to you directly. As a native of the Kingdom of Naples, I know where to get good horses there, and will let you know of any. London

Signed Italian Addressed: 'All^e Illmo Sr Roberto Dudley.' *Endorsed*: 'July 1559.   Donato Rullo.' 1 p. (Dudley Papers I/39)

LORD STAFFORD TO LORD ROBERT DUDLEY

1559, July 18.   Regarding his dispute, as Deputy-Keeper of royal parks and forests in Staffordshire, with Mr Litleton, Keeper of Teddesley Park. He complains that the latter is cutting timber and killing deer for his own use.   Stafford Castle.

Signed Wafer seal Endorsed: 'July 1559.   H. Stafford.' 2 pp. (Dudley Papers I/40)

SIR HENRY PAGET TO LORD ROBERT DUDLEY

1559, July 18.   I send you news of this country, though you may know it already through my Lord Ambassador. 'The chefe rulers that are at this present about the Kinge are the Duke of Guise, the Cardinal of Lawreyne and all that House, who seme to shew a stowt cowtenance as though they feared nothing but that they shalbe able enough to goe thorough with theyre matters and bear styll the greatest swaye.   But when the Duke of Vandosme shall arrive it wilbe quickly veary apparent who shall beare the greatest authorite in this Courte; for he is a man vearye well liked and beloved amonge the greater sorte, and the rather for his religion whereunto veary many are well enclined here.   It is thought that the Cownestable, for that both he and his howse and all his doinges are utterly defacid, will leane unto Vandosmes parte, whereby he shalbe so much the stronger.

The Duke of Guise and the Cardinall of Lawreyne, to shew theyre great courage, have synce the Kinges death burnt three or fower in this towne and made strayte orders and proclamations for the suer punishing of all such as shall seme to professe the Gospell.

The Cownestable and the Marshall of Saint Andrewes with the Admirall and all that howse are cleane out of credit, and it is thought there shalbe as much done as may be to deprive them of theyre offices if by any convenient meanes it be possible to bringe it to passe.

The Duchesse of Valentinoys, a great favourer of that syde and the late Kinges minion, both she and all hirs are alreadie banished the Courte.

Theye have not yet proclaimed there Kinge, and some secret taulke here is that one of theyre chefest stayes is for that they are in consultation whither it be best for them in theyre proclamation to augment his style and to adde any tytle therunto towchinge Englonde.' But I cannot think that in the impoverished and divided state of this realm, and considering the rising in Scotland, that they will be so foolish.

'The Erle of Arrans youngest brother was yesterday committed to prison.' The French are preparing 10,000 men to send to Scotland, but it is doubtful if they can find the money. 'They seeke as much as is possible to entertayne and nourish the league betwixt King Philip and them. It were vearye good if some meanes were used for the breakinge of it. It would be the greatest cuttynge of theyre combes of anythinge that ever happened unto them, and it would give them occasion not onely not to give us cause to breake with them, but also to seke more frendship as much as might be.

But the hope of havinge and continuinge him there frende puttith them in such a braverye as that they thinke themselves stronge enough for all the world, which doth well apeare by theyre doinges here; for though they have not yet proceded so farre, as the Quene of Skots cam from hearinge evensonge, the gentlemen made place for hir by the name Queene of Englonde, which showith that they meane but unhappily to us warde, what cowntenance so ever they show to such as the Quenes Majestie sendeth hither.

Well I dowbte not but theyre disposition being knowne to be such towards us shalbe well enough provided for and the better by your Lordships helpe.' Paris.

Holograph Seal Endorsed: 'July 1559. H. Paget.' 2 pp. (Dudley Papers I/42)

JOHN YERWOURTH TO LORD ROBERT DUDLEY

1559, July 19. Giving an account of the manor house of Walton, and recommending Dudley to acquire the property from Mr Hongate. Chester.

Holograph 2 pp. (Dudley Papers I/44)

THOMAS BENGER TO LORD ROBERT DUDLEY

1559, July 23. 'Althoughe I lyve from her Highnes as I take yt lyke a banysshed man, yet wolde no worme fayner creype to his ffoode then I on the knees of my harte desyer to serve and ffollowe her.' He implores Dudley to persuade the Queen to take him back into her favour. Berkhamstead.

Holograph Seal 2 pp. (Dudley Papers I/46)

THE EARL OF ORMONDE TO LORD ROBERT DUDLEY

(1559) July 24. In favour of the bearer 'for the rome of a grom of the stable.' Bristol.

Holograph Endorsed: 'July 1559. Ormond.' 1 p. (Dudley Papers I/48)

BERNARDIN DE GRANADA TO LORD ROBERT DUDLEY

(1559) July 27. I have delivered the letters and the hounds to the Duchess of Lorraine. It would be well to send some hounds to 'Don Allownso de Agular; he ys one that may doo your Lordship pleasure here and lovythe you well.' I hope to buy some horses here when the King departs hence within the next three weeks. Gawnte.

Holograph   Endorsed: 'July 1559.   Bernardine Granada.'   1 p.   (Dudley Papers I/50)

DOMINICO CONNCINO TO LORD ROBERT DUDLEY

1559, July 28.   Setting forth his services to Dudley's father, and begging him to secure a renewal of a pension of £200 granted to him by King Edward and suspended by Queen Mary.   Genoa.

Signed   Italian   Seal   Addressed: 'Al molto maj^{co} Sor Sor Milord Roberto Dudle.'   *Endorsed:* 'July 1559. Dominick Consino.'   1 p.   (Dudley Papers I/52)

SIR THOMAS CORNWALLIS TO LORD ROBERT DUDLEY

1559, July 29.   Sends his servant Waterhouse 'to be a sewtor to my Lords for my furder liberty.'   London.

Signed   Seal   1 p.   (Dudley Papers I/54)

LORD COBHAM TO LORD ROBERT DUDLEY

1559, August 1.   Expresses a hope to see Dudley on the morrow.   Cobham Hall.

Signed   1 p.   (Dudley Papers I/57)

SIR NICHOLAS THROCKMORTON TO LORD ROBERT DUDLEY

1559, August 2.   Requests instructions for the purchase of 'mulets' for the Queen.   Paris.

Signed   Wafer seal   1 p.   (Dudley Papers I/58)

THE EARL OF WESTMORLAND TO LORD ROBERT DUDLEY

1559, August 4.   Solicits Dudley's interest in obtaining the pardon of Captain Brode concerned in the killing of 'one James Babington.'   York.

Holograph   Seal   1 p.   (Dudley Papers I/59)

HENRI DE FOIX TO LORD ROBERT DUDLEY

1559, August 5.   He sends him *des garnitures doyseaulx* and a glove with *des coleurs de mamye (ma mie) lequel je vous prie porter pour lamour delle.*   London.

Signed   Seal   Endorsed: 'August 1559. From Monsieur.'   1 p.   (Dudley Papers I/61)

MARQUESS OF WINCHESTER TO LORD ROBERT DUDLEY

1559, August 6.   Recommending a footman for the Queen's service.

Holograph   1 p.   (Dudley Papers I/62)

LORD AMBROSE DUDLEY TO LORD ROBERT DUDLEY

1559, August 9.   'For that Sir Richard Sowthwell dothe entende to go outt of thys towne towarde Norfolk upon Frydaye nextt, I thoughtt itt good to advertise you of ytt afore his departure, for that he having so greatt an accompt to make abowt hys office, ytt wer nott fytt he shold so lyghttlye departt, nor yett to make hys deputye to answer for hys doinges, for ytt is no small charge that he hath had under his handes all this whylle.   Wherfor yff ytt be the

Quenes Majestyes pleassure I shall injoye hys office. I wold be lothe to enter so earlye unto ytt as that peradventure hereafter to be called to rehersall for any partt of hys doinges.' At my house.

Holograph 1 p. (Dudley Papers I/64)

LORD AMBROSE DUDLEY TO LORD ROBERT DUDLEY

1559, August 15. He asks for a gift of some hawks, 'for that I am so destytute.' Att my howse in Holborne.

PS. 'Pray you good brother, provide some good lodging for me when the Quenes Majestye commeth to Wynesore, for that I wold be lothe to come afore her Highnes wer settled in some place.'

Holograph 1 p. (Dudley Papers I/68)

LORD AMBROSE DUDLEY TO LORD ROBERT DUDLEY

1559, August 17. 'I am dessyred by an old chapleyne of my fathers and now servauntt to Mr Willybe to wrytt to you in his behalffe, thatt ytt will please you to be a meane for hym to my Lorde of Canterburye, for that he havinge so many good thinges, to bestowe at this pressentt other with the Archedeaconry of Canterbury or els with the Deanery of Lyncolne. Butt yff yt were possible I wold wisshe hym rather to Lyncolne, for that itt ys in the contrey I dwell in and wold be glad to have hym planted neare me, for that he is bothe honeste and as you know veary well able to dyscharge the cure. I pray you, be earnest in ytt.' At my howse in Holborne.

PS. 'I thought to have herd from you ever this as conserninge my office. I wold be glad to have ytt as sone as were possible.'

Holograph 1 p. (Dudley Papers I/70)

BERNARDIN DE GRANADA TO LORD ROBERT DUDLEY

1559, August 23. I have the horses here for you, but the Duchess of Parma will not grant a passport for them. Pray get the Queen to write to the Duchess on the matter. 'The Marques of Barrow hathe tolde me that he will present a gennet unto the Quenes Majesty, whiche as yet I have neither taken nor yet refused until I shall hear further from your Lordship, and likewise the Ringrave will presente unto hyr Majesty to horses, the one a corser and the other a gennet....He comythe to Inglonde to kisse hyr Majestes hands.' The Duchess of Lorraine is still expecting the 'grewnde' (greyhound). 'If your Lordship wolde sende over too or thre coppel of howndes to bestow amongest the nobell men here....yt shalbe well don.' Flushing.

Signed 1 p. (Dudley Papers I/72)

(JOHN) POYNTZ TO LORD ROBERT DUDLEY

(?1559) August 29. He recommends 'his man Freeman', formerly a servant to Dudley's father, for a vacant prebend at Gloucester. 'He is a very honeste man...and dothe take grete paynes with my children. The prebend was won Munslows in the Minster of Gloceter which is in the Quenes gyfte, and also ther ar 2 more prebendes in the Quenes gyfte of won docter Williams Chanselor, ther late departyd...I hiersay ther is no byschopp in Gloceter as yet, if ther be I beseke yower Lordship to be a mene to gett on of thes of him, for then they be in his gyfte.' Oselworthe.

(?) Holograph, the signature almost obliterated. Wafer seal Endorsed: 'August 1559(?). Jone Pointz' 1 p. (Dudley Papers I/74)

LORD CLINTON TO LORD ROBERT DUDLEY

1559, August 29. Announcing that the death of Sir Thomas Carden took place 'this last nyght about one oclok.' Horsley.

Holograph Seal 1 p. (Dudley Papers I/76)

SIR N(ICHOLAS) POYNTZ TO LORD ROBERT DUDLEY

(1559, August) Excusing his departure on the ground of extreme want and praying Dudley to be his 'sollicitor' to the Queen.

Holograph Endorsed: 'August 1559. Sir Nick[s] Points.' 1 p. (Dudley Papers I/77)

ELIZABETH DUDLEY TO LORD ROBERT DUDLEY

(1559, August) I thank you for the geldings. I had hoped to have seen you ere this, 'butt that I dede here the Quenes Majesty dede nott retorne to Hamton Cortt after Thursdaye or Farydaye...and thatt her Majesty ys nott in suche helthe.' She requests to be informed of the Queen's health and of the date of her return, 'thatt my lord ma nott be absentt att her commynge.'

Holograph Endorsed: 'August 1559. Lord Ambroses wyfe.' 1p. (Dudley Papers I/80)

LORD AMBROSE DUDLEY TO LORD ROBERT DUDLEY

(? 1559, August) Wednesday. Expressing regret that serious ill-health prevents him from coming to Court, and making further application for his 'office'. Holborn.

Holograph 1 p. (Dudley Papers I/82)

THE EARL OF HUNTINGDON TO LORD ROBERT DUDLEY

1559, October 2. Thanking Dudley for news of the Queen's prosperous health and asking him to forward his interests at Court. Kyrby.

Holograph Seal, broken 1 p. (Dudley Papers I/86)

GEORGE GILPIN TO LORD ROBERT DUDLEY

1559, October 22. 'As yet no advertysement is come of thillection of any pope. A Spanyshe Cardinall hadd all most by a subtyll practyse opteyned the same. He fayned him selfe marvelous sycke and his phesyscyon being of his counceyll dyd reporte that yt wasse not possyble for him to lyve ten dayes, soo that by this practyse, as it is reported, he had gotten a 22 or 23 voyses. Afterwards his dyssymulation wasse dyssyfered and as yt is geven owte he (was) expulsed the consystorye. The devysion amongyste the cardynalls is such that men thynke such wilbe chosen pope as least is thowght of.'

An army of 10 to 12,000 men and between 40 and 50 galleys is preparing in Italy for a descent on Tripoli. But the Turks have got wind of the design and have sent 3000 men to Tripoli and armed many more (Arabs).

The Duke of Sarrazoo is dead, it is said 'partely upon a concepte hee tooke thynkynghe that the Cardynall Carpye, whoo is his specyall enymye, should be pope. Lyke as in Italye is gredelye watched whoo shalbe poop, soe heare they harken and harpe wheare the Quenes Maestye will beestowe herre syllfe, marveylyngh much of herr Graces soo longe protractyngh. I thinke they staye thayre prosedynges in som thinghes, they pretendyth, tyll thay see how and wheare herre Grace will matche herre syllfe. Thay are not soo yernyste in prosecution as they weare, but yet dayly doynghe. Yt is thought that the creation of theayre new bysshopes which wasse determyned upon heare will not take place for that nayther the nobyllytie, sprytuallytie nor comunes in generall are contented with yt. How the (y) lyke thayre newe regent I woote not, but smalle courte she hath in comparyson of her predecessors.' Antwerp.

Signed   Seal   2 pp.   (Dudley Papers I/88)

K. SUFFOLK TO LORD ROBERT DUDLEY

(? 1559, October)   Praying for the Queen's mercy for 'me ingnorant cossene' and reflecting on the cruelty of Bonner 'layte bashope of Londone.'
Holograph   Endorsed: 'October.   K. Suffolk.'   2 pp.   (Dudley Papers I/90)
(Printed in *Wiltshire Archaeological Magazine,* Vol. XVIII (1879) p.28)

SIR RALPH SADLEIR TO LORD ROBERT DUDLEY

1559, December 4.   In favour of Thomas Lovell, 'an olde servant of my lorde your fathers' for the office of clerk of the council at Berwick.   Berwick.
Holograph   1 p.   (Dudley Papers I/92)

ACCOUNTS

1559, December 22 to 1560-1, February 28.   'Monny receaved by me Richard Ellys, servant unto Lorde Robert Duddeley'.   Included are:

'Of Sir Harry Sydney Knyght for dept.	£20
Of *(blank in MS)* for money won by your Lo. at Tennys	£12:6:8
Of my Lord Admirall won by your Lordship at play.'	£15:8:4
The whole amounting to	£21,249:19:11

Large paper   1 p.   (Dudley Papers III/28)

ACCOUNTS

1559, December 22 to 1561, April 30.   Book of Accompt of moneys received and paid by Richard Ellis or Ellys on behalf of Lord Robert Dudley from 22 December, 2 Elizabeth to 30 April, 3 Elizabeth.

The receipts include:
(1)   Money borrowed from William Byrde, mercer, for the payment of various persons, £3930:10:5.
Ditto from John Chapman, grocer, £1410:18:3.
Money borrowed during this period amounts to about £14,000.
(2)   Money received 'from your L: lycence and for rentes' etc, including rents of Hemesby and Sidesterne, Amy Robsart's lands.
Money won by your Lordship at tennis from my Lord of Sussex, £12:6:8.
Money won by your Lordship from my Lord Admiral at Greenwich, the 28th of June, £15:8:4.
Received of Sir Harry Sydney, knight, for 12th of March (1561), due unto your Lordship for armour, £241:5.

The payments include:
Paid to William Hide, gent., the 18 of June, £33:6:8.
To Mr Appliard for money due unto him, £100.
To Thomas Lodge, Alderman, for a horse bought of him and given to the Emperor's Ambassador, £20.

To my Lady Sydney at several payments, £65.

Paid to Lord Hunsdon, November 3, to be repaid March 31 next, £200.

To Thomas Whiteley, keeper of the tennis court at Whitehall, for four several bills, £8:10:6.

Payments to various persons entered by months include:

Paid unto a poor man that was stayed by your Lordship's commandment on the suspicion of murder, for his charge and recompence after he had cleared himself, 10^s.

For the setting up of a bathing tent at Hawnce's house, 22^d.

To Thomas Forest for licences and collars for your Lordship's hound, 2^s 6^d.

For 'buttered beare', 8^d.

For horsemeat at Greenwich when the Queen's Majesty rode to Deptford, 8^s.

For a bushel of hemp seed for the quails, 18^d.

For one round and 'joyle' of sturgeon when the Duke of Holkest dined with your Lordship.

For roses and other flowers for your Lordship's chamber by the space of 27 days at 6^d the day, 13^s 6^d.

For 6 beds at Greenwich for your Lordship's gentlemen and yeomen by the space of 11 weeks, 66^s.

There are many expenses in the month of July for a banquet at Kew.

For the provender of your Lordship's horses at Bosome's inn and at the 'Maydens Head' when your Lordship dined at the Mayor's feast, 15^s 4^d.

In November there are details of the expenses of a banquet at Eltham, including a 'bricke of marmalade', 2^s 4^d.

For torches when your Lordship supped with the Emperor's Ambassador, 2^s.

For banqueting stuff bought when the Scottish Ambassador dined with your Lordship at Whitehall, 14^s 6^d.

To Mr Doctor Nevison for his pains coming to the Court to take recognisance of your Lordship and others, 8 French crowns, 48^s.

A list of rewards includes the following:

To divers officers of the Queen's household and to the Buttery, 40^s.

To George Woodhouse, the money disbursed by Mr Hide, 20^s.

To one that kept one of the Queen's jennets, 6^s 4^d.

To a poor woman presenting your Lordship with a carnation gilliflower, the 16th day (of February, 1560), 2^s.

To my Lord Rich's man presenting oysters, 2^s.

To the heralds of Armes when your Lordship and my Lord of Hunsdon were calling, 40^s.

To your Lordship's Cator taking the dog out of the water, 4^d.

To an Italian Cap(tain?) presenting your Lordship with a sword, the 10th of March, £6:3:4.

To Sir Giles Poole's man presenting your Lordship with lamprey pies, 12^s 4^d.

To the woman 'that keepeth Master Bakones house' at Kew, 12^d.

To the armourers at Greenwich when your Lordship should have run at Whitehall, for the (*illegible*) of your armour and mending your headpiece being broken, 10^s.

To a marker at the tennis court of Whitehall, the 25th day of March, 12^d.

To two stoppers in the tennis court at Whitehall, April 2, 10^s.

To a poor woman presenting your Lordship with a nosegay at the privy chamber door, 3ˢ 4ᵈ .

To Barnes presenting a hobby, 10ˢ .

To the Marquis of Elverstone's man in reward for the money delivered to Mr Granado, 61ˢ 8ᵈ .

To my Lord of Westmorland's man presenting your Lordship with a cast of 'Leoneretts', 64ˢ .

To Thomas Langham when he was a prisoner, 40ˢ .

To the children of the chapel in reward, April 14, 12ˢ 4ᵈ .

To the Duchess of Suffolk's man presenting Rhenish wine, 19ˢ .

To my Lord Mayor's man presenting a singing blackbird, 6ˢ 2ᵈ .

To the post of Antwerp for bringing letters and silk hose from George Gilpin, 3ˢ 4ᵈ .

To my Lord Hasting's man presenting your Lordship at Richmond with a red deer baked, 6ˢ 4ᵈ .

To John Johnson the 'phipher' (fife player) in reward, December 25, 10ˢ .

To the Frenchman that kept the Queen's mulets in consideration of his goods lost by the casualty of fire, £6:12:4.

To Henry Mansfield in reward at his going to Berwick, £6.

To Archecrage at his going into France at your Lordship's command, 72ˢ

'Payments for dinners and suppers at sundry times when your Lordship hath dined or supped in the City and at other places'.

Paid for your Lordship's men's dinners the 10th day of January, 1559-60, when your Lordship dined at the Duke of 'Ffynelandes', and they at the *Bear* at Bridge Foot, 24ˢ .

Lord Robert Dudley dined again with this Duke on February 8; with the Marquis of Traynes on February 9 and March 17; with the French Ambassador on the 12th, and the servants at the *Salutation of our Lady* in Tower Street; at the Tower on March 10; with the Emperor's Ambassador on March 24; at the Lord Mayor's with the Duke of 'Ffynelande' on February 18; and with the same Duke at Greenwich on April 17th.

Paid for their dinners the 13th of April, at the Queen's Majesty's being at Deptford and they at Greenwich, 23ˢ .

Lord Robert Dudley dined on April 29 with Lord Windsor; on May 3 at the 'Countye of Russyes'; on May 5 at Mr Stukelie's; on May 15 at Lord Manners's; on June 9 with 'the County of Elverston'; on June 21 with 'my Lady Sydney at Ratcleef'; on July 10 at the 'Frennche pledges'; on July 16 with Mr Alderman Offelay; on July 18 with Lord Pembroke; on July 22 at the Mercers' feast; on October 29 at the Lord Mayor's feast; (no date) at the Scottish Ambassador's; on December 22 with Mr Bird; (no date) in 'Powles Churcheyard with Sir John Masoun'; on February 9, 1560-1, at the Lord Mayor's; on February 10 with Mr Basshe; (no date) at the Tower.

'The charges of christenninge of soundry children'.

'Delyvered to Mr Hugganes, February 8, for the christeninge of Sir Thomas Chamberlaynes child 6 french crownes, 38ˢ.'

Also on March 17 a silver gilt salt and money, £7:5:4.

For Mr Walgrave's child, May 21, a salt, £5.

To Sir Henry Sydney for the christening of Lord Hunsdon's child, £30.

For Mr Richmond's child, November 25, 60ˢ .

For the gardener's child, January 3, at Chelsea, 36ˢ 8ᵈ .

For Mr Anslowe's child, 30ˢ .

Money delivered for your Lordship's purse:

The 12th day of May, delivered unto your Lordship 60 pistolets, £18:10.

June 24, when you played at cards with Mr Stookes, 76ˢ 4ᵈ .

150

June 24, for so much lost by your Lordship to the Duke of Holkest, £6:3:4.
To your Lordship by Fowke Grevell 40 crowns, £14:11:8.
Money paid for boat-hire:
For the carriage of banqueting stuff to Eltham, the Queen being there, 3ˢ 4ᵈ .

Small folio. Vellum covers 42 folios. (Dudley Papers XV)
(The entries relating to the funeral of Amy Robsart are printed in *Wiltshire Archaeological Magazine,* Vol.XVII, 1878, pp.88-9)

LORD ROBERT DUDLEY TO 'MR SHRIVES' (? THE SHERIFF)

(? 1559) December 30. He asks that his servant Langham, in prison on a charge of felony, may be released on bail. 'In veary evell hower is hit happened unto him for that he hath made full provisyon to have served the Quenes Majesty under the Duke of Norfolk in the north partes which this myshapp hath greatly hindered.'
Holograph 2 pp. (Dudley Papers I/2)

INVENTORY

(1559) 'An Inventory of the goodes and cattelles of Sir Andrew Dudley, Knight, * deceased.' The value of the furniture amounts to £582:18:6.
9 pp. (Dudley Papers III/170)

LORD DUDLEY TO LORD ROBERT DUDLEY

(1559) Touching the proposed purchase of Budbrook and the obtaining of the fee simple of Balsall.
Signed 1 p. (Dudley Papers I/84)

ACCOUNTS

1559-61. 'The boke of my lordes servaunttes wages and borde wages from Midsummer, 1 Elizabeth to Lady Day, 3 Elizabeth.'
A list of servants, both stewards and bailiffs, and also of domestic servants with their wages and board wages. A typical extract is the following:

Thomas Davyes. Paid unto him for his wages for one yeare and a half ended at Christmas anno tertio. 60ˢ
Item, paid unto him for his Bord from the first of January anno secundo unto Christmas followyng, beyng 51 weekes whearof was allowed for a xi weekes at Greenwich at 8ᵈ the weeke and the xl weekes besides at 6ᵈ the week. 27ˢ 4ᵈ
Item, paid more to him by severall bills of parcels allowed unto him the sum of' 57ˢ

19 pp. (Dudley Papers III/1)

THE EARL OF BEDFORD TO LORD ROBERT DUDLEY

(1559-1563) June 3. He asks him 'to put your helping hand with Mr Threasurer' for the purchasing of a small piece of land from the Queen. Chenys.

* According to *D.N.B.*, Vol. XVI, p.102, Sir Andrew Dudley died in 1559 without issue.

Holograph Addressed: 'To the right honorable my verye good Lord the Lord Robert Dudley, Master of the Quenes Majestys Horse.' *Endorsed*: 'from F. Bedford.' 1 p. (Dudley Papers I/94)

THOMAS LUCY TO LORD ROBERT DUDLEY

(1559-1563) April 8. He is sending his servant Burnell to help Dudley in shooting matches. Charlcot.

Holograph Seal 1 p. (Dudley Papers I/95)
(Printed in *Wiltshire Archaeological Magazine*, Vol.XVIII, 1879, p.25)

ADRIAN STOCKES TO LORD AMBROSE DUDLEY

(1559-60) January 6. Praying that as 'Brodgat is geven to my Lord Jhon' and he is forced to remove his 'stufe and katell', Lord Ambrose will further his suit with Lord Robert Dudley. Knebworth.

Holograph Endorsed: 'January 1559. A Stokes.' 1 p. (Dudley Papers III/134)

THE EARL OF DERBY TO LORD ROBERT DUDLEY

1559-60, January 9. In favour of his servant Robert Dalton, a suitor for the purchase from the Crown of the manor of Cokerham. Lathom.

Signed 1 p. (Dudley Papers I/98)

THE EARL OF WESTMORLAND TO LORD ROBERT DUDLEY

1559-60, January 21. Offering his services to 'doo that pleasure that might stand your Lordship in stede.' Raby.

Signed Wafer seal 1 p. (Dudley Papers I/100)

THE MAYOR AND ALDERMEN OF COVENTRY TO LORD ROBERT DUDLEY

1559-60, January 22. Touching the case of one Stephen Benet 'lackee to your Lordships servant Owen' (and a native of Coventry) accused of having 'certayne cleppenges of gold.' Benet confesses that he found the clippings in Fleet Street. They would like to know Dudley's pleasure. Coventry.

Signed: Thomas Kyrven, Mayor. 1 p. (Dudley Papers I/102)

P. CHOWTE TO LORD ROBERT DUDLEY

1559-60, January 27. 'I have of late devissed with a Frenchman of myne aquaintance to be informed of his knowledge nowe of the state of Fraunce. He saithe the Marques d'Elbeffe, the brother of Monsiere de Guyse, is acompanied with abowete the number of 1500 men and that he had not above 12 or 14 smale shippes for the traunsporting of them into Skotlonde and they were imbarked at Kalles, John Rosse beinge Admirall of the sayde shippes, and he is in a lowe barke beinge not above the portage of 80 tonne. Also I axed him of the Kinges shippes. He answered that the beste of them be gonne in viadges (voyages) and that there is many shippes nowe a rigginge in Newehaven and in other partes, and the Admiralls great shippe is at Depe to be rigged ther, beinge abowete the portage of 500 or 600 tonne. Also I inquyred if ther sholde come no galles to serve in Fraunce this yere. He saide he thowghte not, answeringe that a brother of hys of late came from Marcelles and ther he said he sawe but 12 galles furnyshed and all the rest laide up and the sklaves set at lyberte.'

He says the state of France is very bad: dear food, divisions in religion, many of the great houses Protestant, 'and that the judge that gave order to burne the greate President was after slayne with a dagge.' Everywhere there is preparation for war. 'I gather the meaning is to make a rebellione ther agaynste the State and that the Constable hathe apointed hime a greate strengthe to caste downe the protestants in all parts within the dominions of Fraunce, and ther goods to restore all them that were taken prisoners by Kinge Phillipe and the reste therof towards the sayde Constables chardges.' At the Castell of the Cambre.

PS. 'I have written to my Lorde Warden for munesoune and men for the better assuraunce of the Quenes Maties Howse nowe under my chardge. I have thoughte yt good therof to informe you for my better dyschardge in your behalfe.'

Signed Seal 1 p. (Dudley Papers I/104)

THE EARL OF BEDFORD TO LORD ROBERT DUDLEY

1559-60, January 29. In favour of the bearer, Mr Elmer, for the Deanery of Windsor. From my house.

Holograph Wafer seal Endorsed: 'Januarii 1559. F. Bedford.' 1p. (Dudley Papers I/106)

LORD DUDLEY TO LORD ROBERT DUDLEY

(1559-60) January 30. Asking Dudley to forward his suit for the obtaining of some piece of his lands. Dudley.

Holograph Seal Endorsed. 'January 1559. E. Duddley.' 1 p. (Dudley Papers I/108)

(JOHN ASTLEY) TO LORD ROBERT DUDLEY

(1559-60) January 30. Excusing himself for not 'waiting at Christmas' Melton in Norfolk.

Holograph Endorsed: '1559. A....y' 1 p. (Dudley Papers I/110)
(Printed in *Wiltshire Archaeological Magazine*, Vol.XVIII, 1879, p.23)

THE EARL OF DERBY TO LORD ROBERT DUDLEY

1559-60, January 31. Asking Dudley to be 'good Lord' to Geoffrey Morley, his servant and late tutor to his children in his suits with Lord Wharton. Lathom.

Signed Seal 1p. (Dudley Papers I/112)

ELIZABETH LADY ORMONDE, TO LORD ROBERT DUDLEY

(1559-60, January) 'My lorde, I do understand by my man Pers Welsh that you are offended with me. Wherefore I am right sory, for that I assure you I never ministred any occasion wherby I shulde posses your disspeasure, but, good my lord, lete me knowe both what hath bine reportide unto you and also who they be that are my accusers, which you say are credable, but I dout not the reprovinge of them yf your Lordshipe will bringe them to my face, and then yf I cannot porge my selfe I will never requiare you to do for me nor for any frende of mine; otherwise I shall dessiare your Lordshipe to ansuer for me as a frende and kinsman in all my rightfull causses, never standinge in more ned of frendshipe then nowe at this pressent, as knowith God, who send your Lordshipe much helth with the increas of honour.'

PS. 'In the meane time yf it will pleas your Lordshipe to send for me, I will take my oth upon a boke that I for my parte never said anythinge tochinge you.'

Holograph Endorsed: 'January 1559. L. Ormond.' 1 p. (Dudley Papers I/114)

(KATHERINE ASTLEY) TO (LORD ROBERT DUDLEY)

(? January, 1559-60) On the disgrace of her husband, John Astley.

Addressed: 'To my very good L(ord).' 1 p. (Dudley Papers I/201)
(Printed in *Wiltshire Archaeological Magazine*, Vol.XVII, 1878, p.21 *See also* p.23)

SIR NICHOLAS THROCKMORTON TO LORD ROBERT DUDLEY

1559-60, February 27. Asking Dudley to favour and credit the bearer who is 'full fraught with all the intellegence and mysteries that we can lerne yn thys Court and countrie.'

'My Lord, now uppon these mens amyable offices wyche I take unfaynyd (as thys bearer shall shewe you), I have alteryd my suspicions of theyr evyll menyngs to hyr Majestie and her realme, and so trust the matters yn dowte woll be well compowndyd. Evyne so I pray your Lordship lest the French Ambassador be perswadyd by you and others yn place of honor and credyts, that I am grettlie inclyned to reduce the innimies ynto goode termes.' Amboise.

Holograph 1p. (Dudley Papers I/116)

JOHN FYSHER TO LORD ROBERT DUDLEY

(1559-60) March 18. Concerning a suit of Dudley's with Sir Robert Throckmorton and his son-in-law, Mr Sheldon, about the Stewardship of Barkswell and other manors.

Holograph 1p. (Dudley Papers I/121)

LORD WILLOUGHBY TO LORD AMBROSE DUDLEY

1559-60, March 23. 'I thought yt good to let your Lordship understand howe ungentely Mr Controwler hathe used me in placing of the Ffrenche Embassadores within my house at London, as allso displaced and troughne oute all my stuffe into an oulde howse of no strength able to kepe any thinge within yt. And my servauntes leikwise beinge torned out to the nomber of vi or vii, not beinge suffered to have there repare into any said howse for the savegard of my stuffe there lying in greate decaie moche to my hindraunce, which I thinke ys more ungentilnes then ever was shewed unto gentilman or nobleman.' He requests him to obtain redress through his brother Lord Robert Dudley. Kneyth.

Signed 1 p. (Dudley Papers III/136)

THE EARL OF DERBY TO LORD ROBERT DUDLEY

1560, March 31. Thanking Dudley for his services in 'his doghter Stourtons causes', and asking him to obtain the Queen's leave for his absence on St George's Day. Lathom.

Signed 1 p. (Dudley Papers I/123)

THE DUCHESS OF SUFFOLK TO LORD ROBERT DUDLEY

(1560, March)   Praying Dudley to help that 'my poor cossen was but out of the Tower. Helpe, helpe, helpe, helpe.'

Holograph Endorsed: 'March 1559. K. Suffolk.'   1 p.   (Dudley Papers I/125)

(Printed in *Wiltshire Archaeological Magazine*, Vol.XVIII, 1879, p. 26, where the date is given as 1556.)

SIR JOHN LEGH TO LORD ROBERT DUDLEY

(1560) April 5.   'I myght confes my selff to be verie ungratfull that I dyd not soner ansuer yower leter browght me by Master John Chamberlayn, if I had not byn stayd so long at Brusels at the request of the Count de Ferya, ffor that is such a testymony off the good opynyon you have concevyd off the good wyll, which allwayes I have to you.'

The Count of Ferya departed from Brussels the first of this month. He was accompanied above a mile out of the town by the Counts of Egmont and Horn and by the Bishop of Arras. That morning the Regent presented the Countess of Ferya with a collar of gold set with diamonds and pearls and worth above 3000 crowns, and other presents. The Regent has never before shown such liberality. King Philip has written to the Count with his own hand to take upon the commission which Monsieur de Glasyon now has in England. He refused it because he is supposed to have no credit with the Queen. Antwerp.

Holograph   1p.   (Dudley Papers I/127)

THOMAS KEYS TO LORD ROBERT DUDLEY

1560, April 5.   Sir Thomas Finch and I have been ordered by the Council to enquire into the question of the export of horses overseas. As your deputy I advise that a proper book should be kept at each port by the Customs officers, in which particulars of horses etc., may be entered, and the number of such exported horses will then be known.   Sandgate Castle.

Holograph   1p.   (Dudley Papers I/129)

SIR THOMAS NEWENHAM TO LORD ROBERT DUDLEY

1560, April 6.   Asking for a grant of a lease for 21 years of the tithes of the parsonage of Tewkesbury.

Signed   1p.   (Dudley Papers I/131)

LORD HASTINGS TO LORD ROBERT DUDLEY

1560, April 9.   In favour of a 'sute which Mr Wyllyame Stokes hathe unto the Quenes Majestie for the confyrmacyon of his lease in Bewmanner' granted to him by the late Duchess of Suffolk.   Ashby.

Holograph Seal   1 p.   (Dudley Papers I/133)

I/135 *is a similar letter (same date and place) from Hastings' father, Francis, Earl of Huntingdon, and signed by him.*

NYNYAN MENVILLE TO LORD ROBERT DUDLEY

(1560, April 13) Easter Eve.   I arrived at Newcastle on the 10th of April from the Firth and (am) attending the Scots hostages, viz, 'a sonne of the Duke of Chatelleroy, a kynesman of the Lorde of Arguyle, one that is half brother to the Lord James; a sonne of the Lord of Glencarns, a sonne of the Erle of

Mentethe, a sonne of the Lorde Rovens, which said hostages is appoynted as yet to remayne at Newcastle. But as well others as my selfe appoynted for there convoy shall hastelie receve vituall and so agayne retorne to the Ffyrthe, in which sarvice by sea my Lorde of Norfoke .... hathe thowghte me to be mete for, notwithstanding I thinke my selfe most unhable, save only that I beare a faithfull mynde and an ernest good will to bestowe my lyfe in the Quenes Majesties sarvice and for your Lordshippes honor. And having occasion to pase alongest the coste of Scotland, I have considered the situation of the most notable places uppon the said coste of this mater.' I would rather make my report to you in speech. 'My cominge from the Fyrthe was before the skyrmishe betwene the congregation and the Frenchemen. The which mater is so trewlie reported to the Counsell that I trust your Lordshippe is satisfied. As I here say it is vearie well and mighte have bene much better.' Newcastle.

Holograph 1p. (Dudley Papers I/137)

THE BISHOP OF WORCESTER TO LORD ROBERT DUDLEY

1560, April 14. I thank you for commending me to your friends and pray you to 'mantain my honest and right causes as hitherto ye have done ..... the defense of me shall not turne to youre dishonor, let the maliceouse report what thei list. I trust my doyngs trewly tryed shall be founde upright, and my hart, faith and obedience to be most syncere to them whom God hath sett over me.' London.

Holograph Seal 1p. (Dudley Papers I/139)

SIR RICHARD VERNEY TO LORD ROBERT DUDLEY

1560, April 20. 'I am very sorie that I can not, according to your Lordshippes expectacion and my dutie, make my repaire presently towards you for two principall causes. Thone health, whiche I possesse not as I could wisshe. Thother wealth, which doth not habond in me as perhappes is thought. But as it is both I and althinges els myn are and alweis shalbe to my best power advaunced in any your affaire or commaundement when oportunytie offereth. I am sorie also to wryte unto your Lordshippe the late myshapp and losse by death of oon cast of hawkes whiche my cosen Davers whom I preferred to your Lordshippes service had in keeping. But lyke as I knowe your Lordshippe can best consider that casuall thinges have many times suche casuell end, so I have good hope you will pleas to lett them passe, and to thinke no wilfull necligence in your man, who I assure you taketh the myschaunce marvelous grevously. Except your Lordshippe by your letters seame somthing to comfort hym, I beleave it woll do hym hurt. He greiveth a great deale the more that they shuld miscarye in his guyding considering that he hath had knowledge and long experience of the keping of hawkes.' Warwick.

Signed Seal Addressed to Dudley: 'at the Court.' 1 p. (Dudley Papers IV/10)

ELIZABETH DUDLEY TO LORD ROBERT DUDLEY

(April, 1560) Complaining of her separation from her husband, and asking Dudley's aid in the matter.

Holograph 2pp. (Dudley Papers I/140)

LORD LUMLEY TO LORD ROBERT DUDLEY

1560, May 16.   Thanking Dudley for the 'furderance of my L(ords) sute for Halfnaked.'

P.S. by Lumley's father-in-law, the Earl of Arundel, in the same sense.

Holograph   1 p.   (Dudley Papers I/142)

SIR HENRY PAGET TO LORD ROBERT DUDLEY

1560, June 2.   Varying reports are current about King Philip's late overthrow at sea.   It is generally said that 35 ships and 32 galleys were lost and only 17 escaped.   The Duke of Medina Celi appears to have escaped and to have arrived in Sicily.   He is much blamed, for he had ample warning of the coming of the Turkish army.   He appears to have tarried so long at Gerba because he thought he could have completed the fortifications in time, but the Turks arrived sooner than he expected when 'neyther his shippes nor his galleyes had gotten from the shallowes in such sorte as that they cowlde have sea rome to shift for themselves.'   The Pope is continuing the fortifications of Civita Vecchia and beginning those of Ostia.   'Thus hath this overthrow of Kinge Philips bredde such a feare in Italy as that every man begenneth to stande on his guarde as well as he can.'

The Pope begged the Venetian Ambassador to get fifty galleys lent him.

'Some saye that the Abbot of St Saluto is alreadie parted from Rome towards England, but if he be not alreadie gone, he hath his foote in the stirrop for to part.   One called Sor Giacomo Malatesta is put in prison in Rome in Castell Saint Angelo for geving, so they saye, the *bastonado* to Cardinall Monte for findinge him in a courtisans house.   Most men are of the opinion here that his falt did rather deserve prayse than imprisonment.'

The floods caused by the River Po have been most serious.   Venice.

Holograph Seal Addressed: 'To the right honorable my vearye good lord my Lord R. Dudeley, Master of the Queenes horse and Knight of the (most) honorable order of the (Garter) in the Courte in England.   *Endorsed*: 'June. Sir H. Pagett.'   2 pp.   (Dudley Papers I/144)

THE EARL OF RUTLAND TO LORD ROBERT DUDLEY

1560, June 4.   'I sent unto your Lordship by this berer, my servant Colby, the best dogg that Mr Cressey had or (as he saith) ever shall have - by the judgement of maynye one of the best dogs that ever hath ben in this contry. Yet notwithstanding, for thenmytie that some berith your Lordship but specially towards me, they found meanes to stele the same dog, so as in tenne daies he culd not be hard of, and besides that they did die him of sundrey cullers, as this berer is able to make relacion unto your Lordship more at lardge.   But I doubt not but to requite there good will therin.

I here also ther is wagiars laied in the Courte that I shuld not kepe promise with your Lordship in sending him unto you.   But whosoever so saith, I wishe they were as honest in there dedes as I am and wilbe in keping my promise.'   Belvoir Castle.

Signed, with a holograph postscript containing courteous commonplaces.
1 p   (Dudley Papers I/146)

THE EARL OF HUNTINGDON TO LORD ROBERT DUDLEY

1560, June 30.   'The 29 of thys present I receyved your gentle letters which were better welcum than any you sent me a great whyle, the newes in theym of your cummyng hythyr was so acceptable; and good my Lord, yf yt may be,

157

performe your promysse so frendlye offeryd, of your selfe, which, be you assured I wolde most yearnestlye before thys tyme have requyred yf I coulde have persuadyd my selfe to thynke yt shoulde have ben grauntyd; and now syns you have geven me som hope of yt I crye even out with open mouth, performe your promysse and Ashbey shalle welcum you with harte and hand as he may thoughe not as he wolde. I have all thys whyle forgotten to geve you thankes for remembryng my sute to the Quens majestye, and wyll for thys tyme cease, deferryng yt tyll your cummyng, at which tyme I trust for all thyngs to doo my true devoyre.

The woofull daye of buryall I have apoynted to be this day fortenyght which shall be the 14th of Julye.'* Ashby de la Zouche.

Holograph Addressed: 'To my good Lord and Brothyr the Lord Robert Dudley.' *Endorsed*: 'June. Huntingdon.' 1 p. (Dudley Papers I/147)

WILLIAM SHELDON TO LORD ROBERT DUDLEY

1560, July 5. 'Today I receaved as well your pryvate letters to Sir Thomas Russell and to me as your other letters to all the Justices with a certyfycate, whiche your letters affyrme to be ratyd amongst the Justices for horsemen. Hyt may pleas you to peruse my former letters wherby hit will appear that the same was but my owne opynyon, and not ratyd amongest us. And that if your Lordshipp shulde have had any lykynge therof, that then hit myght have commen of your selfe. What the gentlemen will nowe gather theruppon I cannot judge. I will aunswere the same as I maye, but I wolde hit had byne otherweyse.' Beoley.

Signed 1 p. (Dudley Papers I/149)

THE EARL OF ARUNDEL TO LORD ROBERT DUDLEY

1560, July 21. On the ratification of the French treaty, 'the opynyon of (about) the Frenche ... beyng suche as our forfathers ever consevyd of them.'

'Theye that shall atend the Quenes Majestie in the progresse shall swer from the highest to the lowest to find solft wayes, how hard soever they fynde ther loging and fare.' Stansted.

Holograph 2 pp. (Dudley Papers I/151)

LORD ROBERT DUDLEY TO MR SHELDON

(1560) August 1. 'I am sorrey to se that the Quenes Majestie is more skantly servyde under me than any other in all Englande, and specyally that whear I put so great trust ther shuld be so many respects and considerations had for the ease of the countrey, as yt were that I my self were with out regard therof, or that her Majestie rather went about a spoylle of her people than a savegarde of her realm .... I perceve that your certyfycate wanteth the syxth parte almoste of that ought to have been certyfyed, but I wyll not receave this hetherto done, nor will have the contrey consydering the tyme troublyd with a new muster, but wyll have the fyrst muster booke that was made sent me, for this was a new maner of certyfycat contrary to all others that ever was made, for ther was as yt wer a note and not a declaracion of that you dyd.' Richmond.

Holograph Endorsed: 'August, 1560. My Lords letter to Mr Sheldon.' 1 p. (Dudley Papers I/4)

---

* Francis Hastings, 2nd Earl of Huntingdon, had died on June 23, 1560 (*Complete Peerage*, VI. 656). This letter is signed by his son Henry, who followed his father as 3rd Earl of Huntingdon.

SIR HENRY PAGET TO LORD ROBERT DUDLEY

1560, August 3. 'Your Lordships letters of the last of June I receyved the 28th of Julii.' I am sorry to hear that my letters to you were opened on the way, upon suspicion as it would seem. But the doers will gain nothing for, 'I shulde doe agaynst my dewtie to deface the proceedings of my superiors', or to oppress my inferior. 'But he who tok uppon him to be your Lordships secretary thought to have trapped me in one of those points, or els I know not what other cause shulde have moved him to be so fickle fingerd. Mary! the best is he was deceyved and I therby cleared. I am glad to heare that the necessite of the French is such as that of force they must come to owre conditions. I dowbt not but that this advantage shalbe so well taken as that this short warre shall procure a longe peace.'

As to King Philip's overthrow the Spaniards put it about that the forts of Gerba are well manned and victualled, and that the garrison has forced the Turks to raise the siege with loss. But the facts seem to be that the garrison is sickly and without proper water supply; nor have the Turks raised the siege.

'From Rome they wryte that the Generall Councell so much taulked of and so lyttyll ment is cleane dashed, but the cawse they declare not. The Pope shortly cometh from Rome to lye at Bononia, and by the waye they say he shall meet with the Duke of Florence and crowne him Kinge of Thoscan. Thus the Duke of Florence is lyke styll to florish and, if fortune styll favor him, lyke to grow so great as that they who have most exalted him shall have most cause to feare him. The Cardinals of Tournon and of Carmignay are parted from Rome towards Fraunce by sea, sent by the Pope to call there a nation Councell and by color thereof (as it is suspected) to catch into there handes all the chief and the heades of the Protestants. I doubt not but that there craftie meaninge is alreadie well enough knowne in Fraunce. The Caraffas doe remayne styll in prison; there case dothe rather decline than amend, and yet it is not knowen what shalbe there ende.' Venice.

Holograph 2pp. (Dudley Papers I/153)

SIR THOMAS GRESHAM TO LORD ROBERT DUDLEY

1560, August 18. 'I sent the Quenes Majestie a Turcke horsse from hens with one of my own servaunts to Dunkirk to be conveyed savely unto you, as likewysse I have maid dew serch for sylke howsse (hose) for the Quenes Majesty, but here ys nowen to be gotten. Therfor I have sent her Highnes messeure in to Spayne and therby to make 20 payre according to her Majesties comandement.'

I ask you to use your influence to procure my friend Mr Appleyard the lordship of 'Wynddamme', and to befriend William Hogan, my cousin Marbery and his brother. Antwerp.

Holograph Seal 1 p. (Dudley Papers I/155)

LADY AMY DUDLEY TO WILLIAM EDNEY

(1560 or before) August 24. Ordering a new velvet gown.* Cumnor.

?Holograph 1 p. (Dudley Papers IV/7)
(Printed in *Wiltshire Archaeological Magazine*, Vol. XVII (1878) p.66)

THE PRIVY COUNCIL TO LORD ROBERT DUDLEY

1560, August 30. Setting forth that since the late reconciliation between the

---

* Lady Amy Dudley died on September 8, 1560.

Queen and the French King, numbers of disbanded soldiers and sailors have given trouble, and ordering Dudley to cause an assembly to be made at which measures may be devised to ensure order, 'that no manner of person that hath served this yere as a souldier, having not freehold or occupation or other notorious good and lefull meanes to lyve by, be suffered to live out of service or without his occupation, or idlely or suspiciouslie, nor to so journie otherwise then by traveling in journey, in anie common innes or victualling houses but that thowners of the houses be answerable for them, nor that any suche souldiers or other be suffered to carry about them handgonne or dag contrary to the forme of the law and of our former proclamations.' Means are to be devised 'that the countrey may be free from such notable felonies and burglaries as the last wynter by overmuch sufferance of such idle persons ... were committed.' We request that a certificate may be sent to us concerning the state of each shire by Christmas next in order that due provision may be made. Basing.

Signed by: The Marquis of Northampton, Earl of Arundel, Edward, Lord Clinton, William, Lord Howard of Effingham, Sir Thomas Parry, Sir Francis Knollys and E. Rogers. *Seal* 1p. (Dudley Papers I/159)

Sir Thomas Chamberlayne to Lord Robert Dudley

1560, September 6. I ask your favour to help me to unburden myself of this charge. 'Trouthe it is I cannot have my helthe in this contrie, which together with that I want apte mynisteres to helpe me to serve this charge, being left destitute of soche as came over with me.' I have only one man who can speak and write, and he is of no great experience. Nor can I any longer afford the money 'to beare the porte of this office.'

'Herewithal I do send your Lordship a mynite wherby you may perceive what is comyng to this Kynge out of hande by subsidie and otherwise.' Toledo.

The last paragraph only in holograph. 2 pp. (Dudley Papers I/161)

Sir Thomas Chamberlayne's Minute on the Revenues of Spain

(September 6, 1560) The people of these countries of Castille have of many years paid for subsidy 800,000 ducats, which of late years in respect of the wars they have been content to increase to 400,000 more, which now amount to one million, two hundred thousand ducats concluded at this time to be paid in 3 years. . . . . . 1,200,000 ducats

They have also granted at this parliament for benevolence or gratuity at his Highness's marriage. . . . . 400,000 ducats

The increase of a custom or tenth called by the name of Alquenalla and at this parliament agreed for 300,000 ducats every year during 15 years, which before they had of his father for the term of 20 years now expired . . . . . . 300,000 ducats

His Majesty shall have of the Pope's Bull called the Crosado granted for six years . . . . 150,000 ducats

His Majesty shall have of the clergy for the term of six years . . . . 600,000 ducats

The Pope has granted and given his Majesty faculty to sell lands of the Church to the value of 25,000 ducats a year, assigning so much pensions yearly in lieu of the same which will be worth to him . . . . 200,000 ducats

The whole amounting to . . . . . . Six millions of ducats.

All this is increase at this time besides his ordinary revenues in this country towards the payment of his Majesty's debts. Besides that from the Indias his Majesty is like to have succession in those lands and revenues and to be able to make disposition thereof from one to another in succession, which before this time they could not do.

1p. (Dudley Papers I/163)

ACCOUNTS

(Before September 8, 1560) William Edney's bill 'to my Lords Robarte Dudles wyffe,' for gowns etc, to the amount of £23:10:8.* *Undated*

3 pp. (Dudley Papers IV/3)

(Printed in *Wiltshire Archaeological Magazine*, Vol.XVII, (1878) pp. 85-8)

THE EARL OF HUNTINGDON TO LORD ROBERT DUDLEY

(1560) September 17. Sending him some pies of a stag and (in a postscript) condoling with him on the loss of his wife. Leicester.

Holograph Seal Endorsed: 'September 1560.' 1 p. (Dudley Papers IV/23)

(Printed in *Wiltshire Archaeological Magazine*, Vol.XVII, (1878) pp. 75-6)

LORD JAMES HAMILTON TO LORD ROBERT DUDLEY

1560, September 28. 'Altho I have of langtyme understand be the L. of Lethingtons report your gude affectioune and grit freindschip, nocht only to this hale natioun in generall, but also above the rest to my self in particular, yet for lak of acquentance culd I nocht be baulde with you in writing before now that I have swa gude occasioun be returnyng of the same gentilman quha can testifie unto you howmickle I do esteme your frendship the mare for that it is altogiddur underservt for ony thing that ever I was able to do to your pleser, and notheless I am baulde to crave it for the gude will I have to recompense you with the lyke gif ever occasioun be offert quharby I may stand you in ony sted. I pray you credit him as you wold do my self, and tak in gude part that I will hereafter be bauld with you, and from this furth employ you familiarly in sic materis as I sall have to do in thar partes as ane of my derest frendes.' Edinburgh.

Signed 1 p. (Dudley Papers I/164)

THE EARL OF HUNTINGDON TO LORD ROBERT DUDLEY

1560, October 13. 'I am nowe forcyd to renew my olde sute which I have often troublyd your Lordship with, and that ys for the stautement of my dette unto the Quens Majestie. This bearer can declare unto you what yt ys, and howe yt hathe rysen. Good my Lord, have me nowe in remembraunce, for yf shortely I make not aunswerr unto the Exchequer proces wyll strayghte cum agaynste me and soche losse to me wyll ensue as I shall not be hable a great whyle to recover, as your Lordship may easelye judge understandyng my state, which I thinke you are not alltogythyr ignorant of.

An other sute I have which I wolde desyre your Lordship to move unto the Quens Majestie for me, and yt ys for the office of the Mastershypp of the harte houndes. Yt ys an offyce of no greate proffytte, but with me I assure you,

---

* See *supra* p.159

more estemyd then any other that bryngeth 10 tymes so moche comodyte. My Lord, my father, had yt restoryd unto hym by the Quens hyghnes that nowe ys, for in Quen Maryes dayes he lost yt, and one except yt was all the offyces he had under the Quen when he dyed. And I doute not but her Majestye wyll also graunte yt unto me as she dyd unto my Lord my father yf your Lordship will speake fore me as my verry trust ys you wyll.' Leicester.

Holograph 1 p. (Dudley Papers I/166)

LORD JOHN GREY TO LORD ROBERT DUDLEY

(1560) October 30. Protesting against projected exchange of lands between the Queen and the Earl of Arundel. Halfe Naked.

Holograph 1 p. (Dudley Papers I/168)
(Printed in *Wiltshire Archaeological Magazine*, Vol.XVIII (1879) P.24)

LORD DUDLEY TO LORD ROBERT DUDLEY

(1560) November 25. Protesting against Lord Robert Dudley's requirement 'to exchange my house and lands and to geafe me as much in fee simple ..... I am the poor head of this house .... (and) I wolde rather forsake fyve tymes as much land then to departe with Duddley as the reste. Also the most parte of mye land is inhereted by my lytle daughter, for unlesse hyt be the Castle and certeyne lands thereabout; els Segyleye, Hymley and Swynford, with the chase of Asshwood and Chaspell are as well to daughter as to sonne; and yt may plese God to sende me a sonne with mo children; but yf I and my wyfe shulde dye without issue, I wysshe hyt to your Lordshippe before any man lyving.' Dudley.

Signed Endorsed: 'November 1560. E. Dudley.' 3 pp. (Dudley Papers I/171)

LORD STAFFORD TO LORD ROBERT DUDLEY

1560, December 1. I send 'my rude booke in his ould coote which as a man in symple apparell maye tell a talle bothe trewe and worthie of remembraunce' which shall declare 'againe the usurped color of lawes to condempne men without there aunswer.'

There follows an account of the sentences on various traitors, the Despensers, Roger Mortimer, etc, which have been compiled from the records lying in the Tower. From my lodgings at Drurie Place.

Signed 2 pp. (Dudley Papers I/173)

SIR THOMAS GRESHAM TO LORD ROBERT DUDLEY

1560, December 16. I have received your letter by your servant John Benyssone. 'Here ys no nother comonycatione but that the Emperor and the Ffrenshe Kinge shold be departed, wherby itt ys thought it wolde bread moche quyettnes thoroweowght Cristendome, by the reason that the[y] judge that Maxemallian shalbe Emperor whome ys a protestayen for his lyffe. As licke wysse yffe the Ffrenche Kinge be dead the(y) have no more tittell to Schotteland, wyche wolle be a occaseone to kepe us in quyettnes. As for the Kinge of Spayen it ys thought that his handes ys full anoffe to ressyst the Turcke, and that he wyll nott nowe be so ardent in religione matters as was thought here of latte he wold bey. As lyche wysse the Kinge Phillipe ys of latte enteryd into great jellosye of the greate amytte that is growen between the Pope and the Duche of Ffloryns, fferinge that the Duche of Ffloryns shuld be this maynes growe to great for hym in Ittallye.'

The 4000 Spanish soldiers who were shipped for Spain have been landed again. The Inquisition of the Order of Spain is proclaimed at Louvain and is likely to be proclaimed generally here 'wyche ys nothinge lickyd.'

'The Quenes creditte dothe ryther augmentt then dimynysshe; and so I trust to keppe itt yff my powre and sympell devysse maye be creadytted and take plasse from tyme to tyme.' Please to remember the Queen's present of greyhounds and geldings for the Landgrave. Antwerp.

PS. 'After sealling here of, the letters of Germany be come but the(y) mache no menssione of the Emperors death, whiche is now moche dowghttid. As also I have secrat intelligens that the Kinge of Spayen mynde ys alltered for the 4000 Spanyardes that shuld remayne here, ffor that now he haythe contermaunded agayen to shipe them for Spayen wythe all the expedycione that maye be, wisshing the(y) werre departid for that ther ys gret account maid of them, the(y) be so expart solldyers.'

Signed Holograph postscript 2 pp. (Dudley Papers I/175)

ACCOUNTS

1560 List of payments made to tradesmen and others.

3 pp. (Dudley Papers III/29)

SIR RALPH SADLEIR TO LORD ROBERT DUDLEY

1560-1, January 24. Regarding his suit to the Queen for the fee farm of the manor of Hunden. 'Had I not ben called to her Majesties service, I ment in myn olde yeres to have lyved an obscure life with my poure famylie according to my naturall affection, and wolde not have mistrusted that which God and her Majesties most noble father had bestowed on me (albeit I was overmoche pynched by her sister) should have contented .me, but this calling to such service unloked for, and the dyversite of service while I was in the North from one charge to a nother, for the tyme dryved me to further expence then I will declare although I thinke it (if it were all I have) well bestowed.' Stonden.

Signed 2 pp. (Dudley Papers I/181)

HENRY KILLIGREW TO LORD ROBERT DUDLEY

(1560-1) February 1. 'I have thought good to troble your Lordship with these feaw lynes from hence, bothe because my lord of Bedford had word here of thimbassadors extreame syknes, and also for that the messenger assured me how ther were many of the late Kings horses to be sold at Paris and elles where .... The Court is at Orleanse, but my Lord of Bedford is apoyntid to tary till he here from the King at Paris. By that I can lerne of the State, the house of Guyses credit decayeth dayly. I here the newes of the Duke de Nemors, I meane conseving the sentence gyven agaynst him, confirmed, and myche talke of the Quyne of Scotlande going into Scotland not a litell desirous to passe through Inglond yf she might to avoyd the danger and troble of the seas.' Bollen.

Holograph Addressed: 'The right honorable and singuler good Lord Robert Dudley at the Courte.' *Endorsed*: 'February 1560. H. Killegrew.' 1 p. (Dudley Paper I/185)

THE COUNTESS OF HUNTINGDON TO LORD ROBERT DUDLEY

(1560-1) February 7. 'My good brother; perceyving that my lorde wyll shortlye goo to London even onlye to doo his duetie to the Quens Majestie, and that by this messenger as I thought he certified you therof, yet because I doute he

163

hathe writtyn nothyng largely of his state I wyll be bolde to tell you the truthe therof, desiryng you as you maye perceyve thear is greate cause to be an helper for his shorte retourne, and in any wyse to kepe me from the Court. I assure you when he shall goo he shall not be hable to carrye fortye poundes in his pursse to beare his charges the hole journey, but yf he spende more I am sure he must borrowe yt theare, and that he neadyth not for I trowe he owyth fyve or sixe thousant pounde of the least and maye not spende a yeare past fyve or sixe hundryth. Good brother, consider his state and helpe that he maye not spend more than he hath.' Kerbye.

Holograph Endorsed: 'February 1560. The Countesse of Huntington.' 1 p. (Dudley Papers I/183)

ROYAL GRANT

(After March 1, 1560-1) List of 'Landes geven by the Queenes Majestie unto the Lorde Robert Duddeley' in tail, viz:

In Kent	Knolle Manor, park etc.	35^s 4$\frac{1}{2}$^{d}
In Leicestershire	Burton Lazar Manor or hospital.	£148:6:5$\frac{1}{2}$
In Yorkshire	The manor, park and borough of Beverley.	
	The manor of Skytby and the site etc. of Meaux Abbey.	£198:4:2
	The whole amounting to	£348:6:3

Undated

1 p. (Dudley Papers III/23)
(See *Cal. of Patent Rolls,* Elizabeth, 1560-3, pp.189-191)

JAMES BASKERVILLE TO LORD ROBERT DUDLEY

(1560-1) March 7. 'I have receaved tow severall letters from your Lordeshippe, the one directed unto me and Sir Thomas Baskerfille my brother, dated the 29th of January, wherin your Lordeshippes pleasure was that wee should owe our good will unto Mr Knolles in his suite unto younge Mistres Lyngen; the other letter, dated the 18th of January, directed only unto me, wherin amongst other thinges your Lordeshippe desirethe the contynuance of my frendshippe and other of my frends in the said suite, and to be advertised from me as occasion served towchinge the same. And for aunsweare unto your honorable letters, these are to advertise your good L^p that even from the bygynnynge I and other of my frends have travayled to the uttermost of our good wills and powers to bringe theffects of Mr Knolles suite to passe, and so doo contynewe the same as Mr Knolles can well reporte. Howbeit olde Mistres Lingen for her parte to geve the repulse of dispache of his said suite, what her meaninge inwardlye is (wee knowe not), awnserethe that shee will performe her promyse made to her husband in his lif time that shee wolde not marye her daughter before the age of 21 yeares, because of the stablysshement of her husbands inheritance, whereuppon restith manye thinges (as she saithe). And at this present I assure your L^p olde Mistres Lingen by her talke unto me semethe to use in the contynuance of Mr Knolles suite muche doblenes as she hathe done to the residewe of sundrye other sutors, as Mr Knolles with Henry Baskerfille my kinsman and others can well reporte unto your L^p at large more plainlie; wisshinge that it might like your L^p by some good devise that olde Mistres Lingen shoulde be called to aunswere before the Privie Counsell for suche sclanders as hath bine reported in her house, both againste the Queenes Majesties honor and her Counsells, wherein she hathe towched the woorshippe of suche gentellmen as have ben ernest in the suite of Mr Knolles that were contynuallie in the companye withe him meaninge noo disorder or evell behavior at any time in sekinge the good will of young Mistres Lingen otherwise then honestye and good humanitie required as well uppon Mr Knolles parte as allso by his frends.' Hereford.

Signed 2pp. (Dudley Papers I/187)

SIR RALPH BAGENALL TO LORD ROBERT DUDLEY

1560-1, March 18. On the trial and acquittal of Edward Dekesone, Dudley's man, at Stafford Assizes. 'All seche evedence that cold be showyd or sed agaynst hym was executyd to the uttermost. So that for the satysfying of the world there was nothing omytyd or left undone. My good Lord, as the Justices of thassizes be knowne to be lerned and most discret men, so have I thoght it my part and duty to advertyse your Lordship that I do find by dyvers resons and arguments that the(y) be the men that doth most honor and love you.' Nevertheless no cunning ways were secretly practised at the trial. Stoke-on-Trent.

Holograph 2pp. (Dudley Papers I/189)

VISCOUNT MONTAGUE TO LORD ROBERT DUDLEY

1560-1, March 25. Thanking Dudley for 'well reportinge my un-fayned dutye and desyer to serve and please her Majestie', and for his friendly advice 'which I mynde, God willing, to followe, intendinge immediatelye after Easter to be at the Court.' Cowdray.

Holograph Seal 2pp. (Dudley Papers I/191)

FARGUS GRAYME TO LORD ROBERT DUDLEY

1560-1, March 26. Complaining that, notwithstanding Dudley's letter in his favour, he has been imprisoned by Lord Dacre for many weeks, and asking that he may be brought to London for trial, especially as Lord Dacre himself is now there. Carlisle.

Holograph 1 p. (Dudley Papers I/193)

BARTOLOMEO COMPAGNI TO LORD ROBERT DUDLEY

1561, March 29. Urgently demanding the return of the £100 lent to Dudley more than a year ago. '*Di casa mia in letto gravemente amalato.*'

Italian Signed 1 p. (Dudley Papers I/195)

THE EARL OF SHREWSBURY TO LORD ROBERT DUDLEY

1561, April 10. On abuses in the Forest of High Peak. The Forester is enclosing the best part with a stone wall, and so overcharges it with sheep that there is scarcely any game. His object is to disafforest it altogether. The result will be that many inhabitants will be greatly impoverished, 'and by that meanes her Majesties servyce in tyme of warr, who hertofore hathe beene of good number and force shulde be muche empayred, and the gayne and comodytye redounde onelye to one man and none advauntage or proffitt to her Majestie.' The disparking of the Park of Skottle under Queen Mary is a warning of what will happen. Sheffield.

Signed Seal 1p. (Dudley Papers I/197)

JOHN JOHNSON TO LORD ROBERT DUDLEY

(April, 1561) On abuses in Customs of Wools and fells. 'According unto your Lordships pleasure I have bene reddy to open unto Mr Secretary my knowledge in soche thinges as it hath pleased hym to conferre. And when the merchaunts have attempted to disprove the reconyng which I exhibited unto your honor, I have affirmed the same to be trewe, proving also by manifest matter that if redresse be not in certayn abuses, and the commodite of wulles and felles taken into the princes hands, the commodite will shortly be defaced and the princes revenue by wulles and felles decreased. Ffurther I beseche your honnor to understande that Mr Secretary demanded of me, if I cowld fynde the meanes to joyne others with me and take for a greater custome than now is paid, thutterans of all the Cotswold wulles. By this I gathered that for some respectes moving the Counsaile, it was not ment to take the thing into the princes hands. But to the question I answered, that althoughe I thought my self able to serve the prince therin, for thavauncement of her revenew, yet I was unable otherwise to compasse any such thing.

But syns having further waied and considered the same, I perceave that ther is meanes greatly to encrease the Quenes Majesties custome by wulles and felles (though nothing so moche as by the former devise) wherof at your honnors pleasure I shalbe reddy to make mention.

And wher it hathe bene signified unto me by some of the merchaunts of the Staple that it hathe bene gathered of some of Mr Secretarys wordes that it is I that have geven intelligens in these matters, I am assewred to have as moche displeasure wrought me as they can desire.' He desires to be taken into Dudley's service, 'by the which I dowte not but to be safe, otherwise for going abowte to proffit the prince I shall receave hurt and displeasure.'

Holograph Endorsed: 'April, 1561. John Johnson' 1p. (Dudley Papers I/199)

LORD AMBROSE DUDLEY TO LORD ROBERT DUDLEY

(Before December 25, 1561) 'I have received your letter wherein I doo perceave you thinke moche in your message the which was sentt to the Quenes Majestye. I assure you for my partt I sentt none, butt ytt might have bene done well inough. I maie thanke my sister Sydney and no body els for the sendynge of my stuffe thether, for that she sentt me worde she had gott me the chambers within the Courtt, and shewed them to my man, willing me therefor to send outt of hande to have them dressed up. I knowe well inough I am able to crave no chamber, but being free I cannott tell how will refuse ytt. Therfor ytt is the beste greffe for me to be turned outt because ytt was never of my sute to be ther. To morrow I will nott fayle butt to be ther and to doe my dewty as I am most bounde to doo.' At my house in Holbourn.* *Undated*

Holograph Addressed: 'To my lovinge brother, the Lord Robert Duddeley.' 1 p. (Dudley Papers I/177)

THE HOUSE OF COMMONS

1562:3, January 28, Address of the House of Commons to Queen Elizabeth urging her to marry.

7 pp. (Dudley Papers III/33)

(*II/37 is the Queen's answer to the Address, and II/39 is the Address of the House of Lords urging the Queen to marry, dated November 10, 1566*)

---

* Lord Ambrose Dudley was created Earl of Warwick on December 25, 1561.

1563, June 29 to October 3. Survey with tenants, rental of manors and lands of Lord Robert Dudley, made by John Dudley and others from 29 June to 3 October, 5 Elizabeth; Kenilworth (ff.1 and 138); Oldbury, Langley and Wallaxhall (f.9); Cleobury (f.17); Snodhill (f.25); Clifford (f.28); Trawalkin in Talgarth (f.33); Landenegwod Vaure (f.35); Penbrin (f.36); Denbigh (f.37); Chirk (f.76); Beverley (f.87); Bentley (f.97b); Skidby (f.103); Hornsey Marre (f.117); Meaux (f.118); Watton (f.118b); Hackness (f.119); Rascall (f.120); Hemysby *or* Hamysby (f.126); Sesterne *or* Sedersterne (f.129); Burton Lazarns (f.130b); Manton (f.133); Halsted and Tilton (f.134); Knoll (f.137). On f.139 is a schedule of 'Landes appointed to the Lord Robert Duddeley by the Quenes Majestie in May 1563'. The value of the above properties amounts to £917:17:6½.

Folio Vellum covers ff.139 (Dudley Papers XVI)

THE UNIVERSITY OF CAMBRIDGE TO LORD ROBERT DUDLEY

(1563) August 19. Praying Dudley to defend the privileges of the University, as his father had done.*

Latin 1p. (Dudley Papers I/179)

LORD ROBERT DUDLEY TO BENEDICT SPINOLA

1564, May 6. I send this bearer, Justin Grymes, unto you for the letter to your brother 'as touching the horsses. I pray you therefore dispatche him accordingly.' At the Court.

Signed Seal Addressed: 'To my loving frende Mr Benedic Spinola.' 1p. (Dudley Papers I/6)

P. CHOWTE TO LORD ROBERT DUDLEY

(1564 or before) June 10. He sends Dudley[†] a sapphire 'to be taken of my gyfte as a poore present, wisshing it to be an oryent diamonde, and so it were worthe gramercie, but as it is, King Henrye the eight ware it in a ring.' At the Castell of the Cambre.

Holograph Addressed: 'Lord Robert Dudley.' *Endorsed:* 'June, Chowte.' 1p. (Dudley Papers I/202)

LORD ROBERT DUDLEY TO ANTHONY FOSTER

(1564 or before) July 16. On the buying of hangings for Kenilworth and preparations for the Lord Keeper's visit.

Holograph 1 p. (Dudley Papers IV/13)
(Printed in *Wiltshire Archaeological Magazine* Vol.XVII (1878) p.92)

WILLIAM DRURY TO LORD ROBERT DUDLEY

(1564 or before) July. I am in the custody of Sir Richard Sackville. I hear that you have been a suitor for my liberty, and beg you to intervene further with the Queen in that regard. 'I understand that not only your L[P] dyd clerely and fully requyte myne offense towards you, yea though yt had ben a hundred tymes gretter,' but promised to 'travell for my liberte as yf I were your owen naturall son.' I acknowledge with grief my offence towards you but

---

* Dudley became High Steward of the University of Cambridge in 1563.
† Dudley was created Earl of Leicester on 29 September, 1564.

I was moved by nature and not by malice. I beseech you also to intercede with the Queen 'in that her Majestye hathe taken with dysplesure thosse rasche woordes which only I ment and spake of your L^P , beyng now of your grete curteyse and good natur by you freely remytted and forgeven. I wisshe the same unspoken with the losse of my blood.' I only ask to be allowed to do the Queen service.

Holograph Addressed: 'To the ryght honorable the Lord Robert Dudley.' *Endorsed:* 'July. W. Drury.' 3 pp. (Dudley Papers I/204)

NOTE

(Before September 29, 1564)   A note by Philip Browne of evidences received to the use of Robert Armiger, his father-in-law, from Lord Robert Dudley relating to the lands of Sir Tyrrye Robsart *temp* Henry VII and of John Robsart *temp* Henry VIII. *Undated*

1 p.   (Dudley Papers III/25)

THOMAS TROLLOPE TO LORD ROBERT DUDLEY

(Before September 29, 1564)   Offering to write in defence of Dudley's father and grandfather; the 'articles' to be revised by Dudley himself and then dedicated to the Queen. These spread abroad will win the hearts of all the nobility and commons to Dudley.   *Undated*

Signed Adressed: 'To the right Honorable Lorde Robarde Dudley.' 2 pp.   (Dudley Papers I/207)

RENTALS

1566, June 29.   Rental of manors, lands etc, of Robert Dudley, Earl of Leicester, 'renewed' before John Dudley and others acting under a commission dated 29 June, 8 Elizabeth, viz: Southwell (f.1); Great and Little Hampton (f.24); Bretforton (f.34); Marston Sicca *or* Dry Marston (f.41); Ewias Lacy (f.46); Cantrecelly (f.67); Weston (f.84); Buckland (f.110); Marnhull (f.133); Denbigh (f.152); Chirk (f.153).   At the end (f.188) is a 'schedule of landes delivered in exchange to the Quenes Majestie by the Erle of Lecester' and of lands received in recompense (1564).

Folio Vellum covers   ff. 189   (Dudley Papers XVII)

WARRANT

1566-7, January 14.   Warrant from Anthony Foster to 'Mr Pecok' to deliver to the bearer 1¼ ells of 'black bullony sersnet to cut the payre of a hose upon.'

Signed   1 p.   (Dudley Papers IV/18)

NOTE

1567, June 4 to 1568, April 18.   'A note of all suche stuffe as I have reseved of the Clarke of the Quenes stable, as also of the sadler, bytmaker and steropmaker, with all suche stuffe as hathe ben gyven by my Lord and what remayneth yn my charge.'   Among the items are 'clothes of vellytt of the Quenes' and 'a riche lyttar covered with vellyt layd upon with golde lase.'   The gifts include horses whose names are given, e.g.:

Jun. 9.   'To the Emperors Ymbasseter "Dun Sydney" with a vellyt sadle layd over with lase of golde, a harnys to the same, a pare of gilt steropes and a gilt bytt, a clothe and a collar.'

Jun. 14. 'To a Scotishe man that brought juells "Cole Lyddington".'

Jun. 14. 'To Sir H. Compton "Bayard" worthe with a Spanishe lether sadle.' *(amount not given)*

Jun. 16. 'To the regents Ymbasseter of Flaunders "Bayarde Knightley".'

Jul. 18. 'To Sir H. Sidney "Gre Sowthwell".'

Jul. 24. 'To the L. Chamberlen "Pyde Grene".'

Aug. 6. 'To the Erle of Arundell "Whyt Lyddington".'

Nov. 28 'To Sir Nicholas Throgmorton "Gre Audley".'

Feb. 6. 'To the Erle of Arundell "Pyde Yonge".'

--- 5. 'To Sir H. Sydney a "moyle".'

7 pp. (Dudley Papers III/43)

LORD DUDLEY TO THE EARL OF LEICESTER

(1569 or after) Thanking Leicester for having obtained 'my very freend Mysteres Haward* leave to cume into me' with protestations of devotion. *Undated*

Holograph 3 pp. (Dudley Papers II/289)

NEWS OUT OF FRANCE

(1570, ? July) It is thought the Diet of Spires will not go onward lightly. The Emperor, the two new queens and his family are there, but the chief princes of Germany, as the Landgrave of Hesse and the Count Palatine, will not come in person, alleging the Emperor to have violated his oath in that he has neither forsaken the Papal alliance nor advanced the Confession of Augsburg.

The Duke of Alva has stopped all the preparations which should have been made when the Queen of Spain came to the Low Countries, and the ships are disarmed which it was thought would take her to Spain. It is hoped that if peace takes effect in France, she may pass through that country. But the Pope's Legate was lately seized, his letters from the Duke of Alva taken. The troops at Valenciennes have mutinied; it is feared they may kill Count Ladron. There have been many executions for religion throughout the Low Countries. 'But under dyvers other pretences ther ys abote all the sayd contry many Englesh men with all there famyles.' *Undated*

Endorsed: 'The newes out of Fraunce.' 1 p. (Dudley Papers I/212)

RICHARD LANE TO THE EARL OF LEICESTER AND LORD BURGHLEY

(? 1570) He petitions to be allowed to make declaration of his proceedings in his design to draw all the Queen's subjects to 'all loialtie', the doings of the late rebels, etc. *Undated*

1 p. (Dudley Papers II/301)

MEMORANDUM

(? Before 1570-1) 'The cawses of my hyndraunce in my ferme this yeare.' A paper by a farmer of the Customs of London, who states that the causes are especially the 'continuance of this restraint.'

The merchants now in commission 'sweare all masters of shippes and maryners comynge into this port of London uppon interrogatories and

* Mary Howard, daughter of William Howard, 1st Lord Howard of Effingham, married Lord Dudley after the death of his second wife in 1569.

lykewise allso the merchants, and fynding any Lowe Countrie or Spanyshe wares they ponyshe the merchaunts by the boddy and pursse by fyne and in under-vallewynge their wares. This order is here verry sevearly don and followed to the great decay of this porte, for that no wheare ells ys the tenth parte of the lik searche used.

By which meanes the merchaunts that wold brynge their wares for London do lande them by the waie, as at Gravesend, Hame, Barckynge, Stratforde, Radclif and some at St Katheryns and other places into beere-houses in the nyght.'

Besides this the 'free butters or venterers' of the Prince of Orange lie in wait in the Channel and seize many ships laden for London; consequently most of the spices are landed at Southampton and Bristol.

'They will brynge in a carte laden withe hey fyve hundreth poundes worthe of merchandises, and likewise somtyme in a collyers carte from the beere houses on their beere cartes or draies: whereas they brynge six barrells usually all for beere, two of them shalbe withe marchandises, and these so fynely handled (with cley about the bonges and otherwise) that you shall not knowe them from thother, and so delyver them at the merchantes houses.'

It is calculated that no less than £627:2:2½ was lost in this year's farm in the 'pettie custom.' *Undated*

1 p. (Dudley Papers III/49)

CLAUDIO CORTE TO THE EARL OF LEICESTER

1570-1. February 4. Asking Dudley for payment of money due to him when he left his service. Informs him that Bernardino is at Paris in the employment of the Duke of Nemours. Paris.

Holograph Italian 1 p. (Dudley Papers I/214)

WILLIAM MAITLAND OF LETHINGTON TO THE EARL OF LEICESTER

(1570-1) February 21. Imploring Leicester's patronage to reconcile him with the Queen, and complaining of the continued efforts of his enemies to discredit him. Balvany.

Signed 1 p. (Dudley Papers I/216)

BARBARA DE LANNOY TO THE EARL OF LEICESTER

(After February, 1570-1) 'Alas! Right noble and honorable Lord, youre honors poore supplyante hath made her humble sute to my Lord Burghley* for her poore husband. His Lordship said to me, your said poore beseecher, that he was displeased in that my poore husband had spent the Quenes Majesties money, which aunswere hath so discomforted me as my herte is lyke to fayle me. Wherby I with my poore husbande and small enfante ar utterly lyke to be undone or cast away.' She asks Dudley to take pity on poor strangers banished from their country for religion's sake.

Holograph Directed to: 'The Earle of Leicester.' 1 p. (Dudley Papers I/209)

(See *Cal. S.P. Dom.*, 1547-1580, pp. 275-77)

SIR HENRY SIDNEY'S 'REMEMBRAUNCE'

(Before March, 1570-1) A 'Remembraunce to deale with my Lord of

* Sir William Cecil was created Baron Burghley on February 25, 1570-1.

Leacester and Mr Secretarie'. He declares his intention of coming 'from hence' before the 20th of March next if not countermanded, and expresses his desire in any case to leave with speed.

He proposes to describe the general state of Ireland, not only a general truce with Turlough Lynagh, but between all lords who are involved in disputes about which commissioners have travelled since Christmas.

A good part of the army is sent to Connaught 'to make the sword to work with lawe, so as the one maie bring to passe that thother can not, using them both as instrumentes of justice.' Consequently the President can keep his sessions, and the Scots who were there are either fled or offer to come in upon pardon. The Earl of Thomond is ordered to submit himself to that state which by his revolt he disturbed.

Lord Ormond reports James FitzMaurice to be in small force and hopes 'to have a good daie uppon him'. The Earl of Clancarr has submitted without conditions: 'it was thought convenient to use him with all favour we could.' His submission is a matter of great consequence for the peace of Munster.

'That generallie ther is no towerdnes at this present of any trouble to growe within the realme, nor certentie of any from abrode; never wynter hath passed with fewer stealthes nor lesse dessorder in all partes of the realme.'* *Undated*

Signed 2 pp. (Dudley Papers III/47)

SIR FRANCIS WALSINGHAM TO THE EARL OF LEICESTER

1570-1, March 5. 'I leave to my Lord of Buckhurst to shewe unto you how every waye he hath ben honorably interteyned. Therfor herein, this only wyll I saye, that sooche hath ben my Lords good demeanour and of the gentlemen of his trayne as the Kinge and his coorte restethe verey well satysfyced, and gyvethe both him and them great commendatyon, protestyng that sythence the King comyng to the Crowne thar was not so honorable an ambassage here; which I do not learne of them which report that which may best content, but of thos which advertyce trewly what they heare, which for the encrease of this good reporte he sparethe to use no lyberalyte towards sooche as by the Kings appoyntement have geven ther attendaunce uppon him.

Towching the state of thinges here the Duke of Longevile is lately departed from the Coorte with dyscontentement, for that the precedenship is adjudged unto the Duke of Nemours, protestynge that so long as Queen Mother lyveth he wyll not retorne to the Coorte, whom he judgeth his ennemye in this case.

I heare secretly that ther is not the best lieking betwene the two Quenes here; wherof the yonge Quene is lieke to have the woorste by common judgement, for that here whatsoever our Mother commaundethe takethe place and standethe for lawe. And yf her Majestye therfore desyre to take proffyt of Ffraunce, she must only be used as mestras and mediator here. I coolde therfor have wysshed that her Majestye amongest others had bestowed some present uppon her.

The Kings request unto the Pope for C(ount) Galeazzo his delyverye is quite rejected, whoe protestethe that yf all the Hugenots in Ffraunce were encamped about Roome he woolde not delyver him. The Kinge with this proude and disdaynefull awnswer is verry myche offended. I woolde therfore he woolde geve the Hugenots leave to make some tryall what they coolde doe for his delyverye.

Concerninge a Bull set upp agaynst her Majestie, the Kinges miscon-

* Sir Henry Sidney returned from Ireland in March, 1571. (See *Cal. S.P. Ireland*, 1509-1573, pp. 441, 442, and *D.N.B.*, p. 214)

tentement therwith and certayne requestes presented by the Spanyshe Imbassador, I refer your Lordship to Mr Secretaryes letters.' Paris.

PS. 'I have advertysed Mr Secretarye of a Roomyshe practyce. I can learne nothing as yet therof in particular. Your Lordship shall doe well to have an eye to thos that are suspected ther with you.'

Signed Endorsed: 'Mr Walsingham concerning matters in France. 5 Martii, 1570.' 2 pp. (Dudley Papers II/62)

ACCOUNTS

1570-1, March 7 to 1573-4, March 3. Account of stuffs, etc. delivered out of the Wardrobe of Robert Dudley, Earl of Leicester, to use as materials for articles of clothing, etc.

Folio Ff.33. (Dudley Papers XII)

COUNT LOUIS OF NASSAU TO THE EARL OF LEICESTER

1570-1, March 9. On behalf of Guillaume Dembize, a subject of the Prince of Orange, his brother, who with his ship had been arrested and imprisoned in London. La Rochelle.

Signed French 1 p. (Dudley Papers I/218)

HENRY GOODYERE TO THE EARL OF LEICESTER

1570-1, March 14. Asking aid in a suit to the Queen touching the validity of certain letters patent. London.

Signed 1 p. (Dudley Papers I/220)

THE BISHOP OF LINCOLN TO THE EARL OF LEICESTER

(Before 1571) March 23. Expressing his intention not to depute to any other the collection of the Queen's tenth with which he was charged by statute.* Bugden.

Holograph 1p. (Dudley Papers I/211)

LORD BERKELEY TO THE EARL OF LEICESTER

1570-1, March 24. 'Whereas by occasion of sickenes as well of my self as of my wief, before I had eny knoledge of the parliament, I procured by great entreatye and promisse of Mr Michell the phisician that he would come into the countrey and take some paynes for my recovery to health, the which his promise he hath performed and is now at Calloughden. And ther he is contented to show what pleisuer he (could) before his departure aswell to my self as to my wief. And except he now take me in hand I dowt lest my longe sought health will not by his help be recovered, for that it semeth he is not mynded to make any long abode here in England.' He hopes to cure him in nine weeks, and Dudley is asked to procure the Queen's licence for Berkeley 'to be absent sompart at the beginning of this parliament.' Calloughdon.

Signed Endorsed: 'The Lord Berkeley to be forborne from the Parliament. 24 March 1571.' 1 p. (Dudley Papers I/222)

THE MAYOR AND ALDERMEN OF BRISTOL TO THE EARL OF LEICESTER

1571, March 28. Setting forth that in the last Parliament a private Statute

---

* Nicholas Bullingham, Bishop of Lincoln, was translated to Worcester in 1571.

was passed incorporating the Merchant Adventurers of Bristol and 'excluding all other the inhabitants from intermedling in the trade of the sea'; that this Statute was only passed by the 'sinister dealing' of the two members for the city who were themselves merchants and who misrepresented the wishes of the inhabitants generally. But experience has shown that as a consequence of the Statute the common state of the city has greatly decayed, that the price of corn and other commodities has gone up as the result of their export by the merchants. They finally ask that the Statute in question may be repealed in the present Parliament by Leicester's influence 'of whome next the Quenes Highnes we have made our specyall choyse to be our chief governor and patron', and that the corporation in question may be dissolved.

Signed: W. Tucker, Mayor, David Harris, William Pepwall and Roger Joneys, Aldermen. 1 p. (Dudley Papers I/224)

THE EARL OF DERBY TO THE EARL OF LEICESTER

1571, April 16. Praying Leicester to join with Burghley to procure the Queen's licence for him to be absent from Parliament on the ground of ill-health. 'Though I can walk in my gallery I durste not give the adventure to take on me to remove to any of my howses nere me, beyng here in a colde howse not fytte for my disease, destitute of provision of fyer and other thinges, where I was not accostomyd to lie in wynter when I had my health.' He could only go to London in peril of his life. Knowsley.

Signed Wafer seal 1 p. (Dudley Papers I/226)

HENRY COBHAM TO THE EARL OF LEICESTER

1571, May 2. 'At my first entring in to Spaine I was most favorably entertained by Don Juan d'Acunya, Captain of the province of Guypuscoa, in sutch sorte as that with curtes woordes he did earnestly intreat me to lodge in his house, and when with excuse of my evill health I yelded not to him, he sent hys offesers to go in my company to my apointed lodginge to se me provided of all thinges necessary. Afterward he himself camme thether and presented me with cofertures and I had his letters of commendacion to pleasure me upon my occasion by the waie.

As I passed furder into Spaine towards the Court I reseved no cause of discontentacy, and when I was cumme to Madryd, Secretary Cayas did visyt me at my lodging, geving me to understand that the Kinge receved contentacy by hearing of my being here. Also that shortly his Majesty would geve me audiens and a speedy dispatche. After the Kinge did cumme hether I was admitted to his presens and now living in hope to receve answer of my negotiations.

As touching Stuclie he kepeth howse 3 leags from Madrid, not of the Kings chardges but on his owne despence and that in bountifull a manner.' Madrid.

Holograph 2 pp. (Dudley Papers I/231)

THOMAS SUTTON TO THE EARL OF LEICESTER

1571, May 6. He requests Leicester to intercede with Sir John Forster to obtain for him the hand of Forster's second daughter.

'My Lord of Hunsdons mallyce against me I suspect hathe not yett taken ende, whose good nature is, I knowe, suffycientlie knowne to your Lordship. I cannot accuse myself but to have done to him the dewtie of an honest man.' He asks Leicester to deal favourably with him.

'I stay the shipp here which should carrye your ordonance onlie for lack of the warrant from my Lord of Sussex. Pray send my cousin Thomas Dudley to him for it and in 20 days you shall have it all in London.' Berwick.

Holograph Seal 2 pp. (Dudley Papers I/228)

LEONARD WEST TO THE EARL OF LEICESTER

1571, May 8. 'This vile fleashe of myne cannot beare quietly these unnaturall dealengs of my nephewe the Lord Laware, to whom I offred my annuytie to sell because I would have paid Gilbert.' He bought it but will not now pay. He asks Leicester's help in the matter on behalf of his poor wife and children. London.

Holograph 1 p. (Dudley Papers I/234)

WILLIAM OVERTON TO THE EARL OF LEICESTER

1571, May 22. 'It dismayeth me very muche (right honourable) whan I consyder with my self that amongest all the frends that I have to leane unto in this lif, your Lordshipe beynge alwayes esteamed one of the chiefest and greatest I have, yet not one amongest them all of whom I am more afrayde at this present than of you; not that I doubt of your frendship towards me, which I am sure is firme and stable, but because I see it counterpoised and weighed downe with as great or greater frendship towards others which stand agaynst me. Ffor as your nature is to be loving and frendly to every man, even to your very enemies (which indeed is a good nature and well to be liked of all good and godly men), so whan I see that your frendship is divided betwene two contrary partes and peradventure not indifferently divided betwene them bothe, but with some inclination more to the one syde than to the other, I am afrayde (as I say) of your frendship, not of your frendship towards me which is great and needeth not to be proved, but of your frendship towards others which is greater than myne, and therefore may be feared, bycause it may do me hurte. Wherfore if your Lordship will algates divide your frendship amongest divers your frends, yet let me crave thus muche at your handes that most frendship be there employed wher it is most due and best deserved. I shall speake somewhat foolishly (O honourable) but yet playnly and truly and with all humblenes of hart and mynd as it becometh me unto such a state. Consyder with yourself, I besech you, what I am and what I have ben towards your Lordship. I am your chapleyn of olde, I have ben alwaies servisable at your commandement, I have ben plyable to your letters and suytes. I have ben and am in such case both able and ready to do you honor if you will use me. And though I have not done you much honor in the Court, wherin I have not so muche ben, yet in the country where I have most contynued and where I have ben by your owne goodwill and assignement, I have done you most honour of all the chapleyns you have, both by preaching and houskepinge, which two thinges are the chief poynts of honour and best piece of service that any chapleyn can do you. Ffor what greater honour can you receave than to be knowne and bruted abrode that you keepe suche chapleyns about you as both can and will sett furth the honour of God, whose honour both you and all men els ought chiefly to seeke. Or what better service can any man doe you than whan by your meanes and in your name he seeth that Lord and Kinge well served in his kingdome, I meane God in his Church, unto whom both you and all states els, yea all Kinges and Emperours, doe owe their whole and best service. Would you not take it in good part and think well of it, yf any gentleman of yours or chapleyn that is about you should by your meanes and at your appoyntment doe suche service to the Queenes Majestie in their severall vocation and calling as she for doyng the same wold well like of and commend. Would you not think it muche for your honour and take his service so done unto her to be done unto your owne self. I dare say you would, and good cause why, ffor she is your Lady and Maistres whom you your self doe honour and serve. And can you so well accept the service of your servaunt done by your meanes and in your name to an earthly and mortall Queene, and will not accept as well or better the service which he doth under your name and by your appoyntment unto the eternall God which is King over all Kings and Lord and ruler over all the states of the earth. If therfore I have served God in the country, I have served you also both in the country and in the Court; if I have honoured him there I have honoured you both there and everywhere, for as muche as it is everywhere thought, howsoever it be true, that in all such my doyngs I have ben supported and borne by your Lordships meanes, whose name of Chapleyne I beare. And yet to speak more playnly, I have done you honour in the Court indede, so often as I have ben called unto doyng (as your Lordship doth well know), and would have done you more if I had ben called oftener, neither wanteth there any forwardnes in me, but good will rather and inclination in your Lordship to call me forward. Besydes this, I am a gentleman borne and of aliaunce unto your Lordship, at lest wyse unto those that are alied unto you, as unto my Lord Deputie of Ireland and such others whose nighnes in affinitie you doe acknowledge. And therfore as you are your self a noble gentleman worthily called to great honour, so I trust you will regard me a poore gentleman nurtured and brought up alwaies at my booke, called by continuaunce of study to the highest degree in schole, a longe professor of the Gospell, a traveller in the Churche of Christ, a preacher of hys word and such a one as have suffered many stormes for the truethes sake, finally your owne Chapleyne, or at least wise the Queenes Majesties Chapleyn by your only meanes put and preferred unto her. Now what other men have ben and are, for whom you have done most, besydes that they were straungers unto you, I could say muche more of them if I would and could tell you straunge thinges if I listed. But I meane not to commend myself by depraving of others as other men I know have done by me, whom also you have easely harkened unto, which greveth me most. I am no papist (O, my Lord) nor half papist as they informe you, and as you suppose, neither may I dispend fyve hundreth pounds by the yeare, as they say, nor am I so riche and wealthy as they report me. I would I might spend but the one half onwards or were worth the one half to begyn withall. But they are papists themselves that have so tould you, and they may themselves spend a great deale more than either for their learning they are not worthy of, or for their good life and conversation may well keepe and continue with; whiche thing I will easely prove if the matter might ones come to hearing. But alas, your Lordship is to sone seduced and caried away with the paynted hypocrisie of slie and subtill serpents, which seeke to lurk in your bosum that they may sting you ere you be ware. O, take heede of dissembling enemies and chaunge not away your old frends for new flatterers. Speake they never so fayre, looke they never so smoothe, pretend they never so muche good will and frendship towards you, theyr meaning is to creepe within you craftely, and will deceave you whan you trust them most, be you assured of it, and they stick not so to say in corners whan they meetetogether, as by some of their own blables I have learned. And this is the cause that I marvell awhytt at their false and subtill dealings with me behynd my backe, whan I see they deale so slylie and subtilly with my betters whom they have founde their frends. And worse is he that can spie himself to be sought whan he seeth his faithfull frends and welwillers to be assaulted, and happy is he that can take warning whan he seeth his trusty servaunts shott at, that suche shooters seeke for a better marke; ffor be you out of doubt, right honourable, that whan the enemy striketh me and suche as I am which use to stand in your defence, and have oure eares abrode to heare of you that you can not heare of your self, and have our mouthes often tymes occupied in aunswering for you whan you heare not what is objected nor can aunswere in your owne behalf, be you out of doubt, I say, that the enemy so striking us meaneth the blow towards your owne self, and you shall feele the blow at the last be it never so long er it come, except in your authoritie now whan you may you defend those your poore frends which defend you at all tymes as farre as they may agaynst your closse and secreat enemies.

Alas! why should your Lordship so easely conceave of me to be a papist, which have always abhorred papistry from my hart, and upon the reports only of those that are but papists themselves, or, worse than papists, men of noe religion which serve the tyme for advauntage sake. Or why should your Lordship so definitively judge or say of me that I may spend so muche and so muche, or that I am worth so many and so many hundreth pounds only upon the malitious talkes of myne adversaries, which care not what and how untruly they speake of me, so it may turne to my shame and hynderance. I have ben a protestaunt now these six or seven and twentie yeares and never revolted from the truthe synce I first professed it. I have suffered muche persecution, for I was the first in all Oxford that forsoke my College and the Universitie in Queene Maries tyme for my conscience sake, and did put my nose into the storme whan other men strayned courtessie. I am and have ben continually synce the beginninge of the Queenes Majesties raigne that now is a constaunt and earnest setter furth of the truthe and have not cloked my religion but uttered my judgment and conscience freely in all places whersoever I came, the Court will beare me witnes of it, Paules Crosse will beare me witnes of it, Oxford, Cambridge, Winchester, Chichester, all that know me, yea your Lordships owne self, will beare me witnes of it, and yet they say I am a papist, and you beleeve them. Agayne I have ben a continuall houskeper since I might first spend any thing and have spent according to myne abilitie freely and frankly that which I had, and so freely indede that I am at this houre, I take God to my record, above two hundreth pounds in debt, and yet they report me to be a covetous man of marvelous wealth, and you beleeve them. Surely I am not ashamed at their sayings, bycause God and myne owne conscience doth acquite me of these slaunders, yea and they themselves doe know that they slaunder me; but yet I am greeved with myne evill lucke that your Lordship which knoweth me as well as they doe, and hath always ben my good Lord and thought well of me, doth now con-demne me without cause and chardge me with that which I most abhorre and am least giltie of.

Wherfore I beseeche your Lordship pawse awhyle in your opinion, consyder the premisses advisedly, and weighe every man as he is, bothe them and me. Let not subtill undermeyners abate your good will towards your poor frends and wellwillers. Let not their false tales be a stay of your frendship towards us for they hate you for your sake and so shall you fynd it in the end. O, my Lord. Let your dedes and premisses goe togyther for all their false packinge that are your flattering foes, and whan I deserve ill let me receave it but not afore. I have had your amiable words from tyme to tyme and have ben glad

of them. I have had and have in store your sweet and comfortable letters, and
I delight myself with them whan I reade them. Let not that now make me
heavy that hath so gladded my hart before. Let not that now be soure unto
me which hytherto hath ben so pleasaunt and sweete. Turne not, I say, your
hony into gall for you shall have no cause. Use me as you shall neede me, and
if you fynd noe use of me than reject me as nothing worth. But yet trye me er
you reject me, otherwise you can not know what use you may have of me.
And beynge ones tryed, if you fynd me not to have both will and abilitie for
that kynd of place and calling wher in I am to be used, than reject me most
worthily. And surely for goodwill I dare bragg with hym that bearethe you
lest; as for abilitie, I will say nothing but leave it to your owne judgment whan
you have tryed. But whether abilitie be such in me or noe as my goodwill is
and as I desyer to expresse by dedes, yet I trust you will recompence me with
goodwill for goodwill, though also I tast not of the abilitie that is in you to
expresse the same by like effects. And surely if I might desyer of your
Lordship any good dede at all as fruit of your goodwill towards me, it should
be this or to this effect, that by your good helpe I might fynd the meanes to be
removed not only from the ill will of those myne illwillers and adversaries that
so slaunder me, but also from the place it self where I dwell beyng always
subject to their ill will and malice, bycause I am there continually amongest
them. Neither seeke I so muche preferment of lyvinge therin as quietnes of lif
and opportunitie to serve God in my callinge. Whiche thinge if your
Lordship would bring to passe howsoever it be by exchaunge of my lyvings or
otherwise, I should thinke my self to have receaved at your hands the
singularst benefite, and to have tasted of the excellentest fruit of your good
will towards me that I ever could desyer, yea all men would commend you
for it that knoweth our case, and God himself will reward it unto you,
which loveth peace and unitie in his churche and liketh well of them that
make it. At leastwise let me receive this good dede at your hands as the fruit
of your good will towards me that by your protection I may be defended
from such mischief and malice here after of these pretense frends of yours
and open enemies of myne, as they by the continuall practise of their busy
braynes shall still fourge and frame agaynst me. And so I have at your
Lordships hands as muche as I desyer, though I never have more.
Th'almightie God that hath advaunsed you to this honourable state and
made you a great and excellent member in his Churche, keepe and preserve
you in continuall health and prosperitie, to the glory of his owne name, the
great praise and commendacion of your self, the utilitie and profitt of his
holly congregation, the common joy and comfort of all those that live under
your honourable protection and defence.' Chichester.

Holograph Torn in one place 2½ pp. (Dudley Papers I/237)

GUIDO CAVALCANTI TO THE EARL OF LEICESTER
1571, May 23. The state of the negotiations is now most favourable. The
Princes hold you to be most favourable in this great business, particularly
from the writings of Monsieur de la Mothe. All who are not swayed by
private interests judge the affair to be honourable, commodious and secure
for all parties, the prudence and virtue of her Majesty are praised, as well as
her good government. I hear nothing but praise of Monsieur. Monsieur de
Montmorenci has spoken to me most favourably, and he has great influence;
so also the Count of Foix and many others. I shall remain at Court to help the
Ambassador, of whose discretion and diligence it is impossible to speak too

highly. No ambassador before him has been in such favour at this Court. Monsieur de Foix salutes you. Gaglioni.

Holograph Italian 2 pp. (Dudley Papers I/239)

THE EARL OF LENNOX, REGENT OF SCOTLAND, TO THE EARL OF LEICESTER

1571, May 26. 'I have directed the gentleman bearer herof, James Cunningham, my servant, towardes the Quenes Majestie to declare unto her Hienes and the Lordes of her Honourable Councell the estaiit of this contrie and how matters therin be fallen out far otherwise, I belief, nor was the meaning and opinion of her Hienes and your Lordship at the dispatch of the Erll of Morton and others the Kings Commissioners. Off the ilk I doubt not but your Lordship sall thinke meatt that consideration be spedily taken and due provision made as the present occasion requires. And seing I have once found your Lordships favor and gudewill, not onlie in my awn privat matters but in the affaires of this state since I tuke upon me the regiment therof... I will not now make long discourse but pray you to give credit to the bearer herof.' Stirling.

Signed Wafer Seal 1 p. (Dudley Papers I/243)

THE EARL OF MORTON TO THE EARL OF LEICESTER

1571, May 29. On the troubles in Scotland and especially in Edinburgh. Dalkeith.

Signed Wafer Seal 1 p. (Dudley Papers I/247)

(This letter is a copy of Morton's letter to Burghley. See Cal. S.P. Foreign, 1569-71, No. 1746, p. 458)

JOHN BUTLER TO THE EARL OF LEICESTER

1571, June 17. On legal and other business. Mr Goodyere has delivered the possession of Blackwell to Dockwra and him. An inquisition has been held at Warwick concerning Sir Francis Englefield's lands. He asks for instructions with regard to fitting up the house. Kenilworth.

Holograph Wafer seal 1 p. (Dudley Papers II/4)
Another letter of June 25 on the same matter. 1 p. (II/6)

ROGER YONGE TO EDMUND DOCKWRA

(? 1571) June 18. Asking his interest with the Earl of Leicester that Anthony Stephyns may be made schoolmaster at Ewelme. Bastleden.

Holograph 1 p. (Dudley Papers II/2)

THE DUKE OF MONTMORENCY TO THE EARL OF LEICESTER

1571, June 19. On the satisfaction of the King of France with the good offices of Leicester in furthering a treaty of alliance between England and France. Gaillon.

Signed French Wafer seal 1 p. (Dudley Papers II/7)

J. BARNABY TO THE EARL OF LEICESTER

1571, June 26. I am here on business, and have had opportunity of talking with an Irishman calling himself Archbishop of Cashel. He declared to me the cause of his 'flieing out of Ireland.' He feared to return to England notwithstanding the Queen's letter of safeconduct, and he wished to go straight back to Ireland. Rone.

Holograph Almost illegible in parts through damp 4 pp. (Dudley Papers II/12)

JOHN YONGE TO THE EARL OF LEICESTER

1571, July 12. Applying for the farm of the Customs at Bristol. Melbury.

Holograph Seal 1 p. (Dudley Papers II/17)

SIR 'JOHN OF DESMOND' TO THE EARL OF LEICESTER

1571, July 14. Thanking Leicester for his good offices and asking that he may have liberty to wait upon him. St Leger House, Southwark.

Signed 1 p. (Dudley Papers II/19)

THE BISHOP OF ROSS TO THE EARL OF LEICESTER

1571, July 16. 'This present is to remember your Lordship I wret before the Quenes Maties removing to your Lordship be this gentleman bearer hereoff, as also to my Lord Burghley, wheroff I received answer that no resolution was ther taken but delayed till her Highnes cuming to Hampton Court. Synce the which tyme thair is no answer maid to my sutte that is cuming to my knowlege, through the which I am constrayned to preasse your Lordship again with new remembrance. Praying most humbly your Lordship to move the Quenes Highnes with the assistance of my Lord Burghley to tak sum good and expedient advyse that I may have her Majesties favorable answer with liberte.' Ely House.

Holograph Seal 1 p. (Dudley Papers II/23)

WILLIAM GERRARD TO THE EARL OF LEICESTER

1571, July 16. Concerning legal matters in Wales and the miserable estate in which Sir Roger Vaughan died. All his goods and chattels were not worth £100, no money, in debt to more than £2000; he also left various daughters and sons without clothes or even place where they could get meat and drink. Leicester would do a charitable act if he could get Sir Thomas Gresham to have compassion on them. Presteigne.

Signed Seal, broken 1 p. (Dudley Papers II/25)

EDMUND DOCKWRA TO THE EARL OF LEICESTER

1571, July 17. Protesting against the felling of woods. Windsor.

Holograph 2 pp. (Dudley Papers II/27)

THE EARL OF HUNTINGDON TO THE EARL OF LEICESTER

1571, July 19. Commends the bearer. Informs Leicester that he is almost ready 'to goo towards Coventree about *dedi* and *Concessi*.' London.

Holograph Seal 1 p. (Dudley Papers II/29)

SIR WILLIAM FITZWILLIAM TO THE EARL OF LEICESTER

1571, July 21. 'Forasmuch as by some advertisementes from my ffrendes owt of England, I heare that the L. Deputye aplieth himself to receive dischardge of his Ireland service and the L. Grayes bruted repaire hither to wex cold, wheare through I am wrought the rather into some thinking that I shall be stayed in the office that I beare of government for longer tyme then fyve monethes which was the promysed space of my abode here and then that I shold retourne. I am become rather a right humble servitor to your Lordship that considerenge howe I stonde nowe chardged with honest keping in doble maner, my wiff being in Englond and I here.' The cost of living here is too high for his purse. His lands in England are going to decay, 'and furthermore th'exquisite partes of learning, wytt, pollecie and good skill to govern being in me wanting and my sickness make me unfit for this calling.' He asks Leicester to move the Queen to discharge him from his post. Dublin.

Signed Seal 2 pp. (Dudley Papers II/30)

JOHN MARSH TO THE EARL OF LEICESTER

1571, July 25. On behalf of one Kemp of Windsor whose ships and goods have been detained, and on behalf of the liberty of the city of London in this wise: 'Wheare the Company of Vintners have of late helped themselves and their posteritie by the Quenes Majesties graunt to be owte of the daunger of the Statute of Anno 5° E.VI, other honest cittizens that be not free of this Company have used to retayle wynes and wear never brought upp in other sciences or trad, and their apprentizes and posteritie are unprovided for and by meanes of that statute shall be secluded from occupyinge.' He asks for remedy 'for it hathe bene all wayes the custome of the cittie of London that he that is free of one company is free of all.' Refers to the dangers of giving the Vintners' Company a monopoly.

Signed Seal 2 pp. (Dudley Papers II/36)

THE EARL OF DERBY TO THE EARL OF LEICESTER

1571, July 30. 'I ffynde myself verrey moche bounden unto your Lordship as well for the comfortable letters whiche I lately receyved from your Lordship and others of her Majesties Prevey Counsaill upon my son Thomas his commyttement to warde, as for many others your grette ffrendshippes and curtesies. And perceyvyng by the same letters that he hath incurred her Majesties displeysour and indignacion by summe unadvised and indyrecte dealyng: evin as nature moveth me to be sorie to understande that this oversight and dealyng have given occasyon of offence unto her Highnes, so havyng alwayes found your Lordship faythfull unto me and myne, am now bolde to desyer the same that (as convenyent tyme may serve) your Lordship wolle pleyse (for my sake) to be a meane to qualifye her Highnes indignacion concyved agaynst my said son in suche sorte as you shall perceyve your Lordship may without offence. I have sent my servaunt Sir Rychard Sherburne to your Lordship to put you in remembraunce herof.' Knowsley.

Signed Seal 1 p. (Dudley Papers II/42)

M. DUPIN TO THE EARL OF LEICESTER

1571, August 1. I have received your letter which you sent by Cavalcanti. Mon. de Montmorenci shows more and more good will in promoting the friendship between the two Crowns, and if he and his friends like Monsieur de Foix had the sole ordering of matters, all would be secure. Fontainebleau.

Holograph French 1 p. (Dudley Papers II/44)

SIR JOHN OF DESMOND TO THE EARL OF LEICESTER

1571, August 3. Asking Leicester to procure his liberty and that he may be received by the Queen before she goes on her progress. St Leger House, Southwark.

Signed 1 p. (Dudley Papers II/46)

LORD BURGHLEY TO THE EARL OF LEICESTER

1571, August 10. 'I am here fully occupied lyke a herbenger to procure a lodgyng for Monsieur de Foix. Mrs Onslowes house can not be had, all thyngs being locked up by hir and he is in hurry. I have sent to obteyn Serjeant Manwoods house or Blackwells.

I write to my Lord Cobham to cause on of his brethern to accompany Monsr de Foix to London.

Sir William Pikeryng is in York Shyre and the *(torn)* use Henry Knolls and H. Killigrew.

The Bishop of Ross sent me by Mr Kyngsmill this inclosed and lasteward pressed to spek with me and so I have done and fynd hym better disposed to utter the matter of Halls being with hym, and dealyng with the other night he wold not be knowen of to my Lord of Sussex.

I have also spoken to the B(ishop) of Ely who hath no meaning to go down to Ely until Bartlemewtyde, being so occupyed with the B(ishop) of Canterbury by her Majesties orders, and I see it is not mete that he should soner depart.

I think the B(ishop) of Ross may surely remayn with hym without the attendance of Mr Skypwith or Kyngsmill, and so in my opinion he may be as well kept by the Bishop of Elys own ordre as now he is.

As I shall here from your Lordship of hir Majesties plesure so will I also procede.

I pray your Lordship, except necessary matter shall move you to *(torn)* ... all for me, lett me staye amongst my dusty laborors untill de Foix shall be sent for hyther for my *(torn)*... being in the middest to be fyneshed forceth me to assure your Lordship to hasten to gett it covered. In dede wholly and only with borrowyng here in the Cite wherby as I take plesure in my fond humor of buyldyng, so have I a stay and stopp from to much rejoysyng whan I behold the cost to be doone by borrowyng, and so had I rather doo my Lord and leave my heyre less land to repaye it then by bribery in an office. I have to sett upp on bryckston or by beyng to importune to hir Majesty to seke furder relief of hir Majesty. You see under what disease I labor not unlyke your own in my opinion. From my house in Westminster, as mery with my own as the Q. busynes will permyt me which followyth me where soever I go.'

Holograph Damaged 2 pp. (Dudley Papers II/47)

THE EARL OF BEDFORD TO THE EARL OF LEICESTER

1571, August 12. Enquiring as to the Queen's health and saying that he 'will attend upon her Majeste this progresse.' From my house at Garrdon.

Signed 1 p. (Dudley Papers II/49)

THE EARL OF DERBY TO THE EARL OF LEICESTER

1571, August 26. 'I was so bolde (in respect of some bruts made in the countrey that my son Edward shuld be send forre) to send this bearer by waie of credence to my servaunt Sir Richard Sherburne, knight, then beyng at Court, to troble your Lordship with desier of your private and ffrendly advise whether it myght stande with your lyking I shuld send hym uppe to prevent the speches that myght have ensued by his ffetchyng, as cheffely to declare my reydynes and obedience to offer his attendaunce dutyfully for his better triall of his loyalty and truth toward her Majestie, and the said Sir Richard beyng retorned homewards before my messenger came uppe, my servaunt this (by whom I sent my message) I persave hath presumed to deale with your Lordship to lyke effect, and hath also largely told me your Lordships opynyon for his cummyng uppe, and of your most ffavorable direction for his stay at Solham tylle suche tyme as he shall here from your Lordship more of your pleysour. As this your Lordships curtesse and frendly dealyng giveth me cause of assured hoape of good segnelie by your Lordships meane, so am I bounde for ever and shalbe reydy to make requytall, nothing dowtyng but your Lordship wille consider how grevose it is to me in these my old and unhelthfull yeres to understand that my sonnes have any waye demeryted her Majesties dyspleysour.' I ask that my son Edward be sent home to me, 'who I shall assuer your Lordship upon any request or commandement shalbe reydy to give his attendaunce and answere wher he shall be called. I am the more bolde to ask this request as well for thatt he is not as yet to my knowledge tutched by publyke authoritie, as for that also his present paynes and diligence in servyng me in my chamber was suche as now I fynde ther great wante.' Knowsley.

Signed Seal, broken. Endorsed: '26 August, 1571. The Earle of Derby for his sonnes.' 1 p. (Dudley Papers II/51)

LEWYS EVANS TO THE EARL OF LEICESTER

(1571) August 28. 'I have sythence my last coming unto the countrey searched out some fonde prophecieng bookes and I delyvered them to the Busshop of Bangor; the man that had them ys in prison ... Yf the man were sent for unto your honors he wolde betraye the rest. The prophecies are marvaylous sedicouse and trayterouse. There cam hyther of late a Welshe booke wrytten by some of Rome and prynted at Avyllen. At the Busshops request I translated yt into English, and soe doe aunswere yt.' Denbigh.

Holograph Endorsed: '28 August, 1571. Lewys Evans towching books of prophesie.' 1 p. (Dudley Papers II/53)

THE BISHOP OF ROSS

(August, 1571) 'Memorie of certane heades to be moved to my Lord of Burghly in name of the Bishop of Ros.

He hath spoken with me	First, synce it is the Quenes Majesties plesure that he sal remane with my Lord of Ely and that the most of his company which did attend upone him should depart; therefore he desyres that he may have the comoditie to speak with my Lord of Burghley to ye effect that some ordre may (be) taken as may most comodiously satisfie the Quenes Majesties plesure in that behalf.

Item, that ane passport be granted to ane of the Quene his Maisters servaunts to pas with his wretinges to certifie her of the said

182

If he remove not this may stay.

determination, and to the effect that she may advertis him agane of her plesour, principally touching her servantes whan they shalbe sent and in what maner salbe furnesed, and that in the pasport to be specified that the said servant may remayne for thre or four dayes at least at her plesour to ye effect she may the better resolve tharupon.

Item, that notwithstanding he douttis not but he salbe well and honorable used (by) my Lord Ely, yet he desyres that it be provydit that he may have of *(torn)* free ayre about his houses and paliceis in the towne *(torn)* whan they sal happen to remayne for him sum certane space (at the) Lord of Elys discretion, being alwayes accompanied with such of his servandes as he pleses to appointt.

The discretion of on Bishop may answer the other with circumspection to avoyd all intelligence.

Item, synce it is the Quenes Majesties plesour to discharge the most part of his company he desyris that four at least of his servandes may remayne in company with him with ane cook boy and lackay, conforme to the Counselles appointtment which sal not be chargeable in any waye to my Lord of Ely.

Six are to many for the chardge of the host.

Item, that he may frelie speik with the gentlemen and servandes that has attendit apon him, in respect thay ar to depart and with his other servandis for taking thare comptes and putting ordour thareto as apertinis.

In presence of Mr Skipwith and Kyngsmill.

Item, that he himself might have libertie to pas to his logeing and put ordour to his letters and sic uther furniture as he has in his house, seing he is to depart and incertane of his returne.

To medle with no wrytyngs but by right of others.

Item, that he may speik with the Ambassador of France principally to sollicit the treaty already begune to take effect, as also that he be his *(illegible)*.

He may wryte.

Item, to have libertie to wreit to the Quene.

An oppen letter.
He is sufficiently served and nede not now to go to Cambridge.
If he shall not remove after Bartellmewtyde, these answers are superfluous.

Item, that he may (have) wise camarage.'

Marginal notes in Lord Burghley's hand   2 pp.   (Dudley Papers II/48)

THE EARL OF ARUNDEL TO THE EARL OF LEICESTER

1571, September 14.   'I most hartely thanke your Lordship for your letter, and I am sory to perceve therby that Her Majestie is so fully persuadyd of my Lord of Norfolkes unduteyfull delynges towards her Hyghnes.   I praye God that his trothe may be layed open to the full satysfaction of her Majestie and to the benyfyte of him self (yf he have nott deservyd the contrarye). Hyt aperythe your Lordship knowythe nott his casse and for my part I am utterlye ignorant therof; wherfor tyll I shall see his ontrothe aparant I cannott but hoope that God left him not soo naked of his grace to deserve so evyll as that he is nott to receve her Majesties grace and favor agayne. And in the meane tyme I wyll praye for her Majesties quyett and happenes in all her causys, and to your Lordships good helthe and aswell to doo as any frende maie wyshe to an other.' Arundel Place.

Holograph Seal 1 p. (Dudley Papers II/55)

SIR FRANCIS WALSINGHAM TO THE EARL OF LEICESTER

1571, September 15. 'I conceyved great hope by your letter of the 16th of Auguste that her Majestye woolde have taken proffyt of the late affares, but fyndyne in her Majesties letters lately receyved not so myche as any mentyon made therof makethe me utterly to dysspayre therof. The expectatyon of her Majesties intentyon in that behalfe makethe them here to staye from resolving, wherby I feare the opportunyte of the entreprise wyll be loste, and so the unkyndenesses betwene the two princes put up: which no dowbte of yt wyll turne to owre mischefe. I beseeche your Lordship, do not geve over to doe what good you may, for yt concearnethe as well Gods glory as her Majesties savetye.

Towching my last negotyatyons I am referred over unto Monsieur de Ffoyx, comminge for Ambassador.

This gentleman, the bearer hereof, can informe your Lordship how honorably the Admiraule hathe ben used by the King, Queen Mother and Monsieur, whom I have thorroughely (*illegible*) of that I know.' Blois.

PS. 'Touching my desease and state I beseech your Lordship to credyt this bearer.'

Signed, only postscript being holograph Seal Addressed: 'To the ryght honorable and my veary good lorde the Erle of Lycester: at the Court.' 1 p. (Dudley Papers II/59)

'OCCURRENTES'

1571. A paper of news from the following places:

(1) Strassburg. The Emperor's appeal to the Princes for help against the Turks, the imprisonment of King Eric, and the prevalence of the plague. April 7.

(2) Paris. Suspicions that the House of Guise is falling out of favour with the King. Quarrels for precedence between the Dukes of Nevers and Guise. 'Newes cum this morning that the Cardinall of Guise is dead and the only grief is that the Cardinall of Lorrayne did not supplie his place.' The King's determination to have the Edict in favour 'of those of the Religion' carried out at Toulouse. *Undated*

(3) Lyons. Preparation for war in Italy, especially on the part of the Venetians. April 12.

2 pp. (Dudley Papers III/53)

1571-2, February 5.   I rejoice in your zeal for God's truth and religion, as set forth in your letters to me.   'But whereas you declare at large your good likinge and allowance of the (exercise) and conference of the Ministers of Gods worde and sacraments at Northampton, wher Mr Wyborn is, I knowe you wold doo the same of two other places where Mr Wyborn cometh not, and yet the clergie of my dioces hath conference and exercise also if you had bene therof enformed, I meane in Rutland and Stamford wher the Ministers of Lincolne Dioces in parte with certain others of my dioces have conference and exercise also.   And by the grace of God I promis your honour that good and godlie exercise at Northampton shalbe mainteined at Northampton either with Mr Wybornes help or without it.   And I assure your Lordship of my credit also ther was conference in some partes of my dioces amonge the Ministers even in Rutland before they hard Mr Wyborne named.   But to come more particularlie to your originall cause of writing, which is for assistance to Mr Wyborne and that he may prech at Northampton, ther be two thinges that withdrawe me from the same as to the author therof.   One is the authoritie of my superiors who have by *(torn)* ... out and by orders taken at this late Convocation of the clargie in *(torn)* ..... parliament time as also by speciall letters to the same effecte *(torn)* ... me that I shall licence none to prech in my dioces that doo *(torn)* ... geve their assent and subscription unto certain articles knowen *(torn)* ... enough unto Mr Wyborne, whereunto he hath not assented and *(torn)* ... before me.   And the other cause is because he is, as it seemeth to me over studious of innovation, for although as your Lordship doth like the substance of his doctrine or the most part therof, even so doo I yet knowe, you not peradventure as I doo, that the contention and con(ference) that is in Northampton betwen townesmen themselves and him ther is about externe matters, ceremonies and things indifferent about which he sheweth as much vehemency as about the prin(cipal) groundes of religion, and wold remit no parte of his contention as farre as I can gather when he preched.   Therfore I trust your honour will consider that it is not my parte to procede further with him, and to stand more of his parte then with others, his and my superiors, whom I am bounde to thinke as well of as of Mr Wyborne.   He never had any licence from me in writing, but from my Lord of Canterburie.   Let him get licence nowe where he had it in times past receved in writinge, as I know he may have upon his conformity unto the lawes, and I shall not nede to be anie moved in his behalf, but he may doo as his learning and conscience leadeth him.'   Peterborough.

Signed, with marginal notes containing the headings of the various parts of the letter apparently in the Bishop's hand.   Damaged in places.   2 pp.   (Dudley Papers II/60)
(See *H.M.C. Pepys MSS*, p.177 for Leicester's letter.)

SIR ROBERT CHESTER TO THE EARL OF LEICESTER
(Before March, 1572)   Concerning his suit to the Queen 'for the recovery of th'office of Receyvourship' with objections to the claim of Lord Lough-borough.*   *Undated*
Holograph   2 pp.   (Dudley Papers II/285)
(See *Cal S.P. Dom*, 1547-80, p.118)

* Sir Edward Hastings, Lord Loughborough, died on 5 March 1571-2.

John Yonge to the Earl of Leicester

1572, April 14. Ever since the 11th of this month a large fleet of ships - some think 300 sail - has been observed off Portland. It is working eastwards, but is delayed by contrary winds. Wilton.

Holograph 1 p. (Dudley Papers II/71)

Sir Thomas Smith to the Earl of Leicester

1572, April 15. I thank you for your letter of April 5. As to the negotiation, 'I do not dowte but all here shalbe done as her Majestie wisheth, except that mater of Scotland do hinder which hitherto we can not conclude because we are bownde to our instructions which they will not agree unto. But I think we shall come to it in the end, for they desire it heartily, for they distrust Spain as much as we do.'

It would be a great advantage to all if you would come over to France. Blois.

Signed Seal 1 p. (Dudley Papers II/109)

Edward Southworth to the Earl of Leicester

1572, April 16. Praying Leicester to protect one Ralph Prune from one of his harsh creditors. Rudforth.

Signed 1 p. (Dudley Papers II/82)

The Countess of Southampton to the Earl of Leicester

1572, April 20. Praying to be allowed to go to her husband in the Tower. From my Lord my fathers house (Cowdray).

Holograph Seal 1 p. (Dudley Papers II/78)

The Earl of Morton to the Earl of Leicester

1572, April 25. On behalf of John Tristane, one of the merchants of the Staple, ruined by the loss of Calais. The bearer is Captain Cockburn.

Signed Seal 1 p. (Dudley Papers II/69)

The Titular Archbishop of Cashel to the Regent of Scotland

1572, April 26. Complaining of his arrest. Dundee.

Copy, enclosed in II/69. (Dudley Papers II/90)
(*For the original,* see *Cal. S.P. Foreign,* 1572-74, p.92, No.296.)

The Earl of Morton to the Earl of Leicester

1572, April 28. He asks Leicester to remember the cause of him and his friends; and that Fergus Graeme, who has gone to London, may not be suffered to return. He encloses a copy of a letter from the Archbishop of Cashel to him in order that Leicester may understand 'what the man is and his suspitions.' Leith.

Signed Seal 1 p. (Dudley Papers II/87)

Sir Thomas Gresham to the Earl of Leicester

1572, April 29. Regarding the custody of Lady Mary Grey. Gresham House.

Holograph Seal, broken 2 pp. (Dudley Papers II/91)

(Printed in *Notes and Queries,* 4th Series x, p.71.)

SIR THOMAS RANDOLPH TO THE EARL OF LEICESTER

(1572 ?) May 2. On the difficulties of 'compoundinge the controversis betwene so greate parties as have longe contendid in Scotland.' Berwick.

Signed Almost illegible from effects of damp 4 pp. (Dudley Papers II/310)

SIR WILLIAM PYKERYNG TO THE EARL OF LEICESTER

1572, May 4. Complains of Oswald Metcalf, 'the furst and onely seducer of the Earle of Northumberland,' the author of the most traitorous publications. At the time of the rebellion he and his dear friend Roger (?) Danell entered Pickering's lands at Byland, and committed damage there to the extent of £300. London.

Signed Nearly illegible through damp 3 pp. (Dudley Papers II/95)

SIR VALENTINE BROWNE TO THE EARL OF LEICESTER

1572, May 8. Promising good will to Roger Marbeck who 'is hartely welcome to me.. for your Lordships sake.' He is sorry that in coming into that region Marbeck had had such hard fortune, 'ffor comyng safely within one daies journy to Berwick, he was between Morpit and Anwick violently assaulted by certeyn lewde disposed persons, and being by them forcibley carried towards the Scottish borders was by them pitifully spoiled of all suche furniture and provision as he had, and being stripped to his dublet and hose, not without great peril of his life (came) the next daie to Anwick, where for your Lordships sake he was the better intreated, as well of the Lord Warden himself, who gave him 20ˢ towards his journey, as also of Master Nicholas Ffoster, his soon, who bestowed a cloke upon him for the same purpose.' The offenders should be sought out and punished severely. Berwick.

Signed 1 p. (Dudley Papers II/98)

RICHARD FARMOR TO THE EARL OF LEICESTER

1572, May 8. Reporting speeches and doings of prisoners in the Tower implicated in the Duke of Norfolk's plot. From the Tower of London.

Holograph 2 pp. (Dudley Papers II/100)
(Printed in *Wiltshire Archaeological Magazine,* Vol XVIII (1879) p.28.)

SIR THOMAS SMITH TO THE EARL OF LEICESTER

1572, May 8. 'I am sorie I shall not se your Lordship here in Ffraunce, ffor I understand now my Lorde Admirall doth com. Nevertheless so far as yet I can learne, the Duke de Montmorency, Marshall of Ffraunce, continueth his purpose into England, and with him Monsieur de Ffoix and de Bataille, both of the privie Counsell. De Bataille is a wise and well learned man; de Foix is well enough known to your Lordship..... How the league is estemed there with you, I know not; suer I am the King here estemeth it much, and will not stick to saie that he estemeth it more then eny other, yea then we our self wold think. He accompteth the peace making with his subjects, the mariage of his sister to the Prince of Navarre, and this league of streighter amitie and mutuall defence with the Quenes Majestie to be the thre happines which hath com to him for the establishment of his Crowne; all the which he hath done and brought to pas, he saith, against the will of many of his Counsell. And more than onis or twice hath said 'thanks be to God, these three God hath geven me the grace to do, and to strike the stroke in all difficulties because I wold have it so. And therfor now I know God loveth me, and so I might obteyne the fourth I wold think me the happiest prince in this world.' This prince hath had trouble which hath made him wise in his yong age. Yet I pray God we may have the same or the like grace to know his benefits and still to folow that which shalbe to th'assurance of her Majesties rayne over us in all peace and quietnes both within and without the realme.' Paris.

Signed Seal 1 p. (Dudley Papers II/104)

SIR THOMAS WROTH TO THE EARL OF LEICESTER

1572, June 12. On his committal of John Rawlins *alias* Yonge for playing an unlawful game called 'riffe' (ruff). Enfield.

Holograph 3 pp. (Dudley Papers II/106)
(Printed in *Wiltshire Archaeological Magazine,* Vol XVIII (1879) p.31)

JOHN BULLINGHAM TO THE EARL OF LEICESTER

1572, June 21. Offering to exchange his benefice of Brington for that of Upton-on-Severn. Worcester.

Holograph 1 p. (Dudley Papers II/111)
(Printed in *Wiltshire Archaeological Magazine,* Vol XVIII (1879) p.33)

LORD DE LA WARR TO THE EARL OF LEICESTER

(1572) June 27. Urging his ability to serve Leicester in Hampshire as well as either Mr Horsey or Mr Wallop; and protesting against the 'arrogant speechis' of the Queen of Scots. White Friars.

Holograph 2 pp. (Dudley Papers II/113)

THE EARL OF LEICESTER TO SIR JOHN ZOUCH, SIR JOHN THINNE AND OTHER THE COMMISSIONERS FOR THE SURVEYS OF FUGITIVES' LANDS

1572, July 7. Requesting them to expedite the survey of Wootton Basset, late Sir Francis Englefield's lands. At the Court.

Signed Seal 1 p. (Dudley Papers I/8)

ROBERT FYLLES TO THE EARL OF LEICESTER

1572, July 18. With particulars as to the manor of Clun. Kingsland.

Holograph 1 p. (Dudley Papers II/115)

ELLIS PRICE TO THE EARL OF LEICESTER

(1572) July 22. 'Wheras my very lovinge ffreind Mr John Owen Esquier delivered of late a certen leas or patent of the townshippe of Dolgelley with the appurtenances within this countye of Merioneth, being but of a small thinge of 33s 4d of rent to the Quenes Majestie or there abouts to the hands of his nephew Hugh Lloyd, your Lordships howshold servant, to be renewed and taken agayne from the Quenes Majestie to the said John Owen, after which delivery and before your Lordships said servant had entred into the same sute, one Sir Robert Constable, knight, as is reported, hath by some malicious procurement presentlye obteyned a certen graunt to him made of the same townshippe for certen yeres in reversion of the Quenes Majestie, which is not only somewhat to the discomfort of the said John Owen, but also partelye to the foyle and reproch of his said nephewe, your honors servant, in that behalf, of which townshippe by comyn brute the said Mr Constable hath made half a graunt or promes to John Salisbury, Esquier, who procured him to enterprise in the same sute, the which John Salisburye, as is not unknowen in England and Wales, hath of long tyme, as also of late, bourne unto me malice and displeasure and to my ffrend the said John Owen, as well for that I did as much as in me laye and as to me of dutye apperte255ned, ffurther aswell your affayres as my Lord your brothers within the Lordshippes of Denbigh and Ruthin, at the request of your honorable sister, my Ladye of Warwicke, agaynst the said Salisburye within the same lordshippe of Ruthin; but also that I did lately geve th'ellection and voyces of me and my ffrends within the countey of Merioneth to Hugh Owen, Esquier, brother to the said John Owen, to be knight of the parliament for the said countye agaynest the said Salisburye, who stood in triall with the said Hugh Owen for the same rowme and ellection agaynste the last paste parliament, wherin the said Salisburye was overthrown, by reason whereof and the causes aforesaid he doth contynue and persever in malice and envye to displeasure me and my ffrendes.'* He asks Leicester to prevent the grant from passing the Great Seal. From North Wales.

Signed   2 pp.   (Dudley Papers II/307)

'THE QUEENES MAJESTIES FESTES'

(1572) August 23 to September 24.   List of stages in the Queen's progress from Kenilworth to Windsor.

'Saturday, August 23, from Killingworth to Sir Thomas Lucies to dine and to Compton to suppe and there 3 days. 14 miles.

Tuesday the 26th from thence to Mr Raynsfordes to dyne and to Woodstock to sup and there 11 days. 12 miles.

Tuesday the 9th from thence to Wallingforde and there 2 days.

Thursday the 11th from thence to Yattenden to dine and to Newbury to sup and there 4 days.

Monday the 15th from thence to Englefield and Aldermaston and there 2 days.

Wednesday the 17th from thence to Reading and there 7 days.

Wednesday the 24th from thence to Windsor and there during the Queens Majestys pleasure. 13 days.'

1 p.   (Dudley Papers III/57)

GUNPOWDER

1572, August.   Quantities of powder and other materials for fireworks for the Earl of Leicester to be used at Kenilworth (Killingworth), August, 1572.

2 pp.   (Dudley Papers III/55)

JOHN YERWORTH TO THE EARL OF LEICESTER

1572, October 2.   Explaining the methods employed in the election of new officers in 'your' town of Denbigh, with the view to destroying the influence of the Salisbury family who were accustomed to name the officers. 'I made my repare Denbigh upon thes ellecion days, and findinge the chef of the towne ther assembled in the open and common hawle, signified unto them your Lordships plesure towching theyre officers to be made, and dyd name unto

---

* Hugh Owen represented Merioneth in the parliament of 1571, his brother John Lewis Owen in the parliament of 1572.

them Mr Hugh Lloyd and Mr Latham your Lordships servant to be the Aldermen, John Ireland and Thomas Walter burgesses, Mr William Clough and Thomas Lloyd your Lordships servant coronors, which persons were presently ellectyd with great contentment of all the burgesses ther present.' The Salisbury faction was absent. Sir John Salisbury treats your tenants as if they were his bondsmen. He is shortly coming to London with his wife and 4 sons to seek Leicester's favour, especially in respect of a proposed marriage between his nephew and Sir Nicholas Bagnall's daughter. Denbigh.

Holograph 2 pp. (Dudley Papers II/117)

Sir Thomas Wroth to the Earl of Leicester

1572-3, January 14. Objecting to Mr Astley's valuation of his offices in Enfield. 'From my powre howse in Warwicke Lane.'

Holograph 2 pp. (Dudley Papers II/119)

The Earl of Huntingdon to the Earl of Leicester

1572-3, January 20. I thank you for telling me of the good state of her Majesty, 'which Almyghtye God contynew longe to the comforte of the good and confusion of the rest that wylle not be convertyd. Your Lordships request for Townelye I dyd sollycyte to my Lord of Yorke, but before I sent he had at the sute of my deare brother takyn order for hys delyverye, upon condition that wythyn 40 dayes after he shulde repayre to hym to London, and cum hyther agayne in June nexte, and for the performance therof he ys bounde in 500 markes, as yeasterdaye hym selfe dyd tell me, for I did taulke with hym a good whyles. And truelie I feare yt that conference with hys brothyr wylle doo hym but lyttel good, for he thynketh well of him selfe and hathe a more delyghte to fortyfye hym selfe in hys error then desyre to be better instructed. Surelye yf I weare worthye to geave advysse soche choyse men as he ys shulde be offeryd the othe. I tell you, my Lorde, yt wylle more pearse in to hym and to soche lyke then all the dyvynitie that Mr Nowell and the best doctor in England can shew hym. He ys one that hathe a greate offyce, and excepte he wolde accepte the othe, trewelye he ys farre unfytte for yt. He ys the Steward of Blakeburne in Lankyshyre, wheare he may comaunde as I heare ten thousand men. Yf he weare my brother, beyng geaven as Mr Towneley ys, I wolde wyshe an other to have that charge. I must tell your Lordship of an other thynge, which I wyshe shulde be lookyd to. I heare hathe ben of late greate speache that Sir H. Pearcye was put to hys fyne and that shortelye he wolde be in the cuntrye, whearat I fynde that mannye dyd rejoyse. I hope it be not so as was reportyd, neythyr let yt be yf you can let yt; truelye I wyshe the gentleman to doo well, and yf by the lawe he be an earle, God make hym a better earle then hys brothyr was. And althoughe I doubte not but he be well warnyd, yet surelye, my Lorde, yf he shulde cum heare wheare the vayne opinion of hys aune force and credytte, with soche prettye persuasion as he shulde fynde plentyfully heare, excepte he be wonderfullye armyd in God hys grace, because he ys a man I may feare hys fallyng and therefore theas thynges dothe make me to thynke yt farre better to let him dwell in Sussex then in the North. Sure I am that thys can not harme hym, and thus her Majesty shulde never neade to doubte hym. And to thys end wolde I wyshe an exchange of all hys northern landes or the chefe and principall of them. He shoulde not have one housse in thys northe to dwell in. God ys witnes, tho I chefelye respecte the servys of hyr Majesty as my deutye ys, yet in utteryng thus my opinione I wysshe hym good and no harme, and I thynke hym to be so wyse that yf yt

190

shoulde please hyr Majesty to make hym thys offer, he wolde upon hys knees with most humble thankes accepte yt; surelye I woulde yf hys case weare myne. I wylle not longer trowble your Lordship with thys matter; you can see farthyr in to thys matter then I, but I am so bolde to utter sum parte of my mynde, and I leave yt to your good consideration. And now I may not forget to thank your Lordship for the good comforte you have geaven me of my sute. I truste that by your good meanes hyr Majesty wylle not myslyke yt, because the lande lyeth in my contrye, and so neare my housse, I am the more desyrous of yt.' York.

Holograph 2 pp. (Dudley Papers II/121)

THE EARL OF HUNTINGDON TO THE EARL OF LEICESTER

1572-3, February 8. Urging the granting of the 'olde Castell aamoste ruinated' in Sheriff Hutton for a residence for the President of the North. York.

Holograph 1 p. (Dudley Papers II/123)

THOMAS ASHETON TO THE EARL OF LEICESTER

1572-3, February 8. On behalf of John Vernon and his wife, sister of the Earl of Essex, engaged with Vernon's cousin in a suit against 'one Graye'. 'Your Honour workes for Sir Henrye Sydneys sonne Philippe by name; yf you do so, besydes the wrong you do them, the matche is shamefull as well for the inequality as the basterdye therof. I understand my Lord of Essex is also about to matche ther (whos doing nether in that behalffe I lyke not). I wyshe in my hert my Lord of Essex for his honors sake had taken a better mater in hand, when he considered with Graye. Yf you noblemen wyll seake gaine without respect of your honor, doubt you not but God can blow away in a moment the profytt with your honor.' Stockton.

Holograph Seal 1 p. (Dudley Papers II/125)

O'CONNOR SLIGO TO THE EARL OF LEICESTER

1572-3. February 23. Asking Leicester to inform the Queen of the state of Ireland and saying that his brother, unable to pass through the lands of the rebels, has made his way to France, and will thence cross over to England to see the Queen. Sligo.

Latin Endorsed: '23° Februarii. 1572. O'Connor Sligo.' 1 p. (Dudley Papers II/127)

RICHARD MYLLER TO THE EARL OF LEICESTER

1572-3, March 2. Regarding the authority of the High Stewards of the Honour of Grafton, with a speech of Henry VIII's to the then Steward, Sir John Williams. The King 'spoke unto him thes woordes ffolowinge: John Wylliams, thou shalt have elbowe roome; wee will have no man shall have enny thing to doe within this honour nor no officer wee have shall interupte the. But thou shalt have the whole rule thereof thyself.' Syrsham.

Holograph 1 p. (Dudley Papers II/129)

SIR HENRY SIDNEY TO THE EARL OF LEICESTER

1572-3, March 2. I am sorry to hear that you are displeased with my proceedings towards (Hugh) Shadwell. He was only appointed to a petty office under the Council temporarily because there was a dispute as to whom it rightly belonged, and now he wants to keep it.

He has also been imprisoned for debt. I had him set at liberty, gave him the privilege of the house and dealt with his creditors. 'And this is the unfrendlie dealinge those that you recommende finde at my handes.' Ludlow Castle.

Signed, with a postscript in Sidney's hand recommending the bearer, Captain Floyd. Wafer seal 3 pp. (Dudley Papers II/131)

THE EARL OF THOMOND TO THE EARL OF LEICESTER

1572-3, March 8. Asks that 'er any fearther determination be past then is already concluded touching Ireland, I may by your Lordships meanes optayne a pasport to com to England, at which tyme I trust to disclose such matters as may give some direction to the accomplishing of matters concerning this pore state to the honour of the prince and the wealth of the contrey.' He requests also security for his tenants in his absence, 'for in the last rebellion of Connaught, while I attended uppon my Lord Deputie at Dublin to procure the suppressyon of th'enemy, I have lost above a thousand pounds by the Erle of Clanricherd and his sonnes meanes; for as the state of this pore contrey do now stand, no man is more shott at then he that is founde most faythfull to our princes in useful service, notwithstanding I will never desist to hazard the losse of lyfe and all.' Limerick.

Signed 1 p. (Dudley Papers II/135)

PHILIP SIDNEY TO THE EARL OF LEICESTER

1572-3, March 8. In favour of the bearer. Frankfort.

Holograph 1 p. (Dudley Papers II/48)
(Printed in *Wiltshire Archaeological Magazine,* Vol.XVIII (1879), p.34.)

THE BISHOP OF DURHAM TO THE EARL OF LEICESTER

1572-3, March 10. Asking for time to make answer to the case of Mr Sutton. Auckland.

Signed 1 p. (Dudley Papers II/137)

HENRY MEVERELL TO THE EARL OF LEICESTER

1572-3, March 11. Praying for letters to 'Mr Chauncelour' for relief. 'I have laied my dublett and my hose to gauge alredie.' From Ffrauncis Barker his howse in Flete Street.

Holograph Seal 1 p. (Dudley Papers II/139)

SIR ROGER MANWOOD TO THE EARL OF LEICESTER

1572-3, March 13. On a dispute as to title between Sir John Pollard and Humphrey Walrond, and enclosing a copy of a letter of March 2 from Exeter to Pollard.

Holograph 1 p. (Dudley Papers II/140)
The enclosure: a copy of a letter written by J. Jeffrey. 2 pp. (Dudley Papers II/140)

SIR WILLIAM FITZWILLIAM TO THE EARL OF LEICESTER

1572-3, March 16. 'Since my laste of the 19th February by the which I declared my fancye agreeing with yours for the best form of government of this lande, these be all the accidents that have happened.'

James FitzMaurice has come in to the President of Munster. This is very satisfactory. Things in Ulster go not so well, 'for where upon Mr Smithe and Malbies draught undertaking to mak Syr Bryan either small inoughe or no body ... they are returned leaving hyher mynded then they founde him.' Tirlagge Lenaghe also begin 'to brable.' Experience teaches that 'here is no good governing but by force.' He urgently requires more men as he has already told the Queen.

The state of Queen's County. 'Roger Og falles to sharing owte the cuntrey, allotting the chief of his septe to the severall partes thereof. Himself desireth but a yeares protection or twoe, within the whiche he nothing doubtethe to hit on a tyme for his purpose to roote owte all the Englisherie thence.' Dublin Castle.

Signed Seal 1 p. (Dudley Papers II/144)

ARTHUR DUDLEY TO THE EARL OF LEICESTER

1572-3, March 16. I delivered the Queen's letters which you had promised for me to the Dean of Lichfield, 'and the chapter beyng assembled together in the Chapter house, the sayd Deane readyng the letters hymselfe gave but verye smalle reputation there unto, nothyng regardyng the same as he ought to doe accordyng to his bounden dutie. Butt with great arogancie he sayde that he woulde answer the letters before the Quenes Majestie hym selfe, ffor no cause that he can aleage ryghtfully to be proved butt onlye to wythehoulde my pore lyvynge ffrome me, which the Quene her grace hathe gevyn me throughe your honors grete goodnes.' I beg you will not suffer me to be molested by the Dean, 'who ys a man ffull unmete to be heade of suche a churche, yf your honor dyd knowe hys conditions throughly. I woulde desyre of God that we had a more soberer and a quyeter man to be a heade over hus, which woulde be a very greate commodytie and a quyetnes bothe to the towne and the churche of Lychefelde.' This is the general opinion here, 'for that there ys no truste of his amendment onles there be summe ponyshement layde uppon hym, and especially ffor his unsymelye arogance nott regardyng the Quenes Majesties commandments.' Lichfield.

Signed 1 p. (Dudley Papers II/146)

WILLIAM ROWE TO THE EARL OF LEICESTER

1572-3, March 20. 'God hayth guided me to Heydelberg, where I have for the moste part wintered and mynd by the grace of God to stay this sommer within Doctor Immanuell the Ebrew Professor his house, attending what soever service your Lordshippe shall commande me. The Prince of Palatine will not lye with the French murderer; the Prince him self in personne daylie laboreth reformation of religion, as also in civill government he personally assists with his counsayle, descideth all matters even those which are of litle in importaunce, soe trulie dothe he first seake the glorie of God, and then the welth publique. I beseche your Lordship in Christ Jesu to build with bothe handes the church of God in England, to the rooting out of all tirannye which as yet (most lamentable in our state) lurketh, wheyting the like opportunitie to that of Ffraunce, ffor noe doubt the papist is false when he is courteous, while he is under, humble; but when he reyneth, tirannous. There is noe one noble man that they so pushe at as at your Honor. The Lord God send curst Kynne shorte hornnes, and preserve your Honor long to his Churche.' Frankfort.

Holograph Seal Endorsed: '20 Marcii, 1572. William Rowe.' 1 p. (Dudley Papers II/154)

THE EARL OF PEMBROKE TO THE EARL OF LEICESTER

1572-3, March 22. I will do my best to requite your 'selled fryndshipp'. 'I will supply the same which, God willing, I have not that frynd nor servant at whose mouthes I will hire any thinge otherwyse then comelye touching your Lordship.' I will esteem any such knaves and no better. My servant asks me to intercede with you for him; I assure you he has been wrongfully accused of ill-behaviour towards you. As to the authors of this device I could name one who 'forswears hymselffe damnably and wilfullye, it is the frut of his religion, his maner of lyffe and behavior .... He will not styke to take uppon him any thinge ... that shall anger me or fayle my howse .... This plott hathe byn leyd in my howse any tyme thes 2 yeares, for the which he and his fraternitie are but instruments.' I had to discharge his brother and others for their factious devices, of whom William Harbard was one. 'But good my Lord they dance in a net that thinks to throw stones and hide their handes.' These eight years they have tried to disinherit me both in my father's time and since. But nothing they can do can throw any bone between me and those that I love dearly. Ramsbury.

Signed Seal, broken 2 pp. (Dudley Papers II/150)

PHILIP SIDNEY TO THE EARL OF LEICESTER

1572-3, March 23. On an interview with 'Counte Ludovik, the Prince of Oranges second brother.' Frankfort.

Holograph Seal 1 p. (Dudley Papers II/152)
(Printed in *Wiltshire Archaeological Magazine*, XVIII (1879) p. 35)

LORD LATYMER TO THE EARL OF LEICESTER

1572-3, March 26. Permitting that Jasper Chomley should 'have the serche of my evydences towching the Lord Barkeleys landes, wherof your Lordships ancestors and myne were coparceners.' Snape.

Signed 1 p. (Dudley Papers II/156)

SIR NICHOLAS BACON TO THE EARL OF LEICESTER

1573, March 27. Asking Leicester's favour for the bearer, his servant, 'in the obteyning of his bill to be signed.' From my house beside Charing Cross.

Signed 'Bacon c.s. (*custos sigilli*)' 1 p. (Dudley Papers II/158)

SIR HENRY NEVILL TO THE EARL OF LEICESTER

1573, March 28. Asking on behalf of Lord and Lady Huntingdon for interest 'to gett them ... tenne accers of Mr Inglefelds woodes .... for theayr money' in order to burn bricks for a 'little bylding' at Stoke, 'for that my Lady hathe a liking unto that howse.' He has indicted several men (for forest offences) according to Leicester's pleasure, and has 'a shrewde byble' (bill) against some of the keepers to show Leicester. He hears that the latter will be at Windsor on Tuesday. Pillingbere.

Signed Seal 1 p. ¡Dudley Papers II/160)

HUGH SHADWELL TO THE EARL OF LEICESTER

(1573) March 28. Stating his claim and reporting what 'favour I have

founde with my Lord President (of Wales) for your sake uppon delivery of your honourable letters and what I may attayne unto by your furder favour.'
'There be many attendants here that might be better employed in London or wher they might lerne ther duties.' I want my cause known 'as Josephs and Susannas were' and if I lie to you 'I shuld sedenly dye as Ananias and Saphira his wief did.' He has two mortal enemies there, the secretary Mr Fox and Thomas Sackfourd. 'I wold wisshe of God my Lord President were not so moche ruled by' the latter. Ludlow.
Holograph Seal Endorsed: '28 Marcii, 1573. Hugh Shadwell.' 3 pp. (Dudley Papers II/162)

LORD WINDSOR TO THE EARL OF LEICESTER
1573, March 31. Giving the character of his man, William Jemanes, whom Leicester desires to have if Windsor can spare him. Hewel.
Holograph Seal 1 p. (Dudley Papers II/164)

THE BISHOP OF HEREFORD TO THE EARL OF LEICESTER
1573, April 14. Complaining of being assaulted on his way to Parliament. Whitborne.
Signed Seal 1 p. (Dudley Papers II/168)
(Printed in *Wiltshire Archaeological Magazine*, Vol.XVIII (1879) p.36)

SIR FRANCIS JOBSON TO THE EARL OF LEICESTER
(Date illegible but before 5 June 1573*) In favour of Henry Monoux.
Signed 1 p. (Dudley Papers II/299)

NEWS FROM FRANCE
1575, October 12. 'Frenshe occurrentes' by letters from Paris.
3 pp. (Dudley Papers III/58)
(*This is a copy of Dr Dale's correspondence with Walsingham.* See *Cal. S.P. Foreign*, 1575-7, pp. 154-6, nos. 401 and 402.)

HECTOR NUNEZ TO THE EARL OF LEICESTER AND LORD BURGHLEY
(? c January 1575-6) He petitions for letters to the Judge of the Admiralty to cancel his bond as surety that Captain Bartholomew Bayon should not sail to any place prohibited by the Kings of Spain and Portugal. He sets forth that the Spanish Ambassador had informed his master that Nunez had sent Bayon 'into Novey Spayne with two shippes to spoil his subjects' and that consequently Nunez's servant was imprisoned in Seville and 1700 ducats taken from him, and that another was robbed of 200 ducats at Bilbao. He adds that Bayon himself was robbed of 1500 ducats in goods in the Canary Islands, and that he has now gone to the West Indies. *Undated*
1 p. (Dudley Papers II/279)
(See *Cal. S.P. Foreign*, 1575-7, p.230, no.577.)

THE COUNTESS OF SHREWSBURY TO THE EARL OF LEICESTER
(? Before 1577) June 27. 'My honorabell Lord. Albeyt one of my greatest

* Sir Francis Jobson died on 4 June 1573.

195

comfortes ys to here frome your Lordship and nothynge cane be more acseptabelle unto me then to here of your well lykenge the bathe and helthe recovered therby, yet notwithstandinge I have forborne wrytynge for that I wolde geve your Lordship no ocasyon, herynge yt was wysshede by lerned advyse you shulde not yousse yt otherwysse. I shulde altogeder forgett myselfe, which shall never apeare towardes so nobell a frende as I fynde by good proffe your Lordship ys bothe to me and myne, but wyll rest ever moust faythefoull as many your most honorabell favors may justely challenge. Yn the meane tyme my Lord and I aconte all we cane do or procure nothynge ansorabell to owre good wylle yf yn dede theys baranne partes gave any thynge worthy your Lordship. My Lorde thynkes my sone Gelberte for want of experyence hathe sofered hys conterey cokes (cocks) to be overmatched. I beseche your Lordship desyre my very frend Mayster Julio to presente unto her Magystye my moust humbell dewty, for whose prosperyte I wyll ever pray, as one moust bounde, that we may longe leve under her gracyous and happy goverment, and so my good lorde, praying to God to sende you helthe and your hartes desyre, I ende. Your Lordships lovynge cossen and moust faythefoull frende.'* Sheffield.

PS. 'Hary Cavendysshe hathe desyred me by hys letters to move your Lordship for your erneste letters to the Prince of Orange yn hys favore, and yt wyll plese you to show you acounte of hym.'

Holograph 1 p. (Dudley Papers II/313)

THE EARL OF SHREWSBURY TO THE EARL OF LEICESTER

(? Before 1577) Friday morning. 'My Lord. Althow I perseve by your letter you can nott contente yourselfe with our goodes, but you call us doggry, which standeth us upon to seeke the revenge; and be you assured althow for a tyme we must contente ourselves, yett shall you not reste unchalenged. Agen defend you rather if you dare. And rather then fail, our hartburning is such we wyll come to Killingworth gates this tyme twelmonth, God, and the Quenes Majestie, giving us leve to perform our chalenge ther if your harte faint nott afore the time. And in the mean whyle I shall pray for your Lord-ships helthe and all happynes as I wold desyer for my selfe.' Sheffield.

PS. 'Notwithstanding my losse at the carts beinge £xxiii, my pursbearer used conyng to gyve it me befor my wife, she by forse toke it from me, which was £xlii; thus is simpell men served and spoyled of ther goods.' *Undated.*

Holograph Addressed: 'To the right hon^le my very good Lord and cosin th'erle of Leycester.' 1 p. (Dudley Papers II/318)

GUNPOWDER

1577-8. 'The chardges of your Lordships gunpowder made at Kenilworthe Castell' Michaelmas, 1577 to April 8, 1578. The quantity of gunpowder amounts to 12 hundred weight 100 pounds at the cost of £46:7.

1 p. (Dudley Papers III/60)

THE COUNTESS OF SHREWSBURY TO THE EARL OF LEICESTER

(? 1578) May 23. 'My good lord and brother. Yt ys wrete to me at lenth by my sone Gelberte Talbott how honorabley your Lordship contenewes your wontyed care to do good styll to me and myne, and theryn ys expressed your

---

* See *supra* p.22.

Lordships honorable provydence now extended for my dowter Lennox* yn maryage. I shall ever acknolege besydes ane enfynytte nomber your goodnesses to me and myne, the latte good speede and prefarment my sonne Charles hade brought to pass by your Lordships only wysdome. And as your Lordships nobell mynde ys ever workenge nobell effectes and of the same frewtes by good fourtune I and all myne amongst otheres to owre great comfortes do (wholly) raste. I beynge of no poure nor abelyte any (wayes) to make apeare the dewty of thankes (to) your Lordship the greatter by me and myne ought (to sende) your Lordship worthey fame whyche ys all the recompense I cane make and the beste servis all myne are abell to do unto your Lordship all the dayes of ther lyves. And for my dowter Lennox of whome your Lordship plecythe to have that especyall care, and we most bonde to your Lordship for yt, yeldynge humbyll thankes to your Lordship, she dothe styll fynde her selfe so many wayes bonde to your Lordship for yt, as wyl be advysed by your Lordship more then any man, and I hartely desyre your Lordship contenew that honorabell mynde towardes her ether for the Lord Sandes or any other that shalbe thought metyste, and yf yt plese your Lordship to comende any to Chattysworth as a place for sundery causes, I desyre fourst to enter ther aquentance; he or whome else your Lordship comendes shalbe as frendly welcome as I am beholdyng to geve one sent by your Lordship, wereyn as yn althynges elles I do refare her happy mache. Her well bestoynge ys my greatys care; some of my frendes have heretofore wyshed sondery good maches for her. Yf I coulde have founde yn her the lyste lykenge more to one then another, I wolde have trobeled your Lordship therewith without whose specyall helpe I knewe yt colde take no good affect. She sayth ever to me she cane nott determyne har selfe to lyke of any for a hosbande whome she never sawe nor knowethe not hys lykenge of har. I defare all to your Lordships honorabell consederacyon of whome as of vary nobelyte hym selfe I take my leve with my prayer for all hapenes to you and yours. Your Lordships faythefull syster. E. Shrouesbury.' Sheffield.

   PS. *in the Earl of Shrewsbury's hand*: 'I cannott contente my selfe my wyfes letters .... without rememberinge and commendynge my selfe unto your Lordship, my derest frende, with my most hartyste thankes for the honorable care of us and ours, wherby if it colde .... more and more bynde me to be yours.'

Holograph   Seal   2 pp.   (Dudley Papers II/173)

SIR THOMAS HENEAGE TO THE EARL OF LEICESTER

1578, June 4.. On the suits of Justice Manwood and himself to the Queen. 'The Ladye that moste esteemes you and I honor, dyd tell me of this bearers jorney, and willed me to wryte her commendacions to your Lordship.'   From the Court.

Holograph Seal   1 p.   (Dudley Papers II/176)

SIR CHRISTOPHER HATTON TO THE EARL OF LEICESTER

1578, June 18.   On the Queen's 'contynuall great melencoly. She dremethe of mariage that might seeme injurious to her.'

Holograph   2 pp.   (Dudley Papers II/178)
(Printed in *Wiltshire Archaeological Magazine*, Vol. XVIII (1879) p. 36)

* Her husband, Charles Stuart, Earl of Lennox, died in 1576.

SIR CHRISTOPHER HATTON TO THE EARL OF LEICESTER

1578, June 28.   Touching the Queen's regret at Leicester's absence.   At the Court at Greenwich.

Holograph   Seal   Illegible in places   2 pp.   (Dudley Papers II/181)
(Printed in *Wiltshire Archaeological Magazine*, Vol.XVIII (1879) p.38)

THOMAS AGLIONBY TO THE EARL OF LEICESTER

1578, July 30.   I send you by this bearer '2 dublettes, i paire of boote-hosen, a newe cloke-bagge, patterns of wrought velvet for your night gownde ....
The rydynge cloke your Lordship spake to me of, although your Lordship saide you wolde have it of velvet, yet did you not resolve how you wolde have it trimmed, whether garded with the same or garnished with golde, silver or silke lace.   I thinke it wolde be very prety and faire to be welted downe right somwhat thick with sattin, turned in and snipte on the edges, with some prety lace of golde and silk, or silver and silke, down the midst of the welte ....
Your Lordship semed to blame me for boot-hosen.   And having left in your wardrobe a litle before your going to Bukstone 14 or 15 paire of linen boot-hosen, all as then serviceable, I did not think I shold nede to have provided any more for this sommer .... I was spoken to for a horne for your Lordship. The bawdrike I have bespoken, but when to have the horne or what horne to provide I know not, nor they that spake could tell me.'   Harnesey.

Holograph   2 pp.   (Dudley Papers II/184)

THE EARL OF PEMBROKE TO THE EARL OF LEICESTER

1578, August 14.   I have been ill since my return from Buxton.   I send my duty to the Queen, and ask you to favour the bearer, Philip Williams. Claringdown.

Signed   Seal   1 p.   (Dudley Papers II/185)

THE COUNTESS OF PEMBROKE TO THE EARL OF LEICESTER

(c August, 1578) Friday.   Excusing herself for not writing to Leicester about her husband's illness.   *Undated*

Holograph   Seal   1 p.   (Dudley Papers II/187)

WILLIAM HERLLE TO THE EARL OF LEICESTER

1578, September 3.   I had hoped to hear from you 'towching the transporting of Pyero hither, and for your Lordships warrant to the coste syde to have ayded the party to bryng hym on shore, assuryng your Lordship that yf you so vowched, he shalbe brought over without rumor, to which effecte I have stayed here so long to see what it may plese you to command.'   I have given the bearer four days to go and return with your answer.

It is important that Silvanus Scorye's licence be renewed.   I enclose my letter to Mr Secretary Wilson for you to read and seal up.   'Ytt plesed hym to write me a letter somewhat bytterlye sawced, which I know procedes nott from hym butt from another humor', for he has hitherto treated me more like a son 'than on of so mene callyng.'

'Ytt is a grett observatyon howe your Lordship will carye your sellf bettwen the two personages that squeared att Burye in wordes.   The on is grett and mightye, and the other noble, who only depends of your Lordship, which makes the greater expectacyon in the worlde.   But your wisdom .... is rare and singular and of grett experyence in Court affayres, wherunto your Lordships frends and ffollowers have a consyderacyon one waye and the rest another waye.' I will let you have further news, desiring your advancement 'with the Queens Majestie before all others.' London.

Holograph 2 pp. (Dudley Papers II/189)

FRANCIS HASTINGS TO THE EARL OF LEICESTER

1578, October 10. Thanking Leicester for a warrant 'for a stag at Killingworth', and saying that he has kept watch for 'one Owen a Welchman.' Bosworth.

Holograph 1 p. (Dudley Papers II/191)

HENRY BESBECHE TO THE EARL OF LEICESTER

1578, October 23. On business matters at Kenilworth.

Holograph Seal 2 pp. (Dudley Papers II/193)
Other letters from Besbeche on the same subject are: II/195 (November 20, 1578); II/212 (March 22, 1579) and II/214 (March 28, 1580), all printed in *Wiltshire Archaeological Magazine*, Vol. XVIII (1879) pp. 39-42.

JOHN THYNNE TO THE EARL OF LEICESTER

(1578) December 12. He is writing in the name of his father, Sir John Thynne, and asks for Leicester's aid in his (the writer's) suit against Lord Stafford. Longleat.

Copy Endorsed: 'A copie of the letter which I wrote to my Lord of Leicester in my Fathers name, 1578.' 1 p. (Dudley Papers II/199)
II/201 *is a copy of another letter by Thynne on the same subject and dated* January 3, 1578-9.

THOMAS SMYTHE TO THE EARL OF LEICESTER

1578, December 12. As to a purchase by Leicester of pearls. London.

Signed 1 p. (Dudley Papers II/197)
(Printed in *Wiltshire Archaeological Magazine*, Vol. XVIII (1879) p. 43)

GABRIEL HARVEY TO THE EARL OF LEICESTER

1579, April 24. Praying for 'your favorable and gracious meanes ... for the procuring of Doctor Byddles prebende' at Lichfield, 'for your good Lordshippes poor schollar and servant that only in respect of some hinderances thorough wante of sufficient hability (cannot) undertake those services that otherwise have been often purposed and might shortly by any sutche helpes in sum reasonable sorte be performed ... I have often showed openly ... that this little body of myne carriethe a greate mynde towardes my good Lord and is evermore to attempte or indure any kynde of travayle ... either towards the strengthening of his lordshippes estate or the advancing of his most honorable name... I speake it without vanity that a poore litle schollar would do your Lordshippe more honour in his speciall respects then sum of your gallants and courtlyest servants. It is no greate matter that would suffyr for the mayntenance of on litle body.' He therefore begs for this prebend as also for the vacant chancellorship. 'Your Lordshippe hath a very lernid and wyse chapleyne, Mr Doctor Styll, a man of very good governemente, and in all respects very mete and sufficientley furnisshed for sutch a place as your Lordshippe of your syngular wysdom can judge (which did evydently appeare by makyng choyce of him for the voyage to Smalcaldy) and the common opinion and speciall lyking of all men doth testyfy. If your Lordshippe thought good to prefer him to the Byshhopprick (as is allreddy greately desired of many, esspecially of us unyversity men and sum others of judgmentes, who fynde a greate wante of sutche hable men in lyke places of autoritye), I knowe of all men my oulde Tutor and continuall frende would make choyce of no other chancellor.' Trinity Hall, Cambridge.

Holograph 2 pp. (Dudley Papers II/202)

THOMAS WAGSTAFF TO (LETTICE, COUNTESS OF LEICESTER) AS 'COUNTESSE OF ESSEX'

1579, May 21. Asking her to remind Dudley to obtain for him a prebend at Westminster.

Signed Seal 1 p. (Dudley Papers IV/31)

SIR THOMAS WROUGHTON TO THE EARL OF LEICESTER

1579, May 23. Denying the use of 'any such speache to my brother Thynne or my sister' accusing Leicester of being the cause of the Earl of Pembroke's trouble. Wilton.

Copy Endorsed: 'The copie of Sir Thomas Wroughtons letter to my Lord of Leyster, 1579.' 1 p. (Dudley Papers II/203)

SURVEYS

1579, May 25 to 1581, September 1. Surveys of manors, lands etc. of Robert Dudley, Earl of Leicester, viz: the Manor and Castle of Kenilworth, viewed by William Beinham, the Earl's Surveyor-General, 1 September, 1581 (f.2); Rudfen (f.21); Drayton Basset, 25 May, 1579 (f.23); Stonidelf, May 1579 (f.36); Shuttington and Alvecote, 25 May, 1579 (f.40); Cleobury (f.43).

Folio Imperfect and (from f.41) damaged by fire) ff.52. (Dudley Papers XVIII)

ROGER EDWARDES TO THE EARL OF LEICESTER

1579, June 20. 'Humbly cravinge pardon for requesting your honourable letters to the Bishop of Lincolne: for so sone as the letters weare past my handes I considered that the satisfyinge of my desire should be a *premunire* in the Bishop. What your Lordship doth conceive concerninge the high matters that I wrot unto you and the lordes, I wot not. It behoveth you and bothe prince and people to harken carefully to the matter, as you shall well understande by such devines as the lordes shall believe in the same. And as I fynde the affaires of God to be embraced, so shall you knowe things that I knowe: but furst the prophetes must be opened and received. The lorde maketh hast, and so will I. You maye not be slowe that must forther the cause. Thearefore, good my lord, believe in your God, and I will come to you so sone as I cann myself. But I would furst conferre privately with my Lord Beshop of London, my Lord Be(shop) of Sarum and with the Deane of Paules by your direction and my Lord Treasurers.' I make bold to recommend the bearer Thomas Smyth.

Holograph 1 p. (Dudley Papers II/204)

WILLIAM HERLLE TO THE EARL OF LEICESTER

1579, August 14. Asking for a passport to leave England to escape from creditors. Lack of employment is the reason for this bad state of his affairs, 'yett I can serve with a pyke or harkebuse as well as another.' He encloses 'a discourse ... touching a mene to annoye and divert K. Phillip therby to loke homewards.' It must be kept secret for fear of the Spanish spies. 'Butt yf itt were ones set down and concluded with the sayd King of Barbary, the very drede therof would bryng the K. of Spayne to offer composition to her Majestie. I acquainted the Lord Treasurer and Mr Secretary with the scheme, and most fully to Sir William Wynter, who would willingly have joined me in it. Mendoza, the Spaynish Ambassador, goeth lightlye eche evenyng disgised to Baptist Sempetoryes house. Surely, my Lord, you had nede to loke to mani practises that ar on ffoote agaynst our State, and to persuade your self that the rebellyon of Ireland is even a handling and incresing here by instruments in England, and that as Waterfford hath written to have shott and supplye and to have excuse to rebell thereby belyke yf they be not satisfied as they would in an instant, so the other places of that contrey have Spayneshe ffyrebrandes cast to that effect, wherof our own natyon are the worst buniphieters of all.

I went this daye, being requested by Mr Pryce of Eglussye to speke with hym at Salisburye Courte by water, wher ffinding Mall(visye) *(torn)* yn the way walking under his lodging with D. Lopez, he compelled me, being eleven of the clock, to dyne with hym whether I wolld or no. He told me that your Lordship dyd christen to morow my Lady Danvers (child) *(torn)* and that Monsieur would be here within these 20 days, and that Cymie lodged in Mr Lightes house. Yt is reported abrode that your Lordship and Cymie ar entred into a very grete leage and ffamilyaritye which ys nott a lytell observed.

Ffor the cheyne of perlle that Cymie ware, ytt is known that he gayged ytt for two hundred and odde poundes and yett to show that he wolld cover the same with some good grace he ware a littell parcell of a chayne of perlle as a ffastenyng of his dagger to his girdell in manner of chayne. The wordes that Mallvisye spake of cutting the grasse under your ffeete your Lordship will have them al redy (as I have) by Sir E. Horsey, butt Mallvisye useth the lyke to others. They saye that du Vraye wilbe here to morrow.

I must nedes give your Lordship an advertisement of importance beffore I departe, which requires substancial looking unto; otherwise you will (for so the brute is given owtt) bryng the K. of Denmarke to an open quarrell with her Majestie, who is resolved (as they saye), yf he be not presently well ansererd touching his compleynts made for the depredacions that ar daylye exercised uppon his subjects, to stay all our merchants in the Sound till full satisffaction be made, which what sclander and offense ytt will be to our Government your Lordship best knows. And this is cheefflye sollicited (though ynderectlye) in Denmarke by men of our own natyon, and by som of the Steleyarde crying owtt that there is no justice to be had here, making us more ynffamous for tolleratyon of pyrates than for pyracye ytt self.'

You would do well to place some preachers in North Wales, 'the deffawt wherof (which is to give shame to the Bisshops that your Lordship sholld be remembered of it) brings all things to irreligion, confusion' and becomes the very mother to rebellion and conspiracy with extreme offence to God and Justice. London.

Holograph Seal 3 pp. (Dudley Papers II/170)

JOHN YERWORTH TO THE EARL OF LEICESTER

1579. October 8, He has collected the Earl's rents in Wales, and requests that he be appointed Sheriff of Carnarvonshire, Merionethshire or

Cardiganshire. He has served Leicester loyally and industriously for twenty years or so. He refers to his legal proceedings against Mr Gleseor, the Earl's deputy, for debt.

Holograph 2 pp. (Dudley Papers II/206)

PETITION FROM CANTERBURY TO THE EARL OF LEICESTER

1579, November 1. William Crowmer and twelve others of Canterbury pray for letters to James Nethersole, the Mayor (who has been made an Alderman at Leicester's request) to reinstate William Cooke as gaoler.

Thirteen signatures 1 p. (Dudley Papers II/208)

JANE STAFFORD TO THE EARL OF LEICESTER

1579-80, February 13. Craving Leicester's 'favorable licence to have some free speche with yourself to discharge my conscience towards your Lordship.' From my poor lodging.

Signed 1 p. (Dudley Papers II/210)

WILLIAM HERLLE TO THE EARL OF LEICESTER

1580, May 24. Asking leave to correspond in cipher with one du Vraye at Paris, being an honest man and 'desposed to advertis me of matters of moment.'

Herle is in a grievous state. 'God hath visited me here in prison' with a hectic fever 'as he dyd Sir John Throckmorton'. He has now been in prison 15 weeks and 2 days. The Counter.

Holograph 3 pp. (Dudley Papers II/216)

SIR EDWARD STAFFORD TO THE EARL OF LEICESTER

1580, July 2. 'Beinge arrived hither and havinge presented bothe my letters and that which her Majestie derected me to utter by speaches, I did finde Monsieur greatly joyenge of her dispatche, entending presently to dispatche from himself his Commissioners and also to wryte to the King to prepare his to be sent away with all the spede possible to be in Ingland abowte the ninth or tenth of August. To advertise your Lordship what I finde of the state of Ffraunce, all the way as I came I fownde still compagnies marching to La Fere and great preparation for the siege, and wholly preparing for the field, only this to the contrarye that a couple of Monsieurs gentlemen beinge comme from the Kinge of Navarre (who hath sent full commission to Monsieur to conclude a peace) and gonne to the Frenche Court, Monsieur hopeth by this meane to be a mediator of a peace, who before my repaire to him hath employed himselfe in all that he canne and since hath promised to follow yt more and more.' Tours.

Signed Addressed: To the Earl of Leicester 'at the Courte.' 1 p. (Dudley Papers II/218)

INVENTORY

1580, July 18. Inventory of the plate etc. at Leicester House. It is arranged under the following heads: 'Gold plate; Basons; Livery pottes; Bowlles; Spowte potts; Cuppes; Saltes; Spice boxes; Spoones; Candlestickes; Trencher plates; Vessel.' Most of this plate is silver-gilt and is noted as having 'a beare' graven on it.

Hangings, bed-furniture etc. E.g. 'Fowre peeces of hangengs of the storye of the twoe women that contended for the child; seven peeces of the historie of Latinus and Aeneas; seven peeces of the story of King David; eight peeces of hangengs of storie with the Quenes armes bought of my Lady Lennes.' Among the 'Night-quoyfs' is one 'of lynnen wrought with crimson silke and striped with a chayne lace of silver.' There are also carpets, chairs, close-stools etc.

Weapons. Swords, rapiers and daggers, e.g. 'an arminge sworde with a hilt and pummell gilt and cut lyke open worke.' Also standard-banners and guidons. (P.10).

Instruments. 'A payre of Rigalles with bellowes in a blacke wodden case.' 'A payre of harpe virgenalles covered with yellowe lether.' 'Two settes of vyalles in 2 chestes.' 'A litle treble lute in a case.' 'A white bone horne flewed and garnished with copper and gilte.' (p.11)

The pictures are 42 in number, as follows:

'A picture of the Frenche Kinge in seare clothe in a round case of tinne.

Two pictures of the Duke of Alanson in a wainscote frame with a curteine of yellow sarcenet fringed with green silke.

The picture of the Duke of Askot in clothe without frame.

The picture of the Duchess his wife in lyke manner.

The picture of Cardinall Chatillion upon clothe in a frame.

The picture of his wife in lyke sorte with a curtein of yellow sarcenet

The picture of my La. Sheffield enclosed in a wainscot case.

The picture of the Emperour Charles bareheaded in a frame.

The picture of Fryer Peyto.

The image of Faythe sett fourthe in a table with a frame and certeine verses.

A table of my lordes armes painted under glasse in a blacke frame parcell gilte with the ragged staffe and letters upon the cover.

A painted table with an ape, owles, fisshes, flyes and byrdes in a gilte frame with a case of blacke lether.

A table entitled *Divenorum operum tabula* in a woodden frame with a curteine of purple sarcenet.

The picture of the Quenes Majestie.

The picture of King Henry the Eight with a curteine.

The picture of Quene Mary.

The picture of the King of Scottes that nowe is.

The picture of my La(dy) of Lennes sonne.

The story of Susanna in a table.

A table of the murder of the King of Scottes with a curteine.

My La(dy) of Lennes picture with a curteine.

The picture of Duke Cassimere.

The picture of his father

The picture of his mother.

The picture of my Lady Dorithie.

The picture of Venus and Cupide.

The picture of the Marquis of Berghes.

The picture of Sr Brederode.

The picture of the Counte Mannsfelde and his wife.

The picture of the Counte Degmont and his wife.

The picture of the Counte of Horne and his wife.

The picture of the Reingrave and his wife.

The picture of a Venetian Mayden.

The picture of the bakers daughter.

The picture of an Italian curtisan.

The picture of a Sataian.

A table of the cuttinge of St John Baptistes heade.

A faire great painted table of a story.

The portraictures of the Quenes Majestie and my Lord cut in alablaster.

Nine portraictures of Emperours cut in white marble.

A counterfet of a gentlewoman in crimson and yellowe satten and a gowne of blacke velvet trimed with golde and silver lace.

A woodden boxe with the portraicture of an armed man on horsse backe.'

Among the 'Cardes or Mappes' are:

'2 mappes of the Kingdome of Ffraunce.

A mappe of the northe parte of Englande in vellum.

A mappe of the counties of Oxon., Bucks., and Barks. in clothe.

A globe of all the worlde standing in a frame.' (p.11b)

Among the 'Bookes' are:

'An booke of Common Prayer, stamped with my Lordes armes, Statutes of the Realm and a bible covered with yellow lether.'

Robes of creation, of parliament, of the Garter and of the order of St. Michael.

Apparell. Doublets and hats, including 'a fine strawne hatt.'

Other items of interest include: 'a payre of playenge tables of blacke ebany and white bone, with a sett of tablemen white and blacke in a case of green cotten.' 'A devise lyke a chariot goinge uppon wheeles with a woman sittinge on it.'

29 pp. or 16 ff.   (Dudley Papers V)

THE DUCHESS OF SUFFOLK TO THE EARL OF LEICESTER

(Before September 19, 1580)   Asking to be excused from attendance at the Court.*   *Undated*

Holograph   1 p.   (Dudley Papers II/323)

(Printed in *Wiltshire Archaeological Magazine*, Vol.XVIII (1879) p.27.)

SCHEDULE

(*c* 1580)   A schedule of deeds and evidences of Robert Dudley, Earl of Leicester, relating to lands etc, in various counties, together with patents for offices etc. drawn up about 1580: with additions of 'wrytinges brought by Nuttall the ii of June 1581.'

36 pp.   *Imperfect, the first leaf being numbered* 10.   (Dudley Papers III/177)   *The additions (f. 199 and numbering 6 pages) are in the Earl's handwriting.*

CHARLES ARUNDELL

(? 1580)   The deposition of Charles Arundell.

'On Sondaye last, being Christmas Daye, the Earell of Oxenford desired secred conference with me, as he had done the night before, wherunto I assentinge, we mett in the evening at the maydes chamber door, and after long speech in secrett between him and my cosine Vavaserr (who was the meane of our meetings) we departed thence to have gone to the garden, but the dore being dubble locked or bolted we could not gett in. Then we returned to the tarris, and there in the farthest part of the lowe gallery the sayde Earell used

* Katherine Brandon, Duchess of Suffolk, died on September 19, 1580.

this speche unto me: 'Charles, I have ever loved the and as you have alredie geven your worde to my mistresse, so now I crave it to my self', and after some assurance geven he unfolded to me all his trecherie and what had passed betwene her Majestie and him, usinge many cunning perswasions to make me an instrument of dishonest practice against my Lord Harrie and Francis Southwell, with the proffer of one thowsand pounds to afferm that they were reconciled by one Stevans a prest. I so much misliked of this motion as I perswaded the Earell from so dishonourable a purpose, protesting before God what is most trewe, I nether knewe nor ever hard of any suche thinges. 'Well, Charles,' sayde the Earell, 'Stevens is taken and racked, and hath confessed, and therefore I wishe you as a friend to take flight and depart the realme if you have faulted (?) as farre others.' Wherunto I answered 'God I take to witnes, myself am free of such offence, and so I am perswaded of others.' 'You are deceaved,' sayd the Earell. 'Southwell hath bewrayed all, and to morrow which is to long a time for you to abide, I will show you the articles. Therfore yf you wille go (which I wishe for your safetie), Litchfield my man shall shifte you awaye, and you shall remayne for a time at a house of myne in Norfouk (or Suffouke, I do not well remember whether, but nere the sea), and you shall have a thowsand pounds ether with you or billes for so much, for as yet ther remaynes more then that in the Ambassadors of Spaynes hand.' He further promised that yf the sale of a hundred powndes land myght do me good, I shuld not want it, and he wuld find meane to send unto me, still urging my going. I mislikend so much of this unsownd cownsell as I utterlie refused it. Then the Earell fell to a playnnesse and told me that he had confessed to the Quene that he was reconciled, which I never hard before, and that he had his pardon, and yf I wold be ruled by him to appeche my Lord Harrye or Southwell he would save me. I tanked (sic) him much, but rejected his cownsell; then he concluded that there was not any man culd do him harme but myselfe, wherunto I answered, 'that will I never yf you touche me not with falsehode, but then will I touche you with truthe', and having conceaved his drifte, which was that by my flighte he might be fred of his monsterous dealinges, and others brought to more suspicion, I did not utterlie refuse to yeld to his request, but prayed him I might thynke upon it, and theruppon departed and wrote answer and delivered it to Poore, his boye, the coppye wherof I exhibited to the Lords of the Cownsell. Touching Stevens, as I confessed before your honors, I will confirm it on my othe that a five yeares since the Earell, being greved in conscience about killing of a man, desired conference with a lerned man, wheruppon I brought him to the Earell: and what after happened withoute concealement of any thing, I have playnlie and trewlie disclosed to you.' *Undated*

Copy(?) 2 pp. (Dudley Papers III/203)

THE EARL OF LEICESTER'S MARRIAGE

1580-1, February 18. Deposition of Humphrey Tyndall, B.D., of his having secretly married the Earl of Leicester to Lettice, Countess of Essex, at Wanstead on September 21, 1578.

The deponent testifies 'that uppon a Saterday being as this deponent now remembreth the 20th day of September 1578, the right honourable Robert Dudley, Earle of Leycester, brake with this deponent (being then attendant uppon him at Wainstede nere London as his chappelin) to the effect following: viz, he signified that he had a good seazon forborne marriadge in respect of her Majesties displesure and that he was then for sondry respectes and especially for the better quieting of his owne conscience determined to marry with the right honorable Countesse of Essex; but for as much as it might not be publiquely knowne without great damage of his estate, he moved this deponent to solempnize a marriadge in secret betwene them, and finding this deponent willing therunto, he appointed him to attende for the dispatch therof the next morninge about seaven of the clock, which he, this deponent, did accordingly, and theruppon (betwixt seaven and eight of the clock on the next morning being Sonday) was conveyed up by the Lord North into a litle gallery of Waynstede howse opening uppon the garden, into which gallery their came, within a while after together with the aforsayed Earle of Leycester, the right honorable the Earle of Penbroke, the Earle of Warwick and Sir Francis Knowlles, and, within a litle after, the Countesse of Essex her self attired, as he now remembreth, in a loose gowne. And then and ther he, this deponent, did with the free consente of them both marry the sayd Earl and Countess together in suche maner and forme as is prescribed by the communion booke, and did pronounce them lawfull man and wife before God and the worlde according to the usuall order at solempnizacion of marriadges: and farther this deponent sayeth that he well remembreth Sir Francis Knowlles did at that time give the sayd Lady Letice for wife unto the sayd Earle.' The parties present were the Earls of Pembroke and Warwick, Lord North, Sir Francis and Mr Richard Knowlles and no more. The deponent was a 'full minister', having been ordained by the Bishop of Peterborough in 1572.

On reverse: an unfinished three line deposition by Lord North to the same effect.*

Signed 2 pp. (Dudley Papers III/61)

HANS VON MANSFELDEN AND ANOTHER TO THE EARL OF LEICESTER

(Before 1582) On behalf of a claim of 'the Counte Dolrado of Mansfeld'† for expenses incurred in 1560, in trying to raise a loan for the Queen (Sir Thomas Gresham being the intermediary), and for his failure which had resulted in his being deprived of his pension. *Undated*

Signed 4 pp. (Dudley Papers II/302)

SIR FRANCIS WALSINGHAM TO THE EARL OF LEICESTER AND LORD HUNSDON

1581-2, February 14. 'Her Majesty understanding of the great dearthe of vittalls that is said to be in that countrie did greatly pittye th'opressyve chardges that youe should therebie be dryven to be at there, wheruppon I tould hir Majesty that I thoughte your Lordships meane not to staie there above fower or fyve dayes, wherof I have thought good to geve your Lordships knowledge to th'end that since your abode there is to no greate purpose ether to the Duke (of Anjou) himself, or for any cause that may concerne the beneffit of the countrye, youe may make your returne as soone as in your owne wisdome yt shall seeme meete unto your Lordships.' Feversham.

Signed Addressed: 'To the right honorable my verie goode lords, the Earle of Leicester and the Lord of Hunsdon.' 1 p. (Dudley Papers II/222)

---

* In Dudley Papers, Box IV, no 84 is the certificate of Edward Barker, D.D., the Queen's Registrar that the marriage took place on September 21, 1578. The certificate itself is dated March 4, 1591-2.

† Died *c* or before 1582.

ALEXANDER NEVILE TO THE EARL OF LEICESTER
1582, July 23. Desiring, with his brother, to be taken into Leicester's service. London.
Signed 2 pp. (Dudley Papers II/224)

INVENTORY

1584, September 8 (with notes and additions to March 22 1587-8) 'An inventorie of Guardrob stuffe, hangings and other furniture of ... the Earle of Leicester remai(ni)ng in the charge of Thomas Egeley, his Lo. servant, at Leicester Howse .... September 8, 1584.'
This inventory is practically identical with that of Dudley Papers VI.* The following pictures are in addition:
'A picture of Sir Francis Knolles the elder, half proportion.
Diana bathing herself with nemphes.
One of a mariage in Venice.
A naked boye with a ded mans scull in his hand and an hower glasse under his arme.
Another of an ould woman.
Two smale pictures of Dutch women.
One of my Lord Admirale in black armor, whole proportion, with a ship painted by him and the ancher within the garter.
A picture of Bewchamp.
Mary Magdalin.
One of Sir Thos. Knolles leaning on a holbert with his armor lying by him.
My Lady Darcyes daughters picture.
The Prince of Oranges sonne with a rechet and a ball in his hand.
The picture of Mistress Lettice Garrett.
The picture of Lawra.
The picture of my Lady with blackamores by hir.
My Lady Garrett.
Of Petrarch.
My Lord of Warwicke, whole proportion.
A little picture of a stranger with a chaine of perle about his neck.
A picture of Sir Humfrey Gilbert in armor.
A picture of the Governor of Layden.
Three pictures of my Lord, one with Stewards staff in hand.
One picture of the King of Portingalles sonne.'

One of the Earl of Leicester's portraits is noted as having been sent to the King of Scots.
Folio Vellum covers, the arms of the Earl of Leicester stamped in gilt on each side. ff. 56. (Dudley Papers VII)

SURVEYS

1584. 'A booke of Survey .... of the mannor of Drayton Bassett, co Stafford,' belonging to Robert Dudley, Earl of Leicester, 'lyinge in Drayton, Faseley, Bonehill, Bitterscourt and Dunstall, accordinge to a perfecte plott thereof made' in 1584. At the end (f.25b) are the arms of Goodere in colours with a dedication to the Earl by 'Henricus Gooderus' and two complimentary Latin couplets.
Folio Vellum covers, stamped with the Earl of Leicester's arms. ff. 25.

* See *infra* pp.221-2

(Dudley Papers XIX)

INVENTORY

1584-5, February 24.   Inventory of the household effects of Robert Dudley, Earl of Leicester, at Wanstead, noted as 'perused' on February 24, 1584-5, with additions, ending with a note that 'the charge and custody of all her honours (Lettice, Countess of Leicester's) howshold stuff at Wanstead' was committed to William Witheredge on November 15, 1588.

The inventory is arranged roughly under the same heads as the inventory of Leicester House and includes *inter alia*:

A list of tapestry 'in the Queens beddchamber.' (f.4)

Among the books is a copy of Foxe's 'Acts and Monuments.' (f.31)

The pictures number sixty and consist chiefly of portraits, most of which were at Leicester House in 1580 (*cf* Dudley Papers V). The additions are: 'Cardinal Grandevile', and a map of Sir Francis Drake's 'viage.'

Folio Vellum covers   ff. 33   (Dudley Papers VIII)

Dudley Papers IX *is another copy of this inventory which was delivered into the charge of Nicholas Webber on April 1, 1588.*

NOTE

(? 1585)   'A Note of the number which are to attend your Lordship in yor jorney into the Low Countries.'

The total number of attendants is 227, including 2 barons, 20 knights and gentlemen, a secretary, a steward, a treasurer, a physician, a surgeon, an apothecary etc.

1 p.   (Dudley Papers III/63)

INVENTORY

1585-6, January 29.   Two inventories of plate at Leicester House, the heading of the first torn away, the other headed 'Delivered to the kepinge of Margaret Sacheverell at Lecster House, the 29th Jan. 1585/86.' (ff.1,6)

'Sertayne perseles of stuffe lefte in a chest within the closett att Lester Housse the 28 of Jan. 1585 (?)' including clothes, needlework, prayer-books with embroidered covers, 'sweett bagges' and miscellaneous articles. (f. 9b)

The following was originally separate from the above:

'Inventorie of Leicester House, Wansteede and Kenellworthe' taken after the Earl of Leicester's death on September 4, 1588. The Leicester House inventory is on f.2; that of Wanstead on f.12b; and that of Kenilworth on f. 25, and includes 'all the household stuff, armor, ordinaunce and other goodes within and about the castell.'

The 'pictures and mappes' (f.33b) include:

'Twoe greate tables of pictures of the Queene', valued at 40 shillings.

'Two great pictures of the Earle in whole proportion, £4.'

One ditto of the Countess of Leicester, 40 shillings.

A picture of Alexander the Great, valued at 40 shillings.

15 lesser pictures 'of lesser sorte' at 2^s 6^d apiece.

20 cards and maps.

Small folio   ff. 10 and 41   (Dudley Papers X, a and b)

THE EARL OF RUTLAND TO THE EARL OF LEICESTER

1586, August 7.   He is sending this letter by Mr York. 'I dout not but that your Lordship is advertised of the League concluded on betwixt Her Majestie and the King of Scottes, wherin Her Majestie, as hertofor I wrote to your Lordship, employed me.' Richmond.

Holograph 1 p. (Dudley Papers II/226)

NOTE

(Before August 12, 1586) 'A Note of the Lord Dudleys land.' This relates to the property of Edward Sutton, Lord Dudley,* including Dudley Castle and manor, with the charges upon it amounting to £5070. *Undated*

2 pp (Dudley Papers III/31)

DEEDS

(After 1586.) Schedule of deeds and evidences of Robert Dudley, Earl of Leicester, arranged under counties, drawn up after 1586, with additions (f.64b) dated 3 July, 1590. On f.63 are 'writinges generally' unconnected with lands, but chiefly lists of wills.

Folio Vellum covers ff.66. (Dudley Papers XX)

FORFEITURE OF A BOND

1586-87, January 29. Assignment by William Smith of the Inner Temple to William Burden of £20 forfeit on a bond from Christopher Blount and others. 29 Jan. 20 Eliz.

1 p. (Dudley Papers IV/48b)

ACCOUNTS

(Before December, 1587) Note of 'The Master of the Horssy† alowance in the grate warrante for 2 yeres.' This contains a list of harness and horse furniture. *Undated*

1 p. (Dudley Papers III/19)

THE EARL OF SUSSEX TO THE EARL OF LEICESTER

1587-8, January 22. Saying that he has redeemed 'xiii Frizland horses' taken in a prize, and asking whether they shall be sold in England or allowed to depart on repayment of his £60. Portsmouth.

Signed 1 p. (Dudley Papers II/228)

THOMAS FOWLER TO JOHN MONTGOMERY

(1588 or before) Easter Day. 'John Mongomery. This idill verlet gave me over the fyrst few myles I rode and was fayne to tarry for him, and now he told me playne he could not run, his running was gon, but in truthe he can run if he lyst. Therefore I have sent him to you with this letter enclosed which I pray you deliver out of hand, and that done take off this knaves coate and kepe it. Geve him 2 shillings (?) in his pursse and his old cassok of fryese and turne him away presently without fayle, but take the keyes of the stable and all the things there in frome him before. Get up all the mony you can with spede.' Reading.

Holograph 1 p. (Dudley Papers II/291)

II/293, *dated August 5, but no year concerns the delivery of some Rhenish wine to the Countess of Shrewsbury.*

---

* Buried August 12, 1586.

† Dudley was Master of the Horse to Queen Elizabeth from January 1559 to December 1587.

1588, May 28. I have already given you to understand 'in what sorte certain comyssioners had proceded to the prejudice of her Majestie in favoure of Donnoghe Mac Cale Oge O'Connor. I have (notwithstanding all the reasons and causes alleadged by me to the contrary) receaved expresse commandement from this Lord Deputie to deliver the possession of the Castell, towne and landes of Sligo togeather with all suche landes as Sir Donnell O'Connor died seysed of, to the fore-said Cale, his supposed heire.' The delivery of such land would be to her Majesty's prejudice, yet 'yf I deliver yt not, I shalbe towched with contempte, for so my Lord Deputie hath geven yt fourth.' It will only be by compulsion that I deliver 'unto the handes of an Irishman one of the best playces of importance .... in all this realme, bothe in respecte of the haven and the streighte', a place to which her Highness 'hath great right aswell by aencient inheritance as by a late escheate. The country and province hear standeth wholye upon peaceable tearmes.' Athlone.

Signed 1 p. (Dudley Papers II/230)

FRANCIS BACON TO THE EARL OF LEICESTER

1588, June 11. Praying Leicester to 'back and assist' Lord Essex in pressing his 'longe depending sute' to the Queen. Grays Inn.

Signed 1 p. (Dudley Papers II/232)

THE EARL OF HUNTINGDON TO THE EARL OF LEICESTER

1588, June 12. I have asked the Queen through Lord Essex to give me leave to come to London for 14 days, 'which I desyre to doo upon verrye greate occasion as your Lordship shalle heare after knowe, tho' I wyll not now wryte yt. Yf I had not set all thynges heare under my chardge, of late comaundyd to bee don, in good order, or yf I sawe any lykelyhoode of iminent trobles thys waye, I wolde not nowe make thys sute, but God be thankyd for yt, heare ys nothynge but quietnes apparante thys waye, and yt ys lyke so to holde yf the southe partes be occupyed as yt ys reportyd.' I pray you to further this suit. York.

Holograph 1 p. (Dudley Papers II/234)

INVENTORY

1588, June 15. Inventory of the Wardrobe of Robert Dudley, Earl of Leicester, entitled 'The Booke of all his Lo. Robes at Courte or elsewhere in the charge of Thomas Edgeley and Alford Johnson, the 15th of June, 1588,' with the note (f.1) that 'this booke was perused by my Lo. himself 31 May, 1588.'

The separate headings are: (f.1) 'Night gownes', 10; (f.2) 'short gownes', 14; (f.3) 'Cape Cloakes', 5; (f.4) 'short Cloakes, long cloakes and riding cloakes', 19; (f.6) 'Ryding slops', 6 pairs; (f.7) 'Coates', 5; (f.8) 'Cassocks', 12; (f.9) 'Hose paned and slops', 28 pairs; (f.11) 'Dublettes', 48; (f.14) 'Jerkins', 6; (f.15) 'Buttons, brooches and tags of poincts' of gold; (f.16) 'Caps and hatts', 37; (f.18) 'Bootehose and stockings', 27 pairs; (f.20) 'Rapiers and daggers with their girdles and hangers', 28. Many of these are gifts, 7 from the Earl of Sussex and from Sir Edmund Carye; (f.22) Hangers, Fawchions and Woodknives, 16; (f.23) Buskins, 20 pairs; (f.24) 'Shooes, pumps, pantophels, slepers and bootes', 58 pairs; (f.25) Hunting horns etc. At the end of each list is a note that the articles were delivered to the use of 'My Lady' after the Earl's death, in October and November, 1588.

Folio Vellum covers with leather strap. ff.25, a large number of additional leaves being left blank.   (Dudley Papers XIII)

1588, June 23. 'Advertizements from Cales of the 23 of June, 1588, with others from Sir Edmond (Edward) Stafford at Parrys.'

The Prince's preparations still continue, and all his men come towards the sea coast with intent to do something shortly.

By a letter of Cardinal Allen sent to one at Douai that the Spanish preparations were in readiness to set out, bidding them be of good comfort, that they should shortly be at home with their countrymen in these parts.

That all Englishmen and Scotsmen in the parts of Italy and Spain were embarked in the Armada, saving Sir Francis Englefield and Mr Prideaux, who stayed to come by France.

That all Englishmen and Scots in the Prince of Parma's government are commanded to be in readiness to put forth with the fleet, and to do their endeavour to work all their countrymen serving the States or in the United Provinces.

Two small ships from Spain lately arrived at Dunkirk with treasure, which comforts the soldiers very much.

Many wagers laid that they will be in England before Michaelmas Day to say Mass 'of which wager this partie hath taken £20.' This from Calais.

The Duke of Parma's forces, both of horse and foot, are encamped from 'Bridges to Blattenboroug' to the seaside and thence in the country round about 'Newporte'.

On Monday last at twelve of the clock at night Signor Petro Gaitano arrived at Bruges from Spain with news that the King's Armada would presently arrive on the coast of France. Whereupon the King's forces here are presently to embark and take their journey for England.

The Earl of Westmorland and other English fugitives that were in France are by commandment already come to Bruges, and such others as are 'in the Parties' are likewise charged to be in readiness for the journey.

Within these three days 200 boats have passed through Bruges to Dunkirk.

It is resolved the Treaty of peace shall turn to nothing. The Prince is well content it shall hold a little longer until this whole approach be made.

Cardinal Allen is hourly looked for at the Prince's Court. He has sent there letters of embassage among his friends to encourage their undertaking this journey, and promises to cross, bless and sanctify the way before them.

There is one lately come out of England to Sir William Stanley and two at this present go from him thither.

They have perfect intelligence of her Majesty's forces that are in readiness and yet hope 'of greater partie.'

The officers and 'ffurryours' of the Archduke of Austria are come to Bruges, and the Duke himself is expected there within these 3 days at the furthest with 7000 reiters.

The noblemen of the country who have long hoped and laboured for peace now utterly despair of it.

Cardinal Allen has printed a great number of traitorous books against her Majesty's honour and our nation to stir up rebellious minds to mutiny; such number as they can they will send before and the rest they will disperse upon their arrival. Not known from whence this news came.

Today the League sent to the King from the clergy's deputies to ask the grant of those articles they have demanded. From Paris. Sir Edm. (*sic*) Stafford.

They of Rohan do what they can to make the King have a delight to dwell among them, 'they of this towne fearing it are mad at hitt.'

The League made an unsuccessful attack on Melun. Three great boats full of wounded men are sent to this town.

'The Spanish army be certeynely owte, as I wrote unto you in my last letters, though there be no courier come theyther ordynary nor other.'

Lord Paget, Charles Paget and Morgan took their leave of the Duke of Guise yesterday to go to embark for England with the army as they say. Great company of gentlemen of quality pass this way out of Italy in post to go into Flanders to embark, being assured of the enterprise for England.

3 pp.   (Dudley Papers III/65)

THE KING OF NAVARRE TO THE EARL OF LEICESTER

(1588) July 13. In favour of the Sieur de Clermont d'Amboise, his ambassador. La Rochelle.

?Holograph French   1 p.   (Dudley Papers II/238)

SEIGNEUR DUPLESSIS TO THE EARL OF LEICESTER

1588, July 13. To the same effect as the preceding letter. La Rochelle.

Holograph French   1 p.   (Dudley Papers II/239)

C. PERSEVAL TO H. KILLIGREW

(1588) July 30. 'Hit shall please your worship to understand that as conserninge the cawse of the presydent and the rest whome her Majestie hath wryten for, as yet is not determyned, then theye have delyvered over unto him abowt 43 articles the which he shold answer, and he hathe therof made his answer at lardge and delyvered the same over, which maketh some of them ashamed that ar his adversaries. The resolution therof I doe lie wayting for. Soe that if the matter maye not be ended here, that as then I shall come with the same unto you. I wisshe that it myght be here ended, also your worship shall understand that here is a grete contreversie betwene the land and the towens, so that I fere ther will arise gret inconvenience unles it be intyme loked unto, and that thorowe this means that the land sitting whollie under contribusion with the enyme, the borgers of the towens maye not frelie travell from towen to towen without convoye. So hath the towens with the Governor agreed together that all the enymes that they take comynge so for boote (booty) shall presentlie be executed without mercie as for exampell. On Fridaye last hath Cownt William executed 33 in Leeuwarden, there hedes beinge all cut of by one man in 3 howers, and hath set all theyre hedes upon a gallowes in order, which execution hathe made the enyme in suche a radge that he will doe the lyke with all that he takethe. Yet is there neverthelesse a grete contreversie betwen the land and the towens therfore, for the land will not in any case consent therunto, and besides Cownte William is come in grete hatred for suche a cruell blodshedinge. Here is also this present daye writinge come from the Generall Stattes unto the States here, that the Spaynierts are at Falmouthe with 110 ships, and that my Lord Admirall is by there with 80 ships and Sir Frances Drake is with an other flete after Irland, soe that here are maynie hevye harts. I hope that it is not true, but if it be I trost God will worke and fyght for his folke, and without all dowght overthrowe the grete hore of Babelon. I beseche God to geve our navie good sucses.' Leeuwarden.

Holograph 1 p. (Dudley Papers II/241)

TRANSLATION OF A PLACARD PUBLISHED IN THE
NETHERLANDS AGAINST CALUMNIATORS OF
QUEEN ELIZABETH

1588, August 3. Setting forth the lies which have been spread by open enemies and false friends about the Queen of England's motives in giving succour to the inhabitants of the Low Countries. The peace negotiations are represented as having been entered into for her advantage. Yet the Queen has done more for the United Provinces than any prince in Europe, and has sent an infinite number of her subjects to fight for them. Yet because she negotiates with the King of Spain on the subject of liberty of conscience and abolition of the Spanish Inquisition, she is represented as desiring to restore the places she holds 'pour son assurance' to the Spaniards. A reward of a thousand 'livres d'artois' is offered for the apprehension of the author of these lies. Utrecht.

3 pp. (Dudley Papers II/242)

AMBROSE MARTINI TO THE EARL OF LEICESTER

1588, August 8. I am sending you an account of the state of things in the Low Countries. A great many favour you *(sont affectioné à votre service)*, but those of Holland, particularly those in the government, are otherwise. They think of nothing but the interests of their own province without considering their companions who have suffered so much for them. Their ideal is a popular republic; they hate the noblesse and chafe at all discipline and authority which alone would enable them to make head against Spain, and they will perish according to the common saying *Liberté perit par la liberté*. The greater part of the people are given over to avarice and debauch and have abandoned all rules of religion; they do not in the least understand what war with Spain entails. They are so impatient of authority that they will not admit anyone in office who has been faithful to, or served under, your Excellency, as I myself have experienced. I was only auditor to the judge for the troops, and because I refused to take the oath to the States they banished me ignominiously from Holland, and they have despoiled me of my office, so that I nearly starve. The Hague.

Signed French 1 p. (Dudley Papers II/244)

THOMAS FOWLER TO JOHN MONTGOMERY

(1588) Sunday, August 11. 'I cam in hast yesternight from the Camp upon some bussynes, my Lord being with the Quene at Erythe, but I must returne this nyght and wold not that any body shold have knowne of my comming, because our newse on Fryday, the Quene being at diner, in the campe that the Prynce of Parma was imbarked with 50 thousand men fote and 6000 horse, and that he put to sea yesterday, and it was suerly expected he wold land here or somwhere upon this iland to-morow, being the heyghthe of the sprynge (tide). Wherupon I meane to be at campe thys nyght agayne, God willing, to see the end of so unhappi a matter. I wold have you bye me sum good gloves of 12ᵈ or 15ᵈ a payre and send me 2 payer, and send me word what is become of Mr Roger, as to whether gon to Court at the Leger.' Going to the Leger.

Holograph 1 p. (Dudley Papers II/246)

THE EARL OF HUNTINGDON TO THE EARL OF LEICESTER

1588, August 12. 'I am wyllynge to accompanye thys knyghte with a few lynes to your Lordship, beeynge desyrous rathyr to heare from you then of you.

Howe all thinges doo stande here and of my weake state he can suffycyentlye shew your Lordship. But yf there bee dowthe of the enemye hys lookynge thys waye, I thinke yt wyll soone bee repayryd. Yf I thought otherwyse, my myslyke of my case heare wolde bee greater then yet yt ys, tho' in truthe yt bee soche as happelye your Lordship wolde not thynke yt to bee.' Newcastle.

Holograph 1 p. (Dudley Papers II/249)

ANNE ASKU TO THE EARL OF LEICESTER

(1588 or before) August 15. Expressing good will and a hope 'that herby I myght styrre you sumwhat again to dystribute of your good remembrance among suche as lysten therafter, who neyther wold you harme or can be satysfied to dwell ignorant of your good ... Your Lordships loving kinswoman.' Lambeth Marsh.

Holograph Addressed: 'E. of Leicester.' 1p. (Dudley Papers II/277)

HENRY KILLIGREW TO THE EARL OF LEICESTER

1588, August 16. I thank you for having 'moved Her Majestie so effectually for my revocation.' I have no great matter to report about affairs here, 'considering the two fleetes and the Duke of Parmas preparations hold us in suspense. But all my endevres are to persuade theis men to a mutuall ayde in this extremity and to furnish out what shipping they can, wherein I find them verie willing and they do daily send more supplie to Dunkerke. It hath bene thought good by the Councell and States Generall to raise an extraordinary contribution of 100,000 florins towardes the setting forth of more shippes, to which end the Chancellor of Guelders and I made a journey to Utrecht as from the Councell to persuade them to contribute their portion, and have obtained awnser of 10,000 florins. Touching her Majesties Commissioners in Flaunders, whereas your Lordship signifieth theie are stayed, we understand here theie are safelie come to Cales, and, as some say, arrived in England. It is also reported that the Duke of Parma hath in great furie slain 16 of his men and caused a Colonnell to be hanged, and the Burgomaster of Dunkerke to be beheaded, besides Montiegny, la Mote and Wachter the Viceadmirall of Flaunders to be cast in prison. But Champigny, they say, hath escaped; hereof, notwithstanding ther is no certainetie, I thought good to advertise your Lordship.'

I enclose a letter from Percevall concerning the affairs of Friesland. Colonel Senoy has arrived at Alkmaar; his soldiers are mutinous. Sir Martin Skenck is here, waiting to get his despatch for the relief of Bergh, which is in some extremity. Bonn is still besieged.

A herald from the King of Scots threatened the Council with reprisals unless, within 40 days, they satisfy Colonel Steward for his services. They referred him to the States General. The Hague.

PS. Sir Martin Skenck has departed for Bergh and Bonn. Captain Blane and Captain Sherley are arrived from Berg. Lord Willoughby has ordered them to go to Ostend. 'The controversies of theis provinces are now partly

appeased, and particularly for that of Utrecht. I hope the worst is past .....
But yet theie are so weake of themselves and have so small meanes to
maintayne their cause against the great power of the enemy.' Without liberal
assistance from her Majesty I fear all will be gone. I am glad the enemy has so
manifestly discovered himself and his malice against England.

Holograph 3 pp. (Dudley Papers II/251)

HENRY KILLIGREW TO THE EARL OF LEICESTER

1588, August 21. To recommend the bearer, Thomas Lovell, for an office -
the charge of the Ramekens, which Nicholas Errington is understood to be
vacating. The Hague.

Holograph 1 p. (Dudley Papers II/253)

THE EARL OF SUSSEX TO THE EARL OF LEICESTER

1588, August 24. Announcing the death of Captain Highfield, and asking
Leicester's good word for his (Sussex's) cousin, Edward Radclyffe, to succeed
him in the command of Portsmouth Castle. Portsmouth.

Signed 1 p. (Dudley Papers II/255)

SIR WILLIAM RUSSELL TO THE EARL OF LEICESTER

1588, August 25. Praying to be relieved of his command if the 'forces of this
garrisson be weakened' as the States desire, and begging Leicester to get such
a reduction prevented. Flushing.

Signed 1 p. (Dudley Papers II/257)

LORD BUCKHURST TO THE EARL OF LEICESTER

1588, August 26. 'Though I know you wilbe very hard of belefe in the
opinion of my skill in hunting, yet I hope your Lordship will not reafuze to
geve credit unto profe of demonstration: for that maner of profe was never yet
reapeld by any. And therfore, having striken a stag with mine own hand,
although I wot well your Lordship may comaund many hundreds, I am bold
yet to present him to your good Lordship as a pore token of my skillful
cunning.' Buckhurst.

Holograph 1 p. (Dudley Papers II/259)

ARTHUR ATYE TO THE EARL OF LEICESTER

1588, August 27. As to a proposed conveyance by Sir Thomas Cecil to
Leicester of the Lordships of Westacre and Strickeston, to be given by the
latter to the Queen. And as to the proposed sale of the manor at Kingsmead,
'one of the things of the Bishopricke of Oxon neare Oxon', to Mr Huddlestone.
He has sent the latter to Leicester, 'being nowe in those partes.' At the
Court.

Holograph 2 pp. (Dudley Papers II/261)

SIR FRANCIS WALSINGHAM TO THE EARL OF LEICESTER

1588, August 28. Yesterday there arrived here the Burgomaster of Ostend
with advertisements that the garrison of Ostend was fallen into a mutiny,
'taking occasion uppon the arrivall of certain bad victualles provided by one
Cox, and have made prisoners both the Governor, Sir John Conwey and all
their Captaines and officers, in steed of whom they have chosen an electe
among themselves. There is also one of them come over who seamyth to be an

honest man with ther demaundes in writting, whare sett down in very duetifull sort with protestation of all obedience to her Majestie and to spend ther lyves in her service so as they may be satisfied in such thinges as they required, that is six monethes pay, pardon for their offence and redresse of divers abuses of their captaines, whereof they offer to make proofe. Hereuppon her Majestie hath caused us of her Councell who are here to enter into consultation what remedy is meet to be used for preventing of further misconducting, which we are in hand withall.

I have been earnestly requested by Mr Comptroller and his frends to be a suter to your Lordship that it wold please you in your absence to recommend his case unto her Majestie in consideration of his yeares, long service and poverty, that at the least he may obtain so much favor as to be prisoner in his own house.' From the Court at St James.

Signed 1 p. (Dudley Papers II/263)

The Earl of Essex to the Earl of Leicester

1588, August 28. 'Since your lordships departure her Majestie hath bene ernest with me to ly in the Court, and this morning she sent to me that I might ly in your lordships lodging, which I will forbeare till I know your lordships pleasure, except the Q. force me to yt. And so offering to you my best services now or at any tyme els, I humbly take my leave.' York House.

Holograph 1 p. (Dudley Papers II/265)

Sir James Croft to the Earl of Leicester

1588, August 29. Asking Leicester's assistance, being 'forced to lye in this lothsome prison', in procuring his 'enlargement' from the Queen. At the Fleet.

Signed 1 p. (Dudley Papers II/267)

The Earl of Warwick to the Earl of Leicester

1588, August 29. 'I cannot choose but even in very pitie among the rest be a meane to your Lordship in the behalfe of Mr Comptroller for your good favoure and helpe towardes his enlargement, or at the leaste that he may be removed to some sweeter place. His age is greate and his case lamentable, considering the course he hath runne from his youthe, who without some speedie good order for his reliefe is like to perish in prison. Wheurin I do very earnestly entreate your Lordship to have in honorable consideration of his weake yeares, and assure yourselfe theare can be noe greater honour then to forgive and helpe to raise uppe againe such as are fallen so deeplye as of themselfe they are in noo hope to rise uppe againe.' From the Court at St James.

Signed 1 p. (Dudley Papers II/269)

Sir Thomas Heneage to the Earl of Leicester

1588, August 29. 'Her Majesties pleasure ys that I shold write unto your Lordship of the state of Ostend, which I need not moch now to troble you with, considering I have wrytten to your Lordship therof allredy this mornyng; only I have now to let your Lordship knowe that her Majestie can not be drawen by the opinyon of her whole Councell that be hear, to grante them pardon or to gyve any man she will send authoretie to promes them pardon, yf necessety shold so require, which we greatly feare may proove the losse of the towne to her Majesties both dyshonor and dysavantage. The man they have chosen to governe them ys one Paine. The man they have sent of their erand is called Colman, It lyeth betwyxt Sir Charles Blunte and Sir Edward Norres to be presently sent to her Majesty for the helpe of their myschief. What will falle owt hearof, your Lordship shall hearafter knowe. The whilst and ever the Lord Jesus keape and blesse your Lordship.' At the Court.

Holograph 1 p. (Dudley Papers II/271)

THOMAS DROPE TO THE EARL OF LEICESTER

(1588 or before) August. Denying charges of having reflected upon Leicester in a sermon.

Torn 1 p. (Dudley Papers II/287)

SIR FRANCIS KNOLLYS TO THE EARL OF LEICESTER

1588, September 2. 'I receyved your Lordships letter upon Ffrydday nighte last, and upon the Satterday in the morning I did showe the same also to Mr Secretarye. Whereupon they hayd conference and upon Satterday nyghte late they sent Mr Mylls unto me, Mr Secretaryes man, with this message from them. That they thoughte it not meete that your lordshippe should allow Mr Comptroller any chamber messe or lyveray for his men, whereupon on Sonday morning I made all the offycers of Howshould acquaynted both with your lordshippes letter and with my Lorde Treasorer and Mr Secretaryes opynyon in that behalffe and so we have defawlked all allowance to Mr Comptrollers men accordinglye.

I have harde synce that your lordshippe hathe bene troubled and stayed with an ague at Corneberry Parke whereof I am very sory. Neverthelesse I truste in God that throughe your lordshippes foresyghte and good order of dyet, that you will easylie and soone dyspatche your selfe thereof with good recoverye of your healthe agayne in short tyme.

I do not thinke my Lord Chamberlyn without danger, saving for that his harte wyll not yeelde unto deathe.' At the Court at St James.

Signed Seal 1 p. (Dudley Papers II/273)

A GREY (?ARTHUR GREY LORD DE WILTON) TO THE EARL OF LEICESTER

(Before 4 September 1588) With thanks for favours and complaints of negligence.* *Undated*

Holograph Seal 3 pp. (Dudley Papers II/296)

RICHARD BETTS TO THE EARL OF LEICESTER

(Before 4 September 1588) A petition complaining of the seizure of his cattle on the ground of Kenilworth Church for tenths, notwithstanding that by Leicester's means the church 'hathe byn discharged of the late interdiction without any money paid therfore.' *Undated*

1 p. (Dudley Papers II/283)

THE QUEEN'S FOOTMEN

(Before 4 September 1588) The list is as follows:

James Russell.

---

* Robert Dudley, Earl of Leicester, died on September 4, 1588.

John Rade.
Griffin Jones.
Richard Clerk.
Thomas Edmonds.
John Ventrice.
Edmond Ducke.
Richard Hogge.
John Gurden.
John Hedd.
Bryan Howson.
Humfrey Colby.
Francis Broughton.
John Cooke.
Robert Case.

Undated   1p. (Dudley Papers III/21)

ROYAL PARKS

(Before 4 September 1588)   A list of the Crown's parks in the counties of Nottingham and York, the Earl of Leicester being Ranger of Forests North of the Trent. *Undated*

1 p.   (Dudley Papers III/51)

FINANCIAL MATTERS

(Before 4 September 1588)   Four sets of papers:

(1) Abstract of the rents and revenues of the Earl of Leicester. 22 pp. (Dudley Papers III/69)

(2) Miscellaneous notes and papers chiefly on business matters. 6 pp. (Dudley Papers III/80)

(3) An item of interest and importance is a list sent to the Earl of Leicester of exceptions against the commissioners in the case of John Salisbury, on the death of Robert Lloyd. Among the six names is that of 'Ellis Pryce, doctor of Lawe', and the comment is: 'Albeit they sayed a Doctor and he be now frends and lovers and so deale together: yet for that this Lloyd was his kinsman and that the same doctor but a reconseyled enemy, therefore not indifferent.' (Dudley Papers III/82)

(4) Concerning the offer of Sir Simon Musgrave and Thomas Warcoppe for the 'custom inwardes' of the ports of Hull, Newcastle and Boston. The offer is to increase the yearly custom by £200, on condition that the Privy Council directs that the orders appointed for payment of customs in the city of London should be enforced in the above ports. (Dudley Papers III/86)

Undated

TRACT

(Before 4 September 1588)   Tract on 'godlie fame' in the form of a letter addressed to Robert Dudley, Earl of Leicester, signed by the author Thomas Lupton. The tract which consists of a fulsome eulogy of the Earl begins 'Though the Ethnyckes ... thought there were but twoe kindes of fame, that is to say good or evell, yet we may justlie say that there is a third called godlie fame ..... which godlie fame your honor sekes dailie to acquyre, as it semes by the way you walke yn.' *Undated*

Three leaves, small 4 ^{to} in vellum covers. On the upper cover is written in another hand: 'of vertuous life.' (Dudley Papers III/206)

DEBTS

(After 4 September 1588) 'The state of the debte charged upon the deceassed Earl of Leicester for exceeding his allowance in the time of his lieutenancy generall in the Lowe Contreis.'

The sum owing for 'allowance by him taken at £4:14 *per diem* more then was conteyned in the Quenes list was £3619', but against this debt Sir Christopher Blount urges that no list was ever ratified by the Queen or Council limiting to 'a certen stent or rate' of allowance: that the Earl had been authorized by letters patent dated November 27, an° 28, to command out of the Treasure there any sums at his pleasure: that the Earl in taking £10:14 a day only imitated the Earl of Pembroke, Queen Mary's lieutenant general at St Quentin. Sir Christopher asks therefore that the debt may be discharged. *Undated*

1 p. (Dudley Papers III/91)

INVENTORY

(After 4 September 1588) 'The generall inventory of all such goods of ... the Earl of Leycester as remayned at Killingworth, Leycester House, Grafton Court and Wainstead upon the laste viewes taken' comprising the Earl's household and other effects at his death.

The inventories are as follows:

(a) f.2. Household goods in charge of Thomas Underhill at Kenilworth, 13 October, 1588.

(b) f.25. Bedding, hangings and other stuffs 'in charge of the same at Grafton', 17 October, 1588.

(c) f.28. Plate, glass etc at Kenilworth in the charge of Thomas Cole, 1584 and 1588.

(d) f.31. 'Naperie' etc in the charge of Anne King at Kenilworth, 16 October, 1588.

(e) f.35. 'Ordnaunce and Municion' at Kenilworth 12 October, 1588. Three sakers, one minion and two falcons are noted as having been sent to the Earl of Leicester's ship at Bristol.

(f) f.37. Sheets etc sent from Kenilworth to Leicester House, 17 October, 1588.

(g) f.38. 'An inventory of such golde plate, parcell gilte plate and plaine plate as remained in the charge of Martyn Gonslin at Leicester House, 29 September, 1585.' Among the donors are mentioned the Countess of Warwick, the Archbishop of York, the Bishops of Salisbury and Bath and Wells, Mr Francis Throgmorton, the farmer of the impost of sweet wines at Bristol, 1584, the Merchant Adventurers, 1581. In 1584 Sir Walter Ralegh gives 'the boddie of a strainge shel of a fishe garnished with silver and gilte, the foote embossed, a Manachin standing therupon and supporting the shell, Neptune sitting on the top of the shell with his trident in his hand.' In 1581 'Lady Salopp' gives two double bowls without covers; the Earls of Shrewsbury and Bedford French bowls. Lady Burghley gives two small salts in 1583.

(h) f.50. 'An inventory of such jewells as Collers, Georges, aggatts, Brootches, Garters, Ringes, Buttons etc' remaining at Court, including one gold chain given by Monsieur; 'a ring of gold enameled black with a fayer table diamond in it cutt lozeng wise with these letters on it E.R.' (*noted as* 'not prised'); and 'the brooche of a Turkey graven with the Queenes picture besett with 14 rubies.' The list also contains sweetbags, six books, including 'a discourse of the safetie of the realme', pictures, maps (f.65), globes and robes (f.84).

(1) f.93. Such robes as remained at Court, 1588, including gowns, 'clokes', 'hattes and cappes' etc.

(j) f.105. All such stuff as remained in the custody of Nicholas Webber at Wanstead, 1588, including pictures, books, etc.

Folio. Vellum covers ff.126 *with.many blank* (Dudley Papers XI)
(The inventories of pictures in this volume are printed in *Notes and Queries*, 3rd ser ii 201-2, 224-5)

LORD NORTH TO THE EARL OF LEICESTER

(1588 or before) September 5. Enquiring after Leicester's health. 'We here that your exchange goeth forward, God send yt to your good, therby yt appeareth that change some time doth good. If the parliament be adjorned till some longer time, I will see your Lordship yf yt may be before Bartlemas, wishing to have some knowledge of the Commissioners coming that I may do my dutie and attend hir Majestie at that time.'

Holograph Addressed: 'To the Earle of Lester at Coorte.' 1p. (Dudley Papers II/304)
(*This letter may possibly refer to the proposed exchange of lands between the Queen and the Earl of Leicester. See Cal S.P. Dom, 1581-1590, p.501*)

THOMAS FOWLER TO MR BARKER

(September 16, 1588) 'I pray you informe my Lady that I have not at this present any mony reddy for that I cam home but on Satterday last, and since that I have sent to dyvers that owethe mony, who are slaker to pay now then when he lyved. They aunswer that thayre wynes layes on there hand and cannot sell them.' *Undated*

Holograph Endorsed: 'Mr Ffowlers letter touching mony for the sweete wines. 16 Sept. 1588.' 1 p. (Dudley Papers II/275)

BONDS

1588, October 21. List of bonds, 35 in number, 'brought to my Lady' by Richard Williams.

3 pp. (Dudley Papers IV/50)

WARRANT

1588, November 11. Privy Council warrant for the search of the house at Bishopsgate of Thomas Fowler, servant to the late Earl of Leicester, who had fled to Scotland with £7000 or £8000, and for the imprisonment of John Montgomery, his servant, if he refused to answer questions.

Signed by: Burghley, Walsingham and four others. *Seal Addressed to:* Richard Yonge, William Baynam and Edward Barker. *Endorsed:* 'The letter of the Countessis warrant towching Mr Fowler and Montgo. xi Novem. 1588.' 1 p. (Dudley Papers III/89)

ELIZABETH SUTTON TO THE COUNTESS OF LEICESTER

(?1588) December 29. Praying her to pay 'the great charge I was at when you wyth the young lord* and other your honors frynds and company lay with

* Robert, Lord Denbigh, son of the Earl of Leicester who died in 1584.

me', which the late Earl of Leicester had faithfully promised to do.

Holograph   Endorsed: 'Mrs   Dudleys   demaunde   for   £393:6:8.'   2
pp.   (Dudley Papers IV/33)

THE EARL OF LEICESTER'S DEBTS

1588 to 1590-1.   Papers relating to the Earl's debts.   They include *inter alia:*

(1)   'Mr Brograves answer to our questions.'   The Earl 'dieth in depte to
the valewe of £20,000 more then his goods and chattelles are worthe.'   He has
made his wife his sole executrix, and the question is whether she would be wise
in the circumstances to accept the office.   *Undated* 1 p.

(2)   The 'errors' of the commissioners inquiring into the state of the Earl's
lands in Shropshire.   January 1590-1.   2 pp.

9 pp.   (Dudley Papers IV/94)

INVENTORY

March 23, 1588-9.   Inventory of the household stuff at Leicester House 'first
perused' on May 24, 1583 and perused for the 11th time on March 23,
1588-9.   Many additions and notes to the original inventory are duly noted.
The list includes:

Hangings, e.g. 'Four peeces of Hangings of the Historye of Moses founde
in a basket by the riverside amongest the flags and bulrushes, the border of
Antique and ffrutage, quarter lyned with canvas.'   The hanging with the
history of Latinus and Eneas is marked 'sent into Holland' (p.2).

Bedsteads with their furniture.   Many of these later marked 'at Court' and
'in Flanders' (p.5).   Also 'silke quiltes' (p.8); 'lynnen quiltes' (p.9); 'beddes'
(p.10); 'Fustians' (p.12b); 'wollen blanketes' (p.13); 'rugges' (p.14); 'Counter-
poynts' (p.14b); 'Pilloes' (p.16); 'Mattresses' (p.16); 'Clothe of State' (p.17);
'Carpetts' (p.19); Chairs with their furniture (p.22); 'Lowe stooles' (p.25);
'Long cushens' (p.25); 'Curteins' (p.28); 'Close stooles' (p.28b); 'Looking
glasses, skreens' (p.29); Tables and cupboards, including a 'billiard boorde
for the Scottish game' (p.29b); 'Instrumentes of music' (p.30); 'Andirons'
(p.30); 'Warderobe stuffe' (p.31); 'Apparell' (p.31b); 'Sadles and sadel
clothes', of which one is described as 'a faier saddell cloth verie richely
embrothered with gould, perle, turquoies, two counterfeict rubies,' and has a
note to the effect that 'all the pearle taken of by my Lady the 19th of March
1586' (p.33); 'Cofers boxes' (p.35); Weapons, including a 'Turkey bowe with
45 arrowes within a case.'   Another Turkish bow and arrows is noted as having
been given 'to the Turck that cam with Sir F. Drake' (p.36).

Maps and globes, including one of Africa and America (p.38); 'Ensignes'
(p.39).

Books, including 'one greate historicall booke in latten of creation of the
worlde and the genelogee of the creatures.'   Also Boetius's *de Consolatione* in
Latin; Seneca's tragedies in Latin; Nova Silva in Italian; Cicero's offices in
Latin; Xenophon's *Cyropedia* in Italian (p.40).

Pictures.   The additions since 1580 are:

'A faire long table of the picture of Christ calling Matthew out of the
Custome house.

The historie of the body of Christ after he was taken from the Crosse, with
the iii Maries and their mother (*noted as being at Wanstead*).

The historie of Cookery in a frame of woode all gilt aboute the border with
a curteine of silke.

221

The table of the history of St John preaching in the wilderness.
One other of harrowing hell.
One other of Elias taken up in the fyery chariot.
One other of the birthe of Christ, howe he was borne in an Oxe stall, with 2 leaves to foulde and unfoulde.
One other of the Duke of Alva.
One other of the Cardinal of Lothereng.
One other of the picture of a naked woman with 3 babes about her.
One picture of an ould man looking on his booke and a lady lying by him entising him from ytt in a frame of wood.
One picture of my young Lord of Denbigh.
The picture of the Duke of Savoy.
The picture of the Prince of Orange.
A picture of a gentlewoman with verses under her.
A counterfect of a gentlewoman in a petecote of yellow sattin (*with note:* 'all broken and quite defaced by my yonge lord, *ut dicitur.*')
One smale picture of therle of Essex father.
One of my lord with a little curteine of green sarcenett.
One large one of Mr Henry Knolles.
One of Mr Phillip Sydney when he was a boy.
One of my lord in armoure in cloth in a frame.
One of my lords whole proportion without a frame with Boy his dog by him.
A newe table of the persecution of Saule given by Cutler the painter.
My lords whole proportion on clothe made by Hubbard 1583, *with note:* 'send to the King of Scots.'
A device made by Hubbard on clothe of a butcher and a maide buying meate and a knave making love unto her.
A picture of a naked lady sleeping and Cupid menacing her with his darte.
My Ladys whole proportion in cloth and my yong lorde standing by hir made by Hubard 1584.
A picture of Julius Caesar.
A picture of Penelope.
A picture of my Lady Rich.
An old picture of my Lord.
A picture of my Lord made before his going into Holland.
A picture of the Lady Pembroke.' (p.42)

Folio In vellum covers (Dudley Papers VI)

LORD BURGHLEY TO THE COUNTESS OF LEICESTER

1589, June 28.   Ordering her to give up certain evidences relating to the late Earl of Leicester's lands to the Earl of Warwick.

Signed 1 p. (Dudley Papers IV/35)

T. DOWNHALE TO EDWARD BARKER

1589, July 4.   On his services to the late Earl of Leicester. 'I served his Lᵒ iii yeares, for I came to him in October before his first going over (to the Netherlands) and never left him alive nor dead untill I performed my last service unto him, helping to laye his noble corps in the earth.' He requests that the Countess of Leicester pay what is due to him.

Signed 3 pp. (Dudley Papers IV/212)

THE WILL OF LORD AMBROSE DUDLEY, EARL OF WARWICK

1589-90, January 28. This is a copy of his will.

16 pp. (Dudley Papers III/138)

THE COUNTESS OF LEICESTER TO LORD BURGHLEY

1589-90, March 7. Praying for time to answer the statement of debts of the late Earl of Leicester to the Crown. Leicester House.

Holograph Seal 1 p. (Dudley Papers IV/38)

THE EARL OF ESSEX TO THE COUNTESS OF LEICESTER

1590, March 27. 'Madam. I have sent your Ladyship a letter to my Lord Chauncelor which your Ladyship, when you have read yt, may seale and please you and other send by this bearer or whom els you please. To resolve your Ladyship that I will stand firme in this and in all other your causes, I do send you here mine owne to be a witnes against me yf I do not. For your Ladyships own which you say is uncertaine, I will defend you otherwiles with all the witt, creditt and frendes that I have, and for that which your Ladyship hath of my land I will not refuse to confirme yt when your Ladyship shall say your desire, that ther may be so free dealing on both sides as kindnes may be deerer than anything els. For Wansteed, though I confesse I do greatly affect yt, yet I will not desir yt so as your Ladyship shall loose one penny profitt or one hower of pleasure that you may have ther. The Quene hath divers tymes within these 4 dayes asked me whether I had yt, and I doubt not but to have her there ere May Day yf my lease were made. Yf your Ladyship thinke so good I will receave the conditions from any officer of yours, for whatsoever you aske I will agree unto yt. The Quene hath stayed me here this day, but to-morrow I will see you yf I can. And so I commend your Ladyship to Gods best protection.' Greenwich.

Holograph 1 p. (Dudley Papers IV/40)

THE EARL OF ESSEX TO THE COUNTESS OF LEICESTER

(1590) July 20. 'Madam. I see a disagreement betweene your Ladyships officers and mine for the drawing of the assurances betweene us. In some thinges I thought my officers to curious and therfore I yelded to that which they wold not consent too. Now I must needes thinke your Ladyships officers do deale a great deale too partially for to aske £200 allmost for a £150. If your Ladyship will reforme this second error as I have done the former, we shall have a present agreement, or els I see not any end and so breake of from the bargin I have made for the sale of Tollsbury with great trouble for me and as much losse. I referr all to your Ladyships best and kindest judgment. I pray your Ladyship tell this berer now your plesure, and that which is done lett yt be done with speede. And so I commit your Ladyship to Gods best protection.' Greenwich.

Holograph Seal Endorsed: 'July 20. My l. of Essex, 1590' 1 p. (Dudley Papers IV/41)

THE COUNTESS OF LEICESTER TO LORD BURGHLEY

1590, July 25. Is sending the 'book of Denbigh' by the bearer, for whom she requests the restoration to his office of Recorder of the Barony of Denbigh. Leicester House.

Holograph Seal 1 p. (Dudley Papers IV/42)

INVENTORY

1590, November 21. 'Chargg of Lester House nowe in use and to remayne for my La(dys) service this XXI of November, 1590' under the charge of Michael Peckover. It contains a list of furniture, hangings etc, in Leicester House, e.g.:

In the High Gallery

'Item, three larg picktwers, namely King Hary, Quene Marye and the Quenes Majestie.

Item, seven large picktwers, namely my Lord and Lady, Casymer, the Prynce of Oring, my Lord of Warike, my L. Admirall and Sir Frances Knowles.

Item, 2 spesyall picktwers, namely Julyous Ceaser and Penelopea.

Item, two mappes of the larger making in frames.

Item, three picktwers, namely the French King, two ladyes in one picktwer, my La. Rych and my La. Doryt, the King of Skottes, Mr Hary Knowles.

Item, two picktwers of my young lordes.

Item, six small mapes in frames.

Item, twelve small picktwers.

Item, two other picktwers, namly the Prynce of Orindges youngest sonne and the picktwer of Bewcham.

Item, two other picktwers, my Lord of Esseckes and my Lady Darsyes daughter.

Item, a gren velit chayre and long cushin imbroidered with my Lordes Armes that served in the great chamber at Wansted.'

Among the items in the High Wardrobe is a cloak, hood and little boots of the Order of St Michael of France.

21 pp. (Dudley Papers IV/52)

SIR CHRISTOPHER BLOUNT TO LORD BURGHLEY

(1592) June 20. Concerning 'my boke of debtes' and craving 'some end of my troble.' Leicester House.

Signed Seal, broken Endorsed: '20 Junii 1592. Sir Christopher Blount.' 1 p. (Dudley Papers IV/44)

CERTIFICATE

1595, September 30. Certificate of Sir Christopher Blount to the Warden of the Fleet that Richard Smarte, committed for 'divers slaunderous petitions' against him to the Privy Council, had duly submitted and asked forgiveness. Drayton Bassett.

Signed 1 p. (Dudley Papers IV/214)

ACQUITTANCE

1600, October 13. Acquittance from Margery Garnett to Sir Christopher Blount and Lady Leicester for £15 for all annuities due out of Itchington.

1 p. (Dudley Papers IV/64)

WARRANT

1601, April 2. Warrant from Lord Buckhurst, Lord Treasurer, to the tenants of the manors of the late Earl of Leicester, under an extent for his debts to the Crown, ordering them to pay rents to Edward Barker to whom the said manors had been demised under bond at the request of the Countess of Leicester.

Signed Seal 1 p. (Dudley Papers III/103)

LEGAL PAPERS

1602, August 23 to 1604, October 10. Seven papers relating to cross-suits between the Countess of Leicester and John Crompton, Ralph Lyon and others for 'divers great riottes and mysdemeanours.'

9 pp. (Dudley Papers IV/65)

W. SPARKE TO THE COUNTESS OF LEICESTER

(Before 1603) On questions between her and her daughter-in-law, Lady Essex,* touching Chartley, Leicester House and Taynton. *Undated*

Signed 2 pp. (Dudley Papers IV/46)

PETITIONS

(*temp* Elizabeth) Petitions, dated and undated, to the Earl of Leicester with a few to the Queen.

(1) Robert Atkyns 'grolme of the Queenes Majesties powltrey' for payment of £3:17:9 for poultry. (Dudley Papers III/104b)

(2) James Beamont *or* Beaumont for the continuance of an allowance of 12 d a day made to his brother, now dead. (Dudley Papers III/106b)

(3) John Bradley, merchant adventurer 'and consarge of the Englishe howse in Barrow' for compensation for losses inflicted upon him in the Netherlands for having aided in conveying Dr Storye to England. 'In the monthe of July 1570, arryved at the saide towne of Barrow Roger Ramsden and Martin Bragge, boathe brethren of the saide companye beinge sent from a thirde personne (an English gentleman) to conferre with me about a certaine practise or enterprise for provydinge or hyringe of a shippe for the conveighinge over of Doctor Storye, whiche practise had bene attempted at Andwarpe and theare lyke to have bene revealid and so utterly frustrate: further by wrytinge receavid from the saide gentleman playnelye appeared' that he had a licence from England and from Mr Mershe, and thinking 'the said Storye to be no lesse then a ranche traytour and (to his power) an extreme ennemye to God and the Queen'; the petitioner 'employed his service and helpenge hande to the pretendid premisses, usinge all the servise he could devyse, and falling in talke with one Cornelis Adrianson, a shipper of Barowe, throughe much persuasion caused him to serve with his shippe' under oath not to reveal anything until the enterprise had been completed, which it was. Besides this the petitioner 'assested the saide Ramsden and Bragge and the said Storyes sendinge from thence, hath also entertained and lodged him in the saide Englishe howse, and in the ende accompanied him to the shippe, sawe him imbarked.' The result was that the petitioner had to flee the country. (Dudley Papers III/108b)

* Married Richard de Burgh, 4th Earl of Clanricarde in 1603.

(4)   Henry Dames, 'straunger', for the release of a hawk seized by a Customs officer.   (Dudley Papers III/111)

(5)   Sir Valentine Browne, Treasurer of Berwick, to be recouped for losses amounting to £5205:2:6 in victualling Berwick.   Petition addressed to the Queen.   (Dudley Papers III/112b)

(6)   Hans Franke, goldsmith, for payment of £46 for 'certeyne jewelles' before September, 1564.   (Dudley Papers III/114)

(7)   John Hetherley, Yeoman of the Queen's Chamber, for aid to obtain a Crown lease.   (Dudley Papers III/115b)

(8)   Henry Hovenn to the Queen, for the redelivery of 'a jewell of diamondes in forme of a combe to the value of £180' supplied to the late Earl of Leicester on approval and detained by the Countess. Endorsed with a note by William Aubrey that 'of her owne gratiouse remembraunce her hyghenes did knowe that the late Earle of Leicester hadd the jewell ... and that the peticioner hadd neither solde it nor given it unto him, and promised her prencelie aide therein' that it should be restored.   (Dudley Papers III/117)

(9)   The Mayor and burgesses of Leicester, praying that in any Crown lease of the pasture called Beamount Leas the inhabitants of Leicester may have agistment for their milch kine and riding horses as in the lease to Michael Corbett granted in 1 Edward VI.   (Dudley Papers III/119)

(10)   Sir William Malory to the Queen, for a grant of 'the towne of Lertyngton and Cotsterton' in Yorkshire, or equivalents, in consideration of his services against the rebels in the North and in Scotland.   (Dudley Papers III/121)

(11)   Elizabeth Massye, to be 'so good lorde' to her and her husband 'persoune within the Tower of London' as to obtain from the Queen a lease of 'a salte-house that was sumtyme of the churche landes within the Nomptewyche conteynyng iii dozen leydes' for 21 years; she and her late husband Richard Ynce 'that was her graces servant and in his graces affare at the Newehavyn' having been the former tenants of the same. 'God save Quene Elyzabeth and confounde hyr enymes.'   (Dudley Papers III/124)

(12)   The Earl of Leicester's Players, six in number, asking to be retained in his household. *Signed by*: James Burbage, John Perkin, John Laneham, William Johnson, Robert Wilson and Thomas Clarke.   (Dudley Papers III/125)   (This petition is printed in *Notes and Queries* 3rd ser xi 350.)

(13)   Ralph Shelton, praying Leicester to prefer one of two suits to the Queen, either for a licence to import wines without paying the impost, or for a grant of concealed lands.   (Dudley Papers III/128)

(14)   Symon Jewkes, 'one of them that broughte over Doctor Story', for relief in the way of a licence to buy some Spanish prize 'taken on the seas by the Prince of Orenges aucthoreste which bringe in prices dailly.'   (Dudley Papers III/131)

CLAIM TO LANDS

(?*temp* Eliz.)   Papers concerning the Countess of Leicester's claim to lands at Wyford, co. Stafford.   *Undated*

24 pp.   (Dudley Papers IV/157)

ARTICLES OF AGREEMENT

1607, September 5.   An agreement between the Countess of Leicester and Robert Devereux, 3rd Earl of Essex, her grandson and Frances, his wife, that until the said Earl be of full age the Countess shall hold the Myrevall, co. Warwick, with other lands, paying to the said Earl £400 yearly.

Copy   3 pp.   (Dudley Papers IV/81)

DEPOSITIONS

1608, April 7.   Depositions on behalf of the Countess of Leicester against Sir Thomas Dilke and others for non-payment of rent on a lease of Ryton Manor, co. Warwick.

37 pp.   (Dudley Papers IV/83)

DEVEREUX PAPERS
1533-1659

ACCOUNTS

1533, October 17 to 1534, September 25.   Book of Accompt of receipts and payments of William Clopton, Steward of the Household to Henry Bourchier, 2nd Earl of Essex, kept apparently at Stansted Hall in Halstead, co. Essex, and dated 17 Oct. 25 Henry VIII to 25 Sep. 26 Henry VIII.

The receipts down to December 6, 1533, are missing, and the whole volume has been much damaged by damp. The receipts amount to £282:17:2 and the payments to £275:8:1$\frac{1}{4}$.

The payments, chiefly for provisions, are entered day by day, e.g.:

'Mercurie, the 19th of November:

Item, a mutton of store.	Item, a porke, price 2s. 8d.	
	Item, in eggs, 2d.	2s. 10d.

Jovis:

Item, two muttons of store.	Item, a porke, price 2s. 8d.	
	Item, a pygge, 4d.	
	Item, two curles, two wodcocks and four redeshankes, 22d.	6s. 4d.
	Item, fuve dussen larkes, 15d.	
	Item, in eggs 2d., in appells 1s. 3d.	
Crestmas Day:	Item, 4 duckes and mallardes, 14d.	
Item, a stere of store.	Item, a wodcock 3d., a crane 6s., a heron	
Item, 4 muttons of store.	10d.	
Item, a veale of store.	Item, six dussen larkys, 2s. 3d.	
	Item, a plover 3d., 2 snyghtes 2d., 5d.	
	Item, 7 wodcocks 2s. 4d., 4 ducks and mallards, 12d. 3s. 4d.	
	2 woodcoks the pece 2d. 4d.	17s. 6d.
	4 hottes and a plover, 5d.	
	7 teales and 10 redshankes, 2s. 2d.	
	a whyg, a plover and 2 oxbyrdes, 4d.' f.10-.	

Other payments are for, *inter alia*:

'Lynge, saltfyshe and stockefyshe bowght,
Item, 5 copell of olde lynge, 25s.
Item, a hundred stockefishe, 13s. 4d. 58s. 4d.
Item, a hundred salt fyshe, 20s.'   ff.26-7.

Wheat, e.g.

'Ffor xv seme of wheate from Lyston the 24th daye of Maye, price the seme 7s., £5:5:0.'

Spices and fruit, e.g.   f.28

Sunday, November 9.		
	Pepper 3 lb.	5s. 6d.
	Dates, 12 lb.	4s.
	Cloves and maces, a lb.	4s.
	Isornglasse, a lb.	2s. 8d.
	Tornesall, a lb.	14d.
	Gynger Casse, 1 lb.	3s. 4d.
	Corrantes, 12 lb.	2s. 6d.
	Gynger Case, 1 lb.	2s. 8d.
	Gynger Venyse, 1 lb.	2s. 4d.

Socade, 8 lb.	5$^{s.}$ 4$^{d.}$	
a barrell.	2$^{d.}$	
Ryses, 8 lb.	16$^{d.}$	49$^{s.}$ 1$^{d.}$
Almondes, 12 lb.	2$^{s.}$ 6$^{d.}$	
Comfettes, 6 lb.	3$^{s.}$ 0$^{d.}$	
Carawayes, 2 lb.	16$^{d.}$	
Byskettes, 1 lb.	8$^{d.}$	
Annessedes, 4 lb.	8$^{d.}$	
Lykores, 1 lb.	3$^{d.}$	
Synamonde, 1 lb.	5$^{s.}$ 8$^{d.}$'	f.30.

Costs, expenses, rewards and repairs. *Inter alia:*

October 24. At London 'ffor the matter betwene my lorde and my lady of Oxenforde, £4:3:11.

To Mr Ryche, solicitor, 6$^{s.}$ 8$^{d.}$

Sabbato, the 10 day of Januarie:

Item, to William Waffen of Halsted, for the hyre of hys barne to laye tharein my Lordes barlye, 2$^{s.}$ 4$^{d.}$

Item, in rewarde to Master Gunwells clarke to call upon hys master ffor my lordes busynes, 5$^{s.}$

Item, ffor my costes, my meate and drynke and horsemeate ffor 7 dayes at London before the Parlyament in my lordes busynes, 14$^{s.}$

Item, to a carryer of Sudbery ffor carryenge of serteyne spyces, 30 orrenges, a hundred appells, carrott rotes and navy rootys with other thynges, 2$^{s.}$'

February 23. 'To Richard the Minstrels coste to London for the vyalls', and his costs homewards by water, 4$^{s.}$ 2$^{d.}$

Wages of Servants, including:

For half a year ending at May Day, eight gentlemen at 26$^{s.}$ 8$^{d.}$, one chaplain, Nicholas Wastelyn, 40$^{s.}$, £12:13:4.

Twenty one yeomen, 20 at 20$^{s.}$, 1 at 26$^{s.}$ 8$^{d.}$, £21:6:8.

Eighteen grooms at 13$^{s.}$ 4$^{d.}$, £12.

Two women of the laundry, 11$^{s.}$ 8$^{d.}$ f.41b.

August 3. For drink for the Children of the Chapel, 8$^{d.}$

To 'Master Cowke, pryst, for hys borde-wayges for a monythe', 5$^{s.}$4$^{d.}$ f.46

Folio.   ff.48   (Devereux Papers X)

MARRIAGE SETTLEMENT

1536, July 1.   Settlement on the marriage of Richard Devereux, son and heir of Walter Devereux, Lord Ferrers of Chartley, and Dorothy, daughter of George Hastings, Earl of Huntingdon, 1 July, 28 Henry VIII.

Copy   7pp.   (Devereux Papers III/1)

ACCOUNTS

1559, October to 1561, May.   'My Lorde Herefords reckning'. A tailor's bill for Walter Devereux, 2nd Viscount Hereford, amounting to £158:9:9.

23 pp.   (Devereux Papers III/14)

ACCOUNTS

1570, March 30.   Receipt by John Vernon for £40 in part payment of 300 marks due to him from Lady Dorothy Devereux, his mother-in-law.

Signed   1 p.   (Devereux Papers III/26)

1571, Michaelmas. 'A brief of the nombre of the garaisons there (in Ireland) with the chardges thereof for one month.'

The garrison consists of 2031 men at the yearly charge of £32,442:10:0¼.

11 pp. (Devereux Papers II/1)

(See *Cal.S.P. Ireland*, Vol.34, p.459)

NETHERLANDS

1572, July 26 to August 11. An account of the proceedings of an English force in the Netherlands against the Spaniards, with news from Flushing, August 13.

'The 26th of July we landed in Suyd Beverland where at our fyrst cominge fortye or fiftye of our men were skyrmyshed with all by two or thre hundred Spanyardes. In this skirmysh there were slayne 4 or 5 of our men wherof yonge Argall and More were two. And of the Spanyards 6 or 8, and the French men and other Wallons that shold have backt our men ran awaye at this skirmysh.

The 28th of July we marched towards Tergose, where at a lytle villadge caled Nisckirk one Englishe myle distaunt from Tregose our forlorne hope, being under the leadinge of Captayn Thomas Morgan, were skirmyshed with all by 3 or 400 Spanyardes who had ambushed them selves so closly on eyther syde of a strayght, by the which we must passe, that they were undescryed by our scowtes, and so setting upon our men at unawares they inforced them somwhat to retyer, which being sene I caused divers gents to the number of 12 with sordes and targettes accompayned with some halbartes to charge them afresh, who executed the same so valiantly as that they drove the Spanyardes into the towne of Tregose, following them to the gattes, beinge a longe Englyshe myle distant from the place where the skirmysh first begane; and stade under the wales the space of an hower or more. In all which tyme neyther Ffrenchmen nor Walons wold come in daunger of thenemye, but contynualye persuaded us to retyer, otherwise they profered to leve us in the felde. Whereupon we retorned our selfes to a towne caled Barland, from which we cam in the morninge. There were slayne in this skirmyshe of the Spanyardes 30 gentle and brave soldiers, besydes two or three of the galantest Capt (aynes) amongst them; there were hurt of them about 50.

There were slayne of thenglyshe 12 or 14 besydes 40 hurte, amongst whome there was none of any countenaunce but only Captayne Stanton and Mr Rowland Yorke, who are neythyr in danger of mayme or lyfe. The gents that charged them in the face with sordes and targettes were these, viz:

Mr Cotton, Lyvestenaunt generall; Mr Lyster; Mr Edward Jobson; Mr George Gascoigne; Mr Keymyshe; Mr Waye; Mr Selynger, with others.

All the Capitaynes served valyauntly this day and in especiall Capitayn West, Capitayn of my privy bande, and with hym these gents being shot, viz: yong Mr Henry Jobson, Mr Anthony Poynes, Mr Sampson of Kent, Mr Ruben Senton, Mr Brokesby, Mr Edward Jobson, with others.

These breakinge through a great garde charged the enemy on the fflanke and were a great cause of their retyeringe.

The 30th of July the army departed from suyd Beverland over agayne into Fflaunders, my selfe going to Fflushinge.

This day cam news to Fflushinge that the Prince had gotten Remund in Gelderland and was in it.

That the Grave van Bergh, brother-in-law to the Prince, entered into

Delphe the 29th of July.

Also it was informed me this daye by one of this towne caled Ffox, who cam from the Counts campe the 27th of this moneth of the strengthes of tharmye here underwryten:

The Princes poure	The Prince of Orenge	Footemen aboute 13,000	23,000
		Horsemen aboute 10,000	
	Casimeres	Fotemen 2000	
		Horsemen 1600	
	Count Ludowike	Footemen in Monts 2200	3,300
		Item, goten at the overthrow of Jeniis 500	
		Horsemen 600	
			29,900

The Duke D'Alvas power	Ffootmen 7560	Wallons, 13 ensing at 120 per ensing 1560
		Germains, 19 ensing at 300 per ensing 5700
		Spanyardes, 2 ensinges at 150 per ensing 300

	Horsemen 2200	The band of thordynaunce 150
		Spanyardes 6 cornettes at 100 per cornett 600
		Wallons 100
		Ruytters 1500

10,900 *(sic)*

The 4 of August tharmy cam over owte of Fflaunders into this llande and encamped at a towne called Zellonde nere the sea coste two leagues from the towne.

The 6th daye newes cam from Andwerpe by a letter dated the 3 of August and sent to the Balyffe of this towne, as foloweth: that the shippes at Andwerpe be in redynes and that dyvers shippes are prepared to come from Slues, Newporte, Dunkerke and other places, wherefore he wisheth diligent watch to be hadd. That the Governors brother of this towne is prysoner with D. D'Alva.

That he who sent this letter cam latly from the campe of Count Lodowike, where althinges be in very good case, and that during his beinge there these townes folowing were taken, viz: Gelders, Walgalen, Dunicke, Arthalens, Buckesina, Reum.

Item, that since, he understandeth the Counts power to have taken Vendolle about mydnyght.

Also he writeth the newes is at Andwerpe that the Wallons, which were in Germany, be retyered towards Harlem in Hollande, whereupon the townesmen of Germine had utterly rased the castell begone by the Spanyardes and will no more have any Spanyardes or Wallons to come there.

Bomelle, a very stronge towne, being two myles from Bolduke, was taken the day before the date of this letter without any slaughter by reason of 2 wagons laden with haye, thone entringe in and thother steinge without, betwene which wagons 400 soldiers entered and possest the towne for the Prince.

There cam to ayde the Duke 13 ensignes of Almayns of which 600 were slayne and three of the chefest capytaynes taken prysoners; and to conclude he wryteth there were coming oute of Ffraunce soldiers innumerable to ayde the Prince.

The 8th of this moneth, Mounsieur de Benvoyse, Governor of Myddelborough, upon false reporte of his spyes perswaded with the soldiars that at Zootland, where our men were encamped, we had not above 500 men and they to be the symplest, for he was enformed that 4 or 500 were sent to Camphier and the rest with the best gents to be at Fflusshinge. Upon this persuasion ther came to the campe about 5 of the clocke in the morning betwene the discharginge of the wach and the setting of the warde 600 Spanyardes and Wallons, so that if by the provydence of God a boure of the contry goinge from the campe of Fflushinge with his wagon for victualls had not discryed them and recovered upon one of his horses with spede geveng the larome to the campe, assueredly they had spoyled the whole army in their lodgings accordinge to their intentes, for they made sure accompt thereof as appeared by dyvers that had there hose full of halters, whome our men toke and hanged with theire owne haulters.

By meanes of this alarm everyman put hym selfe in a redynes so sone as he coulde, and whereas the enemye had placed certayne of theire shot upon a sand hyll hanginge over the towne most fytt for theire purpose and they havinge wonne a trenche from our men, the same was recovered agayne quickly.

The skirmysh was so whote upon a soden that our men at the furst did somwhat retyer, and had not the valiaunt myndes of the gents caused them perforce to charge them afresh, yt had bene worse with us. But this charge was so valyauntly executed that the Spanyardes torned their faces and went theire way, our men followinge them till they cam within two myles of Mydleborough. They killed, hanged and hurte of them 200.

In this skirmyshe were slayne 15 or 20 Englysh men, namelye:

Capitayn Bowsor: Capitayn Bedow; Mr Bostocke, Lyvt to Mr Capt. Cotton; Mr Lyle; Mr Gunter.

Theire served very valiantly all the Capytaynes as Mr Chester, Mr Evors and Capytayne Handly, Capitayn West, Mr John Crookes, Mr Philpott, Mr Hamon, Mr Lovell and Mr Merricks with others.

There was one Capitayne of the French slayne whose name was Capytayn Ryveyre, a propper man, besydes 7 or 8 others.

The 11th of this present the Admyrall of this towne, a very valyaunt man, sent one of his hoyes hether to informe the townesmen that he had taken Surrepe and the whole iland and that he had cut the throtes of 150 Spanyardes and gave lyfe to 200 Wallons that offered to serve hym, whome he disarmed and sent awaye.

This day cam dyvers letters to the chefe of this towne from Andwarpe dated the 8th of this present, the effects of which ar thus:

That the 7th of this moneth the Prince vanquished 6 ensinges of the Grave van Everstons company, who came to the ayde of the Duke, and hath taken many prysoners.

That Amsterdame in Holland is revolted to the Prince without doubt.

Extract of the newes wryten from Flusshinge the 13th of August 1572.

The towne of Andwerpe prepares shippes and men to set upon Flusshinge, which they of Flusshinge ar nothinge in feare of.

Certayne horsemen of the Prince of Orenges about Hassell have overthrowne 6 ensinges of Germayns. The chefe therof was the Count Oversten, wherof 200 are taken prysoners.

The Prince of Orenge hath agreyed with the State of Gelderlande.

A new supplye is makinge redye in Ffraunce of 15 ensinges and 4000 horsemen, which in hast ar cumminge, and letters thereof wryten by thadmyrall of Ffraunce to some in Fflusshinge.

Amsterdam is with the Prince of Orenge.

The Prince of Orenge was the 7th of August at Stoken. The towne of Nericksea is taken by Captayne Worston. The Spanyardes and Walowns saved themselves in the churche, which were about 300. The Spanyardes after were slayne and the Walons saved.

Upon Saterday last at a place called Zootland, where thenglisshe and Ffrench were incamped, the company of Beauvois to the number of (600) men cam from Mydleborough in the morning aboute 5 of the clocke when the watch was paste, and upon a sodeyn our men were so furiously assayled by the Spanyardes that they drove our men above 200 foote from theyre trenches, but thenglyshe gents as men of great corage gave a recharge of the Spanyardes with such a fury that glad was he that coulde runne faste awaye, and so overcam the Spanyardes, slewe 150 and hanged 13.'

6 pp. (Devereux Papers II/7)

FRANCIS KNOWELLS TO THE EARL OF ESSEX

(1572) November 11. Regretting his neglect of his friends, promising to write while he is in France, and commending himself to Essex and to 'Madame ma soeuer et vostre femme.' * Paris.

Holograph French Addressed: To the Earl of Essex 'at the Court'. 1 p. (Devereux Papers I/108)

THE EARL OF LINCOLN TO THE EARL OF ESSEX

1572-3, March 16. Desiring Essex to admit the bearer, John Kiste, to the office of Marshal of the Admiralty in co. Pembroke. Purforde.

Holograph 1 p. (Devereux Papers I/1)

JACQUES DE MONTGOMERY TO THE EARL OF ESSEX

1573, March 27. Announcing his arrival at Plymouth, and his intention to sail (for La Rochelle) as soon as possible. Plumue.

Holograph French Endorsed: 'Letter to Walter, Earle of Essex from the Comte de Montgomery and others.' 1p. (Devereux Papers I/2)

RICHARD VAUGHAN TO THE EARL OF ESSEX

1573, April 1. Sending Essex a note of his rents, etc, from Monckton, with 'an auncient parchment boke' showing that many rights had been 'withdrawen, loste and curteiled.' Whitlond.

Holograph 1p. (Devereux Papers I/3)

SIR FRANCIS KNOLLYS TO THE EARL OF ESSEX

1573, April 15. 'Yf your Lordships jorney to London had not drawne youe to an other cowrse, I wold have ben gladde youe had taken my howse in youre waye, but yf youe had so done, then I must nedes have wayted uppon youe to London before my busynes here had ben parfytted: wher as nowe I meane to dispatche my busynes here before my commyng upp, so that I mean not to be at London nowe before Monday next at nyght.' Rotherfield Greye.

PS. 'Robin Knollys wold have hastened me to London but my busynes dothe wythe holde me.'

Holograph Seal 1p. (Devereux Papers I/5)

* Walter Devereux was created Earl of Essex in May, 1572, and embarked for Ireland in July, 1573.

MORGAN PHILLIPS TO THE EARL OF ESSEX

1573, April 20. Reminding Essex of his suit 'concerning the office of peace to me and my brother Francis Lagharne.' From my poore house at Picton.

Holograph Addressed: To the Earl of Essex 'at London.' 1 p. (Devereux Papers I/7)

HENRY CLYFFORD TO THE EARL OF ESSEX

1573, May 3. Sending the rent of Keyston, and craving forbearance for his own rent. Keyston.

Holograph 1p. (Devereux Papers I/9)

RICHARD BRADFORD TO THE EARL OF ESSEX

(? 1573) May 15. On the provision of six 'costlettes' (corslets) for the musters of the Lordship of 'Dimoke'. Dimoke.

Holograph 1 p. (Devereux Papers I/11)

SIMON HARCOURT TO THE EARL OF ESSEX

1573, May 25. On the killing of one of his son Robinson's men by a man of Mr Richard Chamberlynne. 'Myn enymyes with some lacke of good nature in my soon-in-law will seme to chardge my soon therwith.' Rontoon.

Enclosing some of the evidence as given at the inquest. The murder was committed in a fray arising out of a private quarrel between Lichfield and Drayton on Friday, May 20. The name of the victim was John Bate.

Holograph 1p. (Devereux Papers I/13)

G. PRETIER TO THE EARL OF ESSEX

1573, June 1. Praying that he may enjoy his lease of the parsonage of Little Mondon without hindrance. 'From the Benche where I remayne a poore prysoner.'

Signed 1p. (Devereux Papers I/16)

ROBERT RYCHE TO THE EARL OF ESSEX

1573, June 1. 'I have only taryed and mynd to morrow to pass homeward iff I heare no furder off sum lykelyod off your jurney or sum fynall dyspatche which your good frendes expect, for delayes bryngeth perell and the yeare well spent wheare bye provision off mony and nessarye (*sic*) forrage, with provision off wynter store wolde be provyded, prayinge your good Lordship to impart how far you have proceeded and what resolute answer you have receaved, and whether you hope itt wyll take effect. I leave you to the eternall God as one redye to spend bothe lyffe and land att your devoted ffrend.' Saynt Bertlemeus.

Holograph Seal 1p. (Devereux Papers I/18)

(SIR) THOMAS COKAYNE TO THE EARL OF ESSEX

(1573) June 10. Asking Essex to take his son, 18 years of age, into his service for Ireland, and saying he has also 'a very perfecte sodyor (soldier) for him.' Pooley.

Holograph Addressed: 'To the Earl of Essex in London.' *The autograph of Essex and of Henry Sydenham scribbled several times on the back.* 1 p. (Devereux Papers I/20)

HUMFREY FOSTER TO THE EARL OF ESSEX

(1573) June 12. Craving pardon from Essex for not accomplishing his expectation.

Holograph 1p. (Devereux Papers I/22)

ROWLAND BULKELEY TO THE EARL OF ESSEX

(1573) June 12. On the provision of 'bisket' and beer for Ireland. Chester.

Holograph Addressed; To the Earl of Essex at 'Dorome house at London.' 1 p. (Devereux Papers I/24)

ANDREW MYCHYLSON TO THE EARL OF ESSEX

1573, June 13. As a tenant of Essex's in Maldon, he expresses his inability to serve, being the Queen's 'servante sworne in the Tower of London', or to send 'any man of myne owne chardge.' Maldon.

Signed, with holograph postscript concerning his losses and debts. 1 p. (Devereux Papers I/26)

THOMAS RIDGELEY TO THE EARL OF ESSEX

1573, June 13. 'I receaved your honours letters dated the 4th of June the 12th day of this munthe, and havinge dutifully considered the contents therof, doe this signifie to your honour, that all excuses and impedimentes wherewith uppon this soden I ame diverslie drawen sette on side, by Gods sufferance I will attende upon your honor att my day appoynted as a horseman, att the Quenes Majesties or your honors charges, if hit so please you. And rather then my own service in that order sholde be over chargeable to your honour, I will furnishe my self accordinge to the contents of your honors letters, and on or two with me, whom I will prepare to be caliver shotte.' Normanton.

Holograph 1p. (Devereux Papers I/27)

GABRIEL DE MONTGOMERY TO THE EARL OF ESSEX

(? 1573) June 14. Thanking Essex for taking his son with him (? to Ireland). Onyntene.

Signed French Seal 1p. (Devereux Papers I/28)

THE TENANTS OF KEYSTON TO THE EARL OF ESSEX

1573, June 14. 'Whereas we understand by your letter derected unto us that your honor dothe demaund of us your honors tenaunts a certain number of men furnisshed for to serve in Ireland (which demaund in verye dede we are bound to doo by our leasses), yet notwithstandyng we most humble beseche your honor to be good unto us and to our wyves and to our children, ffor we are not able to doo yt. And whereas your honour demaundethe owr determynation herein, owr determynation is this, that we reffer our matter unto Master Clyffard who knoweth what we are able to doo, ffor louke what order he taketh with your honor, we wyll accomplysshe, God wylling, to the uttermost of owr power.'

1p. (Devereux Papers I/30)

EDWARD BERYSFORDE TO THE EARL OF ESSEX

(1573) June 16. He informs Essex that he is willing to serve, but cannot provide or pay for his 'furnyture.' Enstone.

Holograph 1 p. (Devereux Papers I/32)

THOMAS TRENTHAM TO THE EARL OF ESSEX

1573, June 17. He will 'furnishe iiii horsemen for Ireland,' but cannot find any other 'that is that waye minded.' Charteley.

Holograph 1 p. (Devereux Papers I/34)

GEORGE DEVEREUX TO THE EARL OF ESSEX

(1573) June 18. I send the names of as many of your men as have made answer as to what they will do in the matter of the Irish expedition. The bark you spoke of is ready as regards the trimming of her hull, but she has no tackle, sails, etc yet, and these you must buy. And 'for ordenaunse for hir ther ys a barke of the Quenes att Lirpole which was brocken in peases ther, and all her ordenanse lyes ther still, and yf your Lordeship can get a warraunte from the master of the ordenansse for the ordenanse that lyes ther, schee wilbe abell to doe you good servisse divers wayes, and yff ytt schall please you I will serve in her my selfe.' I have pressed a hoy for the carriage of your horses. 'Yf your Lordshippe will have her you must sende a coeninge man to gide hir, for ther is non canne tell howe to gide hir heare.' James Barret's ship is ready. 'You must sende me a commission for the staying of hir, and for the taking uppe of marryneres to serve your owne barke, for they will nott sticke heare to aske what commission I have to doe this.' I cannot get salt, but I can get a good store of oats and barley at a reasonable price. Caermarthen.

Holograph 2 pp. (Devereux Papers I/36)

1/39 *enclosed is a list in another hand of the* 'wantes or lackes of the bark lyeinge in Carm'then', *and the names of the Pembrokeshire tenants who have been* 'spoken with' *and are willing to serve as horsemen, viz, Mr Laugharne and his man and Mr Gillie Smith, and as footmen, viz, Mr George Colton and himself (the writer). The Mayor of Pembroke, Richard Minton, will furnish a footman, and it is likely that Morgan Phillips will send 2 or 3 horsemen.* 'Yf anie of the rest want furniture they be to blame, for I willed them all to certyfye me, and for money they shulde be served.'

THE ARCHBISHOP OF ARMAGH TO THE EARL OF ESSEX

1573, June 19. 'This shalbe to desier you to send me by this berer, my boye, the trewthe of your honors prosedinge into Ireland, which is the honorablest jornay that ever was taken this two hundereth yeres of any subject, and I trust in God your Lordshep shal spead as well as ever dyd any, which I desier God from the ground and bothome of my harte prosper, for it is honorable, and I trust to his glorie, the Quens Majesties honor and your owne commodiete, and al those that shal goo with you, amongest whome I wyll be one, with all I cane make, yf your honor send me word when I shal repayr unto you.' Salisbury.

Holograph Addressed: 'To the Earl of Essex at Court.' 1 p. (Devereux Papers I/40)

EDWARD WYRALL TO WILLIAM BARROLL

1573, June 20. Expressing readiness to serve the Earl of Essex 'with one other as horsemen and to make of my companye besides 11 others to be fotte men and shotte, and to importe my owne chardges throwghlie', if Essex will give him the money now raised on the manor. English Bicknor.

Holograph 1 p. (Devereux Papers I/170)

REDDI GWYN TO THE EARL OF ESSEX

1573, June 20. I have received your letter of the 11 of June requiring me to furnish as many footmen as I can from this shire. I cannot get any such unless I have some authority, 'to take them out and to rate their severall furnitures, for they will not voluntarylye go from home, nor yet furnish them selfes without they be there unto compelled'. Your own men shall be duly ready if you will give them a place of assembly. I ask leave to accompany you myself. Carmarthen.

PS. 'If it might please your Lordship and your leasure to come your selfe into Wales, you might have more horsemen and footmen than I or any other for you can gett, for all the men of worship and gentlemen would mete your honor and willingly furnishe every of them a horseman or foteman.'

Holograph 1 p. (Devereux Papers I/42)

SIR GILES POOLE TO THE EARL OF ESSEX

1573, June 21. As to finding men, his son is sick and his country men 'are vearie loth to goe of them selves, except yt were with such a one as they have greate good liking of and well acuaynted with all, as your Lordship shall understand at your cominge to Chertley.' Saperton.

Signed Seal 1 p. (Devereux Papers I/44)

THE TENANTS OF KEYSTON TO THE EARL OF ESSEX

1573, June 21. To the effect that they cannot give £100, the sum demanded by Essex, but offer £40.

1 p. (Devereux Papers I/46)

WILLIAM CRADOCK TO THE EARL OF ESSEX

1573, June 21. Concerning his grievances against one Chapman to whom he has to pay £120. Stafford.

Holograph 1 p. (Devereux Papers I/48)

EDMUND TYRELL TO THE EARL OF ESSEX

1573, June 22. He sends £5 'towardes your greate charges in this voiage', with particulars as to the intentions of the other tenants of Ramsden Manor. Ramsden.

Signed Endorsed: 'Letters at my coming into Ireland'. 1 p. (Devereux Papers I/50)

T. BASKERVYLE TO THE EARL OF ESSEX

(1573) June 22. Recounting his efforts to raise men for the Irish expedition. 'My sonnes George, Richard and Thomas Baskervyle shall wayte upon your Lordship furnished ... theyre desyre ys to wayte upon your owne person as your houshold men ..... they do not mynde to loke for any commodytie of anye farmes in Ireland, but to wayte upon your honor and to adventure theire lyves with you.' The sums paid by the tenants in Bodenham, but there is nobody there who will serve. Those at Lyonshall and Weobley will provide money after Leominster fair on St Peter's Day. The Lyonshall money will serve to furnish the five men spoken of by Essex. But Weobley is doubtful; there are few payers and many beggars. Baskervyle will do his best at the Assizes to send the men, duly furnished, to Liverpool. 'Also, I would know your Lordships pleasure whether the money that I shall receve of your tenaunts shalbe delyvered to those men that shalbe apoynted to serve, at the begynynge, or els the money to be brought to the waters syde, and they to have some in their purses as 20^s a pece of eyther of them to bringe them to Lyverpoole.' Essex has appointed 12 footmen from his lands, viz, 5 from Lyonshall, 5 from Weobley and 2 from Bodenham. Netherwood.

Signed Adressed: 'To the Earl of Essex at Durham House, London.' 2 pp. (Devereux Papers I/52)

SIMON HARCOURT TO THE EARL OF ESSEX

1573, June 23. Promising aid for 'the advauncement of your Lordships journey', and to come himself if able to travel. Lekhamsted.

Holograph 1 p. (Devereaux Papers I/54)

EDWARD HALFHYDE TO MR BARROLL

1573, June 23. Asking his aid to procure a lease from the Earl of Essex of Bennington Park.

Holograph 1 p. (Devereux Papers I/56)

ADRIAN STOCKS TO THE EARL OF ESSEX

1573, June 24. 'Yf it maye please your Lordshipp I have receyved your letter and the notes of your order which I perseave you meane to followe, and although there be some, that loveth your lordshipp well, doth not like of the jorney, yet I assuer your lordshipp, I thank God for it, because I am fullye perswaded your jorney shalbe greatlie to the service of God, for that you shall drive out those which knoweth not God and plant in those that shall lyve in his feare, and shewer I ame, as great a service to the Quens Majestie as maye be, and more then yet can be conceived by those that understand it not. I am verie glad your lordshipp is so well accompayned and specially of two men, who I have great knowledge of: thone for his understanding of the warres, that is Sir Peter Caro, and thother for his honestie and his upright dealinge, not an honester man within the realme of England, I meane Mr George Carlton. Inn my opinyon, Sir Peter Caro is the odest man in this realme for matters of the warre, and so I am shewer your Lordshipp shall find him or ye retorne. I asshewer your Lordshipp I had perswaded my wief and fullie resolved myselfe to have wayted upon your Lordshipp, but seeing you are so well accompayned your lordshipp shall have no nedd of me, which I am glad of. I will not faille, God willing, to travell with all my neyghbours and frendes and will not faill to send men furnished or money. And thus praying to God contynewallye to hould his holie hand over you that your jorney may be to thadvancement of his honor and trewe serving of him, I humblie take my leave.' Beaumanoir.

Holograph 1 p. (Devereux Papers I/58)

RICHARD FYTON TO THE EARL OF ESSEX

1573, June 24. Excusing himself for not having, since landing at Plymouth, waited upon Essex. Trentham.

Holograph Addressed: 'To the Earl of Essex at Durham House.' 1 p. (Devereux Papers I/60)

RICHARD BAGOTT AND THOMAS TRENTHAM TO THE EARL OF ESSEX

1573, June 26.   On the measures to be taken for 'the shewe of horses' at Stafford on July 13.

Signed   1 p.   (Devereux Papers I/62)

WILLIAM HAWTREY TO THE EARL OF ESSEX

1573, June 27.   Thanking Essex for taking his kinsman Philip Hawtrey into his service, and promising to furnish him with horse, armour and weapons. 'At my pore house at Chekkers.'

Holograph   1 p.   (Devereux Papers I/64)

THOMAS MIGHT TO THE EARL OF ESSEX

1573, June 28.   'I have appointed this bringer ... for the receipte of three score sixteene poundes, ten shillinges which of force, as your honor knoweth, muste bee payde, for the which somme I have lefte with him my bill, mooste humbly beseching your honor that the same maye bee paide accordingly, for those hoppes of force I muste nedes have.'   London.

Holograph   1 p.   (Devereux Papers I/66)

LORD NORTH TO THE EARL OF ESSEX

(1573) June 28.   'My good Lord. The mean estate I ame yn doth kepe me backe from doeng that which yn my harte I ame willing to do. And that ys to ventur my purss and my parson with you. But seing I cane not do the one I will not fayll to wish and pray to God that he will geve unto your noble mind good success and victorye. For trewly my Lord (without flattering of you) yf you miscarrye, God and the Queen shall lose a principal piller for both their services. And to be plain with you, I am sorry with my harte that you goe.'

I commend a young Kentishman, my servant, to you. 'He ys furnished yn the best manner and praieth to be partenor of your good and badd.'   Kirtling.

Holograph   Seal   1 p.   (Devereux Papers I/68)

THE ARCHBISHOP OF ARMAGH TO THE EARL OF ESSEX

1573, June 29.   'I have reseaved your honors letters where in I persave you intend to be at Learpoll aboute the fyrst of August, whare I intend to meate your Lordship by Gods grace yf I can bring my charge to passe. I am glad your honor hathe entertayned my tenant, Davye Etherington, who is not only a good sodyer and valiant innowght in the feld, but also is well knowne in all the partes of the Northe.'   Salisbury.

Holograph   1 p.   (Devereux Papers I/70)

JOHN WIRLEY TO JOHN BRETON

1573, June 30.   Praying Breton, who is his son-in-law, to obtain from the Earl of Essex letters to three of his tenants at Bugbrook, who were on the panel of a jury for the trial of an action at Northampton between himself and one Morgan, bidding them not to appear at the Assizes, 'whearby the wholl jury myght be quashed.'   Dodford.

Holograph Seal Addressed: 'To the right worshipfull Mr John Breton of Towcester, esquier, geve these.   Enqueare for him at the *Rose* in Smythfield and at all the Innes in Holburne, and at the Innes abought the Straunde, and at Mr Rotherhams in Chauncery Lane, and at the *Sarazons heade* without Newgate.' 1 p. (Devereux Papers I/154)

RICHARD BEYNHAM TO THE EARL OF ESSEX

(1573) July 1. According to your directions, 'I have mustered your tenauntes of Bicknor where I finde small choyse of able men, and have travelled also with them for the furnyshinge of five caliver shott, whom I fynde very willinge ther unto. And for that they have no furnyture in a readines are contentyd to geave your Lordship thyrtie poundes.' Saperton.
Signed 1 p. (Devereux Papers I/72)
 Underneath is a note in Essex's (?) *hand*: '£30. Mr Beynham, a man; Mr G. Wyrrall him self.'

SIR GILES POOLE TO THE EARL OF ESSEX

(1573) July 1. Reporting that he has 'musterid and put in redyness ten men' at Dymock, that at Teynton he cannot find one able man, but they are willing 'to be at the charge of setting forth two.' He hopes to meet Essex at Chartley 'yf I be able to light uppon my horse.' Saperton.
Signed 1 p. (Devereux Papers I/74)

SIR GILES ALLINGTON TO THE EARL OF ESSEX

1573, July 2. Craving favour for the bearer, Rowland Argall, sheriff of co. Down, who is one of his wife's sons. Horsheth Hall.
Holograph 1 p. (Devereux Papers I/76)

SIR THOMAS BROMLEY TO THE EARL OF ESSEX

1573, July 4. Asking Essex to employ the bearer as his secretary, having been 'ever brought up in good letters' at the University, Clement's Inn and the Temple, and knowing Latin, French and Italian. London.
Signed, with a holograph postscript 1 p. (Devereux Papers I/78)

THOMAS MIGHT TO THE EARL OF ESSEX

1573, July 7. Promising to be 'redy with my victualls redy ymbarked' on the 16th inst., with ships for 400 men by the 4th of August. Westchester.
Holograph 1 p. (Devereux Papers I/80)

LORD RICH TO THE EARL OF ESSEX

1573, July 7. 'I would gladly receave advertisement from your Lordship wheather you have taken your leave of the Quenes Majestie or not, that I may determyne of some tyme for my selfe to the same purpose. Ffurther, when I may nexte assure my selfe to fynde your Lordship at your howse in the contry, and also what order your Lordship hathe taken for your affayres by sea. I am determyned, by Gods leave, my horsemen shall set forwarde on with my fotemen the 14th of this instant moneth, and thus leaving your Lordship to the tuition of Almyghty God, I ende.' Leez.
Signed 1 p. (Devereux Papers I/82)

EDWARD PENNTE TO EDWARD BURRE

1573, July 7. Requesting him to procure more money from Essex, since the sum he had brought with him was exhausted.   Chester.

Holograph Addressed: 'To his lovinge fellowe Edward Burre at Durham Place nere unto Charing Crosse.'   1 p.   (Devereux Papers I/84)

I/85 *is a similar letter of the same date to the Earl of Essex.*

JOHN BRETON TO THE EARL OF ESSEX

(1573) July 9.   Promising that 'the 20 ploves (ploughs)wyth theyr whole furniture' shall be ready in four days and asking for instructions as to their conveyance.   Tamworth.

Holograph   1 p.   (Devereux Papers I/88)

I/87 *is the Earl of Essex's draft giving orders for the supply of the above ploughs.*

ROBERT LAWSON TO THE EARL OF ESSEX

1573, July 13.   Excusing himself for not having sent Essex a larger sum for the Irish expedition.   Prytwell.

Holograph   1 p.   (Devereux Papers I/90)

THE EARL OF ESSEX TO

1573, July 15.   On the slowness of his 'despatche hence', and asking him to meet him at Hereford on July 21 with 'suche of my servauntes and frendes as meane to adventer with me, to thende I may take order for shipping.'   London.

Draft in Essex's hand   1 p.   (Devereux Papers I/92)

I/93 *is another draft but not in Essex's hand, of the same date and place, asking recipient to meet him at Brecknock on July 22.*

THOMAS MONINGTON TO MR BARROLL

(1573).   Begging him to move the Earl of Essex that he may serve as a footman for 'of truthe I cannot for money in all our contrey provyd a horse suffycyent for that servyce.'   Chartley.

Holograph   1 p.   (Devereux Papers I/94)

(THE EARL OF ESSEX) TO JOHN TALBOT

(1573)   Asking him to accompany Essex to Ireland.   *Undated*

Draft   1 p.   (Devereux Papers I/71)

THE TENANTS OF RAMSDEN BARRINGTON TO THE EARL OF ESSEX

(1573)   Sending a list of their contributions towards the Irish expedition, viz, three tenants at 10 ⁶ each, one at 4 ˢ, the four copyholders having not yet answered.   *Undated*

1 p.   (Devereux Papers I/96)

IRELAND

1573.   Heads of 'Articles and Instruccions' apparently for Walter Devereux, Earl of Essex, on his expedition to Ireland.

The instructions are under 28 heads and relate to the provision of men and material, discipline, the choice of companions, etc, e.g. 'to divide the state into pollycie, some only to devise and others to execute'; 'never to attempt any

241

thinge withoute deliberation, to use secrecye and expedition, to execute to thuttermoste, to be unremovable in resolution, and leave the successe to God and his good ffortune'; 'the service of God dailye to be ffrequented'; 'to refuse none that proffer submission, nor to credit any their promises, but to think of them as of wolves or ffoxes.' There are also directives on the necessity of building and fortifying towns and of increasing the number of husbandmen; and 'to be provided of meet men and tacle for fisshing which wilbe no small commodytie.'

2 pp. (Devereux Papers II/13)

IRELAND

1573. Accounts of the cost of the Irish expedition, *inter alia:*

'The Erle (of Essex) is to be allowed for the whole chardges as by the bookes therof appeareth £63,000 sterling, making Irish £84,000.'

2 pp. (Devereux Papers II/24)

IRELAND

1573. Papers relating to the transport, victualling etc. of the forces sent to Ireland, e.g:

'For a shipp called the *Black Bark* bought of Thomas Warcopp. £160
Provision of victuals for the same shippe for 2 moneths. £60:11:9
Wages to 30 mariners to serve in the same shippe ten days. £5'

8 pp. (Devereux Papers II/15)

IRELAND

1573. 'Remembrances for Mr Waterhouse', and, as endorsed, 'Instructions for my Lord of Essex from Mr Auditor Jenison' relating to the pay, victualling, building works etc. of the Irish expedition.

2 pp. (Devereux Papers II/27)

IRELAND

1573. 'Deviseis how ye Q(ueen's) Majesty may have half ye commodities and proffittes of ye Erle of Essex voyage into Ulster, bearyng also half ye charges that ar susteaned and shall be by hym susteaned in ye same.

For ye charges:

Imprimis, ye said Erle shall within (blank) dayes delyver to such as ye Q(ueen) shall appoynt a perfect declaration in wrytyng of all manner his chardges which he hath susteaned from ye begyning of his sute in these poyntes followyng, viz, in provisions of victell, of powdre shott and all kynd of armrie, of shippes and vessells for ye sea as well for transportation of men, horses and victells, as for to serve uppon ye sea, of sendyng of men in any kynd of messadg by sea or by land about the sayd service.

And after such declaration made and ye same so well and sufficiently proved hir Majesty shall paye to ye sayd Erle ye on half of all ye sayd charges, so farr furth as ye same shall also sufficiently appere to have bene spent for ye use of ye sayd Erle towardes ye furderance of ye voyadg into Ireland.

Item, the sayd Erle shall also for all other provisions to be from thence furth made for any of ye forsayd thynges tendyng to ye furderance of ye sayd service, mak declaration befor hand to such persons as shall be appoynted by hir Majesty what the same shall be, and what the allowance of ye sayd persons, the sayd provisions being made at ye most resonable price yt the same

Erle can mak with the advise of some on to be appoynted by ye Q(ueen's) Majestes agent, hir Majesty shall also from tyme to tyme cause imprestes and payementes to be made of ye moyte and half part of such somes of monny as ye same shall amont unto, and so shall contynew for ye space (blank) yeres, or untill ye sayd Erle shall have by force or otherwise reduced ye three contreys of Clandeboy, ye [*illegible*] and ye Glyns with ther membres, iles and territoryes direct by land or by sea, to such quietnes as he shall be hable to mak division of ye sayd landes, territoryes and iles to tenantes to hold ye same by rentes and services in estates or any frehold or other estate what so ever. And as soon as ye sayd Erle shall be well hable so to doe, he shall for ye devision of ye same use ye advise of Hir Majestes depute and counsell in Ireland for ye devision of ye sayd contries into Shyres, and of ye shyres into Hundredes, cantredes, wapentakes or such lyke, and of ye sayd Hundredes etc into towns to be made corporat, and other towns to be constituted mannors, yt is to saye, to consist part of in demeane and part in service, and furder shall assent to such other devisies for ye devision of ye sayd countries and of any part of them for ye reducyng of them to be mete for cyvill government, accordyng to ye most usuall manner of ye commen lawes of England and as to ye Lord depute and consell of ye realme or otherwise to Hir Majesty shall be found most mete and convenient.

Item, in this division the Erle shall in every of ye sayd 3 contries appoynt ii principall places which shall be not distant asondre above xii myles, nor nearer than vii myles, to be buylded mete for ye state of a Baron of ye realme, and shall limitt to ye same placies landes and territoryes convenient for to be a demeane to ye sayd placies for ye expencies of a Barron to kepe at ye lest yerly L persons in household with meat and drynk, and L horsies for service, and shall also appoynt to every of ye sayd placies so manny tenantes next adjoyning therto as shall have landes assigned to them to hold ye same by such servicies as shall seme metest to ye Depute and Counsell for defence of ye sayd places, and for the attendance of ye Lord of ye sayd place in all lefull services, and furder to hold by such kynd of rentes to be reserved and payd in monny or victell as may yerly serve to susteyne ye nombre of L other persons dwellyng in yt place.

Item, ye sayd Erle shall also, as soon as he may, conveniently buyld upon ye sayd placees such houses for habitation and in such forme for strength and commodite as shall be thought mete to ye sayd Erle with ye advise of ye depute and consell.

Item, after yt the same houses shall so be buylded and redy to inhabitt, ye sayd Erle shall permitt and suffer ye Queen Majesty to make chois which of ye sayd 2 houses in every of ye sayd iii contrees she will to remayn to hir and to ye Crown or otherwise as she shall please to dispose.

Item, ye sayd Erle shall also in places nedefull mak such castells or houses of force and strength for defence of those contrees, as shall seme to hym nedefull with the advise of ye depute of ye realm, and in those being buylded he shall place such constables and soldiors with such enterteymens and wages as for ye space of vii yeres he shall thynk mete with the advise of ye said L(ord) depute, and at ye sayd vii yeres ye same shall be at ye disposition of ye Q(ueen) if she will make payement to ye sayd Erle and his heyres of ye whole of ye buyldynges thereof and will make grantes etc to ye sayd Erle of half so much landes in some other place within the same shires as shall be annexed and made appurtenant to ye sayd castells or houses of strength if otherwise he shall be allowed or recompenced before in ye lymitation of his moytie.

Item, ye sayd Erle shall in all other thynges convenient to mak ye sayd contrees habitable with cyvell and loyall subjectes, follow such directions as hir Majesty shall within ye tyme of ii yeres gyve unto hym not being prejudyciall to tak away the inheritance and frehold that shall grow and come to hym without resonable recompence to be made to him for ye same. And in consideration of all ye premissees yt shall be chargeable to ye sayd Erle or his heyres, the Q(ueen's) Majesty shall from tyme to tyme uppon just declaration therof to be made to such persons as hir Majesty shall therto appoynt, as well befor ye chardges shall begyn as after they shall be ended, cause due payementes by imprestes and payementes to be made to ye sayd Erle and his heyres of ye on half of ye whole charges or estymat of ye charges to be made, accordyng as it shall justly appere yt the sayd Erle and his heyres shall susteane and beare.

Item, in consideration yt hir Majesty shall beare ye sayd half charges in all thynges equally with the sayd Erle in ye premissees, hir Majesty shall at hir pleasure as soone as ye sayd contrees or any part of them shall be redy to be lymitted and granted to any persons to inhabett, mak chois in every of ye sayd 3 contrees and their (*illegible*) of so many towns corperat, haven towns, man(ors), villages, hamlettes, rectoryes, fishynges, housees made for strength and to be kept with garrysons as shall in every of ye sayd three contrees amount in nombre and quantite of soyle and in......'

Draft Imperfect Amended and illegible in parts 2 pp. (Devereux Papers II/11)

W. Goodere to the Earl of Essex

1573-4, February 11. Praying the Earl to assign to the tenants of Stretton in Monk's Kirby a lease of the tithe corn in the same granted to him by Trinity College, Cambridge. Monk's Kirby.

Holograph 1 p. (Devereux Papers I/98)

The Earl of Ormond to the Earl of Essex

1574, June 26. 'My veray good Lord. Even nowe being redy to go to horse, having appointed to parle with O'Karroll and others my bad neghbors uppon the borders of Ormond and other places, I recevid your Lordships letter touching therle of Desmond. And do not a litle mervayle what put my Lord of Desmond in this vayne feare that I shold meane to invade his country, for that I never ment any suche matter, nether assembled any company other then to appoint sume of my men to put them selfes in a redynes to wait on me to this sarvice with my Lord Deputie. And for putting him out of all doubt I wrot to him by your Lordships man, that he and his shall stand sure I will not invade his contry till I heare farther of my Lord Deputies pleasure.' Kilkenny.

Signed 1 p. (Devereux Papers I/110)

'The Hole Band of Footemen under the Leading of Capten Georg Boilsher' to the Earl of Essex

1574, July 12. Praying Essex to procure the release of their captain 'captive in the handes of the Earle of Desmond.' Kilmallock.

1 p. (Devereux Papers I/102)

1575, March 29. 'My good lords. I have of late sene a letter signed by the
Queenes Matie and jointly endorsed to my Lord Depute and me concernyng
myne enterpryse in the province of Ulster, which although it cary a shewe of a
present proceding herin and of a consent to all my petitions, yet hath it
brought forth none other efforts but the present discharge of all that served
under me and a fynall dissolving of my enterprise. Whereunto what answer I
have made to her Ma^{ty} may appear unto you by the copy of my letter herin
closed. And although it become me to stand contented with any thing that
her Majesty shall signify to be her will (yet do I think this a strange kind of
dealing)*, when I compare this conclusion to the whole cours that hath beene
taken with me since my coming hither I cannot but think the dealing very
strange.

Ffirst, I came with the good liking of all your lordships with the allowance of
the Counsell here, so as by the consente of both realmes I toke my jorney, the
matter being first thoroughly debated and so onestlie as thoughe no scruple
shuld at any tyme arise. I had not bene here iii monethes but that it was given
forth that the contynuaunce of the enterprise was a question and in that stay
hath it remayned ever since, till now that in all appearaunce the proceding
therein is agreed uppon and all my petitions graunted, and yet the same letter
that doth so assure me of all the gracius favors is a warrant to my Lord
Deputy, as he taketh it, to overthrow the hole.

My lords, I humbly desier you to consider well of this matter. It is somwhat to
me, tho litell to others, that my house which suffering me to run my self out of
breth with expenses shall be overthrown. It is more that in the word of the
Quene I have as it were undone, abused and bewitched with fair promises
O'Donell, MacMahone and all others that pretend to be good subjects in
Ulster. It is most that the Quenes Majesty shall adventure this estate, for will
not all partes of this realme take hold of this dissolution, or can any in Ulster
or in any parte of the realme hope of defense heraftter. But to retorne to myne
owne estate, let my lief here, my good lords, be examined by the straightest
commyssioners that may be sent. I trust in examining my faults they will
alledge this for the chief, that I have unseasonably tolde a plaine, probable,
honorable and effectuall way how to do the country good, for of the rest they
can say nothing of me but witnes my mesyry by plague, famyn, sycknes, contynuall toyle and contynuall wants of men, money, cariages, vittells and all
things meat for great attempts. And if any of this have growen by my default,
they condemn me for the whole.

I pray you, my lords, pardon myne ernestnes. I thynk I have reason that am
thus amased with an oversoddeyn warning that must take a discharge before I
am made acquainted with the matter. Do ye not think it had bene a better
course that I might have had tyme to have made some profitable pease with
Turlo, which hath beene sought at my handes, but that I must at one instant
loose my travell, my money and my credit, and with the same hasard the
honor of her Majesty and of the realm of England. I trust, my lords, my plain
dealing shall not do me hurt. With you for your owne part a solitary lief is
best for a disgrased person, but because there is none of you but hath
professed favor towards me, and some of your lordships next with me in blud
and alliance, I crave of you all that as I have enterid into this action with your
good liking and advices, so now the faillency being in way to be laid uppon

* crossed out in MS.

245

me, ye will all be meanes to her Majesty to deal well with me for my charges as in honor, conscience and justice ye shall think good, and so committing myself and my posterity to her Majestys favor and your persuasion in this point, I commytt your lordships to God and humbly take my leave.' Dublin.

Holograph Copy Endorsed in Essex's hand: 'Copy to the Lords, 29 March 1575, when the enterprise was first dissolved.' 6 pp. (Devereux Papers I/104)

THE DUCHESS OF SUFFOLK TO THE EARL OF ESSEX

(?Before 1576) 'I have resaved your lordships corteus letter and thanke you for it, but I am sore that you shold so understand off myen that I shold seeke any meanes to make you do any theng to offend her highnes, No, my good lorde, I have benne always, I troste, clere from any suche towche, bothe for my nowen doings or procurings off any me frendes, and I troste be Gods lyve so to continue. For the taking off the mane, I wol no forder presey your lordship, but for my self I pray your lordship to have a better jugement off me. Iff I had not knowen his true harte and humble obaydens to her Majeste I wold not have wrytten for him, nyther have kepett him me selffe al this tym off his meyssere, without wyche hele, he, his wyffe and poore cheldren myght have deyd in the strettes, and that I am sure wold not have plesed her Majeste. And on the other seyd I thenke off any worthe of juste cryme cold have bene proved agenst him. My howes colde not have savede hym from feling the smart of his desserts.'* *Undated*

Holograph 1 p. (Devereux Papers I/112)

THE EARL OF ESSEX, TO RICHARD BROUGHTON, JOHN STIDMAN AND WILLIAM BARROLL

1576, July 12. 'I have attended for an esterlie wind at Helbrie, Chester, Beaumaris and Holiehead almost this month and have bene in all these places at verie great charges, for all the companye of gentelmen have and doe lie onlie upon my pursse, themselves not having any money to defraye their owne charges. My provisions that Pennant hath made for corne, coles and the fraughtes of ships hath come almost to £200. These thinges have greatlie consumed my money so that I shall hardlie carrie with me into Ireland £1200, and I here I shall have for a while of the Deputie but smale imprest, for a man of his which is come over for money tells me he is utterlie without money: and besides that, there is such an occasion happened in Ireland as will spend much. This I writ unto you because I would have you not to accompt of the havinge of any parte of my rentes at Michaelmas towardes the payment of my debtes, but must have them sent over to me, or els to be spent at Lanfey, which I think the rather of the two will happen. Stidman must therefore make some provision there and money must by some meanes be gotten for the same purpose. Beefe, mottons and wyne must be provided beforehand, and that with as moch speede as maye be. I woulde have some Englishe strawe-dried malt gotten to make ale for myself. I desire to here from you as sone as is possible. It shall not be longe before I will send one over with advertisement of the tyme of my comming.' Holyhead.

Copy 1 p. (Devereux Papers V/18b)

---

* The Earl of Essex returned to Ireland from London in July 1576 and died there in September of the same year.

THE EARL OF ESSEX TO RICHARD BROUGHTON

1576, September 13. 'Upon receipt of some letters out of England the 29th of August, I purposed to take shippinge with speede to repare thither. The last daye of the same moneth a disease tooke me and Hunninges my boye and a third person to whom I dranck, which maketh me suspect of some evill receaved in my drincke, for ever sins I have bene greatlie troubled with a flux and vomittes, and my page extreamlie ill also till now of late he is recovered, and I from ill to worse for ought that I yet feele in myself. Neverthelesse I will presentlie, God willinge, embarke for Milforde and repose myself at my house at Lanfey till I shall understand howe God will worke his will in me. To that place I have directed Doctor Peny to come to me with all speed by letters from Mr Waterhouse, whose coming to me I pray you further; and let me see yourself there also. Upon Sonday or Monday next I purpose, God willing, to embarke. And so till God shall shape our meetinge, I committ you to him.' Dublin.

Copy Headed: 'The copie of my Lords letters for warrant of Mr Doctors Penyes expences.' 1 p. (Devereux Papers V/20b)

EDWARD WATERHOUSE TO DOCTOR PENY

1576, September 13. 'Mr Doctor, whereas upon the last daye of August last past the Erle of Essex fell into a great laske which hath ever sithes contynued with hym, after 20 or 30 stooles every daye, and is alredie many tymes bluddie and the rest of his stoles black burnt color. He hath had the advise of all the physicions of this contrey and cannot be stopped. But all counsaill hym to goe into England as sone as is possible, whether he had determined to goe before he fell sick.' He asks you at be at Lanfey near Pembroke 'where he purposeth to be, God willing, if this wind doth contynue' about Tuesday next. Please bring all things necessary for this disease. His apothecary goes with him and two physicians, of small experience, one Irish and the other English. He asks me to say that 'he doth the more mistrust himself because he is in extreme weakeness, and that the page that wayted on his cup and a thirde person to whome he dranke weare all taken after one manner. They be well agayne, but he extremelie ill and taketh litle sustenaunce or non.' Dublin.

PS. After 7 days' sickness he took unicorn's horn which has made him vomit many times.

Copy Headed: 'The copie of Mr Edward Waterhouses letter to Mr Doctor Peny.' 1 p. (Devereux Papers V/20b)

ACCOUNTS

(September 1576) 'Debts due .... by Walter, Earle of Essex, at the tyme of his deceas', including £6190 due to the Queen, followed by a list of 'legacies', payments for board-wages, etc. *Undated*

16 pp. (Devereux Papers V/9)
(See *Lives of the Devereux*, Volume II, pp 485-6, Appendix C)

ACCOUNTS

1576, Michaelmas to 1586, Michaelmas. Richard Broughton's accompt of receipts and disbursements including the expenses of the young Earl, Robert Devereux, at Cambridge.
Inter alia:
(f.22b) The account of Thomas Newport for the Staffordshire estates, John

Stidman for the Welsh estates, William Barroll for the Herefordshire estates, and sundries such as legal expenses, cost of messengers to Ireland and Wales, e.g. 'Two horses bought and spoyled in riding in hast to Lanfey and the seaside', £7:3:0.

Memorandum, the residue of plate worth 1000 marks given away by the Earl in Ireland, as directed, 'to many that deserved litle afterwards.'

'A color of SS of the order of the Garter by direction of the lords and other feoffees sold to pay debts and legacies rather then (erased) to be kept, £85:18:9.'

'The Erle Marshalls staffe of Ireland remayneth in the custodie of Mr Bagott at Blithfaild.'

(f.22)   Payment of the funeral charges of Walter Devereux, Earl of Essex, and the transportation of his body from Dublin to the castle of Carmarthen, where he was born, amounting in all to £1760:17:9, including:

Transportation of the corps, £9:10:0.	For the charges of the transportation of the Earl's body to Carmarthen, viz by sea from Dublin to Pwllheli in Carnarvonshire, and from thence with most painful labour of his servants in extreme tempestuous weather upon their backs, where horses with litters could not go.
Blackes Heralds' fees, etc, £830:4:1.	The funeral charges upon accompts finished at Carmarthen, £769:19:6. To the Countess to buy black for her Ladyship and her servants by direction of the Lords, £40. For the Earl and his brother and their servants, £20:4:7.
Boardwages, £119:4:7.	Board wages of servants attending the corpse at Carmarthen from the 6th of October to the 25 of November, for 50 days until the funeral were performed according to his degree.*

(f.27b)   For the copy of attainder of An: Mason, a freeholder in Bodenham, by whose attainder lands ought to escheat, 5ˢ·

(f.40b)   For the exhibition of Mr Walter Devereux at the oversight of the Earl of Huntingdon, £10.

(f.52b)   To Robert, Lord Rich, and the Lady Penelope his wife, of parcel of £2000 to the said lady for her marriage, £500. On f.56b is a note of the marriage in November 1581, and of the amount of Lady Penelope's exhibition, £66:13:4.

(f.66b)   An item dated November 3, 1583. To Sir Thomas Parot (Perrot) parcel of the legacy of £2000 due to the Lady Dorothy, his wife, £40. A further £200 paid on December 2.

(f.73b)   Notes of deaths in 1586 and 1586-7. Sir Henry Sidney, 5 May; Sir Philip Sidney, wounded 22 September, died 12 October; Sir Henry Jones of

---

* The account is in much less detail than that printed in *Lives of the Devereux*, Vol. II, pp.481-2, and differs as to the amount.

Abermarles, 24 September; Mary, Queen of Scots, 8 February; John Broughton of the Inner Temple, 6 March.

(Devereux Papers V)

RICHARD BROUGHTON

(c September, 1576) A statement by Richard Broughton how, upon a 'speciall letter of entreatie' from the late Walter Devereux, Earl of Essex, and 'at the instance and entreatie' of Lord Burghley and others his trustees, he 'did take upon him the burthen and care of the now younge Earle of Essexs causes during the Earles mynoritie'. This is followed by a copy of the letter referred to and addressed by the Earl to Broughton and four of his servants from Dublin on September 18, 1576. 'My generall request to you all is to be loving to my children and not to grieve yourselves with the discontented newes of my death.' *Undated*

2 pp. (Devereux Papers V/3)

LAW SUITS

(After September 1576) Notes on suits and disputes following the death of Walter Devereux, Earl of Essex.

(1) A suit for dower by Lettice, Countess of Essex, who 'by some froward advise did utterlie renounce and refusse the jointure to her assigned by her late husband.' She claimed one third of his lands, but was adjudged to be content with the jointure, with £60 *per annum* by her demanded.

(2) A claim by the Earl of Worcester for Sir John Perrot for the Stewardship of the possessions of the Bishopric of St David's.

(3) A claim by Thomas Baskerville to the parks of Weobley and Lyonshall. *Undated*

5 pp. (Devereux Papers V/24)

TITLE TO LANDS

(1576 or before) The title of Walter Devereux, 1st Earl of Essex, to certain manors willed by Edmund Mortimer, Earl of March, to Isabel his niece, afterwards wife of Henry Bourchier, Earl of Essex.

3 pp. (Devereux Papers III/5)

ESSEX PROPERTY

1576. Schedule of the 'honors, lordships, manors, landes, tenementes and hereditamentes' of Walter Devereux, Earl of Essex, at his death, with their yearly value and disposition.

9 pp. (Devereux Papers V/4)
(See *Lives of the Devereux* II, pp.483-5, Appendix C.)

ACCOUNTS

1576-77, January 20 to 1577, Michaelmas. Expenses of Robert Devereux, Earl of Essex, at Cambridge. *Inter alia*:

To Mr Wright, the Earl's tutor, upon bills £71:4:10½.
(f.34b) June 27th, for silk £14:13; for lace 60ˢ 2½ᵈ; for stockings, gloves and prints, 67ˢ·; for a hat and velvet cap, 25ˢ·; tailor's bill, £4:16:9; shirts and handkerchief, £9:8. For sheets, table cloths, napkins provided at the Earl's going to Cambridge, £9.

(f.35b)   1578. September 23. To R. Wright at Cambridge to the Earl's use, £4.

Diet and ordinary at Cambridge, besides 26 weeks at Keyston, £26:10:11.

Charge of a horse kept, £6.

(Expenses) at the Court at Walden attending on her Majesty, 60ˢ·

(f.38b)   For Gabriel Montgomery's charges at Cambridge and Keyston.

The accounts of R. Wright, the Earl's tutor at Cambridge, from November 9, 1578 to May 3, 1579, £83:12:6½.

(f.43b)   The accounts of the said R. Wright from May 3, 1579, till Michaelmas, 1579, £75:14:4.

1578, 23 January, 40ˢ·

Item, more 15ˢ·

Item, more 40ˢ·

Item, repaid 40ˢ his Lordship borrowed then, 40ˢ·, 2 March at going to Cambridge, 40ˢ·

Item, in March, 40ˢ·

6 April, 40ˢ·

3 May, £4.

1 June, £4.

15 July, 100ˢ·

Item, repaid to Mr Napper £5 borrowed of the Lord Treasurer in Northamptonshire.

1579, October 2. Paid for the debts of the Earl as money borrowed of divers by him, £11.

10 November, 1579, 100ˢ·

1 December, 1579, 60ˢ·

To a hackney man, 10ˢ·

For Gabriel Montgomery's expenses, £12.

For dress, £141:15:3.

(Devereux Papers V)

ACCOUNTS

1576-86.   A book kept by Richard Broughton, or his clerk, concerning the financial and legal affairs of Robert Devereux, Earl of Essex.   *Inter alia:*

f.47b   The expenses of the Earl for one year ending at Michaelmas (above his allowance of £210), £153:7:11½.

f.47b   The Earl's expenses at Cambridge from Michaelmas 1579 to Michaelmas 1580, which included 'extraordinarie expenses' of £69:8:8.

Mr Wright's reckoning from Michaelmas 1579 to April 20, 1580.

His Lordship's diet, £32:12:1.

Books, 16ˢ 10ᵈ

Apparel, £4:11:2.

Wood, coal, candles, etc, £14:3:8.

Reader and laundress, £1:1:0.

Riding charges, £8:2:8.

To a Frenchman 7 months 'to parle Frenche', £1:3:4.

Rent of chamber for a year, £2:5:0.

Diet and other necessaries, £2:18:6.

Diet for Mr Anthony Bagot for half a year, £4:10:0.

Diet for servant for 7 weeks, £1:8:4.

Wages, £1:0:0.

For keeping his Lordship's gelding at Cambridge, £4:15:0.
For the second half year the Tutor's charges are £29:12:9½.
The tailor (John King's) bill, £67:16:11.
The 'Milliner' for silk stockings, £10:10.
The expenses for the whole year came to £339:3:4⅓. of which there was allowed by warrant in the Court of Wards for the Earl's exhibition £140, and the fees of office in South Wales £70. So his expenses exceeded his allowance by £129:3:4⅓.

ff.53-54   In the next year, 1580-1, expenses exceeded allowance by £424:5:6. Items include:

> To riding to Newmarket for the horse-race, 16ˢ·
> Books, viz: Romain History, 4 volumes, 10ˢ·
>   Plutarch's *Opera* 16ˢ·
>   Beza's works, 15ˢ·
>   Mulcaster's *Positions*, 2ˢ·
> The tailor's bill is £144:14:10.

On f.55b there is the following note: 'Mem: that by reason of the said great expenses of the Earle of Essex, anno 1581, amounting to £634:5:5, and the contynuall occasions sollicited and ministered by sundrie meanes to withdraw the saide Earle from his studie in Cambridge; upon consultation had amongest the Right honorable William, Lord Burghley, Lord Treasurer of England, Thomas, Earl of Sussex, Henry, Earl of Huntingdon, Sir Francis Knollys, Knight and other feoffees in truste for the behoufe of the said Earle of Essex, it was thought requisite, with the consent of her Majestie obtained, that the saide Earl of Essex should be residente at Yorke under the oversight of the said Earle of Huntingdon, and to that end to reduce the saide Earle from excessive expences. On the 22nd of November, 1581, the said Earle was commended to the household oversight of the said Sir Francis Knollys, Knight, with whome he remained untill the 20th day of February 1581-2. And then shortly after went under the oversight of the saide Earle of Huntingdon to Yorke, where he continued for the space of one yeare and half or therabouts with his ordinarie allowance of £210 per annum, having diett for him and his servantes allowed by the saide Earle of Huntingdon and manie extraordinarie charges above the said allowance defrayed by the said Earle of Huntingdon.'

f.62b   The expenses of the next year only exceeded the allowance by £21:18:7 (f.59b), and the year after by £30.

On f.63b there is the following note: 'Memorandum that the Erle of Essex against Michaelmas 1584, findinge occasion to him and his honorable frendes best knowen; did repayre to his house at Lanfey in the countie of Pembroke, and there did very honorablie and bountifullie kepe house with many servantes in liverie and the repaire of most gentlemen of those partes to attend his lordship: by reason of which keeping of household, the rents of sundry lordships were paid to his officers of household.'

f.64b   Among the household expenses for 1584, £45:7:9 were spent on the reception of the Earl of Leicester when he came from Buxton to Chartley (f.64), and 6ˢ· given to a guide to Eardisley with letters out of France from the Duke of Bouillon.

f.67   Expenses from Michaelmas 1583 to Michaelmas 1584 include:

> December 24, 1583. To King, tailor, as parcel of a great debt due to him by the Earl, £10.

(Devereux Papers V)

1585 - 1608.   Copies of Treaties between England and the United Provinces, 1585, 1598 and 1608.*

French   64 pp.   (Devereux Papers II/31)

DEBTS

(? 1589)   Statement of 'Debtes owinge by the Right Ho. Roberte (Devereux, 2nd) Erle of Essex unto the Q(ueen's) Majestye', amounting to £11,145, the chief item being £6000 due out of a loan of £10,000 by the Queen to Walter Devereux, 1st Earl of Essex.

1 p.   (Devereux Papers II/29)

ACCOUNTS

1589, October 21 to 1592, April 26.   Note of a loan from Queen Elizabeth to the Earl of Essex of £3000 made in 1590, and allowed in the accompt of Thomas Freake, son and executor of Robert Freake, Receiver 'of the moneys growinge by sale of her Majestes lands' from 21 October, Eliz.31 to 26 April, Eliz.34.

1 p.   (Devereux Papers II/79)

ACCOUNTS

1589-1590.   Bill of Peter van Loow for jewels supplied to the Earl of Essex to the amount of £1305:8, with two signatures of the Earl.

'In primis, delyvered one poynted dyamond of £7.   £7
Item, for mendinge of garters and stones put in place where
they were lost.   £10
Item, delievered the 17 of November, 1590, 5 pendants of
diamonds at £32 per pece.   £160
Item, one greate jewill with 20 greate dyamondes and with
one greate rubye in the middest and with 2 other rubies in
the sides and fowre lesser diamondes all in fasshion lyke a
a flower de luce. *(Against this entry is a note in Gelly
Meyrick's hand* (?) 'Peter hath this jewel in pawn for your
Lo: in partt of payment.')   £800
Item, one George with 113 dyamonds the peice being no
lesse then   £100
Item, one hommer solde unto your Lordship.   £8
Item, one cuppe of sylver all gilte weyenge 76 ounces at 8^s·
per ounce.   £30:8
Item, one other flowerdeluce with 40 dyamondes and one
greate cabyson rubye.'   £140

There are also some observations in Sir Gelly Meyrick's (?) writing, e.g.: 'Ther was a hundred poundes borrowed uppon the garters which I charge myself with all.'

1 p.   (Devereux Papers III/47)

---

* The vellum covers of this manuscript contain a deed-poll of Ludowick Stuart, Duke of Lennox, appointing Raphael Powell of Upminster, co. Essex, his deputy as Alnager and Collector of subsidies and alnage of 'the olde as of the newe draperies', in Hertfordshire. It is imperfect and the date has been cut away.

1589-90, January. Survey of the manors of Swell and Prestbury 'latelye graunted by her Majestie to (Robert Devereux) the Erle of Essex.'
17 pp. (Devereux Papers III/37)

THE DEAN AND CHAPTER OF LICHFIELD TO THE EARL OF ESSEX

(1589-90 or later) February 23. Praying that certain 'covenantes which concern the payment of the Bushoppes rent' may be inserted into a grant which they are called upon to pay. Chapter House, Lichfield.

Signed: the Dean and three prebendaries, E. Merrick, John Bagshawe * and Symon Cocks. *Imperfect* 1 p. (Devereux Papers I/150)

THE QUEEN'S NAVY

(February 26, 1589-90). 'The names of all her Majestes shippes and other vesselles with their nombers of men to serve in warrlyke mannour.' With estimates of charges etc. Signed by Sir John Hawkins, William Borough and B(enjamin) Gonson.

The number of ships is 40 and of men 6854, viz: 5371 mariners, 767 gunners, 1716 soldiers, at a charge of £39,985:16:8. The charge of 40 merchant ships 'taken up to serve with her Majestys armye for 3 months' is £16,276:13:4, making a total of £56,262:10:0.

7 pp. *Endorsed:* 'February 26, 1589.' (Devereux Papers II/65)

INSTRUCTIONS TO SIR JOHN HAWKINS

(May, 1590) 'Instructions to be observed by Sir John Hawkins, Knight, in his jeorney to the Southward by Her Majesties Order.

Inprimis, You shall with as convenient speede as maye be take into your charge syxe of her Ma^ts shippes with their ordenaunce and furniture, viz: the *Marie Rose*, the *Hope*, the *Nonperely*, the *Rainebow*, the *Swiftesure* and the *Foresight*, and saile with them directly to Plymouth. And there aswell joyne such smale vesselles with you as shalbe meete for the service you have in hande. As allso furnish your self with convenient nombers of mariners and other servitors fitte for your saide shippinng. And then with all convenient speede to repayre to Cape Finister where lyinge some convenient time, you maie seeke to understande what provision of shippinge are prepared in the Groyne, in Farral, or enye other porte of Galizia or Biscaye.

And if you shall perceave that there be any stronge fleete or army in enye readines to sette forwarde towardes the coastes of Englande, Fraunce, Irelande or Scotlande, then you shall attende and accompany them, and forthwith send some swyfte and nymbel barque with intelligence before.

And uppon suche occasion the charge of the wages and victuals of suche as serve with you in suche shippes as you have under your charge, shalbe borne by her Majestie untill you shalbe putte at libertie by writinge from us to follow your owne adventure.

Item, if when you shalbe uppon that coast some reasonable time and shall not finde by your intelligence that any preparation shalbe in eny great forwardnes or readines to sette to the seas, then you may ravage the coast of Spain when you shall thinke fittest, to impeache such as traffique in and oute

* Made prebendary on February 14, 1589-90.

uppon that coaste, and restrayne and impeache such as relyeve the domynyons of the Spanish Kinge eyther with victuall, munycion or eny kynde of furnyture fitte for his shippinge or for his forraine traffique.'

Endorsed: 'Instructions to be observed by Sir John Hawkins in his voiage to the Southwarde'. 2 pp. (Devereux Papers II/70)

THOMAS MONYNGTON TO GELLY MEYRICK

(After 1590) June 28. Denouncing Mr Harley, a Justice of the Peace* for most 'barbarous ymmanity to a woman (the wife of Roger Weale) and her suckyng child' and stating his intention of calling Mr Harley before the Lords of the Council. Sarnesfield.

Holograph 3 pp. (Devereux Papers I/291)

ACCOUNTS

1591, April 12. Expenses of the Earl of Essex 'for the entertaining of the Imbasator of Fraunce' at Wanstead.

The Ambassador was entertained to supper on Friday, April 9, and to dinner on Saturday the 10th, at a total cost of £53:6:11.

1 p. (Devereux Papers II/72)

ACCOUNTS

1591, August 12 to October 26. 'A note of certeyne disbursementes when my Lo. (the Earl of Essex) was before Roane.'

Begins: 'The x of September we came to Diep from the journeye to the Kyng.'

The payments are chiefly for hay, repair of wagons, harness etc.

9 pp. (Devereux Papers II/73)

JAMES BASKERVILLE TO GELLY MEYRICK

1592, October 5. Asking for the refusal of Ashperton Park, if the Earl of Essex 'shall be pleased to departe with it.' It lies 'necessary to my manor of Westhide'. Hereford.

Signed Seal (not the Baskerville arms or crest) 1 p. (Devereux Papers I/159)

ACCOUNTS

1592, November 24 to 1593, December 14. 'The declaration of the accompte of Gelley Mericke, esquier, Steward of the Earle of Essex houshold, and Receivour Generall of all his rents and revenewes'. The receipt amounted to £5189:1:10 and the payments to £5182:2:7.

Among the payments are £32 for entertaining the Earl of Pembroke at Wanstead in November, 1592.

'More at the same place the 21st and 22nd of May', and many days before and after at the entertainment of the Vidame and the French Ambassador, £193:14:7.

A dinner at Hampton Court for the entertainment of the 'Erles of Empden' in July, 1593, £67:16:9.

For diet and charges at Greenwich, his Lordship being there exercising himself at pastime in the Tilt yard, £74:10.

For a supper at Essex House, 25 March, 1593, the Italian gent being there, £16:4:8.

* Made J.P. in October, 1590. (See *Acts of the Privy Council*, 1590-1, p.38.)

Dinner for 200 of his retainers when his Lordship dined with the Lord Mayor, 25 April, 1593, £19:18.

To Ralph Abnett 'for a paire of stockinges given by his Lordship to her Matie', £6.

To Otwell Smith for certain 'ingines', £6:13:4.

For a 'paire of white pompes for his Lordships page', 7^s.

To the French Ambassador's man that presented his Lordship with a sturgeon pie, 22^d.

To Mr Baker, the Queen's chirurgeon, 100^s.

To Sir John Wingfield to give the nurse and midwife at the christening of Mr Savile's son at Oxford, with other his charges, 100^s.

To Joseph Lupo and other her Majesty's musicians, £16.

An annuity to Mr Thomas Purslowe of St Marie Hall in Oxford of £10. Annuities also to Anthony Pembridge, Henry Bourchier, Mrs Dorothy Wroughton.

To Thomas Watwood for interest of his Lordship's plate pawned for £200 for half a year.

10 pp.   (Devereux Papers III/72)

PARLIAMENTARY ELECTION

1592-3, February 1.   Thomas Davies, Mayor, and eleven burgesses of Carmarthen to the Earl of Essex, sending a blank 'nomination of one burgesse of Parliament...leavinge the appointment of the person to your lordships best liking.'

1 p.   (Devereux Papers I/125)
(Printed in *Lives of the Devereux*, Vol.I., p.279, note 1.)

SIR ROGER WILLIAMS TO THE EARL OF ESSEX

(1593) June 4.   Protests the loyalty of officers and men to Essex. 'We hire still the Duke of Parmas army is entered the Lowe Countries and that the Spanis faction is gretly in fere of this pese, but when so ever the pore King enter Pary I pray God he may be well accompanid, fiering booth himself and folowers be not intertainid as they were at his mareig in the sayd towne. For my part I see no reson the liguers has to crave a pese, considering their fortunes of late unles the (*torn*)....resolves to clere this cuntrie from there great aflictions, or that the princes of the lige diskovere sum gret practises by the princes against them. Your Lordship may be assuryd that the princes be prone unto a pese hire, it is to withdrawe all there forces againste England; therefor your Lordship may do well to remember her Majesty to looke well unto it.' He will take care to inform Essex of further developments.

Holograph Seal   2 pp.   (Devereux Papers I/127)

MARY HERBERT TO LAWRENCE JOHNSON

1593, June 8.   Acknowledging receipt of letter 'by the which I perseve you have acquanted Mr Herberts good cosin Mr Thomas Powell and his good frend Mr Messinger with some letters of myne written unto you touchinge the obstenant coursis that menye of Mr Herberts unlovinge tenauntes of Powes have taken laietlye againste him.'

Holograph   1 p.   (Devereux Papers I/165)

SIR THOMAS LEIGHTON TO THE EARL OF ESSEX

1593, June 20.   Concerning the complaints of the inhabitants of Alderney

against 'Johan Chamberlen' and his servants, and of the latter against the inhabitants. The special cause of complaint is that the 'conyes off the waren are sofrid so mightily to encris and to stray over the contre as a grete quantitie of grounde is spoyled.' Leighton has sent 14 soldiers for the better guard of the place, and would have sent more but that the country has no corn to feed them. He has heard nothing of Captain Goring. Castle Cornett.
Holograph 1p. (Devereux Papers I/129)

THE EARL OF ESSEX TO THE LORD KEEPER

1593, July 9. Asking that Thomas Monington 'may be placed in the Commission of the peace and subsidie' for Herefordshire, and that one 'Robert Vaughan, beinge a man of verie contentious and unquiet disposition' may be displaced and put out of Commission. From the Court.
Copy Endorsed: 'Copy of my Lords letter to my L. Keper for Mr Monington.' 1 p. (Devereux Papers I/114)

MICHAEL MOLEYNS TO GELLY MEYRICK

1593, July 10. Praying that the Earl of Essex will use his favour with the Queen to further a certain suit. 'No sute can passe from her highnes to him with lesse shew or countenaunce of gayne than this.'
Holograph 2 pp. (Devereux Papers I/173)

SURVEY OF THE EARL OF ESSEX'S LANDS

1593, July 31. William Knollys, Henry Unton and Charles Wednester to the Earl of Essex on a survey of 'your landes in theis partes', with particular mention of Shiplake, Englefield House and Sindlesham.
1 p. (Devereux Papers I/131)

GEORGE HORDE TO THE EARL OF ESSEX

1593, August 22. Urging the Earl to procure one of the two daughters and co-heiresses of Robert Corbett, deceased, of Moreton, Salop, in marriage for Robert Vernon his cousin. At the Temple.

Holograph 1 p. (Devereux Papers I/133)

1/135 *is a letter to Gelly Meyrick on the same subject, dated June 20, 1593, with a schedule of Corbett's lands in co. Salop.*

IMPOST OF WINES

1593, December 14 to 1594, December 12. 'The Booke of the Impost of Wynes', containing particulars of wines imported into England, with names of ships, captains, consignees, etc. The 'farm of sweet wines' was granted to Robert Devereux, Earl of Essex, in succession to his step-father, Robert Dudley, Earl of Leicester, in 1590.

At the end are receipts given by Henry Lindley, esquire, for wages 10 and 13 May, 1594, the last signed by Samuel Franklin 'servant to Gelly Meyrick.' A typical entry is the following:

' Roads and Jones, 22 December 1593.
The *White Lyon de Edam* oneris 100 doll:
Hayme Simonson, Master, at Cadix.
Nicholas Bowdenson 171 buttes sack.
The Master and Mariners 3 buttes sack.

Nicholas Bowdenson 171 buttes sack.
The Master and Mariners butts sack 3.
Allowed to the Master for portage, 17ˢ˙

Small quarto Vellum covers ff.62 (Devereux Papers VI)

WARRANT

1593, December 17. Warrant from the Earl of Essex to Gelly Meyrick to pay £20 half yearly to his servant, Thomas Uvedale.

Signed Endorsed: 'A warrant to me to pay Mr Udalls annuitie half yearly.' 1 p. (Devereux Papers I/116)

CHARLES CHESTER TO GELLY MEYRICK

(*c* 1593) On his affection for the Earl of Essex and dislike of the Earl of Cumberland, 'which is the rudest Earll by reson of his northerly bringen up.'

Holograph 1 p. (Devereux Papers I/177)
(Printed in *Wiltshire Archaeological Magazine*, Vol.XVIII (1879) p.269)

ACCOUNTS

(*c* 1593-8.) Papers relating to the debts of Robert Devereux, Earl of Essex, and the means proposed for paying them off, ff.107-9 and 116-24.

According to the first paper (f.107) Essex owed £29,993:4:6 of which £4000 was secured to Peter Van Lore out of the profits of the 'lease of swete wynes'. It was proposed to raise the balance by the sale of lands valued at £30,520, leaving to the Earl a yearly rental of £1787:5; or with 'the countesse revenue' of £1300, in all £3087:5. *Undated*

17 pp. (Devereux Papers III/107)

NICHOLAS GEFFE TO GELLY MEYRICK

1593-4, February 6. As to the right of Mr Dyer to 'all laye fees and appropriacons' of the College of Aberguilley.

Holograph 1 p. (Devereux Papers I/186)

EDWARD BARKER TO GELLY MEYRICK

1593-4, February 13. Praying him to give order that he may receive a 'butte of sacke of the best sorte' allowed him yearly by the Earl of Essex 'at his first entrance into the impostes of the sackes and sweet wines.'

Holograph 1 p. (Devereux Papers I/191)

SIR RICHARD BINGHAM TO THE EARL OF ESSEX

1593-4, February 15. In favour of the bearer, 'Mr Holmes, a most godlie and learned minister.' Athlone.

Holograph 1 p. (Devereux Papers I/136)

SIR HENRY DUKE TO THE EARL OF ESSEX

1593-4, February 17. Reporting 'the late bourninge, spoillinge, praieinge and the meare wasting of all your honnors landes in Ferny by the traitors Ever McCooloes sonnes, Collei McBryans sonnes and Rory McHewe Ogge McMahowne, upon which outradge the Lord Deputie and Councell have appointed me with a bande of Irish footemen and xxx horsemen and myne owne 30 kearne to procecuitt the traitors, in which service, with Gods assistance, I will do my uttermoste indeavour boothe night and day, and will alsoo certefie your Lordship from time to time as ofte as anie newe accourants worth the certefieing shall fall onto'. Dublin.

Holograph 1 p. (Devereux Papers I/138)

WILLIAM PRATT TO THE EARL OF ESSEX

1593-4, February 17. 'By the inclosed letter your Lordship shall perceive what Constantyne McMahon your servaunt hath written unto me as touching the estate of your countries of Fferney and Clancarroll. Since the date whereof newe mischeiffs are growen, the countries being on Sonday, Monday and Tuesday last wholye wasted, burnt and spoyled, having not left one howse therin, soch a hedd is the rebellious route growen unto, being supported, as your Lordship may perceive by the enclosed letter. The miserie of soch poore tenauntes as are left (being but a fewe in comparison of the rest), which are of the sept that Constantyne your man is off, and some others of the sept of Manus McRorie, is so great that above 100 of theim are come into the Pale to seeke relieffe of meate and drinke. Constantyne is an humble sutor to the Lord Deputye and Councell here to have commission to take meate and drinke for theim, wherein howe farre he shall prevayle I doubt, but if they be not relieved they must of necessitie either joyne with the rebells or starve. Their be of them, as Constantyne informeth me, above 80 swoordes and targetters which were pittie but shold ben holpen. Constantyne intendeth if he be not relieved to attend upon your Lordship hymselfe, and to informe you perticulerly of all thinges. The rebells are nowe growen so strong as they do dayly and nightlye nowe pray the adjoyning borders of the country of Lowth, unto which as well as unto your landes they do nowe all the spoyles they may: for the preventing whereof and the relieffe of Mr Talbott in Fferney the Lord Deputie and Councell, after Mr Talbotts long sute for the same, have apointed Sir Henry Duke to be commaunder of 100 soldiers, 30 horsemen and the kerne under his leading of her Majestys pay, to lye on those confynes both for the relieffe of the Pale and your landes. I beseach your Lordship, according as I have formerly written to your Lordship, to remember the good knight who I know in this imployment is most willing to do your Lordship (what) service he may.' Dublin.

Holograph 1 p. (Devereux Papers I/140)

ANDREW BLUNDEN TO GELLY MEYRICK

1593-4, February 24. 'Mr Meyrick. There is on Edward Lyngen, who is heire apparant to Mrs Lyngen nowe Mrs Shelley, in some troble at York and in prison with the Counsell there. His offence is that he hath served in the warres with the Kyng of Spayne and under Sir William Stanley, and his fortune was to come into England in company with a Jesuyt. The man, I hope, is free from all trechery and cam over into Inglond by appoyntement and suyt of his brother. Thexpectauncye of the man as in respect of his appearaunce to the lyving is great, and yf extremetie of lawe be usyd against him, yet the Quene neither any other shall gayne by his death, the lands being intayled as they are. I wold wish therefor that some consideration were had for his present delivery, and that which is to be doen must be doen out of hand for thaffairs in Yorkshire draw nye.'

PS. 'Fyftye poundes wilbe given for his delyverance.'

Holograph 1 p. (Devereux Papers I/204)

JOHN LACY TO THE EARL OF ESSEX

1593-4, February 24.   Praying that he may have his promised security for a debt.   London.

Holograph   1 p.   (Devereux Papers I/144)

WALTER VAUGHAN TO THE EARL OF ESSEX

1593-4, February 24.   Asking that if among the evidences of Sir Thomas Parott, deceased, the jointure made at the marriage of his (Vaughan's) wife's mother can be found, it may be given to him, 'if any thing therein doeth or may in any wise concerne the honorable ladye your lordships sister or her daughter.'   Golden Grove.

Holograph   1 p.   (Devereux Papers I/142)

EDWARD PHYTON TO THE EARL OF ESSEX

1593-4, March 11.   On an application to 'Mr Justis Beamond' and offering to disclose a matter (of concealed lands) 'that may be worth to your lordship without damage to any, six or seven thowsand pond.'   Essex House.

Holograph   1 p.   (Devereux Papers I/146)

SIR THOMAS THROCKMORTON TO GELLY MEYRICK

1593-4, March 12.   Offering the Earl of Essex his cousin Guyese's lease 'of the libertyes of the forrest of Deane' with 'the ayres of goshawkes which ar two besydes the Earle of Pembroke his ayerye belonginge to his office of the Constalbshipe(*sic*)'.

Holograph   1 p.   (Devereux Papers I/212)

THOMAS WILKES TO GELLY MEYRICK

1593-4, March 23.   On behalf of 'the Examiners of the Chancery', suitors to the Earl of Essex for his 'furtherance of her Majestie in a matter of their right to certaine thinges usurped from them by the sixe clarkes of the Chancery.'   London.

(?)*Holograph Seal*   1 p.   (Devereux Papers I/226)

THOMAS POWELL TO GELLY MEYRICK

1594, April 1.   'We doe understand heare that thear goes some horse to Brytany: if there doe any goe ther well be new captaynes made, and the bearer hereof hopes to have a company, desiringe you to prefer me unto some of them as Leftenaunt or Auncient if youe doe.'   Ostend.

Holograph   1 p.   (Devereux Papers I/240)

G. LISLE TO GELLY MEYRICK

1594, April 3.   'My Ladie Walsingham doth here that Sir Nicholas Clifforde is remooved from the Fleet to the Tower and therfore praies you to take order that her bedd (which was carried to the Fleet for his use) maie bee brought backe againe and sent home to Walsinghame House, which her Ladyship saith shee hath present use of.'   London.

Holograph Seal   1 p.   (Devereux Papers I/244)

FRANCIS HASTINGS TO GELLY MEYRICK

1594, April 5.   Deprecating favour from the Earl of Essex to Sir Harry

Barkley, and asking support for the suit of the 'Examiners of the Chancery.' The letter is headed 'Immanuel.' Cadbury.

Holograph 1 p. (Devereux Papers I/248)

ANNE BOYLE TO GELLY MEYRICK

1594, April 6. Asking for the favour of the Earl of Essex in the hearing of a cause before the Council between her cousin Henry Boyle and William Duppa, clerk. Hereford.

Signed 1 p. (Devereux Papers I/249)

MARGARET (LLOYD) TO GELLY MEYRICK

1594, April 10. With thanks for kindness shown to her son. 'And whereas you have recomended unto me one Mr Edmunde Morgan, an honeste gente in my conceite and worthy to match with a better woman then myself: yett soe hit is, whether hit be for my crosse or otherwise I knowe not, ther is in me no motion or inclination to match with him, restinge indede resolute as yett not to marreye with anie man for certein yeares ...... prainge you to holde me excused in that I cannot soe kindlie affect the gentleman as you wisshe, wherin I can yelde noe reason but that evrie woman, I think, hath her peculiar affection, be hit ffor her good or ill, and claime the pryviledge tochinge the matter of her choise to match after there owne fancie .... I praie you to desiste to perswade me anie forther in this matter.' Llanvayr.

Holograph 1 p. (Devereux Papers I/258)

EDMUND MORGAN TO GELLY MEYRICK

(1594, April) 'Your continuall sarvice towardes me is my warrant for these my presumtions in that I shall be both tedious and troublesome in relatinge the discreses offered to my Lord of Essexs letters wich were kontempteustly refused by the gentlewoman.'

Holograph 1 p. (Devereux Papers I/294)

ACCOUNTS

1594, November 13 to 1595, July 19. Accompt of moneys received to the use of Robert Devereux, Earl of Essex.

7 pp. (Devereux Papers III/111)

THE EARL OF ESSEX TO DR GYFORD

(c 1594) Informs him that Signor Antonio Peres has fallen ill at his (Essex's) house, and requests him urgently to attend him. *Undated*

Holograph Torn Addressed: 'To my assured good frend Mr Dr Gyfford.' 1 p. (Devereux Papers I/120)

PETITION

(? 1594) A petition to the Earl of Essex from John Garnons, of Garnons, co. Hereford against 'the malice of your honors servaunte Geylley Meyricke' who is alleged to have said that 'your petitioner hadd not more religion than his horse, threatenynge him that this somer he woulde playe a Walshemans trycke or parte and would drive all your petitioners cattall awaye.' *Undated*

Endorsed: 'Garnons petition to my Lord.' 1 p. (Devereux Papers I/151)
On fol. 263 is the copy of an order out of the Chancery against John

Garnons, dated November 23, 1594 showing that he had been committed to the Fleet on October 31 for non-payment of arrears of rent.

ACCOUNTS

1594. Estimate of the expenses of the Earl of Essex in the Queen's service etc, drawn up by Gelly Meyrick, apparently in or about 1594, with a draft of a letter from Meyrick on the subject.

3 pp. (Devereux Papers II/82)
(Printed in *Wiltshire Archaeological Magazine,* Vol.XVIII (1879), p.271.)

ACCOUNTS

1594-95. Book of Accompt of household and other expenses of Robert Devereux, Earl of Essex. It includes the following *inter alia:*

(1) Gifts. To Sir Nicholas Clyfford at his going to Cambridge £5, and at his coming from thence, £5.

At Trinity College. To her that was your Lordship's laundress 'when your Lo: contynued at Cambridge', 20ˢ·

To Mr Doctor Neville's Steward.

To the Manciple, 10ˢ·

To the Butler of the College, 20ˢ·

To the Porter of the College, 10ˢ·

At Queen's College. To the poor there (? Cambridge), £7.

Towards building the steeple of St Mary's, £10:10.

(2) Reward. To the Players at Essex House at the marriage of the Earl of Northumberland, £10.

To Sir Robert Cecil's man, your Lordship lodging there, the Queen being at the Lord Treasurer's, 30 January, £4.

To Mr Anthony Bacon's coachman who carried your Lordship, 17 January, from Essex House to the Lord Treasurer's and so to Walsingham House, 10ˢ·

To one that keeps the monuments at Westminster, your Lordship being there to see them, 20ˢ·

For Mon. Perez, a month's salary, £20.

'To him, 26 Dec and 5 Jan towards his furnishing into France', £300.

(3) Play. 'To a linen draper', your Lordship playing with him at chess and lost at that time £10.

To your Lordship to play at cards with the Lord Sheffield on New Year's day at night in the Presence, your Lordship giving him odds at Noddy, £20.

To your Lordship at Sir Robert Cecil's, 26 Jan, in 20 pieces of gold, £20.

To the Countess of Leicester when your Lordship lost at chess to Sir Robert Carewe, £8.

(4) Extraordinary. To a fellow come lately out of the galleys, having been out of England 7 years, £20.

For a yard of white taffeta to fold the cristal in (for) her Majesty, 5ˢ·

For boat hire from Sion to London with two scholars of Oxford, 3ˢ·

In January many charges for boat hire to and from Walsingham House.

In February, expenses of Sir John Wingfield riding post from Cambridge to London and back, £5.

To Saunders the foot, 5ˢ·

(5) Debts paid. 'To Sir Thomas Baskerville I have the bond of £315.'

(6) Annuities. Including those paid to Sir Nicholas Clifford, Mrs Elizabeth Vernon, Mr Bourchier, Mrs Wroughton, Thomas Perrot.

(7) Diet. For supper for the Lady Rich at Essex House that night she came thither, 42s·

For diet at Gravesend at such time as Senor Anthony Perez departed for France, £11:9:10.

56 pp. *Much injured by damp in places* (Devereux Papers III/78)

THE EARL OF ESSEX TO THE LORD CHIEF JUSTICE

1594-5, January 29. In favour of his kinsman, Sir Thomas Knyvett of Norfolk. London.

Copy ½p. (Devereux Papers I/118)
(Printed in *Wiltshire Archaeological Magazine*, Vol. XVIII (1879) p.270)

RICHARD BURGON TO GELLY MEYRICK

(? 1594-5) March 5. 'Here is no newes to write for this bad contry afords nothing good, for the most part of the nobellite hear is all papist and very disobedient, especially thei which be in the North of Skootland. Hontley, Axall, Angus are the principall Earls which offers be to eade (aid) the Spanyerds. All Skootland asks for their coming, the which maks them not a litle proud, for then thei say thei will be revenged of there oulld ennymyes. The death of their quene they forget not. The King is a man that executeth no justis, the cause that thei are so badly governed. His Counsell is hafe papist, and to himself is nathere houtt nor could. He has a young sone at the which all skoots rejoyced. They touldd us planely there rejoycing was for there King and ours. They are a hatefull proud peopell as leaves. God knowes when the King will despach my Lord, for we suppose he drues (draws) him of and till he heare out of Spayne, look for no peace with them, if they can have any.' Edinburgh.

Holograph 1p. (Devereux Papers I/278)

SIR FULK GREVILLE TO THE EARL OF ESSEX

(?1595) Begging for his interest with the Queen. 'From solytary Broxborne'. *Undated.*

Holograph 1p. (Devereux Papers I/123)
(Printed in *Wiltshire Archaeological Magazine*, Vol.XVIII (1879) p.268)

RYS AP HUGH, ROBERT NEWCOMEN AND ZACHARY PEERS TO THE EARL OF ESSEX

1595-6, January 10. On business connected with Essex's lands in Ireland. 'As for your Lordships lands and territories of Fernie they lie all wast, and wee do not see howe in any short time they will yeld that benefitt to your Lordship that Mr Talbot is to answere, unles the Northern rebellion be suppressed.' They ask Essex to persuade the Lord Deputy to have garrisons and fortifications on them 'being the fittest place for defence of the borders of the Pale, espetially the counties of Lowth and Meath.' Dublin.

Signed Seal 2 pp. (Devereux Papers I/148)

ALBAN STEPNETH TO GELLY MEYRICK

1596, April 28.   Sending a 'pore present of fiftie poundes in golde' to furnish soldiers for the Cadiz expedition.   Prendergast.

Holograph Seal Addressed: To Meyrick as Essex's Steward, 'or in his absence to the worshipfull Mr Lyndeley, his lordships Comptroller, or to the worshipfull Mr Reynolds, his lordships Secretarie, these be delivered at Plymouth.'   1 p.   (Devereux Papers I/309)

THE CADIZ EXPEDITION

1596, April 28 to September 17.   Discharges, passes, certificates, etc, of soldiers who served in the Cadiz expedition and elsewhere, with lists of sick, etc, signed by officers, mayors and others between 28 April and 17 September, 1596 mostly undated, *inter alia*:

'*Villa et Com. Southampton.*   To all people to whome these presents shall come, Paul Ellyot, Mayor of the Towne and Countey of Southampton sendeth greeting.   Whereas the bearer herof, George Walnut, hath arrived at this port out of her Majestes forces in Spayne very sick and weak, where he hath served a gent. of a Companie under Capteyn Throgmorton under the regiment of Sir Thomas Gerrat, as he sayeth, and now being desirous to go to the Citie of London there to obteyn his pey: these are to desire all ye to whome it shall appertayne quietly to permit and suffer him to passe thither without any your lettes or molestations, he behaving himself accordingly as apperteyneth.   In witnes whereof I, the sayd Mayor, the seale of the sayd Towne for Passports used, have unto these presents caused to be affixed.   Dated the 5th day of August A.D. 1596 in the 38th yere of the Quenes Majesties regne.'   (f.110)

Signed: the Mayor.   1 p.   (Devereux Papers II/97-264)
   There are in all 143 of these documents, many with seals and signatures, e.g. of Sir Francis Vere, Sir Edward Norris, Sir Oliver Lambert, Sir Richard Wingfield and others.

JAMES BASKERVILLE TO GELLY MEYRICK

1596, April 30.   On an invitation by the Earl of Essex to his 'frendes or followers of the countey of Hereford' to accompany him in 'this intendid voiage' (the Cadiz expedition).   The writer regrets that reasons of health prevent him from taking part in the expedition, but promises to use his influence to induce his neighbours to go.   Bristol.

Signed Endorsed: 'Mr James Baskerville.'   1p.   (Devereux Papers I/265)

THOMAS CANON TO GELLY MEYRICK

1596, May 3.   Sending a 'poor testemonie' of his duty to the Earl of Essex in the way of a contribution towards the cost of the Cadiz expedition. Haverfordwest.

Holograph   1p.   (Devereux Papers I/267)

WARRANT

1596, May 23.   Warrant from the Earl of Essex to John Lynewraye, Clerk of the Ordnance, to deliver pikes out of the Tower to the 'severall coronells' commanding in the Cadiz expedition, viz: the 'Lord Marshall', the Earl of Sussex, Sir John Wingfield, Sir Christopher Blount, Sir Thomas Gerrard, Sir Conyers Clifford and Sir Richard Wingfield. Plymouth.

Copy   1p.   (Devereux Papers II/84)

(June, 1596)   News from Spain and the Low Countries, viz:

That upon Sunday, the 20th of June last, our fleet arrived before Cadiz, which was taken the next day.   Our men found the great *St Philip* of 1600 tons and the *St Paul* of 1400 tons burden, which fought for a while and were then forced to fire themselves, many of the crews being killed or drowned.   Our men took 70 great ships richly laden with silk, velvet etc, 'estemed by merchauntes of deepe judgement no leesse worthe then' two millions, of which ships 40 were over 1000 tons burden.   If our ships had but stayed at sea one day and night longer, they could have taken 18 more, but these received the alarm and fled up the river towards Seville.

On the 23rd our men took San Lucar.   There were 21 great galleys in the harbour, 16 manned.   They fought well being supplied with fresh men from the shore, but were at last 'spoyled'.   On the 24th and 25th our men took three neighbouring towns, 'Port St Marie, Port Riale and Sherys where veray miche sackes be usually made'.   They have also taken 12 of the King's 'great armadoes' laden with powder etc. for Lisbon, where the King had made great provision 'thinkinge in deede our men had shott at that marke'. This news was brought to Bristol by one Matthew Rize, a Bristol man, who had been taken prisoner by the Spaniards in March last.   He left San Lucar on June 28 and arrived at Bristol on July 20, having been an eye-witness of our men's prowess and also of the lamentations of the Spaniards, wringing their hands and crying 'that the Englishe will never leave us tyll theye have subdued our country.'

From the Low Countries it is reported that Count Maurice had gained a victory over the Cardinal and slain 3000 Spaniards, men, women and children.

A ship of St Malo, coming from Spain, reports our army near Seville, and that 16,000 Moors had been landed in Spain to assist our army, but the General refused to let them camp with our men fearing 'some jarres'.

'Yt may please your worshippe not to make these newes comon, but only to your deere frends, bycause there be proclamations sett owte agaynst the reporters of newes.'

Endorsed: 'Newes of the Earl of Essexs voyage 1596.'   3 pp.   (Devereux Papers II/89)

JAMES RETHELTH TO SIR GELLY MEYRICK

1596, August 13.   Complaining of the contempt shown for the men he had provided for the Cadiz expedition.   Llandewy.

Holograph   1p.   (Devereux Papers I/271)

SIR JOHN STANHOPE TO SIR GELLY MEYRICK

1596, September 8.   'This bearer Ffrauncis Whitfeilde was recommended to me to Sir Robert Sydneye to serve under him in Her Majestys garryson of Fflushinge, and was from thence drawne to serve in Her Majestys warres in Spayne under the bloody collers, where he was sore hurte.'   He requests that he may receive the pay due to him.   Grenwich.

Signed   1p.   (Devereux Papers I/273)

THE CADIZ EXPEDITION

1596.   List of regiments with names of Colonels and Captains, and number of men in each company, amounting in all to 6300, engaged in the Cadiz expedition, 1596, followed by a note 'of the severall dayes that the Colonells and Captains receaved entertaynment for their Companyes'.

The General's Regiment, 1050. 'My lords owne companie, 200 men.' 150 men each, Sir Matthew Morgan, Sir George Carew, Sir Oliver Lambert. 100 men each, Sir Clement Higham, Captains Goring, Hunbridge and Edkircke.

The Lord Marshal's Regiment, 750. The Lord Marshal's own Company, 150 men. 100 men each, Sir Samuel Bagnal, Captains Constable, Haiden, Daniel Vere, Upcher, Carewe.

The Earl of Sussex's Regiment, afterwards disposed to Sir Edward Conway, 750. The Earl of Sussex's own Company, 150 men. 100 men each, Sir Edward Conway, Captains Fulk Conway, Terret, Rishe, Harvie, Williams, Evans.

Sir Christopher Blount's Regiment, 750. Sir Christopher Blount's own Company, 150 men. 100 men each, Sir Charles Blount, Captains Brett, Boulsrett, Harcott, Williams, Ffoliett.

Sir Thomas Gerard's Regiment, 750. Sir Thomas Gerard's own Company, 150 men. 100 men each, Captains Throckmorton, Lloid, Billinges, Collier, Salesburie, Mullinex.

Sir Conyers Clifford's own Regiment, 750. Sir Conyers Clifford's own Company, 150 men. 100 men each, Captains Meyrick, Davis, Dansie, Wilton, Poolie, Tolkarne.

Sir Richard Winckfield's Regiment, 750. Sir Richard Winckfield's (Wingfield) own Company, 150 men. 100 men each, Captains Cunnye. Jackson, Hopton, Ffleming, Sir George Gifford, Smithe.

Sir Horatius Vere's Regiment, 750. Sir Horatius Vere's own Company, 150 men. 100 men each, Captains Laurence, Sir Gerrard Harvie, Maunsfield, Charles Morgan, Richards and Gibbon.

7 pp.   (Devereux Papers II/85)

THE CADIZ EXPEDITION

1596.   Miscellaneous papers connected with the expedition to Cadiz comprising lists of soldiers, payments to several companies, etc.

6 pp.   (Devereux Papers II/92)

PETITIONS

1596.   Petitions to Robert Devereux, Earl of Essex, chiefly from soldiers and others who had served in the expedition to Cadiz. Many of them are endorsed with orders signed by the Earl.

14 documents   (Devereux Papers II/290-316)

CONVEYANCE OF PROPERTY

(1596 or after)   Release by Robert Devereux, Earl of Essex, to Sir Gelly Meyrick,* Robert Wright and Thomas Crompton of the manors of Fanhope and Ross. Undated

Draft 12 pp.   (Devereux Papers III/49)

THE SECOND SPANISH EXPEDITION

1597, October 28 to November 5. Discharge of seamen of the Bonaventura, Dreadnought, Lyon, and Nonpareil after the return of the Earl of Essex's

*Knighted by Essex after the capture of Cadiz in June 1596.

second expedition to the coast of Spain.

Signed: Lord Thomas Howard, Vice-Admiral, Captain George Fenner and other officers.

24 *documents*   (Devereux Papers II/265-289)

SIR THOMAS SMITH TO SIR GELLY MEYRICK

(? 1598) June 27. 'My Lord hath commanded me to send for you to the Courte: and if he had not commanded, I would have advised you myselfe. Why his Lordship sendeth for you I cannot tell, but I wishe you to be there speedily because the matter of Lieftenantship* is followed earnestly of all hands. His Lordship hath bin sicke this night and is not well yet. I commend me to you, and wishe myself no other wise beloved of you then I love you.' Windsor.

Holograph   1p.   (Devereux Papers I/304)

PETITION

(*c* 1598)   A petition from Peter Cooke, Mayor of Portsmouth,† and Mark James, Postmaster, against 'one Mr Herbert, a gentelman belonging to your lordship' who had taken a post-horse and ridden him 'no man knoweth whether.' *Undated*

Endorsed: 'Certificatt of the Maior of Portsmouth.'

Signed   1 p.   (Devereux Papers I/153)

ANTHONY BACON TO THE EARL OF ESSEX

(After November 29, 1599)‡ 'My singuler good Lo: Her Majesties proceedings with your Lordship thus by gradacion doth make mee in my love towards you jealous least you dooe somewhat that amounteth to a new error, ffor I suppose that of all former matters there is a ffull expiracion for anie thing your Lordship doth. I for my parte whoe am remote cannot cast nor devise wherein anye error should bee, except in one pointe which I dare not censure nor disswayde which is (as ye prophet sayth) in this affliction you looke up *ad manum percutientis* and so make your peace with God. And yet I have heard it noted that my Lord of Leycester whoe wolde never get to bee taken for a sainte, yet in the Queenes disfavoure waxed seeming religious, which may be thoughte by some and used by others as a case resembling yours, yf men doe not see the difference betwixt your twoe dispositions. But to be plaine with your Lordship, my feare rather is because I heare how some of your good and wise ffriendes not unpractised in ye Court and supposing themselves not to bee a little seen in that deep and inscrutable center of ye Courte (which is her Majesties minde) doe not onely toule the bell, eaven ring out peales, as if your ffortune were dead and buried, and as if there were no possibilitie of recoveringe her Majesties ffavor, and as if the best of your condition were to live a private lief, out of want, out of perill and out of manifest disgrace; and so in theis perswasions of theyrs include a perswasion to your Lordship ward to fframe and accommodate your minde and actions to that ende: I feare, I say, that this untimely dispaire causeth your Lordship to slaken and break of your wise, loyall and seasonable endevors for reintegration to her Majesties ffavoure. In comparison whereof all other circumstaunces are but atoms, or rather as vacuum without anie substaunce

---

* Of Ireland, to which the Earl of Essex was appointed in March 1599.

† Elected Mayor in September, 1597. (See *Records of the Corporation of Portsmouth*, ed. R.J. Murrell and R. East, 1884, p. 197

‡ The Earl had been censured in the Star Chamber on 29 November 1599.

at all against this opinion. It maie please your Lordship to consider of theis reasons which I have collected, and to make judgment of them neyther out of the melencholly of your present fortunes nor out of the infusion of that which cometh to you by relation, which is subject to much tincture, but *ex rebus ipsis*, out of the nature of the persons and actions themselves as the trewest and least deceaving groundes.

Ffirst, thoughe I am soe unfortunate as to be a straunger to her Majesties eye, much more to her nature and manner, yet by that which is extant I doe manifestlye descerne that she hath that character of ye devine nature and goodnes as *quos amavit amavit ad finem*: and where she hathe a creature she doth not deface nor defeat it: insomuch (as if I observe rightly in theis personnes whome heretofore shee hath honored with her speciall ffavoure) shee hath cured and remitted not only defections in affections but errors in state of service.

Secondlie, if I can schollerlike spell, I put together her Majesties proceedinges towardes your Lordship, I cannot but make this construction: that her Majestie in this royall intention never purposed to call your Lordships doeings into publique question, but only to have used a cloude without a shower in censuring them by some restrainte of liberty and debarring you from her presence; ffor bothe the first handling of your cause in the Star Chamber was enforced by violence of libellinge and rumoures wherein the Queen thought to have satisfied the worlde and yet spared your apparaunce. And then after when that means which was intended for the quenchinge of so malicious brutes tourned to kindle them because it was said your Lordship was condempned unheard and your Lordships sister wrote that piquaunt, then her Majestie did see plainlie that theis roundes of rumoures could not bee commaunded down without a handling of the cause by making yowe partie and addmitting your defence: and to this purpose I soe assuer your Lordship that my brother Ffrauncis Bacon whoe I think is too wise to be abused and too honest to abuse, though he bee more reserved in particulers then is needful, yet in generallitye hath ever constantlye and with great assuraunce affermed to me, 'That both daies, that of ye Starchamber and that at my Lord Keepers, there went one from the Queen merely upon necessitye and point of humour against her owne inclination.'

Thirdlie, in the last proceedinges I note three pointes which are directlye signifyed that her Majestie did expresslie forbeare anie pointe which was irreparable or might make your Lordship in anie degree uncapable of the retourne of her favoure, or might ffixe anie character indeleable of disgrace upon you; ffor she feared the publique place which caried ignominye, she limited your chardge precisely not to touch disloyaltye, and noe recorde remaineth to memorie of chardge or sentence.

Ffourthlie, the verie distinction which was made in the sentence of sequestration from the place of service in State and leavinge to your Lordship the place of Master of the Horse dothe in understandinge indicative pointe to this: that her Majestie meant to use your Lordships attendaunce in Courte while the excersises of ye other places stoode suspended.

Ffifthlie, I have heard that your Lordship knoweth better nowe that since you were in your owne custodie her Majestie *in verbo Regiae* and by his mouth to whome she comitteth the fframinge of her roiall grauntes and decrees hath assured your Lordship shee will forbid and not suffer your ruine.

Sixtlie, as I have hearde your (*sic*) Majestye to bee a prince of that magnanimitye that shee can spare the service of ye hablest subject or peere when shalbe thought to stand in need of it, so shee is of that policy that shee will not loose the service of a meaner man than your Lordship when it shall depend merely upon her choyse and will.

Seaventhly, I holde it for a principle those diseases are hardest to cure whereof the cause is obscure, and those easiest whereof the cause is manifest; whereupon I conclude that since it hath been your error in your course towardes her Majestie that hath prejudiced you, that your refourminge and conformitye will restore you and so that you maie *faber fortunae propriae.*

Lastlie, considering that your Lordship is remooved from dealing in causes of State and lefte onlie to a place of attendaunce, mee thinkes the ambition of anie that can endewer no partener in State matters may bee so quenched as those shoulde not oppose themselves to your being in Courte. So as upon the whole matter I cannot finde eyther in her Majesties person or in your owne person or in anie third person, or in anie former presidentes, or in your case anie cause of dyre and peremptorie despaire. Neyther doe I speak this but that if her Majestie out of her resolution should designe you to a privat lief, you should be as willing upon her appointement to goe into the wildernes as into the land of promise: onlie I wish that your Lordship will not preoccupate dispaire, but trust next to God in her Majesties grace and not to bee wanting to your self. I know your Lordship may justlye interpreth that this which I speak may have some reference to my particuler because I may truly say *testante vivebo* I am withered in my self, but I shall in some sorte bee or holde it out. But your Lordships yeares and health maie expect retourn of grace and ffortune, yet your eclipse for a time is an *ultimum vale* to my fortune, and were it not that I desier and hope to see my brother in some sorte established by her Majesties ffavoure, as I think him well worthie for that hee hath doon and suffered, it were tyme I did take ye course which I disswayde to your Lordship, thoughe in the meane time I cannot but perfourme theis honest duties unto you to whome I have ever been so deeply bounde.' *Undated*

Copy 5 pp. (Devereux Papers VII/105)

THE EARL OF ESSEX TO ANTHONY BACON

(After November 29, 1599) 'I thank yow for your kinde and carefull lettre. It perswaides that which I wish stronglie but hope weaklie, that there is possibility of restitution to her Majesties favour. Your arguments which should cherish hope tourn into dispayre. You say the Queen never meant to call me to publique censure, which sheweth her goodnes, but you see I passed that, which sheweth others power. I believe most stedfastlie that her Majestie never meant to bring my cause to a sentence, and believe as nerely that since the sentence she meant to restore me to attend upon her person. But they that coulde use occasion (which was not in mee to lett) and could amplifie occasions and practise occasions to represent to her Majestie a necessitie to bring me to the one, can and will dooe the like to stop mee from the other. You say my errors were my prejudice, and therefore I can mend myself. It is true, but they that knowe I can mend myself and that if ever I recover the Queen I will never loose hold of her, they will never suffer mee to have interest in her ffavoure. Againe you saie the Queen never forsooke utterlye where shee hath inwardly ffavoured, but you know not whether the hower-glasse of time hath altered her. Once I am suer the ffalce glasse of others informations must alter her both *in re creationis*, for I am her creature, and *jure redemptionis*, for I know shee hath saved me from overthrowe, but for her first love and last protection and all her great benefittes I can but praie for her Majestie, and my endevoure is now to make my praier for her and my self better heard; ffor thankes be to God they which can make her Majestie beleeve that I counterfeyte with her cannot make God beleeve I counterfeyte with him, and they which can lett me from coming nere to her cannot lett me from draweing nere to him as I hope I dooe dalye. Ffor your brother I holde him an honest gent, and wish him all good, much rather for your sake. And I assuer you I think no more hurt of him then I dooe of my Lord Chief Justice. Yourself I knowe have suffered more for mee and with mee then anie ffreend I have, but I cann but lament freely as you see I dooe and advize you not to dooe that which I dooe, which is despaire. You knowe letters what hurt they have doone mee and therefore make suer of this. And yet I could not (as having no other pledge of my love to give you) but communicate openly with you for the ease of my hurt and yours.' *Undated.*

Copy 2 pp. (Devereux Papers VII/108)

EVIDENCES

1599 and after. Schedule of evidences of Robert Devereux, Earl of Essex, at Essex House, with additions to 1599.

Signed: Anthony Pembridge. 14 pp. (Devereux Papers III/126)

THE TRIAL OF THE EARL OF ESSEX

5° die Junii, 1600. 'On Thursdaie ye 5th of June about viiith of ye clocke in the morninge was the Earle of Essex brought to the Lord Keepers, where theis honorable persons here under written were by commission from her Majestie appointed to heare his cause, viz: the Lord Archbushopp of Canterbury, the Lord Keeper, the Lord Treasurour, the Lord Admirall, the Earles of Shrewesburie, Worcester, Comberland and Huntingdon, the Lord Darcey, Lord Zouche, Sir William Knowles, Mr Secretarie Cecill, Sir John Fortescue, the Lord Cheif Justice of England, Lord Anderson, Lord Cheef Barron, Justice Gawdye and Justice Walmesley.

Theis comissioners being sett in the greate chamber at York howse, there were there admitted to the hearing of his cause many and, I thinke, all the noble men about London and the Corte, many knyghtes of the best accompt and other choise gent(lemen), both courtiers and others, yt were about the towne, order being taken ye daye before amonge ye Lordes yt noe multitude shold be brought in but every counceller and comissioner to have a man or twoe.

The auditorie consisted of almost 200 persons, and the Earle in pleading for himself thanked God for soe ho(norable) and soe choise an assemblie as he confessed he had.

The matters laied to the Earles chardge by Mr Yelverton, the Queenes Serjaunt, Mr Coke, her Majesties Attorney, Mr Sollicitour Mr Bacon, were theis 5 followinge:

1. The first, that before his going into Ireland he was a suytour to her Majestie yt the Earle of Sowthampton might be gennerall of the horse, which her Majestie, in regarde of his late contempte which he had rune into by marriadg of his wief and his little exsperience in marciall affaires, denied unto the Earle; notwithstanding ye Earle of Essex made him at his coming over into Ireland Lord General of the Horse; which when ye Queene understoode she comaunded the Lords of ye Councell to writte unto him in her name signifying her dislike thereof, and required yt the Earle should be againe displaced; notwithstanding which letters the Earle of Essex contynewed him in the place still and wrotte back againe a passionate and indiscreete letter.

2. Secondlye, that the Earle before his going into Ireland had layed the

projecte himself of an army of 16 thowsand foote and 16 hundred horse for Ulster where the rebell was, and by making warre uppon him he should putt the axe to ye roote which being cutt downe the rest of ye braunches would falle or wither, and soe thereby bringe an end of the warre. This projecte being his owne was confirmed before his departure hence by all the councell of warre about London, and approved by her Majestie and the Lordes of the Councell heare, and afterwardes alsoe approved by the Councell of Ireland and likewise by letters afterwards from her Majesties Councell againe requiring him to goe to Ulster. Never the lesse the Earle diverted his purpose to Munster where he spent 8 weekes, lost many of his forces upon many unnecessary attemptes, weakned and consumed his army by soe longe and contynuall a marche, in soe much as when he retorned noe accompt colde be rendred of anie good he had done in those twoe moneths jorney, no not bringinge in so much as one rebell. And then with his feeble and consumed army, the traytor Tyrone being in his greatest strengthe and pride, hee marcheth towards him with a purpose to fight uppon soe manye and greate disadvantages, and by his letters sent unto ye Queene, he promised to pull down ye pryde of yt baze traytor Tyrone, and if he cold fynd him uppon firme grownd to ma(ke) yt to tremble under him, at which tyme Capten Lea was sent by the Marshiall to taulk with Tyrone, and neither the Marshiall nor Capten Lea punished. Soe as Master Attorney thought in his conscience that what so ever ye Earle pretended, yet he never meant to fight with Tyrone. Moreover her Majestie, before his goinge over, forgave him 14 thowsand poundes and gave him 8 thowsand more besides 3 monethes paye, which was delivered unto him before hande, and he spent her Majestie during the tyme of his beinge in Ireland 300 thowsand powndes. Her Majesties mercyfull dealinge with him in this kind of proceeding was by many argumentes theire manifested; in soe muche as to satisfie ye people who reported yt he was clapt up for nothing. She meante to have had his cause harde in the Starr Chamber, which when the Earle perceyved he begged by his humble letters at her Majesties handes to be spared from that tryall. And she to save him from ruyne whose offences tended to the ruyne of a kingdome, spared his cominge thither.

3. Thirdlie, that yt was a question disputable and in greate consultacon before his goinge over, whether by reason of his making soe many knightes in former ymploymentes, he shold have yt authoritye in his commission or noe; yet afterwardes (having a commission farr larger in other pointes then any whatsoever that was imploied in theis partes heretofore, as both for pardoninge of all manner of treasons and traytours and the disposition of theire landes in Ulster), yt was thought very fytt yt he shold not be debarred of yt point; never the les he was by the Queene herself required to (be) verie sparinge in that pointe and to make verie fewe, and those of verie good dezert and qualitie, notwithstanding which warninge, after his cominge over into Ireland, he made a greate number of knightes which being by the Queene verie much disliked he was afterwardes by letters in the Queenes name required to hold his hand; and yet after the receipt of those letters he made many more whereof 3 were of his owne domesticall servauntes, and the nomber of the whole knightes by him made were almost 60, one of which he had not longe before his goinge over bin a suytor to her Majestie to knight him, which she did not onlie refuse soe to doe but also gave him a caucon not to do it, which not withstandinge he did afterwardes knight him in Ireland.

4. Fourthlie, that beinge Lo(rd) Lyevetenaunte and Generall under soe greate a prince, who had righted and upphelde other princes in theire seates

and kingdomes, had made warre against the greatest prince of Ewrope, become glorious and renowned through owte the wordle (*sic*) for her power, vertues, wisdomes and prowesse of her nation, that a generall to soe mightie a prince shold so dishonorablie conferre with a misbegotten, baze traytour, the sonne of a blacksmith and a bushe kerne, being in his greatest pride and, as he then termed himself, master of the field, was most intollerable without comission. And in this conference with him required the Earle of Sowth (ampton) to be the guarde to kepe backe all men from cominge neere to them or hearinge theire conferences, and then to receyve such condicons for cessacon of armes as were not fytt to be receyved from anie equall prince much lesse from soe baze a traytour, was not to be indured.

5. Fiftlie, that receyving a letter from her Majestie comaunding him uppon his duty not to leave the countrey untill he had signified unto her whom he meante to leave the government unto, and receyved her allowaunce and approbacon or some other ho(nest) person from hence to supplie the place, not withstanding contrarie to her highnes comaund (which letters he confessed he receyved) he came over into Ingland, and not having deliberated it howres before his cominge awaye, sendeth his comission fourthe and with owte conferringe with the parties, comitteth the government of a kingdome to the Lo(rd) Chauncellor and Earle of Ormond against whome he had not long before protested for theire misgovernment.

The inconveniences which happened immediatlie after the Earles departure owte of Ireland and suspicous imputacons were thies followinge:

1. Sir William Warren and Mr Bremingham confering with Tyrone the 14th of October, Tyrone asked what was said in the English armye of the Earle of Essex his going into England, who answered that yt was said that Tyrone shold tell the Earle he would alsoe be in England shortlie. Nay, saide Tyrone, I never told the Earle anie such thinge, but I meane shortlie to be in England and to have a good share theire. And he further said that they shold see shortlie such an alteracon theire as they did never see.

2. Besides, Tyrone in his demaundes and speeches was verie insolent requiringe a generall pardon for all traytours.

3. A tolleracon for religion throughe owte all Ireland. An establishment of all such as were possessed of anie landes which were gotten by stronge hand and in possession of anie traytour or rebell.

4. And those that either by right of inherytaunce or which had bought and paide for them, shold not be restored hereafter to them.

Tyrone allso protested that he would be content to put himself into a monasterie soe theire cause might be uppheld and theire countreye at freedome and libertie of conscience.

Tyrone, after the Earle of Essex his departure into England, sendeth fourth his edictes and letters with his name written on the topp as the Queene doth, shewing his victories, that he fighteth for the Catholike faithe to be planted and intymateth to be kinge of Ireland, termeth the Queene to be deprived of all her kingdomes beinge excommunicated by the Popes bull which was still of force.

That he was proferred manie condicons which for his pryvat respectes he cold not refuse, but that he still woulde mayntayne the warres for freedome of conscience and theire ancient libertie. Tyrone threatneth by his edictes and letters the nobilytie and others that will not come in to him, that he will overrune and destroie theire countreye and people.

For the more substanciall proofe of the 5 first contemptes wherewith the Earl of Essex was chardged, he cold not denie her Majesties severall comaundementes and receipt of her letters. And the rest were partelie proved by his owne letters written to the Lords of the Councell, for in his letters in answere of the Lords letters concerninge the removinge of the Earle of Sowthampton from being Generall of the Horse, and in other former letters he saieth that he most discouradg his frendes, dismaye the army and give harte to the enemie by ye disgraces which were heaped uppon him when he had well deserved.

That theire was noe tempest to the passionat indignacon of a prince.

That her Majesties harte was obdurated.

That he is made of fleshe and bloode.

What, cannot princes err?

Cannot subjectes receyve wronge?

Lett those yt meane to make profytt of princes faultes fawne and flatter them in their follies.

I am sorie to lyve to see theis daies wherein I cannot serve and please the Queene at once.

Is yt treason for the Earle of Sowthampton to marrye my kingeswoman? I dare not doe that which will overthrowe me and the accon that yf Misenas and Agrippa had lived they would have said *O tempora, O mores.*

The Earle of Essex, after all theis thinges uttered by her Majesties learned councell, the letters shewed and the contentes inforced, with imputacons and shrewde collecons made of his secrett conference with Tyrone and Tyrones bragges and insultacons to Sir William Warren and Mr Bremingham; the Earle (I saye) on his knees desired to be harde purposinge, as he protested, not to contest with her Majestie for anie thinge where with he was by her in pryvate speeche or by her letters chardged withall, neither did he come with a minde to excuse himself for the rest of the 5 first thinges where with he was by his owne letters and other wise chardged withall, but confessed his manie errours in that behaulf; and that his exsperience since taught him he was in a wronge course which if it were to begine againe he would alter; yet nevertheles he desired to touche everie one of the first 5 pointes with the reasons that lead him to doe as he did. And then leavinge them and himself to theire Lordshipps further censure with umble (sic) and hartie confession of his offenses and errours in that behaulf to her highnes, and his contricon and unfayned repentance therefore; besought forgivnes at her Majesties handes and that theire Lordships would be his intercessors and make knowne unto her highnes his earnest and umble desire of pardon. And for the imputacons and inferences laied uppon him concerninge yt damnable traytor Tyrone his speeches to Sir William Warren and Master Bremingham, he desired to answere to everie particuleritie of yt, and would bothe approve and mayntayne his integrytie and lyolltie to her sacred Majestie, and wold rather with his owne handes and nayles rent his fleshe and teare fourthe his harte then he would either make confession or aske forgivenes for anie thought of disliolltie, and would (he made no doubt) both cleere himself and satisfie theire Lordshipps for anie imputacon or inference in that behaulf to be laide uppon him.

Whereuppon everye of ye Lords particulerley cleered him either of the matter itself or of any suche imputacon or inference, wherewith the Earle being much satisfied with theire Lords good opinion in yt pointe delivered his resons, not by way of justifycacon but as being then much misled by his owne conceyte of doing thinges for the best though the successe fell owte contrarie.

1. To the first he said yt indeede he was suytor to her Majesty for the Earle of Sowthampton to be Generall of the Horse and she rejected his desire, which he rather supposed she did at that tyme because she would not, by allowing his mocon, discouradg or discontenance others about her who at that tyme

were suytours for that place. But at his second mocon made to her Majestie bothe in the presence of ye Lord Admiral and Mr Secretary, he delivered such reasons for his being made Generall of the Horse as her Majesty made noe replie, and therefore he supposed her highnes had rested satisfied and pleased therewith, and because her Majestie nominated no other for that place (he having comission to make his owne choise) made him Lord Generall of the Horse.

And for his contynewance after the receipt of their Lordships letters, he hoped that his reasons in his letters then and since his retorne in answere thereof would have satisfied the Queene and theire Lordships, which reasons were to this effecte; yt the Earle of Sowthampton having excercysed the place for 8 weekes and gotten to greate comendacon and good opynion by his famylier and curteous carriadg amonge the voluntaries who were gent(lemen) of ye best forwardnes and resolucon, he must by displacinge him discouradg his frendes (with whome by reason of his owne contynewall imploymentes and other cogitacons he cold not be soe familier with as in former tymes), dismaie the army and give harte to the enemy by ye disgraces heaped uppon him that for his carriadg and late service had desserved.

At the receite alsoe of theis letters he had none of the nobilitie of England with him fitt for the place unles he should have placed such a one as might have given occacon of offence to the Irish nobilitie for superioritie and dignitie of place, and the Irish Lords having comaundes otherwise and some of them as greate place as ye Earle of Sowthampton he thought fytt for his best comfort to have his neerest frendes about him, from whom he might hope for most asistance. And therefore said in his letters to the Lordes, I dare not doe yt which will overthrowe me and the accon.

2.   To the 2 he saied yt he confessed the projecte to be laied by himself and confirmed by the Queene and the Lordes of the Councell for the going with his armye into Ulster. And that he had all thinges performed which he had before his departure required, that her Majestie had dealt graciouslie with him for the somes given him and bestowed uppon him before his goinge over, and that he had receyved 3 moneths paie or treasere before hand; that his instrucons were verie large both for pardoninge of traytours and disposing of landes in Ulster, that the Counsell of Ireland approved his goinge to Ulster after his first aryvall there; but at the next sitting laying before him the impossibility then to undertake yt journey and wantes he should both of victualls and horsemeate have, if hee went soe soone before the grasse was growen with soe greate an armie, and also looking to his proporcons yt he had brought for soe waightie an enterprise, being advized to make 3 several fortificacons towardes ye frontyres of Tyrone his countrey, and therefore supposing before but by bare conjecture what wold serve his torne, (he) founde himself shorte of the trewe proporcon which indeede should be had for soe waightie an enterprize, and of his shipping and men yt should land at Lafoyle to keepe the seas and to anoye Tyrone by making contynewall rodes on the backe of the enemy, and to hinder his passadg if he should offer to come that waye; and therefore bothe for the better hope of victualls to supplie so greate an armye he resolved to staie for a while, and in the meane tyme he sent to England for a supplie of 2000 men more. And soe stayinge for shippinge and men to land at Lafoile and for a better season to marche on with his armie, he was advised by the Councell of Ireland in this meane tyme, and because he would not alsoe hold his army in ydleness, to marche for 8 daies to Waterford and theire to conferre with the President and councell of Munster for the well guidinge and settlinge of that province, which

course having signified to the Lords of the Councell of England when he sent for the supplie of 2000 men, the Earle said that theire Lordships did also approve the Councell of Irelandes advise and comended his care in performinge the same. When he was come to Waterford where he mett with the President of Munster, he was by the Councell of Warr for that province perswaded to hould one to Carre Castle, and then with unanswerable reasons importuned to go to Limbrick which they told him was but 8 daies journey the next waie from Dubblin, to the end that that province might see her Majesties goodlie armye, whereby afterwards ye better to keepe that countrey in awe. And being at Lymbrick he then desired to be directed the neerest waie, but being then perswaded by the Earle of Irmond, Sir George Bourcher and Sir Warrham St Leger with unanswerable reasons for the performaunce of manie services to marche the further waie about, which through theire perswacons he did.

Then this disaster of Sir Coniers Cliffordes overthrow and the cowardize of manie runnawayes at small skirmishes and encounters, besides the feeblnes of his army having marched daie by daie for 2 monethes space, wrought theis unhappie successes afterwardes.

3. To the thirde the Earle said and protested not to contest with her Majestie, and that she comaunded him to be sparing in making of knightes, but having many gallant gent(lemen) voluntaries who had spent themselves very farre in followinge him this weriesome journey, havinge noe imployement for them and having bestowed amonge them all that he was able to make, and fearing theire discontentment and shrinking awaie, having (as hee said) noe ymployement for them, no other treasere or guifes to bestowe uppon them, he rewarded manie of them for theire valure and forwardnes in divers enterprises that he passed with the honour of knighthoode, thereby to hold the rest on with the like hope of the same rewarde hereafter. And for the gent(leman) whom her Majestie had refused to make knight and gave him a like caution, he was tould both by a nobleman and an ho(norable) la(dy) about the Queene that they had againe moved her Majestie in his behaulf who seemed attentyve enough to the mocon, and although she had not in expresse wordes yeelded unto the same, yet they would warrant him if he would make him knight, the Queene wold not be displeased.

4. To the iiiith, for his conference with Tyrone, he said that he first went to him with that feeble army yt he had and proffered to fight even uppon his owne grownd, though to greate disadvantage. He made manie skirmishes uppon him and he alwaies refused the fight and still sought to pryvate parlie, which consideringe the weaknes of his owne armye, some of them consisting of baze cowardes that were beaten and rune awaie, who having desire to be gone into England by stealthe and there to perswade others rather to suffer imprysoment and deth then to come into soe wreached a countrey where nothing but miserie was to be hoped after; theis reasons together with Tyrones earnest desire to imparte his minde to no man lyving nor to adventure nor relye uppon anie mans worde but uppon his, caused the Earle to parlie with him, and knowing the distresse of the countrey and the weakenes of his owne army supposed (as the case then stoode) the condicons which Tyron proposed to be reasonable, offering himself to come into her Majesties obedience and protecon without proposinge anie of those condicons, either for tolleracon of religion or generall pardon or establishment of such as were possessed of other mens landes. But absolutlie offerred himself to be her Majesties obedient subject if she would accept of him. And for those proposicons made to Sir William Warrham and Mr Bremingham they were but florishes and vauntes,

assuring me that whatsoever he should speake or vaunte to others in open conference he did it in due pollicy, as fearing yf his souldiers or partakers should suspecte him to make anie peace they would forsake him. And 2 other spialls, one from Spaine and another from the Pope, being a fryer or religious person, they alsoe watched and observed what passed from him in theis open conferences, and therefore if they should suspecte his making of peace theis forren asistantes would quicklie leave him. And therefore wished what vauntes or demaundes soe ever he should heare him make openlie of others, he should conceyve him in what respectes he did yt. And uppon this conferennce the Earle yeelded to a cessacon of armes.

5. To the fifte and last he saied that for his coming over, being uppon his dutie comaunded to the contrarie, he presumed that the hope of the condicons which he brought from Tyrone would have appeazed her highnes for that offence; or the delivery of a new projecte which he had conceyved by his industrie and exsperience, therefor the more effectuall overthrowe of that wicked traytor; besides, when he remembred that in like case Leicester beinge imployed by her Majestie in the Lowe Countreis and receyvinge from her Majestie by Sir Thomas Gorge the like letters of comaundement for his staie and contynewaunce theire, notwithstanding presuming of her Majesties favour he came over for safegarde of his lief and receyved grace and pardon, much more did Essex hope for mercie and forgivenes coming over for the safgard of a kingdome. Mr Secretary denied the sending of anie such letters to the Earle of Leicester to this effecte, but would not gaynsaie the messagdge which being verball might admitt many interpretacons and construcons. Agayne the Earle of Essex beinge by the last clause of her Majesties letters stricken into such an amazement and mellancholly concerning his obedience that, being rapt with fury and passion, adventureth desperatlie over into England to render an accoumpt of his doings and hoping that all former matters of disobedience as her highnes had promised him, when he tooke his leave at Richmond, should never be imputed unto him, emboldened him the rather thus to do.

Replie beinge made by Mr Secretarie, the Lord Treasurour and Lord Keeper and others of her Majesties most princlie care for the expeditinge of such further supplies as he sent for and the disavowing of the Councell of Irelandes approbacon of his goinge further to Munster then for the 8 daies first proposed, besides shewinge her Majesties letters comaundinge him to goe to Ulster according to his first projecte and resolucon of all councells and opynions; as also stayinge of his handes from making anie more knightes. All which said 5 first contemptes being partlie by his owne letters proved and in other parte confessed by himself to proceede of error and not of willfullnes or disloyalltie, and if they were againe to doe, having nowe a more sensible feelinge of his former passions, imperfecons and errours, he would not committ the like transgressions as he had donne; and therefore once more besought (on his knees) pardon of her Majestie for his offences in yt behaulf, and desired theire Lordships to signifie unto her highnes his confession of his faultes and contricon with protestacon of his loyalltie and fedelitie to her highnes, and howe ready he would be to hazard and adventure that poore carcas of his, even to obteyne this favoure, to prostrate himself once againe at her Majesties feete, whose unspeakeable favoures towardes him was the cheif occacon of theis his errours and presumpcons.

He was by all the Lords and otheres freede from imputacon of disloyalltie, and for his 5 first contemptes thus sentenced:

That he shold hereafter forbeare to take uppon him the name or tytle of a councellor or meddle in matteres of councell.

That he shold alsoe forbeare to take uppon him the name or tytle of Earle Marciall.

That he shold likewise refrayne the execucon of the office of Master of the Ordynance or take uppon him that tytle.

And lastlie that he shold retorne to the place from whence he came and there remayne prysoner as before untill her Majesties further pleasure were signified.'

14 pp.   (Devereux Papers II/318)

NAMES OF PRISONERS

1600, July 2.   'The names of the prisoners taken the second of Julye, 1600 (Newe Stile) by Grave Morris.'

'The Admirall of Aragon	Counte de Salines
Counte de la Ffere	Don Luis de Valasco
Don Charles de Sapina	

Those which were slain:

Count de Buckoy	Count de Barlamont
LaBarlott	Don Ambrose Landrina
Monsieur de Ffrehingam	Count Ffrederiques van Bergh
The Governor of Dunkirk	Traytor Stanley, commander of the
Don Juan de Reynas	Flemings

Of the Archduke Albertus, of the Duke de Aumall is not knowen whether they be slain or no. The enemy was stronge betwene 11 or 12,000 footemen and 17 cornets horse, which also all their chiefe captaines are moste slaine and taken.

Eight peeces of ordinauns taken.

There weare brought before the tent of his Excellencye 125 ensignes and banners.

The Infanta came with the campe to Brugges.'

1 p.   (Devereux Papers II/328)

NEWSLETTER

(c July 2, 1600)   Count Maurice landed between Ghent and Bruges, warned those of Bruges not to stir or he would ravage their country. He sat down before Nieuport, but hearing that the Archduke had marched he ordered a retreat, leaving behind a regiment of Scots to guard a bridge. The enemy cut the Scots in pieces and were so encouraged thereby that they attacked the States' forces. After two hours' fighting, during which the issue seemed doubtful, victory went to the States, who had the killing of about 5000 and took 1000 prisoners. All the chief commanders were taken or slain, as the Admiral of Aragon, Barlotto, Barlomonte, etc; and all artillery and baggage taken. The like overthrow had not been suffered by the Spaniards these forty years by any knowledge or remembering.

Count Maurice had 11,000 foot and 1000 horse, the Archduke 8000 foot and 500 horse, so that after the defeat of the Scots they were equal in force, except as to horse. The States lost not above 1600 and not a commander. Sir Francis Vere and Lord Grey were wounded. This overthrow was chiefly due to the valour of the English.

The usurper of Desmond is said to be taken by Sir G. Carew. The White Knight is also reported to have come in, and with him one of the Namid O'Neales. The rest of Munster should soon be 'lymitted'. The Earl of Ormond is delivered 'upon hostages put in and conditions promised.'

The King of France is gone 'in post' from Paris to Lyons to punish the Duke of Savoy for breaking peace with him in the matter of the Marquisate of Saluzzo.

One named Nolanus Jordanus, a Neapolitan, a notable, learned and fantastical fellow, who was in England with Monsieur the Ambassador, fell into the hands of the Inquisition at Venice, sent to Rome, tried, found guilty and handed over to the secular arm to be burned.

Mrs Russell mended.

A warrant signed for the Earl of Essex and his knights.

The Earls of Shrewsbury and Rutland's horses were embarked yesterday. *Undated*

2 pp. (Devereux Papers II/326)

R. Petchford to Sir Gelly Meyrick

(Before 1601) 'My Lord commands me to send you word that he will dyne at Essex house to morowe, being Frydaye. You must provide a table that will hould 14 or 15 persons. He will dyne in the chamber next his bed-chamber. Ther comes the Lord Admirall and Sir Ro. Sissell, the reste I knowe not nor I care not.' *Undated*

Holograph 1 p. (Devereux Papers I/299)

On fol.300 there is another undated letter from Petchford to Meyrick which runs as follows: 'My Lord hathe taken order with me and sayeth he will be sicke this 3 or 4 dayes. I demaunded of him yf you should provide dinner at Essex house and he answered, Yes, as well as yf he weare there present. He sayeth my Lord Admirall and Sir Ro. Syssill and others shall dyne ther. Looke not for my Lord for he will not come.' 1p.

Roger Vaughan to Sir Gelly Meyrick

(Before 1601) On behalf of James Lewis, who had served 'under Sir Philip Sidney as on of his gard and after his dethe under Sir William Russell' and was now being unjustly accused of robbery. *Undated*

Holograph 1 p. (Devereux Papers I/312)

The Earl of Essex's Rebellion

1600-1, February 8. 'The first proceedings of ye Earles of Essex and South(amp)ton, together with some speeches that passed between them and ye Lord Admiral, her Majesties Lieftenaunt Generall for that time and Sir Robert Sydney on Sondaie ye viiith of Feb. 1600, anno regni Eliz regine 43.

Upon Sondaie morneinge aboute ix of ye clock being ye viiith of Febr. 1600, as aforesaid, the Lord Keeper, the Earle of Worcester, Sir William Knowles and the Lord Chief Justice were sent from the Courte (then lyeing at Whitehall) to Essex house with message from her Majestie that the Earle of Essex shoulde speedelye dissolve his companie and himself to come to the Courte, with promise that his griefes shoulde bee gratiouslie heard. At whose comming thether the gates were shut and well guarded, yet they themselves were suffered to enter, but not one of their followers admitted thereto. Comminge into the courte at Essex house the Earle of Essex met them and led them throughe twoe roomes well guarded with musketteres into a third roome as well guarded, where atter some few wordes past between them, the Earle left them as prisoners to the chardge of Sir Gilly Merrick, Sir Jo. Davies and Frauncis Tresham, the Earle himself yssueinge forthe with the Earles of Rutland, Southhampton and Bedforde, the Lords Sands and Mounteagle, Sir Charles Davers and Sir Christofer Blounte with manie other knightes and gent(lemen) to the number of iiii^{xx} or thereaboutes, making towardes Ludgate cryeing out for the Queen, for the Queen my masters, giveing out besides that the Earle of Essex that nighte before shoulde have been murthered by the Lord Cobham, Sir Walter Rayleigh and others. Cominge to Ludgate the gates were shutt against them, but at theyr cryeing they were for the Queen and menconing ye intended murther with protestacon that they came into ye cittie for safegarde of their lives, the gates were opened unto them and so they marched into the cittie all on foote, armed onely with swordes and daggers, some having targetes and moste of them French pistoles, through Cheapside untill they came to Sherriffe Smithes house in Fanchurch streete where they stayed some small while, and then came back againe to Gracious streete where they made a stand, and there his companye were increased well nighe to 300. In which time tydinges were brought therof to the Courte. And thereupon the Lorde Burghley was presently dispatched with a King of Herrauldes into London to proclaime the Earle of Essex and all his company traytours with promise of 1000^{li} to him that shoulde take his personne and pardonne to all such as wolde forsake him. Soe cominge in this sorte into Gratious streete they were forced by the Earles side to retyre, the Lord Burleghes horse being hurt under him with shott. At which proclamacon the Earle of Bedford and Lord Cromwell and manie others came back towardes Essex house, and comminge to Ludgate thinking to have passed home againe that waye hee was chardged about Saint Paules churchyarde and his page there slayne. And his father in lawe Sir Xpoffer Blount sore hurt in the head. Then was the Earle of Essex with his companie driven back from thence into Cheapside againe where hee was assaulted by the Knighte Marshalles menn and so enforced to take his waye downe to Queen Hyethe. And there taking as manie boates as they could get, cut the ropes and rowed themselves to Essex house, where when hee came hee founde not ye Lordes whome hee had left presoners there as aforesd, for that they were a little space before delivered by Sir Ferdinando Goudge whoe, as it seemeth, in pollicy to save his owne lief came with a fayned message from the Earle of Essex to Sir Gilly Merrick whereby they were set at libertye, and being suffered to departe after they had been restrained about 2 howers they tooke Sir Ferdinando Goudge to Courte with them by water. And the same Lordes were no sooner comed to ye Courte but newes were broughte thether that the Earle of Essex was comde to Essex house with the Earle of Southampton. Whereupon the Lord Burghley was sent to force the house on ye street side. And the Lord Admiral, Lieutenant Generall, Sir Robert Sidney and Sir Robert Mansfield on the waterside, whoe soone after possest themselves of the gardeyn. The Lord Burghley on the other side had broken the gate and entred the courte wherein were twoe common souldiers onely slayn. The Earles, when they saw the gardeyn possessed with the Lord Admirall accompanied as aforesayde, shewed themselves on the leades, and flourishinge with their drawne swordes above their heades, walked 3 or 4 turnes there and went in againe. The dores of the house were so fortifyed within that no violence wolde break them open. And they had set bookes in the windowes by which the shot lighting on their bookes was so strangled that it was little fencive unto them. Yet Captaine Owen Salisburie was slayne by a shott from St Clementes church steeple as hee was upon the gallerie towards the streete. The resistaunce continewed untill about vi of the clock at nighte. And then the Lord Admirall sent Sir Robert Sydney to summon the Earle of Essex and those that were with him to yeeld themselves. And after the drum had summoned a parley the Earle of Southampton came forthe and shewed himself upon the leades, and asked Sir Robert Sydneye (calling him cossen Sydney) what hee wolde have, who aunsered that hee summoned them for the Lord Admirall her Majestes Lieftenaunte Generall to yeelde themselves, whereupon Southampton replyed thus, Deare cossen Sydneye, to whome wolde yow have us yeelde, to our enemyes? That were to thrust ourselves into perill willinglie. No, said Sir Robert, but yow must yeeld yourselves to her Majestie. That wold wee willinglie dooe, sayde Southampton, but that thereby wee should confesse ourselves guiltie before wee had offended; yet if my Lord Admirall wolde yeelde us honourable hostages for our safe retourne to the place wee will goe and present our selves before her Majestie to whome (God knowes) wee never intended the least harme, and whose royall disposicon wee know to bee such that if wee might but freely declare our mindes before her Majestie, shee coold pardon us and blame those that are moste blame worthie. Theis aethist caterpillers I meane, whoe have layde plottes to bereave us of our lives for safegarde whereof (as the law of nature willeth us) wee have taken up those armes, thoughe wee both dooe and will acknowledge all dutie and obedience to her Majestie unto our lives end. For it is not lykely that wee who have so often adventured our lives in defence of her Majestie and this realme shoulde now proove traytours to the Queen and State. Noe, cossen, no, we detest that name and all traytourous accons. My Lord, quoth Sir Robert Sydney, you must not capitulate with your prince. I know my Lord Admiral will not yeeld to anie such condicons of hostages. Good cossen of Southampton (*sic*), I doe not capitulate with my prince. I do but expostulate with yours. You are a man of armes and know well what belonges therto, yow know wee are bound by nature to defend ourselves against our equalls much more against our inferiours. And cossen, yow cannot but know or at least wise conjecture that if wee should yeeld ourselves, wee should willinglie put ourselves into the wolves mouthes, I mean their handes who will keep us farr inoughe from coming to her Majestie to speak for our selves, or if yt wee were admitted, yet coming before her as captives there lyes (throughe the greatnes of her favour towardes them) will over ballence our truthes. Then, good cossen, what wolde yow doe if you were in our cases. Good my Lord, quoth Sir Robert Sydney, put no such questions. I holde it your best waye to yeelde for yow know this house is of no such force as it can long preserve you. And my Lord Admirall hath alredye sent for pouther and ordinaunce for batterie. And if that prevayles not, hee is purposed to blowe yow up and then there is noe way but one with yow. Well, quoth the Earle of Southampton, let his Lordship dooe his pleasuer, wee purpose not to yeelde without hostages, for wee will rather make choice to dye lyke men with our swordes in our handes then 9 or 10 daies hence to end our lives upon a scaffolde. By standing out, quoth Sir Robert Sydney, there is noe hope, but by yeelding there is some hope afforded you. Well cossen, aunswered Southampton, that is little hope except wee may have hostages. Wee will rather make choice of this wee hope then of yt wee hope. And at theis wordes the Earle of Essex came forthe to the Earle of Southampton and said to Sir Robert Sydney, Good brother Sydney and yow my loving countrimen, nothing doth so much greeve mee as that yow, whome my conscience telleth mee dooe all love mee and for whose safetie I have so often exposed myself to perill, that yow, I say my friends, whose least dropp of bloud-shed wold exceedinglye perplex mee, whoe wold rather fling myself downe headlong from hence then that yow should be endaungered; and those aethistes, myne enemyes, keep aloofe from perill and dare not once approche mee; in fighting against whome if I mighte end my lief, I wold think my death moste honourable that by my death I might end their lives, and that I had done both God and my prince and countrye good service by rooting out such aethistes and caterpillers from the earth. I hope, quoth Sir Robert Sydney, yow doe not meane my Lord Admirall. No, God knowes, quoth the Earle againe, I never tooke him but to bee as honourable in minde as in byrth, though there hath been betwixt us some publique jarrs, which I know on his parte came more throughe others provocacons then anie waies of his owne disposicon. But I mean men of more base condicon, though in greater favoure with her Majestie, who had layde secrett plottes and dampnable devises to bereave mee of my lief, from which purpose my conscience lykewise tells me my Lorde Admiral is most free. Yet, good brother, excuse me if I yeelde not for I will stand to my Lord of Southamptons resolucon. For as for my lief I hate it and have loathed to live anie tymes this xii monthes and more. And I have thoughte it one of the greatest punishmentes that ever God layde upon mee, to suffer me to esscape the daunger of that sicknes which then attacked me. For judge yow, brother, whether it can bee grief or not to a man desscended as I am to have lived in action and ye estimacon as I have doone, to be penned up so long together as I was, to be trodden under foote by such base upstartes, yea and more then that, to have my lief nerely soughte by them; woulde it not trouble yow, yes I am suer it wolde. Well, it is no matter. Death will end all and death shalbe welcome to me. And sith I must dye, and they injoy their wishes, I will dye so honorable as I may and so, good brother, enfourme my Lord Admiral. Well, my Lord, quoth hee, I will retourne your aunswere to his honour. So hee departed and tolde the Lord Admirall the effect of their parley, but he wold yeelde noe hostages to rebells (hee sayd), but sent Sir Robert back againe unto them with another message, which hee, after the drum had sounded the second parley, delivered to Southampton after this sorte. My Lord Admiral will yeeld no hostages, but because hee understandeth that your ladyes are in the house with yow, to thend that the innocent (for so esteemeth your ladies with the gentlewoemen) may not perishe with the guiltye, hee willeth yow to send them forthe and they shalbe safelye and honourablye receaved and conveyed to some other place which they shall best lyke of. Whereunto Southampton replyed sayeing, Wee thank his Lordship for his honourable care of our ladies which sheweth him to bee honourablye desscended. But wee desier him to pardon us also in this case; we prefer our safetie before their freedome. For wee have now fortiffied our doores which stoode us in a good whiles work, and if wee shoulde unfortifye ourselves to let our ladies forthe wee shoulde by that meanes make an open passage for your forces to enter. Yet if my Lord Admiral will graunte us but one howers space to open the passage of our ladyes and another howers space after they bee gone to make it good againe, with promise upon his honour not to make anie attempt upon us in ye mean season, then will wee willingly suffer our ladies to departe. Sir Robert Sidney retourned this their aunswere to the Lord Admiral whoe yeelded to them therein. But by this time, which was about 9 of the clock, was store of powther, shott and ordinance brought thether from the Tower to batter the house, but when Sir Robert brought worde back unto them that they should have their twoe howers space graunted them as they demaunded, and tolde them besides of the provision broughte from the Tower to beate the house, the Earle of Essex requested a time of resolucon which was graunted him: and after they had a while consulted together, the Earles came forthe againe upon the leades, and then the

Earle of Essex tolde Sir Robert Sidney that they wolde yeelde upon theis condicons, viz:

(1) That they mighte bee used as honorable prisoners.

(2) That the Lord Admiral should promise to make faithfull relacon to her Majestie of whatsoever they should say from themselves in their owne defence.

(3) That they might have an honourable and just tryall.

Lastlie, that during their imprisonment they might have such devines for their soules health as were well able to instruct them in matters of religion.

Theis condicons the Lord Admiral promised upon his salvacon and honour to bee perfourmed, whereupon they went downe and opening the dores, eech of them upon their knees surrendered their swordes into the Lord Admirals hands. And the Earl of Essex requested him to desier her Majestie to inflict all ye tormentes upon him that could bee invented, for ye punishment of the rest mighte bee diminished who entred into that action with him, some for friendship, some for kinred, some for affection and some as servantes to their masters. And Southampton requested that thinges doubtfully sayde or doone mighte be construed to the best, which the Lord Admiral sayd should bee doone. Soe from thence they and theyr followers went to their severall places of committmentes as appereth in folio 11 in the latter end of this booke.'

10½ pp. (Devereux Papers VII/124)

THE EARL OF ESSEX'S REBELLION

1600-1, February. 'The names of those that weare committed to the Tower for the Earl of Essexs cause.'

The Tower

Earl of Essex	Lord Rich
Earl of Rutland	Lord Sandes
Earl of Southampton	Lord Mountegle
Earl of Sussex	Lord Cromwell
Earl of Bedford	Greye Brydges

G(atehouse)

Sir Ferdinando Gorge

T(ower)

Sir Charles Danvers

T(ower)

Sir Christopher Blunte

G(atehouse)

Sir Robert Vernon   Sir Henry Linley

F(leet)

Sir Charles Percye

N(ewgate)

Sir John Davis

N(ewgate)

Sir Gellye Merricke

M(arshalsea)

Sir Edward Michelborne   John Tymme
Sir Edward Baynhame   Francis Lyster

Sir William Constable
Sir Thomas Weste
Sir Henry Carye of Kent
Sir Christopher Haydone
Sir John Haydon
Sir George Manners
Sir Edward Littelton
Francis Manners
Mr Tresham
Robert Catesbye
John Littelltone
Mr Downewell
Edmund Burkewell
Mr Gosenall
Francis Smith
William Spratte
Ambrose Clundell
Edward Harte
Edward Reynolds
William Temple
Henry Chensefelde
Anthony Russell
William Grantham
Francis Kinnersley
Edmond Kinnersley
Edward Hanmer
Richard Chomleye
John Arden

Thomas Cundall
Thomas Typpin
Robert Rudall
William Greenall
William Greene
John Morris
John Kemer
Robert Detston
Francis Tredar
John Lymericke
George Cheffyede
John Roberts
John Lymericke
Stephen Men
John Toster
William Perkyn
Bryan Dawson
Thomas Crompton
Symon Johnson
(erased) Vaughan
John Bonnell
Ellis Jones
John Lloyd
Richard Herteforde
Christopher Jarryngtone
John Wheeler
Thomas Medlen
John Wrighte
John Graunte

Christopher Write

Endorsed: 'The names of those that were committed to the Tower for the Earle of Essexs cause.' 1 p. (Devereux Papers II/329)

ACCOUNTS

1607, May 10 to November 20. Accompt of sums paid to Peter Van Lore for jewels, etc, and to others headed: 'A noate of such somes of mony as I have received towardes my debett concernynge the jorny into the Lowe Cuntryes.' The total sum paid was £5575:15:8 of which Van Lore's bill accounted for £3640:7:6.

3 pp. (Devereux Papers III/168)

ANDREW ARCHER TO THE COUNTESS OF CLANRICARDE

1609, August 26. Respecting a proposed marriage between his son, Simon, and her daughter, Lady Dorothy Devereux. Tamworth.

Holograph ½p. (Devereux Papers I/317)

SURVEY

[*c* 1610] Survey of the lands of Robert Devereux, 3rd Earl of Essex, in the counties of Pembroke and Carmarthen.

Survey of the Lordships of Hodson and Laugharne, co. Pembroke, in which shire the Earl held 3706 acres at a rent of £434:8:1 and of the granges

282

of *inter alia* Escoyd, Castle Cossam, Llanreball, Havodwin, Morva Moure and Henneniocke, co. Carmarthen.

A typical entry is: the grange of Morva Moure (f.193).

'Mr Thomas Gwyn houldeth there a ffaire house with 868 acres of lande whereof 180 at 2^s, 200 at 16^d, 170 at 12^d, and 398 at 6^d the acre come to £51:19 *per annum*.

He hath two corne mills with in saide grainge worth £10 *per annum*.

Jenkin David one tenement, Pen a bant cont. 113 acres whereof 28 at 2^s, 28 at 18^d, and 57 at 6^d the acre cometh to £6:6:6 *per annum*.

Morgan Thomas one tenement, Fwerne a merth, conteyninge 66 acres whereof 34 at 2^s, 20 at 18^d, and 12 at 12^d the acre cometh to £5:10 *per annum*.

The thirde of the tithe of the grainge is worth £8 *per annum*.

The acres conteyned in this grainge amounteth to 1241 acres. The rent at these rates cometh to £110:11:6 *per annum*. *Undated*

33 pp. (Devereux Papers III/176)

ACCOUNTS

1612, November 26. Statement of the Earl of Essex's 'receytes after bothe audites' viz, £8000:6:7¾, and of his debts, viz, £20,315:2:4, with further note of debts, October, 1613. The chief creditors are Mr Van Lore, Sir Goddard Pemberton, Sir William Kingsmill, Mrs Tryon, Sir William Harvie, Lady Fortescue, Alderman Bowles, Lord Dudley, Sir Edward Francis and Sir Gilbert Prynne.

3 pp. (Devereux Papers III/203)

SIR ROBERT DIGBY TO THE EARL OF ESSEX

1614-15, February 8. On the means taken to delay a patent to the Primate of Ireland, alleged to be prejudicial to the rights of the Earl, and on an offer of Sir Adam Loftus to purchase the Earl's Irish lands. Dublin.

Holograph Seal 3 pp. (Devereux Papers I/318)

RORY MCMAHON AND COWLO MCMAHON TO THE EARL OF ESSEX

1618-19, February 15. Praying for an addition of better land to their holding on the Earl's estate of Ferney. Ferney.

Signed 1 p. (Devereux Papers I/320)

ACCOUNTS

1619. A copy of a report on the accompt of Thomas Gardiner, Teller of the Exchequer, as 'Receivour of the money coming and growing of the sale' of Crown lands 'made by two severall commissions', dated 20 October 3 Eliza. (1561) and 19 May 5 Eliza. (1563), the accompt being declared 10 March 13 Eliza. (1571). The report bears no date nor name but was apparently made in 17 James 1 (1619).

The accompt showed Gardiner to be indebted to the Crown in £24, 283:9:1½ taken as £24,000, and the report goes on to explain the means taken to secure payment by seizing Gardiner's lands and assigning them to certain persons who took over the debt, under bond to pay it by instalments.

The report gives surveys of the manors of Pembridge, Eardisland, Shobdon, Atforton, Newton, Letton and Stanwey, lands in Tibberton and the Castle of Bromeshall, Wollashall Manor, Sowtham Manor, lands in Trumpington, lands in Kew all granted to Thomas Handford of Wollashall, whose estates at Pembridge, etc, passed to Robert Devereux, 3rd Earl of Essex. *Folio Vellum covers* 62ff. (Devereux Papers VIII)

Sir William Ryves to the Earl of Essex

1619-20. February 23. As to a suit with one Garnon concerning the Earl's rights to certain lands in Ireland. Dublin.

Holograph Damaged by damp 1 p. (Devereux Papers I/322)

Estates and Families

[*c* 1620-30.] Notes concerning the estates and families of Bourchier, Ferrers and Devereux, with copies of deeds, etc.

The volume includes surveys of the Herefordshire estates and of Lamphey; notes of births and deaths of the Ferrers family, *temp* Edward 1 - Henry VI; and the names of 'all the townes of the (3rd) Earle of Essex in his countrey of Farney in Ireland.'

64 ff. (Devereux Papers IX)

Thomas Petre to the Earl of Essex

1623, April 30. As to the terms of a lease to him from the Earl of lands in Ireland 'for plantacion.'

Holograph 1 p. (Devereux Papers I/325)

Lord Cromwell to William Wingfield

(February 1627-8) On a dispute between the Primate of Ireland and the Earl of Essex as to the title of certain lands, and on money matters affecting the Earl. *Undated*

Holograph Endorsed: 'The Lo. Cromwell. Ffeb.1627.' 1 p. (Devereux Papers 1/333)

Similar letters as follows: I/337, *dated February* 9, 1628-9, *Dublin*, 2 pp.; I/339, *dated April* 29, 1629, 1 p.; *and* I/340, *dated June* 20, 1629, *Throwley*, 1 p. *In the third letter he writes*: 'I am for want of company contented to be a sport that I understand not, cockinge (*sc* cock-fighting). An honest papist in Lycke is com to me called Mr Beddel with his cocks, and I have lost 5 battells at 40^s a battel.'

Rentals

1627-39. Rentals of the lands of Robert Devereux, 3rd Earl of Essex, in co. Monaghan, Ireland.

91 pp. (Devereux Papers IV/1)

Accounts

1629, June 18. Certificate of the payment by Sir Thomas Love, knight, deceased, of £130 'in preste to the said Erle (of Essex) as Collonell generall of the Foote in the late expedicion to Cadiz in the yeare 1625.'

1 p. (Devereux Papers IV/73)

Exchequer

1631. Plea in the Exchequer against Robert Devereux, Earl of Essex, for not having taken up his knighthood in accordance with the King's writ of 5 January, 1 Charles 1. Michaelmas Term 7 Charles 1.

Four copies (Devereux Papers IV/76, 81, 85, 89)

WILLIAM SHERBORNE TO THE EARL OF ESSEX

1632, September 27. On business connected with the Earl's estates in Herefordshire. Ross.

Holograph 2 pp. (Devereux Papers I/341)
  Three other letters on similar business are: I/343, *dated April* 25, 1633, *Pembridge*, 2 pp; I/345, *dated April* 17, 1635, *Hereford*, 1 p.; and I/355, *dated August* 20, 1639, *Pembridge*, 2 pp.

LADY HONORA BURKE TO THE EARL OF ESSEX

(Before 1633) November 10. On her father's regret that 'I should settle an affection wheare he had so great a dislike', and her conclusion that 'if he and my frends could find out a fitt one for me and one that I could affect, I would give way.' *

Holograph 2 pp. (Devereux Papers I/363)

LICHFIELD

1636, September 28. Copies of records in the Registry of the Dean and Chapter of Lichfield respecting the liberties of the Canons and their tenants, produced at Lichfield in a cause between Robert Devereux, Earl of Essex, and Michael Biddulph and others, with other papers in the same suit.

Three copies (Devereux Papers IV/153, 169 and 205)

SIR ROBERT TALBOT AND JOHN TREFOR TO SIR WALTER DEVEREUX

1637, May 17. Concerning an allotment of 'tenn tates' of land in Ireland reserved to them by Sir Walter and the Commissioners.

Signed 1 p. (Devereux Papers I/369)

THE COMMISSIONERS FOR THE PRINCIPALITY OF WALES TO THE EARLS OF ESSEX AND SUFFOLK

1638, June 15. 'Whereas uppon the takeinge of the accompt of John Rouse, Esquire, wee find severall great fees allowed unto your lordships as Stewards of severall lordshipps or mannors in South Wales, yett wee find the proffittes at Courts to be of very small value, which (we conceave) is the fault of your lordships deputie Stewards. Wherefor wee have thought fitt hereby to desier your lordshipps that you will make choyse of carefull and honest men to be your deputie Stewards, and to require them to keepe courtes and make forth estreates to the severall bayliffs to the end his Majestie be duly assueared the casuall proffitts within the said mannors; otherwise wee shall be inforced to make stay of your lordshipps fees, which wee doubt not but your lordshipps will prevent.' From his Majestys Commission Howse in Fleet Street, London.

Signed: Lumley, Richard Wynn, James Bagg, D. Cuningham and C. Harbord. 1 p. (Devereux Papers I/347)

CHRISTOPHER WANDESFORDE TO THE EARL OF ESSEX

1638, November 28. Informing him that his cause against Patrick Gernon would be heard on January 27.

Signed Endorsed: 'Delivered by a boye to his Lo. at the Playehouse in Black Friers, the 10th of January.' 1 p. (Devereux Papers I/349)

* She married John Paulet, 5th Marquess of Winchester, in October, 1633.

1638-9, January 28. Enquiring on behalf of a friend whether the Earl had 'any purpose to part with' his Irish lands. Dublin.

Holograph 1 p. (Devereux Papers I/351)

1/371 is a similar letter addressed to Sir Walter Devereux on this subject, and is dated 22 March 1638-9, from Dublin.

CHRISTOPHER WANDESFORDE TO SIR WALTER DEVEREUX

1639, March 28. Expressing his readiness to serve the Earl of Essex in all his affairs in Ireland. Dublin.

Holograph Seal 1 p. (Devereux Papers I/373)

STAR CHAMBER

1639, July 8. Declaration by Robert Devereux, Earl of Essex, of the terms on which he will drop a suit in the Star Chamber against certain persons engaged in a riot against his servants when collecting his tithes at Walton.

3 pp. (Devereux Papers IV/230)

JOHN TREFOR TO THE EARL OF ESSEX

1639, July 29. Reporting on the backwardness in the payment of Irish rents.

Holograph 2 pp. (Devereux Papers I/353)

COLLO MCMAHON TO THE EARL OF ESSEX

1640, August 10. Complaining of harsh treatment by the Commissioners as tenant of Ferney. The arable land has been taken and only the barren land left. Anaghmore.

Holograph Seal 2 pp. (Devereux Papers I/359)

RICHARD HERBERT TO THE EARL OF ESSEX

1640, August 18. 'We are now, my Lord, to march away the 19th of this moneth for Newcastle, where I am perswaded the Scottish army will be before us. Understand me now I pray, my Lord, as among the foote; the horse are in the Bishopricke or about Newcastle long agoe; the reason of my Lord Generalls troope and my troope were commanded hither, my last did expresse. We shall march from hence with 8000 foote armed, beside officers; these regiments which are but halfe armed do notwithstanding take their men entirely with them. Newcastle affourding them armes, the rest are left behind. Co. Will. Vavosuor and Sir Jacob Ashley and Co. Astons regiments are not come up at all; those who are unarmed and left behind are Co. Wentworth regiment and Sir Thomas Culpeper who executs Sir Jacob Ashleys place. Those of the Marquess regiments about Hull once ordered to be cash sherd were taken on againe the same day by an expresse from my Lord Conway unexpectedly received. The Lord Generall being sicke of a ffeavoure gives little hope of seing him here; in his care he is sending word. Yesternight £20,000 was upon the way hither to content the army, 14 dayes being already gained upon the souldier and counsel taken to pay the countrey againe, and this will undoubtedly sound well in a Parliament.

The Scotch army is said to consist of 30,000 foote and 2000 horse, as this is of the most to beleeve. I am apt to credit them strong or else the designe where to mightie for them, as it is now layd. They bring with them 6000 sheepe and 1000 heade of cattle, declaring noe purpose in them at all to injure us in provision, much lesse in person or state. They passe the Tweede at Warke, Carhill & Carram, and purpose the first night to lodge at Fflowden, the second at Hedgley Moore, the third at Burkenfield Moore, where it may chance they will in their own phrase offer again their first complaints unto his Majestie. It is beleeved Newcastle is in great danger for all the force, Northumberland and Bishoppricke, the two regiments already there, Glemmon and Luncefourd and the towne it self cannot exceede five thousand ffoote; the horse are 2500. And as the Scotch do now ly, they are nearer Newcastle then wee are. There are twelve small peeces in the towne, 3lb or 6lb the bullet, a faire traine of artillarie, but happily proportioned to the care taken for draught horses not above 200, as I heare of, and without doubt the foote commanders are much to seeke for waggons, and as yet to whom the charge of one or other shall be commended, I neither see or know.

That grant a disposition in our men to fight, the promptnesse and knowledge how to use their armes, minds quieted in the justnesse of the cause and pay, I cannot perceive how being drawen together in a little cirquit, the meanes to keepe them soe doth appeare. No store of corne, fforredge, maggozins or generall accommodation at any time, so much as falling into deliberation; no wonder the things are not done, and to confesse a truth, I beleeve there is not two companies in the army who have exercised with musketts duly laden; the King husbanding his powder to loose a kingdom.

It is considerable then whither delay makes more against the generall safety or for his Majesties perticular ends, ffor from a purpose of an offensive war wee are fallen uppon the passive part. Consider then how the assertions of many the Scotts would not invade are inverted with prejudice and the miseries threatened by an incredilous hearte (among them) against his Majesties care and foresight for the common good; so now neither person or estate stands cleare against the Kings pleasure or displeasure. That laying the meane consideration aside of compounding them out againe, deare in the dishonorable, purse and vaines of the nobility must bleede and those who most opposed his Majesty, or see a publique ruine.

I confesse Lashley hath done honestlie for the souldiers, giving the King meanes to raise monies and reasons to keepe us together.

Northumberland is given already lost and all intended is defence of Newcastle and Yorke by making good the River Tyne.

As I was closeing this letter the packet came from Newcastle with certaine newes, the Scotch passed the river yesterday and entered England, they declaring themselves resolved to carry both Newcastle and Yorke.

So expecting very shortly your lordship here in the honour of a just commande.' Yorke.

Signed 2 pp. (Devereux Papers I/357)

THE SCOTTISH INVASION

1640, September 8. 'Copie of a letter sent from an alderman of Newcastle concerning the Scotch Invasion.'

3 pp. (Devereux Papers I/361)
(See *Cal. S.P. Dom*, 1640-41, p.28)

1641, July 31.   On business connected with the Irish properties of the Earl of Essex.   Carrick.

Holograph   Seal   2 pp.   (Devereux Papers I/375)

THE EARL OF ESSEX'S WILL

1642, July 4.   Three copies of the will of Robert Devereux, Earl of Essex, dated at the top 4 July 1642, and at the end 1 August 1642.

6 pp.   (Devereux Papers IV/252, 256 and 260)

VERSES

(After September 14, 1646)   Verses in memory of Robert Devereux, 3rd Earl of Essex, and in honour of his sister and co-heir Frances Seymour, Marchioness of Hertford, with the initials T.J. at the end, and marginal notes in the same hand.

'Paynte mee a Mother weeping att ye tombe
Of ye sole hopefull yssue of her wombe,
Now growne to full maturity displaye
Great Agamemnons Iphigenia;
Ledd to ye Altar when by a wyllfull night
And veyled countenance hee shunns ye sight.
Paynte mee a Kingdome burning, and who'd save
It from its ashes carryed to his grave,
Lett flayming Troye appeare, and midst it bee
Sadd Hecuba, sadder Andromache,
Raving att theyre deare champion Hectors fall
And him dragd round about ye fatall wall.
Thow hast not yett exprest our greife, wee have
All these layd in one universall grave.
Not one man but a tribe falls, a tribe knowne
A terrour through Cristendome alone.
Ireland and Spayne and ruyned Germany
Will thinke in him extinct nobilitye.

W.E. of Essex

The grandsire first subdude that nation

Irelande

And hew'd ye way for his victorious sonne,
Who fill'd his fathers tryumphs, was't not hee

Robt E of Essex

Atcheived the famous Cadiz victorye.
When fiercely crossing on the boysterous mayne
Hee surfitts bloody Phillip with his owne slayne.

Robt, ye last

Aske butt ye Neatherlands what there has don
What hee and this, this his renowned son.

E of Essex

Aske butt ye now undone Palatinate
How long hee did uphold that drooping State.
And England knows his valour, such we cou'd
Wish had bene spent upon a forreighne blood.
Tis easy to vanquish an unarmed foe,
Through beaten paths and shallow waters goe.
Hee first cutt through ye Alps and alone stood
Against ye surges of ye highest flood.
Butt this I neede not tell you, lett's but see
What other virtues crown'd his chivalrye,
Without which Valour's brutish: This ye sonn

Had's fathers sweetness and Religion
Of his saint grandsyre, these wee seldome see
Amidst ye ruder camps debaucherye.

His ordering
his soldiers

No undone Tradesman nor exhausted Boore
Ffelt his unjust exactions, or were
Marks of his sword, to him ye injured came
As to a courte of justice, and his name
Did awe from rapine, nor did his souldiers feele
The rigid force of his inraged steele.
Hee ledd them as a father, looke and worde
Did keepe from violence and make accorde
Order, and courage his example moves
And each man fights because hee Essex loves.
All his were men of warr, not any there
Hermaphrodite, parte preist, parte souldier.
He suffers no unhallowed libell flye
Against ye sacred regall dignitye;
Both blasphemyes from campe and pulpitt fright
And made them severall things, to preach and fight.

His carriage
to his
enemye

These to his gallantryes of courtesyes,
Meeknesse and justice shows to his enemyes.
He was ye same to them, none ere does knowe
Him tread ye neck of his newe vanquisht foe;
Counts them as freinds and brethren and preferrs
The Patrons title fore the Conquerors;
And whensoere to battle hee proceeds
Compassion melts his valour, his heart bleeds;
As wee a sweete and tender Virgin see,
Oft skill'd in med'cnall hearts and surgery
When shee doth ope and launce and search a wound
Now shreeks and trembles, ready now to swound;
Her gentle heart doth feele her patients greife
And mercy makes her feare to give releife.
Hee with this meekness marcheth to ye warr
Considers those hee fights with brethren are,
And that which fills his and his souldiers veyne
Is ye same blood that issues from ye slayne.
Soe in this both ye adverse parts agree
Wish such a generall such an enemy.

His carriage
to ye King

But when ye altered face of things appears,
And whither tend those jealousyes and fears,
With indignation lays his gauntlett downe
Raged hee had fought so long putt on his gowne
And now appears true Essex, one that wou'd
For truth and freedom sacrifice his blood.
As when in flight ye King hee did espy
Awed with ye reverend sence of Majestye
The flying bullets peirce his loyall heart,
Trembles for him more then himselfe should smart.

Upon ye motion
of committing
ye King

Soe now hee stands his champion and dares here
Professe hee would not bee his conqueror
Nor captivate him whome they must obeye

289

Hands manacled, ye scepter hardly swaye.
Twould be a shame to noble souls to have
Him bee theyre King that once had bene theyre slave,
That his just priviledge att least must bee
Which every subject challenged, *Libertye*.
This hee decrees, and no man dares it breake,
They knewe that hee could fight as well as speake.
By this to his greate honour itt appears
His warr was still against ill counsellors.
Howe hee obstructs wylde motions! How he aws
The subtle undermyners of ye laws!
A reall publique man, whilst there he sate
Sole ballast of ye uneven tottering State.

To ye Kings party Aske but ye wyddowe, whose continuall tears
With laden hands and justice he still chears.
Aske wee butt those whome warrs calamity,
And ye Allmightye's secrett just decree,
Wasted and broaken now does captivate;
Hee was theyre patron and theyre advocate;
And well considered that ye powerfull God
Gives not ye leave of judgement to his rodd,
Or that his people scourged should trampled be
And buy themselves or lose theyre libertye.
But when ye Instruments doe savage growe
He can ye rodd into ye burning throwe;
Will be avenged on him whose brother tears
When hee himselfe is deepe to in arrears.
These needs must wayte, this fatall exequie
And feelingly recorde his memorye.
Sadd tears and silence all does overspread
Not cause hee only, but his house is dead.
Butt stay, for though ye name of Essex bee
Extinct, his father has posteritye.

His 2 wives Heaven would that House should fall rather than bredd
By an adulterous or a spurious bedd,
A Saynt should nurse itt up, one that should bee
A patterne att ye least of Chastity.

Wm Ms Hertford E.D. of Somerset beheaded by ye Papists treachery for the advancing Prot Ma(ry) Q of France, dr to H(enry) 7 La. Marchiones of Hertford Joyn'd unto such a family as might
Rather increase then darken theyre great light,
Such as hee is whose blood and honour come
From Somersets renowned martyrdome;
From her fayre wombe whose fathers royall lyne
Does our divided roses still combyne,
Such as his noble sister whome ye courte
Hath taught no other vanity or sporte
Then faste and weepe and praye, whose spirritt appears
As greate in suffring as in doing theyrs.
What ere in all that House could gallant bee,
Exceeds in her and her posteritye.
Walter and Roberts there you'l easily fynde
These like in shape, all in theyre noble mynd.
She cam an Heyre, upon an heyre afford

2 sonns And should these fayle, wants not a threefold cord.

3 daughters

Lett butt these sonns and these sweet daughters live,
Essex greate memory will still survive.'*

4 pp. (Devereux Papers IV/300)

Essex Property

1646-7, March 19. 'A view of writings and evidences concerning the estate of Robert, late Earl of Essex, taken at York House 19° Martii, 1646-7.'

48 pp. (Devereux Papers IV/275)

Narrative of the Earl of Essex's Bailiff

(1659) 'A Booke of severall concer(n)ments': narrative by the bailiff of the Earl of Essex for Ross, Ross Farran and Fownhope of the troubles that befell him in his office during the Civil War, the decay of rents, etc. It was apparently written in 1659, when the manors had descended to Frances, Marchioness of Hertford.

When my dear lord and master was made choice of by the Parliament to be general of their army and he, coming down to Worcester in the head thereof, sent to Ross to Walter Kyrle, esquire, and myself to come to him thither. A little before the fight at Edgehill in 1642 he conferred on Kyrle the stewardship of all his manors in Herefordshire and on me the bailliwick of Ross, Ross Farran and Fownhope, displacing one Toby Payne. I collected the rents from the several tenants till Prince Maurice came to Ross, to which town I had sent the money and books for safety. This was the worst thing I could have done for I had not only lost £100 but was forced to flee. Before I paid in the money to the Steward I was taken prisoner to Goodrich Castle by soldiers sent from their captain whose name was Giffard, and forced to enter bond not to stir in that business any more. The soldiers made havoc of the books. Soon afterwards I was ordered to go to Hereford to the Commissioners of Array to be examined about the rents: but the books were either in Prince Maurice's or Captain Giffard's hands. They sent me to Goodrich to copy out what was there, and afterwards gave the charge of collecting the rents to Captain Wigmore. This continued till 1645 when I was appointed by letters from his Lordship to Colonel Birch to settle me in the place again, which he did. But the people of that part being most addicted to the King's party were very backward in paying in their rents. Never any of the King's party came into the forest but I was sure to be plundered by them. My health was so much affected that in 1649 Mr Kyrle persuaded me to resign. I now ask to be reinstated with a fit man as deputy, because I alone can get things straight. There follow details of arrears, etc.

13 pp. (Devereux Papers IV/266)

Collections relating to Robert Dudley, Earl of Leicester and Robert Devereux, 2nd Earl of Essex

(1) 'The Copie of a letter written by a Master of Arts in Cambridge to a friend in London,' (i.e. 'Leicesters Commonwealth'). ff.1-100.

(2) Copies of letters and papers of or relating to Robert Devereux, 2nd Earl of Essex, viz:

(a) Earl of Essex to Queen Elizabeth beginning 'My dutifull affection to your Majestie'. *Undated* (Printed in *Cabala* 1691, p.215) f.101.

---

* Robert Devereux, 3rd Earl of Essex, died on 14 September 1646.

(b)   Sir Thomas Egerton, Lord Keeper, to the Earl of Essex beginning 'It is often seen that a slander by'.   *Undated* (Printed in *Cabala* p.216) f.102.

(c)   'The aunswere of the Earl Marshal (Essex) to ye Lorde Keeper' beginning 'There is not a man'.   *Undated* (Printed in *Cabala*, p.217) f.102b.

(d)   Anthony Bacon to the Earl of Essex after he was censured in the Star Chamber (November 29, 1599), beginning 'Her Majesties proceedings'. *Undated* (See *infra* p.266) f.105 b.

(e)   The Earl's answer to the above beginning 'I thank you for your kinde and carefull letter'.   *Undated* (See *infra* p.268) f.108.

(f)   Speeches by the Lords of the Council in the Star Chamber 'the last sitting in ye end of Michaelmas Term 1599'.   (See *Cal.S.P.Dom 1598-1601*, pp.347-51) f.109.

(g)   The Lord Keeper's speech in the Star Chamber, February, 1600-1, beginning 'The Consideracions of these late accidents'.   (See *Cal.S.P.Dom 1598-1601*, pp.553-4) f.115b.

(h)   'Mr Secretaries (Sir Robert Cecil's) speech there the verie same daye', beginning 'Iff I had knowne I should have spoken'. (See *Cal.S.P.Dom 1598-1601*, pp.554-5) f.118.

(i)   The Earl of Essex to the Earl of Southampton 'whilest he was prisoner at York House with the Lord Keeper', beginning 'As neyther nature nor custome'.   *Undated* (Printed in T.Birch, *Memoirs of the reign of Queen Elizabeth*, Vol. II, p.484) f.121.

(j)   'The first proceedings of ye Earles of Essex and Southampton, together with some speeches that passed between them and ye Lord Admiral, her Majesties Lieftennant generall for that time, and Sir Robert Sydney in London ye 8th of February, 1600-1.' (See *Lives of the Devereux*, Vol. II, pp.141-7 and *infra* pp.279-80) f.124.

(k)   The arraignment of the Earls of Essex and Southampton, 19 February, 1600-1. (See *Lives of the Devereux*, Vol. II, pp.149-164 and *Cal.S.P.Dom 1598-1601*, p.587) f.129b.

(l)   The manner of the Earl of Essex at the time of his death, 25 February, 1600-1. (See *Lives of the Devereux*, Vol. II, pp.186-190 and *Cal.S.P.Dom 1598-1601*, pp.592-4) f.147b.

Small Quarto Vellum covers Early 17th Century 149ff. (Devereux Papers VII)

A

Abergwili (Aberguilley), Carms.
  College of, 257
Abermarlais (Abermarles), Carms., 249
Abnett, Ralph, 255
Acunha (Acunya), Don Juan d',
  Captain of Guipuzcoa.
  entertains Cobham, 173
Adforton (Atforton), Herefs.
  manor of, 283
Admirall, The. See Coligny.
Admiralty, Judge of, 195
Adrianson, Cornelis, shipper of
  Bergen-op-Zoom.
  involved in kidnapping of Story, 225
Aerschot, Jeanne Henriette,
  Duchesse d', wife of following.
  her portrait at Leicester House, 203
Aerschot (Askot), Philippe de Croy,
  Duc d'.
  his portrait at Leicester House,
  203
Africa.
  globe of, at Leicester House, 221
Agard (Agar), William, of Foston.
  dispute with Henry Cavendish,
  102, 126
Aglionby, Thomas, of Hornsey.
  letter from, 198
Aguilar (Agular), Don Alonso
  (Allownso) de, 144
Alanson, Duke of. See Anjou,
  François, Duc d'.
Alava, Don Francisco de, Spanish
  Ambassador to France, 172
Albert (Albertus), Cardinal Archduke
  of Austria, Governor of the Spanish
  Netherlands, 276
  defeated by Count Maurice at
  Nieuport, 264, 276
Aldermaston, Berks.
  Queen at, 189
Alderney, Island of.
  complaints of inhabitants of, 255
Aldersgate Street, London.
  letter dated from, 50
Alkmaar, in Holland, 214
Allen, Cardinal William, 211
  subversive books printed and
  distributed by, 211

Allington, Mr., 21
Allington, Sir Giles, of Horseheath.
  letter from, 240
Allington, Margaret, Lady, wife of
  preceding, 240
Almayns. See Germany.
Alnwick (Annewick), Northumb.
  letter dated from, 44
Alps, The.
  mentioned in verses, 288
Alquenalla.
  Spanish tax called, 160
Alva, Fernando Alvarez de Toledo,
  Duke of, 169, 231
  his portrait at Leicester House, 222
  details of his forces, 231
  defeat of his mercenaries, 231, 232
Alvecote, Warwicks.
  survey of Earl of Leicester's lands
  at, 200
Alyson, ------, of Fleet Street,
  London, 124
Ambassadors, Envoys, etc.
  Emperor, The:
    to England. See Preyner; Stolberg.
  England:
    to France. See Cobham, Sir Henry;
    Dale, Dr. Valentine;
    Howard, Sir George; Sackville,
    Sir Thomas; Stafford,
    Sir Edward; Walsingham,
    Sir Francis.
    to Low Countries. See Gresham,
    Sir Thomas.
    to Scotland. See Randolph,
    Sir Thomas.
    to Spain. See Chamberlain, Sir
    Thomas; Cobham, Sir Henry.
    to Turkey. See Barton, Edward.
  France:
    to England. See Bellièvre; Foix;
    La Mothe-Fénélon; La Noele;
    Montmorency; Noailles;
    Vieilleville.
    to Scotland. See Courcelles.
  Navarre, King of:
    to England. See Clermont
    d'Amboise.
  Scotland:
    to England. See Keith; Maitland;
    Stewart.
    to France. See Seton.

Spain:
to England. *See* Glajon; Guaras; Mendoza.
to France. *See* Alava.
Amboise, in France.
letter dated from, 154
America.
globe of, at Leicester House, 221
Amsterdam, in Holland.
adheres to Prince of Orange, 232, 233
Amurath III, Sultan of Turkey.
refuses to meet Spanish and Catholic League envoys, 116
prepares military action against Spain, 116
Anaghmore, Ferney, co. Monaghan.
letter dated from, 286
Anderson, Sir Edmund, Lord Chief Justice of Common Pleas.
case between Earl and Countess of Shrewsbury heard before, 54, 60
Commissioner at trial of Queen of Scots, 74
takes part in Earl of Essex's trial, 269
Andrews (Andrewe, Andrewes), Thomas, of Charwelton, Sheriff of Northamptonshire.
charged with duty of bringing Queen of Scots to her execution, 80
signs letter to Earl of Shrewsbury, 92
Andwarpe. *See* Antwerp.
Angus, Earl of. *See* Douglas, William.
Anhuniog (Henneniocke), Cards.
grange of, 283
Anjou, François, Duc d'Alençon, later Duc d', 28, 36, 206
his visit to England, 24
his agent dines with Earl of Leicester, 24
reported offers of land and marriage to, 24
his devotion to Queen stressed, 24
Low Countries reported to be inclined to entrust themselves to, 28
reference to agreement with Low Countries, 30
sends de Buhy to England, 30
discusses peace terms with Henry of Navarre at Jarnac, 30
at Bruges, 37
problem of payment of his forces, 37
expected in London, 201, 202
desirous of arranging peace between his brother and King of Navarre, 202
his portrait at Leicester House, 203
his agent. See Simier; Vray.
Anjou, Henri, Duc d'. *See also* Henry III, King of France.

negotiations for Queen's marriage with, 177
his honourable treatment of Coligny, 184
Anne of Denmark, Queen, wife of James VI and I, 133
Anne, Princess, daughter of Emperor Maximilian II and wife of Philip II of Spain, 169
Annewick. *See* Alnwick.
Anslowe, Mr., 150
Antonio, Don, Prior of Crato and claimant to the throne of Portugal.
not expected to hold out against Spanish forces, 28
in London, 36
some opinions of, 36
his preparations for expedition to Azores, 36, 40
Antwerp (Andwarpe, Andwerpe), in Belgium, 225, 231
letters dated from, 142, 147, 155, 159, 232
surrenders to Parma, 45, 57
River Scheldt blocked at, 116
post of, 150
news from, 231, 232
Appleyard (Appliard), John, half-brother of Amy Robsart, 148
Appleyard, Philip, of Wymondham, 159
Apricot trees.
cultivation of, 131
Arabella, Lady. *See* Stuart, Lady Arabella.
Aragon, Admiral of. *See* Mendoza.
Archecrage, ------.
sent by Lord Robert Dudley to France, 150
Archer, Andrew, of Tamworth.
letter from, 282
Archer, Simon, son of preceding.
proposed marriage with Lady Dorothy Devereux, 282
Archers.
Earl of Leicester's request to Earl of Shrewsbury for, 63
Arden, John, partisan of 2nd Earl of Essex.
imprisoned in the Marshalsea, 282
Argall, -----, of the English expeditionary force in South Beveland.
killed in skirmish with Spaniards, 230
Argall, Rowland, stepson of Sir Giles Allington and Sheriff of co. Down, 240
Arguyle, Lord of. *See* Campbell, Archibald.
Armada, Spanish.
sets sail for England, 91

dispersed by bad weather, 92
reported to have landed men in
    Moray Firth, 93
said to be on its way home, 94
ships wrecked on Irish coast, 94, 95
premature celebrations in Spain and
    Italy of its falsely reported
    victory, 95
defeat celebrated in England and
    Protestant countries, 95
expected to arrive off coast of
    France, 211
reported to be at Falmouth, 212
Armagh, Archbishop of. *See* Lancaster,
    Thomas.
Armagnac (Carmignay), George d',
    Cardinal d'.
sent by Pope to France, 159
Armiger, Robert, father-in-law of Philip
    Browne, 168
Arnold, Richard, Gloucestershire tenant
    of Earl of Shrewsbury, 56
Arran, Earl of. *See* Hamilton,
    James.
Arras, in France, 115
Arras, Bishop of. *See* Perrenot.
Arthalens (?), in Netherlands.
captured by Dutch, 231
Arundel, Earl of. *See* Fitzalan, Henry;
    Howard, Philip; Howard, Thomas.
Arundel Place *or* House, Strand,
    London.
letter dated from, 184
Arundell, Charles, recusant, later exile
    and conspirator, brother of
    following.
involved in Earl of Northumberland's
    intrigues to release Queen of
    Scots, 48
deposition of, 204
Arundell, Sir Matthew, of Wardour
    Castle.
letter from, 126
Ashby de la Zouch, Leics.
letters dated from, 155, 158
Asheton, Sir Walter. *See* Aston, Sir
    Walter.
Ashford, Derbys., 48
letter dated from, 66
Ashley, Sir Jacob. *See* Astley, Sir Jacob.
Ashperton Park, Herefs., 254
Ashton (Asheton), Thomas, of Stockton.
letter from, 191
Ashwood, Staffs., 62
Aske, Robert, Sheriff of Yorkshire.
seminary priests to be sent under
    guard to, 92
Askew (Asku), Anne.
letter from, 214
Askot, Duke of. *See* Aerschot.
Asthall (Astle), Oxon.
letter dated from, 45

Astley, Mr. *See* Atslowe, Edward.
Astley (Ashley), Sir Jacob, of Maidstone.
his regiment, 286
Astley, John, Steward of the manor of
    Enfield, 190
letter from, 153
reference to his disgrace, 154
Astley, Katherine, wife of preceding.
letter from, 154
Aston, Yorks.
letter dated from, 73
Aston, Colonel Arthur, Sergeant-Major-
    General of Royalist army.
his regiment, 286
Aston (Asheton), Sir Walter, of Tixall.
his dispute with Kynersley, 96
Astronomy.
reference to purchase of 'instrument
    of', 136
Atforton. *See* Adforton.
Athlone, co. Westmeath.
letters dated from, 210, 257
Atkins, Robert, Groom of the Queen's
    Poultry.
petition to Earl of Leicester, 225
Atslowe (Astley), Edward, of London,
    physician.
at Buxton, 21
Atye, Arthur, secretary of Earl of
    Leicester.
letter from, 215
Aubigny, d'. *See* Stuart, Esmé.
Aubrey, William, Master in Chancery,
    226
Auckland. *See* Bishop Auckland.
Augsburg, Confession of, 169
Aumale (Aumall), Duc d'. *See*
    Lorraine, Charles de.
Austria, Archduke of. *See* Charles.
Avignon (Avyllen), in France.
reported to have been offered by
    Pope to Duke of Anjou, 24
Welsh book printed at, 182
Avylay. *See* Wailly.
Avyllen. *See* Avignon.
Axall, Earl of. *See* Stewart, John.
Aylmer, John, Bishop of London, 200
probably the 'Mr. Elmer'
recommended for Deanery of
    Windsor, 153
Azores (Isles of Azorres).
Don Antonio's preparations in France
    and England for expedition to, 36

B

Baarland (Barland) in South Beveland,
    Zeeland.
English expeditionary force's base
    at, 230
Babington, James

295

reference to killing of, 145
Bacon (Bakone), Mr., of Kew, 149
Bacon, Anthony, brother of following, 261
letter from, 266
letter to, 268
Bacon, Francis, later Viscount St. Alban, 267
letter from, 210
Earl of Essex's opinion of, 269
assists prosecution in trial of Earl of Essex, 269
Bacon, Sir Nicholas, Lord Keeper.
letter from, 194
Bagenal, Sir Nicholas. See Bagnall, Sir Nicholas.
Bagenall, Sir Ralph. See Bagnall, Sir Ralph.
Bagg, Sir James, of Saltram, Commissioner for the Principality of Wales.
signs letter to Earls of Essex and Suffolk, 285
Bagnall (Bagenal), Sir Nicholas, of Carlingford, Marshal of the English army in Ireland.
letter from, 141
Sir John Salusbury's wish to marry his nephew to daughter of, 190
Bagnall (Bagenall), Sir Ralph, of Barlaston, 138
letter from, 165
Bagnall, Sir Samuel, later Chief Commander in Ulster and Governor of Newry.
commands company in Cadiz expedition, 265
Bagot, Anthony, of Blithfield, later in the service of 2nd Earl of Essex, 250
Bagot (Bagott), Richard, of Blithfield.
letter from, 239
appointed collector of Queen's loan in Staffordshire, 98
Earl of Essex's Earl Marshal staff in custody of, 248
Bagshaw (Bagshawe), John, prebendary of Lichfield.
signs letter to Earl of Essex, 253 and n
Baker, George, surgeon to the Queen, 255
Baldwin, Baldwyne. See Bawdewyn, Thomas.
Balsall, Warwicks., 151
Baltinglass, Lord. See Eustace, James.
Balvenie (Balvany), Banffshire.
letter dated from, 170
Bangor, Bishop of. See Robinson, Nicholas.
Barbary, King of, 201
Barkeley, Lady. See Berkeley, Katherine.
Barker, Edward, Registrar to the Queen, 206n, 220, 225
letter from, 257
letters to, 220, 222
Barker, Francis, of Fleet Street, London.
letter dated from house of, 192
Barkley, Sir Henry. See Berkeley, Sir Henry.
Barking (Berckynge), Essex, 170
Barkswell. See Berkswell.
Barlamont, Count of. See Berlaymont.
Barland. See Baarland.
Barnaby, J.
letter from, 178
Barneby, Thomas, of Burnby.
appointed guardian to Bosevile, 29
Barn Elms (Barne Lands), Surrey, residence of Sir Francis Walsingham.
letters dated from, 56, 73, 76
Barnes, -----, 150
Barnet, Herts., 102
Barney (Blane), Captain Edward de, renegade and spy.
ordered to Ostend, 214
Barret, James, 236
Barroll, William, in the service of Earl of Essex.
letters to, 236, 238, 241, 246
his account for Earl of Essex's estates in Herefordshire, 248
Barrow. See Bergen-op-Zoom.
Barton, Edward, English Ambassador to Turkey.
sends information concerning Franco-Turkish collaboration, 116
Barwyke. See Berwick.
Basildon (Bastleden), Berks.
letter dated from, 178
Basing, Hants.
letter dated from, 160
Baskerville, George, son of Sir Thomas Baskerville of Brinsop.
to join Earl of Essex's expedition to Ireland, 237
Baskerville (Baskerfille), Henry, kinsman of following, 164
Baskerville, Sir James, of Eardisley (d1573).
letter from, 164
Baskerville, James, of Westhide.
letters from, 254, 263
Baskerville (Baskervyle), Richard, brother of following.
to join Earl of Essex's Irish expedition, 237
Baskerville (Baskervyle), Thomas, son of following.
to join Earl of Essex's Irish

expedition, 237
Baskerville (Baskervyle), Sir Thomas, of
  Netherwood in Thornbury, Herefs.
  letter from, 237
Baskerville (Baskerfille), Sir Thomas,
  of Brinsop, brother of Sir James
  Baskerville, 164, 262
  his claim to certain parks, 249
Basseford. See Beresford, Henry.
Bassett, Sir Arthur, of Umberleigh, J.P.
  dies of gaol fever, 68
Bassett, John, of Fledborough, Sheriff
  of Nottinghamshire, 117
Basshe, Mr.
  Lord Robert Dudley dines with, 150
Bastledon. See Basildon.
Bataille, Monsieur de, French
  diplomatist and privy councillor.
  to go to England, 187
Bate, John, in the service of Robinson
  Harcourt.
  killed in an affray, 234
Bath, Somerset.
  Earl of Leicester at, 196
Bath and Wells, Bishop of, 219
Bathing.
  reference to erection of bathing tent,
  149
Bawdewyn (Baldwin, Baldwyne),
  Thomas, in the service of Earl of
  Shrewsbury, 50
  letters from, 24, 29, 44
  letter to, 34
  sent to Walsingham, 46
Bawkin, -----, 29
Bayard.
  name of horse bestowed on Sir Henry
  Compton, 169
Bayarde Knightley.
  name of horse bestowed on Flemish
  Ambassador, 169
Baylie or Bayly, Thomas, in the service
  of Earl of Shrewsbury, 41
  letter from, 71
Baynard's Castle, London.
  Don Antonio lodged at, 36
Baynham, Sir Edmund (Edward), of
  Boxley.
  imprisoned in the Marshalsea, 281
Baynham (Baynam, Beinham),
  William, Surveyor-General to the
  Earl of Leicester, 200, 220
Bayon, Bartholomew, Captain, 195
Beale, Robert, brother-in-law of Sir
  Francis Walsingham.
  letters from, 46, 91
  to examine proposals made by Queen
  of Scots, 42
  to convey sentence of death to Queen
  of Scots, 78
  given commission for execution of
  Queen of Scots, 79

signs letter to Earl of Shrewsbury, 92
  his speech in House of Commons on
  pluralities disliked by bishops, 100
Beamond, Justice. See Beaumont,
  Francis.
Bear, The, inn, Bridge Foot, London,
  150
Beaumanoir (Bewmanner), Leics., 155
  letter dated from, 238
Beaumaris, Anglesey.
  Earl of Essex at, 246
Beaumont (Beamond), Francis, Judge
  of the Common Pleas, 259
Beaumont, James.
  petition to Earl of Leicester, 225
Beaumont Leas, Leics.
  lease of pasture called, 226
Beauvais, Elizabeth de Hauteville,
  Dame de Lore, styled Comtesse de,
  wife of Odet de Coligny, Comte de
  Beauvais.
  her portrait at Leicester House, 203
Beauvois, Company of, in the Spanish
  Army of the Low Countries.
  defeated near Middelburg, 233
Beckwith, Roger, of Selby, 38, 40
Beddel, Mr., of Leek, recusant, 284
Bedell (Byddle), Dr. Arthur, canon of
  Lichfield, 199
Bedford, Earl of. See Russell, Edward;
  Russell, Francis.
Bedford, Lady. See Russell, Bridget.
Bedford, F. See Russell, Francis.
Bedow, Captain, of the English
  expeditionary force in Walcheren.
  killed in action near Middelburg, 232
Beeston (Beson), -----, in the service of
  Earl of Shrewsbury, 70, 74
Belvoir Castle, Leics.
  letter dated from, 157
Bellièvre (Bellyevre), Pomponne de,
  French Ambassador to England.
  sent to intercede for Queen of Scots,
  76, 77(2), 78
  his audience with Queen, 78
Benche, The. See King's Bench.
Benet, Stephen, of Coventry.
  charged with possessing gold
  clippings, 152
Benger, Sir Thomas, of Berkhamsted.
  letter from, 144
Bennington Park, Herts., 238
Bennison (Benyssone), John, in the
  service of Lord Robert Dudley, 162
Benthall (Bentall), George, in the
  service of Earl of Shrewsbury.
  Queen opposes his appointment as
  Gentleman Porter to Queen of
  Scots, 52
Bentley, Yorks.
  survey of Lord Robert Dudley's lands
  at, 167

Benvoyse, Monsieur de, Governor of
Middelburg, 231
defeat of his troops, 232
Beoley, Worcs.
letter dated from, 158
Berckynge. *See* Barking.
Beresford (Berysforde), Edward, of
Enstone.
letter from, 235
Beresford (Basseford, Berisforde),
Henry, in the service of the
Countess of Shrewsbury, 41, 69
Queen forbids Earl of Shrewsbury to
proceed by law against, 67
Berg (Bergh), Count Frederick van den,
cousin of Count Maurice of
Nassau, and Colonel-General in the
army of the Archdukes.
reported killed in action at Nieuport,
276
Berg (Bergh), Count William van den,
brother-in-law of Count Maurice of
Nassau.
reported to have entered Delft, 230
Bergeinie, Lord. *See* Nevill, Henry.
Bergen-op-Zoom (Barrow), in Brabant,
225
Marquis of, 146
Keeper of the English House in. *See*
Bradley, John.
Bergh. *See* Rheinberg.
Bergh, Grave van. *See* Berg.
Berghes, Adrien, Marquis de (*d*1572).
his portrait at Leicester House, 203
Berisforde. *See* Beresford, Henry.
Berkeley, Henry, 7th Lord Berkeley,
194
letter from, 172
Berkeley (Barkley), Sir Henry, of
Bruton, 260
Berkeley (Barkeley), Katherine, Lady,
wife of 7th Lord Berkeley, 172
mourner at funeral of Queen of
Scots, 83
Berkhamsted (Berkhamstead), Herts.
letter dated from, 144
Berkshire.
Campion arrested in, 35
map of, at Leicester House, 204
Berkswell (Barkswell), Warwicks.
dispute over stewardship of, 154
Berlaymont (Barlamont, Barlomonte),
Floris, Count of, Spanish
commander, 276
said to have been killed in battle at
Nieuport, 276
Bernadino, -----, in the service of the
Duke of Nemours, 170
Bernet, Raymond Roger de, Captain of
Boulogne, 93
Bertie, Peregrine, 13th Lord
Willoughby of Eresby, Commander

of the English forces in the Low
Countries, 214
directed to investigate complaint
against Stanhope, 103
Berwick (Barwyck, Barwyke),
Northumb., 44, 90, 148, 150, 226
letters dated from, 139, 140, 141,
148, 174, 187(2)
Privy Council criticised for curtailing
expenditure on defence of, 140
office of clerk of the council at, 148
Treasurer at. *See* Browne, Sir
Valentine.
Bery, -----, brother of the landlord of
the *Three Tuns* inn in Fleet Street,
London, 122
Berysforde, Edward. *See* Beresford,
Edward.
Besbeche, Henry, steward of the Earl of
Leicester at Kenilworth.
letter from, 199
Beson, Mr. *See* Beeston.
Betts, Richard, minister of Kenilworth.
petition to Earl of Leicester, 217
Beveland, South (Suyd Beverland), in
Zeeland.
English force lands in, 230
English troops return to Flanders
from, 230
Beverley, Yorks.
Lord Robert Dudley granted manor
and borough of, 164
survey of Lord Robert Dudley's lands
at, 167
Bewchamp.
picture of, at Leicester House, 207,
224
Bewmanner. *See* Beaumanoir.
Beynham, Richard, of Sapperton.
letter from, 240
Beza, Theodore, French Protestant
writer and minister in Geneva.
his works, 251
Bicknor, Glos.
Earl of Essex's tenants at, 240
Biddulph, Michael, of Elmhurst.
case between Earl of Essex and, 285
Bilbao, in Spain, 195
Bilborough (Bylbrowe), Notts., 22
Billiards.
table at Leicester House, 221
Billingbeare (Pillingbere), Berks.
letter dated from, 194
Billings, Captain.
takes part in Cadiz expedition, 265
Bingham, Sir Richard, Governor of
Connaught.
letters from, 210, 257
Birch, Colonel John, Parliamentary
commander, 291
Bird, Mr.
dines with Lord Robert Dudley, 150

Bird (Burd), Edmund, 136
Bird (Byrde), William, of London, mercer.
Lord Robert Dudley borrows money from, 148
Birkhead, Martin, of Wakefield and Gray's Inn.
letter from, 37
Biscay (Biscaye), in Spain, 253
Bishop Auckland, co. Durham.
letter dated from, 192
Bishopsgate, London, 220
Bishopsgate Street, London.
letter dated from, 102
Bitterscote (Bittercourt), Staffs., 207
Black Bark, The.
soldiers conveyed to Ireland in, 242
Blackburne (Blackurne), Launcelot, seminary priest, formerly of Douai College.
to be sent to London for trial, 80
Blackfriars, London.
Playhouse at, 285
Blackurne, Lancelot. See Blackburne, Launcelot.
Blackwell, -----, of London.
his house considered suitable to accommodate French envoy, 181
Blagrew, Mrs.
her death and burial, 128
Blaklenborough. See Blankenberge.
Blane, Captain. See Barney, Captain Edward de.
Blankenberge (Blaklenborough), in Belgium.
Parma's forces encamped at, 211
Blithfield (Blithfaild), Staffs., 248
Blois, in France.
letters dated from, 184, 186
Blondeston (Blundeston), Christopher, of Haughton.
signs evidence concerning Stanhope's defamation of Earl of Shrewsbury, 105
Blount (Blunte), Sir Charles, later 8th Lord Mountjoy and Earl of Devonshire, commander of company of foot at Ostend, 217
commands company in Cadiz expedition, 265
Blount, Sir Christopher, Gentleman of the Horse, Marshal of Earl of Essex's army in Ireland, 209, 219, 224(2)
letter from, 224
commander in Cadiz expedition, 263
composition of his regiment, 265
sends Lee to have talks with Earl of Tyrone, 270
takes part in Earl of Essex's rebellion, 278
wounded in skirmish at St. Paul's

Churchyard, 278
imprisoned in the Tower, 281
Bluemantle Pursuivant. See Thomas, James.
Blunden, Andrew, of Bishop's Castle and the Middle Temple.
letter from, 258
Blundeston, Christopher. See Blondeston.
Blunte, Sir Charles. See Blount, Sir Charles.
Blythman, Jasper, of Burton, Yorks.
letter from, 39
Bockenfield Moor (Burkenfield Moore), Northumb.
Scottish forces plan to camp at, 287
Bodenham, Herefs.
Earl of Essex's tenants at, 237, 238, 248
Boethius, Anicus Manlius Severinus, Roman scholar and statesman.
copy of his *De Consolatione Philosophiae* at Leicester House, 221
Boilsher, Georg. See Bourchier, Sir George.
Bois-le-Duc (Bolduke) or s'Hertogenbosch, in Brabant, 231
Boleyn, George, Dean of Lichfield.
signs letter to Earl of Essex, 253
Bollen. See Boulogne.
Bologna (Bononia), in Italy.
Pope expected in, 159
Bomelle. See Zaltbommel.
Bonaventura, Bonaventure, The, of the Queen's Navy.
described as 'the best conditioned shipp of the world', 72
takes part in Earl of Essex's second expedition to Spain, 265
Bonehill, Staffs., 207
Bonn (Bonna), in Germany.
held by Colonel Schenk, 86
besieged, 214
Bonnell, John, partisan of 2nd Earl of Essex.
imprisoned in the Marshalsea, 282
Bonner, Edmund, Bishop of London.
his cruelty condemned, 148
Bononia. See Bologna.
Books.
at Leicester House, 204, 221
at Wanstead, 208
at Cambridge University, 251
Booth (Bouth), John, steward to Earl of Shrewsbury, 129, 130
Borgaruccio (Borgarucci), Dr. Julio, Court physician, native of Italy, 196
Borough, William, navigator, author and Comptroller of the Queen's Navy.

signs naval estimates, 253
Bosevile (Bosevyle), -----, 29
Bosevile, Godfrey, of Beighton.
  his will proved, 29
Bosomes, 149
Bostocke, Mr., of the English
    expeditionary force in Walcheren.
  killed in action near Middelburg, 232
Boston, Lincs., 218
Bosworth, Leics.
  letter dated from, 199
Bothal (Bothall Castle, Bothole),
    Northumb.
  letters dated from, 42, 63, 125
  description of Lord Ogle's house at,
    44
  Barony of, 44
Bouchain, in France.
  Prince of Orange blamed for loss of,
    30
Bouchier. See Bourchier.
Bouillon, Henri de la Tour d'Auvergne,
    Duc de, Marshal of France, 251
Boulogne (Bollen, Bullein), in France.
  letter dated from, 163
  adheres to King of France, 99
  capture by League of lower town of,
    99
  Captain of. See Bernet.
Boulsrett, Captain.
  takes part in Cadiz expedition, 265
Bourbon, Cardinal of. See Bourbon-
    Vendôme.
Bourbon, Antoine de, Duc de Vendôme
    and King of Navarre, 143
Bourbon, François de, Prince Dauphin
    of Auvergne.
  expected to arrive at Bruges with
    horse and foot, 38
Bourbon, Henri de. See Henry.
Bourbon, Henri de, Prince de Condé.
  in England, 27
  thought to be at St. Jean d'Angely, 31
Bourbon-Vendôme, Charles de,
    Cardinal de Bourbon.
  seized by order of King of France, 97
  reported to be ill, 97
Bourbourg, in France.
  reference to peace negotiations at,
    211
Bourcher, Sir George. See Bourchier,
    Sir George.
Bourchier (Bouchier).
  estates and family, 284
Bourchier (Bourcher, Boilsher), Sir
    George, Master of the Ordnance in
    Ireland, 274
  captured by Earl of Desmond, 244
Bourchier, Henry, 1st Earl of Essex
    (d1483), 249
Bourchier, Henry, 2nd Earl of Essex
    (d1539), 228

his Steward of the Household. See
    Clopton, William.
his Chaplain, See Wastelyn, Nicholas.
Bourchier, Henry.
  given annuity by Earl of Essex, 255,
    262
Bourchier, Isabel (d1484), wife of Henry
    Bourchier, 1st Earl of Essex, and
    niece of 5th Earl of March.
  title of Earl of Essex to lands of, 249
Bourchier (Bowssor), Lady Susanna,
    daughter of 2nd Earl of Bath.
  at Buxton, 21
Bouth, Jhon. See Booth, John.
Bovy, John, of Nottingham.
  letter from, 125
Bowdenson, Nicholas, 256, 257
Bowles, George, Alderman of London.
  Earl of Essex in debt to, 283
Bowssar (Bowsor), Captain, of the
    English expeditionary force in
    Walcheren.
  killed in action near Middelburg, 232
Bowssor, Lady Susans. See Bourchier,
    Lady Susanna.
Boy, Earl of Leicester's dog.
  painted with his master, 222
Boyle, Anne, cousin of following.
  letter from, 260
Boyle, Henry, of Bidney and the Middle
    Temple.
  case between Duppa and, 260
Bradborn, Sir Humphrey, of Burrows
    in Langley, J.P.
  Privy Council's directive to, 23
Bradford, Richard, of Dymock.
  letter from, 234
Bradley, John, Merchant Adventurer
    and Keeper of the English House
    in Bergen-op-Zoom, Brabant.
  petition to Earl of Leicester, 225
Bragge, Martin, member of the
    Company of Merchant
    Adventurers.
  involved in kidnapping of Story, 225
Brandon, Katherine, Duchess of
    Suffolk, wife of (1) Charles
    Brandon, Duke of Suffolk,
    (2) Richard Bertie, 150
  letters from, 148, 155, 204, 246
Branthwait, Robert.
  letter from, 288
Brecknock, 241
Brederode, Henri de, Viscount de
    Brederode.
  his portrait at Leicester House, 203
Bremingham, Mr. See Brimeghan,
    Edmond.
Bretforton, Worcs.
  rental of Earl of Leicester's lands at,
    168
Breton, John, of Towcester, son-in-law

of John Wirley.
letter from, 241
letter to, 239
Brett, Captain.
takes part in Cadiz expedition, 265
Bridge Foot, Southwark, London, 150
Bridges. *See* Bruges.
Brimeghan (Bremingham), Edmond,
secretary of Earl of Tyrone, 271
Brington, Hunts.
benefice of, 188
Bristol, 264
letters dated from, 144, 263
spices landed at, 170
letter from Mayor and Aldermen of,
172
Merchant Adventurers of, 173
Customs at, 179
ordnance sent from Kenilworth to
Earl of Leicester's ship at, 219
Brittany (Brytany), France, 259
visited by Edward and Henry Talbot,
43
Broadgates (Brodgat), Essex, 152
Broad Street, London, 124
Brode, William, Captain of infantry
at Berwick.
implicated in the killing of
Babington, 145
Brodgat. *See* Broadgates.
Brograve, Mr., 221
Broke, William, of Lew.
letter from, 48
Broken Wharf, Upper Thames Street,
London, 122
Brokesby, Mr., member of the English
expeditionary force to South
Beveland.
wounded in skirmish near Goes, 230
Bromeshall. *See* Bronsil.
Bromley (Bromeley), Sir Thomas,
Solicitor-General, later Lord
Chancellor, 55, 60, 61, 62, 69(2),
70. 75, 76. 81, 92, 99, 125.
letters from, 55, 74, 240
Campion examined before, 35
to try Earl of Shrewsbury's suit
against Countess of Shrewsbury,
53, 60
issues order in Earl of Shrewsbury's
suit against Cavendishes, 53
Commissioner at trial of Queen of
Scots, 73
speaks in favour of Parliament's
petition for execution of Queen of
Scots, 77
Bronsil (Bromeshall), Herefs.
castle of, 283
Brooke, Henry, 11th Lord Cobham.
accused of trying to murder Earl of
Essex, 278
Brooke, William, 10th Lord Cobham,

Lord Warden of the Cinque Ports,
153, 181
letters from, 93, 145
Broughton, Francis, footman to the
Queen, 218
Broughton, John, of the Inner Temple.
date of his death, 249
Broughton, Richard, of the Inner
Temple.
letters to, 246, 247
his accounts, 247, 250
statement by, 249
Browne, Anthony, 1st Viscount
Montagu, 186
letter from, 165
Commissioner at trial of Queen of
Scots, 74
Browne, Philip, son-in-law of Robert
Armiger, 168
Browne, Sir Valentine, of Kirton,
Treasurer at Berwick.
letter from, 187
petition to Queen, 226
Broxbourne (Broxborne), Herts.
letter dated from, 262
Bruce, Christian, daughter of following.
her marriage with William
Cavendish, 134, 135
Bruce, Edward, 1st Lord Kinloss,
Master of the Rolls.
marriage of his daughter with
William Cavendish, 134, 135
Brudenell, Thomas, of Deene.
mourner at funeral of Queen of
Scots, 83
Bruges (Bridges), in Belgium.
letter dated from, 38
Duke of Anjou and Prince of Orange
at, 37
spies arrested in, 38
Parma's forces encamped at, 211
Gaetano arrives in, 211
English political refugees reported at,
211
Infanta Isabella at, 276
Count Maurice's warning to, 276
Bruno, Giordano (Nolanus Jordanus),
of Naples, philosopher
burnt at Rome, 277
Brussels, 155
letter dated from, 139
King of Spain sends Fuentes to, 116
Bryan, Syr. *See* M'Felim, Bacagh.
Brydges, Grey (Greye), 5th Lord
Chandos.
imprisoned in the Tower, 281
Brytany. *See* Brittany.
Buckden (Bugden), Hunts.
letter dated from, 172
Buckesina, in Netherlands.
captured by Dutch, 231
Buckhurst, Sussex.

301

letter dated from, 215
Buckhurst, Lord. *See* Sackville,
Thomas.
Buckinghamshire.
map of, at Leicester House, 204
Buckland Newton (Buckland), Dorset.
rental of Earl of Leicester's lands at,
168
Buckoy, Counte de. *See* Bucquoy.
Bucquoy (Buckoy), Charles de
Longueval, Comte de, *Maître de
Camp* in the Archduke's army.
reported killed in action at Nieuport,
276
Budbrooke, Warwicks., 151
Bugbrooke, Northants.
Earl of Essex's tenants at, 239
Bugden. *See* Buckden.
Bukstone. *See* Buxton.
Bulkeley, Launcelot, Archbishop of
Dublin and Primate of Ireland.
his dispute with Earl of Essex, 284
Bulkeley, Rowland, of Beaumaris.
letter from, 235
Bull, Papal.
issued against Queen, 171
Bullein. *See* Boulogne.
Bullingham, John, canon of Worcester
and rector of Brington, later
Bishop of Gloucester.
letter from, 188
Bullingham, Nicholas, Bishop of
Lincoln.
letter from, 172
Buntingford, Herts., 137
Burbage, James, member of the Earl of
Leicester's Company of Players.
signs petition to Earl of Leicester, 226
Burd, Edmund. *See* Bird, Edmund.
Burden, William, 209
Burgen (Burgon), Richard.
letter from, 262
Burgh, Frances de, Countess of
Clanricarde, wife of 4th Earl of
Clanricarde and widow of 2nd Earl
of Essex.
letter to, 282
Burgh (Burke), Lady Honora de,
daughter of preceding.
letter from, 285 and *n*
Burgh, Richard de, 2nd Earl of
Clanricarde (Clanricherd), 192
Burgh, Richard de, 4th Earl of
Clanricarde, 285
Burghley, Northants.
Burghley invites Earl of Shrewsbury
to make use of his house at, 79
Burghley unable to attend his
mother's funeral at, 88
Burghley, Lord. *See* Cecil, Thomas;
Cecil, William.
Burghley, Lady. *See* Cecil, Mildred.

Burghley House, Strand, London, 102
Burgon, Richard. *See* Burgen, Richard.
Burke, Lady Honora. *See* Burgh, Lady
Honora de.
Burkenfield Moore. *See* Bockenfield
Moor.
Burkewell, Edmund, partisan of 2nd
Earl of Essex.
imprisoned in the Marshalsea, 282
Burnby, Yorks., 29
Burnell, -----, 25
Burnell, -----, in the service of Sir
Thomas Lucy, 152
Burre, Edward, of Durham Place near
Charing Cross, London.
letter to, 240
Burton Lazars (Lazarns), Leics.
Lord Robert Dudley granted manor
of, 164
survey of Lord Robert Dudley's lands
at, 167
Bury, 198
Busshe, -----, niece of Elizabeth
Wingfield, 128
Butler, Elizabeth, Countess of Ormond,
1st wife of 10th Earl of Ormond.
letter from, 153
Butler, Elizabeth, Countess of Ormond,
2nd wife of 10th Earl of Ormond,
71
Butler, John, of Kenilworth.
letter from, 178
Butler, Thomas, 10th Earl of Ormond,
71, 73, 171, 274, 277
letters from, 144, 244
Earl of Essex commits government of
Ireland to, 271
Buttery, The Queen's, 149
Buxton (Bukstone, Buxstons, Buxtons),
Derbys., 25, 26, 27, 29, 198(2), 251
letter dated from, 39
list of persons at, 21
Queen of Scots at, 40, 49
Buy, Monsieur de. *See* Mornay, Pierre
de.
Byddle, Dr. *See* Bedell, Arthur.
Byland, Yorks.
Northern rebels damage Pickering's
estate at, 187
Bylbrowe. *See* Bilborough.
Byrde, William. *See* Bird, William.

C

Cadbury, Somerset.
letter dated from, 260
Cadiz (Cadix).
Earl of Essex's expedition against,
263(5), 264(3), 265(3)
capture of, 264
reference to second expedition

against, 284
English success at, mentioned in
  verses, 288
Caermarthen. *See* Carmarthen.
Caernarvon (Carnarvon), 141
Cahir Castel (Carre Castel), co.
  Tipperary, 274
Calais (Cales, Calice, Calles, Callesse,
  Kalles), in France, 77, 93, 186, 214
adheres to King of France, 99
peace talks jeopardised by French
  refusal to surrender, 138
French troops for Scotland embark
  at, 152
news from, 211
Governor of. *See* Gourdain
Callowden (Calloughden, Calloughdon),
  Warwicks.
letter dated from, 172
Camber Castle (Cambre), Sussex.
letters dated from, 153, 167
Captain of. *See* Chute, Philip.
Camberwell (Camerwell), Surrey, 136
Cambrai (Cambray), in France, 36
Cambre, Castell of the. *See* Camber
  Castle.
Cambridge, 176, 261(2)
Cambridge, University of.
letter from, 167
letter dated from Trinity Hall, 200
Earl of Essex's expenses at, 247, 249,
  250(2), 251
Earl of Essex's gift to poor at, 261
Trinity College, 244, 261
Queens' College, 261
Camerwell. *See* Camberwell.
Campbell, Alexander, son of 3rd Earl of
  Argyll.
sent to England as hostage, 155
Campbell, Archibald, 5th Earl of
  Argyll, 155
Camphier. *See* Veere.
Campion, Edmund, English Jesuit.
arrested in Berkshire, 35
his interrogation, 35
Campton (Cambton), Beds.
manor of, 69
Canary Islands.
attacked by Drake's fleet, 71, 195
Candale, Frédéric de Foix, Comte de,
  a French hostage.
Lord Robert Dudley dines with, 150
Candale, Henri de Foix, Comte de, 177
letter from, 145
Candysh, Mr. *See* Cavendish, Henry;
  Cavendish, William.
Canon, Thomas, of Haverfordwest.
letter from, 263
Canterbury.
petition to Earl of Leicester from, 202
Gaoler of. *See* Cooke, William.
Mayor of. *See* Nethersole, James.

Canterbury, Archbishop of. *See* Parker,
  Matthew; Whitgift, John.
Canterbury, Archdeaconry of, 146
Cantreselyf (Cantrecelly), Brecon.
rental of Earl of Leicester's lands at,
  168
Cape Finisterre (Finister), in Spain.
English naval force to proceed to, 253
Cape Verde Islands (Capo Verde).
attacked by Drake's fleet, 71
Caraffa, Carlo, Cardinal, Legate of
  Bologna, nephew of Pope Paul IV.
banished by Pope from Rome, 139
Caraffas, The, nephews of Pope
  Paul IV.
still held in prison, 159
Carden, Sir Thomas. *See* Cawarden,
  Sir Thomas.
Cardinal, The. *See* Albert.
Cardinall, William, J.P. and member of
  the Council of the North, 117
Cards, 138, 151
illegal game called 'riffe' (ruff), 188
Earl of Shrewsbury's losses at, 196
Earl of Essex loses at, 261
game called 'Noddy', 261
Care, Mrs., 101
Carew (Carye), Sir George, Marshal of
  the Queen's Household.
his diplomatic mission to Scotland, 39
Carew, Sir George, Lieutenant-General
  of the Ordnance, later President of
  Munster and Earl of Totness.
commands company in Cadiz
  expedition, 265
reported to have captured the Sugan
  Earl of Desmond, 277
Carew (Caro), Sir Peter, of Mohun's
  Ottery, 238
Carewe, Captain.
takes part in Cadiz expedition, 265
Carewe, Sir Robert. *See* Carey, Sir
  Robert.
Carey, Anne, Lady Hunsdon, wife of
  1st Lord Hunsdon, 97
Carey, Sir Edmund, of Kennington,
  Esquire of the Queen's Body.
his gift to Earl of Leicester, 210
Carey, Henry, 1st Baron Hunsdon,
  Lord Chamberlain, 90, 101, 104,
  107, 114, 149, 173
letter to, 206
to go to Berwick, 44
signs letters, etc., from Privy Council,
  46, 94, 96, 98
chosen to be responsible for Queen's
  safety, 92
Lord Robert Dudley's gift at
  christening of his child, 150
said to be gravely ill, 217
Carey, Sir Henry, partisan of 2nd Earl
  of Essex.

imprisoned in the Marshalsea, 282
Carey (Carewe), Sir Robert, Warden of
the East and Middle Marches, 127
Earl of Essex loses at chess to, 261
Carham (Carram), Northumb.
Scottish forces cross Tweed at, 287
Carhill.
Scottish forces cross Tweed at, 287
Carlingford, co. Louth, 141
Carlisle, Cumberland.
letter dated from, 165
Carlton, George, 238
Carlton-in-Lindrick, Notts., 80
Carmarthen (Caermarthen).
letters dated from, 236, 237
preparations for Earl of Essex's Irish
expedition at, 236(2)
Earl of Essex's body conveyed from
Dublin to, 248
his burial at, 248
Earl of Essex invited to nominate
burgess M.P. for, 255
Mayor of. See Davies, Thomas.
Carmarthenshire.
no volunteers for Earl of Essex's
Irish expedition in, 237
survey of Earl of Essex's lands in, 282
Carmignay, Cardinal. See Armagnac.
Caro, Sir Peter. See Carew, Sir Peter.
Carpi (Carpye), Rodolfo Pio de,
Cardinal.
mentioned as possible Pope, 147
Carraffa, Cardinal. See Caraffa, Carlo.
Carram. See Carham.
Carre Castle. See Cahir.
Carrick, in Ireland.
letter dated from, 288
Cartagena, in Colombia.
plundered by Drake's fleet, 71
Carye, Sir George. See Carew, Sir
George.
Case, Robert, footman to the Queen,
218
Cashel, Titular Archbishop of. See
Macgibbon, Maurice.
Casimir (Casymer, Cassimere), Duke
John, Prince Palatine (d1592).
his portrait at Leicester House, 203,
224
details of his forces, 231
his father. See Frederick III.
his mother. See Palatine, Marie,
Electress.
Castell Saint Angelo. See Sant'Angelo.
Castile (Castille), in Spain.
amount of subsidy paid to King of
Spain by, 160
Castle, The, inn, Fleet Street, London,
24
Castle Cornet, Guernsey.
letter dated from, 256
Castle Cossam or Castell Cossam,

Carms.
grange of, 283
Caswell, Mr.
letter dated from his house near
Clement's Inn, 100
Casymer. See Casimir.
Catesby (Catesbye), Robert, of
Lapworth.
imprisoned in the Marshalsea, 282
Cavalcanti, Guido, of Florence,
diplomatic agent to Catherine de
Medici, 180
letter from, 177
Cave, Sir Ambrose, of Kingsbury,
Chancellor of the Duchy of
Lancaster, 141
letter from, 142
Cavendish family, 41, 80
letters from members of, 129
commission issued to deal with
dispute between Earl of Shrewsbury
and, 66
Earl of Shrewsbury ordered to cease
all legal proceedings against, 67, 69
Earl of Shrewsbury to meet all
financial claims of, 69
Cavendish, Sir Charles, of Welbeck,
3rd son of Elizabeth Talbot,
Countess of Shrewsbury, by her
former marriage with Sir William
Cavendish, 48, 54, 57, 58, 59, 60,
66, 67, 80, 104, 115, 125, 127,
128, 129, 131, 133, 197
letters from, 22, 73
letter to, 127
order issued in Earl of Shrewsbury's
legal proceedings against, 53
Queen forbids Earl of Shrewsbury to
proceed by law against, 67, 69
elected M.P. for Nottinghamshire,
117
summary of letters passed between
Stanhope and, 118
forbidden by Privy Council to pursue
quarrel with Stanhope, 118
his challenge to duel accepted by
Stanhope, 118
account of abortive duel
arrangements with Stanhope, 120
his servants take part in street
assault on Stanhope, 122, 123
visits Burghley's house at Cheshunt
with Earl of Shrewsbury, 124
reference to incident between
Stanhope and, 127
Cavendish, Elizabeth, later Countess of
Devonshire, 2nd wife of 1st Lord
Cavendish, 134
Cavendish, Frances, daughter of 1st
Lord Cavendish, 133
Cavendish, Lady Grace, daughter of 6th
Earl of Shrewsbury, wife of

following.
letters from, 34(2)
Cavendish (Cavendysst, Candysh),
Henry, of Tutbury, eldest son of
Elizabeth Talbot, Countess of
Shrewsbury, by her former marriage
with Sir William Cavendish, 34(2),
196
letters from, 84, 132, 134(2)
letter to, 131
dispute between Agard and, 102, 126
his servants take part in street assault
on Stanhope, 122, 123, 124
rejects his brother's offer, 132
Cavendish, Katherine, Lady, daughter
of 7th Lord Ogle and wife of Sir
Charles Cavendish, 42, 125, 133
Cavendish (Candysh), William, 1st Lord
Cavendish of Hardwick, later 1st
Earl of Devonshire, 2nd son of
Elizabeth Talbot, Countess of
Shrewsbury, by her former marriage
with Sir William Cavendish, 48,
51, 54, 60, 67, 80, 132, 133, 134,
135
letter from, 21
criticised by Earl of Shrewsbury, 52
order issued in Earl of Shrewsbury's
suit against, 53
allegations made by Earl of
Shrewsbury against, 131
his financial offers rejected by his
brother, 132
Cavendish, William, son of preceding,
later 2nd Earl of Devonshire, 132,
133
his marriage with Christian Bruce,
134, 135
Cavendysst, Mr. See Cavendish, Henry.
Cawarden (Carden), Sir Thomas, joint
Lieutenant of the Tower of
London.
his death, 147
Cayas, Gabriel de, Secretary to
Philip II, King of Spain, 173
Cecil, Mistress. See Cecil, Elizabeth.
Cecil (Cicill), Dorothy, Lady, wife of Sir
Thomas Cecil, 25
at Buxton, 21
mourner at funeral of Queen of Scots,
83
Cecil, Elizabeth, later Lady Cecil, of
the Queen's Privy Chamber, wife of
Sir Robert Cecil.
informs Queen of Earl of
Shrewsbury's death, 102
Cecil, Jane, widow of Richard Cecil of
Burghley and mother of 1st Lord
Burghley.
Burghley's grief at her death, 88
Cecil, Mildred, Lady Burghley, wife of
1st Lord Burghley.

her gift to Earl of Leicester, 219
Cecil (Sissell, Syssill), Sir Robert,
later 1st Earl of Salisbury, son of
1st Lord Burghley and Secretary of
State, 261(2)
Earl of Shrewsbury pays compliment
to his son, 124
takes part in trial of Earl of Essex,
269
his answer to allegations by Earl of
Essex, 275
replies to Earl of Essex's defence, 275
to dine with Earl of Essex, 277
Cecil, Sir Thomas, later 1st Earl of
Exeter, eldest son of following, 25,
215
Queen stays at his house in
Wimbledon, 45
at Buxton, 20
receives gift of beer, 20
mourner at funeral of Queen of
Scots, 83
proclaims Earl of Essex a traitor in
London, 278
forced to retreat by Earl of Essex's
followers, 278
leads attack on Essex House, 278
his wife. See Cecil, Dorothy.
Cecil, William, 1st Lord Burghley,
Lord Treasurer and principal
minister to the Queen.
letters from, 28, 35, 36, 40, 74,
75(2), 77(2), 78(2), 80, 81, 85,
86, 87, 88(2), 95, 96, 105, 116,
181, 222
letters to, 40, 53, 66, 70, 71,
95, 102, 106, 107, 112, 115,
117, 124, 169, 195, 222(2), 224
signs letters from Privy Council,
22, 46, 86, 89, 93, 98, 220
troubled by gout, 45, 92, 96
summoned to conference with Queen
after fall of Antwerp, 45
signs money order for Earl of
Shrewsbury, 54
Commissioner at trial of Queen of
Scots, 73
his opinion on Queen of Scots'
case, 75
places his house at Burghley at
disposal of Earl of Shrewsbury, 79
welcomes overtures for peace from
Duke of Parma, 80
appeals to Earl of Shrewsbury to give
financial help to Lord Talbot, 82,
87
complains of being overworked, 85
his grief over his mother's death, 88
refuses Queen's offer of higher rank
in peerage, 97
receives news of Earl of Shrewsbury's
death, 102

New Year's gift from Earl of
Shrewsbury to, 117
serious illness of, 118
Earl of Shrewsbury visits his house at
Cheshunt, 124
warned by Walsingham of plot
against Queen, 172
pleasure in building results in
financial difficulties for, 181
his marginal comments on Bishop of
Ross's memorial, 182, 183
his mother. *See* Cecil, Jane.
Chaloner, Thomas, in the service of
Earl of Derby.
request on behalf of, 88
Chamberlain (Chamberlayn), John, of
Alderney.
dispute between inhabitants of
Alderney and, 256
Chamberlain (Chamberlayn), John, 155
Chamberlain (Chamberlynne), Richard,
of Astley.
one of his men implicated in a
murder, 234
Chamberlain (Chamberlayne), Sir
Thomas, English Ambassador to
Spain.
letter from, 160
Lord Robert Dudley's gift at
christening of his child, 150
wishes to be relieved of his post, 160
sends details of King of Spain's
revenues, 160
Champagny (Champigny), Frédéric
Perrenot, Seigneur de, a Peace
Commissioner.
escapes being imprisoned by Duke of
Parma, 214
Chancellor, Mr. *See* Sadler, Sir Ralph.
Chancery, 260
Masters of, 41
commission from, 66
Examiners of, 259, 260
Six Clerks of, 259
Chancery Lane, London, 46, 122, 240
Chapel, Children of the, 150, 229
Chapman, -----, 237
Chapman, John, of London, grocer.
Lord Robert Dudley borrows money
from, 148
Charing Cross, London, 241
letter dated from Sir Nicholas
Bacon's house near, 194
Charlecote (Charlcot), Warwicks.
letter dated from, 152
Charles V, Emperor (*d*1559), 24
his portrait at Leicester House, 203
Charles I, King of England, 287(5)
said to be economizing with his store
of gunpowder, 287
Earl of Essex commended in verses
for his courteous treatment of, 289

Charles IX, King of France, 163, 178
extends warm welcome to Lord
Buckhurst, 171
his request rejected by Pope, 171
Coligny honourably treated by, 184
House of Guise reported to be losing
his favour, 184
three objectives of his policy, 187
adheres to alliance between England
and France, 187
his sister. *See* Valois, Marguerite de.
Charles, Archduke of Austria and
Margrave of Burgau, son of
Ferdinand, Archduke of Austria.
expected in Bruges, 211
Charles Emmanuel, Duke of Savoy.
Henry IV leads punitive expedition
against, 277
Chartley (Charteley, Chertley), Staffs.,
225, 237, 240, 251
letters dated from, 236, 241
Chartres, Jean de Ferrières, Vidame de,
Huguenot leader.
entertained by Earl of Essex, 254
Chasepool (Chaspell), Staffs., 162
Chatelleroy, Duke of. *See* Hamilton,
James.
Chatillon (Chatillion), Odet de Coligny,
Comte de Beauvais, Cardinal de.
his portrait at Leicester House, 203
his wife. *See* Beauvais.
Chatsworth (Chatyssworth), Derbys., 20,
26, 29, 51, 132, 197
household stuff removed by William
Cavendish from, 51, 52
'Chauncelour', Mr. *See* Mildmay, Sir
Walter.
Chaunsye *or* Chancy, William, Receiver
to Lord Robert Dudley.
his accounts, 136, 138
Chaworth, Sir George, of Annesley.
appointed collector of Queen's loan in
Nottinghamshire, 98
Chaworth, Henry, of Lindley, Sheriff
of Nottinghamshire, 127
Cheak, Lady. *See* Cheke, Mary.
Cheapside, London, 24, 122, 278
Earl of Essex and his followers
forced to retreat from, 278
Chedell, Humphrey, in the service of
Mary, Countess of Shrewsbury.
conveys offensive message to
Stanhope, 119
Cheffyede, George, partisan of 2nd
Earl of Essex.
imprisoned in the Marshalsea, 282
Cheinie, Lord. *See* Cheney, Henry.
Cheke, John, son of Sir John Cheke,
former Secretary of State.
killed at Smerwick, 31
Cheke (Cheak), Mary, Lady, mother of
preceding, 137

Chekkers. *See* Chequers.
Chelsea, Mddx., 150
  letters dated from, 54(2)
  Queen rowed to, 136
Chenesfelde, Henry, partisan of 2nd
  Earl of Essex.
imprisoned in the Marshalsea, 282
Cheney (Cheinie), Henry, Lord Cheney
  of Toddington.
Commissioner at trial of Queen of
  Scots, 74
Chenies (Chenys), Bucks.
  letter dated from, 151
Chenys. *See* Chenies.
Chequers (Chekkers), Bucks.
  letter dated from, 239
Chertley. *See* Chartley.
Cheshire.
  Papists in, 24
Cheshunt, Herts.
  Lord Burghley's house at, 124
Chess.
  Earl of Essex's losses at, 261
Chester (Westchester), Cheshire, 246
  letters dated from, 144, 235, 240, 241
Chester, -----, formerly in the service
  of Earl of Shrewsbury.
his alleged duplicity, 20
Chester, Captain, of the English
  expeditionary force in Walcheren.
his conduct in action commended,
  232
Chester, Charles, of London.
  letter from, 257
Chester, Sir Robert, of Royston.
  letter from, 185
Chester, Sir William, Lord Mayor of
  London, 150
Lord Robert Dudley attends banquet
  of, 150
Chester Herald. *See* Knight, Edmund.
Chichester, Sussex, 176
  letter dated from, 177
Chichester, Sir John, of Raleigh, J.P.
  dies of gaol fever, 68
Chirk, Denbighs.
  survey of Lord Robert Dudley's lands
  at, 167
  rental of Earl of Leicester's estates
  at, 168
Chomley, Jasper, 194
Chomleye, Richard, partisan of 2nd
  Earl of Essex.
imprisoned in the Marshalsea, 282
Chowte, P. *See* Chute, Philip.
Christian, Prince of Denmark.
  succeeds his father, 90
Christs Church, 136
Chute (Chowte), Philip, Captain of
  Camber Castle.
letters from, 152, 167
sends gift of jewel to Lord Robert

Dudley, 167
Cicero, Marcus Tullius, Roman orator
  and writer.
copy of his *De Officiis* at Leicester
  House, 221
Cicill, Lady. *See* Cecil, Dorothy.
Civitavecchia (Civita Vecchia), in Italy.
  Pope fortifies, 157
Clancarr, Earl of. *See* More, Donald
  Maccarty.
Clancarroll, co. Monaghan.
  devastation of Earl of Essex's lands
  at, 258
Clandeboye, Ulster.
  Earl of Essex to establish English
  shire system in, 243
Clanricarde, Countess of. *See* Burgh,
  Frances de.
Clanricherd, Earl of. *See* Burgh,
  Richard de.
Clarenceux King of Arms. *See* Cook,
  Robert.
Clarendon (Claringdown), Wilts.
  letter dated from, 198
Clarke, Nicholas, of Chesterfield.
  released from prison, 80
Clarke, Thomas, member of the Earl of
  Leicester's Company of Players.
signs petition to Earl of Leicester,
  226
Cleare, Sir Edward. *See* Clere, Sir
  Edward.
Clearke, -----, 64
Clement VIII, Pope.
  talks between Earls of Essex and
  Tyrone observed by spy of, 275
Clement's Inn, London, 100, 240
Cleobury, Salop.
  survey of Lord Robert Dudley's lands
  at, 167, 200
Clere (Cleare), Sir Edward, of Blickling.
  to be made a baron, 97
Clergy.
  bill in House of Commons against
  non-residence of, 100
Clerk, Richard, footman to the Queen,
  218
Clermont d'Amboise, Georges de, Baron
  de Bussy, Ambassador from the
  King of Navarre to England, 212(2)
Clifford, Herefs.
  survey of Lord Robert Dudley's lands
  at, 167
Clifford, Sir Conyers, soldier, late
  Governor of Connaught.
commander in Cadiz expedition, 263
composition of his regiment, 265
his defeat and death in Ireland, 274
Clifford, George, 3rd Earl of
  Cumberland.
Commissioner at trial of Queen of
  Scots, 74

Chester's opinion of, 257
takes part in Earl of Essex's trial, 269
Clifford (Clyfford, Clyffard), Henry,
    of Keyston, 235
    letter from, 234
Clifford, Sir Nicholas, nephew of 2nd
    Earl of Essex, 261
    moved from Fleet prison to Tower,
    259
    annuity paid to, 262
Clifton, Sir Gervase, of Clifton.
    complaint against, 80
Clinton (*otherwise* Fiennes), Edward,
    Lord Clinton, later 1st Earl of
    Lincoln, Lord High Admiral, 138,
    148
    letters from, 147, 233
    signs letters from Privy Council, 22,
    46, 160
    to go to France, 187
Clinton, Elizabeth, Lady, later Countess
    of Lincoln, 3rd wife of preceding,
    137
Clinton, Elizabeth, Countess of Lincoln,
    daughter of Sir Richard Morrison,
    2nd wife of following.
    as Mrs. Morreson, 21
    mourner at funeral of Queen of
    Scots, 83
Clinton (*otherwise* Fiennes), Henry,
    2nd Earl of Lincoln.
    Commissioner at trial of Queen of
    Scots, 74
    mourner at funeral of Queen of
    Scots, 83
Clopton, William, Steward of the
    Household to Earl of Essex.
    his accounts, 228
Clough, William, of Denbigh.
    nominated by Earl of Leicester to be
    coroner of Denbigh, 190
Clun, Salop.
    manor of, 188
Clundell, Ambrose, partisan of 2nd Earl
    of Essex.
    imprisoned in the Marshalsea, 282
Clyffard, Mr. *See* Clifford, Henry.
Clyfford, Henry. *See* Clifford, Henry.
Coal.
    pits in Northumberland, 44
Cobham, Kent, 138
    Queen at, 137
Cobham, Lord. *See* Brooke, Henry;
    Brooke, William.
Cobham, Sir Henry, diplomatist.
    letters from, 43, 48, 173
    replaced as ambassador to France by
    Stafford, 44
    sends gifts to Earl of Shrewsbury, 48
Cobham Hall, Kent.
    letter dated from, 145
Cockburn, Captain, 186

Cockerham (Cokerham), Lancs.
    manor of, 152
Cockfighting, 196, 284
Cockin, Sir T. *See* Cokayne, Sir
    Thomas.
Cocks, Simon (Symon), prebendary of
    Lichfield.
    signs letter to Earl of Essex, 253
Cokayne (Cockin), Sir Thomas, of
    Ashbourne, J.P.
    letter from, 234
    Privy Council's directive to, 23
Coke, Sir Edward, Attorney-General.
    takes part in trial of Earl of Essex,
    269, 270
Cokerham. *See* Cockerham.
Colborne, -----, in the service of Henry
    Cavendish, 124
Colbruck. *See* Colnbrook.
Colby, -----, in the service of Earl of
    Rutland, 157
Colby, Humfrey, footman to the Queen,
    218
Coldharbour (Colharbor, Cowlharbor,
    Coleherbent), London
    letters dated from, 41, 64
    Lady Mary Sidney's request for loan
    of Earl of Shrewsbury's house at, 21
Cole, Thomas, Keeper of the plate at
    Kenilworth, 219
Cole Lyddington.
    name of horse bestowed on Scotsman,
    169
Coleherbent. *See* Coldharbour.
Coleman Street, London.
    letters dated from, 90, 92
Colepeper (Culpeper), Sir Thomas, of
    Hackington.
    his regiment, 286
Coleshill (Collehull), Warwicks., 143
Colharbor. *See* Coldharbour.
Coligny, Gaspard de, Admiral of
    France, 232
    discredited at the French Court, 143
    honourably treated by French Royal
    family, 184
Collehull. *See* Coleshill.
Collen. *See* Cologne.
Collier, Captain.
    takes part in Cadiz expedition, 265
Colman, -----, of the English garrison
    at Ostend.
    brings grievances and demands of
    mutineers to England, 217
Colnbrook (Colbruck), Oxon., 71
Cologne (Collen), 86
Colton, George, Pembrokeshire tenant
    of Earl of Essex, 236
Colville, John, Scottish divine and
    diplomatist.
    his audience with Queen, 42
Comberford (Comterforde), Henry,

precentor of Lichfield.
reported to be in hiding, 142
Commission for Sewers, 106, 107, 109,
113, 114, 115(2)
Commission House, Fleet Street,
London.
letter dated from, 285
Commissioners for peace, 1588.
embark at Dover, 86
arrive in Ostend, 87
general expectation of their success,
90
Commissioners of Array.
in Herefordshire, 291
Common Prayer Book.
bill submitted to House of Commons
for reform of, 100
Compagni, Bartolomeo, of St.
Christopher's, Broad Street,
London, Italian merchant.
letter from, 165
Compton. See Compton Wynyates.
Compton, Sir Henry, later 1st Lord
Compton.
Commissioner at trial of Queen of
Scots, 74
mourner at funeral of Queen of
Scots, 82
receives gift of a horse, 169
Compton Wynyates, Warwicks.
Queen sups at, 189
Comptroller, Mr. See Croft, Sir James;
Parry, Sir Thomas.
Comterforde, parson. See Comberford,
Henry.
Concino, Dominico, of Genoa.
letter from, 145
Condé, Prince de. See Bourbon,
Henri de.
Conduit, The, Cheapside, London, 123
Congregation, Lords of the (Scottish).
skirmish between French forces and
supporters of, 156
Connaught, Ireland.
troops sent to pacify, 171
reference to late rebellion in, 192
President of. See Fitton, Sir Edward.
Consistory, Papal.
Spanish cardinal expelled from, 147
Constable, Captain.
takes part in Cadiz expedition, 265
Constable, Sir John, of Holderness, 66
Constable, Sir Robert, of Flamborough,
188
Constable, Sir William, of
Flamborough.
imprisoned in the Marshalsea, 282
Constantinople, in Turkey, 116
Convocation, 185
Conway, Sir Edward, later 1st Viscount
Conway.
commands regiment in Cadiz
expedition, 265

Conway, Edward, 2nd Viscount
Conway, General of the Horse, 286
Conway, Captain Fulk.
takes part in Cadiz expedition, 265
Conway, Sir John, Governor of Ostend.
taken prisoner by mutinous garrison,
215
Cook, Robert, Clarenceux King of
Arms.
mourner at funeral of Queen of
Scots, 82, 83
Cooke, John, footman to the Queen,
218
Cooke, Peter, Mayor of Portsmouth.
signs petition, 266 and n
Cooke, William, of Canterbury.
request that he be reinstated as
gaoler, 202
Cooper, Thomas, Bishop of Lincoln,
200
Copley, Christopher, of Sprotborough,
in the service of Earl of
Shrewsbury, 54, 70
letters from, 64, 66
Corbet, Michael, of London, merchant,
226
Corbet, Robert, of Moreton, deceased,
256
Cordell, Edward, of London, 99
Cordell, Sir William, of Long Melford,
Master of the Rolls, 136
Cornbury Park (Corneberry Parke),
Oxon.
Earl of Leicester detained by illness
at, 217
Cornwallis, Sir Thomas, of Brome Hall.
letter from, 145
not imprisoned as recusant because of
ill health, 92
Coroner.
election at Derby of, 43
Corte, Claudio, formerly in the service
of Earl of Leicester.
letter from, 170
Cortes, Spanish.
grants money to discharge debts of
Philip II, 160
Corunna (The Groyne), in Spain, 253
Cotherstone (Cotsterton), Yorks., 226
Cotton, Thomas, Lieutenant-General of
the English expeditionary force to
South Beveland, 232
his conduct in action commended,
230
his lieutenant. See Bostocke.
Council of the North, 191
President of. See Hastings, Henry.
Council of State of the United
Provinces.
levies contribution for building ships,
214
threatened by King of Scots, 214
Count Maurice. See Nassau, Count

Maurice of.
Counter *or* Compter, The, prison,
  Southwark.
  letter dated from, 202
  Herle imprisoned in, 202
Courcelles, Camille de Preau, Monsieur
  de, French Ambassador to
  Scotland.
  given passport in London to go to
  France, 46
Court, English, 23-269 *passim*
  letters dated from, 20-256 *passim*
  optimism regarding peace between
  England and Spain at, 90
  rivalries and intrigues at, 110, 111,
  112, 113
  Lord Robert Dudley accompanies
  French Ambassador to, 136
  Earl of Essex invited by Queen to
  stay in Earl of Leicester's lodging
  at, 216
  at Walden, 250
  at Whitehall during Earl of Essex's
  rebellion, 277
Court, French, 171, 177, 202
  at Orleans, 163
  Lord Buckhurst warmly welcomed
  at, 171
Court, Spanish, 173
Covent Garden (Garrdon), London.
  letter dated from Earl of Bedford's
  house at, 181
Coventry (Coventree), Warwicks., 143,
  179
  letter from Mayor and Aldermen of,
  152
  Mayor of. *See* Kyrven, Thomas.
Cowdray, Sussex.
  letters dated from, 165, 186
Cowke, -----, a priest, 229
Cownestable, The. *See* Montmorency,
  Anne de.
Cowoppe, Richard, 119
Cox, Henry, victualler of the garrison
  at Ostend.
  mutiny sparked off by arrival of poor
  provisions from, 215
Coxe, Richard, Bishop of Ely, 92,
  181(2), 182
Cradock, William, of Stafford.
  letter from, 237
Cressey, Mr., 157
Croft, Sir James, Governor of Berwick,
  later Comptroller of the Queen's
  Household, 24
  letters from, 139, 140, 216
  Commissioner at trial of Queen of
  Scots, 73
  signs letters, etc., from Privy Council,
  86, 98
  entertained at Dunkirk and Nieuport,
  87

critical of Privy Council's decision to
  effect economies at Berwick, 140
  his imprisonment in the Fleet, 216
  appeal to Earl of Leicester on behalf
  of, 216(2)
  his servants deprived of household
  allowance, 217
Crompton, John.
  Countess of Leicester's lawsuits
  against, 225
Crompton, Thomas, of London,
  partisan of 2nd Earl of Essex.
  manors conveyed by Earl of Essex to,
  265
  imprisoned in the Marshalsea, 282
Cromwell, Edward, 3rd Lord Cromwell.
  takes part in Earl of Essex's
  rebellion, 278
  imprisoned in the Tower, 281
Cromwell, Mary, Lady, mother of
  preceding.
  mourner at funeral of Queen of
  Scots, 83
Cromwell, Thomas, 4th Lord
  Cromwell.
  letter from, 284
Crookes, John, Captain, of the English
  expeditionary force to Walcheren.
  his conduct in action commended,
  232
Crosado, The.
  Papal Bull called, 160
Crowmer, William, of Canterbury.
  signs petition to Earl of Leicester, 202
Culpeper, Sir Thomas. *See* Colepeper,
  Sir Thomas.
Cumberland, Earl of. *See* Clifford,
  George.
Cumnor, Berks.
  letter dated from, 159
Cundall, Thomas, partisan of 2nd Earl
  of Essex.
  imprisoned in the Marshalsea, 282
Cunningham, Alexander, 4th Earl of
  Glencairn.
  his son sent as hostage to England,
  155
Cunningham, Sir David, Receiver-
  General of the Prince of Wales's
  revenue and Commissioner for the
  Principality of Wales.
  signs letter to Earls of Essex and
  Suffolk, 285
Cunningham, James, son of 4th Earl
  of Glencairn.
  sent as hostage to England, 155
Cunnye, Captain.
  takes part in Cadiz expedition, 265
Curzon (Curson), Francis, of
  Kedleston, J.P.
  Privy Council's directive to, 23
Custos Rotulorum, office of.

in Derbyshire, 125
in Nottinghamshire, 125
Cutler, Arthur, Warden of the
    Company of Painter-Stainers of
    London.
    presents picture to Earl of Leicester,
    222
Cymie. See Simier.

D

Dacre, William, 3rd Lord Dacre,
    Warden of the West Marches.
    imprisons Fergus Graham, 165
Dale, Dr.Valentine, Master of
    Requests, English Ambassador
    to France, 25
    correspondence with Walsingham,
    195 and n
Dalkeith, Midlothian.
    letter dated from, 178
Dalton, Robert, in the service of Earl
    of Derby.
    request on behalf of, 152
Dames or Dams, Henry, of East
    Smithfield, London, alien.
    petition to Earl of Leicester, 226
Danell (?), Roger, of Yorks.
    takes part in northern rebellion, 187
Dannett (Dannet), Audley, secretary of
    John Norris in the Netherlands.
    letter from, 37
Dansie, Captain.
    takes part in Cadiz expedition, 265
Danvers (Davers), Sir Charles, of
    Dauntsey.
    takes part in Earl of Essex's
    rebellion, 278
    imprisoned in the Tower, 281
Danvers, Elizabeth, Lady, wife of
    following.
    Earl of Leicester to attend
    christening of her child, 201
Danvers, Sir John, of Dauntsey.
    letter from, 45
Darby. See Derby.
Darcy, Elizabeth, Lady, widow of 1st
    Lord Darcy of Chiche, 207
    letter from, 141
    portrait of her daughter at Leicester
    House, 207, 224
Darcy, John, 2nd Lord Darcy of
    Aston.
    letters from, 73, 99
    assesses Earl of Shrewsbury's lands,
    29
Darcy, Robert, son of 1st Lord Darcy
    of Chiche.
    taken into Earl of Leicester's
    service, 141
Darcy, Thomas, 3rd Lord Darcy of

Chiche.
    takes part in trial of Earl of Essex,
    269
Dartford, Kent, 137
Davers, -----, 156
Davers, Sir Charles. See Danvers, Sir
    Charles.
David, Jenkin, tenant of Morfa Mawr
    grange, Cards.
    his rents, 283
Davies, Sir John, of Tisbury and the
    Middle Temple, 278
    takes part in Earl of Essex's
    rebellion, 278
    imprisoned in Newgate, 281
Davies, Richard, in the service of Lord
    Strange, 66(2)
Davies, Thomas, Mayor of
    Carmarthen.
    sends blank nomination paper for
    Parliamentary election to Earl of
    Essex, 255
Davies (Davyes), Thomas, in the
    service of Lord Robert Dudley,
    151
Davis, Captain.
    takes part in Cadiz expedition, 265
Davison, William, secretary to the
    Queen.
    signs letter to Earl of Shrewsbury, 92
Davy, Watkin, of Bampton.
    alleged to have defamed Earl of
    Shrewsbury, 48
Dawson, Bryan, partisan of 2nd Earl
    of Essex.
    imprisoned in the Marshalsea, 282
Dean, Forest of, 259
    Constable of. See Herbert, Henry.
Dearolme. See Durham.
Dekesone, Edward. See Dickenson,
    Edward.
Delft (Delphe), in Holland.
    Van Berg reported to have entered,
    231
Dembize, Guillaume, Dutch shipper
    imprisoned in London.
    appeal on behalf of, 172
Denbigh.
    letters dated from, 182, 190
    election of Earl of Leicester's
    nominees at, 189
    reference to 'the book of', 223
    survey of Lord Robert Dudley's
    lands at, 167
    rental of Earl of Leicester's lands at,
    168
Denbigh, Lordship of.
    Recorder of, 224
Denbigh, Lord. See Dudley, Robert.
Denmark.
    importance to England of naval
    strength and friendship of, 90

defeat of Armada celebrated by
Protestants in, 95
complaints of attacks by English
pirates on merchants of, 201
Denmark, King of. *See* Frederick II;
Christian.
Denmark, Prince of. *See* Christian.
Depe. *See* Dieppe.
Deptford, Kent.
Queen at, 149, 150
Deputy Lieutenants.
of Derbyshire, 59
to assist in raising of loan by privy
seal for Queen, 98
Derby (Darby), 43, 108, 109(2), 112,
115, 129
quarrel between Zouche and
Stanhope at, 22
election of coroner at, 43
musters to be held at, 59
Archdeacon of. *See* Walton, John.
Steward of. *See* Talbot, Gilbert.
Derby, Earl of. *See* Stanley, Edward;
Stanley, Henry.
Derbyshire, 35, 41, 58(2), 59, 60,
84, 91, 93, 98(2), 107, 128
lower value of property in
Northumberland than in, 44
Earl of Shrewsbury appointed
Commissioner of Horse in, 46
state of harvest interferes with
musters in, 59
Deputy Lieutenants of, 59
Assizes in, 67
Lord Lieutenant of. *See* Talbot,
George.
Desmond, Earl of. *See* Fitzgerald,
Gerald.
Desmond, Usurper of. *See* Fitzgerald,
James FitzThomas.
Desmond, Sir John of. *See* Fitzgerald,
Sir John.
Despenser, Hugh, the elder, Earl of
Winchester (*d*1326), 162
Despenser, Hugh, the younger (*d*1326),
162
Detersall, -----, 136
Dethick, William, Garter King of
Arms.
mourner at funeral of Queen of
Scots, 83(2)
Detston, Robert, partisan of 2nd Earl
of Essex.
imprisoned in the Marshalsea, 282
Devereux.
estates and family, 284
Devereux, Lady Dorothy, daughter of
2nd Earl of Essex.
proposed marriage with Simon
Archer, 282
Devereux, Lady Dorothy, daughter of
1st Earl of Huntingdon, wife of

Sir Richard Devereux (*d*1547),
229(2)
Devereux, Lady Dorothy (Doryt)
(*d*1619), daughter of 1st Earl of
Essex, wife of (1) Sir Thomas
Perrot (*d*1594), (2) 9th Earl of
Northumberland.
her portrait at Leicester House, 203,
224, 259
her legacy, 248
her second marriage, 261
Devereux, Frances, daughter of Sir
Francis Walsingham, wife of
(1) Sir Philip Sidney, (2) 2nd Earl
of Essex, (3) 4th Earl of
Clanricarde, 225n, 257
Devereux, Lady Frances, daughter of
1st Earl of Suffolk, wife of 3rd Earl
of Essex.
agreement with Countess of Leicester,
227
Devereux, George, brother of 1st Earl
of Essex.
letter from, 236
Devereux, Lettice, daughter of Sir
Francis Knollys, wife of (1) 1st
Earl of Essex, (2) Earl of Leicester,
(3) Sir Christopher Blount, 208,
211, 220, 221, 222, 224, 225(2),
226, 227(3), 261
letters from, 223(2)
letters to, 200, 220, 222, 223(2),
225
deposition regarding secret marriage
with Earl of Leicester, 204
her portrait at Leicester House, 207,
222, 224
made sole executrix, 221
her suit against Crompton and others,
225
agreement with Earl and Countess of
Essex, 227
her suit against Dilke, 227
attends Earl of Essex's funeral at
Carmarthen, 248
her suit for dower, 249
Devereux, Sir Richard, son of 1st
Viscount Hereford, father of 1st
Earl of Essex.
his marriage with Lady Dorothy
Hastings, 229
Devereux, Robert, 2nd Earl of Essex,
101, 102, 103, 210(2), 249-282
passim
letters from, 216, 223(3), 256, 260,
262, 268
letters to, 255(2), 256, 257(2), 258,
259(3), 262(2), 266
at Buxton, 21
invited by Queen to stay in Earl of
Leicester's lodging at Court, 216
his portrait at Leicester House, 224

his expenses at Cambridge, 247, 249, 250
attends his father's funeral at Carmarthen, 248
placed under supervision of Earl of Huntingdon, 251
goes to Lamphey, 251
his debts to Queen, 252
Queen's loan to, 252
jewels delivered to, 252
survey of manors of, 253
manors bestowed by Queen on, 253
entertains French Ambassador, 254(2)
in action near Rouen, 254
invited to nominate burgess M.P. for Carmarthen, 255
survey of his lands, 256
farmer of sweet wines, 256
warrant for payment from, 257
his debts, 257
devastation of his Irish estates, 257, 258, 262
petition from Garnons to, 260
estimate of his expenses in Queen's service, 261
account of money received for use of, 261
household and other expenses of, 261
visits historical monuments in Westminster Abbey, 261
his losses at chess and cards, 261
his expedition to Cadiz, 263(5), 264(2), 265(3)
his warrant to Linwray,263
contributions towards expedition of, 263(2)
Cadiz captured by forces of, 264
General of the English expedition to Spain, 265
composition of his regiment, 265
petitions to, 265, 266
his second expedition to Spain, 265
schedule of deeds and evidences of, 269
trial of, 269-276 *passim*
his reply to indictment, 272
defends his negotiations with Tyrone, 274
verdict pronounced against, 276
account of rebellion of, 277-281 *passim*
parleys with Sidney, 279, 280
imprisoned in the Tower, 281
mentioned in verses, 288
copies of papers relating to, 291
Comptroller to. See Lindley, Sir Henry.
Secretary of. See Reynolds, Edward.
Steward of. See Meyrick, Sir Gelly.
Devereux, Robert, 3rd Earl of Essex, 284, 286
letters to, 283(2), 284(2), 285(4), 286(4)
agreement between Countess of Leicester and, 227
goes to Low Countries, 282
survey of his lands, 282
receipts and debts of, 283
his estates in Ireland, 258, 262, 283(2), 284(4), 286(3), 288
his dispute with Primate of Ireland, 284
Colonel of foot in second expedition to Cadiz, 284
plea in Exchequer against, 284
case between Biddulph and, 285
his declaration in Star Chamber, 286
his will, 288
verses in memory of, 288-291 *passim*
estate of, 291
mentioned in his bailiff's narrative of events, 291
reference to his appointment as General of Parliamentary army, 291
Devereux, Walter, 3rd Lord Ferrers, later 1st Viscount Hereford, 229
Devereux, Walter, 2nd Viscount Hereford, later 1st Earl of Essex, 191, 229(2)
letters from, 241(2), 245, 246, 247
letters to, 233-246 *passim*
his portrait at Leicester House, 222
request to, 239
asked to send more money to Chester, 240
directives relating to his Irish expedition, 241
cost of his Irish expedition, 242
his agreement with Queen regarding expenses and profits of Irish expedition, 242
reference to his fatal illness, 247(2)
his debts to Queen, 247, 252
his body conveyed from Dublin to Carmarthen, 248
his funeral at Carmarthen, 248
his request to Broughton, 249
matters affecting estate of, 249(3)
Queen's loan to, 252
mentioned in verses, 288
Devereux, Walter, son of preceding.
attends his father's funeral at Carmarthen, 248
Devereux, Sir Walter, of Castle Bromwich, cousin of 3rd Earl of Essex.
letters to, 285(3), 288
Devonshire.
Assizes in, 68
Dicing, 138
Dickenson (Dekesone), Edward, in the service of Lord Robert Dudley.
acquitted at Stafford Assizes, 165

Dickenson, Francis, of Rotherham, 129, 130, 131

Dickenson, Gilbert, of Sheffield, in the service of Earl of Shrewsbury, 129, 130, 131

Dickenson, William, of Wincobank, 130, 131

Dickenson, William (d1606), late Bailiff of Sheffield, father of the three preceding.
his papers placed under lock and key, 129, 130

Dieppe (Depe, Diep), in France, 254
adheres to King of France, 99
French Admiral's ship being refitted at, 152

Digby, Mr.
at Buxton with his wife, 21

Digby, Mrs. Elizabeth, 132
in attendance on Dowager Countess of Shrewsbury, 133

Digby, Sir Robert, of Coleshill.
letter from, 283

Dilke, Sir Thomas, of Maxstoke.
Countess of Leicester's lawsuit against, 227

Dimocke. See Dymock.

Djerba (Gerba), in Tunisia.
Turks defeat Spanish naval forces at, 157
Spanish garrison besieged by Turks, 159

Dockwra, Edmund, of Chamberhouse, M.P. for Aylesbury, 178
letter from, 179
letter to, 178

Dodding, Henry.
attests copy of offensive message sent by Countess of Shrewsbury, 119

Dodford, Northants.
letter dated from, 239

Dolgellau (Dolgelly), Merioneth, 188

Dolman, Thomas, of Shaw House, Newbury.
Queen and Court lodged with, 103

Dolrado, Count. See Mansfeld, Count Wolrad of.

Dolynville. See Ollinville.

Domingo, in Cape Verde Is.
sacked by Drake's fleet, 71

Donington Castle, Berks., 71

Dorking, Surrey, 46

Dorome House. See Durham House.

Doryt, Lady. See Devereux, Lady Dorothy.

Dottin, Andrew, senior, of Bampton.
letter to, 48

Douai, in France, 211

Douglas, James, 4th Earl of Morton, 178
letters from, 178, 186(2)

Douglas, Robert, half-brother of Lord James Stewart.
sent as hostage to England, 155

Douglas, William, 10th Earl of Angus.
alleged to be in favour of Spanish intervention in Scotland, 262

Dover, Kent.
English Peace Commissioners embark at, 86, 87

Down, County, Ireland, 240

Downewell, Mr. See Downhall, William.

Downhall (Downhale), Thomas, in the service of Earl of Leicester.
letter from, 222

Downhall (Downewell), William, in the service of Earl of Essex.
imprisoned in the Marshalsea, 282

Drake, Sir Francis.
news of his expedition to West Indies, 68
returns to Portsmouth, 71
details of his success, 71
ordered to patrol coast of Spain, 86
at court, 90
his fleet in readiness, 90
reference to his and Norris's expedition against Spain, 99
map of his voyage at Wanstead, 208
reported to be sailing with his fleet to Ireland, 212
gift to Turk 'that cam with', 221

Drayton Bassett (Drayton), Staffs.
survey of Earl of Leicester's lands at, 200, 207
certificate dated from, 224
fatal quarrel on road between Lichfield and, 234

Dreadnought, The, of the Queen's Navy.
takes part in Earl of Essex's second expedition to Spain, 265

Drogheda, co. Louth.
captured Armada men brought to, 95

Drope, Thomas, prebendary of Wells.
letter from, 217

Drury, -----, 48

Drury, Sir Drue, of Riddlesworth, 79
sent to Fotheringhay to assist Paulet, 77, 78

Drury, William, a prisoner in the custody of Sir Richard Sackville.
letter from, 167

Drury Place, London,
letter dated from, 162

Dry Marston. See Marston Sicca.

Dublin, 192, 274
letters dated from, 180, 246, 247(2), 249, 258(2), 262, 283, 284(2), 286(2)
Earl of Essex's body conveyed to Carmarthen from, 248

Dublin Castle.
letter dated from, 193

Duck (Ducke), Edmond, footman to the
Queen, 218
Duckett, Everard. *See* Haunse, Everard.
Duddeston, Warwicks.
letter dated from, 143
Dudley, Staffs.
letters dated from, 153, 162
Dudley, Lady. *See* Sutton, Theodosia.
Dudley, Lord. *See* Sutton, Edward.
Dudley, Lord Ambrose, later Earl of
Warwick, Master of the Ordnance,
222, 236
letters from, 145, 146(2), 147, 166
and *n*, 216
letters to, 152, 154
goes to the Wells, 28
Privy Council letter signed by, 46
Commissioner at trial of Queen of
Scots, 73
not present in Star Chamber to
pronounce sentence ●n Queen of
Scots, 75
his wife complains of being separated
from, 156
present at secret marriage between
Earl of Leicester and Countess of
Essex, 206
his portrait at Leicester House, 207,
224
appeals on behalf of Sir James Croft,
216
his will, 223
Dudley, Amy, daughter of Sir John
Robsart, 1st wife of Lord Robert
Dudley, later Earl of Leicester,
137(2)
letter from, 159 and *n*
Edney's bill to, 161
reference to her death, 161
Dudley, Sir Andrew, formerly Captain
of Guisnes, brother of Duke of
Northumberland.
inventory of his goods, 151
Dudley, Anne, Countess of Warwick,
3rd wife of Earl of Warwick, 189,
219
goes to the Wells, 28
Dudley, Arthur, residentiary canon of
Lichfield.
letter from, 193
Dudley, Edmund, Councillor of
Henry VII and grandfather of Earl
of Leicester, 168
Dudley, Edward. *See* Sutton, Edward.
Dudley, Elizabeth, *suo jure* Baroness
Tailboys, 2nd wife of Lord
Ambrose Dudley, later Earl of
Warwick.
letters from, 147, 156
letter to, 140
complains of being separated from
her husband, 156

Dudley, John, Duke of
Northumberland (*d*1554),
father of Lord Robert Dudley, 139,
145, 146(2), 148, 167, 168
Dudley, John, auditor to Lord Robert
Dudley, 138, 167, 168
Dudley, Lettice, Countess of
Leicester. *See* Devereux, Lettice.
Dudley, Lord Robert, later Earl of
Leicester, Master of the Horse and
Lord Steward of the Household,
33-291 *passim*
letters from, 20, 24, 25(2), 31, 36,
38, 41, 47, 50, 55, 57, 63, 68, 69,
81, 86, 89, 91, 158, 167(2)
letters to, 20-220 *passim*
Privy Council letters signed by, 46,
86, 89, 93,
his advice to Earl of Shrewsbury, 33
Campion examined before, 35
regains Queen's favour, 44
summoned to conference by Queen
after fall of Antwerp, 45
mentioned as probable commander
of English forces in
Netherlands, 45
hint of attempt to destroy friendship
between Earl of Shrewsbury and,
47
commends Lord Talbot's conduct,
48, 50
refers to death of his son, 50
to command in Netherlands, 57
prepares to go to Netherlands, 63, 64
arrives in Netherlands, 65, 222
criticised for accepting Governorship
of United Provinces, 68
expected in England, 77
prepares to return to Netherlands,
80, 81
deputy to Earl of Shrewsbury in
office of Earl Marshal, 89
ill at Wanstead, 90
Queen's grief at death of, 94
his New Year's gift to Queen, 136
dines with French Ambassador, 136,
137
installed as Knight of the Garter at
Windsor, 136
financial accounts of, 136, 148, 163
wins wager from Earl of Pembroke,
137
dines with notable foreign persons
and envoys, 150
intervenes for release of his servant
from prison, 151
wages of his servants, 151
grant of lands by Queen to, 164
surveys and rentals of lands of,
167, 168, 200, 207
High Steward of Cambridge
University, 167*n*

receives gift of jewel from Chute, 167

bestows horses as gifts, 168

inventories of his wardrobe, 172, 207, 208, 210

asked to intervene on behalf of Stephens, 178

asked to intercede with Queen for Earl of Derby's son, 180

requests that survey of Englefield's lands be expedited, 188

reference to his visit to Bath for health reasons, 196

pearls purchased by, 199

to attend christening of Lady Danvers' child, 201

deposition regarding his secret marriage, 204, 205

portraits of, 207, 208, 222(6), 224

description of people attending upon him in Low Countries, 208

deeds and evidences of, 209

his allowance as Master of the Horse, 209

hostility in Holland towards, 213

with Queen at Erith, 213

Ranger of Forests north of Trent, 218

tract on *Godlie Fame* addressed to, 218

ordnance sent to his ship at Bristol, 219

debts of, 219, 221, 223, 225

reference to death of, 220(2)

petitions to, 225, 226

travels from Buxton to Chartley, 251

late farmer of sweet wines, 256

Chaplain to. *See* Hoverton, William; Tyndall, Humphrey; Willoughby.

Company of Players of. *See* Burbage; Clarke; Johnson; Laneham; Perkin; Wilson.

father of. *See* Dudley, John.

grandfather of. *See* Dudley, Edmund.

Steward to, at Kenilworth. *See* Besbeche, Henry.

Surveyor-General to. *See* Baynham, William.

son of. *See* Dudley, Robert.

servant of. *See* Bennison, John.

Dudley, Robert, *styled* Lord Denbigh (*d*1584), son of preceding, 220*n*

his death, 50

his portrait at Leicester House, 222(2), 224

breaks and defaces pictures at Leicester House, 222

Dudley, Thomas, cousin of Thomas Sutton, 174

Dudley Castle, Staffs., 209

Duke, Sir Henry, General of the Queen's Kerns in Ireland.

letter from, 257

appointed to deal with disturbances in Ulster, 258

Dun Sydney.

name of horse bestowed on Imperial Ambassador, 168

Dundee, Angus.

letter dated from, 186

Dunicke (?), in Netherlands.

captured by Dutch, 231

Dunkin, -----, in the service of Lord Robert Dudley, 137

Dunkirk (Dimkerke, Dunkyrk), 159, 211, 214, 231

Croft entertained at, 87

peace with England desired by inhabitants of, 87

Spanish ship arrives with money at, 211

Duke of Parma reported to have ordered execution of Burgomaster of, 214

reported death in battle of Governor of, 276

Dunstall, Staffs., 207

Du Pin, Monsieur, French diplomatist.

letter from, 180

Duppa, William, vicar of Dilwyn, Herefs.

case between Boyle and, 260

Durham (Dearolme), 29, 141

Durham, Bishop of. *See* Pilkington, James; Tunstall, Cuthbert.

Durham, Bishopric of, 286, 287

Durham House (Dorome House), Strand, London, 241

letters addressed to Earl of Essex at, 235, 238(2)

Dyer, Lady.

mourner at funeral of Queen of Scots, 83

Dyer, Mr., 257

Dyer, Sir Edward, of Weston, Somerset.

mourner at funeral of Queen of Scots, 83

Dymock (Dimocke), Glos., 240

letter dated from, 234

lordship of, 234

E

Eakring (Ekring), Notts.

parsonage of, 54

Eardisland, Herefs.

manor of, 283

Eardisley, Herefs., 251

Eastofte (Eastoft), John, of Eastoft, Yorks., 99

Edam, in Holland.
 ship called *White Lyon de*, 256
Edgehill, Warwicks.
 reference to battle at, 291
Edinburgh, 178
 letters dated from, 161, 262
Edkircke, Captain.
 takes part in Cadiz expedition, 265
Edmonds, Thomas, footman to the
  Queen, 218
Edney, William, of Tower Royal,
  London, tailor.
 letter to, 159
 his bill to Lady Amy Dudley, 161
Edward VI, King of England, 49, 141,
  145, 180, 226
Edwards, Roger.
 letter from, 200
Edzard II, Count of Emden.
 dines at Hampton Court, 254
Effingham, Lord Howard of. *See*
  Howard, William.
Egeley *or* Edgeley, Thomas, Keeper
  of Leicester House.
 his inventories, 207, 210
Egerton, Sir Thomas, later 1st Viscount
  Brackley, Lord Keeper, 125, 267,
  277
 takes part in Earl of Essex's trial, 269
 replies to Earl of Essex's defence, 275
 kept prisoner in Essex House during
  Earl of Essex's rebellion, 278
 released by Gorges, 278
Egmont(Egmond), Lamoral, Count of.
 accompanies Duke and Duchess of
  Feria out of Brussels, 155
 his portrait at Leicester House, 203
Egmont (Egmonde), Philippe, Count of.
 reference to Spanish sympathies of,
  38
Egmont, Sabine de Bavière, Countess
  of, wife of Lamoral, Count of
  Egmont.
 her portrait at Leicester House, 203
Ekring. *See* Eakring.
Elbeffe, Marquis d'. *See* Lorraine,
  René de.
Elboeuf, Marquis de. *See* Lorraine,
  Charles de.
Elections for Parliament.
 in Merioneth, 189
 in Nottinghamshire, 116, 117
Elizabeth I, Queen of England, 20-262
  passim
 letters from, 67, 70, 84, 85, 90, 91,
  94, 95
 letters to, 54, 60, 64, 85
 her marriage negotiations with Duke
  of Anjou, 24, 28, 30, 177
 sends reinforcements to Ireland, 24
 grants wardship to Jones, 24
 Duke of Anjou said to be devoted to,
  24
 Burnell examined by, 25
 distressed by quarrel between Earl
  and Countess of Shrewsbury, 25, 40
 Prince of Condé sees, 27
 suffers from a cold, 28
 orders greater security in the
  guarding of Queen of Scots, 28
 new ships added to her navy, 28
 advised by Walsingham not to abate
  Earl of Shrewsbury's allowance, 29
 refuses to reconsider her decision on
  allowance, 32
 financial cost of her policy in
  Scotland, 32
 grants land to Tasser, 35
 prevented by plague from going to
  Richmond, 35
 Parliament grants subsidy to, 36
 critical of freedom allowed by Earl
  of Shrewsbury to Queen of Scots,
  40
 her audience with Scottish envoys, 42
 proposed talks with Queen of Scots,
  42, 43
 Earl of Leicester regains her favour,
  44
 perturbed by surrender of Antwerp,
  45
 at Wimbledon, 45
 at Nonsuch, 45
 commends hospitality shown by Earl
  of Shrewsbury to Walsingham, 47
 offended by Earl of
  Northumberland's intrigues to
  release Queen of Scots, 48
 requests Earl of Shrewsbury to ignore
  rumours of her alleged suspicions
  of him, 48
 orders Earl of Shrewsbury not to
  assemble freeholders of the Peak,
  50
 suggests that Queen of Scots be
  removed to Wingfield, 51
 opposes appointment of Bentall as
  Gentleman Porter to Queen of
  Scots, 52
 requests Earl of Shrewsbury to
  provide victuals for Queen of
  Scots, 53
 her decision in dispute between
  Earl and Countess of Shrewsbury,
  55, 69, 70, 71, 72
 proposes to send Earl of Leicester
  to Netherlands, 57
 Lord Talbot's account of his interview
  with, 60
 Earl of Shrewsbury's gift of jewel
  to, 60
 snubs Countess of Shrewsbury, 64
 commends Earl of Shrewsbury's
  conduct towards Lord Talbot, 65

indisposition of, 68
revises her opinion concerning Earl
of Leicester's acceptance of
Governorship of United Provinces,
68
at Lambeth, 75
Scottish and French envoys sent to
intercede on behalf of Queen of
Scots with, 76, 77(2), 78, 79
Parliament's petition for execution
of Queen of Scots presented at
Richmond to, 77
her audience with Bellièvre, 78
pleased with Earl of Shrewsbury's
concern about her security, 79
her exchange of views with
Parliament over death sentence
on Queen of Scots, 79
requests Earl of Shrewsbury to
visit his wife, 80
appoints Earl of Huntingdon as
Lieutenant-General of the North,
84, 85
takes steps to defend frontiers of
Scotland against invasion, 84
prepares to meet naval threat from
Spain, 86
visits Earl of Leicester during his
illness at Wanstead, 90
grieved by death of King of
Denmark, 90
Earl of Shrewsbury mentioned as
possible guardian of her person,
92
her grief at Earl of Leicester's death,
94
to give public thanks for defeat of
Armada, 95
commends Earl of Shrewsbury's
kindness to his daughter-in-law, 95
proposes to create new earls and
barons, 97
Burghley refuses her offer of higher
rank in peerage, 97
measures for raising loan by privy
seal for, 97, 98(2)
orders restraint in eating of meat at
Lent, 98
her dislike of certain members of
House of Commons, 99
forbids discussion of doctrinal matters
in House of Commons, 100
much affected by Earl of
Shrewsbury's death, 101
estimate of her aid in men and
money to King of Navarre, 101
at Woodstock, 107
displeased with Earl of Shrewsbury,
108
at Chelsea, 136
Lord Robert Dudley's New Year's Gift
to, 136
at Greenwich, 137

at Gillingham, 137
at Cobham, 137
at Horsley, 137
Low Countries interested in her
marriage prospects, 139, 147
reference to her blood-letting, 140
at Deptford, 149, 150
at Eltham, 151
on progress, 158
Gresham sends to Spain for silk hose
for, 159
her gift of geldings and greyhounds to
Landgrave of Hesse-Cassel, 163
her grant of lands to Lord Robert
Dudley, 164, 167, 168
urged by House of Commons to
marry, 166
her reply to this request, 166
reference to Papal Bull issued
against, 171
Earl of Derby's son incurs her
displeasure, 180
persuaded of Duke of Norfolk's
disloyalty, 183
French King's enthusiasm for
friendship with, 187
her progress from Kenilworth to
Windsor, 189
reference to her melancholy, 197
her regret at Earl of Leicester's
absence from Court, 198
danger of quarrel between King of
Denmark and, 201
her portrait at Leicester House, 203,
224
her portraits, 208
her bedchamber at Wanstead, 208
treaty concluded between King of
Scots and, 209
placard published in Netherlands in
defence of, 213
reference to peace talks between King
of Spain and, 213
with Earl of Leicester at Erith, 213
orders Privy Council to deal with
mutiny of Ostend garrison, 216
invites Earl of Essex to stay in
Earl of Leicester's lodging at Court,
216
Earl of Leicester asked to intervene
on Croft's behalf with, 216(2)
disinclined to pardon mutinous
English garrison at Ostend, 216
list of her footmen, 217, 218
petitions to, 225, 226
her agreement over Irish expedition
with Earl of Essex, 242
her loans to Earl of Essex, 252(2)
her grant of manors to Earl of
Essex, 253
her instructions to Hawkins, 253
opposes Earl of Essex's appointment
of Earl of Southampton as General

of Horse, 269
summons Earl of Essex to court, 277
Groom of the Poultry to. *See* Atkins,
Robert.
Master of the Horse to. *See* Dudley,
Robert.
Registrar to. *See* Barker, Edward.
Yeoman of the Chamber to. *See*
Hetherley, John.
Elizabeth of Austria, daughter of
Emperor Maximilian II, wife of
Charles IX, King of France, 169
uneasy relations with Catherine de
Medici, 171
Elliot (Ellyott), Paul, Mayor of
Southampton.
his certificates in favour of Walnut,
263
Ellis *or* Ellys, Richard, Receiver to
Lord Robert Dudley.
his accounts, 148(2)
Elmer, Mr. *See* Aylmer, John.
Elmes, Edward, of Lilford.
mourner at funeral of Queen of
Scots, 83
Eltham, Kent, 138(2), 149
Queen at, 151
Elverston, County of. *See* Helfenstein.
Elverstone, Marquis of. *See* Helfenstein.
Ely, Cambs., 181
recusants imprisoned in Bishop's
house at, 92
Ely, Bishop of. *See* Coxe, Richard.
Ely House, Holborn, London.
letters dated from, 85(2), 179
Emmanuel Philibert, Duke of Savoy.
his portrait at Leicester House, 222
Empden (Emden), Earls of. *See*
Edzard II; John XVI.
Emperor, The. *See* Charles V;
Ferdinand I; Maximilian II;
Rudolph II.
Empire, The.
King of Spain reported to be
requesting help against Duke of
Anjou from Princes of, 38
Diet of, 38
Enclosures.
in Derbyshire, 165
Enfield, Middx.
letters dated from, 188, 190
England, 253, 255, 256, 258, 261,
277
Don Antonio hires men and ships in,
36
defeat of Armada to be celebrated
throughout, 95
King of Spain disinclined to make
peace with France without, 138
anxiety in Low Countries because of
impending religious changes in,
139

circulation in Low Countries of
adverse reports about, 142
Queen of Scots regarded by French
Court as Queen of, 144
Duke of Feria refuses to take over
Glajon's mission in, 155
reference to ratification of treaty
between France and, 158
disorders caused by demobilized
soldiers and sailors in, 160
Queen of Scots desires to return to
Scotland through, 163
negotiations for treaty of alliance
between France and, 178, 187
map of northern, at Leicester House,
204
preparations in Low Countries for
invasion of, 211
copies of treaties between United
Provinces and, 252
Scottish forces invade, 287
Englefield, Berks.
Queen at, 189
Englefield, Sir Francis, of Englefield,
194, 211
inquisition concerning his lands, 178,
188
Englefield House, Berks., 256
English Bicknor, Glos.
letter dated from, 237
Enstone, Oxon.
letter dated from, 236
Epinac, Pierre, Archbishop of Lyons.
seized by order of King of France, 97
Erasmus, Desiderius.
his works banned from Low
Countries, 139
Eric, Duke, of Sweden and Finland,
later Eric XIV of Sweden.
Lord Robert Dudley dines with,
150(4)
reference to imprisonment of, 184
Erith (Erythe), Kent.
Queen and Earl of Leicester at, 213
Errington, Captain Nicholas, in charge
of the English company at
Rammekens, 215
Erskine, John, Earl of Mar, Regent of
Scotland.
letter to, 186
Erythe. *See* Erith.
Escoyd. *See* Iscoed.
Essex, Earls of. *See* Devereux.
Essex House, Strand, London, 254,
261, 262, 269, 277(2)
letter dated from, 259
players at, 261
Queen's representatives kept prisoner
in, 278
besieged by Queen's forces, 278
Etherington, Davye, tenant to the

Archbishop of Armagh, 239
Eure (Ewry), William, 2nd Lord Eure.
    deputises for Lord President of
        Council of the North, 29
Eure, William, son of preceding.
    letter from, 141
Eustace, James, 3rd Viscount
        Baltinglass.
    heads rebellion, 28
    English casualties in attack on, 30
Evans, Captain.
    takes part in Cadiz expedition, 265
Evans, Lewis, Popish (later Protestant)
        controversialist and divine.
    letter from, 182
Everstons, Grave van. See Helfenstein.
Every or Eure (Evers), in the service
        of Earl of Shrewsbury, 112, 113,
        114, 115
Evors, Captain, of the English
        expeditionary force in Walcheren.
    his conduct in action commended,
        232
Ewden, Yorks., 131
Ewell (Hewel), Surrey.
    letter dated from, 195
Ewelme, Oxon., 178
Ewias Lacy. See Ewyas Lacy.
Ewry, Lord. See Eure, William.
Ewyas Lacy (Ewias Lacy), Herefs.
    rental of Earl of Leicester's lands
        at, 168
Excellency, His. See Dudley, Lord
        Robert.
Exchange, The, London.
    Latin verses found in, 90
Exchequer, 98, 128, 161
    bill in House of Commons against
        abuse in, 99
    plea against Earl of Essex in, 284
    Chancellor of. See Mildmay, Sir
        Walter.
Exchequer Chamber, 129
Exeter, Devon, 192

F

Fadys (Fades), Henry, of Cheshunt, in
        the service of Lord Burghley, 124
Falmouth, Devon.
    Spanish Armada reported to be at,
        212
Fanchurch Street. See Fenchurch
        Street.
Fanhope. See Fownhope.
Farmor, Richard, an officer in the
        Tower of London.
    letter from, 187
Farnese, Alessandro, Prince of Parma,
        Governor of the Low Countries,
        214, 255

Antwerp surrenders to, 45
    overtures for peace from, 80
    sends Mansfeld to recapture Bonn,
        86
    severely criticised for alleged
        inaction, 93
    ready to assist League in France, 99
    description of his sudden death, 115
    likely consequences of his death, 116
    his preparations to invade England,
        211
    rumour of imminent invasion by,
        213
    report of his severity towards
        soldiers and officials, 214
Farney. See Ferney.
Farral. See Ferrol.
Faseley. See Fazeley.
Faversham (Feversham), Kent.
    letter dated from, 206
Fazeley (Faseley), 207
Fenchurch (Fanchurch) Street,
        London, 88
    Sheriff of London's house in, 278
Fenner, Captain George, naval
        commander, 266
Ferdinand I, Emperor.
    false news of his death, 162
Feria (Ferya), Gomez Suares de
        Figueroa y Cordova, Duke (Count)
        of.
    leaves Brussels, 155
    refuses to take over Glajon's mission
        in England, 155
Feria (Ferya), Jane Dormer, Countess
        of, wife of preceding.
    presented with gifts by Regent of
        Low Countries, 155
Ferney (Farney, Fernie, Fferny), co.
        Monaghan, 258(2), 283, 284, 286
    letter dated from, 283
    spoliation by Irish of Earl of
        Essex's land at, 257, 258, 262
Ferrers.
    estates and family, 284
Ferrers, Lord. See Devereux.
Ferrol (Farral), in Spain, 253
Feversham. See Faversham.
Ffere, Count de la. See La Fère.
Ffleming, Captain. See Fleming,
        Captain.
Fflowden. See Flodden.
Ffoliett, Captain. See Foliett, Captain.
Ffrehingam, Monsieur de.
    reported killed in battle at Nieuport,
        276
Ffynelands, Duke of. See Eric.
Fiennes (Ffynes), Richard, later 7th
        Lord Saye and Sele, 91, 97
Finch, Sir Thomas, of Eastwell.
    to inquire into export of horses, 155
Fireworks.

at Kenilworth, 189, 196
Firth, The. *See* Forth.
Fitton, Sir Edward, President of
 Connaught (*d*1579), 171
Fitton (Phyton), Sir Edward, son of
 preceding.
 letter from, 259
Fitton (Fyton), Richard, of Trentham.
 letter from, 238
Fitzalan, Henry, 12th Earl of Arundel,
 157, 160, 162
 letters from, 158, 183
 receives gift of horses, 169
Fitzgerald, Gerald, 11th Earl of
 Kildare.
 takes the field against Baltinglass, 28
Fitzgerald, Gerald, 14th Earl of
 Desmond.
 takes refuge in mountains of
 Munster, 28
 his fear of being attacked by Earl of
 Ormond, 244
 Bourchier taken prisoner by, 244
Fitzgerald, James FitzThomas, *known
 as* the Sugan Earl of Desmond.
 said to have been captured by
 Carew, 277
Fitzgerald, Sir John, brother of 14th
 Earl of Desmond.
 letters from, 179, 181
Fitzgibbon, Sir Edmund, the White
 Knight, 277
Fitzherbert, Anthony, recusant, son of
 John Fitzherbert.
 to be removed to gaol from Earl of
 Shrewsbury's house, 94
Fitzherbert, John, of Padley, recusant.
 to be removed to gaol from Earl of
 Shrewsbury's house, 94
 his son. *See* preceding.
Fitzherbert, Sir Thomas, of Norbury.
 his house forfeited because of his
 recusancy, 93
Fitzmaurice, James, Irish rebel, cousin
 of Gerald Fitzgerald, 14th Earl of
 Desmond, 171
 submits to Perrot, 193
Fitzwilliam, Anne, Lady, wife of
 following and sister of Sir Henry
 Sidney, 180
Fitzwilliam, Sir William, of Milton,
 Northants., Lord Deputy of
 Ireland, 192, 243(6), 244, 245, 246,
 257, 258, 262
 letters from, 179, 192
 takes up his office in Ireland, 87
 leads forces against shipwrecked men
 of Armada, 95
Fitzwilliam, William, of Dogsthorpe,
 son of preceding.
 mourner at funeral of Queen of
 Scots, 83

Flanders, 138, 212, 221, 231
 Spanish forces reported to have
 entered, 38
 Earl of Leicester bestows gift of
 horse on ambassador from, 169
 English peace commissioners return
 from, 214
 English expeditionary force returns
 from South Beveland to, 230
 Vice-Admiral of. *See* Walters.
Fleece, Order of the Golden.
 King of Spain postpones bestowal of,
 142
Fleet, The, prison, London, 259, 261
 letter dated from, 216
 Warden of, 224
Fleet Street, Coventry, 152
Fleet Street, London, 24, 192, 285
 affray in, 122, 123, 124
Fleming (Ffleming), Captain.
 takes part in Cadiz expedition, 265
Fletcher, Mr., of Gray's Inn, father of
 following, 106
Fletcher, Francis, of Stoke Bardolph,
 106
 signs evidence concerning Stanhope's
 defamation of Earl of Shrewsbury,
 104
Fletcher, Richard, Dean of
 Peterborough.
 mourner at funeral of Queen of
 Scots, 82
Flodden (Fflowden), Northumb.
 Scottish forces plan to camp at, 287
Florence, Duke of. *See* Medici,
 Cosimo de.
Florida, 72
Flowerdew, Edward, Baron of
 Exchequer.
 dies on circuit of gaol fever, 68
Floyd, Captain, 191
Floyd, Mr., 'the saltpeter man', 100
Flushing, in Zeeland, 230, 231, 232(2)
 letters dated from, 146, 215
 St. Phillipo captured by men of, 93
 States General desirous of reducing
 garrison at, 215
 news from, 230, 232
 Admiral of, 232
 English garrison at, 264
Fodrynghay. *See* Fotheringhay.
Foix, Count of. *See* Candale.
Foix, Henri de. *See* Candale.
Foix, Paul de, French Ambassador
 Extraordinary to England.
 reference to his Anglophile
 sentiments, 180
 arrives in England, 181, 184, 187
Foliett (Ffoliett), Captain.
 takes part in Cadiz expedition, 265
Foljambe, Sir Godfrey, of Walton,
 Derbys., 43

letter from, 44
Fontainebleau, in France.
　letter dated from, 180
Foresight, The, of the Queen's Navy.
　to take part in Hawkins's expedition, 253
Forrest, Thomas, 149
Forster, Mr., 137
Forster (Foster), Anthony, of Cumnor Place, steward to Lord Robert Dudley, M.P. for Abingdon.
　letter to, 167
　warrant from, 168
Forster, Sir John, of Bamborough Castle, Lord Warden of the Middle Marches, 173, 187
Forster (Foster), Nicholas, son of preceding, 187
Fortescue, Lady.
　Earl of Essex in debt to, 283
Fortescue, Sir John, Chancellor of the Exchequer.
　takes part in the trial of Earl of Essex, 269
Fortescue, Thomas, of London.
　appointed collector of subsidy, 36
Forth, Firth of, Scotland, 156
Foster, Mr., 102, 136
Foster, Humfrey.
　letter from, 235
Foster, Nicholas. *See* Forster, Nicholas.
Fotheringhay (Fodrynghay), Northants., 77, 80
　list of Commissioners present at trial of Queen of Scots at, 73
Fowler (Fouller), Thomas, political agent, in the service of Earl of Leicester.
　letters from, 44, 209, 213, 220
　flees to Scotland, 220
Fownhope (Fanhope), Herefs.
　manor of, 265, 291
Fox, -----, of Flushing.
　supplies information about Prince of Orange's forces, 231
Fox, Mr., servant of Henry Cavendish, 135
Fox, Charles, Secretary of the Council in the Marches of Wales.
　regarded by Shadwell as his enemy, 195
Foxe, John, martyrologist.
　copy of his *Acts and Monuments* at Wanstead, 208
Foyle, Lough (Lafoyle, Lafoile), in Ulster, 273
Foyntes, Count of. *See* Fuentes.
France, 40, 43, 44, 46, 116, 150, 191, 193, 233, 251, 253
　news of events in, 28, 30(2), 57, 59, 65, 68, 99
　Don Antonio hires men and ships in, 36

36
Walsingham goes to, 36
reinforcements arrive in Bruges from, 37
Cobham brings gifts to Earl of Shrewsbury from, 48
intervention on behalf of Queen of Scots by, 76, 77(2), 78, 79
Parma's death advantageous to, 116
collaboration between Turkey and, 116
gardener at Kew a native of, 138
death of Henry II expected to lead to changes in, 141
Scottish expedition being organised in, 144
state of affairs in, 153, 202
reference to ratification of treaty between England and, 158
cardinals sent by Pope to call national council in, 159
suspected manoeuvre to catch Huguenot leaders in, 159
newsletters from, 169, 195, 211
negotiations for treaty of alliance between England and, 178, 187
Lord Admiral to go to, 187
maps of, at Leicester House, 204
Spanish Armada expected to arrive on coast of, 211
Prince of Orange expects soldiers from, 231, 232
Perez leaves England for, 261, 262
France, Admiral of. *See* Coligny.
France, King of. *See* Charles IX; Francis I; Francis II; Henry II; Henry III; Henry IV.
France, Marshal of. *See* Montmorency.
France, Queen of. *See* Elizabeth; Louise.
France, Queen Mother of. *See* Medici, Catherine de.
Francis I, King of France (*d*1547), 24
Francis II, King of France, 160
　under influence of Guise family, 143
　his proclamation as King postponed, 144
　news of his death, 162
　his horses to be sold, 163
Francis (Frances), 136
Francis, Sir Edward, of Petworth.
　Earl of Essex in debt to, 283
Franke, Hans, of London, goldsmith, originally a native of Antwerp.
　petition to Earl of Leicester, 226
Frankfurt am Main (Frankfort), in Germany.
　letters dated from, 192, 193, 194
Franklin, Samuel, in the service of Sir Gelly Meyrick, 256
Frankpledge.
　view of, 48

Freake, Thomas. *See* Freke, Thomas.
Frederick II, King of Denmark.
  his death, 90
  well affected towards England, 90
  threatens to detain English merchant ships, 201
Frederick III, Elector Palatine (*d*1576).
  refuses to attend Diet of Spires, 169
  engaged in religious and civil reforms, 193
  his portrait at Leicester House, 203
Freeman, -----, in the service of John Poyntz, 146
Freke (Freake), Robert, Receiver of sale of Crown lands, 252
Freke (Freake), Thomas, son of preceding, 252
French, Margaret, 97
French Pledges, The. *See* Candale; Laval; Nantouillet; Trans.
Friesland, Netherlands.
  news concerning affairs of, 214
Frobisher (Frobyshyr), Martin, navigator and naval commander, 90
Fryer Peyto.
  picture of, at Leicester House, 203
Fuentes (Foyntes), Don Pedro Henriquez de Azevedo, Conde de, Spanish General.
  sent by King of Spain to Brussels, 116
Fulwood, John, in the service of Sir Thomas Stanhope.
  his disclosures, 124
Fylles, Robert, of Kingsland.
  letter from, 188
Fynes, Richard. *See* Fiennes, Richard.
Fysher, John, 142
  letter from, 154
Fyton, Richard. *See* Fitton, Richard.

G

Gaetano (Gaitano), Pedro, member of the Prince of Parma's Council of War.
  arrives in Bruges, 211
Gaillon (Gaglioni), in France.
  letters dated from, 178(2)
Gainsborough, Lincs., 105, 109, 115
Gaitano, Petro. *See* Gaetano, Pedro.
Galeazzo, Count, 171
Galicia (Galizia), in Spain, 253
Galleys.
  reference to English prisoner in Spanish, 261
  English forces take San Lucar and destroy, 264

Gaming, 138, 151
  gaming tables at Leicester House, 204
  See also Cards; Dicing.
Ganua. *See* Genoa.
Gaol Fever.
  Justices of Assize and of Peace die of, 68
Gardiner, Thomas, Teller of the Exchequer, 283
Gargrave (later Sir) Coton, of Nostell, 29
  letter from, 38
Garnett, Margery, 224
Garnon *or* Gernon, Patrick.
  his suit against Earl of Essex, 284, 285
Garnons, Herefs., 260
Garnons, John, of Garnons, 261
  petition to Earl of Essex, 260
Garrdon. *See* Covent Garden.
Garret, Lady.
  her portrait at Leicester House, 207
Garret, Lettice.
  her portrait at Leicester House, 207
Garter, Order of the.
  Lord Robert Dudley installed as Knight of, 136
  robes of, at Leicester House, 204
  sale of Earl of Essex's collar of SS of, 248
Garter King of Arms. *See* Dethick, William.
Gascoigne, George, member of the English expeditionary force to South Beveland.
  his conduct in action commended, 230
Gatehouse, The, prison, London.
  Earl of Essex's partisans imprisoned in, 281
Gawdy, Sir Francis, Justice of Queen's Bench, 269
  takes part in trial of Earl of Essex, 269
Gawdy (Gowdie), Sir Thomas, Justice of Queen's Bench, 269
  Commissioner at trial of Queen of Scots, 74
Gawnte. *See* Ghent.
Geffe, Nicholas, of London.
  letter from, 257
Gelderland (Guelders), in Netherlands, 214, 230
  agreement between Prince of Orange and, 232
  Chancellor of. *See* Leoninus.
Geldern (Gelders), in Germany.
  captured by Dutch, 231
Gemynie, a Frenchman.
  an instrument of astronomy bought from, 136

General, The. *See* Devereux, Robert, 2nd Earl of Essex.
General Council of Catholic Church.
  not to be held, 159
Genlis (Jenliis), Jean de Hangest, Seigneur de, Huguenot commander, 231
Genoa (Ganua), in Italy.
  letter dated from, 145
  death of Santa Cruz reported from, 87
Gerard, Sir Gilbert, Master of the Rolls.
  Lord Henry Howard committed to his custody, 99
Gerard (Gerrat), Sir Thomas, of Gerard's Bromley, Knight Marshal.
  his regiment in Cadiz expedition, 263
  commander in Cadiz expedition, 263
  composition of his regiment, 265
  forces Earl of Essex to retreat from Cheapside, 278
Gerard (Gerrard), (later Sir) William, Vice-President of the Council in the Marches.
  letter from, 179
Germany, 163, 231
  reiters expected in Bruges from, 38
  Kings of France and Navarre hire mercenaries from, 65
  French Huguenots expect military assistance from Protestant Princes of, 68
  defeat of Spanish Armada celebrated in, 95
  Emperor's appeal for help against Turks to Princes of, 184
  defeat of Duke of Alva's recruits from, 231, 232
  references in verses to 'ruyned', 288
Germine (?), in Netherlands.
  anti-Spanish action of townsmen of, 231
Gerrat, Sir Thomas. *See* Gerard, Sir Thomas.
Ghent (Gawnte), in Belgium, 276
  letter dated from, 144
  Duke of Anjou promises to visit, 37
  celebration of mass considered odious in, 37
  King of Spain at, 142
Gibbon, Captain.
  takes part in Cadiz expedition, 265
Giffard, Captain, Royalist officer, 291
Giffard (Gyford), Roger, physician to the Queen.
  letter to, 260
Gifford, Sir George. *See* Gyfford, Sir George.
Gilbert, -----, 174
Gilbert, Dr. *See* Gilbert, William.

Gilbert, Sir Humphrey, navigator.
  his portrait at Leicester House, 207
Gilbert (Gylbert), Thomas, in the service of Sir Thomas Stanhope, 104, 119
Gilbert, William, of St. Peter's Hill, London, physician and physicist.
  letter written at his house, 71
Gildford. *See* Guildford.
Gill, -----, fishmonger, of Broken Wharf, London, 122
Gilling Castle, Yorks., 125
Gillingham, Kent.
  Queen at, 137
Gilpin, George, English Agent in Zeeland, 150
  letters from, 138, 141, 147
Glajon (Glasyon), Philippe d'Estade, Seigneur de, Spanish Ambassador Extraordinary to England.
  Duke of Feria refuses to take over mission from, 155
Glemham (Glemmon), Colonel Sir Thomas, of Little Glemham.
  his regiment in Newcastle, 287
Glencarns, Lord of. *See* Cunningham, Alexander.
Globes.
  of the world, at Leicester House, 204
  of America, at Leicester House, 221
Gloucester (Gloceter).
  Minster of, 146
Gloucestershire, 45
Glover, Robert, Somerset Herald, 25
  his death, 89
Glynn (Glyns), Ulster, 243
  Earl of Essex to establish English shire system in, 243
Goes (Tergose, Tregose), in Zeeland.
  English troops in action against Spaniards near, 230
Golden Grove, Carms.
  letter dated from, 259
Gonslin, Martin, Keeper of the plate at Leicester House, 219
Gonson, Benjamin, Treasurer of Naval Causes.
  signs naval estimates, 253
Gonzague, Louis de, Duc de Nevers (d1595).
  quarrel between Duke of Guise and, 184
Goodere (Gooderus, Goodyere), Sir Henry (Henricus), of Polesworth, 178, 207
  letters from, 84, 172
Goodere, William, of Monk's Kirby, brother of preceding.
  letter from, 244
Goodrich Castle, Herefs.
  occupied by Royalists, 291

Goodyere, Mr. *See* Goodere, Sir Henry.
Gordon. *See* Gourdain.
Gordon, George, 6th Earl of Huntly
  (Hontley).
  alleged to be in favour of Spanish
    intervention in Scotland, 262
Gorges (Goudge, Gorge), Sir
  Ferdinando, of Plymouth.
  tricks Meyrick into releasing prisoners
    at Essex House, 278
  imprisoned in the Gatehouse, 281
Gorges (Gorge), Sir Thomas, of
  Longford, Wilts., 275
Goring, Captain.
  takes part in Cadiz expedition, 265
Gosenall, Mr., partisan of 2nd Earl of
  Essex.
  imprisoned in the Marshalsea, 282
Goudge, Sir Ferdinando. *See* Gorges,
  Sir Ferdinando.
Gourdain (Gordon), Girault de
  Mauléon, Seigneur de, Governor
  of Calais.
  Queen asked to write to, 93
Gowdie, Justice. *See* Gawdy, Sir
  Thomas.
Grace, Lady. *See* Cavendish, Grace.
Gracechurch Street (Gracious Street),
  London.
  Londoners join Earl of Essex in, 278
  Lord Burghley forced to withdraw
    from, 278
Grafton, Northants.
  Honour of, 191
Grafton, Worcs., 45
Grafton Court, Northants, 219
Graham (Grayme), Fergus (Fargus).
  letter from, 165
Graham, George, son of following.
  sent as hostage to England, 156
Graham, John, 4th Earl of Menteith.
  his son sent as hostage to England,
    156
Graie, Lady. *See* Grey, Jane.
Graie, Lord. *See* Grey, Arthur.
Granada (Granado), Bernardin de,
  Gentleman Esquire of the Queen's
  Stables.
  letters from, 144, 146
Grandevile, Cardinal. *See* Granvelle.
Grantham, William, partisan of 2nd
  Earl of Essex.
  imprisoned in the Marshalsea, 282
Granvelle (Grandevile), Antoine
  Perrenot de, Cardinal.
  his portrait at Wanstead, 208
Graunte, John, partisan of 2nd Earl
  of Essex.
  imprisoned in the Marshalsea, 282
Grave Morris. *See* Nassau, Count
  Maurice of.
Gravesend, Kent, 170, 262

Gray, Lord. *See* Grey, Arthur.
Gray, Edward, of Buildwas.
  suit with Vernon, 191
Grayme, Fargus. *See* Graham, Fergus.
Gray's Inn, London, 106
  letters dated from, 100, 210
Gre Audley.
  name of horse bestowed on Sir
    Nicholas Throckmorton, 169
Gre Southwell.
  name of horse bestowed on Sir
    Henry Sidney, 169
Green, William, partisan of 2nd Earl of
  Essex.
  imprisoned in the Marshalsea, 282
Greenall, William, partisan of 2nd Earl
  of Essex.
  imprisoned in the Marshalsea, 282
Greenwich, Kent, 129, 137(3), 148,
  149(3), 150(2)
  letters dated from, 22, 36, 43, 65,
    67, 68, 70, 79, 80, 81, 86, 87,
    88, 89(2), 91(2), 127, 198, 223(2),
    264
  court at, 89, 127, 198
  Princess Mary to be christened at,
    128 and *n*
  Queen at, 137
  tilt yard at, 254
  Perez leaves for France from, 262
Gregory XIII, Pope, 28, 35
  reported to have offered money and
    land to Duke of Anjou, 24
  said to have closed English House in
    Rome, 30
Grenville (Grenefield), Sir Richard,
  naval commander, 72
Gresham, Anne, Lady, of Osterley,
  widow of following.
  at Buxton, 21
Gresham, Sir Thomas, English
  Ambassador to the Regent of the
  Low Countries (*d*1579), 179, 206
  letters from, 159, 162, 186
  Lord Robert Dudley dines with, 137
Gresham House, London.
  letter dated from, 186
Gresley, (later Sir) Thomas, of
  Drakelow, 43
Grevell, Fowke. *See* Greville, Sir Fulke.
Greves, Thomas, of Buxton, 130
  letter from, 20
Greville (Grevell), Sir Fulke (Fowke),
  poet and statesman, 151
  letter from, 262
Grey (Graie), Arthur, 14th Lord Grey
  of Wilton (*d*1593), 31, 179
  letter from, 217
  appointed Lord Deputy of Ireland, 28
  requests reinforcements for Earl of
    Kildare, 28
  reference to his victory at Smerwick,

31
Commissioner at trial of Queen of
Scots, 74
named as deputy to Earl of Leicester
in Netherlands, 77
Grey, Frances, Duchess of Suffolk,
daughter of Charles Brandon,
Duke of Suffolk and Mary Tudor,
wife of (1) Henry Grey, Duke of
Suffolk, (2) Adrian Stokes, 155
Grey, Henry, 6th Earl of Kent, 24
Commissioner at trial of Queen of
Scots, 74
commission for execution of Queen
of Scots to be first shown to, 79
signs letter to Earl of Shrewsbury, 91
Grey, Sir Henry, of Enville.
to be made a baron, 97
Grey (Graie), Jane, Lady, 2nd wife of
14th Lord Grey of Wilton.
train-bearer to Countess of Bedford
at funeral of Queen of Scots, 83
Grey, Lord John, brother of 3rd
Marquess of Dorset and uncle of
Lady Jane Grey.
letters from, 140, 162
Grey, Lord John, of Pyrgo, 152
Grey, Lady Mary, daughter of 3rd
Marquess of Dorset and widow of
Thomas Keyes, former Serjeant
Porter.
in the custody of Sir Thomas
Gresham, 186
Grey, Robert, in the service of Sir
Thomas Stanhope, 104
Grey, Thomas, 15th Lord Grey of
Wilton.
reported to have been wounded in
battle at Nieuport, 276
Griffin (Griffyn), Edward, of Dingley.
mourner at funeral of Queen of
Scots, 83
Grindal, Edmund, Archbishop of
York, 190
Groyne, The. See Corunna.
Grymes, Justin, of Greenwich, 167
Guaras, Antonio, Spanish Ambassador
to England, 195
Guelders. See Gelderland.
Guildford (Gildford), Surrey, 46
Guipuzcoa (Guypuscoa), in Spain.
Captain of the province of. See
Acunha.
Guise, House of. See also Lorraine.
reference to collaboration between
King of Spain and, 144
losing its power in France, 163
said to be forfeiting favour of
French King, 184
Gunpowder.
supplied for fireworks at Kenilworth,
189, 196

Gunter, Mr., of the English
expeditionary force in Walcheren.
killed in action near Middelburg, 232
Gunwell, Mr., a lawyer, 229
Gurden, John, footman to the Queen,
218
Guyese. See Gyse.
Guypuscoa. See Guipuzcoa.
Guyse, Monsieur de. See Lorraine,
François de.
Gwyn, Rhydderch (Reddi), of
Manordeilo.
letter from, 237
Gwyn, Thomas, tenant of Morfa Mawr
grange, 283
Gyfford (Gifford), Sir George, of
Weston Subedge.
takes part in Cadiz expedition, 265
Gyford, Dr. See Giffard, Roger.
Gylbert, Thomas. See Gilbert,
Thomas.
Gyse (Guyese), -----, 259

H

Haarlem, in Holland, 231
Hackness, Yorks.
survey of Lord Robert Dudley's
lands at, 167
Hafodwen (Havodwin), Cards.
grange of, 283
Hague, The, in Holland.
letters dated from, 213, 214, 215
Haiden, Captain. See Heydon, Sir
Christopher.
Half Moon, The, a grocer's shop
in Westminster.
letter dated from, 33
Gilbert Talbot lodges at, 33
Halfhyde, Edward, of Aspenden.
letter from, 238
Halfnaked. See Halnaker.
Halifax, Yorks.
letter dated from, 29
Hall, -----, 181
Hallamshire, Yorks., 28
Halnaker (Haufnaker, Halfnaked) in
Boxgrove, Sussex, 157
letters dated from, 140, 162
Halstead, Essex, 228
Halstead (Halsted) and Tilton, Leics.
survey of Earl of Leicester's lands
at, 167
Ham (Hame), Essex, 170
Hamilton, Claude, 4th son of James
Hamilton, Duke of Chatelherault.
sent as hostage to England, 155
Hamilton, Lord David, brother of
following.
imprisoned in France, 144
Hamilton, Lord James, 2nd Earl of

Arran and Duke of Chatelherault, 144
letter from, 161
his son sent as hostage to England, 155
Hamilton, James, 3rd Marquess of Hamilton, Master of the Horse to Charles I.
his regiments, 286
Hamlet (Hanlett), William, messenger of the Queen's Chamber, 112
Hamon, Captain, of the English expeditionary force in Walcheren.
his conduct in action commended, 232
Hamon, Mr., servant of Earl of Shrewsbury, 135
Hampden, Mr., 136
Hampshire, 188
Hampton, Great and Little, Worcs.
rental of Earl of Leicester's lands at, 168
Hampton Court (Hamton Cortt), Middx.
letter dated from, 128
Counts of Emden dine at, 254
Hamysby. See Hemsby.
Handford, Thomas, of Woollashill.
his estate at Pembridge passed to Earl of Essex, 284
Handly, Captain, of the English expeditionary force in Walcheren.
his conduct in action commended, 232
Hanlett, William. See Hamlet, William.
Hanmer, Edward, partisan of 2nd Earl of Essex.
imprisoned in the Marshalsea, 282
Harbard, William. See Herbert, William.
Harbord, Sir Charles, Auditor of the Prince of Wales's revenue and Commissioner for the Principality of Wales.
signs letter to Earls of Essex and Suffolk, 285
Harcourt (Harcott), Captain.
takes part in Cadiz expedition, 265
Harcourt, Robinson, son of following.
one of his men killed in an affray, 234
Harcourt, Simon, of Stanton Harcourt.
letters from, 234, 238
Hardwick, Derbys., 108, 117, 131, 132
Harington, James, M.P. for Rutland.
Lord Robert Dudley loses at play in his house, 138
Harley or Harleigh, Thomas, of Brampton Bryan.
denounced for his 'barbarous

ymmanity', 254 and n
Harnesey. See Hornsey.
Harpur (Harper), John, of Swarkeston, 43
Harrie, Lord. See Howard, Lord Henry.
Harris, David, Alderman of Bristol.
signs letter to Earl of Leicester, 173
Hart (Harte), Edward, partisan of 2nd Earl of Essex.
imprisoned in the Marshalsea, 282
Hart, Sir John, Lord Mayor of London.
to enforce restraint on eating of meat in London, 98
Hart, Sir Perceval, of Lullingstone, M.P. for Kent.
Queen dines with, 137
Harvey (Harvy), -----, in the service of Earl of Shrewsbury, 38
Harvey (Harvie), Captain.
takes part in Cadiz expedition, 265
Harvey, Gabriel, poet, Fellow of Trinity Hall, Cambridge.
letter from, 199
Harvey (Harvie), Sir Gerard, of Thurleigh.
takes part in Cadiz expedition, 265
Harvey, Sir William. See Hervey, Sir William.
Harwood.
letter dated from, 30
Hasselt (Hassell), in Belgium.
Helfenstein's troops defeated near, 232
Hastings, Catherine, Lady, later Countess of Huntingdon, wife of 3rd Earl of Huntingdon, and sister of Lord Robert Dudley, 194
letters from, 139, 163
Hastings (Hastinges), Dorothy, Lady, wife of Sir George Hastings.
mourner at funeral of Queen of Scots, 83
Hastings, Lady Dorothy. See Devereux, Lady Dorothy.
Hastings, Edward, Lord Hastings of Loughborough, 185
Hastings, Francis, 2nd Earl of Huntingdon, 155, 162
reference to his funeral, 158 and n
Hastings, Sir Francis, son of preceding.
letters from, 199, 259
Hastings, George, 1st Earl of Huntingdon.
his daughter marries Richard Devereux, 229
Hastings, Sir George, later 4th Earl of Huntingdon.
mourner at funeral of Queen of Scots, 83
takes part in trial of Earl of Essex, 269
Hastings, Henry, Lord Hastings, later

3rd Earl of Huntingdon, President of the Council of the North, 25, 29, 37, 93, 150, 163, 194, 248
letters from, 93, 139, 155, 157, 161(2), 179, 190, 191, 210, 214
expected in Wakefield, 29
appointed Lieutenant-General of the North, 84, 85
wishes to be made Master of the Hart Hounds, 161
Earl of Essex placed under his supervision, 251
Hatfield, Herts., 141
Hatfield, Yorks, 29
letters dated from, 47, 99
Hatfield Chase, Yorks.
dispute over, 131
Hatton, Sir Christopher, Vice-Chamberlain of the Household and later Lord Chancellor, 23, 33, 39 66, 86, 92, 100, 223
letters from, 35, 65(2), 70, 88, 197, 198
Prince of Condé visits, 27
Campion examined before, 35
signs letters from Privy Council, 46, 86, 89, 93(2), 94, 96, 98
Commissioner at trial of Queen of Scots, 73
Lord Chancellor, 88
Haufnaker. See Halnaker.
Haunse, Everard, alias Duckett, Everard, Catholic priest (executed 1581).
charged with treason, 35
Haverfordwest, Pembs.
letter dated from, 263
Havering, Essex.
letter dated from, 24
Havodwin. See Hafodwen.
Haward, Mistress (Mysteres). See Howard, Mary.
Hawkins, Sir John, naval commander.
signs naval estimates, 253
Queen's instructions to, 253
Hawnce, -----.
bathing tent erected at house of, 149
Hawtrey, Philip, kinsman of following, 239
Hawtrey, William, of Chequers.
letter from, 239
Haydon, Sir John. See Heydon, Sir John.
Haydone, Sir Christopher. See Heydon, Sir Christopher.
Heathcock, -----, of Buxton.
Walsingham's meals prepared in house of, 26
Hedd, John, footman to the Queen, 218
Hedgeley Moor, Northumb.
Scottish forces plan to camp at, 287

Heete, Richard, of Sheffield, 129
Heidelberg (Heydelberg), in Germany, 193
Heigham (Higham), Sir Clement, of Barrow, Suffolk.
commands company in Cadiz expedition, 265
Helbry (Helbrie), Cheshire, 246
Helfenstein (Elverston, Elverstone, Everston, Oversten), George, Count of, Imperial Ambassador to England and military commander, 150
Lord Robert Dudley dines with, 150
his troops defeated by Prince of Orange, 232(2)
Hemsby (Hamysby, Hemesby, Hemysby), Norfolk, 148
survey of Earl of Leicester's lands at, 167
Hendon, Middx.
letter dated from, 140
Heneage, Ann, Lady, wife of following, 114
Heneage, Sir Thomas, Vice-Chamberlain of the Household, 101, 105, 110, 111, 113
letters from, 102, 105, 110, 114, 197, 216
letters to, 109, 112, 113
signs letters from the Privy Council, 86, 89, 93(2), 94, 96, 98
Henneniocke. See Anhuniog.
Henry II, King of France.
refuses to surrender Calais in peace negotiations, 138
death of, 141
Henry III, King of France, 40, 49, 212
La Fère expected to surrender to, 28
at siege of La Fère, 30
reported to be dangerously ill, 30
sends his mother to Ollinville, 30
comment on his policy, 65
intervenes on behalf of Queen of Scots, 76, 77(2), 78, 79
orders assassination of Duke and Cardinal de Guise, 97
his other measures against Guise supporters, 97
reported to be proceeding against King of Navarre, 97
towns in Normandy and Picardy declare for and against, 99
said to be treating with Pope, 99
Duke of Anjou desirous of arranging peace between King of Navarre and, 202
his portrait at Leicester House, 203, 224
Henry, King of Navarre, later Henry IV of France, 28, 68, 97, 254, 255

letter from, 212
discusses peace terms with Duke of
Anjou at Jarnac, 30
said to enjoy general support in
France, 57
hires mercenaries from Switzerland
and Germany, 65
reported to have captured many
towns during troubles in France,
97
Parma's death advantageous to, 116
Sultan complies with request from,
116
reference to his marriage with sister
of King of France, 187
authorizes Duke of Anjou to arrange
peace terms between him and King
of France, 202
leads punitive expedition against
Duke of Savoy, 277
Henry VIII, King of England, 163,
167, 191
his portrait at Leicester House, 203,
224
Hepple, Northumb.
Barony of, 44
Heralds, Kings of Arms and
Pursuivants.
Bluemantle, 95
Chester, 95
Clarenceux (Clarencieux), 82, 83
Garter, 83
Lancaster, 95
Norroy (Norrey), 95
Portcullis, 89
Rouge Croix (Rougecrosse), 95
Somerset, 25, 89(2)
Herbert, Mr., 68, 266
Herbert, Mr. See following.
Herbert, (later Sir) Edward, of Powis
Castle, 255
Herbert, Henry, 2nd Earl of
Pembroke, 136, 200, 254
letters from, 39, 194, 198
requests payment of his sister's
jointure, 39
Commissioner at trial of Queen of
Scots, 74
Lord Robert Dudley dines with, 136,
150
loses wager to Lord Robert Dudley,
137
present at secret marriage between
Earl of Leicester and Countess of
Essex, 206
Constable of Forest of Dean, 259
his sister. See Talbot, Anne.
Herbert, Mary, Countess of Pembroke,
wife of preceding.
letter from, 198
her portrait at Leicester House, 222
Herbert, Mary, Countess of Pembroke,

daughter of 7th Earl of
Shrewsbury and wife of 3rd Earl
of Pembroke, 134
Herbert, Mary, later Lady Herbert,
wife of Sir Edward Herbert.
letter from, 255
Herbert, Richard, later 2nd Lord
Herbert of Cherbury.
letter from, 286
Herbert, William, 1st Earl of
Pembroke, 136, 219
letter from, 139
Herbert, William, 3rd Earl of
Pembroke, 134
letter from, 128
Herbert, Sir William, of Red Castle.
letter from, 98
Herbert (Harbard), William, in the
service of 2nd Earl of Pembroke.
dismissed from service, 194
Hereford, 241, 291
letters dated from, 165, 254, 260,
285
Hereford, Bishop of. See Scorby,
John.
Hereford, Viscounts. See Devereux.
Herefordshire, 263
Assizes in, 238
Earl of Essex's estates in, 248, 284,
285, 291
Justices of the Peace in, 254, 256
Commissioners for Army in, 291
Steward of Earl of Essex's manors
in. See Kyrle, Walter.
Herle (Herlle, Hurlle), William, in the
service of Earl of Leicester, later
M.P. for Callington.
letters from, 198, 200, 202
imprisoned in the Counter, 202
Herne, Mr., 99, 102
Hertford, Earl of. See Seymour,
Edward.
Hertford (Herteforde), Richard,
partisan of 2nd Earl of Essex.
imprisoned in the Marshalsea, 282
Hertfordshire, 252n
Deputy Aulnager of. See Powell,
Raphael.
Hervey (Harvey), Sir William, of
Kidbrooke (d1642).
Earl of Essex in debt to, 283
Hesse-Cassel, Philip, Landgrave of,
163
refuses to attend Diet of Spires, 169
Hetherley, John, Yeoman of the
Queen's Chamber.
petition to Earl of Leicester, 226
Hewel. See Ewell.
Hewett, Sir William, Lord Mayor of
London, 150
Lord Robert Dudley attends banquet
of, 149

Heydelberg. *See* Heidelberg.
Heydon (Haiden, Haydone), Sir
    Christopher, of Baconsthorpe.
    commands company in Cadiz
        expedition, 265
    imprisoned in the Marshalsea, 282
Heydon (Haydon), Sir John, brother
    of preceding.
    imprisoned in the Marshalsea, 282
Hide, William, *See* Hyde, William.
High Peak, Derbys.
    Forest of, 165
Higham, Sir Clement. *See* Heigham,
    Sir Clement.
Highfield, Captain John, Commander
    of Portsmouth Castle.
    his death, 215
Himley (Hymley), Staffs., 162
Hinton, Richard, Mayor of Pembroke,
    236
Hispaniola, West Indies, 71
Hodgeston (Hodson), Pembs.
    survey of Lordship of, 282
Hogan, William, 159
Hogg (Hogge), Richard, footman to
    the Queen, 218
Holborn (Holburne), London, 240
    letters dated from Lord Ambrose
        Dudley's house in, 146(2), 147,
        166
Holkest, Duke of. *See* Holstein.
Holland, Netherlands, 231, 232
    Queen considers measures for
        defence of, 45
    no desire for peace shown by people
        of, 87
    criticism of people of, 213
    antipathy towards Earl of Leicester
        in, 213
    hangings sent from Leicester House
        to, 221
    Earl of Leicester's departure for, 222
Holland, Robert, preacher, 91
Holland, Seth, Dean of Worcester.
    reported to be in hiding, 142
Holles (Hollice), John, of Haughton,
    son-in-law of Sir Thomas
    Stanhope, 107, 127
    quarrel between Markham and,
        117(2)
    chosen to be second in duel, 120
Hollywell, John, of Shelford.
    attests copy of offensive message
        sent by Countess of Shrewsbury,
        119
Holme, Roger.
    attests copy of offensive message
        sent by Countess of Shrewsbury,
        119
Holmes, Mr.
    described as 'a most godlie and
        learned minister', 257

Holmes, Mr.
    assesses Earl of Shrewsbury's lands,
        29
Holstein (Holkest), Adolph, Duke of.
    dines with Lord Robert Dudley,
        149
    wins money off Lord Robert Dudley
        at gaming, 151
Holstein (Hulster), Ulrich, Duke of.
    to be godfather to Princess Mary,
        128
Holt, George, of Stanton, Derbys., in
    the service of Countess of
    Shrewsbury.
    delivers offensive message from
        Countess of Shrewsbury to Sir
        Thomas Stanhope, 119
Holyhead (Holiehead), Anglesey, 246
    letter dated from, 246
Hongate, Mr., of Walton, Cheshire.
    his property recommended for
        purchase to Lord Robert Dudley,
        144
Hontley, Earl of. *See* Gordon, George.
Hope, The, of the Queen's Navy.
    to take part in Hawkins's expedition,
        253
Hopton, Captain.
    takes part in Cadiz expedition, 265
Horde, Mr., 131
Horde, George, of the Middle Temple,
    London.
    letter from, 256
Horden, R., auditor to Lord Robert
    Dudley, 138
Horn, Philippe de Montmorency-
    Nivelles, Count of (*d*1568).
    accompanies Duke and Duchess of
        Feria out of Brussels, 155
    his portrait at Leicester House, 203
Horn, Walburge de Nieunaer,
    Countess of Horn, wife of
    preceding.
    her portrait at Leicester House, 203
Hornsea Mere (Hornsey Marre),
    Yorks.
    survey of Lord Robert Dudley's
        lands at, 167
Hornsey (Harnesey), Middx.
    letter dated from, 198
Horsebreeding, 126
Horseheath (Horseth) Hall, Cambs.,
    240
Horseracing.
    at Horsley, 137
    at Newmarket, 251
Horses.
    Privy Council orders inquiry into
        export of, 155
    Earl of Leicester's gifts of, 168
    Friesian, 209
Horsey, Sir Edward, of Great Haseley

in Arreton, M.P. for Hampshire, 188, 201

Horsley, Derbys., 123

Horsley (Horsely), Surrey.
  letter dated from, 147
  Queen at, 137
  racing at, 137

Houghton, Peter, collector of subsidy, 88

House of Commons.
  represented at presentation of petition for execution of Queen of Scots, 77(2)
  speech in favour of petition made by Speaker of, 77
  Queen's dislike of certain members of, 99
  bills passed by, 99, 100
  criticism of House of Lords by, 99
  Speaker refuses to read bill for reform of Common•Prayer Book introduced in, 100
  urges Queen to marry, 166
  Speaker of. See Puckering, Sir John; Snagg, Thomas.

House of Lords.
  represented at presentation of petition for execution of Queen of Scots, 77
  criticised by House of Commons, 99
  urges Queen to marry, 166

Hovenn or Hovenner, Henry, of Thames Street, London, jeweller.
  petition to Queen, 226

Howard, Colonel. See Stewart, Sir William.

Howard, Alethea, Countess of Arundel, daughter of 7th Earl of Shrewsbury and wife of 14th Earl of Arundel, 134

Howard, Anne, Countess of Arundel, wife of 13th Earl of Arundel, 134
  confined to her house, 99

Howard, Charles, 2nd Lord Howard of Effingham, later 1st Earl of Nottingham, Lord High Admiral, 104, 105, 110, 114, 277(2)
  letters from, 107, 110, 111, 115
  letters to, 112, 113
  prepares to meet Spanish Armada in Narrow Seas, 86
  signs letters from Privy Council, 89, 93, 94, 96, 98
  at court, 90
  his fleet in readiness, 90
  his portrait at Leicester House, 207, 224
  reported to be facing Armada at Falmouth, 212
  takes part in trial of Earl of Essex, 269
  attacks Essex House, 278

delegates Sidney to parley with Earl of Essex, 279

Howard, Sir George, English Ambassador to France, 143

Howard, Lord Henry, brother of 4th Duke of Norfolk, 205
  committed to custody of Master of the Rolls, 99

Howard, James, Lord Maltravers, son of 14th Earl of Arundel, 134

Howard (Haward), Mary, daughter of 1st Lord Howard of Effingham, later 3rd wife of 4th Lord Dudley, 169 and n

Howard, Philip, 13th Earl of Arundel.
  order given for his indictment, 100

Howard, Theophilus, 2nd Earl of Suffolk.
  letter to, 285

Howard, Thomas, 4th Duke of Norfolk (executed 1572), 136, 138, 151, 156
  Queen persuaded of disloyalty of, 183
  reference to conspiracy of, 187

Howard, Thomas, 14th Earl of Arundel, 134

Howard, Lord-Thomas, later 1st Earl of Suffolk, Vice-Admiral, 266

Howard, William, 1st Lord Howard of Effingham, Lord Chamberlain (d1573), 137, 160
  receives gift of horse, 169

Howard, Lord William, son of 4th Duke of Norfolk.
  committed to custody of Cordell, 99

Howland, Richard, Bishop of Peterborough.
  mourner at funeral of Queen of Scots, 82

Howson, Bryan, footman to the Queen, 218

Hubbard, ----.
  his portrait at Leicester House, 222

Huddlestone, Richard, of Thame Park, M.P. for Lichfield, 215

Hugganes, Mr., 150

Hugh, Rhys (Rys) ap, a commissioner in Ferney.
  signs letter to Earl of Essex, 262

Huguenots, 171
  treatment of, 28
  expect military assistance from Protestant Princes of Germany, 68
  measures taken by the Guises to punish, 143
  threat of Constable of France to suppress, 153
  suspected manoeuvre to catch leaders of, 159
  King of France supports edict in favour of, 184

Hull, Yorks., 218, 286
Hulster, Duke of. *See* Holstein.
Humfreson, Mrs., 128
Hunbridge, Captain.
  takes part in Cadiz expedition, 265
Hundon (Hunden), Suffolk.
  manor of, 163
Hungatt, Mr., 22
Hunnings, -----, page of 1st Earl of
  Essex.
  illness of, 247
Hunsdon, Lady. *See* Carey, Anne.
Hunsdon, Lord. *See* Carey, Henry.
Huntingdon (Huntyngdon), 76
  postal endorsements at, 31, 76
Huntingdon, Earls of. *See* Hastings.
Hurlle, William. *See* Herle, William.
Hyde (Hide), William, later M.P. for
  St. Germans, 138, 148, 149
Hymley. *See* Himley.

I

Immanuel, Dr., Professor of Hebrew
  at Heidelberg, 193
Imposts.
  of sack and sweet wines, 256
Ince (Ynce), Richard, late husband
  of Elizabeth Massy, 226
Indians, Red.
  reported to have been armed by
  Drake, 68
Indies (Indias), The.
  King of Spain's revenues and lands
  in, 161
Infanta, The. *See* Isabella.
Inglefield, Mr. *See* Englefield, Sir
  Francis.
Inner Temple, The, London, 249
Inquisition, The.
  proclaimed in Louvain, 163
  Queen seeks its abolition in peace
  talks with Spain, 213
  in Venice, 277
Inventories.
  at Leicester House, 202, 207, 219,
  221
Ireland, 29, 179, 191, 234, 235(2),
  236, 242(3), 245, 246, 248(2), 253,
  262, 284, 285, 286, 288
  reinforcements sent to, 24
  Lord Grey appointed Lord Deputy
  of, 28
  news from, 28, 30, 31(2)
  defeat and massacre of Spanish and
  Italian forces at Smerwick in, 31
  Drake to prevent Spanish move
  against, 86
  post of herald in, 88
  soldiers for, 89
  Armada ships wrecked in north of,

94, 95
  information on state of, 171
  rebellion in, 171, 272
  Drake goes with fleet to, 212
  garrisons in, 230
  Earl of Essex's tenants at Keyston
  bound by their leases to serve in,
  235
  preparations for Earl of Essex's
  expedition to, 236(2), 237(6), 238,
  239. 240(3), 241(3)
  contributions towards his expedition,
  237(3), 238(2), 240, 241(2)
  directives issued to Earl of Essex
  concerning his expedition to, 241
  cost of his expedition to, 242
  Council of, 243(4), 245, 257, 258,
  270
  Earl of Essex protests against
  decision to halt operations in, 245
  Earl of Essex's estates in, 258, 262,
  283(2), 284(4), 286(3), 288
  Earl of Essex charged with
  misdemeanors in, 269, 270, 271
  Earl of Tyrone's ambition to
  become King of, 271
  plantation in, 284
Ireland, Auditor General of. *See*
  Jenison, Thomas.
Ireland, Lord Chancellor of. *See*
  Loftus, Sir Adam.
Ireland, Lord Deputy of. *See*
  Fitzwilliam, Sir William; Grey,
  Arthur; Perrot, Sir John; Sidney,
  Sir Henry.
Ireland, Marshal of. *See* Bagnall,
  Sir Nicholas; Stanley, Sir George.
Ireland, Primate of. *See* Bulkeley,
  Launcelot; Jones, Thomas.
Ireland, John.
  nominated by Earl of Leicester to
  be burgess of Denbigh, 190
Ireton, Germayne, in the service of
  Earl of Shrewsbury, 23
Irmond, Earl of. *See* Butler, Thomas.
Isabella, Infanta of Spain, daughter of
  Philip II, later wife of Archduke
  Albert.
  reported to have been offered in
  marriage to Duke of Anjou, 24
  at Bruges, 276
Iscoed (Escoyd), Carms.
  grange of, 283
Isleworth (Thestelworthe), Mddx.
  Lord Robert Dudley's Company of
  Players lodged at, 137
Italy.
  false reports of victory of Armada
  circulating in, 95
  forces for assault on Tripoli
  assembled in, 147
  Turkish victory over Spanish forces

alarms people of, 157
Duke of Florence's growing power
    in, 162
preparations for war in, 184
reported embarkation in Armada of
    English and Scots from, 211
Itchington, Warwicks., 224

J

Jackson, Captain.
    takes part in Cadiz expedition, 265
Jakes *or* Jaques, Francis, of Towton,
    in the service of the Stanhope
    family, 124
Jakes *or* Jaques, James, in the service
    of John Stanhope.
    wounded in assault by Earl of
        Shrewsbury's partisans, 122
James VI, King of Scots, later James I
    of England, 44, 49, 68, 133, 134,
    222
    Walsingham's opinion of, 39
    said to be opposed to Lennox's
        policy, 40
    his ambassador's audience with
        Queen, 42
    intervenes on behalf of Queen of
        Scots, 76, 77(2), 78, 79
    visits Scottish borders, 90
    treaty concluded between Queen
        and, 209
    his warning to Council of State of
        United Provinces, 214
    his portrait at Leicester House,
        203, 224
    criticism of, 262
James, Lord. *See* Stewart, James.
James, Mark, Postmaster of
    Portsmouth.
    signs petition, 266
Jaques, James. *See* Jakes, James.
Jarnac (Jarnacke), in France.
    discussion of peace terms between
        Duke of Anjou and King of
        Navarre at, 30
Jarrington, Christopher, partisan of
    2nd Earl of Essex.
    imprisoned in the Marshalsea, 282
Jeffrey, J.
    letter from, 192
Jemanes, William, in the service of
    3rd Lord Windsor, 195
Jenison, Thomas, Auditor-General of
    Ireland, 242
Jenliis. *See* Genlis.
Jerez de la Frontera (Sherys), in
    Spain.
    captured by English forces, 264
Jesuits, 258
Jewels.

delivered to Earl of Essex, 252, 282
Jewkes, Simon. *See* Jukes, Simon.
Jhon, Lord. *See* Grey, Lord John.
Jobson, Edward, member of the
    English expeditionary force to
    South Beveland.
    his conduct in action commended,
        230
    wounded in skirmish near Goes, 230
Jobson, Sir Francis, Lieutenant of the
    Tower of London.
    letter from, 195 and *n*
Jobson, Henry, member of the English
    expeditionary force to South
    Beveland.
    wounded in skirmish near Goes, 230
John XVI, Count of Emden.
    dines at Hampton Court, 254
Johnson, Alford, in the service of
    Earl of Leicester, 210
Johnson, John, merchant.
    letter from, 166
Johnson, John, fife player, 150
Johnson, Lawrence, in the service of
    Mary Herbert.
    letter to, 255
Johnson, Simon, partisan of 2nd
    Earl of Essex.
    imprisoned in the Marshalsea, 282
Johnson, William, member of Earl of
    Leicester's Company of Players.
    signs petition to Earl of Leicester,
        226
Jones, -----, 256
Jones, Ellis, partisan of 2nd Earl of
    Essex.
    imprisoned in the Marshalsea, 282
Jones, Griffin, footman to the Queen,
    218
Jones, Sir Henry, of Abermarlais.
    date of his death, 248
Jones, Owen, in the service of Lord
    Burghley.
    receives gift of wardship, 24
Jones, Thomas, Archbishop of Dublin,
    283
Joneys, Roger, Alderman of Bristol.
    signs letter to Earl of Leicester, 173
Jordanus, Nolanus. *See* Bruno.
Joyeuse, Anne d'Arques, Duc de.
    his negotiations over seignorial dues
        with Queen of Scots, 49
Jukes, -----, tailor to Queen of Scots,
    33
Jukes (Jewkes), Simon, member of the
    Company of Merchant Adventurers.
    involved in kidnapping of Story, 266
    petition to Earl of Leicester, 266
Julio, Mayster. *See* Borgarucci.
Justices of Assize, 165
    in Derbyshire, 22
    in Devon, 68

in Oxford, 68
in Yorkshire, 69, 92
Justices of the Peace, 98
in Derbyshire, 23
in Devon, 68
in Herefordshire, 254, 256
in Nottinghamshire, 117, 125
in Pembrokeshire, 234
in Worcestershire, 158

Kalles. *See* Calais.
Katherine, daughter of Sigismund I of
    Poland and wife of John III of
    Sweden.
    her son chosen to be King of
        Poland, 87
Keith (Kyth), William, Scottish
    Ambassador to England.
    sent by James VI to intercede for
        Queen of Scots, 76, 77(2), 78, 79
Kellam, -----, of Sheffield, locksmith,
    129
Kemer, John, partisan of 2nd Earl of
    Essex.
    imprisoned in the Marshalsea, 282
Kemish (Keymyshe), Mr., member of
    the English expeditionary force to
    South Beveland.
    his conduct in action commended,
        230
Kemp, -----, of Windsor, 180
Kendall, -----, in the service of Lord
    Darcy, 99
Kenilworth (Killingworth), Warwicks.,
    28, 167, 196, 199(2)
    letters dated from, 57, 178
    survey of manor of, 167, 200
    Queen's progress to Windsor from,
        189
    fireworks at, 189
    inventories at, 208, 219
    minister of. *See* Betts, Richard.
Kent, Earl of. *See* Grey, Henry.
Kerbye. *See* Kirby.
Kew, Surrey, 137, 149, 283
    Earl of Leicester entertained by his
        musicians at, 137
    French gardener at, 138
Keymyshe, Mr. *See* Kemish.
Keys, Thomas, Serjeant Porter at
    Dover.
    letter from, 155
Keyston, Hunts., 250
    letter dated from, 234
    letters from Earl of Essex's tenants
        at, 235, 237
Kidman (Kydman), Robert, in the
    service of Earl of Shrewsbury,

106, 127
    signs evidence concerning Stanhope's
        defamation of Earl of Shrewsbury,
        104
Kildare, Lord. *See* Fitzgerald, Gerald.
Kilkenny, Ireland.
    letter dated from, 244
Killigrew, Sir Henry, diplomatist,
    member of the Council of State
        of the United Provinces, 181
    letters from, 163, 214, 215
    letter to, 212
    to be recalled from Netherlands, 214
Killingworth. *See* Kenilworth.
Kilmallock, co. Limerick.
    letter dated from, 244
Kimberworth, Yorks., 73
Kimbolton (Kymelton), Hunts.
    letter dated from, 66
King, Anne, Keeper of the linen at
    Kenilworth, 219
King, John, tailor.
    his bill, 251(2)
King's Bench, prison, Westminster.
    letter dated from,. 234
Kingsland, Herefs.
    letter dated from, 188
Kingsmead, Oxon.
    manor of, 215
Kingsmill (Kyngsmill), Mr., 181
Kingsmill, Sir William, of Sydmonton.
    Earl of Essex in debt to, 283
Kingswinford (Swynford), Staffs., 162
Kinnersley, Edmond. *See* Kynersley,
    Edmond.
Kinnersley, Francis. *See* Kynersley,
    Francis.
Kirby (Kerbye, Kyrby), Leics.
    letters dated from, 147, 164
Kirkby, Notts., 117
Kirkby Woodhouse (Woodhouse),
    Notts.
    letters dated from, 39, 44
Kirtling, Cambs.
    letter dated from, 239
Kiste, John, Marshal of the Admiralty
    in Pembrokeshire, 233
Kitson, Thomas, in the service of Earl
    of Shrewsbury.
    letter from, 102
Knaith (Kneyth), Lincs.
    letter dated from, 154
Knebworth, Herts.
    letter dated from, 152
Knevett, Mr. *See* Knyvett, Mr.
Kneyth. *See* Knaith.
Knight, Edmund (Edward), Chester
    Herald, later Norroy King of
        Arms, 95
Knight Marshal, The. *See* Gerard, Sir
    Thomas.
Knole (Knoll), Kent.

Lord Robert Dudley granted manor and park of, 164
survey of Lord Robert Dudley's lands at, 164
Knolles, Mr., 164
Knollys, Sir Francis, of Rotherfield Greys, Vice-Chamberlain, later Treasurer, of the Household, 251(2)
letters from, 217, 233
signs letters from Privy Council, 22, 160
present at secret marriage between Earl of Leicester and Countess of Essex, 206
his portrait at Leicester House, 207, 224
Knollys (Knowells), Francis, of Battel near Reading, son of preceding.
letter from, 233
Knollys, (Knowles), Henry, of Kingsbury, brother of preceding, 181
his portrait at Leicester House, 222, 224
Knollys, Richard, of Stamford-in-the-Vale, brother of preceding.
present at secret marriage between Earl of Leicester and Countess of Essex, 206
Knollys, Robert (Robin), brother of preceding, 233
Knollys, Sir Thomas, brother of preceding.
his portrait at Leicester House, 207
Knollys, Sir William, of Rotherfield Greys, brother of preceding, 256, 277
takes part in trial of Earl of Essex, 269
kept prisoner in Essex House, 278
released by Gorges, 278
Knot (Knott), John, 106
signs certificate concerning alleged offensive behaviour of Sir Thomas Stanhope, 104
Knowells, Francis. See Knollys, Francis.
Knowsley, Lancs.
letters dated from, 142, 173, 180
Knyvet (Knevett), Mr.
Lord Robert Dudley's gift at christening of his child, 137
Knyvet (Knyvett), Sir Thomas, of Ashwellthorpe, 262
Kydman, Robert. See Kidman, Robert.
Kydmore, Mrs., 101
Kyen, Cornelis, Burgomaster of Ostend.
brings news of mutiny of English garrison at Ostend, 215
Kyllose, Lord. See Bruce, Edward.

Kymelton. See Kimbolton.
Kynersley (Kynnerslie), Anthony, of Loxley, 96
Kynersley (Kinnersley), Edmond, partisan of 2nd Earl of Essex.
imprisoned in the Marshalsea, 282
Kynersley (Kinnersley), Francis, partisan of 2nd Earl of Essex.
imprisoned in the Marshalsea, 282
Kyngsmill, Mr. See Kingsmill, Mr.
Kynyatt, William, auditor to Lord Robert Dudley, 138
Kyrby. See Kirby.
Kyrle, Walter, of Ross.
appointed steward of Earl of Essex's manors in Herefordshire, 291
Kyrven, Thomas, Mayor of Coventry.
signs letter from Coventry corporation, 152
Kyth, Mr. See Keith, William.

La Bourlotte (La Barlott), Colonel Claude de, Commander of the Spanish infantry in the Archduke's army, 276
reported killed in battle at Nieuport, 276
Lacock or Lawcock, George, of Burton, Notts., 119, 124
Lacy, John, of Brierley, Yorks., 39
Lacy, John.
letter from, 259
Ladron, Count. See Lodron.
La Fère, in France.
expected to surrender, 28
still resisting, 30
preparations for siege of, 202
La Fère (La Ffere), Colas, Comte de, French commander in the service of Spain.
taken prisoner by Prince of Orange, 276
Lafoyle. See Foyle, Lough.
Lagharne, Francis. See Laugharne, Francis.
Lambert, Sir Oliver, of St. Mary's near Southampton, 263
commands company in Cadiz expedition, 265
Lambeth, Surrey.
Queen at, 75
Lambeth Bridge, Surrey, 120
Lambeth Marsh, Surrey.
letter dated from, 214
Lambeth Palace, Surrey, 130
Lamens, -----, member of the Earl of Leicester's Company of Players, 136
La Mothe-Fénélon, Bertrand de

335

Salignac, Marquis de, French
Ambassador to England, 27, 46,
177, 183
La Motte (La Mote), Valentine
Pardieu, Seigneur de, Governor
of Gravelines.
criticised for alleged inaction, 93
reported to have been arrested by
Parma, 214
Lamphey (Lanfey), Pembs., 246,
247(2), 248, 251, 284
Lancashire.
Papists in, 24
Lancaster, Duchy of.
Chancellor of. *See* Sadler, Sir Ralph.
Lancaster, Thomas.
letters from, 236, 239
Lancaster Herald, 95. *See also* Paddy,
Nicholas.
Landenegwod Vaure. *See* Llanegwad.
Landgrave, The. *See* Hesse-Cassel.
Landrina, Don Ambrose, of the
Archduke's army.
reported killed in battle at Nieuport,
276
Lane, Richard.
letter from, 169
Lane, Thomas. *See* Lant, Thomas.
Laneham *or* Lanham, John, member of
the Earl of Leicester's Company
of Players.
signs petition to Earl of Leicester,
266
Lanfey. *See* Lamphey.
Langham, Thomas, in the service of
Lord Robert Dudley, 150
Lord Robert Dudley intervenes for
his release from prison, 151
Langley, Worcs. (formerly Salop).
survey of Lord Robert Dudley's
lands at, 167
Lannoy, Barbara de, wife of following.
letter from, 170
Lannoy, Cornelius de, native of
Burgundy, now of Dowgate Ward,
London, musician, 170
La Noele, Beauvoir de, French
Ambassador to England.
entertained by Earl of Essex,
254(2), 255
Lant (Lane), Thomas, later Portcullis
Pursuivant and Windsor Herald.
recommended by Walsingham as
Portcullis Pursuivant, 89(2)
Lartington (Lertyngton), Yorks., 266
Lascelles, Brian, of Sturton and
Gateford, Sheriff of
Nottinghamshire, 92, 128
Lascelles (Lassells), Edmund, of
Gateford.
letter from, 128
Lashley, -----, 287

Lassells, Edmund. *See* Lascelles,
Edmund.
Latham, Mr., in the service of Earl
of Leicester.
nominated and elected as alderman
of Denbigh, 190
Lathom, near Ormskirk, Lancs.
letters dated from, 66(2), 152, 153
Latymer, Lord. *See* Nevill, John.
Laugharne, Carms. (formerly Pembs.).
survey of Lordship of, 282
Laugharne (Lagharne), Francis, of St.
Bride's, brother-in-law of Morgan
Phillips, 234, 236
Laurence, Captain.
takes part in Cadiz expedition, 265
Laval, Louis de Sainte Maure, Marquis
de Nesle, Comte de, a French
hostage.
Lord Robert Dudley dines with, 150
Laware, Lord. *See* West, William.
Lawreyne, Cardinall of. *See* Lorraine,
Louis de.
Lawson, Robert, of Prittlewell.
letter from, 241
Layden. *See* Leiden.
Lea, Captain. *See* Lee, Captain
Thomas.
Lead, 35, 41, 67, 100
League, The.
chief towns in Normandy and
Picardy adhere to, 99
Parma ready to assist, 99
demand to French King addressed
by, 212
unsuccessful attack on Melun by
forces of, 212
Leake (Leek), Sir Francis, of Sutton
Scarsdale (*d*1578), 125
Leake, Henry, of Sookholme, 120
takes part in assault on Stanhope,
122, 123, 124
Learpoll. *See* Liverpool.
Leckhampstead (Lekhamsted), Berks.
letter dated from, 238
Lee, Sir Richard, military engineer.
invites inspection of fortifications
at Berwick, 140, 141
letter from, 141
Lee (Lea), Robert, of Hatfield, Yorks.
Lord President of Council of the
North stays with, 29
assesses Earl of Shrewsbury's lands,
29
letter from, 99
Lee *or* Lea, Captain Thomas, partisan
of 2nd Earl of Essex.
his talks with Earl of Tyrone, 270
Leek (Lycke), Staffs., 284
Leek, Sir Francis. *See* Leake, Sir
Francis.
Leeuwarden, in Friesland.

letter dated from, 213
Spanish prisoners of war executed at, 212
Leez. *See* Leighs.
Legh, Sir John.
letter from, 155
Le Havre (Newehaven), in France, 266
French ships refitted at, 152
Leicester (Leycestre), 26
letters dated from, 161, 162
petition to Earl of Leicester from Mayor and burgesses of, 226
Leicester, Earl of. *See* Dudley, Robert.
Leicester House, Strand, London, 225
letters dated from, 223, 224(2)
inventories at, 202, 207, 219, 221, 224
Leicestershire.
Lord Robert Dudley receives grant of land in, 164
Leiden (Layden), in Holland.
portrait of governor of, at Leicester House, 207
Leighs (Leez), Essex.
letter dated from, 240
Leighton, Sir Thomas, Governor of Guernsey.
letter from, 255
Leith, Midlothian.
letter dated from, 186
Lekhamsted. *See* Leckhampstead.
Lennox, Duke of. *See* Stuart, Esmé.
Lennox, Earl of. *See* Stuart, Matthew.
Lennox (Lennes), Lady. *See* Stuart, Elizabeth; Stuart, Katherine.
Leominster, Herefs.
fair held on St. Peter's Day at, 237
Leoninus, Elbertus, Chancellor of Guelders, 214
Lertyngton. *See* Lartington.
Leslie, John, Bishop of Ross.
letter from, 179
memorial by, 181, 182
Letton, Herefs.
manor of, 283
Leveret, Mr., 21
Lew (Lewe), Oxon.
letter dated from, 49
Lewis, James, formerly on active service in the Netherlands, 277
Lichfield, Staffs., 199, 285
letters dated from, 193, 253
fatal quarrel on highway between Drayton and, 234
Lichfield, Dean of. *See* Boleyn, George; Nowell, Lawrence; Rambridge, John; Warner, John.
Light, Mr., of London, 201
Limerick (Limbrick), 274
letter dated from, 192
Limerick (Lymericke), John, partisan of 2nd Earl of Essex.

imprisoned in the Marshalsea, 282
Lincoln, Bishop of. *See* Bullingham, Nicholas; Cooper, Thomas; Wickham, William.
Lincoln, Deanery of, 146
Lincoln, Diocese of, 185
Lincoln, Countess of. *See* Clinton, Elizabeth.
Lincoln, Earl of. *See* Clinton, Edward; Clinton, Henry.
Lincolnshire, 107
Lindley (Lyndeley, Linley), Sir Henry, comptroller to 2nd Earl of Essex, 256, 263
imprisoned in the Gatehouse, 281
Lingen (Lyngen), Edward, of Sutton, Herefs.
detained in prison at York, 258
Lingen, Isabel, widow of John Lingen of Sutton.
opposes Knolles's suit for her daughter's hand, 164
Lingen (Lyngen), Jane, daughter of preceding and wife of William Shelley of Michelgrove, 164, 258
Lingen, John, brother of Edward Lingen, 258
Linwray (Lynewraye), John, Clerk of the Ordnance, 263
Lirpole. *See* Liverpool.
Lisbon.
thought by King of Spain to have been objective of English expedition in 1596, 264
Lisle, G.
letter from, 259
Lister (Lyster), Francis, partisan of 2nd Earl of Essex.
imprisoned in the Marshalsea, 281
Liston (Lyston), Essex, 228
Litchfield, -----, in the service of Earl of Oxford, 205
Littelltone, John. *See* Littleton, John.
Littelton, Sir Edward. *See* Littleton, Sir Edward.
Little Munden (Mondon), Herts.
parsonage of, 234
Littleton (Littelton), Sir Edward, of Pillaton.
imprisoned in the Marshalsea, 282
Littleton (Litleton), Edward, Keeper of Teddesley Park.
his dispute with Lord Stafford, 143
Littleton (Littelltone), John, of Frankley, partisan of 2nd Earl of Essex.
imprisoned in the Marshalsea, 282
Liverpool (Learpoll, Lirpole, Lyverpoole), 236, 238, 239
Llanddewi (Llandewy), in Wales.
letter dated from, 264
Llanegwad (Landenegwod Vaure),

Carms.
survey of Lord Robert Dudley's
lands at, 167
Llanfair (Llanvair), in Wales.
letter dated from, 260
Llanfair-is-Gaer (Llanver), Caerns.
letter dated from, 141
Llanreball. *See* Llwynyrebol.
Lloyd (Lloid), Captain.
takes part in Cadiz expedition, 265
Lloyd, Hugh, in the service of Earl
of Leicester, 188
nominated and elected as alderman
of Denbigh, 190
Lloyd, John, partisan of 2nd Earl of
Essex.
imprisoned in the Marshalsea, 282
Lloyd, Margaret, of Llanfair.
letter from, 260
Lloyd, Robert, 218
Lloyd, Thomas, in the service of
Earl of Leicester.
nominated and elected as coroner
of Denbigh, 190
Llwynyrebol (Llanreball), Carms.
survey of grange of, 283
Lodge, Thomas, Alderman of London, 148
Lodron (Ladron), Alberico de Lodron,
Count, Spanish commander.
held captive by mutinous Spanish
troops, 169
Loftus, Sir Adam, Lord Chancellor of
Ireland.
Earl of Essex commits government
of Ireland to, 271
offers to purchase Earl of Essex's
lands in Ireland, 283
London, 23-270 *passim*
letters dated from, 34-262 *passim*
optimism regarding prospects of
peace in, 90
recusants sent to prison at Ely
from, 92
Bishop of Durham sets out for, 141
foreigners in, 143, 165, 170
memorandum on trade malpractices
by farmer of Customs of, 169
Company of Vintners of, 180
Burghley forced to borrow from city
of, 181
Earl of Essex's military failure in
streets of, 278
Bishop of. *See* Aylmer, John.
Lord Mayor of. *See* Chester, Sir
William; Hart, Sir John;
Hewett, Sir William; Row, Sir
William.
London, Tower of, 49, 99, 155,
186, 235, 259, 263
letter dated from, 187
Campion imprisoned in, 35
Lord Robert Dudley dines at, 150(2)

medieval records in, 162
northern rebels committed to, 187
threat to batter Essex House with
artillery from, 280
names of Earl of Essex's partisans
imprisoned in, 281
parson of. *See* Massy, Roger.
London and Westminster and environs.
See also Aldersgate Street;
Baynard's Castle; *Bear*;
Bishopsgate; Bishopsgate Street;
Blackfriars; Broad Street; Broken
Wharf; Burghley House; *Castle*;
Chancery Lane; Charing Cross;
Cheapside; Clement's Inn;
Coldharbour;
Coleman Street; Commission
House; Conduit; Court, English;
Covent Garden; Drury Place;
Durham House; Ely House; Essex
House; Exchange; Fenchurch
Street; Fleet; Fleet Street;
Gatehouse; Gracechurch Street;
Gray's Inn; Gresham House;
Holborn; Inner Temple; King's
Bench; Leicester House; Ludgate;
Maiden's Head; Mile End;
Moorgate; Newgate; Newgate
Street; *Old Swan*; Playhouse;
Queenhithe; *Rose*; St.
Bartholomew's; St. Clement's
Church; St. James; St. James's
Park; St. Katharine's; St. Martin-
in-the-Fields; St. Paul's; St. Paul's
Cross; St. Paul's Churchyard;
Saracen's Head; Savoy;
Shrewsbury House; Smithfield;
Somerset House; Strand; *Talbot*;
Temple; *Three Tuns*; Tower Hill;
Tower Street; Tower Wharf;
Walsingham House; Warwick
Lane; Westminster Abbey;
Westminster Hall; Whitefriars;
Whitehall; York House.
Longleat, Wilts.
letter dated from, 199
Longueville, Leonor d'Orléans, Duc de.
regards Catherine de Medici as
personal enemy, 171
Lopez, Roderigo (D.), Jewish
physician from Portugal, resident
in the parish of St. Peter the
Poor, London, 201
Lord Admiral. *See* Clinton, Edward;
Howard, Charles.
Lord Chamberlain. *See* Carey, Henry;
Howard, William; Radcliffe,
Thomas.
Lord Chancellor. *See* Bromley, Sir
Thomas; Hatton, Sir Christopher.
Lord Chief Baron of Exchequer.
See Manwood, Sir Roger; Peryam,

Sir William.
Lord Chief Justice. *See* Popham, Sir
John; Wray, Sir Christopher.
Lord Chief Justice of Common Pleas.
See Anderson, Sir Edmund.
Lord Deputy of Ireland. *See*
Fitzwilliam, Sir William; Grey,
Arthur; Perrot, Sir John; Sidney,
Sir Henry.
Lord General. *See* Percy, Algernon.
Lord Keeper. *See* Bacon, Sir Nicholas;
Egerton, Sir Thomas; Puckering,
Sir John.
Lord Marshal. *See* Vere, Sir Francis.
Lord Steward. *See* Dudley, Robert.
Lord Treasurer. *See* Cecil, William;
Paulet, William; Sackville,
Thomas.
Lord Warden of the Cinque Ports. *See*
Brooke, William.
Lord Warden of the Middle Marches.
See Forster, Sir John.
Lorde, Mr., 55
Lords Lieutenant, 98
Lorraine (Lothereng), Charles de,
Cardinal de Lorraine (*d*1574), 38,
143, 184
his portrait at Leicester House, 222
Lorraine, Charles de, Duc d'Aumale
(*d*1631).
escapes from Paris, 97
takes part in battle at Nieuport, 276
Lorraine, Charles de, Marquis (later
Duc) d'Elboeuf (*d*1605).
seized by order of King of France,
97
Lorraine, Charles de, Duc de Mayenne
(Maine) (*d*1611).
escapes assassination ordered by
French King, 97
Lorraine, Christine of Denmark,
Duchesse de, widow of following,
144, 146
report of proposed marriage with
Duke of Anjou, 24
Lorraine, François de, Duc de Guise
(*d*1563), 152
holds dominating position at French
court, 143
Lorraine, Henri de, Duc de Guise
(*d*1588), 57, 212
assassinated by order of French
King, 97
quarrel between Duc de Nevers and,
184
Lorraine, Louis de, Cardinal de Guise
(*d*1578).
rumour of his death, 184
Lorraine, Louis de, Cardinal de Guise
(*d*1588).
assassinated by order of French
King, 97

Lorraine, René de, Marquis d'Elboeuf
(*d*1566).
in command of projected French
expedition to Scotland, 152
Lothereng. *See* Lorraine, Charles de,
Cardinal de Lorraine.
Loughborough, Lord. *See* Hastings,
Edward.
Louise, Queen of France, wife of
Henry III.
reported to be dead, 97
Louth (Lowth), County, Ireland, 258,
262
Louvain, in Belgium.
Spanish Inquisition proclaimed in,
163
Love, Sir Thomas, Captain of the
Anne Royal in the Cadiz
expedition, 284
Lovell, Thomas, formerly in the service
of Duke of Northumberland, 148
Lovell, Thomas, Captain, on active
service in the Low Countries.
Killigrew's request on behalf of, 215
his conduct in Walcheren action
commended, 232
Low Countries, The, 56, 57, 64, 80,
213, 219, 255, 282
reported to have been offered to
Duke of Anjou by King of Spain,
24
said to be inclined to give themselves
to Duke of Anjou, 28
agreement between Duke of Anjou
and, 30
threat of mutiny amongst Spanish
forces in, 37
Earl of Leicester to be sent to
command in, 57
Earl of Leicester arrives in, 65
defeat of Armada celebrated by
Protestants in, 95
threat of religious persecution in,
139
Erasmus's works banned from, 139
Queen's prospects of marriage a
subject of interest to, 139, 147
King of France's death expected to
influence state of affairs in, 141
heretics executed in, 169
English families in, 169
sale in London of goods from, 170
description of people attending on
Earl of Leicester in, 208
preparations for invasion of England
in, 211
state of affairs in, 213
news from, 264
Regent of. *See* Margaret.
Lowth. *See* Louth.
Lucy, Sir Thomas, of Charlecote.
letter from, 152

Queen dines at house of, 189
Ludgate, London.
  Earl of Essex and his followers enter London by, 278
Ludlow, Salop.
  letter dated from, 195
Ludlow Castle, Salop.
  letter dated from, 192
Ludovik, Ludowike, Count. *See* Nassau, Count Louis of.
Lumley (Lumleie), John, 1st Lord Lumley, 127
  letter from, 157
  Commissioner at trial of Queen of Scots, 74
Lumley, Richard, Viscount Lumley of Waterford. Commissioner for the Principality of Wales.
  signs letter to Earls of Essex and Suffolk, 285
Lunsford (Lunce Fourd), Colonel Thomas, later Lieutenant of the Tower of London.
  his regiment in Newcastle, 287
Lupo, Joseph, of Blackfriars, musician to the Queen.
  receives gift of money, 255
Lupton, Thomas, miscellaneous writer.
  addresses his *Godlie Fame* to Earl of Leicester, 218
Lycke. *See* Leek.
Lyle, Mr., of the English expeditionary force in Walcheren.
  killed in action near Middelburg, 232
Lymericke, John. *See* Limerick, John.
Lyndeley, Mr. *See* Lindley, Henry.
Lynewraye, John. *See* Linwray, John.
Lyngen, Mrs. *See* Lingen, Jane.
Lyngen, Edward. *See* Lingen, Edward.
Lynne, George, of Southwick.
  mourner at funeral of Queen of Scots, 83
Lyon, Ralph, of Tamworth.
  Countess of Leicester's lawsuits against, 225
Lyon, The, of the Queen's Navy.
  takes part in Earl of Essex's second expedition to Spain, 265
Lyons, in France, 277
  Duke of Mayenne escapes from, 97
  news from, 184
  Archbishop of. *See* Epinac, Pierre.
Lyonshall, Herefs.
  Earl of Essex's tenants at, 237, 238
  park of, 249
Lyster, Mr., member of the English expeditionary force to South Beveland.
  his conduct in action commended, 230
Lyster, Francis. *See* Lister, Francis.
Lyston. *See* Liston.

M

M'Brien (McBryan), Collo (Collei), of co. Monaghan.
  his sons pillage Earl of Essex's estates, 257
Macclesfield, Cheshire.
  Royal Forest of, 59
McCooloe, Ever. *See* M'Mahon, Ever M'Coley.
M'Felim Bacagh, Sir Bryan, Chief of Clandeboye, co. Antrim, 193
MacGibbon, Maurice, Titular Archbishop of Cashel, 186
  letter from, 186
  at Rouen, 178
Mackwyllyames, Mrs., 101
M'Mahon (MacMahone), -----, of Ulster, 245
M'Mahon (McMahon), Collo (Cowlo), of Ferney, uncle of Rory M'Mahon.
  letters from, 283, 286
M'Mahon (McMahon), Constantine (Constantyne), in the service of Earl of Essex.
  reports on devastation of Earl of Essex's lands in Ulster, 258
M'Mahon (McCooloe), Ever M'Coley, of co. Monaghan.
  his sons pillage Earl of Essex's estates at Ferney, 257
M'Mahon (McMahowne), Rory M'Hugh (MacHewe) Oge (Ogge), of co. Monaghan, 257
M'Mahon (McMahon), Rory, of Ferney.
  letter from, 283
M'Rory (McRorie), Manus, chief of sept in co. Monaghan.
  his tribesmen flee to the Pale, 258
Madrid.
  letter dated from, 173
  Cobham arrives in, 173
Maiden's Head, The, inn, London, 149
Maine, Duke of. *See* Lorraine, Charles de.
Maitland, William, of Lethington, Scottish envoy to England.
  letter from, 170
  dines with Lord Robert Dudley, 149, 150
Malatesta, Giacomo, of Rome.
  imprisoned for thrashing Cardinal Monti in a courtesan's house, 157
Malby, Captain (later Sir) Nicholas, one of the Commissioners in the North of Ireland.
  employed in Ulster, 193
Maldon, Essex.
  letter dated from, 235
Mallvisye. *See* Mauvissière.
Malory, Sir William, of Studley, Yorks.

petition to Queen, 226
Manners, Lord. *See* Manners, Henry.
Manners, Edward, 3rd Earl of
Rutland, 24, 88, 108
letters from, 34, 208
Commissioner at trial of Queen of
Scots, 74
negotiates treaty between Queen and
King of Scots, 209
Manners, Elizabeth, Countess of
Rutland, wife of 4th Earl of
Rutland.
mourner at funeral of Queen of
Scots, 83
Manners, Francis, son of 4th Earl of
Rutland, partisan of 2nd Earl of
Essex.
imprisoned in the Marshalsea, 282
Manners, Sir George, son of 4th
Earl of Rutland, partisan of 2nd
Earl of Essex.
imprisoned in the Marshalsea, 282
Manners, Henry, 2nd Earl of Rutland.
letter from, 157
dines with Lord Robert Dudley, 150
Manners, John, 4th Earl of Rutland,
81
mourner at funeral of Queen of
Scots, 83
his dispute with Earl of Shrewsbury
over Sherwood Forest, 88
Manners, John, of Shelford and
Haddon Hall, son of 1st Earl of
Rutland, 44, 125
letter from, 66
Deputy Lieutenant for Derbyshire,
79
appointed collector of Queen's loan
in Derbyshire, 98
Manners, Roger, 5th Earl of Rutland,
81
takes part in Earl of Essex's
rebellion, 278
imprisoned in the Tower, 281
Manners, Roger, of Uffington, Lincs.,
son of 1st Earl of Rutland, and
uncle of 7th Earl of Shrewsbury,
63, 71, 100
Manners, Sir Thomas, Constable of
Nottingham Castle, brother of
preceding, 88
Mansell (Mansfield, Maunsfield), Sir
Robert, of Pentney.
commands company in Cadiz
expedition, 265
his troops attack Essex House, 278
Mansfeld, Count Charles of.
sent by Parma to recapture Bonn, 86
Mansfeld, Count Dorado of. *See*
Mansfeld, Count Wolrad of.
Mansfeld, Marie de Montmorency,
Countess of, wife of following.

her portrait at Leicester House, 203
Mansfeld, Count Peter Ernest of.
his portrait at Leicester House, 203
Mansfeld, Count Wolrad (Dolrado) of,
206
Mansfelden, Hans von, agent of
preceding.
letter from, 206
Mansfield (Mansfylde), Notts., 127
Mansfield, Henry, 150
Mansfield, Sir Robert. *See* Mansell, Sir
Robert.
Manton, Rutland.
survey of Lord Robert Dudley's
lands at, 167
Manwood, Sir Roger, Serjeant-at-Law,
later Justice of Common Pleas
and Chief Baron of Exchequer,
181, 197
letter from, 192
Commissioner at trial of Queen of
Scots, 74
Maps, 204
at Wanstead, 208
at Leicester House, 224(2)
Marbeck, Roger, of London,
physician, 187
Marbery, -----, cousin of Sir Thomas
Gresham, 159
his brother, 159
Marcelles. *See* Marseilles.
Margaret, Duchess of Parma, Regent
of the Low Countries, daughter of
Emperor Charles V.
prohibits transport of horses for
Queen's service, 146
her gifts to Duchess of Feria, 155
Marie Rose, The, of the Queen's
Navy.
to take part in Hawkins's expedition,
253
Markham, Gervase (Jarvis), of
Dunham.
quarrel between Holles and, 117, 118
chosen by Cavendish to be his
second in duel with Stanhope, 120
Markham, Godfrey, in the service of
Earl of Shrewsbury.
prominent in assault on Stanhope,
122, 123
Markham, Sir Thomas, of Kirkby
Woodhouse.
letter from, 39
Markham, Thomas, of Ollerton, 102,
108, 109, 126(?)
reconciled with Stanhope, 108
supports Stanhope in Parliamentary
elections at Nottingham, 117
Marmalade.
'bricks' of, 149
Marnhull, Dorset.
rental of Earl of Leicester's lands

at, 168

Marquess, The. *See* Hamilton, James.

Marseilles (Marcelles), in France.
state of French galleys at, 152

Marsh, John.
letter from, 180

Marshal, The. *See* Blount, Sir
Christopher.

Marshalsea, The, prison, Southwark.
names of Earl of Essex's partisans
imprisoned in, 281, 282

Marston Sicca *or* Dry Marston, Glos.
rental of Earl of Leicester's lands at,
168

Martinengo, Abbot of St. Saluto.
appointed Nuncio to England, 157

Martini, Ambrose, former auditor to
the Dutch military judge.
letter from, 213
his criticism of Dutch people, 213

Martyn, -----, 31

Marvell, Sir Andrew, 82

Mary, Queen of Scots, 20, 52, 53, 74,
76, 249, 262
Earl of Shrewsbury ordered to
exercise greater supervision over,
28
his allowance for guarding, 29, 32
Queen critical of freedom allowed by
Earl of Shrewsbury to, 40
proposals made by, 42, 43, 49
reference to schemes for her release,
48, 49
negotiations over seignorial dues
between Duke of Joyeuse and, 49
to go to Buxton, 49, 50
Earl of Shrewsbury forbidden to
assemble freeholders of Peak
because of his responsibility for,
50
Sir Ralph Sadler to take charge of,
51, 52
her removal to Wingfield proposed,
51
reluctant to leave Wingfield, 52
money order for her maintenance, 54
reference to quarrel between
Countess of Shrewsbury and, 55
list of Commissioners at her trial, 73
opinions of Burghley and Earl of
Shrewsbury on her case, 75
sentence pronounced in Star
Chamber on, 75, 76
intervention by Scotland and France
on her behalf, 76, 77(2), 78, 79
Parliament to petition for her
execution, 76, 77
Parliament's petition presented to
Queen, 77
sentence of execution to be conveyed
by Lord Buckhurst and Beale to,
78(2)

her request to make her will granted,
78
Parliament insists upon her
execution, 79
Beale given commission for her
execution, 79
beheaded, 80
order of cortège at her funeral, 82
regarded by French Court as Queen
of England, 144
said to be returning from France to
Scotland, 163
reference to 'arrogant speechis' of,
188
Secretary to. *See* Nau, Claude.
Tailor to. *See* Jukes.

Mary, Queen of England (*d*1559), 139,
145, 162, 163, 165, 176, 219
her portrait at Leicester House, 203,
224

Mary, Princess, daughter of Henry VII
and wife of Louis XII of France,
later wife of Charles Brandon,
Duke of Suffolk.
mentioned in verses, 290

Mary, Princess, daughter of James VI
and I, 128 and *n*

Mary Magdalen.
picture at Leicester House of, 207

Mason, Anthony, of Bodenham.
attainted, 248

Mason (Masoun), Sir John, Clerk to
the Privy Council and diplomatist.
Lord Robert Dudley dines with, 150

Massy (Massye), Elizabeth, wife of
following.
petition to Earl of Leicester, 226

Massy, Roger, parson of the Tower
of London, 226

Master of the Rolls (Rowells). *See*
Cordell, Sir William; Gerard, Sir
Gilbert.

Masters, Richard, physician, 25

Matravers, Lord. *See* Howard, James.

Maunsfield, Captain. *See* Mansell, Sir
Robert.

Maurice, Prince, military commander,
nephew of Charles I.
at Ross-on-Wye, 291

Mauvissière (Mallvisye), Michel de
Castelnau, Sieur de, French
diplomatist, 201(2)

Maximilian (Maxemallian), Archduke
of Austria, later Emperor
Maximilian II (*d*1576), 162
attends Diet of Spires, 169
appeals to German Princes for help
against Turks, 184

Maximilian (Maximillian), Archduke of
Austria, brother of Emperor
Rudolph II.
defeated and taken prisoner by

Chancellor of Poland, 87
Maynard, Henry, secretary to Lord
  Burghley, 102
Meath, County, Ireland, 262
Meaux Abbey, Yorks.
  Lord Robert Dudley granted site
  of, 164
  survey of Lord Robert Dudley's
  lands at, 167
Medici, Catherine de, Queen Mother
  of France.
  sent to Ollinville, 30
  her death, 97
  regarded as his enemy by Duke of
  Longueville, 171
  uneasy relations between Queen of
  France and, 171
  her dominating influence in France,
  171
  her honourable treatment of
  Coligny, 184
Medici, Cosimo I de, Duke of Florence
  (d1574).
  expected to be crowned King of
  Tuscany by Pope, 159
  King of Spain suspicious of
  friendship between Pope and, 162
Medina Coeli (Celi), Juan de la
  Cerda, Duke of.
  defeated by Turks, 157
Medlen, Thomas, partisan of 2nd Earl
  of Essex.
  imprisoned in the Marshalsea, 282
Melbury, Dorset.
  letter dated from, 179
Melton, Norfolk.
  letter dated from, 153
Melun, in France.
  unsuccessful attack by Catholic
  League on, 212
Memorancie, Duke. See Montmorency.
Men, Stephen, partisan of 2nd Earl of
  Essex.
  imprisoned in the Marshalsea, 282
Mendoza (Mendosa), Don Bernardino
  de, Spanish Ambassador to
  England, 205
  denies that Terceira supports Don
  Antonio, 36
  spreads false reports of victory of
  Armada, 95
  goes about disguised, 201
Mendoza, Francisco de, Admiral of
  Aragon, 276
  taken prisoner by Prince of Orange,
  276
Mentethe, Erle of. See Graham,
  John.
Menville, Nynyan, of Sledwick.
  letter from, 155
Mercers, Company of.
  Lord Robert Dudley attends banquet
  of, 150
Merchant Adventurers, Company of.
  their gift of plate to Earl of
  Leicester, 219
Merevale (Myrevall), Warwicks., 227
Merioneth, 188
  Parliamentary elections in, 189
Merrick, Edmund, prebendary of
  Lichfield.
  signs letter to Earl of Essex, 253
Merricks, Captain, of the English
  expeditionary force in Walcheren.
  his conduct in action commended,
  232
Mershe, John, Governor of the
  Company of Merchant
  Adventurers, 225
Messinger, Mr., 255
Metcalfe, Oswald, of Wildon Grange.
  reference to his traitorous
  activities, 187
Metham, Francis, of Wigginthorpe,
  125
Metham, Thomas, of Metham, 125
Meverell, Henry.
  letter from, 192
Meyrick, Sir Gelly (Gilly), of
  Gladestry, Steward of 2nd Earl of
  Essex, 252, 256, 257, 261, 263, 265
  letters to, 254-267 passim
  his accounts, 254
  warrant for payment to, 257
  complaint against, 260
  takes part in Cadiz expedition, 265
  in charge of Queen's representatives
  committed to Essex House by Earl
  of Essex, 278
  tricked into releasing Queen's
  representatives, 278
  imprisoned in Newgate, 281
Michelborne, Sir Edward, of Hackney,
  partisan of 2nd Earl of Essex.
  imprisoned in the Marshalsea, 281
Michell, Mr., a physician.
  attends on Lord Berkeley, 172
Middelburg (Myddelborough,
  Mydleborough), in Zeeland.
  defeat of Spanish forces of, 232, 233
  Governor of. See Benvoyse.
Might, Thomas, Surveyor of Victuals
  in Ireland.
  letters from, 239, 240
Mildmay, Mary, Lady, wife of
  following and sister of Sir
  Francis Walsingham.
  at Buxton, 2
Mildmay, Sir Walter, Chancellor of
  the Exchequer, 21, 44, 46, 192
  signs money order for Earl of
  Shrewsbury, 54
  Commissioner at trial of Queen of
  Scots, 74

Mile End, London.
  letter dated from, 54
Milford Haven, Pembs., 247
Mills (Mylls), Francis, secretary to
  Sir Francis Walsingham, 217
Mitcham, Surrey.
  letter dated from, 54
Moleyns, Michael, of Mackney.
  letter from, 256
Molineux (Mollineux), John, of Carlton-
  in-Lindrick, 80
Monaghan, County, Ireland.
  Earl of Essex's estates in, 284
Moncado, Francisco de, former
  Viceroy of Valencia (d1587), 93
Moncado, Hugo de, Captain of the
  galleasses in the Spanish Armada,
  son of preceding.
  his galleasses driven on to sands
  at Calais, 93
Monckton. See Monkton.
Mongomeri (Montgomery), Gabriel de
  Lorge, Comte de, Huguenot leader
  and refugee.
  letter from, 235
Mongomeri (Montgomery), Jacques de
  Lorge, Comte de, son of
  preceding, 235
  letter from, 233
Monington (Monyngton), Thomas, of
  Sarnsfield, 254, 256
Monington, Thomas, of Chartley.
  letter from, 241
Monk's Kirby, Warwicks.
  letter dated from, 244
Monkton (Monckton), Pembs., 233
Monnox (Monoux), Henry, of
  Leominster, 195
Mons (Monse, Monts), in Belgium,
  138, 231
Monsieur. See Anjou, Duc d'.
Montagu (Mountague), Sir Edward
  (Edwarde), of Boughton.
  mourner at funeral of Queen of
  Scots, 83
Montagu (Mountague), Elizabeth,
  Lady, wife of preceding.
  mourner at funeral of Queen of
  Scots, 83
Montague, Viscount. See Browne,
  Anthony.
Monte, Cardinal. See Monti.
Montgomery. See Mongomeri.
Montgomery, Gabriel, gentleman
  companion to 2nd Earl of Essex.
  his university expenses, 250(2)
Montgomery, John, in the service of
  Thomas Fowler.
  letters to, 209, 213
  Privy Council issues warrant for
  arrest of, 220
Monti (Monte), Christophle de,

Cardinal.
  thrashed by Malatesta in a
  courtesan's house in Rome, 157
Montigny (Montiegni), François de la
  Grange, Seigneur de.
  reported to have been imprisoned by
  Parma, 214
Montmorency, Anne, Duc de, Constable
  of France (d1567).
  discredited at French court, 143
  threatens to suppress Huguenots, 153
Montmorency, François de, French
  Ambassador to England, son of
  preceding.
  met by Lord Robert Dudley at
  Tower Wharf, 136
Montmorency, Henri, Duc de,
  Constable and Marshal of France,
  65, 177
  letter from, 178
  reference to his Anglophile
  sentiments, 180
  to go to England, 187
Monts. See Mons.
Monyngton, Thomas. See Monington,
  Thomas.
Moorgate, London, 90
Moors.
  reported to have landed in Spain to
  assist English forces, 264
Moray Firth, Scotland.
  Spanish Armada reported to have
  landed men in, 93
Mordaunt (Mordant), Lewis, 3rd Lord
  Mordaunt.
  Commissioner at trial of Queen of
  Scots, 74
  mourner at her funeral, 83
More, -----, of the English
  expeditionary force in South
  Beveland.
  killed in skirmish with Spaniards,
  230
More, Donald Maccarty, Earl of
  Glancar.
  submits unconditionally, 171
Moreton, Salop, 256
Morfa Mawr (Morva Moure), Cards.
  grange of, 283
Morgan, -----, 239
Morgan, Captain (later Sir) Charles,
  of Pencarn, brother of Sir
  Matthew Morgan.
  takes part in Cadiz expedition, 265
Morgan, Edmund, later M.P. for
  Wilton and Monmouthshire, 260
  letter from, 260
Morgan, Sir Matthew, of Pencarn.
  commands company in Cadiz
  expedition, 265
Morgan, Thomas, Catholic exile and
  conspirator, 212

Morgan, Captain (later Sir) Thomas, M.P. for Shaftesbury, member of English expeditionary force in South Beveland.
leads attacking party in skirmish near Goes, 230
Morley, Geoffrey, former tutor in the service of 1st Lord Wharton, 153
Morlie, Lord. *See* Parker, Edward.
Mornay, Philippe de, Seigneur du Plessis-Marly, 30
letter from, 212
Mornay, Pierre de, Seigneur de Buhy, brother of preceding.
sent by Duke of Anjou to Queen, 30
Morpeth (Morpit), Northumb., 187
Morreson, Mrs. *See* Clinton, Elizabeth.
Morris, John, partisan of 2nd Earl of Essex.
imprisoned in the Marshalsea, 282
Mortimer, Edmund, 5th Earl of March (*d*1425), 249
Mortimer, Isabel. *See* Bourchier.
Mortimer, Roger, Lord of Chirk (*d*1326), 162
Mortlake (Mortlack), Surrey.
plague at, 35
Morton, Earl of. *See* Douglas, James.
Morva Moure. *See* Morfa Mawr.
Mounslow (Munslow), Richard, late prebendary of Gloucester (*d*1558), 146
Mountague, Lady. *See* Montagu, Elizabeth.
Mountague, Viscount. *See* Browne, Anthony.
Mountague, Sir Edward. *See* Montagu, Sir Edward.
Mounteagle, Lord. *See* Parker, William; Stanley, William.
Mulcaster, Richard, schoolmaster and author.
his *Positions*, 251
Mullinex, Captain.
takes part in Cadiz expedition, 265
Munslow. *See* Mounslow, Richard.
Munster, Ireland, 171, 273, 277
Earl of Desmond takes refuge in mountains of, 28
Earl of Essex's activities in, 270
Council of War of, 274
President of. *See* Norris, Sir Thomas; Perrot, Sir John.
Murrey, Erle of. *See* Stewart, James.
Musgrave, Sir Simon, of Bewcastle, 218
Music *and* Musicians.
Richard 'the Minstrel', in the service of Henry Bourchier, 2nd Earl of Essex, 229
Queen's musicians, 255
Musical Instruments, 229

at Leicester House, 203, 221
Musters.
in Derbyshire, 59
in Worcestershire, 158
at Dymock, 234
Mychylson, Andrew, of Maldon.
letter from, 235
Myddelborough. *See* Middelburg.
Myller, Richard, of Syresham.
letter from, 191
Mylls, Mr. *See* Mills, Francis.
Myrevall. *See* Merevale.

N

Nantes, in France, 43
Nantouillet, Antoine du Prat, Sieur de, Provost of Paris, a French hostage.
Lord Robert Dudley dines with, 150
Naples, Kingdom of.
complaint of native of, 143
Napper, Mr., 250
Narrow Seas.
Lord Admiral prepares to meet Spanish Armada in, 86
Nassau, Count Henry Frederick of, youngest son of William I of Nassau, Prince of Orange.
his portrait at Leicester House, 207, 224
Nassau, Count Ludovic (Ludovik, Ludowike) *or* Louis of, brother of William I of Nassau, Prince of Orange.
letter from, 172
Sir Philip Sidney's interview with, 194
details of his forces, 231
successes of his army, 231
Nassau, Count Maurice of, Prince of Orange, son of following.
defeats Archduke Albert at Nieuport, 264, 276
names of Spaniards killed and captured by, 276
his warning to Bruges, 276
Nassau, William I of, Prince of Orange, 170, 172, 194, 196, 266
blamed for loss of Bouchain, 30
King of Spain offers reward for his death or capture, 30
accompanies Duke of Anjou to Bruges, 37
his appeal for money to pay French forces, 37
his portrait at Leicester House, 222, 224
captures Roermond, 230
details of his forces, 231
expects soldiers from France, 231
Amsterdam adheres to, 232, 233
defeats Helfenstein's troops, 232(2)

345

his agreement with Gelderland, 232
at Stokkem, 233
Nassau-Dillenburg, Count William of,
Governor of Friesland.
orders execution of Spanish prisoners
of war, 212
Nau, Claude, secretary to Queen of
Scots, 52
Navarre, King of. See Bourbon,
Antoine de; Henry.
Navy, The Queen's.
new ships added to, 28
names and crews of, 253(2)
Needham, Francis, of Melbourne, 104
Nemours (Nemors), Jacques de Savoie,
Duc de, 163, 170, 171
Nericksea. See Zieriksee.
Nether Haddon, Derbys., 44
Netherlands, The, 225
Earl of Leicester in, 208, 222
account of activities of English
expeditionary force in, 230
mentioned in verses, 288
Nethermill (Neythermylle), John, M.P.
for Coventry, 142
Nethersole, James, Mayor of
Canterbury, 202
Netherwood, Herefs.
letter dated from, 238
Nevell, Henry, of Grove, Notts., in
the service of Earl of Shrewsbury,
100
Nevell, John, 34
Nevers, Duc de. See Gonzague, Louis
de.
Nevill (Nevile), Alexander, of South
Leverton.
letter from, 207
Nevill (Nevyle), Edward, later 7th
Lord Bergavenny, 91
Nevill, Henry, 6th Lord Bergavenny.
Commissioner at trial of Queen of
Scots, 74
Nevill, Sir Henry, of Billingbear.
letter from, 194
Nevill, John, 4th Lord Latimer.
letter from, 194
Nevill, Dr. Thomas, Master of
Trinity College, Cambridge, 261
Neville, Charles, 6th Earl of
Westmorland.
reported to be in Bruges, 211
Neville, Henry, 5th Earl of
Westmorland.
letters from, 145, 152
presents Lord Robert Dudley with a
'cast of leonecattes', 150
Nevyle, Mr. See Nevill, Edward.
Nevynson (Nevison), Dr. Stephen,
Commissary-General for the
Diocese of Canterbury, 149
New Park, Lathom, Lancs.

letter dated from, 59
Newark, Notts., 109, 117
hunt meets at, 118
offence committed against Earl of
Shrewsbury at, 118
Newbury (Newberry), Berks., 71, 103
Queen at, 189
Newcastle upon Tyne, Northumb., 94,
218, 286(2), 287(4)
letters dated from, 156, 214
Scottish hostages expected at, 155
King's forces march towards, 286
letter on Scottish invasion from
alderman of, 287
Newcomen, Robert, officer for the
victuals in Ireland.
signs letter to Earl of Essex, 262
Newehaven. See Le Havre.
Newenham, Sir Thomas, of Oxton.
letter from, 155
Newfoundland.
Spanish fishermen at, 72
Newgate, London.
The Saracen's Head inn at, 240
Newgate, prison, London, 124
names of Earl of Essex's partisans
imprisoned in, 281
Newgate Street, London.
letter dated from, 84
Lady Arabella Stuart lodged in, 84
Newhall, Boreham, Essex, seat of the
Earls of Sussex, 28
Newmarket, Cambs.
horseracing, 251
Newport. See Nieuport.
Newport, Thomas, in the service of
1st Earl of Essex.
his account for Earl of Essex's
estates in Staffordshire, 247
Newton, Herefs.
manor of, 283
Neythermylle, Mr. See Nethermill,
John.
Nicholson (Nycholson), Thomas, in the
service of Francis Fletcher.
signs evidence concerning Stanhope's
defamation of Earl of Shrewsbury,
104
Nieuport (Newport), in Belgium, 231
Croft entertained at, 87
peace with England desired by
inhabitants of, 87
Parma's forces encamped around, 211
Archduke Albert defeated by Prince
of Orange at, 276
Nisse (Nisckirk), in Zeeland.
skirmish between Spanish and English
soldiers at, 230
Noailles, Gilles de, French Ambassador
to England, 154
Lord Robert Dudley dines with, 136,
137, 150

Noddy.
card game called, 261
Noel (Nowell), Mabel, Lady, wife of
Sir Andrew Noel of Brooke.
mourner at funeral of Queen of
Scots, 83
Nonpareil (Nonperely), The, of the
Queen's Navy.
to take part in Hawkins's expedition,
253
takes part in Earl of Essex's second
expedition to Spain, 265
Nonsuch (Nonsuche), Surrey, 137
letters dated from, 57, 58, 59, 80(2)
Queen at, 45
Court at, 58, 59, 80
Norfolk, 145, 262
Norfolk, Duke of. *See* Howard,
Thomas.
Normandy, France.
adherence to Catholic League of
towns in, 99
Normanton, Derbys.
letter dated from, 235
Norris (Norres), Sir Edward, Governor
of Ostend, 217, 263
Norris, Sir John, military commander,
90
reference to his and Drake's
expedition against Spain, 99
Norris, Margaret, Lady, wife of 1st
Lord Norris of Rycote.
at Buxton, 20, 21
Norris, Sir Thomas, President of
Munster, 273
Norroy (Norrey) King of Arms, 95
North, Council of the, 37, 78, 258
letter from, 25
sitting at York, 37
President of. *See* Hastings, Henry.
Secretary of. *See* Bede, Henry.
North, Lieutenant-General of the, 84,
85
See also Hastings, Henry.
North, Roger, 2nd Lord North.
letters from, 220, 239
at Zutphen, 73
present at secret marriage between
Earl of Leicester and Countess of
Essex, 206
Northampton.
clerical conference at, 185
Assizes at, 239
Northampton, Marquess of. *See* Parr,
William.
Northumberland, 287(2)
value of property higher in
Derbyshire than in, 44
Northumberland, Earl of. *See* Percy,
Henry; Percy, Thomas.
Norton, Edmund, son of following, 25
Norton, Richard, of Rilston.

letter to, 25
Norton, William, brother of preceding,
25
Nostell, Yorks.
letter dated from, 38
Nottingham, 115, 116, 124, 129
letter dated from, 125
Parliamentary elections at, 117
Assizes at, 125
Mayor of. *See* Scot, William.
Nottingham Castle, 88
Parliamentary elections held in, 117
Keeper of. *See* Manners, Sir Thomas.
Nottinghamshire, 98(2), 107, 112, 113
reluctance to provide money for
Queen's household shown in, 100
report of Earl of Shrewsbury's
intention to influence election
of M.P.s of, 116
election of knights of, 117
Sir Charles Cavendish elected M.P.
for, 117
Crown parks in, 218
Sheriff of. *See* Bassett, John;
Chaworth, Henry; Lascelles, Bryan.
Nova Silva, 221
Novey Spayne. *See* Mexico.
Nowell, Lady. *See* Noel, Mabel, Lady.
Nowell, Alexander, Dean of St. Paul's,
190, 200
Nowell, Henry.
his account of abortive duel
arrangements between Cavendish
and Stanhope, 120, 121
Nowell, Lawrence, Dean of Lichfield.
criticism of, 193
Nunez, Hector, of London, merchant
and physician. native of Portugal.
letter from, 195
Nuttall, -----, 204

O

Oatlands (Otelandes), Surrey, 35
letters dated from, 46(2), 52
O'Brien, Conor, 2nd Earl of Thomond,
171
letter from, 192
O'Carroll (O'Karroll), Sir William,
Chief of Ely, King's County, 244
O'Connor, Donough (Donnoghe)
M'Cahil (Mac Cale) Oge.
acknowledged as heir to Sir
Donough O'Connor Sligo, 210
O'Connor, Owen, brother of following,
191
O'Connor Sligo, Sir Donough (Donnell).
letter from, 191
discussion regarding inheritance of
his lands, 210

O'Donell, 245
Offeley (Offelay), Sir Thomas,
Alderman of London.
Lord Robert Dudley dines with, 150
Og, Roger. *See* O'More, Rory Oge.
Ogle, Northumb.
Barony of, 44
Ogle, Catherine, daughter of following.
See Cavendish, Katherine.
Ogle, Catherine, Lady, wife of
following, 44(2), 125
Ogle, Cuthbert, 7th Lord Ogle, 125
letters from, 42, 63
negotiates terms for marriage of
his daughter with Edward Talbot,
44
in debt to Earl of Northumberland,
44
Ogle, Jane, daughter of preceding, 42,
63
negotiations for marriage of Edward
Talbot with, 44
O'Karroll. *See* O'Carroll, Sir William.
Oldbury, Worcs. (formerly Salop).
survey of Lord Robert Dudley's lands
at, 167
Old Swan, The, inn, London.
Lord Robert Dudley and French
Ambassador dine at, 137
Ollinville (Dolynville), French royal
residence near Paris.
Queen Mother of France sent to, 30
O'More, Rory Oge (Roger Og), Captain
of Leix, 193
O'Neill, Hugh, 3rd Earl of Tyrone.
Earl of Essex indicted for his
dealings with, 270, 271
talks with Lee, 270
his peace conditions, 271
his alleged ambition to become King
of Ireland, 271
Earl of Essex justifies his negotiations
with, 274
O'Neill (O'Neales), Namid, 277
O'Neill, Tirloch Luineach (Tirlagge
Lenaghe, Turlo, Turlough
Lynagh), Chief of Tyrone, 171,
193, 245
Onslowe, Mrs., 181
Onyntene.
letter dated from, 235
Orange, Prince of. *See* Nassau,
William I of.
Ordnance.
sent from Kenilworth to Earl of
Leicester's ship at Bristol, 219
Ordnance, Clerk of the. *See* Linwray,
John.
Ordnance, Master of the. *See* Dudley,
Lord Ambrose.
Orleans, in France, 43
rebels against King of France, 97

French court at, 163
Ormond, Ireland, 244
Ormond, Earl of. *See* Butler,
Thomas.
Ormond, Lady. *See* Butler, Elizabeth.
Orton Longueville (Orton Longvile),
Hunts., 79
Oselworth. *See* Ozleworth.
Ostend, in Belgium, 214
letter dated from, 259
English Peace Commissioners arrive
in, 87
mutiny of English garrison at, 215,
216
Burgomaster of. *See* Kyen, Cornelis.
Governor of. *See* Conway, Sir John.
Victualler of. *See* Cox, Henry.
Ostia, in Italy.
Pope begins fortifications at, 157
Otelandes. *See* Oatlands.
Otford, Kent, 137
Oversten. *See* Helfenstein.
Overton, William, Rector of Stoke-
on-Trent, chaplain to the Earl of
Leicester.
letter from, 174
Owen, -----, in the service of Lord
Robert Dudley, 152
Owen, -----, a Welshman, 199
Owen, Hugh, of Cae'r Berllan, former
M.P. for Merioneth, brother of
following, 189
Owen, John Lewis, of Llwyn near
Dolgellau, M.P. for Merioneth,
188, 189
Oxford, 176(2), 108, 255
letter dated from, 107
Assizes in, 68
presence in Warwickshire of
contumacious priests from, 142
Oxford, Bishopric of, 215
Oxford, University of, 176, 261
St. Mary (Marie) Hall, 255
Oxford (Oxenforde), Countess of, 229
Oxford, Earl of. *See* Vere, Edward de.
Oxfordshire.
map of, at Leicester House, 204
Ozleworth (Oselworth), Glos.
letter dated from, 146

P

Paddy (Padie), Nicholas, Rouge Dragon
Pursuivant.
appointed Lancaster Herald, 95
Paget, Charles, Catholic exile and
conspirator, brother of following.
received by Earl of Northumberland
after his arrival from France, 48
takes leave of Duke of Guise, 212
Paget, Sir Henry, later 2nd Lord Paget
of Beaudesert, brother of following.

letters from, 143, 157, 159
Paget, Thomas, 3rd Lord Paget of
Beaudesert, 24
involved in Earl of Northumberland's
intrigues to release Queen of
Scots, 48
takes leave of Duke of Guise, 212
Paine, -----, of the English garrison
at Ostend.
elected leader by mutineers at
Ostend, 217
Palatinate, Germany.
mentioned in verses, 288
Palatine, Count or Prince. See
Frederick III.
Palatine, Marie, Electress, mother of
Duke John Casimir, Prince
Palatine.
her portrait at Leicester House, 203
Pale, The English, Ireland, 258, 262
Papists.
commission issued by Privy Council
for examination and punishment
of, 24
Paris (Pary), 36, 97(2), 163, 211, 255,
277
letters dated from, 43, 144, 145, 170,
172, 188, 212, 233
murder of Guises leads to uproar in,
97
heretics burnt in, 143
news from, 184
Parker, Edward, 12th Lord Morley.
Commissioner at trial of Queen of
Scots, 74
Parker, Matthew, Archbishop of
Canterbury, 146, 181, 185
Parker, William, Lord Monteagle, later
13th Lord Morley.
takes part in Earl of Essex's rebellion,
277
imprisoned in the Tower, 281
Parliament, 78, 97, 100, 172(2), 173(2),
220, 229, 286
to meet in October 1580, 30
prorogued until November 1580, 30
grants subsidy to Queen, 36, 88
prorogued, 75, 76, 78, 79
to petition for execution of Queen
of Scots, 76, 77
presents its petition to Queen at
Richmond, 77(2)
insists upon execution of Queen of
Scots on grounds of national
security, 79
expected to grant subsidy, 97
Queen proposes to create new earls
and barons for, 97
grants double subsidy, 99, 100
elections for, 116
reference to elections in Merioneth
for, 189

Bishop of Hereford assaulted on his
way to, 195
elections at Carmarthen for, 255
Earl of Essex appointed General of
army of, 291
See also Commons, House of; Lords,
House of.
Parliament, Spanish. See Cortes.
Parma, Duchess of. See Margaret.
Parma, Prince of. See Farnese,
Alessandro.
Parott, Sir Thomas. See Perrot, Sir
Thomas.
Parr, William, Marquess of
Northampton (d1571), 160
Parry, Sir Thomas, Comptroller of the
Household, 138, 154, 160
Partridge (Partrige), -----, 137
Pary. See Paris.
Patten, William, of Aldersgate Street,
London.
letter from, 50
Paul IV, Pope (d1559).
banishes Cardinal Caraffa from
Rome, 139
Paulet (Powlet), Sir Amias, Keeper of
Mary, Queen of Scots.
Sir Drue Drury sent to assist, 77, 78
signs letter to Earl of Shrewsbury, 92
signs letter from Privy Council, 93
Paulet, Lucy, Lady St. John, wife of
William Paulet, Lord St. John,
later 4th Marquess of Winchester.
mourner at funeral of Queen of
Scots, 83
Paulet, William, 1st Marquess of
Winchester, Lord High Treasurer,
140(2), 151
letter from, 145
Paul's. See St. Paul's.
Payne, Tobias (Toby).
dismissed as Steward by Earl of
Essex, 291
Peacock (Pecock), Mr., 168
Peak, The, Derbys., 43
Earl of Shrewsbury forbidden by
Queen to assemble freeholders of,
50
Catholic sympathies of inhabitants of,
50
Forest of, 69
Pearcye, Sir H. See Percy, Henry.
Pearls.
purchased by Earl of Leicester, 199
Pearson, William, in the service of
Francis Fletcher.
signs evidence concerning Stanhope's
defamation of Earl of Shrewsbury,
104
Peckover, Michael, Keeper of Leicester
House.

his inventory, 224
Peers, Zachary.
  signs letter to Earl of Essex, 262
Pemberton, Sir Goddard, of
  Hertingfordbury.
  Earl of Essex in debt to, 283
Pembridge, Herefs.
  letters dated from, 285(2)
  manor of, 283
Pembridge, Anthony, M.P. for
  Hereford, 269
  given annuity by Earl of Essex, 255
Pembroke, 236, 247
  Mayor of. See Hinton, Richard.
Pembroke, Countess of. See Herbert,
  Mary.
Pembroke, Earl of. See Herbert, Henry;
  Herbert, William.
Pembrokeshire, 233, 236, 251
  survey of Earl of Essex's lands in, 282
  Marshal of the Admiralty in. See
  Kiste, John.
Penbryn (Penbrin), Cards.
  survey of Lord Robert Dudley's lands
  at, 167
Pennant, -----.
  supplies provisions for Earl of Essex's
  expedition to Ireland, 246
Pennte, Edward, in the service of Earl
  of Essex.
  letter from, 240
Penny (Peny), Thomas, of London,
  physician.
  letter to, 247
  summoned by Earl of Essex to
  Lamphey, 247
Pepwall, William, Alderman of Bristol.
  signs letter to Earl of Leicester, 173
Perceval (Percevall, Perseval),
  Christopher, Sergeant-Major of
  Harlingen in Friesland, 214
  letter from, 212
Percy, Lord. See Percy, Henry.
Percy, Algernon, 10th Earl of
  Northumberland, Lord General of
  the King's Army, 286
  prevented by illness from going
  to the North, 286
Percy, Sir Charles, son of 8th Earl
  of Northumberland.
  imprisoned in the Fleet, 281
Percy, Dorothy, Countess of
  Northumberland. See Devereux,
  Lady Dorothy.
Percy, Henry, Lord Percy, later 5th
  Earl of Northumberland, 35
Percy, Henry, 8th Earl of
  Northumberland (d1585), 24, 42
  letter from, 35
  Lord Ogle in debt to, 44
  Queen offended by his intrigues for
  release of Queen of Scots, 48

his return to the North deplored
  by Earl of Huntingdon, 190
Percy, Henry, 9th Earl of
  Northumberland, 99
  his marriage to Lady Dorothy
  Devereux at Essex House, 261
Percy, Mary, Countess of
  Northumberland, daughter of 4th
  Earl of Shrewsbury, wife of 5th
  Earl of Northumberland, 35
Percy, Thomas, 7th Earl of
  Northumberland.
  said to have been seduced from
  his allegiance by Metcalfe, 187
Peream, Justice. See Peryam, Sir
  William.
Perez (Peres), Antonio, former Secretary
  of State to King of Spain, later a
  political refugee in England.
  falls ill in Earl of Essex's house, 260
  receives monthly sum from Earl of
  Essex, 261
  leaves England for France, 261, 262
Perkin (Perkinne) John, member of the
  Earl of Leicester's Company of
  Players.
  signs petition to Earl of Leicester,
  266
Perkin (Perkyn), William, partisan of
  2nd Earl of Essex.
  imprisoned in the Marshalsea, 282
Perott, Sir John. See Perrot, Sir John.
Perrenot, Antoine, Bishop of Arras,
  Cardinal de Granvell.
  accompanies Duke and Duchess of
  Feria out of Brussels, 155
Perrot, Dorothy, Lady. See Devereux,
  Lady Dorothy.
Perrot, Jane, Lady, 2nd wife of
  following, 259
Perrot (Perott), Sir John, President of
  Munster, later Lord Deputy of
  Ireland (d1592), 210
  to be called to Parliament or made
  Comptroller of the Household, 97
  Fitzmaurice submits to, 193
  Earl of Worcester's claim on behalf
  of, 249
Perrot (Parott), Sir Thomas, of
  Haroldston (d1594), son of
  preceding, 248, 259
Perrot, Thomas.
  annuity paid to, 262
Perseval, C. See Perceval, Christopher.
Peru, 71
Peryam (Peream), Sir William, Justice
  of Common Pleas, later Chief
  Baron of Exchequer.
  Commissioner at trial of Queen of
  Scots, 74
  takes part in trial of Earl of Essex,
  269

Petchford, R., in the service of Earl of Essex.
letter from, 277
Peterborough, Northants.
letter dated from, 185
Peterborough, Bishop of. *See* Howland, Richard; Scambler, Edmund.
Peterborough, Dean of. *See* Fletcher, Richard.
Petrarch.
his portrait at Leicester House, 207
Petre, Robert, Auditor of the Receipt of the Exchequer, M.P. for Penryn, 54
Petre, Thomas.
letter from, 284
Philip II, King of Spain, 86, 101, 153, 173, 195, 201, 254, 258
reported to have offered Infanta and Low Countries to Duke of Anjou, 24
invades Portugal, 28
offers rewards for capture or death of Prince of Orange, 30
Portugal occupied by, 31
reported to be asking aid of Princes of Empire against Duke of Anjou, 38
military preparations of, 87, 89
his Armada sails for England, 91
Duke of Guise's pension from, 97
sends Fuentes to Brussels, 116
Franco-Turkish collaboration against, 116
forced to request financial aid from Spanish people, 116
returns to Brussels from Mons, 138
disinclined to make peace with France without England, 138
much affected by death of French King, 141
postpones bestowal of Order of the Fleece, 142
his collaboration with Guises, 144
expected to return to Spain, 144
Duke of Feria refuses offer of mission in England from, 155
his forces defeated at sea by Turks, 157, 159
memorandum on revenues of, 160
receives gratuity from Cortes on his marriage, 160
authorized by Pope to sell church lands, 160
Turkish pressure expected to moderate his religious fervour, 162
suspicious of friendship between Pope and Duke of Florence, 162
Cobham's negotiations with, 173
peace talks with Queen, 213
his false assumption that Lisbon would be objective of English

expedition in 1596, 264
mentioned in verses, 288
his secretary. *See* Cayas.
his wife. *See* Anne.
Philipe, 125
Philipes, -----.
attends to Earl of Shrewsbury's apricot trees, 131
Phillips, Morgan, of Picton, 236
letter from, 234
Phillips, William, of London.
appointed collector of subsidy, 36
Philpot, Captain, of the English expeditionary force in Walcheren.
his conduct in action commended, 232
Phyton, Edward. *See* Fitton, Sir Edward.
Picardy, France.
adherence to Catholic League of towns in, 99
Pickering (Pykeryng), Sir William, courtier and diplomatist, 136, 181
letter from, 187
Picton, Pembs.
letter dated from, 234
Pierrepont (Pierpoint), Henry, of Holme Pierrepont, 116, 118
Piers, John, Bishop of Salisbury, 200
Pilkington, James, Bishop of Durham.
letter from, 192
Pillingbere. *See* Billingbear.
Pipe, Mr., 127
Pius IV, Pope.
fortifies Civitavecchia and Ostia, 157
requests loan of 50 galleys from Venice, 157
to go to Bologna, 159
expected to meet Duke of Florence and crown him King of Tuscany, 159
sends cardinals to France to call national council, 159
authorizes King of Spain to sell church lands, 160
King of Spain granted money out of Bull called *Crosado* issued by, 160
King of Spain suspicious of friendship between Duke of Florence and, 162
Pius V, Pope.
his Legate in Low Countries arrested, 169
rejects French King's request with contempt, 171
issues Bull against Queen, 171
Plague, The.
Spanish army in Low Countries ravaged by, 24
prevents Queen going to Richmond, 35
in Europe, 184

Plantation.
Earl of Essex leases land in Ulster for, 284

Plate.
at Leicester House, 202, 208, 219
at Kenilworth, 208
given away by Earl of Essex in Ireland, 248

Players *and* Plays, 285
payment to Lord Robert Dudley's players, 136, 137
petition from Earl of Leicester's Company of Players, 226
at Essex House, 261

Playhouse, The, Blackfriars, London.
Earl of Essex at, 285

Plessy, Monsieur de. *See* Mornay, Philippe de.

Plumue. *See* Plymouth.

Pluralities.
bill in House of Commons against, 100

Plutarch.
his *Opera*, 251

Plymouth (Plumue), Devon, 233, 238, 253, 263
letters dated from, 233, 263

Po, River, Italy.
serious damage caused by flooding of, 157

Poitiers, Diane de, Duchess of Valentinois, mistress of Henry II, King of France.
banished by Guises from French court, 143

Poitou, France, 43

Poland.
reference to war for succession to throne of, 87
Chancellor of. *See* Zamoyski, John.

Poland, King of. *See* Sigismund III.

Pole, Reginald, Cardinal and Archbishop of Canterbury, 130

Pollard, Sir John, of Trelawne, 192

Poole, Sir Giles, of Sapperton, 149
letters from, 237, 240

Poole, Henry, son of preceding, 237

Pooley, Warwicks.
letter dated from, 234

Poolie, Captain.
takes part in Cadiz expedition, 265

Poor, The.
in Derbyshire, 41
Earl of Essex's gift to, at Cambridge, 261

Poore, -----, in the service of Earl of Oxford, 205

Pope, The.
attempted trickery by Spanish cardinal at election of, 147
See also Clement VIII; Gregory XIII; Paul IV; Pius IV; Pius V; Sixtus V.

Popham, Sir John, Lord Chief Justice of Queen's Bench, 269, 277
letter to, 262
takes part in trial of Earl of Essex, 269
kept prisoner in Essex House, 278
released by Gorges, 278

Port Riale. *See* Puerto Real.

Port St. Marie. *See* Puerto de Sta. Maria.

Portcullis Pursuivant. *See* Lant, Thomas; Segar, Sir William.

Portland, Dorset.
large foreign fleet sighted off, 186

Portraits *and* Pictures.
at Leicester House, 203, 207, 208, 222

Portsmouth, Hants., 266
letters dated from, 209, 215
Drake returns from West Indies to, 71
Mayor of. *See* Cooke, Peter.
Postmaster of. *See* James, Mark.

Portsmouth Castle, Hants., 215

Portugal.
King of Spain invades, 28
Spanish occupation of, 31
portrait at Leicester House of son of King of, 207

Portugal, King of. *See* Sebastian.

Powell, Raphael, of Upminster.
appointed Deputy Aulnager of Hertfordshire, 252 *n*

Powell, Thomas, cousin of Sir Edward Herbert, 255

Powell, Thomas, on active service in the Netherlands.
letter from, 259

Powis, Lordship of, 255

Powles. *See* St. Paul's.

Powlet, Sir A. *See* Paulet, Sir Amias.

Poynes, Anthony, member of the English expeditionary force to South Beveland.
wounded in skirmish near Goes, 230

Poyntz (Pointz), John (Jone), of Ozleworth.
letter from, 146

Poyntz, Sir Nicholas, of Iron Acton.
letter from, 147

Praia, in Cape Verde Is.
sacked by Drake's fleet, 71

Pratt, William, a commissioner in Ferney.
letter from, 258

Prendergast, Pembs.
letter dated from, 263

Prestbury, Glos.
survey of manor of, 253

Presteigne, Radnor.
letter dated from, 179

Pretier, C., prisoner in the Queen's

Bench prison, London.
letter from, 234
Preyner, Baron Casper, Imperial
Ambassador to England.
receives gift of horse, 148
Lord Robert Dudley dines with, 149,
150
Price, Dr. Ellis, of Plas Iolyn, 218
letter from, 188
Prideaux, John, English Catholic in
exile, 211
Priests, 205
arrested in Berkshire, 35
execution for treason of, 35
arrested, 86, 92, 94
in Warwickshire, 142
See also Recusants.
Prince Daulphin. See Bourbon, François
de.
Princes of the Blood (French).
favour plan of Duke of Anjou's
marriage, 177
Prine (Prune), Ralph, of London,
grocer, 186
Prittlewell (Prytwell), Essex.
letter dated from, 241
Privy Council, 36, 45, 53, 62, 66,
79, 85, 102(2), 107, 108, 109, 110,
112, 141, 145, 156, 164, 178, 180,
183, 200, 205, 216, 218, 224, 254,
260, 269(2), 270
letters from, 22, 23, 46, 79, 80(2), 84,
86, 89, 91, 92, 93, 94, 96, 98(3),
127, 159
letters to, 103, 121, 245
issues commission to examine and
punish Papists, 24
chooses Lord Hunsdon to be
responsible for Queen's personal
safety, 92
decrees general public thanksgiving
for defeat of Armada, 95
issues order for restraint in eating
of meat at Lent, 98(2)
Stanhope complains about Earl of
Shrewsbury to, 108, 115
forbids Charles Cavendish to pursue
his quarrel with Stanhope, 118
receives account of assault by Earl
of Shrewsbury's partisans on
Stanhope, 122
criticized for curtailing expenditure
on defences at Berwick, 140
orders inquiry into export of horses,
155
ordered by Queen to deal with
mutiny of English garrison in
Ostend, 216
issues warrant for search of Fowler's
house, 220
Clerks to. See Wilkes, Sir Thomas;
Wilson, Thomas.

Privy Council, French.
Charles IX's policy opposed by many
members of, 187
Proclamations.
prohibiting dissemination of news
about English expedition to Cadiz,
264
Prune, Ralph. See Prine, Ralph.
Pryce, Mr., of 'Eglussye', 201
Prynne, Sir Gilbert, of Allington,
Wilts.
Earl of Essex in debt to, 283
Prytwell. See Prittlewell.
Puckering, Sir John, Speaker of the
House of Commons, later Lord
Keeper, 76, 114, 124
letters to, 107, 256
speaks in favour of petition for
execution of Queen of Scots, 77
Puerto de Sta. Maria (Port St. Marie),
in Spain.
taken by English forces, 264
Puerto Real (Port Riale), in Spain.
taken by English forces, 264
Purforde. See Pyrford.
Purslowe, Thomas, of St. Mary Hall,
Oxford.
given annuity by Earl of Essex, 255
Purveyors.
bill in House of Commons against, 99
Pwllheli, Caerns.
Earl of Essex's body conveyed from
Dublin to Carmarthen by way of,
248
Pyde Grene.
name of horse bestowed on Lord
Chamberlain, 169
Pyde Yonge.
name of horse bestowed on Earl of
Arundel, 169
Pyero, -----, 198
Pygin, Robert, in the service of John
Stanhope, 124
Pykeryng, Sir William. See
Pickering, Sir William.
Pyrford (Purforde), Surrey.
letter dated from, 233

Q

Queen Mother, The. See Medici,
Catherine de.
Queenhithe (Queen Hyethe), London.
Earl of Essex and his followers
return to Essex House by boat
from, 278
Queens, The two new. See Anne,
Princess; Elizabeth, Princess.
Queens' College, Cambridge. See
Cambridge.
Queen's County, Ireland, 193

R

Raby, co. Durham.
  letter dated from, 152
Radcliff. *See* Ratcliff.
Radcliffe (Radclyffe), Edward, of
  Elstow, cousin of following, 215
Radcliffe, Henry, 4th Earl of Sussex.
  letters from, 209, 215
  his gift to Earl of Leicester, 210
Radcliffe, Robert, 5th Earl of Sussex.
  commander in Cadiz expedition, 263
  composition of his regiment, 265
  imprisoned in the Tower, 281
Radcliffe, Thomas, 3rd Earl of
  Sussex, Lord Chamberlain, 138(2),
  148, 174, 181, 251
  letter from, 38
  signs letter from Privy Council, 22
  goes to Newhall, 28
Rade, John, footman to the Queen, 218
Ragusa, in Yugoslavia.
  Sultan orders expulsion of Spanish
  and Catholic League envoys from,
  116
Rainbow (Rainebow), The, of the
  Queen's Navy.
  to take part in Hawkins's expedition,
  253
Ralegh (Rayleigh), Sir Walter, military
  commander and author.
  description of his gift to Earl of
  Leicester, 219
  report of his trying to murder Earl
  of Essex, 278
Rambridge, John, Dean of Lichfield.
  reported to be in hiding, 142
Rammekens, in Zeeland, 215
Ramsbury, Wilts.
  letter dated from, 194
Ramsden (Ramsden Barrington), Essex.
  letter dated from, 237
  letter from Earl of Essex's tenants
  at, 241
  manor of, 237
Ramsden, Roger, member of the
  Company of Merchant
  Adventurers.
  involved in the kidnapping of Story,
  225
Randolph, Sir Thomas, English
  Ambassador to Scotland.
  letter from, 187
Ranton (Rontoon), Staffs.
  letter dated from, 234
Raskelf (Rascall), Yorks.
  survey of Lord Robert Dudley's lands
  at, 167
Ratcliff (Radcliff, Ratcleef), London,
  150, 170
Ratcliffe (Ratcliff), Alexander, of
  Gray's Inn, in the service of Earl
  of Shrewsbury, 58, 107, 108
Raven, John, later Richmond Herald.

appointed Rouge Croix Pursuivant,
  95
Rawlins, John *alias* Yonge.
  arrested for playing illegal card game,
  188
Rayleigh, Sir Walter. *See* Ralegh, Sir
  Walter.
Rayner, Elizabeth, daughter of
  following, later wife of Henry
  Talbot, son of 6th Earl of
  Shrewsbury.
  Copley's description of, 66
Rayner, Sir William, of Orton
  Longueville, 66
Raynsforde, Mr.
  Queen dines at house of, 189
Reade, Sir William, general, 90
Reading, Berks.
  letter dated from, 209
  Queen at, 189
Recusants.
  imprisoned in Bishop's house at Ely,
  92
  arrest of, 92
  See also Priests.
Redfern (Rudfen), Warwicks.
  survey of Earl of Leicester's lands at,
  200
Regeley. *See* Rugeley.
Remund. *See* Roermond.
Rethelth, James, of Llanddewi.
  letter from, 264
Reum (?), in Netherlands.
  captured by Dutch, 231
Reynas, Don Juan de.
  reported killed in battle at
  Nieuport, 276
Reynolds, Edward, secretary of 2nd Earl
  of Essex, 263
  imprisoned in the Marshalsea, 282
Rheinberg (Bergh), in Germany.
  Schenk on his way to relieve, 214(2)
Rheingrave (Reingrave, Ringrave),
  Philip Francis, Count of Salm,
  The, 146
  his portrait at Leicester House, 203
  his wife. *See* Salm.
Rhine (Rhyne), River, 86
Rich (Ryche), Mr., a solicitor, 229
Rich, Penelope, Lady, wife of 3rd Lord
  Rich, later 1st Earl of Warwick,
  262
  her portrait at Leicester House, 222,
  224
  her marriage and dowry, 248
Rich, Richard, 1st Lord Rich, 149
Rich (Ryche), Robert, 2nd Lord Rich.
  letters from, 234, 240
Rich, Robert, 3rd Lord Rich, later
  1st Earl of Warwick.
  his marriage with Lady Penelope
  Devereux, 248

imprisoned in the Tower, 281
Richard the 'Minstrel', in the service
of Henry Bourchier, 2nd Earl of
Essex, 229
Richards, Captain.
takes part in Cadiz expedition, 265
Richardson, Edmund, of Nottingham,
shoemaker.
his disclosures, 124
Richmond (Richmounde), Surrey, 50,
60, 75, 78, 150, 275
letters dated from, 27, 30, 31, 40,
50, 60, 63, 78, 79, 84, 96, 97,
158, 209
court at, 30, 31
plague prevents Queen from going to,
35
Queen walks 'on the grene' at, 64
petition from Parliament for
execution of Queen of Scots
presented at, 77
Richmond, Mr.
Lord Robert Dudley's christening gift
to his child, 150
Richmounde. See Richmond.
Ridgeley, Thomas.
letter from, 235
Ringrave, The. See Rheingrave.
Rishe, Captain.
takes part in Cadiz expedition, 265
Rize, Matthew, of Bristol.
brings news of success of Cadiz
expedition, 264
Roads, -----, 256
Roan. See Rouen.
Roberts, John, partisan of 2nd Earl
of Essex.
imprisoned in the Marshalsea, 282
Robinson, Nicholas, Bishop of Bangor,
182
Robsart, Sir John, of Syderstone, 168
Robsart, Sir Terry (Tyrrye), of
Syderstone (d1496), 168
Rochelle, La, in France, 233
letters dated from, 172, 212(2)
victuals prevented from reaching, 31
Rochester, Kent, 137
Rodes, John, of Staveley Woodthorpe,
J.P.
Privy Council's directive to, 23
Roermond (Remund), in Limburg,
Netherlands.
captured by Prince of Orange, 230
Roger, Mr., 213
Rogers, -----, in the service of Earl
of Shrewsbury, 130
Rogers, Sir Edward, of Cannington,
Comptroller of the Household, 160
Rohan, family of.
relations with King of France, 212
Rome, (Roome, Rowme), 99, 171, 182
reported closure by Pope of English

House in, 30
Cardinal Caraffa banished by Pope
from, 139
Cardinal Monti thrashed in
courtesan's house in, 157
Martinengo ready to leave for
England from, 157
Pope's request to Venetian
Ambassador in, 157
news from, 159
Bruno burnt at, 277
Rone. See Rouen.
Rontoon. See Ranton.
Rooe, John, in the service of the
Stanhope family, 124
Roome. See Rome.
Rose, The, inn, Smithfield, London,
239
Ross, Bishop of. See Leslie, John.
Ross Foreign (Ross Farran), Herefs.
manor of, 291
Ross-on-Wye (Ross), Herefs.
letter dated from, 285
manor of, 265, 291
Prince Maurice at, 291
Rosse, John, Scottish naval commander.
in charge of French fleet conveying
expeditionary force to Scotland,
152
Rotherfield Greys (Greye), Oxon.
letter dated from, 233
Rotherham, Yorks., 131
Rotherham, Mr., of Chancery Lane,
London, 240
Rouen (Roan, Roane, Rone), in France,
38
letter dated from, 179
Earl of Essex on active service near,
254
Rouge Croix (Rougecrosse) Pursuivant.
Raven appointed to post of, 95
Rous (Rousse), John, Receiver-General
for South Wales, 285
Roussy (Russye), Louis de Luxembourg,
Comte de.
Lord Robert Dudley dines with, 150
Rovens, Lord. See Ruthven, Patrick.
Row, Sir William, Lord Mayor of
London.
Earl of Essex dines with, 255
Rowe, William.
letter from, 193
Rowme. See Rome.
Rudall, Robert, partisan of 2nd Earl
of Essex.
imprisoned in the Marshalsea, 282
Rudfen. See Redfern.
Rudforth. See Rufford.
Rudolph II, Emperor, 87
Rufford (Rudforth, Rughford), Notts.,
29, 54
letters dated from, 95, 96, 186

Rullo, Donato, a native of Naples.
letter from, 143
Russell, Lady. *See* Russell, Elizabeth.
Russell, Mrs., 277
Russell, Anthony, partisan of 2nd Earl
of Essex.
imprisoned in the Marshalsea, 282
Russell, Bridget, Countess of Bedford,
wife of (1) Sir Richard Morrison, of
Cassiobury, (2) 2nd Earl of
Rutland, (3) 2nd Earl of Bedford.
mourner at funeral of Queen of
Scots, 83
her daughter. *See* Clinton, Elizabeth.
Russell, Edward, 3rd Earl of Bedford.
takes part in Earl of Essex's
rebellion, 278(2)
imprisoned in the Tower, 281
Russell, Elizabeth, Lady, widow of
John, Lord Russell (*d*1584), son
of following, 71
Russell, Francis, 2nd Earl of Bedford,
125, 143, 163
letters from, 153, 181
his employment of Chester criticised
by Earl of Shrewsbury, 20
signs letter from Privy Council, 22
sympathetic towards Zouche, 23
refers in after-dinner speech to Earl
of Shrewsbury's ancestor, 24
his gift to Earl of Leicester, 219
Russell, James, footman to the Queen,
217
Russell, Margaret, daughter of 2nd Earl
of Bedford.
at Buxton, 21
Russell, Sir Thomas, of Strensham, 158
Russell, Sir William, later 1st Lord
Russell of Thornhaugh, Governor
of Flushing, 277
letter from, 215
asks to be relieved of his post, 215
Russye, 'Countye of'. *See* Roussy.
Ruthin, Lordship of, Denbighs., 189
Ruthven, Archibald, son of following.
sent to England as hostage, 156
Ruthven (Rovens), Patrick, 3rd Lord
Ruthven.
his son sent to England as hostage,
156
Rutland, Countess of. *See* Manners,
Elizabeth.
Rutland, Earl of. *See* Manners,
Edward; Manners, Henry;
Manners, John; Manners, Roger.
Rutland.
clerical conference in, 185
Ryche, Robert. *See* Rich, Robert.
Ryton, Warwicks.
manor of, 227
Ryves, Sir William, Attorney-General
for Ireland.

letter from, 284
Ryveyre, Monsieur, a French captain.
killed in action near Middelburg, 232

S

Sacheverell, Henry, of Morley, Derbys.,
23
Sacheverell, Margaret, Keeper of the
plate at Leicester House, 208
Sacheverell, Ralph, of Stanton, Derbys.,
43
Sackfourd, Thomas. *See* Seckford,
Thomas.
Sackville, Sir Richard, Chancellor of
the Exchequer.
Drury in his custody, 167
Sackville, Thomas, 1st Lord Buckhurst,
English Envoy Extraordinary to
France, later Lord Treasurer, 24,
111, 113, 114, 225
letters from, 110(2), 114, 215
letters to, 112, 113
conveys sentence of death to
Queen of Scots, 78(2)
signs letter from Privy Council, 98
warmly welcomed at French Court,
171
takes part in trial of Earl of
Essex, 269
replies to Earl of Essex's defence, 275
Sadler (Sadleir), Sir Ralph, diplomatist,
Chancellor of the Duchy of
Lancaster, 53
letters from, 148, 163
to take charge of Queen of Scots,
51(2), 52(2)
reports reluctance of Queen of Scots
to leave Wingfield, 52
Commissioner at trial of Queen of
Scots, 74
St. André (Saint Andrewes), Jacques
d'Albon, Marshal of.
discredited at French court, 143
St. Augustine, in Florida.
destroyed by Drake's fleet, 72
St. Bartholomew.
reference to massacre of, 38
St. Bartholomew's (St. Bertlemeus),
London.
letter dated from, 234
St. Clement's Church, Strand, London.
Owen Salisbury killed in Essex House
by shot fired from steeple of, 278
St. David's, Bishopric of, 249
St. Domingo. *See* Santo Domingo.
St. George's Day, 154
St. George's Feast, 41
Earl of Shrewsbury excused from
attending, 90
to be held at Whitehall, 129

St. Jago. *See* San Tiago.

St. James, Westminster.
letters dated from, 93, 94
Queen's letter to Earl of Shrewsbury dated from manor of, 47
court at, 93, 216(2), 217(2)

St. James's Park, Westminster.
supper arranged for Queen in, 136
Lord Robert Dudley hunts in, 137

St. Jean d'Angely (St. Jhon d'Angeli), in France.
besieged, 30

St. John, Catherine, Lady St. John of Bletso (Bletsoe), wife of following.
mourner at funeral of Queen of Scots, 83

St. John, John, 2nd Lord St. John of Bletso.
Commissioner at trial of Queen of Scots, 74

St. John of Bassinge, Lady. *See* Paulet, Lucy.

St. Johns, in Florida.
Drake's fleet burns fort at, 71

St. Katharine's (St. Katheryns), London, 170

St. Leger, Sir Warham (Warrham), Commissioner for Munster, 274

St. Leger House, Southwark, London.
letters dated from, 179, 181

St. Malo, in France, 264

St. Martin-in-the-Fields (St. Martin's), London.
letter dated from, 35

St. Mary Hall, Oxford. *See* Oxford.

St. Mary's, Cambridge.
Earl of Essex's contribution towards building steeple of, 261

St. Michael of France.
Order of, 204, 224

St. Paul, The, of the King of Spain's Navy.
set on fire during English attack on Cadiz, 264

St. Paul's (Powles), London, 71, 95, 123

St. Paul's, Dean of. *See* Nowell, Alexander.

St. Paul's Churchyard (Powles Churchyard), London, 150
Earl of Essex and his followers beaten back from, 278

St. Paul's Cross (Paules Crosse), London, 176

St. Peter's Day.
fair day at Leominster, 237

St. Philip, The, of the King of Spain's Navy.
set on fire during English attack on Cadiz, 164

St. Phillipo.
people of Flushing capture Spanish galleass called, 93

St. Quentin (St. Quyntyn, St. Quentans), in France, 136, 219
Walsingham at, 36

St. Saluto, Abbot of. *See* Martinengo.

Salceedoe *or* Salceedo, -----, a Spanish spy.
arrested and tortured in Bruges, 38

Salines, Count of.
reported to have been taken prisoner in battle at Nieuport, 276

Salisburie, Captain.
takes part in Cadiz expedition, 265

Salisbury, Wilts.
letters dated from, 39, 236, 239

Salisbury, Bishop of, 219

Salisbury, Captain Owen, partisan of 2nd Earl of Essex.
killed during attack on Essex House, 278

Salisbury. *See also* Salusbury.

Salisbury Court, Fleet Street, London, 201

Salm, Marie Egyptienne, Countess of Oettingen and of, wife of Philip Francis, Count of Salm *styled* the Rheingrave.
her portrait at Leicester House, 203
her husband. *See* Rheingrave.

Salop, Lady. *See* Talbot, Elizabeth.

Saltpetre.
opposition expected in Nottinghamshire to demand for money to transport, 100

Salusbury (Salisbury) family of Lleweni, 189
election of officers at Denbigh designed to curb influence of, 190

Salusbury (Salisbury), Jane, wife of following, 190

Salusbury (Salisbury), Sir John, of Lleweni.
proposes to come to London to seek Earl of Leicester's favour, 190

Salusbury (Salisbury), John, of Lleweni, 189, 218

Salutation of Our Lady, The, inn, Tower Street, London, 150

Saluzzo, Marquisate of, 277

Sampson, Mr., of Kent, a member of English expeditionary force to South Beveland.
wounded in skirmish near Goes, 230

San Lucar, in Spain, 264
taken by English forces, 264

San Tiago (St. Jago), in Cape Verde Is.
sacked by Drake's fleet, 71

Sandes, Lord. *See* Sandys, William.

Sandgate Castle, Kent.
letter dated from, 155

Sandys, Edwin, Bishop of Worcester, later Archbishop of York.

letter from, 156

Sandys (Sandes), William, 3rd Lord Sandys.
Commissioner at trial of Queen of Scots, 74
his name mentioned as possible husband for Countess of Lennox, 197
takes part in Earl of Essex's rebellion, 278
imprisoned in the Tower, 281

Sant Angelo, Castello di, Rome.
Malatesta imprisoned in, 157

Santa Cruz (Sta. Croce), Alvaro de Bazan, Marquis of, Spanish Admiral.
his death reported from Genoa, 87

Santo Domingo, in Hispaniola.
sacked by Drake's fleet, 71

Sapina, Don Charles de.
reported to have been taken prisoner in battle at Nieuport, 276

Sapperton (Saperton), Glos.
letters dated from, 237, 240(2)

Saracen's Head (Sarazons heade), The, inn, Newgate, London, 240

Sarnsfield (Sarnesfield), Herefs.
letter dated from, 254

Sarrazoo, Duke of.
reported dead, 147

Sarsenet.
cloth of, 168

Sarum, Bishop of. See Piers, John.

Saunders, -----.
mourner at funeral of Queen of Scots, 83

Saunders, -----, footman in the service of 2nd Earl of Essex, 261

Saunders, John, of Lew.
letter from, 48

Savile, Sir George, of Lupset and Barrowby, 37, 115

Savile, Henry, Warden of Merton College, Oxford.
his son christened at Oxford, 255

Savoy, The, Strand, London.
letter dated from Burghley's house near, 85

Savoy, Duke of. See Charles Emmanuel; Emmanuel Philibert.

Sawre, William, of Gainsborough, in the service of Lord Burghley, 109

Say, Lord. See Fiennes, Richard.

Say House (Say Ows).
letter dated from, 28

Scambler, Edmund, Bishop of Peterborough, 206
letter from, 185

Scarsdale, Derbys., 43

Schenk (Shenk, Skynke), Colonel Martin, Sieur de Afferden and Blyenbeek, in the service of the

States General.
takes possession of Bonn, 86
knighted by Earl of Leicester, 90
in London, 90
on his way to relieve Rheinberg, 214(2)

Schmalkalden (Smalcaldy), in Germany.
reference to Diet at, 200

Scory, John, Bishop of Hereford.
letter from, 195
assaulted on his way to Parliament, 195

Scory (Scorye), Sylvanus (Silvanus), son of preceding, 198

Scot, William, Mayor of Nottingham.
requested to maintain order during elections, 117

Scotland (Schottelande, Skotlonde), 29, 77, 94, 127, 144, 162, 178(2), 186, 220, 226, 253, 262
d'Aubigny reported to be in control of, 28
financial cost of Queen's policy in, 32
news from, 39, 40, 43, 44, 68, 262
Walsingham to go to, 44
news expected of Walsingham's negotiations in, 46
cortège at funeral of Queen of Scots includes representatives from, 83, 84
Queen takes steps to defend frontiers of, 84
Drake to prevent Spanish move against, 86
defeat of Armada celebrated by Protestants in, 95
France reported to be organizing military expedition to, 144
Lord Robert Dudley dines with ambassador from, 152
Duc d'Elboeuf in command of French expedition to, 152
hostages from, 155, 156
skirmish between French forces and troops of the Congregation in, 156
Queen of Scots desirous of passing through England to, 163
irreconcilable differences of views between parties in, 187
Scottish army crosses English border from, 286, 287
letter on the invasion from, 287

Scotland, Council of.
said to be half Papist, 262

Scotland, Regent of. See Erskine, John.

Scots, King of. See James VI.

Scott, John, of Camberwell, grandfather of Amy Robsart, 136

Scrimgeour (Scrimger, Scrimgrour), Francis.
guilty of poaching on Earl of Shrewsbury's land, 73

Scrope, Thomas, 10th Lord Scrope,
Warden of the West March, 127
Scryour, -----, in the service of Earl
of Rutland, 88
Scudamore, Mr.
obtains wardship of John Talbot, 45
Sea Dragon, The.
missing from Drake's fleet, 72
Seager, William. *See* Segar, Sir
William.
Sebastian, King of Portugal, 195
Seckford (Sackfourd), Thomas, M.P.
for Bridgnorth, Steward of the
Household of the Council in the
Marches of Wales.
regarded by Shadwell as his enemy,
195
Secretary, Mr. *See* Cecil, Sir William;
Walsingham, Sir Francis.
Sedersterne. *See* Syderstone.
Sedgley (Segyleye), Staffs., 162
Segar (Seager), Sir William, Portcullis
Pursuivant, later Garter King of
Arms.
recommended by Earl of Leicester as
Somerset Herald, 89
Segyleye. *See* Sedgley.
Selby, Yorks., 41, 44
Selynger, Mr., member of the English
expeditionary force to South
Beveland.
his conduct in action commended,
230
Sempetori (Sempetory), Baptista
(Baptist), of Allhallows Staining
parish, London, Spanish merchant.
Mendoza goes disguised to house of,
201
Seneca, Lucius Annaeus.
copy of his *Tragedies* at Leicester
House, 221
Senoy. *See* Sonoy.
Senton, Reuben (Ruben), member of
the English expeditionary force to
South Beveland.
wounded in skirmish near Goes, 230
Sesterne. *See* Syderstone.
Seton, Alexander, son of 5th Lord
Seton.
obtains passport from Privy Council
to travel to France, 46
Seton, Mary (Marie de), daughter of
6th Lord Seton, former lady-in-
waiting to Mary, Queen of Scots,
and now resident at the convent of
St. Pierre in Rheims.
letter from, 133
Seville, in Spain, 195
Spanish ships escape from Cadiz to,
264
English forces reported to be near,
264

Seymour, Edward, Duke of Somerset.
mentioned in verses, 290
Seymour, Edward, Earl of Hertford, 138
Seymour, Frances, Marchioness of
Hertford, later Duchess of
Somerset, wife of following, sister
of 3rd Earl of Essex, 291
verses in honour of, 288-291
Seymour, William, Marquess of ·
Hertford, later 1st Duke of
Somerset.
mentioned in verses, 290
Shadwell, Hugh, Marshal of the Court
of the Council in the Marches of
Wales, 191
letter from, 194
Sheffield (Sheffylde), Yorks., 29(2), 31,
38, 43, 51, 73, 127, 129
letters dated from, 20, 34, 41, 49,
52, 59, 61, 62, 63, 113(3), 132,
165, 196(2), 197
manor of, 21
parish of, 100
Sheffield, Douglas, Lady, wife of 2nd
Lord Sheffield.
her portrait at Leicester House, 203
Sheffield (Sheffeld), Edmund, 3rd Lord
Sheffield, 105, 109
mourner at funeral of Queen of
Scots, 83
Earl of Essex loses at cards to, 261
Sheffield Castle, Yorks., 20, 39, 51, 52
letters dated from, 112, 113, 115
Sheffield Manor, Yorks., 21, 30
letter dated from, 70
Sheffield Park, Yorks., 52
Sheldon (Shelton), Ralph, of Beoley,
son-in-law of Sir Robert
Throckmorton.
his suit against Lord Robert Dudley,
154
petition to Earl of Leicester, 226
Sheldon, William, of Beoley.
letter from, 158
letter to, 158
Shelford, Derbys.
letters dated from, 23, 44
Shelley, Mrs. *See* Lingen, Jane.
Shelton, Ralph. *See* Sheldon, Ralph.
Shenk, Colonel. *See* Schenk, Colonel
Martin.
Sherborne (Sherburne), Sir Richard, of
Aighton, Steward of Earl of
Derby, 182
Sherborne, William, of Ross-on-Wye.
letter from, 285
Sherbrook (Sherbrooke), Robert, son
of Thomas Sherbrook of Oxton.
wardship of, 24
Sheriff Hutton, Yorks.
proposal to build residence for
President of Council of the North

out of ruined castle at, 191
Sherley, Captain, 214
Sherwood Forest, Notts.
  dispute between Earls of Shrewsbury
    and Rutland concerning, 81, 88
Sherys. *See* Jerez de la Frontera.
Shiplake, Oxon., 256
Ships.
  Black Bark, 242
  Bonaventura, Bonaventure, 72, 256
  Dreadnought, 265
  Foresight, 253
  Hope, 253
  Lyon, 265
  Marie Rose, 253
  Nonpareil (*Nonparely*), 253, 265
  Rainbow (*Rainebow*), 253
  St. Paul, 264
  St. Philip, 264
  St. Phillipo, 93
  Sea Dragon, 72
  Swiftsure (*Swiftesure*), 253
  Talbot (*Talbote*), 72
  White Lyon, 72
  White Lyon de Edam, 256
Shobdon, Herefs.
  manor of, 283
Shooting Matches.
  reference to, 152
Shottle (Skottle), Derbys.
  Park of, 165
Shrewsbury, Countess of. *See* Talbot,
    Elizabeth; Talbot, Mary.
Shrewsbury, Earl of. *See* Talbot,
    George; Talbot, Gilbert.
Shrewsbury House, Broad Street,
    London.
  letter dated from, 35
Shropshire *or* Salop, 25, 60, 85, 256
  Earl of Leicester's lands in, 221
Shuttington, Warwicks.
  survey of Earl of Leicester's lands
    at, 200
Sicily, 157
Sidesterne. *See* Syderstone.
Sidney, Sir Henry, Lord Deputy of
    Ireland and later President of the
    Council in the Marches of Wales,
    148, 150, 175, 191, 195
  letter from, 191
  receives gift of horses, 169
  his memorandum, 170
  retires from his post in Ireland, 179
  complaint that he is ruled by
    Seckford, 195
  reference to his death, 248
Sidney (Sydney), Lady Mary, wife of
    Sir Henry Sidney and sister of
    Lord Robert Dudley, 149, 166
  requests loan of Earl of
    Shrewsbury's house, 21
  Lord Robert Dudley dines with, 150

Sidney, Sir Philip, courtier, poet and
    soldier, 89, 191, 277
  letters from, 192, 194
  news of his death, 76, 248
  his interview with Count Louis of
    Nassau, 134
  his portrait at Leicester House, 222
Sidney (Sydney, Sydneye), Sir Robert,
    of Penshurst, Governor of
    Flushing, later Lord Sidney,
    Viscount Lisle and 1st Earl of
    Leicester, 264, 277
  to be made a baron, 97
  attacks Essex House, 278
  parleys with Earl of Essex, 279, 280
Sigismund (Sigismond) I, King of
    Poland (*d*1548).
  his grandson chosen to be King of
    Poland, 87
  his daughter. *See* Katherine.
Sigismund, Prince of Sweden, later
    Sigismund III, King of Poland.
  chosen by majority of Poles to
    be their King, 87
  his proposal of marriage with Lady
    Arabella Stuart, 128
Signet, Clerk of the, 136
Simier (Cymie), Jean de, envoy of
    the Duke of Anjou to the Queen,
    201
Simonson, Hayme, master of the
    White Lyon de Edam, 256
Simpson, Richard, a seminary priest.
  to be committed to trial, 86
Sindlesham, Berks, 256
Sion. *See* Syon.
Sissell, Sir Robert. *See* Cecil, Sir
    Robert.
Sixtus V, Pope.
  King of France said to be
    negotiating with, 99
Skidby (Skytby), Yorks.
  Lord Robert Dudley granted manor
    of, 164
  survey of Lord Robert Dudley's
    lands at, 167
Skottle. *See* Shottle.
Skynke, Captain. *See* Schenk, Colonel
    Martin.
Skypwith, Mr., 181, 183
Skytby. *See* Skidby.
Sligo, 210
  letter dated from, 191
Sluys (Sluce, Slues), in Zeeland, 231
  besieged, 81
Smalcaldy. *See* Schmalkalden.
Smart (Smarte), Richard, prisoner in
    the Fleet, London, 224
Smerwick, co. Kerry.
  surrender and massacre of Italian
    and Spanish soldiers at, 31
Smith, Francis, partisan of 2nd Earl

of Essex.
imprisoned in the Marshalsea, 282
Smith, Gillie, Pembrokeshire tenant
of Earl of Essex, 236
Smith, Sir John, of Little Baddow,
diplomatist.
his mission to Prince of Parma
postponed, 45
Smith, Otwell, of St. Benedict in
Broad Street, London, merchant,
255
Smith, Sir Thomas (d1577), English
Ambassador to France, later
Secretary of State.
letters from, 186, 187
at Buxton, 21
summarizes policy of King of
France, 187
Smith (Smithe), Captain Sir Thomas
(kt 1596).
letter from, 266
takes part in Cadiz expedition, 265
Smith, Sir Thomas (d1625), merchant,
Sheriff of London, son of
following.
Earl of Essex and his followers
surround house of, 278
Smith (Smythe), Thomas (d1591), of
Gracechurch Street, London,
farmer of the Customs.
letter from, 199
Smith, Thomas (d1573), illegitimate
son of Sir Thomas Smith (d1577),
Secretary of State.
employed in Ulster, 193
Smith, William, of the Inner Temple,
London, 209
Smithfield, London.
The Rose inn at, 239
Smyth, Thomas, 200
Smythe, -----, in the service of Lord
Cavendish, 134
Smythe, Thomas. See Smith, Thomas.
Snagge, Thomas, Speaker of the House
of Commons.
refuses to read bill submitted for
reform of Common Prayer Book,
100
Snape, Yorks.
letter dated from, 194
Snodhill, Herefs.
survey of Lord Robert Dudley's
lands at, 167
Sollom (Solham), Lancs., 182
Somers (Sommer), John, Clerk of the
Signet, 48, 52
Somerscales, Robert, Steward of
Pontefract, 109
Somerset (Somersetshire), 45, 63, 92
Somerset, Edward, 4th Earl of
Worcester, 277
takes part in trial of Earl of

Essex, 269
kept prisoner in Essex House at time
of Earl of Essex's rebellion, 278
released by Gorges, 278
Somerset, William, 3rd Earl of
Worcester (d1589), 24
Commissioner at trial of Queen of
Scots, 74
death of, 99
his claim on behalf of Sir John
Perrot, 249
Somerset Herald. See Glover, Robert.
Somerset House, Strand, London, 136
Sommer, Mr. See Somers, John.
Sonnyng Hyll. See Sunninghill.
Sonoy (Senoy), Colonel Dietrich,
Governor of North Holland, 214
Souche, Lady. See Zouche, Mary.
Souche, Sir John. See Zouche, Sir
John.
Souche, William. See Zouche, William.
Sound, The.
King of Denmark's threat to detain
English shipping in, 201
Southam (Sowtham), Glos.
manor of, 283
Southampton, Hants., 263
spices landed at, 170
Mayor of. See Elliot, Paul.
Southampton, Countess of. See
Wriothesley, Mary.
Southampton, Earl of. See
Wriothesley, Henry.
Southorpe, Lawrence.
attests copy of offensive message
sent by Countess of Shrewsbury,
119
Southsex. See Sussex.
Southwark. See Bridge Foot; Counter;
Marshalsea; St. Leger House.
Southwell, Notts., 29
rental of Earl of Leicester's lands
at, 168
Southwell, Francis, recusant, 205
Southwell (Sowthwell), Sir Richard,
of Wood Rising, Master of the
Ordnance, 145
Southworth, Edward, of Rufford.
letter from, 186
Sowtham. See Southam.
Spain, 163, 169, 262, 263, 264(2),
266, 288.
Earl of Desmond's hope of aid
from, 28
news of Drake's exploits in West
Indies transmitted from, 68
attack by Drake's ships on coast
of, 71
Drake ordered to patrol coast of, 86
false reports of victory of Armada
circulating in, 95
expedition of Norris and Drake

against, 99
news of general destitution in, 116
King of Spain delays his return from
   Low Countries to, 141
Gresham orders silk hose for Queen
   from, 159
memorandum on Crown revenues in,
   160
King of Spain authorized by Pope to
   sell church lands in, 160
sale in London of goods from, 170
Cobham's account of his arrival and
   reception in, 173
French suspicions of, 186
reported embarkation in Armada of
   English and Scots in, 211
Hawkins permitted to ravage coast
   of, 253
news from, 264
Earl of Essex's second expedition
   to, 265
talks between Earls of Essex and
   Tyrone observed by spy from, 275
Spain, Infanta of. See Isabella.
Spain, King of. See Philip II.
Sparke, W.
   letter from, 225
Spices.
   landed at Southampton and Bristol,
      170
   prices of, 228
Spinola, Benedict, of Genoa, now
   resident of St. Gabriel Fenchurch
   parish, London, Italian merchant.
   letter to, 167
Spires, in Germany.
   Diet of, 169
Sprat (Spratt), William, partisan of
   2nd Earl of Essex.
   imprisoned in the Marshalsea, 282
Stables, The Queen's.
   Clerk of, 168
Stafford, 239
   letter dated from, 237
   Assizes at, 165
Stafford, Mr. See Stafford, Sir
   Edward.
Stafford, Edward, 3rd Lord Stafford,
   199
   Commissioner at trial of Queen of
      Scots, 74
Stafford (Staffre), Sir Edward,
   diplomatist and courtier, 76, 211
   letter from, 202
   sent to France on matter of Queen's
      marriage with Duke of Anjou, 30
   succeeds Cobham as ambassador to
      France, 44
Stafford, Henry, 1st Lord Stafford.
   letters from, 143, 162
   his dispute with Littleton, 143
   sends Lord Robert Dudley his book

on English law and traitors, 162
Stafford, Jane.
   letter from, 202
Stafford Castle, Staffs.
   letter dated from, 143
Staffordshire, 84(2), 85, 91, 93, 98,
   107, 143
   Earl of Essex's estates in, 247
   Lord Lieutenant of. See Talbot,
      George.
Staffre, Mr. See Stafford, Sir Edward.
Stamford, Lincs., 113
   alleged negligence of post at, 30
   clerical conference at, 185
Standon (Stonden), Herts.
   letter dated from, 163
Stanhope, (later Sir) Edward,
      Treasurer of Gray's Inn, brother
      of following, 93, 119
   letter from, 100
Stanhope, Sir John, later 1st Lord
      Stanhope of Harrington, Treasurer
      of the Chamber.
   letters from, 100, 264
Stanhope, (later Sir) John, of
      Elvaston, son of Sir Thomas
      Stanhope, 119, 124
   letter from, 121
   summary of letters passed between
      Cavendish and, 118, 119
   accepts Cavendish's challenge to
      duel, 119
   called 'rascal' by Countess of
      Shrewsbury, 119
   account of abortive duel
      arrangements between Cavendish
      and, 120, 121
   his statement regarding assault by
      followers of Earl of Shrewsbury,
      122
   made J.P. for Nottinghamshire, 125
   incident between Cavendish and, 127
Stanhope, Michael, of the Queen's
      Privy Chamber, brother of
      following, 112
   reference to his influence at Court,
      108, 109, 110
Stanhope (Stannop), Sir Thomas, of
      Shelford, 96, 105(2), 106, 107(2),
      109, 112, 115, 117, 123, 124
   letters from, 23, 43(2)
   at Buxton, 21
   his quarrel with Zouche, 22, 23
   statement by, 23
   brings a further charge against
      Zouche, 43
   Privy Council examines complaint
      against, 102
   Earl of Shrewsbury protests about,
      103
   Privy Council receives complaint
      about Earl of Shrewsbury from,

362

108, 115
efforts to reconcile Earl of
Shrewsbury and, 110(2), 111
Earl of Shrewsbury rejects
compromise with, 112, 113, 114(2)
leads opposition party at
Parliamentary elections in
Nottinghamshire, 117
receives offensive message from
Countess of Shrewsbury, 119
his complaints to be heard in
Star Chamber, 125
his death expected, 125
his son-in-law. See Holles, John.
Stanley, Edward, 3rd Earl of Derby,
136, 137
letters from, 142, 152, 153, 154,
173, 180, 181
Stanley, Sir Edward, son of
preceding, 181
Stanley, Ferdinando, Lord Strange,
later 5th Earl of Derby, 66
letter from, 66
to be summoned to Parliament, 97
Stanley, Sir George, Marshal of the
army in Ireland, 141
Stanley, Henry, 4th Earl of Derby, 88,
94
letters from, 59, 66
Commissioner at trial of Queen of
Scots, 73
signs letter from Privy Council, 93
Stanley, Sir Thomas, of Winwick,
brother of preceding.
committed to ward, 180
Stanley, William, 3rd Lord Monteagle.
letter from, 30
Stanley, Sir William, of Hooton,
political refugee in Flanders,
maître de camp in the Archduke's
army, 93, 211, 258
reported killed in battle at
Nieuport, 276
Stannop, Sir Thomas. See Stanhope,
Sir Thomas.
Stanstead (Stansted), Sussex.
letter dated from, 158
Stansted Hall, Halstead, Essex, 228
Stanton, Captain. See Staunton.
Stanway (Stanwey), Herefs.
manor of, 283
Staple, The.
merchants of, 166, 186
Star Chamber, The, 55, 267
sentence on Queen of Scots
pronounced in, 75, 76
Stanhope's complaint against Earl
of Shrewsbury to be heard in, 125
Earl of Essex censured in, 266 *n*
Queen grants Earl of Essex's request
not to be tried in, 270
Earl of Essex's declaration in, 286

States General, The, 86, 211, 214(2)
Queen writes on behalf of Earl
of Leicester to, 68
send information to Leeuwarden,
212
levy new contributions for building
ships, 214
desirous of reducing strength of
garrison at Flushing, 215
See also United Provinces.
Statute of Retainers.
charge brought against Cavendish
under, 126
Statutes of the Realm.
copy at Leicester House, 204
Staunton (Stanton), Captain,
member of the English
expeditionary force to South
Beveland.
wounded in skirmish near Goes, 230
Stedman (Stidman), John, of Strata
Florida.
letter to, 246
his accounts for Earl of Essex's
estates in Wales, 248
Steelyard (Steleyarde), London.
English justice criticised by
merchants of, 201
Stephens (Stephyns), Anthony.
requests to be appointed
schoolmaster at Ewelme, 178
Stephenson, Mr., 44
Stepneth, Alban, of Prendergast.
letter from, 263
Stevens, Richard, of New College,
Oxford.
reported to have been arrested and
racked, 205
Steward, Colonel. See Stewart,
Colonel Sir William.
Stewart, Lord James, later Earl of
Mar and 1st Earl of Moray,
Regent of Scotland, 53
his half-brother. See Douglas,
Robert.
Stewart, John, 5th Earl of Atholl
(Axall).
alleged to be in favour of Spanish
intervention in Scotland, 262
Stewart (Steward), Colonel Sir
William, Commendator of
Pittenweem, soldier and
diplomatist.
his audience with Queen, 42
King of Scots demands that Dutch
Council of State satisfies claim
of, 214
Stidman, John. See Stedman, John.
Still (Styll), Dr John, Master of
Trinity College, Cambridge.
Cambridge delegate to Diet at
Schmalkalden, 199

Stilton (Stylton), Hunts, 76
Stirling.
    letter dated from, 178
Stockes, Adrian. *See* Stokes, Adrian.
Stockton.
    letter dated from, 191
Stoke. *See* Stoke Poges.
Stoke Bardolph, Notts., 104
Stoke-on-Trent, Staffs.
    letter dated from, 165
Stoke Poges, Bucks., 194
Stoken. *See* Stokkem.
Stokes (Stocks, Stockes, Stookes),
    Adrian, of Beaumanoir, second
    husband of Frances Grey, Duchess
    of Suffolk.
    letters from, 152, 238
    Lord Robert Dudley plays at cards
    with, 151
Stokes, William, of Abkettleby.
    his suit recommended to Lord
    Robert Dudley, 155
Stokkem (Stoken), in Belgium.
    Prince of Orange at, 233
Stolberg, Ludovic, Count of, Imperial
    Ambassador to England.
    receives gift of a horse, 168
Stonden. *See* Standon.
Stoneleigh (Stonley), Warwicks.
    subsidy commissioners to meet at,
    143
Stonydelph (Stonidelf), Warwicks.
    survey of Earl of Leicester's lands
    at, 200
Stookes, Mr. *See* Stokes, Adrian.
Story (Storye), Dr John, Catholic
    martyr (*executed* 1571)
    kidnapped by English agents at
    Bergen-op-Zoom, 225, 226
Stourton, Anne, Lady, wife of 8th
    Lord Stourton, and daughter of
    3rd Earl of Derby, 154
Stourton (Sturton), John, 9th Lord
    Stourton, son of preceding.
    Commissioner at trial of Queen of
    Scots, 74
Strafford, Yorks.
    Wapentake of, 29
Strand (Straunde), London, 240
    Burghley confined by gout to his
    house in the, 92
Strange, Lord. *See* Stanley,
    Ferdinando.
Strasbourg.
    news from, 184
Stratford (Stratforde), Essex, 170
Stratford-upon-Avon, Warwicks.
    subsidy commissioners meet at, 142
Strelley, Sir Anthony, of Strelley,
    117
Strelley, Philip, son of preceding.
    letter from, 124

elected M.P. for Nottinghamshire,
    117
Stretton in Monk's Kirby, Warwicks.
    request on behalf of tenants of, 244
Strixton (Strickeston), Northants.
    Lordship of, 215
Strozzi, Philippe, Seigneur d'Epernay,
    Lieutenant-Colonel of the infantry
    in France.
    prevents revictualling of La
    Rochelle, 31
Stuart, Lady Arabella *or* Arbella
    (Arbela), 128, 133, 134
    causes quarrel between Earl and
    Countess of Shrewsbury, 26
    lodges in Newgate Street, 84
    collection of her letters to Earl
    and Countess of Shrewsbury, 128
    King of Poland's proposal of
    marriage with, 128
Stuart, Elizabeth, Countess of
    Lennox, widow of 6th Earl of
    Lennox.
    possibilities of future marriage
    of, 197
Stuart, Esmé, 6th Seigneur d'Aubigny,
    later 1st Duke of Lennox.
    said to be in control of Scotland, 28
    King of Scots reported to be
    opposed to policy of, 40
Stuart, Henry, Earl of Darnley, King
    of Scots.
    tableau at Leicester House of his
    murder, 203
Stuart, Katherine, Duchess of Lennox
    (Lennes), wife of 1st Duke of
    Lennox.
    hangings bought of, 203
    her portrait at Leicester House, 203
Stuart, Ludovic, son of preceding,
    later 2nd Duke of Lennox, 252 *n*
    his portrait at Leicester House, 203
Stuart, Matthew, 4th Earl of Lennox,
    Regent of Scotland.
    letter from, 178
Stucley (Stuclie, Stukelie), Thomas,
    English adventurer, 150
    residing near Madrid, 173
Sturton, Lord. *See* Stourton, John.
Styll, Dr. *See* Still, John.
Stylton. *See* Stilton.
Subsidy.
    measures to collect it in
    Warwickshire, 142
Sudbury (Sudbery), 229
Sudeley Castle, Glos.
    letters dated from, 105(2)
Suffolk, 125
Suffolk, Duchess of. *See* Brandon,
    Katherine; Grey, Frances.
Suffolk, Earl of. *See* Howard,
    Theophilus.

Suffolk, K. *See* Brandon, Katherine.
Sunninghill (Sonnyng Hyll), Berks., 46
  letter dated from, 139
Surrepe (?), in Netherlands.
  captured by Dutch, 232
Surveys and rentals, 167, 168, 200, 207,
  253, 256
Susons, Lady. *See* Bourchier, Susanna.
Sussex (Southsex), 125
Sussex, Earl of. *See* Radcliffe, Henry;
  Radcliffe, Thomas.
Sutton, Somerset, 57, 58, 59
Sutton, Mr., 192
Sutton, Agnes, daughter of following,
  162
Sutton *or* Dudley, Edward, 4th Lord
  Dudley.
  letters from, 151, 153, 162, 169, 209
Sutton *or* Dudley, Edward, 5th Lord
  Dudley.
  mourner at funeral of Queen of
    Scots, 83
  Earl of Essex in debt to, 283
Sutton, Elizabeth, wife of John
  Sutton, brother of preceding.
  letter from, 220
Sutton, Theodocia, Lady Dudley, wife
  of 5th Lord Dudley.
  mourner at funeral of Queen of
    Scots, 83
Sutton, Thomas, Master of the
  Ordnance at Berwick.
  letter from, 173
Suyd Beverland. *See* Beveland, South.
Sweden, Prince of. *See* Sigismund.
Swell, Glos.
  survey of manor of, 253
Swethelande, Duke of. *See* Eric.
Swift, Sir Robert, of Doncaster and
  Street Thorpe.
  his dispute with Earl of Shrewsbury
    over Hatfield Chase, 131
Swiftsure (Swiftesure), The, of the
  Queen's Navy.
  to take part in Hawkins's expedition,
    253
Swinnerton (Swinerton), Thomas, in
  the service of Henry Cavendish.
  prominent in the assault on
    Stanhope, 124
Switzerland.
  mercenaries expected in Bruges
    from, 38
  Kings of France and Navarre hire
    soldiers from, 65
  conversion to Protestantism of two
    cantons in, 87
Swyndell, Thomas, in the service of
  Sir Thomas Stanhope, 104
Swynford. *See* Kingswinford.
Sydenham, Henry, 234
Syderstone (Sedersterne, Sesterne,

Sidesterne), Norfolk, 148
survey of Lord Robert Dudley's
  lands at, 167
Sydney, sister. *See* Sidney, Lady
  Mary.
Sydney (Sydneye), Sir Robert. *See*
  Sidney, Sir Robert.
Syon (Sion), Mddx., 261
Syresham (Syrsham), Northants.
  letter dated from, 191
Syssill, Sir Robert. *See* Cecil, Sir
  Robert.

T

Tailor. *See* Taylor, Nicholas.
Talbot, Lord. *See* Talbot, Francis;
  Talbot, Gilbert.
Talbot, Mr. *See* Talbot, Henry.
Talbot, Anne, Lady, daughter of 1st
  Earl of Pembroke and wife of
  Francis Talbot, Lord Talbot, 27,
  39, 95
Talbot, Edward, later 8th Earl of
  Shrewsbury, 63, 86
  recalled by his father from France,
    43
  negotiations for marriage of Jane
    Ogle with, 44
Talbot, Elizabeth, Countess of
  Shrewsbury, daughter of John
  Hardwick, wife of (1) Robert
  Barlow, (2) Sir William Cavendish,
  (3) Sir William St. Loe, (4) 6th
  Earl of Shrewsbury, 20, 39, 48, 52,
  57, 58, 59, 62, 63, 71, 87, 132
  letters from, 22, 45, 195, 196
  letters to, 21(2), 61
  Earl of Bedford writes on behalf of
    Chester to, 20
  Stanhope recommends intervention
    on his behalf by, 23
  quarrel with Earl of Shrewsbury,
    25, 40, 41, 47, 52, 54, 57, 60(2),
    61, 64, 67(2), 69, 72
  Lord Chancellor to try Earl of
    Shrewsbury's suit against, 53, 55
  Queen's decision in the quarrel
    between Earl of Shrewsbury and,
    55, 67, 69, 70, 72
  reference to quarrel with Queen of
    Scots, 55
  relations with Lord Talbot, 58
  her chief complaint against her
    husband, 60
  snubbed by Queen, 64
  Earl of Shrewsbury requested by
    Queen to visit, 80
  certain matters still unresolved
    between Earl of Shrewsbury and
    her sons, 81

her death expected, 131
her gift to Earl of Leicester, 219
her sons. *See* Cavendish, Sir Charles;
    Cavendish, Henry; Cavendish,
    William.
Talbot, Francis, 5th Earl of
    Shrewsbury, 50, 58
Talbot, Francis, Lord Talbot
    (*d*1582), son of 6th Earl
    of Shrewsbury.
    letter from, 27
    at Chatsworth, 27
    severity of Earl of Shrewsbury
        towards, 27
    defended by Earl of Leicester, 27
    reference to his death, 39(2)
Talbot, George, 6th Earl of
    Shrewsbury, Lord Marshal of
    England, 20-197 *passim*
    letters from, 20-197 *passim*
    letters to, 20-100 *passim*
    quarrel with Countess of
        Shrewsbury, 25, 40, 41, 47, 52,
        54, 57, 60(2), 61, 64, 67(2), 69, 72
    matter of his allowance for guarding
        Queen of Scots, 29, 32
    Lady Grace Cavendish desires his
        leave to go to London, 34
    Lord Steward of manors in
        Derbyshire and Yorkshire, 35
    sends Burghley a gift of lead, 35
    requested to pay his part of
        subsidy, 36, 88
    appointed Commissioner for horses
        in Derbyshire, 46
    receives Queen's thanks for his
        hospitality to Walsingham, 47
    hint of attempt to destroy
        friendship between Earl of
        Leicester and, 47
    receives gifts from Cobham, 48
    advised by Queen to ignore rumours
        of her suspicions of his conduct,
        48
    allegations against, 49
    forbidden by Queen to hold
        assembly of freeholders of Peak
        district, 50
    Queen opposes his appointment of
        Benthall as Gentleman Porter to
        Queen of Scots, 52
    requested by Queen to provide
        victuals for Queen of Scots, 53
    his suit against Countess of
        Shrewsbury to be heard by Lord
        Chancellor, 53, 55
    order issued in his suit against
        Sir Charles and William
        Cavendish, 53
    receives money order for
        maintenance of Queen of Scots, 54
    Queen's decision in dispute between

Countess of Shrewsbury and, 55,
    67, 69, 70, 72
promises Queen to give £1,000 a
    year to his son, 60
his gift of jewel to Queen, 60
Countess of Shrewsbury's further
    complaints against, 60, 64(2)
Queen commends his conduct
    towards Lord Talbot, 65
commission issued to deal with
    dispute between Cavendishes and,
    66
forbidden by Queen to proceed by
    law against Sir Charles Cavendish,
    67
sends instructions to Henry
    Talbot, 67
Commissioner at trial of Queen of
    Scots, 73
his opinion on case of Queen of
    Scots, 75, 76
not present in Star Chamber to
    pronounce death sentence on
    Queen of Scots, 75
Queen pleased with his concern
    for her safety, 79
directed by Privy Council to send
    Blackburne to London, 80
requested by Queen to visit
    Countess of Shrewsbury, 80
certain matters still unresolved
    between Countess of Shrewsbury's
    sons and, 81
appealed to by Burghley to give
    financial help to Lord Talbot, 82
Lord Lieutenant of Derbyshire and
    Staffordshire, 84
ordered to furnish soldiers for the
    North, 85(2)
illness of, 87, 89, 90
his dispute with Earl of
    Rutland over Sherwood Forest, 88
ordered to place trained bands in
    readiness to meet threat of
    Spanish invasion, 89
receives special letter from Queen
    concerning defence of country, 91
mentioned amongst those to be
    entrusted with Queen's safety, 92
recusants to be moved to prison
    from house of, 94
his kindness to daughter-in-law
    commended by Queen, 95
reference to his death, 100, 102
his losses at cards, 196
adds postscript to Countess of
    Shrewsbury's letter to Earl of
    Leicester, 197
his gift to Earl of Leicester, 219
his daughter. *See* Cavendish, Grace.
his sons. *See* Talbot, Edward;
    Talbot, Francis; Talbot, Gilbert;

Talbot, Henry.

Talbot, Gilbert, Lord Talbot, later
7th Earl of Shrewsbury, 42-277
passim
letters from, 31-117 *passim*
letters to, 58-116 *passim*
his conversation with Walsingham,
32
called 'my cousin Gilbert' by Earl
of Leicester, 36
becomes Lord Talbot after his
brother's death, 41
his conduct commended by Earl of
Leicester, 48, 50
his debts, 57, 58, 59, 87
relations between Countess of
Shrewsbury and, 58
his account of interview with
Queen, 60
Queen approves of Earl of
Shrewsbury's conduct towards, 65
appeal by Burghley to Earl of
Shrewsbury to give financial help
to, 82, 87
to be given command of soldiers
raised for service in the North, 85
to be summoned to Parliament, 97
Queen displeased with, 108
Steward of Derby, 108
efforts to reconcile Stanhope
and, 110(2), 111
rejects any form of compromise with
Stanhope, 112(2), 113(3)
report of his intention to
influence election of M.P.s, 116
sends New Year's gift to Burghley,
117
attends Parliamentary elections at
Nottingham, 117
assault on Stanhope by partisans of,
122, 123
his coat of arms defaced at Newark,
124
visits Burghley's house at Cheshunt,
124
his dispute with Swift over
Hatfield Chase, 131
his allegations against Lord
Cavendish, 132
takes part in Earl of Essex's
trial, 269

Talbot, Henry, brother of
preceding, 45, 57, 60, 66, 67,
70, 79, 80, 85, 105
letters from, 39, 41
recalled from France by his
father, 43
receives instructions from Earl
of Shrewsbury, 67

Talbot, John, of Grafton, cousin
of Lord Talbot, 45
imprisoned for recusancy, 92

Talbot, John, 113

letter from, 54

Talbot, John, in the service of
Earl of Essex, 258, 262
letter to, 241

Talbot, Mary. *See* Herbert, Mary.

Talbot, Mary. *See* Percy, Mary.

Talbot, Mary, Countess of
Shrewsbury, daughter of Sir
William Cavendish and wife of
7th Earl of Shrewsbury, 50, 57,
58, 63, 101, 103, 105, 126, 129
letters to, 73, 84, 133
sends offensive message to Sir
Thomas Stanhope, 119

Talbot, Sir Robert, of Carton.
letter from, 285

Talbot (Talbote), The.
missing from Drake's fleet, 72

Talbot, The Sign of the, London.
house called, 102

Talboys, Lady. *See* Dudley,
Elizabeth.

Talgarth, Brecon, 167

Tamworth, Staffs.
letters dated from, 241, 282

Tasker, Philip, of London, 102

Tasser, -----, 35

Taylor (Tailor), Nicholas, of
Gainsborough, 105
charged with organizing unfair
complaint against Stanhope, 103

Taynton (Teynton), Glos., 225, 240

Teddesley Park, Staffs., 143
Keeper of. *See* Littleton, Edward.

Temple, The, London, 240
letter dated from, 256

Temple, William, partisan of 2nd
Earl of Essex.
imprisoned in the Marshalsea, 282

Tennis, 136, 148
court at Whitehall, 149
markers, 149
stoppers, 149

Terceira (Terceras), Azores.
said to be holding out for Don
Antonio, 36

Tergose *See* Goes.

Terrett, Captain.
takes part in Cadiz expedition, 265

Tewkesbury, Glos.
parsonage of, 155

Teynton. *See* Taynton.

Theobalds (Thebalds, Tibolles,
Tybells), Herts, 45, 71, 80, 88
letter dated from, 88

Thestelworthe. *See* Isleworth.

Thinne, Sir John. *See* Thynne, Sir
John.

Thomas, James, Bluemantle
Pursuivant, later Chester Herald,
95

Thomas, Morgan, tenant of Morfa
Mawr grange, 283

Thomond, Earl of. *See* O'Brien,
  Conor.
Thornhill (Thornell), Yorks., 37
  parson of. *See* Whitacres, Edward.
Three Tuns, The, inn, Fleet Street,
  London, 122
Throckmorton (Throgmorton), Arthur,
  of Mile End, son of Sir Nicholas
  Throckmorton, 263
  commands company in Cadiz
    expedition, 265
Throckmorton (Throgmorton),
  Francis, 219
Throckmorton, Sir John, of
  Feckenham, late Justice of
  Chester, 202
Throckmorton, Sir Nicholas, of
  Paulerspury, English Ambassador
  to France.
  letters from, 145, 154
  receives gift of horse, 169
Throckmorton, Sir Robert, of
  Coughton.
  his suit against Lord Robert
    Dudley, 154
Throckmorton, Sir Thomas, of
  Tortworth.
  letter from, 279
Throgmorton, Captain. *See*
  Throckmorton, Arthur.
Throgmorton, Francis. *See*
  Throckmorton, Francis.
Throwleigh (Throwley), Staffs.
  letter dated from, 284
Thynne, Dorothy, Lady, wife of
  following and sister of Sir
  Thomas Wroughton, 200
Thynne (Thinne), Sir John, of
  Longleat, 199, 200
  Earl of Leicester's request to, 188
Thynne, John, son of preceding.
  letter from, 199
Tibberton. *See* Tyberton.
Tibolles. *See* Theobalds.
Tickhill, Yorks.
  Wapentake of, 29
Tilt Yard at Greenwich, 254
Tilton, Leics. *See* Halstead.
Tirlagge Lenaghe. *See* O'Neill,
  Tirloch Luineach.
Toledo, in Spain.
  letter dated from, 160
Tolkarne, Captain.
  takes part in Cadiz expedition, 265
Tollesbury (Tollsbury), Essex, 223
Tomson, Lawrence, of London,
  secretary to Sir Francis
  Walsingham, 53
Toster, John, partisan of 2nd Earl
  of Essex.
  imprisoned in the Marshalsea, 282
Toulouse, in France.

Edict in favour of Huguenots to be
  enforced at, 184
Tournon, François, Cardinal de.
  sent to France by Pope to convene
    national council, 159
Tours, in France.
  letter dated from, 202
Towcester, Northants., 239
Tower Hill, London, 99
Tower Street, London, 150
Tower Wharf, London, 136
Townley (Townelye), John, of
  Townley, Steward of Blackburn.
  Earl of Huntingdon deplores
    recusancy of, 190
Townsend (Townesend), (later Sir)
  John, cousin of John Stanhope,
  120, 121
Trained Bands.
  of Derbyshire, 84, 91
  of Staffordshire, 84, 91
Trans (Traynes), Gaston de Foix,
  Marquis de, French hostage.
  Lord Robert Dudley dines with, 150
Trawalkin. *See* Tre Walkin.
Traynes, Marquis of. *See* Trans.
Tre Walkin (Trawalkin), Talgarth,
  Brecon.
  survey of Lord Robert Dudley's
    lands at, 167
Treasurer, Mr. *See* Paulet, William.
Tredar, Francis, partisan of 2nd
  Earl of Essex.
  imprisoned in the Marshalsea, 282
Trefor (Trevor), John.
  letters from, 285, 286
Tregose. *See* Goes.
Trent, Forests north of the, 218
  Ranger of. *See* Dudley, Lord
    Robert.
Trent, River, 107
Trentham, Staffs.
  letter dated from, 238
Trentham, Thomas, of Rocester, 57
  letters from, 236, 239
Tresham, Francis, of Rushton.
  takes charge of Lord Keeper
    Egerton and others kept prisoner
    at Essex House, 278
  imprisoned in the Marshalsea, 282
Trinity College, Cambridge. *See*
  Cambridge.
Trinity Hall, Cambridge. *See*
  Cambridge.
Tripoli, in North Africa.
  land and sea force being prepared
    in Italy for assault on, 147
Tristane, John, a merchant of the
  Staple, 186
Trollope, Thomas.
  offers to write in defence of Lord
    Robert Dudley's grandfather and

father, 168
Trumpington, Cambs., 283
Tryon, Mrs.
Earl of Essex in debt to, 283
Tucker, William, Mayor of Bristol.
signs letter to Earl of Leicester, 173
Tunstall, Cuthbert, Bishop of
Durham.
expected to be deprived of his
temporalities, 141
Tuoscom. See Tuscany.
Turenne (Turynne), Henri de la Tour,
Vicomte de.
result of his mission to London, 101
Turk, The. See Amurath III.
Turkey.
collaboration between France and,
116
Turks, 162
send reinforcements to counter
projected attack on Tripoli, 147
Duke of Medina Coeli defeated by,
157
continue siege of Djerba, 159
Emperor's appeal to Princes of
Germany for help against, 184
gift to a Turk 'that cam with
Sir F. Drake', 221
Turlo, Turlogh Lynagh. See O'Neill,
Tirlogh Luineach.
Tuscany (Tuoscom).
Pope expected to crown Duke of
Florence as King of, 159
Tutbury (Tutberie), Staffs., 53
letters dated from, 34, 84, 132
Tweed, River.
crossed by Scottish army, 287
Tybells. See Theobalds.
Tyberton (Tibberton), Herefs.
manor of, 283
Tymme, John, partisan of 2nd Earl
of Essex.
imprisoned in the Marshalsea, 281
Tyndall, Humphrey, chaplain to Earl
of Leicester.
his deposition regarding secret
marriage of Earl of Leicester, 205
Tyne, River.
English plan to resist Scottish
army along, 287
Typpin, Thomas, partisan of 2nd
Earl of Essex.
imprisoned in the Marshalsea, 282
Tyrell, Edmund, of Ramsden.
letter from, 237
Tyrone, Earl of. See O'Neill, Hugh.

U

Ulster, Ireland.
news from, 193

agreement between Queen and Earl
of Essex over expedition to, 242
Earl of Essex's protest against
policy of ending his attempt to
colonize, 245
invasion and spoliation of Earl
of Essex's lands in, 257, 258, 262
indictment of Earl of Essex's
activities in, 270
his reply to charge of misdemeanour
in, 272
Underhill, Thomas, Keeper of
household goods at Kenilworth
and Grafton, 219
United Provinces, The, 211, 213
Earl of Leicester's acceptance of
Governorship of, 68
mutiny of English soldiers in, 68
controversies between town and
countryside in, 212
copies of treaties between England
and, 252
See also Low Countries and States
General.
Unton, Sir Henry, of Wadley, 256
Upcher, Captain.
takes part in Cadiz expedition, 265
Upminster, Essex, 252 n
Upton-on-Severn, Worcs.
benefice of, 188
Utrecht, in Netherlands, 214
placard in defence of Queen's
policies published at, 213
Uvedale, Thomas, in the service of
2nd Earl of Essex.
his annuity, 257

V

Valasco, Don Luis de. See Velasco,
Don Luis de.
Valenciennes, in France.
Spanish troops mutiny at, 169
Valentinoys, Duchess of. See Poitiers,
Diane de.
Valois, Marguerite de, sister of Charles
IX of France and wife of Henri,
King of Navarre, later Henry IV,
187
Van Bergh, Count Frederick. See Berg,
Van den.
Van Lore (Van Loow), Peter, of
London, merchant and jeweller.
his bill, 252
Earl of Essex's debts to, 257, 283
payments to, 282
Vandosme, Duke of. See Bourbon,
Antoine de.
Varney, Sir Richard. See Verney,
Sir Richard.
Vaughan, -----, partisan of 2nd Earl
of Essex.

imprisoned in the Marshalsea, 282
Vaughan, Letitia, daughter of Sir
John Perrot, wife of Walter
Vaughan, 259
her mother. See Perrot, Jane.
Vaughan, Richard, of Whitland.
letter from, 233
Vaughan, Robert, J.P., 256
Vaughan, Sir Roger, of Talgarth,
Brecon, 179
Vaughan, Roger.
letter from, 277
Vaughan, Walter, of Golden Grove.
letter from, 259
Vaux, William, 3rd Lord Vaux of
Harrowden.
not imprisoned for recusancy
because of ill health, 92
Vavasour (Vavaserr), Anne, cousin of
Charles Arundell, 204
Vavasour (Vavosour), Colonel Sir
William, of Hazelwood.
his regiment, 286
Veere (Camphier), in Zeeland, 232
Velasco (Valasco), Don Luis de,
Master of the Artillery in the
Archduke's army.
taken prisoner in battle at Nieuport,
276
Vendolle. See Venlo.
Venice, 207
letters dated from, 157, 159
Pope requests loan of fifty galleys
from, 157
reported to be preparing for war,
184
Inquisition in, 277
Venlo (Vendolle), in Belgium.
captured by Dutch, 231
Ventrice, John, footman to the
Queen, 218
Vere, Captain Daniel.
takes part in Cadiz expedition, 265
Vere, Edward de, 17th Earl of Oxford.
Commissioner at trial of Queen of
Scots, 74
his secret conversation with Charles
Arundell, 204
Vere, Sir Francis, military commander,
263
Lord Marshal of the expedition to
Cadiz, 263
composition of his regiment, 265
reported to have been wounded in
battle at Nieuport, 276
Vere, Sir Horace (Horatius), later
Lord Vere of Tilbury, brother of
preceding.
composition of his regiment in
Cadiz expedition, 265
Verney (Varney), Sir Richard, of
Compton Verney, Warwicks., 142
letter from, 156

Vernon, Elizabeth, wife of following
and sister of 1st Earl of Essex, 191
annuity paid to, 262
Vernon, Sir John, of Hodnet, 191, 229
Vernon, Sir Robert, of Hodnet, 256
imprisoned in the Gatehouse, 281
Vice-Chamberlain, The. See Hatton,
Sir Christopher.
Vidame, The. See Chartres.
Vieilleville, François de Scepeaux,
Seigneur de, Marshal of France,
French Ambassador to England.
met by Lord Robert Dudley at
Tower Wharf, 136
Vintners, Company of, London.
criticism of trading privileges
granted to, 180
Vray, Jacques de, Sieur de Fontorte,
Agent to the Duke of Anjou, 201,
202
dines with Earl of Leicester, 24

W

Waad (Wade), Armagil (Armigell),
former Clerk to the Privy Council
(d1568), 49
Waad (Wade), William, diplomatist,
later Clerk to the Privy Council,
124
recommended by Burghley, 49
Wachter, Vice-Admiral of Flanders.
reported to have been imprisoned by
Parma, 214
Wade, Armigell. See Waad, Armagil.
Waffen, William, of Halstead, 229
Wagstaff, Thomas, vicar of Lewknor,
later prebendary of Westminster.
letter from, 200
Wailly (Avylay), near Arras, in France.
Prince of Parma dies suddenly at,
115
Wakefield, Yorks., 29
Walden, Herts.
court at, 250
Wales, 95, 179, 237, 248
letter dated from North, 189
letter to Earls of Essex and Suffolk
from Commissioners for, 285
adverse results of lack of preachers
in North, 201
Earl of Essex's estates in, 248
South, 251, 285
Wales, Council in the Marches of, 191
Lord President of. See Sidney,
Sir Henry.
Secretary of. See Fox, Charles.
Walgalen, in Netherlands.
captured by Dutch, 231
Walgrave, Mr.
Lord Robert Dudley's christening
gift to his child, 150

Walinge Welles. *See* Wallingwells.
Wallaxhall. *See* Walloxhall.
Wallingford, Berks.
Queen at, 189
Wallingwells (Walinge Welles), Notts.,
227
Wallop, Sir Henry, of Farleigh Wallop,
M.P. for Southampton, 188
Walloxhall (Wallaxhall), Worcs.
(formerly Salop).
survey of Lord Robert Dudley's
lands at, 167
Walmesley, Sir Thomas, Justice of
Common Pleas.
takes part in trial of Earl of
Essex, 269
Walnut, George, a discharged soldier,
formerly of Captain
Throckmorton's company in the
Cadiz expedition.
receives certificate from Mayor of
Southampton, 263
Walrond, Humphrey, of Sea,
Somerset, 192
Walshe (Welsh), Piers (Pers), of the
Grange, co. Kilkenny, in the
service of Elizabeth, Countess
of Ormond, 153
Walsingham, Sir Francis, English
Ambassador to France, later
Secretary of State, 31, 38, 41, 45,
57, 67, 69, 70, 85, 86, 89, 99,
201, 217(2)
letters from, 35, 39, 42, 43, 46, 48,
50, 51, 52(2), 53(2), 56, 59, 60, 68,
72, 76(2), 79, 80, 86, 88, 89(2),
171, 184, 206, 215
letters to, 33, 49, 51, 62, 66, 90, 93
at Buxton, 21
signs letters from Privy Council, 22,
86, 89, 93, 96, 220
references to his daughter's illness,
25
Prince of Condé sees, 27
interested in purchase of horses, 29
opposes decrease in allowance of
Earl of Shrewsbury for guarding
Queen of Scots, 29, 32
his conversation with Lord Talbot,
32
goes to France, 36
to go to Scotland, 44
news expected of his negotiations in
Scotland, 46
injured by a fall, 46
his kind treatment by Earl of
Shrewsbury, 46, 47
Commissioner at trial of Queen of
Scots, 74
warns Burghley of conspiracy against
Queen, 172
engaged in negotiations for Queen's
marriage with Duke of Anjou, 177

his secretary. *See* Mills, Francis;
Tomson, Lawrence.
Walsingham, Mary, daughter of
preceding.
her illness, 25
Walsingham, Ursula, Lady, widow of
Sir Francis Walsingham, 259
Walsingham House, London, 259,
261(2)
Walter, Thomas.
nominated by Earl of Leicester to
be burgess of Denbigh, 190
Waltham Cross (Walton at Cros),
Herts., 137
postal endorsements at, 31, 76
Walton, Cheshire.
Lord Robert Dudley advised to
purchase manor house of, 144
Walton, Derbys.
letter dated from, 44
Walton, Staffs.
riot against Earl of Essex's
servants at, 286
Walton, John, Archdeacon of Derby.
Earl of Shrewsbury's opinion of,
112, 113
Walton at Cros. *See* Waltham Cross.
Wanchese (Wingandecoa), Roanoke
I., N. Carolina.
Grenville's colonists brought home
by Drake's fleet from, 72
Wandesford (Wandesforde),
Christopher, Master of the Rolls
in Ireland.
letters from, 285, 286
Wanstead (Wainstead, Wansted,
Wansteed), Essex, 220, 221, 223,
224, 254
letter dated from, 89
Earl of Leicester ill at, 90(2)
secret marriage between Earl of
Leicester and Countess of Essex
at, 205
inventory at, 208(2), 219
reference to Queen's bedchamber
at, 208
French Ambassador entertained at,
254
Warcopp, Thomas, 138, 218
ship purchased from, 242
Wardell. *See* Weardale.
Wardour, Wilts.
letter dated from, 126
Wards *and* Wardships, 24, 45, 97
Wards, Court of, 251
Ware, Herts., 137
postal endorsements at, 31
Wark (Warke), Northumb.
Scottish forces cross Tweed at, 287
Warner, John, Dean of Lichfield, 285
Warren, Sir William, captain of
company of horse in Ireland and
Commander-designate at

Carrickfergus.
his conference with Earl of
Tyrone, 271
Warwick, 178
Assizes at, 142
Warwick, Countess of. *See*
Dudley, Anne.
Warwick, Earl of. *See* Dudley, Lord
Ambrose.
Warwick Lane, London.
letter dated from, 190
Warwickshire.
Earl and Countess of Warwick go to
the wells in, 28
report on state of, 142
recusants in, 142
measures to collect subsidy in, 142
Wastelyn, Nicholas, chaplain to Henry
Bourchier, 2nd Earl of Essex, 229
Wastney (Wastness), Gervase, of
Headon.
his wardship, 97
Waterford, Ireland.
request for munitions and provisions
from, 201
Earl of Essex at, 274
Waterhouse, -----, in the service of
Sir Thomas Cornwallis, 145
Waterhouse, Edward, in the service of
1st Earl of Essex in Ireland, 242,
247
letter from, 247
Watson, (later Sir) Edward (Edwarde),
of Rockingham.
mourner at funeral of Queen of
Scots, 83
Watton, Yorks.
survey of Lord Robert Dudley's
lands at, 167
Watwood, Thomas.
Earl of Essex's plate pawned to, 255
Waye, Mr., member of the English
expeditionary force in South
Beveland.
his conduct in action commended,
230
Weale, Roger.
Harley denounced for his barbarous
behaviour towards wife of, 254
Weardale (Wardell), co. Durham.
Stewardship of, 141
Webber, Nicholas, 208, 220
Wednester, Charles, of Bromyard,
Auditor of Prests, M.P. for
Reading, 256
Weeford (Wyford), Staffs., 227
Welbeck, Notts., 54, 92, 95
letters dated from, 127, 128, 131
Welsh, Pers. *See* Walshe, Piers.
Welsh Language.
book printed at Avignon in, 182
Wentworth, Mr.

assesses Earl of Shrewsbury's lands,
29
Wentworth, Henry, 3rd Lord
Wentworth.
Commissioner at trial of Queen of
Scots, 74
Wentworth, Colonel Henry.
his regiment, 286
Weobley, Herefs.
Earl of Essex's tenants at, 237,
238(2)
park of, 249
West, Captain, of the English
expeditionary force in South
Beveland and Walcheren.
his conduct in action commended,
230, 232
West, Leonard, son of 8th Lord La
Warre.
letter from, 174
West, Sir Thomas, later 3rd Lord
De La Warre.
imprisoned in the Marshalsea, 282
West, William, 1st Lord De La Warre.
letter from, 188
complaint against, 174
West Indies, 195
Drake's reported success in his
expedition to, 68, 71
Westacre, Norfolk.
Lordship of, 215
Westhide, Herefs., 254
Westminster.
letters dated from, 33, 49, 75, 76,
77, 78, 99, 117, 181
Queen at, 75
Lord Robert Dudley plays tennis
at, 136
See also London and Westminster
and environs.
Westminster Abbey, 95, 200
Earl of Essex visits monuments
in, 261
Westminster Hall, 85
Westmorland, H. *See* Neville, Henry.
Westmorland, Earl of. *See* Neville,
Charles; Neville, Henry.
Weston, Somerset.
rental of Earl of Leicester's lands
at, 168
Wetherington, Mr. *See* Widdrington.
Wevenho. *See* Wivenhoe.
Wharton, Anne, Lady, widow of
following and daughter of 5th
Earl of Shrewsbury.
reference to her recent death, 54
Wharton, Thomas, 1st Lord Wharton,
153
Wharton, William.
complaint against, 37
Wheeler, John, partisan of 2nd
Earl of Essex.

imprisoned in the Marshalsea, 282
Whitacres, Edward, Rector of
　Thornhill, Yorks., 37
Whitbourne (Whitborne), Herefs.
　letter dated from, 195
White Knight, The. *See* Fitzgibbon,
　Sir Edmund.
White Lyon, The.
　missing from Drake's fleet, 72
White Lyon de Edam, The.
　wine shipped to England in, 256
Whitefriars, London.
　letter dated from, 188
Whitehall, 136, 137, 149
　letters dated from, 35(2), 98(3)
　St. George's Feast to be held at, 129
　tennis at, 149
　tilting at, 149
　court at, 35, 277
　Keeper of tennis court at. *See*
　following.
Whiteley, Thomas, Keeper of the
　tennis court at Whitehall, 149
Whitfield (Whitfeilde), Francis,
　formerly of the English garrison
　at Flushing, 264
Whitgift, John, Archbishop of
　Canterbury.
　signs letter from Privy Council, 94
　takes part in Earl of Essex's trial,
　269
Whitland (Whitlond), Carms.
　letter dated from, 233
Whyt Lyddington.
　name of horse bestowed on Earl of
　Arundel, 169
Whyte, Sir Nicholas, of Leixlip.
　letter from, 286
Wiburn (Wyborn, Wyborne), Perceval,
　Puritan divine.
　regarded with disfavour by Bishop
　of Peterborough, 185
Wickham, William, Bishop of Lincoln.
　mourner at funeral of Queen of
　Scots, 82
Widdrington (Wetherington), Mr., 125
Wight, Isle of, 72
Wigley, John, of Wirksworth.
　Walsingham's letter on behalf of, 35
Wigmore, Captain, Royalist officer,
　291
Wilcock, Samwell, in the service of
　Francis Fletcher.
　signs evidence concerning Stanhope's
　defamation of Earl of Shrewsbury,
　104
Wilkes (Wylkes), Sir Thomas, Clerk
　to the Privy Council and
　diplomatist, 106
　letter from, 259
William, Count. *See* Nassau-
　Dillenburg.

Williams, Sir John, later Lord
　Williams of Thame, Steward of
　Grafton, Northants., 191
Williams, Dr. John, Chancellor to
　the Bishop of Gloucester, 146
Williams, Philip, 198
Williams, Richard, 220
Williams, Sir Roger, of Penrhos,
　soldier and author.
　letter from, 255
Williams, Captain W.
　takes part in Cadiz expedition, 265
Williamson, Nicholas, of Sawley, in
　the service of Earl of Shrewsbury.
　delivers offensive message to
　Stanhope, 119
Willoughby (Wyllobe), Lady.
　at Buxton, 21
Willoughby (Willowby, Willybe), Mr.,
　chaplain to Lord Robert Dudley,
　137, 146
Willoughby (Willoughbie), Charles,
　2nd Lord Willoughby of Parham.
　mourner at funeral of Queen of
　Scots, 83
Willoughby, Sir Francis, of Wollaton.
　letter from, 66
Willoughby, William, 1st Lord
　Willoughby of Parham.
　letter from, 154
Wilson, -----, 130, 131
Wilson, Robert, member of the Earl
　of Leicester's Company of
　Players.
　signs petition to Earl of Leicester,
　266
Wilson, Thomas, Secretary of State,
　32, 33, 198
　letters from, 30(2)
　to go to Durham, 29
Wilton, Wilts.
　letters dated from, 186, 200
Wilton, Captain.
　takes part in Cadiz expedition, 265
Wimbledon (Wymbolton), Surrey.
　Queen at, 45
Winchester, Hants., 176
Winchester, Marquess of. *See* Paulet,
　William.
Winckfield, Sir Richard. *See*
　Wingfield, Sir Richard.
Wincobank (Winkebanke), Yorks., 131
Windsor (Winsor, Wynesore), Berks.,
　30, 35, 82, 136, 180, 194
　letters dated from, 39, 74, 75, 179,
　266
　Lord Robert Dudley installed as
　Knight of the Garter at, 136
　Queen expected at, 146
　Deanery of, 153
　Queen's progress from Kenilworth
　to, 189

373

Windsor, Edward, 3rd Lord Windsor.
  letter from, 195
  Lord Robert Dudley dines with, 150
Wines, 266
  Malmsey, 54
  sweet, 219, 220, 256, 257(2)
  Earl of Essex granted farm of
    sweet, 256, 257
  sack, 257
Wingandecoa. See Wanchese.
Wingfield (Wynckfeld), Derbys., 53, 80
  proposal to move Queen of Scots to,
    51
  Queen of Scots reluctant to leave, 52
Wingfield, Elizabeth, wife of Anthony
    Wingfield and half-sister of
    Elizabeth, Countess of
    Shrewsbury.
  letter from, 128
Wingfield, Sir John, of Withcall,
    255, 261
  commander in the Cadiz expedition,
    263
Wingfield (Winckfield), Sir Richard,
    later 1st Viscount Powerscourt,
    263
  commander in the Cadiz expedition,
    263
  composition of his regiment, 265
Wingfield (Wingfeld), Robert
    (Roberte), of Upton, M.P. for
    Stamford.
  mourner at funeral of Queen of
    Scots, 83
Wingfield (Wingfylde), William, in the
    service of Earl of Shrewsbury, 129
Wingfield, William.
  letter to, 284
Winkebanke. See Wincobank.
Winter or Wynter, Admiral Sir
    William, of Lydney, 201
  death of, 99
Wirksworth, Derbys. (co. Lancaster).
  hundred of, 35
Wirley, John, of Dodford.
  letter from, 239
Wirteley. See Wortley.
Witheredge, William, Keeper of Earl
    of Leicester's house at Wanstead.
  his inventory, 208
Witton (Wytton), co. Durham.
  letter dated from, 141
Wivenhoe (Wevenho), Essex.
  letter dated from, 141
Wollashall. See Woollashill.
Wolley, John, Latin secretary to the
    Queen and Privy Councillor.
  signs letters from Privy Council, 89,
    93, 94, 96, 98
Woodhouse. See Kirkby Woodhouse.
Woodhouse, George, 149
Woodstock, Oxon.

Queen at, 107, 189
Woollashill (Wollashall), Worcs.
  manor of, 283
Wools.
  project to eradicate abuses in
    customs of, 166
Woorsop. See Worksop.
Wootton Bassett, Wilts., 188
Worcester.
  letter dated from, 188
  Earl of Essex at, 291
Worcester, Bishop of. See Sandys,
    Edwin.
Worcester, Dean of. See Holland,
    Seth.
Worcester, Earl of. See Somerset,
    Edward; Somerset, William.
Worcestershire.
  Justices of the Peace in, 158
Worksop (Woorsop, Worshoppe,
    Worsupe), Notts., 131
  letters dated from, 104, 106, 107,
    109, 118
  Walsingham hospitably received at,
    46, 47
Worksop Abbey, Notts., 100
Worsley, John, messenger of the
    Privy Council, 84
Worston, Captain, of the English
    army in the Netherlands.
  captures Zierikzee, 233
Worsupe. See Worksop.
Wortley (Wirteley), Yorks., 131
Wortley, Sir Francis, of Wortley, 37
  letters to Earl of Shrewsbury, 28, 29
Wray, Sir Christopher, Lord Chief
    Justice of Queen's Bench.
  case between Earl and Countess
    of Shrewsbury heard before, 54,
    60
  Commissioner at trial of Queen of
    Scots, 74
Wright (Write), Christopher, partisan
    of 2nd Earl of Essex.
  imprisoned in the Marshalsea, 282
Wright, John, partisan of 2nd Earl
    of Essex.
  imprisoned in the Marshalsea, 282
Wright, Robert, of Trinity College,
    Cambridge, tutor to 2nd Earl of
    Essex.
  his accounts, 249, 250(2), 251
Wright, Robert, 265
Wriothesley, Henry, 2nd Earl of
    Southampton, 24
  his wife requests to visit him in
    the Tower, 186
Wriothesley, Henry, 3rd Earl of
    Southampton.
  appointed General of the Horse by
    Earl of Essex, 269
  takes charge of security during

talks between Earls of Essex and
Tyrone, 271
his appointment as General of the
Horse defended by Earl of Essex,
273
takes part in rebellion of Earl of
Essex, 277
parleys with Sidney at Essex House,
279, 280
surrenders to Lord Admiral, 281
imprisoned in the Tower, 281
Wriothesley, Mary, Countess of
Southampton, wife of 2nd Earl
of Southampton.
letter from, 186
her father. *See* Browne, Anthony.
Write, Christopher. *See* Wright,
Christopher.
Wroth, Sir Thomas, of Durrants in
Enfield.
letters from, 188, 190
Wroughton, Dorothy.
given annuity by Earl of Essex, 255,
262
Wroughton, Sir Thomas, of
Broadhinton.
letter from, 200
his sister. *See* Thynne, Dorothy.
Wyborne, Mr. *See* Wiburn, Perceval.
Wyford. *See* Weeford.
Wylkes, Sir Thomas. *See* Wilkes,
Sir Thomas.
Wyllobe, Lady. *See* Willoughby, Lady.
Wymbolton. *See* Wimbledon.
Wymondham (Wynddamme), Lordship
of, 159
Wynesore. *See* Windsor.
Wynn, Sir Richard, Treasurer of
Queen Henrietta Maria and
Commissioner for the
Principality of Wales.
signs letter to Earls of Essex and
Suffolk, 285
Wynter, Sir William. *See* Winter,
Admiral Sir William.
Wyrall, Edward, of English Bicknor.
letter from, 236
Wyrall, G., of English Bicknor.
to serve under Earl of Essex, 240
Wytton. *See* Witton.

X

Xenophon, Greek historian.
copy of his *Cyropaedia* at Leicester
House, 221

Y

Yate, Francis, of Lyford.

Campion arrested at house of, 35
Yattendon, Berks.
Queen dines at, 189
Yelverton, Sir Christopher, Queen's
Serjeant, later Justice of the
Queen's Bench.
prosecutes in trial of Earl of
Essex, 269
Yerworth (Yerwourth), John, of
Ruardean.
letters from, 144, 189
recommends purchase of Walton,
144
supervises election of Earl of
Leicester's nominees at Denbigh,
189
Ynce, Richard. *See* Ince, Richard.
Yonge, John, merchant, collector of
customs and subsidies at Bristol,
M.P. for Old Sarum.
letters from, 179, 186
Yonge, Richard, 220
Yonge, Roger, of Basildon.
letter from, 178
York, 117, 258, 287
letters dated from, 25, 29, 37, 94,
145, 191(2), 210, 287(2)
Council of the North meets in, 37
Earl of Essex placed under
supervision of Earl of
Huntingdon at, 251
York, Archbishop of, 219
See also Grindal, Edmund.
York (Yorke), Roland (Rowland),
member of the English
expeditionary force to South
Beveland.
his death reported, 87
wounded in skirmish near Goes, 230
York House, Strand, London, 291
letter dated from, 216
Earl of Essex's trial held at, 269
Yorkshire, 23, 35, 38, 87, 258
Papists in, 24
Assizes in, 67, 69, 92
arrest of recusants in, 92
Lord Robert Dudley receives grant
of land in, 164
Crown Parks in, 218
Sheriff of. *See* Aske, Robert.

Z

Zaltbommel (Bommel), in Gelderland.
captured by stratagem, 231
Zamoyski, John, Chancellor of
Poland.
defeats and captures Archduke
Maximilian in battle, 87
Zeeland, Netherlands.
Queen considers measures for

defence of, 45

Zellonde. *See* Zoutelande.

Zierikzee (Nericksea), in Zeeland.
taken by Captain Worston, 233

Zootland. *See* Zoutelande.

Zouche (Zowche), Edward la, 11th
Lord Zouche.
Commissioner at trial of Queen
of Scots, 74
takes part in trial of Earl of
Essex, 269

Zouche, Sir John, of Codnor Castle,
125
his quarrel with Stanhope, 22, 23(2)
charge brought by Stanhope against,
43
Earl of Leicester's request to, 188

Zouche (Souche), Mary, Lady, wife of
preceding.
Stanhope's statement regarding, 23

Zouche (Souche), William.
Stanhope's statement regarding, 23

Zoutelande (Zellonde, Zootland), in
Zeeland, 231
English defeat Spaniards in skirmish
near, 232, 233

Zowche, Lord. *See* Zouche, Edward
la.

Zutphen (Zutfen), in Gelderland.
letter dated from, 73

Printed in England for Her Majesty's Stationery Office by Commercial Colour Press, London E.7.
Dd. 290409 K5 6/80